Lou
and Barb
with Grazia

All in One
Grammar

CAMBRIDGE
UNIVERSITY PRESS

Loescher

Ristampe

8	7	6	5
2014	2013	2012	2011

Nonostante la passione e la competenza delle persone coinvolte nella realizzazione
di quest'opera, è possibile che in essa siano riscontrabili errori o imprecisioni.
Ce ne scusiamo fin d'ora con i lettori e ringraziamo coloro che, contribuendo
al miglioramento dell'opera stessa, vorranno segnalarceli al seguente indirizzo:

Loescher Editore s.r.l.
Via Vittorio Amedeo II, 18
10121 Torino
Fax 011 5654200
clienti@loescher.it

Loescher Editore S.r.l. opera con sistema qualità
certificato CERMET n. 1679-A
secondo la norma UNI EN ISO 9001-2000

Videoimpaginazione: Fregi e Majuscole, Torino
Progetto grafico: Fregi e Majuscole, Torino
Stampa: L.E.G.O. S.p.A.

INDICE

V

INTRODUZIONE

All in One Grammar si propone come uno strumento completo per apprendere la grammatica inglese ed esercitarsi nell'uso della lingua.

Il testo presenta gli elementi principali della lingua dal livello elementare al livello avanzato e si rivolge sia a coloro che studiano inglese per la prima volta, sia agli studenti che vogliono approfondire la conoscenza della lingua e raggiungere un livello avanzato di competenza linguistica e comunicativa (B2 e oltre).

L'organizzazione dei contenuti

I contenuti da apprendere sono specificati in modo dettagliato all'inizio di ogni *Unit*. La progressione dei contenuti riflette l'organizzazione della maggior parte dei corsi di lingua in uso. In questo modo, questa grammatica può accompagnare in modo sequenziale il libro di testo. Non ci sono strutture grammaticali o attività che si discostano in modo significativo dalla sequenza che emerge naturalmente dai corsi generali di lingua. Tuttavia, il testo può anche essere usato, da un lettore più esperto, come strumento di consultazione per rivedere e approfondire regole grammaticali specifiche.

Le spiegazioni

Le spiegazioni sono improntate a criteri di chiarezza e completezza. Tuttavia, si è scelto consapevolmente di non fornire regole troppo dettagliate, per non distogliere gli studenti dagli elementi fondanti della lingua, che hanno un maggiore valore comunicativo. Le spiegazioni in italiano sono sempre accompagnate da numerosi esempi di lingua inglese autentica, immediatamente spendibili in contesti di comunicazione reale. Il raffronto costante tra le strutture inglesi e quelle italiane mira a rendere gli studenti consapevoli degli elementi di specificità delle due lingue.

Le descrizioni grammaticali della lingua sono spesso affiancate da tabelle, schemi e accorgimenti grafici per visualizzare le strutture linguistiche e fornire un confronto tra L1 e L2.

Gli esercizi

Il rapporto tra numero di esercizi e spiegazioni grammaticali è molto elevato, circa di 5 a 1. Uno degli obiettivi fondamentali di *All in One Grammar* è quello di fornire ampie opportunità di pratica per interiorizzare le strutture della lingua.

La spiegazione di ogni regola grammaticale è immediatamente seguita da esercizi specifici, che permettono agli studenti di manipolare e assimilare le strutture trattate.

Alla fine di ogni *Unit*, la sezione **All in One Revision** favorisce l'inserimento delle conoscenze acquisite nel repertorio linguistico dello studente, con una vasta tipologia di esercizi e *tasks* che richiedono l'attivazione delle diverse risorse linguistiche di cui dispone.

Gli esercizi seguono una progressione da elementi grammaticali di base a forme più complesse, da pratica controllata a uso comunicativo della lingua. Questa progressione porta gli studenti a diventare gradualmente più consapevoli dei rapporti inscindibili tra forma e significato.

Esercizi di traduzione sono presenti sia all'interno delle *Unit* che alla fine di ogni sezione di revisione: frasi brevi, mirate a consolidare i punti chiave degli argomenti trattati.

Sviluppo delle abilità di ascolto: context listening

Le attività di revisione sono introdotte da brani di ascolto (contenuti nei due CD allegati al volume) che ripropongono le strutture grammaticali della *Unit* in un chiaro contesto di comunicazione di livello B1 (PET) o B2 (FCE), consentendo agli studenti di riconoscere gli elementi della grammatica in situazioni di uso reale della lingua: dialoghi telefonici, conversazioni tra amici, colloqui di lavoro, programmi radiofonici. L'inserimento di attività di ascolto all'interno della grammatica ha tre funzioni principali, strettamente collegate:

- consolidare l'acquisizione delle strutture della lingua attraverso modalità che si adattano a diversi stili di apprendimento;
- potenziare le abilità di ascolto, per uno sviluppo integrato delle competenze linguistiche oggetto delle certificazioni Cambridge ESOL e TOEFL;
- sviluppare la sensibilità degli studenti nei confronti della cosiddetta "grammatica del parlato".

Aspetto lessicale

Grammatica e lessico sono strettamente collegati. Le frasi che illustrano le descrizioni grammaticali e gli esercizi che forniscono pratica sono esempi di lingua viva, attuale, autentica. Per garantire questa naturalezza le autrici hanno attinto a tre sezioni del *Cambridge International Corpus*.

- *Student errors*
- *Collocations*
- *Natural speech*

Si è scelto in modo deliberato di non avere sezioni specifiche dedicate allo sviluppo del lessico, perché un approccio attento agli aspetti lessicali della lingua è sotteso a tutto il testo.

Terminologia

La questione della terminologia nella descrizione delle strutture di una lingua straniera è molto complessa. In generale, si è scelto di mantenere la terminologia inglese in tutti i casi in cui l'equivalente italiano suona innaturale: per esempio, *past simple* e *present perfect*. Per descrivere l'aspetto delle forme verbali, si è scelto il termine *continuous* invece di *progressive*, coerentemente con le principali grammatiche moderne.

In molti casi ci è sembrato corretto fornire la doppia terminologia, italiana e inglese: per esempio, per descrivere tutte quelle parole ed espressioni che servono per creare legami tra frasi e strutturare le parti di un discorso si è utilizzato il termine **connettivi** affiancandolo all'equivalente inglese *linking words*. Si è ritenuto in questo modo di mantenere la terminologia tradizionale familiare agli studenti, e allo stesso tempo fornire a chi lo desiderasse gli strumenti linguistici per consultare testi di grammatica in lingua inglese.

Exam Practice and Test Booklet

L'esercizio non è mai abbastanza. *All in One Grammar* è accompagnato da un *Exam Practice and Test Booklet* che copre i principali punti grammaticali di ogni *Unit*. I test rispecchiano il format degli esami PET e FCE e mirano allo sviluppo integrato delle abilità linguistiche: *Use of English*, *Reading* e *Writing*. Il livello linguistico di ogni esercizio dei test è specificato: in ogni test ci sono attività PET (B1) e attività FCE (B2). I test possono essere usati come *Exam practice* oppure possono essere utilizzati per la verifica sommativa in classe, selezionando, tra il materiale proposto, gli esercizi più adatti al livello linguistico dei propri studenti.

Nota

I brani di ascolto sono contrassegnati dal logo
1.12

I due numeri sottostanti indicano rispettivamente il CD (1 o 2) e il numero della traccia.
Per un elenco delle tracce, vedi p. 454.

I TEMPI DEL PRESENTE

1.1 IL *PRESENT SIMPLE: TO BE*

Il verbo **to be**, che corrisponde all'italiano **essere**, si usa sia come verbo **principale** che come verbo **ausiliare** nei tempi composti alla forma continua e nella formazione del passivo.

■ In inglese, diversamente dall'italiano, l'**ordine delle parole** segue regole precise:

nella frase **affermativa**, l'ordine è **soggetto + verbo**;

nella frase **interrogativa**, l'ordine si inverte: il verbo essere, ausiliare, **precede** il soggetto: **ausiliare + soggetto**;

nella frase **negativa**, si mette *not* **dopo** il verbo essere: **soggetto + ausiliare + *not***.

Affermativa		Negativa		Interrogativa
I **am**	I**'m**	I **am not**	I**'m not**	**Am** I …?
you **are**	you**'re**	you **are not**	you **aren't** / you**'re not**	**Are** you …?
he **is**	he**'s**	he **is not**	he **isn't** / he**'s not**	**Is** he …?
she **is**	she**'s**	she **is not**	she **isn't** / she**'s not**	**Is** she …?
it **is**	it**'s**	it **is not**	it **isn't** / it**'s not**	**Is** it …?
we **are**	we**'re**	we **are not**	we **aren't** / we**'re not**	**Are** we …?
you **are**	you**'re**	you **are not**	you **aren't** / you**'re not**	**Are** you …?
they **are**	they**'re**	they **are not**	they **aren't** / they**'re not**	**Are** they …?

■ Nella lingua parlata e nei messaggi informali si usano generalmente le forme contratte.

Affermativa

*I**'m** tired.* **Sono** *stanco.*

*My brother**'s** at home.* *Mio fratello **è** a casa.*

Negativa

*The test **isn't** difficult.*
*They **aren't** twins.*

*Il compito **non è** difficile.*
***Non sono** gemelli.*

Interrogativa

***Is** John your cousin?*
***Where's** the post office?*

*John **è** tuo cugino?*
Dov'è l'ufficio postale?

PRACTICE

1 Inserisci negli spazi la forma giusta del verbo *to be*.

1 Where .....is..... your new office?

2 My boyfriend and I ..are... vegetarians. We never eat meat.

3 ..are... you a student?

4 Robin and Katie ..are.... American. They're Canadian.

5 I .'m not. sure what time I'll be home. It depends on the traffic.

6 It only takes five minutes to get to the station. It ..isn't.. far.

7 There ...is..... no food in the fridge. We'll have to eat out.

8 Sorry! ..AM.... I terribly late?

ci vogliono

Saremo costretti a mangiare

2 Riordina queste parole in modo da formare frasi di senso compiuto.

1 are / yours / gloves / these / ? .... Are these gloves yours?

2 what / eyes / his / are / colour / ? .... What color are his eyes?

3 many / people / here / how / are / ? .... How many people are here?

4 too / suitcase / heavy / is / this / . ... This is too heavy suitcase

5 name / 's / what / the / teacher's / ? .... What's the teacher's name?

6 on / mobile / my / 's / desk / my / . ... My mobile's on my desk

7 aren't / exercises / the / difficult / . ... The exercises aren't difficult

8 train / late / 's / again / her / . ... her train's late again

9 shops / are / on / open / the / Sundays / ? .... The shops are open on Sundays?

10 the / not / moment / 'm / hungry / I / at / . ... I'm not hungry at the moment

1.2   USI PARTICOLARI DI *TO BE*

L'uso del verbo *to be* corrisponde sostanzialmente a **essere**. Tuttavia, a differenza dell'italiano, in inglese si usa *to be* nei seguenti casi:

■ per esprimere la **professione**.

*Thomas **is** an architect.*
I'm a teacher.

*Thomas **fa** l'architetto.*
***Sono** insegnante. / **Faccio** l'insegnante.*

■ per esprimere l'**età**.

How old **are** you?   Quanti anni **hai**?
I'm 16 (years old). (**Non** ~~I have 16.~~)   **Ho** 16 anni.

■ per esprimere **fame**, **sete**, **caldo**, **freddo** e altre condizioni fisiche e mentali comuni, si usa **be +
aggettivo**, non *have* + sostantivo.

be hungry	avere fame	be right	avere ragione
be thirsty	avere sete	be wrong	avere torto, sbagliarsi
be cold	avere freddo	be late	essere in ritardo / fare tardi
be hot	avere caldo	be early	essere in anticipo
be afraid	aver paura	be in a hurry	avere fretta

I'm thirsty. Can I have a glass of lemonade?   **Ho sete**. Posso prendere un bicchiere di limonata?
My sister **is afraid** of spiders.   Mia sorella **ha paura** dei ragni.

PRACTICE

1 Abbina a ogni immagine un'espressione nel riquadro.

He's afraid.   He's wrong.   It's hungry.   She's late.   She's thirsty.   They're in a hurry.

1 ......They're in a hurry......

2 ......He's afraid......

3 ......She's thirsty......

4 ......She's late......

5 ......It's hungry......

6 ......He's wrong......

2 Completa i seguenti dialoghi con un'espressione del verbo **to be**.

1 A Would you like some more?

   B No, thanks. It's really delicious but I'm ...not hungry................................... .

2 A Why isn't anybody here yet?

   B We ...are coming................................. . It doesn't start for half an hour.

3

3 A Why don't you go by plane?

B Because I .....'m afraid.............. of flying.

4 A Can I speak to you for a moment?

B Sorry. I ......'m in a hurry.............. . My train leaves in ten minutes.

5 A Look! There's Brad Pitt! **B** Don't be ridiculous!

A No, really. Look! **B** You ......are right.............. ! It's him!

6 A The film's starting. Where's Harry?

B I don't know. He .....is late.............. , as usual.

7 A Take your jacket with you.

B No, I'm fine. I .....'m hot.............. at all.

8 A Kate's sure Kamal likes her.

B She .... He likes Sophie.

3 Traduci.

1 Jenny ha paura dei cani. *Jenny is afraid of dogs*

2 Ho freddo. Possiamo chiudere la finestra, per favore? *I'm cold. Can we close the window?*

3 Hai ragione. Siamo in ritardo. *He's right. We are late.*

4 **A** Quanti anni hanno i tuoi fratelli? **B** Connor ha sette anni e Bill (ne) ha due.

5 Mio padre fa l'ingegnere e mia madre è infermiera.

4. How old are your brothers? Connor has seven years old and Bill has two years old

1.3   IL *PRESENT SIMPLE*: FORMA AFFERMATIVA

In inglese, a differenza che in italiano, tutti i tempi verbali hanno una forma semplice e una forma continua o progressiva che esprimono aspetti temporali diversi. Ci sono quindi due tempi del presente: il *present simple* e il *present continuous* (o *progressive*).

La forma affermativa del *present simple* corrisponde alla **forma base del verbo**, **infinito senza** *to*, a eccezione della 3ª persona singolare, che aggiunge *-s*.

Affermativa	
I **live**	I **work**
you **live**	you **work**
he/she/it **lives**	he/she/it **works**
we **live**	we **work**
you **live**	you **work**
they **live**	they **work**

*I **live** in a small town in Tuscany.*

*He **works** for a travel agency. She **lives** in London.*

*My grandparents **live** in the country.*

5. My father is a ...   and my mother is a nursery.

LA 3ª PERSONA SINGOLARE: VARIAZIONI DI SPELLING

Alcuni verbi presentano delle variazioni di spelling alla 3ª persona singolare.

I verbi terminanti in **-ss**, **-sh**, **-tch**, e **-x** aggiungono **-es**:
mi**ss** → he mi**sses**; bru**sh** → she bru**shes**; wa**tch** → he wa**tches**; fi**x** → it fi**xes**.

I verbi terminanti in **y preceduta da consonante** trasformano **y** in **i** e aggiungono **-es**:
t**ry** → he t**ries**; st**udy** → she st**udies**.

Ma i verbi terminanti in **y preceduta da vocale** aggiungono regolarmente **-s**:
pl**ay** → she pl**ays**; enj**oy** → he enj**oys**.

Aggiungono **-es** anche i verbi **do** → he **does** e **go** → he **goes**.

USI DEL *PRESENT SIMPLE*

Il *present simple* si usa per parlare di:

- **abitudini** e cose che accadono con **regolarità**.

  *Jack **plays** football every Sunday.*   *Jack **gioca** a calcio tutte le domeniche.*
  *I **go** there most weekends.*   ***Vado** là quasi tutti i fine settimana.*

- **situazioni permanenti**.

  *My sister **works** for a bank.*   *Mia sorella **lavora** per una banca.*
  *My parents **live** in Durrington.*   *I miei genitori **abitano/vivono** a Durrington.*

- **verità universalmente riconosciute**.

  *Many tourists **enjoy** coach tours.*   *Molti turisti **amano** le escursioni in pullman.*
  *The Moon **goes** around the Earth.*   *La luna **gira** intorno alla terra.*

PRACTICE

1 Scrivi la 3ª persona singolare dei verbi seguenti.

1 like ......*likes*.......   2 buy ..*buys*.....   3 touch ..*touches*..   4 stay ....

5 kiss ..*kisses*.....   6 marry ..*marries*..   7 catch ..*catches*..   8 go ....

9 rain ..*rains*....   10 finish ..*finishes*..   11 drink ....   12 fix ....

2 Completa le frasi usando i verbi nel riquadro. Usa ogni verbo una volta sola.
Ricorda di aggiungere **-s** o **-es** se necessario.

| pass | fly | ~~do~~ | teach | wash | want | believe | take |

1 In Great Britain children ....*do*.......... a lot of sport at school.

2 My neighbour .... his car every Saturday afternoon.

3 Many people .... that nuclear power is dangerous.

4 I .... my dog out for a walk every day.

5 The government .... to increase taxes.

6 Airline pilots .... about 1,440 km a year.

7 It's a really easy exam. Everybody ....

8 My aunt .... children with learning difficulties.

3 Leggi l'annuncio di un lavoro come truccatore televisivo. Completa l'articolo accanto con la forma giusta del *present simple*.

Do you want to meet lots of famous people? Can you do this?

4 am Get up.

5 am Arrive at the TV studio. Have a coffee.

5.10 Prepare the make-up room.

6 am Do make-up for the newsreaders.

6.30–11.30 Work with guests on morning TV shows. No time for a break.

12 Have lunch with colleagues.

1 pm Order new make-up.

2 pm or later Leave the studio.

Apply to Megalith TV Ltd Box 2343

A hard day at the studio

Sharon usually **(1)** .....gets up..... at four o'clock. She hates that! She **(2)** .... at the TV studio at five and **(3)** .... a coffee. She **(4)** .... her room carefully. At six, she **(5)** .... the make-up for the newsreaders and for the next five hours she **(6)** .... with guests on morning TV shows. She doesn't have time for a break but at noon she **(7)** .... lunch with colleagues. After lunch she **(8)** .... new make-up. She doesn't leave the studio before two o'clock. It's a tiring job!

4 Adesso scrivi un testo analogo su di te.

I get up at...

....

....

....

....

....

1.4 *IL PRESENT SIMPLE*: FORMA NEGATIVA E INTERROGATIVA

Le frasi negative e interrogative in inglese hanno sempre bisogno di un **ausiliare**: l'ausiliare del *present simple* è **do** (**does** alla 3ª persona singolare). Il verbo è sempre alla **forma base**.

Negativa	Interrogativa
I **don't work**	**Do** I **work** …?
you **don't work**	**Do** you **work** …?
he/she/it **doesn't work**	**Does** he/she/it **work** …?
we **don't work**	**Do** we **work** …?
you **don't work**	**Do** you **work** …?
they **don't work**	**Do** they **work** …?

PRACTICE

1 Riscrivi le frasi alla forma negativa, usando le parole fra parentesi.

   1 Helen speaks Italian. (*German*) .... *Helen doesn't speak German.* ....

   2 I like dance music. (*jazz*) ....

   3 My cousins live in Argentina. (*Italy*) ....

   4 It rains a lot in autumn. (*summer*) ....

   5 Jack does the cooking. (*washing up*) ....

   6 We go out at the weekend. (*during the week*) ....

2 Scegli il verbo giusto e completa le frasi alla forma negativa.

   1 Ann ..*doesn't go*.. (*do / play / go*) jogging any more. She's too busy.

   2 I .... (*have / take / get*) coffee after dinner because it keeps me awake.

   3 Simone .... (*do / say / make*) many mistakes when he speaks English.

   4 'Actually' .... (*spell / mean / say*) the same as 'now'.

   5 You .... (*notice / listen / hear*) to anything I say.

   6 We .... (*look / talk / see*) each other often because we live in different cities.

3 Completa gli spazi con **Do** o **Does**.

   1 ....*Do*......... your relatives spend Christmas with you?

   2 .... the London train leave from platform 1?

   3 .... this programme last an hour?

   4 .... we have English lessons on Saturdays?

   5 .... you know the way to Jane's house?

   6 .... David Beckham play for Real Madrid?

4 Riordina queste parole in modo da formare frasi di senso compiuto.

1 does / station / at / this / bus / stop / the / ? ....*Does this bus stop at the station?*........

2 speaks / when / he / quickly / don't / understand / I / . ...

3 everywhere / drive / so / walks / Keith / he / doesn't / . ...

4 to / study / listen / do / when / you / music / you / ? ....

5 French / doesn't / speak / his / dad / . ...

6 evening / to / do / you / out / want / this / eat / ? ....

7 don't / cold / orchids / in / grow / climates / . ...

8 pool / does / a / hotel / have / the / swimming / ? ....

5 In sette di queste frasi c'è un errore nella forma verbale. <u>Sottolinea</u> l'errore e scrivi la forma corretta.

1 I <u>not like</u> shopping for clothes. ....*don't like*..........

2 He isn't fit because he doesn't any exercise. ....

3 The bookshop don't sell magazines. ....

4 You like playing computer games? ....

5 The other students in my class don't speak Italian. ....

6 Does study law your brother? ....

7 A fire don't burn without oxygen. ....

8 Do money make people happy? ....

1.5 AVVERBI DI FREQUENZA

Gli avverbi di frequenza, che indicano quanto spesso si verifica un'azione, si usano generalmente con il *present simple*. (Vedi *Unit* **11**)

always	*usually*	*often*	*sometimes*	*seldom*	*hardly ever*	*never*
sempre	*di solito*	*spesso*	*qualche volta*	*raramente*	*quasi mai*	*mai*

più frequente   **meno frequente**

Gli avverbi di frequenza di norma sono posti immediatamente **prima** del verbo principale, ma **dopo** il verbo essere.

*The tour **usually** lasts about an hour.*   *Il giro turistico **di solito** dura circa un'ora.*
*Do you **often** eat out?*   *Mangiate **spesso** fuori?*
Ma *Jane is **always** late.*   *Jane è **sempre** in ritardo.*

■ Gli avverbi ***never*** (non … mai) e ***hardly ever*** (quasi mai) hanno significato negativo, così **non possono** essere usati con un'altra negazione.

*I **never** drink coffee.*   *Io **non** bevo **mai** il caffè.*
(**Non** ~~I don't never drink coffee.~~)

■ Nelle frasi interrogative, **mai** si traduce con *ever*.

*Do you **ever** go shopping on Monday?*   *Fai **mai** la spesa di lunedì?*

Altre espressioni di frequenza di uso comune sono:

once	*a day/week*	*una volta*	*al giorno / alla settimana*
twice	*a month*	*due volte*	*al mese*
three/four/... times	*a year*	*tre/quattro/... volte*	*all'anno*
every day (**Non** ~~*every days*~~)		*ogni giorno / tutti i giorni*	
every 10 minutes		*ogni 10 minuti*	
every 2 weeks		*ogni 2 settimane*	

*Lucy goes to the gym **twice a week**.*   *Lucy va in palestra **due volte alla settimana**.*
*There's a train to Oxford **every 35 minutes**.*   *C'è un treno per Oxford **ogni 35 minuti**.*

PRACTICE

1 Riordina queste parole in modo da formare frasi di senso compiuto.

1 Monday / often / in / hurry / I'm / on / morning / a / .   I'm often in a hurry on Monday morning.

2 jogging / do / you / before / go / breakfast / ever / ? ....

3 always / clothes / spends / a / lot / she / on / . ...

4 she / grandparents / seldom / sees / her / . ...

5 have / I / usually / in / my / don't / coffee / sugar / . ...

6 are / lunchtime / at / usually / home / at / you / ? ....

7 hardly / there's / interesting / ever / TV / anything / on / . ...

8 Josh / ever / does / up / his / bedroom / tidy / ? ....

2 Riscrivi le frasi seguenti in modo personale, inserendo un avverbio o un'espressione di frequenza al posto giusto.

1 I have a big breakfast. ....

2 I eat Chinese food. ....

3 I stay in bed until 11. ....

4 I fall in love. ....

5 I get headaches. ....

6 I'm polite. ....

7 I do the washing up. ....

8 I feel lonely. ....

9 I go to the dentist. ....

10 I argue with my parents. ....

3 Traduci.

  1 Mio padre gioca a tennis due volte alla settimana.

  2 Di solito vado a scuola in autobus.

  3 Non vado mai a letto tardi.

  4 Guardi mai la televisione di pomeriggio?

  5 Raramente sono a casa prima delle sette di sera.

1.6   ALCUNI PRONOMI E AVVERBI INTERROGATIVI: *WH- WORDS*

I seguenti pronomi e avverbi interrogativi sono usati nelle domande per specificare il tipo di informazione richiesto. (Vedi *Unit* **6.3**)

Who	*What*	*Where*	*Why*	*When*	*What time*	*How*	*How often*
Chi	*Che cosa*	*Dove*	*Perché*	*Quando*	*A che ora*	*Come*	*Ogni quanto tempo*

<table>
<tr><td rowspan="5">Domande</td><td>***Wh- word***</td><td>**ausiliare**</td><td>**soggetto**</td><td>**verbo**</td><td>**complementi**</td><td></td></tr>
<tr><td>**Who**</td><td>do</td><td>you</td><td>want</td><td>to invite?</td><td>***Chi*** *vuoi invitare?*</td></tr>
<tr><td>**What**</td><td>does</td><td>Dean</td><td>teach?</td><td></td><td>***Che cosa*** *insegna Dean?*</td></tr>
<tr><td>**Why**</td><td>don't</td><td>you</td><td>take</td><td>a day off?</td><td>***Perché*** *non prendi un giorno di vacanza?*</td></tr>
<tr><td>**What time**</td><td>does</td><td>the match</td><td>start?</td><td></td><td>***A che ora*** *inizia la partita?*</td></tr>
</table>

<table>
<tr><td rowspan="4">Risposte</td><td>*I want to invite **my school friends**.*</td><td>*Voglio invitare **i miei compagni di scuola**.*</td></tr>
<tr><td>*He teaches **Information Technology**.*</td><td>*Insegna **informatica**.*</td></tr>
<tr><td>***Because** I'm too busy at work.*</td><td>***Perché** sono troppo occupato al lavoro.*</td></tr>
<tr><td>*It starts **at 9 o'clock**.*</td><td>*Comincia **alle 9**.*</td></tr>
</table>

PRACTICE

1 Completa le domande con un pronome o un avverbio interrogativo e la forma corretta dell'ausiliare ***do***.

  1 A .... Who do .... you play tennis with? **B** Lara.

  2 A .... the shops close? **B** 7.30

  3 A .... you go to the gym? **B** Twice a week.

  4 A .... Rob buy his clothes? **B** At Armani.

  5 A .... you think of Amy? **B** She's nice.

  6 A .... you get to school? **B** By scooter.

  7 A .... 'to cough' mean? **B** *Tossire*.

  8 A .... Alex still live with his parents? **B** To save money.

2 Formula domande appropriate alle seguenti risposte.

1 How often do you go to the cinema? ....

Not more than once a month. I prefer watching a DVD at home.

2 ....

E-N-O-U-G-H.

3 ....

Because you can't dance to it. I prefer rock music.

4 ....

Usually in the evening. I can't concentrate during the day.

5 ....

My father. I can't talk to my mother about my problems.

6 ....

In the mountains. I don't like the sea.

7 ....

At about ten to eight. Lessons start at eight.

8 ....

Because he's shy and he doesn't like dancing.

9 ....

Anything, but not pasta again. We always have pasta.

10 ....

I never turn it off. Someone might phone me.

1.7   IL *PRESENT CONTINUOUS*: FORMA AFFERMATIVA, NEGATIVA E INTERROGATIVA

Il *present continuous* (o *progressive*) si forma con il presente del verbo *to be*, che funge da **ausiliare**, e la forma *-ing* del verbo. Il verbo *to be* si traduce con **stare**, la forma *-ing* del verbo con il gerundio presente.

Affermativa	Negativa	Interrogativa
I **am** (**'m**) work**ing**	I **am not** (**'m not**) work**ing**	**Am** I work**ing** …?
you **are** (**'re**) work**ing**	you **are not** (**aren't**) work**ing**	**Are** you work**ing** …?
he/she/it **is** (**'s**) work**ing**	he/she/it **is not** (**isn't**) work**ing**	**Is** he/she/it work**ing** …?
we **are** (**'re**) work**ing**	we **are not** (**aren't**) work**ing**	**Are** we work**ing** …?
you **are** (**'re**) work**ing**	you **are not** (**aren't**) work**ing**	**Are** you work**ing** …?
they **are** (**'re**) work**ing**	they **are not** (**aren't**) work**ing**	**Are** they work**ing** …?

Il *present continuous* si usa per parlare di:

■ azioni che si stanno svolgendo **in questo momento** (= *now, at the moment*).

A *What* **are** you **doing**? **B** *I'm* **listening** *to you.*	**A** *Che cosa* **stai facendo**? **B** *Ti* **sto ascoltando**.
The bus **is** *now* **turning** *into Queens Road.*	*L'autobus* **sta svoltando** *adesso in Queens Road.*

■ **situazioni temporanee**.

I'm **working** *in London* **this week**.	**Lavoro** *a Londra* **questa settimana**.
(= I don't usually work in London.)	(= Non lavoro a Londra di solito.)
He's **studying** *Biology* **this term**.	**Sta studiando** *biologia* **questo trimestre**.

■ **situazioni e processi in evoluzione**.

The Earth's temperature **is rising**.	*La temperatura della Terra* **sta aumentando**.
That group's **becoming** *more well known.*	*Quel gruppo* **sta diventando** *più famoso.*

■ **azioni future certe o già programmate**. (Vedi *Unit* **5**)

What **are** you **doing** *this evening?*	*Cosa* **fai stasera**?
I'm **going** *to the cinema.*	**Vado** *al cinema.*

FORMA -*ING*: VARIAZIONI DI SPELLING

La forma **-ing** normalmente si forma aggiungendo il suffisso **-ing** alla forma base del verbo:

work → work**ing**   **eat** → eat**ing**   **teach** → teach**ing**   **visit** → visit**ing**.

Alcuni verbi presentano delle variazioni di spelling.

■ I verbi **monosillabi** terminanti in **c**onsonante **v**ocale **c**onsonante (**c v c**) **raddoppiano** la consonante finale: **run** → run**ning**   **stop** → stop**ping**   **sit** → sit**ting**.

■ **Raddoppiano** la consonante finale anche i verbi **bisillabi** terminanti in **c v c**, a condizione che l'ultima sillaba sia accentata: begin → begin**ning**.

■ I verbi terminanti in **-e eliminano la -e** e aggiungono **-ing**: **smoke** → smok**ing**   **have** → hav**ing**   **leave** → leav**ing**.

■ I verbi terminanti in **-ie** trasformano **-ie** in **-ying**: **die** → d**ying**   **lie** → l**ying**.

🔦 I verbi terminanti in **-y** seguono la regola generale e aggiungono sempre **-ing** alla forma base, **senza nessuna modificazione**:

study → study**ing**   **enjoy** → enjoy**ing**   **carry** → carry**ing**.

PRACTICE

1 Scrivi la forma **-ing** dei verbi seguenti.

1 clean ....*cleaning*....   2 live ....   3 get ....   4 stay ....

5 fly ....   6 decide ....   7 see ....   8 play ....

9 beat ....   10 tie ....   11 sleep ....   12 forget ....

2 Leggi questa conversazione al cellulare. Completa gli spazi usando i verbi nel riquadro alla forma corretta del *present continuous*.

come	come	do	get	leave	read
shout	sit	talk	wait		

Mandy: Dwayn? This is Mandy.

Dwayn: Hi Mandy. Why aren't you here? What **(1)** .....are you doing. (you)? **(2)** .... (you) to this party?

Mandy: **(3)** I .... on the bus.

Dwayn: What?

Mandy: The bus has broken down. We **(4)** .... for another bus to come and take us to town.

Dwayn: Oh, no.

Mandy: Yes. Some of the passengers **(5)** .... angrily, but what can the driver do?

Dwayn: **(6)** .... (he) to them?

Mandy: No, he **(7)** .... a newspaper. Ah, here's the other bus.
I **(8)** .... on to it now. The bus **(9)** ....
I **(10)** .... to the party!

1.8   VERBI DI STATO (VERBI CHE NON HANNO LA FORMA CONTINUA)

Alcuni verbi, chiamati verbi di stato, di norma si usano solo alla forma semplice, perché indicano **stati permanenti** e non azioni.

*I **like** chocolate ice cream.* (**Non** ~~I'm liking chocolate ice cream.~~)   ***Mi piace** il gelato al cioccolato.*

*...that special CD **you want to get**.*   *...quel CD particolare che **vuoi prendere**.*
(**Non** ...~~that special CD **you are wanting to get**~~)

I verbi di stato più comuni appartengono alle seguenti categorie:

◾ verbi che esprimono **sentimenti** e **stati emotivi**.

adore, hate, love, like, dislike, despise, want, wish, prefer.

*Jeff **adores** his little sister.*   *Jeff **adora** la sua sorellina.*
*I **prefer** not to think about it.*   ***Preferisco** non pensarci.*

◾ verbi che esprimono **opinioni, certezze, idee**.

believe, know, mean, realise, recognise, remember, suppose, understand, feel (= believe),
think (= believe).

*I **think** you are wrong.* (= This is my **opinion**.)   ***Penso** che tu abbia torto.* (= È la mia **opinione**.)
*Ma I'**m thinking** about my holiday.*   ***Sto pensando** alla mia vacanza.* (non è verbo di stato)

■ verbi che esprimono **possesso** e **appartenenza**.

belong, **have / have got** (= quando significa **possedere**, vedi *Unit* **1.9**), **own**, **possess**.

It **belongs** to my father.	**Appartiene** a mio padre.
The manager **has** the biggest company car.	Il direttore **ha** l'auto aziendale più grossa.

■ verbi che indicano **percezione**.

hear, **see**, **smell**, **taste**.

Do you **see** anything you want to buy here?	**Vedi** niente che ti piacerebbe comprare qui?
Ma Are you **seeing** Tom today?	**Vedi** Tom oggi? (in questo caso see = meet, avere un appuntamento, incontrare)

🎤 **Listen to**, **watch** e **look at** non sono **verbi di stato**, perché indicano **azione volontaria**, quindi possono essere usati alla forma continua.

I**'m listening to** music	Io **sto ascoltando** della musica
and Diane **is watching** a DVD upstairs.	e Diane **sta guardando** un DVD di sopra.

PRACTICE

1 Sottolinea la forma corretta del verbo.

1 I *know* / *am knowing* this part of town quite well.

2 Amy *has* / *is having* very small feet.

3 We *go* / *are going* on holiday with my grandparents every summer.

4 My grandmother *stays* / *is staying* in my room this week so I *sleep* / *am sleeping* in the sitting-room.

5 *Do you understand* / *Are you understanding* my situation?

6 Can I phone you back in ten minutes? We *have* / *are having* breakfast at the moment.

7 These CDs *belong* / *are belonging* to my sister.

8 Have you seen John's email? He *has* / *is having* a great time in Tokyo.

2 Completa le frasi seguenti con una forma verbale nel riquadro.

don't think	'm thinking	feel	isn't feeling	see
are seeing		'm not listening	hear	

1 **A** What's the matter with Kay? **B** She ....isn't feeling.......... very well.

2 I'm sorry but I .... you're right.

3 **A** What did he just say? **B** I don't know. I ....

4 I .... that you're doing the right thing.

5 **A** Can you .... that noise? **B** Don't worry, it's only the wind.

6 We .... Ed and Elena this evening. Do you want to come?

7 **A** Have you decided what to do? **B** Not yet. I .... (still) about it.

8 I .... what the problem is, but I don't agree with your solution.

1.9   IL *PRESENT SIMPLE*: *HAVE GOT* E *HAVE*

Come in italiano, in inglese il verbo **avere** si usa sia come verbo **principale**, per esprimere **possesso** in senso generale, sia come verbo **ausiliare** nei tempi composti, o *perfect tenses*.

Come verbo principale, al presente **avere** ha due forme, *have got* e *have*.

Have got		Negativa		Interrogativa	
I **have got**	I**'ve got**	I **have not got**	(**haven't got**)	**Have** I **got** …?	+ *I**'ve got** a new car.*
you **have got**	you**'ve got**	you **have not got**	(**haven't got**)	**Have** you **got** …?	
he she it } **has got**	he**'s got** she**'s got** it**'s got**	he she it } **has not got**	(**hasn't got**)	**Has** he **got** …? **Has** she **got** …? **Has** it **got** …?	— *She **hasn't got** a new car.*
we **have got**	we**'ve got**	we **have not got**	(**haven't got**)	**Have** we **got** …?	
you **have got**	you**'ve got**	you **have not got**	(**haven't got**)	**Have** you **got** …?	
they **have got**	they**'ve got**	they **have not got**	(**haven't got**)	**Have** they **got** …?	? ***Have** they **got** a new car?*

Have	Negativa	Interrogativa	
I **have**	I **don't have**	**Do** I **have** …?	+ *I **have** a new car.*
you **have**	you **don't have**	**Do** you **have** …?	
he she it } **has**	he she it } **doesn't have**	**Does** he she it } **have** …?	— *She **doesn't have** a new car.*
we **have**	we **don't have**	**Do** we **have** …?	
you **have**	you **don't have**	**Do** you **have** …?	
they **have**	they **don't have**	**Do** they **have** …?	? ***Do** they **have** a new car?*

Si usa *have got* o ***have*** al *present simple* (**non** al *present continuous*) per:

▨ esprimere **possesso** in senso generale.

*We**'ve got** a new entertainment centre.*
= *We **have** a new entertainment centre.*   ***Abbiamo** un nuovo centro ricreativo.*

***Have** they **got** a map of the underground?*
= ***Do** they **have** a map of the underground?*   ***Hanno** una cartina della metropolitana?*

*We **haven't got** any money.*
= *We **don't have** any money.*   ***Non abbiamo** soldi.*

■ **descrivere** cose e persone.

It's got a cinema and a concert hall.   **Ha** *un cinema e una sala concerti.*
It doesn't have enough seats.   **Non ha** *abbastanza posti a sedere.*
Has *he got dark hair?*   **Ha** *i capelli scuri?*

■ parlare di **malattie** e **stati di salute**.

I've got a sore throat.   **Ho** *mal di gola.*

PRACTICE

1 Riscrivi ogni frase in modo che il significato non cambi. Usa la forma corretta di **have got**.

1 He's an only child. .... *He hasn't got any brothers or sisters.* ....

2 My head hurts. ....

3 Her hair is long and straight. ....

4 His girlfriend is Brazilian. ....

5 I'm not rich. ....

6 Jane's leg is broken. ....

1.10   USI PARTICOLARI DI *TO HAVE*

Il verbo **have** (**non** *have got*) si usa con valore di **verbo principale** in molte espressioni in cui assume il significato di **fare**, **mangiare**, **prendere** e **divertirsi**. Eccone alcune tra le più comuni:

Fare:	*have a bath/shower*	*fare il bagno / la doccia*
	have a holiday	*fare una vacanza*
	have a swim/walk	*fare una nuotata/passeggiata*
	have a chat	*fare una chiacchierata*
Mangiare:	*have breakfast/lunch/dinner*	*fare colazione/pranzare/cenare*
Prendere:	*have a sandwich/coffee*	*prendere un sandwich/caffè*
Divertirsi:	*have a good time / fun*	*divertirsi*

In questi casi, poiché indica **azioni** e **non possesso**, il verbo **have** può essere usato sia con i tempi semplici che con i tempi progressivi.

Inoltre, ha sempre bisogno dell'ausiliare **do/does** nelle forme negative e interrogative del *present simple*.

*I hope you're **having a good time**.*   *Spero che **ti stia divertendo**.*
*Why **don't** you **have a walk** round there?*   *Perchè **non fai una passeggiata** là intorno?*
*You can **have lunch** in the school canteen.*   *Puoi **mangiare/pranzare** alla mensa della scuola.*

PRACTICE

1 Completa le frasi seguenti usando la forma corretta di **have** e le espressioni nel riquadro.

a chat	fun	a walk	dinner	a swim	a bath	holiday	cereal

1   Why don't we ....have a walk......... when it stops raining?

2   It's great here. We're all ....

3   I hardly ever see her but we often .... on the phone.

4   We .... this summer because we haven't got enough money.

5   Do you usually .... for breakfast?

6   We .... early tonight because we're going to the theatre.

7   He always uses all the hot water when he ....

8   The children are in the pool. They .... before lunch.

2 Traduci.

1   Laura non può sentirti perché sta facendo la doccia.

2   Facciamo sempre una breve vacanza alla fine di settembre.

3   Non ceniamo mai prima delle nove, perché il babbo torna tardi dal lavoro.

4   I nostri vicini stanno cenando nel giardino.

5   Che cosa mangi di solito per colazione?

ALL IN ONE REVISION

1 Guarda queste immagini. Scrivi che cosa sono questi luoghi.

 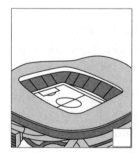  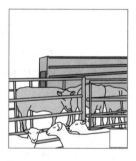

1 ....   2 ....   3 ....   4 ....

2 Adesso ascolterai una guida turistica che si rivolge ad alcuni turisti su un autobus. Sta spiegando quali luoghi d'interesse possono vedere nella città.
Ascolta e segna (✔) i luoghi che vedono, tra quelli indicati nell'esercizio 1.

1.2

3 Ascolta di nuovo e completa le frasi seguenti.

1.3

1   Our tours .usually last. about one hour.

2   The bus .... into Queens Road.

3   We .... the City Theatre.

4   This Cititour bus .... along the High Street into the market place.

5   At the moment some musicians .... for an outdoor concert there.

17

4 La guida usa a volte *have* e a volte *have got* davanti a un sostantivo. Leggi le parole nel riquadro e scrivile nella colonna giusta.

| a good time   a map   a sore throat   a new entertainment centre   a cinema |
| air-conditioning   good shops   a walk   lunch |

have	have got
a good time	

5 Il brano seguente è tratto dalla lettera di uno studente a un amico (*penfriend*). Completa gli spazi con il *present simple* o *present continuous* dei verbi tra parentesi.

Dear Pam

(1) ......I'm...... (*I / be*) a university student. As it's holiday time now, **(2)** .... (*I / work*) in a hotel. At the end of every term **(3)** .... (*I / come*) back to my home town and **(4)** .... (*I / get*) a job in this hotel to earn money.

This summer **(5)** .... (*I / share*) a room in the hotel with another girl.

(6) .... (*It / not be*) as comfortable as my parents' house, but **(7)** ....

(*I / prefer*) it, because **(8)** .... (*I / not want*) to travel home late at night. So this year

(9) .... (*I / save*) more money and **(10)** .... (*I / get*) more sleep.

6 Scegli la frase corretta.

1 **a** My brother lives with us until he can find a flat of his own.
   b My brother is living with us until he can find a flat of his own. ✔

2 **a** Megan goes to Hong Kong every January.
   b Megan's going to Hong Kong every January.

3 **a** I don't have enough money for a long holiday this year.
   b I'm not having enough money for a long holiday this year.

4 **a** Everyone needs a break from work sometimes.
   b Everyone is needing a break from work sometimes.

5 **a** What period of history do you study this term?
   b What period of history are you studying this term?

7 Riempi gli spazi coniugando il verbo tra parentesi al *present simple* o al *present continuous*.

1 My father ....knows....... (*know*) all about mending cars, but nothing about bicycles.

2 **Alex:** Why .... (*you wear*) my coat?

   Ben: Oh, I'm sorry. It .... (*look*) like mine in this light.

3 This pie .... (*smell*) a bit odd. What's in it?

4 I .... (*like*) the jacket of this suit, but unfortunately the trousers ....

   (*not fit*) me any more.

5 You're very quiet this evening. What .... (*you think*) about?

6 Carl: I .... (*have*) no idea what this sentence .... (*mean*). Can you translate it?

Donna: No, sorry. I .... (*not understand*) it either.

7 Eddie: .... (*you see*) those men near the door? They .... (*look*) at us very strangely.

Fergus: Yes. You're right. .... (*you recognise*) them from anywhere?

Eddie: No, but they certainly .... (*seem*) to know us. They .... (*come*) across to speak to us.

8 Gina: What .... (*you do*) in the kitchen?

Hamid: I .... (*just make*) some coffee.

Gina: Well, go away. I .... (*not want*) your help. Our guests .... (*wait*) for their dessert, and you .... (*get*) in my way!

8 Inserisci negli spazi la forma corretta dei verbi nel riquadro.

behave	come	cost	eat	enjoy	feel	go	have	have	have
like	love	realise	say	serve	show	smile	stay	take	visit

Dear Stephanie,

How are you? We're fine. Our trip round the States **(1)** ....is going..... well and we **(2)** .... ourselves very much. One good surprise is that things **(3)** .... less here than back home. For example, this weekend we **(4)** .... in a motel beside a lake. We **(5)** .... a room with a beautiful view for only $35 per night. The only thing we **(6)** .... (*not*) much is the food. Restaurants **(7)** .... dinner rather early. We **(8)** .... (*never*) at six o'clock at home so we **(9)** .... (*not*) hungry then and Americans **(10)** .... very big meals. Apart from that, we **(11)** .... a wonderful time. We **(12)** .... lots of interesting little towns and we **(13)** .... the scenery.

People here **(14)** .... in a very friendly manner towards strangers, all the shop assistants **(15)** .... at us, and everyone **(16)** .... 'Have a nice day!' At home, the TV **(17)** .... (*always*) us bad news stories about the States, but in fact, when you **(18)** .... here, you **(19)** .... it's a really great place.

We **(20)** .... lots of photos to show you.

Much love,

Mick and Mary

9 Scrivi cinque frasi personali, usando le espressioni nel riquadro e un verbo appropriato alla forma corretta.

before breakfast	every day	most weekends	once a year	right now	this term

1 I'm doing my homework right now, and I'm listening to a CD. ....

2 ....

3 ....

4 ....

5 ....

6 ....

I TEMPI DEL PASSATO (1)

2.1   Il *past simple*: *to be*

2.2   Il *past simple*: forma affermativa – verbi regolari e irregolari

2.3   Il *past simple*: forma negativa e interrogativa

2.4   Il *past simple*: quando si usa

2.5   Avverbi ed espressioni di tempo

2.6   Il *past continuous*: forma affermativa, negativa e interrogativa

2.7   Il *past simple* vs il *past continuous*

2.1   IL *PAST SIMPLE*: *TO BE*

Affermativa	Negativa	Interrogativa
I **was**	I **was not** (**wasn't**)	**Was** I …?
you **were**	you **were not** (**weren't**)	**Were** you …?
he/she/it **was**	he/she/it **was not** (**wasn't**)	**Was** he/she/it …?
we **were**	we **were not** (**weren't**)	**Were** we …?
you **were**	you **were not** (**weren't**)	**Were** you …?
they **were**	they **were not** (**weren't**)	**Were** they …?

+ *I was there.*

? *Were you there?*

– *They weren't there.*

Il verbo **to be** ha due forme al *past simple*: **was** e **were**. In italiano queste forme vengono tradotte comunemente con l'imperfetto; altre volte con il passato prossimo o il passato remoto.

*It **was** very hot yesterday.*	***Era/Faceva** molto caldo ieri.*
*John **wasn't** at school this morning.*	*John **non era** a scuola stamani.*
***Were** you in London last week?*	***Eri / Sei stato** a Londra la settimana scorsa?*

PRACTICE

1   Inserisci *was* o *were* negli spazi.

1   Who ...~~was~~.... your favourite singer when you ...~~were~~... a teenager?

2   When I .... your age children .... more respectful.

3   There .... a bus strike yesterday so the traffic .... awful.

4   I .... absent yesterday. .... there any homework?

5   When my grandmother .... young most women .... housewives.

6   .... there any calls for me while I .... out?

7   50 years ago there .... no hotels here and the beach .... clean.

8   I don't know why she .... so upset. It .... only a joke!

2 Riordina queste parole in modo da formare frasi di senso compiuto.

1 any / morning / there / post / this / wasn't / . ...There wasn't any post this morning..........

2 at / because / the / wasn't / ill / party / Sue / she / was / . ...

3 the / there / concert / many / at / weren't / people / . ...

4 teachers / were / primary / school / your / strict / ? ....

5 was / the / man / Armstrong / on / the / first / Moon / . ...

6 student / wasn't / very / Einstein / a / school / good / at / . ...

3 Completa il brano con il *past simple* del verbo *to be*.

LONDON IN THE EIGHTEENTH CENTURY

Life in London at the beginning of the eighteenth century **(1)** ...wasn't... easy. The city

(2) .... crowded and dirty and sanitation **(3)** .... non-existent. The streets

(4) .... safe because there **(5)** .... a lot of thieves and there **(6)** .... any

policemen. There **(7)** .... enough jobs either and people **(8)** .... very poor.

So why **(9)** .... there so many people in the city? Because life in the country **(10)** ....

even more difficult. It **(11)** .... difficult to find work.

2.2   IL *PAST SIMPLE*: FORMA AFFERMATIVA – VERBI REGOLARI E IRREGOLARI

Il *past simple* dei verbi **regolari** si forma aggiungendo il suffisso *-ed* alla forma base. I verbi terminanti in *-e* aggiungono solo *-d*. La forma è uguale per tutte le persone.

Affermativa		
I work**ed**	I phone**d**	*I phoned you.*
you work**ed**	you phone**d**	
he/she/it work**ed**	he/she/it phone**d**	*She worked in New York.*
we work**ed**	we phone**d**	
you work**ed**	you phone**d**	
they work**ed**	they phone**d**	*They phoned me at 2 o'clock.*

IL *PAST SIMPLE*: VARIAZIONI DI SPELLING

■ I verbi **monosillabi** terminanti in **c**onsonante **v**ocale **c**onsonante (**c v c**) **raddoppiano** la consonante finale: ***stop*** → ***stopped***.

■ **Raddoppiano** la consonante finale anche i **bisillabi** terminanti in **c v c**, a condizione che l'ultima sillaba sia accentata: *regret* → *regretted* mentre *visit* → *visited*.

■ I verbi terminanti in **-y** preceduta da **consonante** trasformano **y** in **i** e aggiungono *-ed*:

study → *studied*; *try* → *tried*.

Ma i verbi terminanti in **-y** preceduta da **vocale** aggiungono regolarmente *-ed*: *play* → *played*.

Molti verbi di uso comune sono **irregolari**. Questo significa che non formano il *past simple* aggiungendo *-ed*, ma hanno una forma propria, che va imparata caso per caso.

Verbi irregolari		
Forma base	*Past simple*	
have	had	*I **had** a temperature yesterday.* ***Avevo / Ho avuto** la febbre ieri.*
go	went	*Jen **went** to the cinema with her friends.* *Jen **è andata** al cinema con i suoi amici.*
buy	bought	*I **bought** a black sweater in the sales.* ***Ho comprato** un maglione nero ai saldi.*
make	made	*Mum **made** a chocolate cake for my birthday.* *La mamma **ha fatto** un dolce di cioccolata per il mio compleanno.*
swim	swam	*My brother **swam** in the lake.* *Mio fratello **ha nuotato** nel lago.*
think	thought	*I **thought** it **was** a good idea.* ***Ho pensato / Pensavo** che **fosse** una buona idea.*

Come si può vedere dagli esempi, il *past simple* si traduce comunemente con il passato prossimo o talvolta con l'imperfetto. Il *past simple* corrisponde anche al passato remoto, che però in italiano si usa quasi esclusivamente nelle narrazioni e nelle storie.

*A man and a woman **walked** into a bank and **asked** to speak to the manager.*
*Un uomo e una donna **entrarono** in una banca e **chiesero** di parlare col direttore.*

PRACTICE

1 Scrivi il *past simple* di questi verbi.

1 rob .....robbed.......   2 start ....   3 prefer ....   4 carry ....

5 open ....   6 offer ....   7 clean ....   8 fit ....

9 walk ....   10 agree ....   11 enjoy ....   12 die ....

2 Completa gli spazi con il *past simple* dei verbi nel riquadro.

take   see   lose   get up   spend   go   break   start   buy

1 We ...took... a lot of photos when we were on holiday.

2 I .... my car keys yesterday so I walked to work.

3 Elisa .... two months in California last summer.

4 I went shopping this morning and I .... this T-shirt.

5 Last winter I .... my leg in a car crash.

6 We're late. The film .... ten minutes ago.

7 When we .... to Paris we .... the Mona Lisa.

8 I'm tired because I .... early this morning.

3 Completa gli spazi con il *past simple* dei verbi nel riquadro.

be   begin   come   drink   eat   explain   feed
find   find   give   go   have   know   learn   meet   read
seem   speak   spread   start   tie   write

THE MYSTERY OF CASPAR HAUSER

The mystery of Caspar Hauser **(1)** .....began..... in Nuremburg, Germany, about 200 years ago. One morning, the people of the town **(2)** .... a young man standing alone in the square. He was holding a piece of paper in his hand. The paper **(3)** .... only that he **(4)** .... the son of a soldier. Caspar **(5)** .... how to say a few words and when given a paper and pencil he **(6)** .... his name, but he **(7)** .... completely ignorant about everyday life. At first he **(8)** .... only bread and **(9)** .... only water, but he gradually **(10)** .... to have ordinary meals. He also **(11)** .... to talk properly.

No one ever **(12)** .... out the real truth about his birth, but it is probable that his father kept him in one small room for the whole of his early life. He **(13)** .... him on bread and **(14)** .... him water to drink. He **(15)** .... Caspar up and Caspar never **(16)** .... out, he never

(17) .... to anyone or **(18)** .... other children. In spite of this extraordinary childhood, Caspar was not stupid. He **(19)** .... books and **(20)** .... discussions with teachers and philosophers. News about Caspar **(21)** .... through Europe and visitors **(22)** .... from abroad to meet him. Unfortunately, he lived only a few years, but his strange life story still fascinates many people.

2.3   IL *PAST SIMPLE*: FORMA NEGATIVA E INTERROGATIVA

Come abbiamo già visto a proposito del *present simple,* le frasi negative e interrogative in inglese richiedono un ausiliare: l'ausiliare del *past simple* è **did** (*past simple* di **do**). Il verbo è sempre alla forma base, **infinito senza *to***.

L'ausiliare **did** **non** si usa con **be**, **have got** e i **verbi modali**. (Vedi *Units* **13** e **14**)

Verbi regolari		Verbi irregolari	
Negativa	**Interrogativa**	**Negativa**	**Interrogativa**
I **did not (didn't) work**	**Did** I **work** …?	I **did not (didn't) go**	**Did** I **go** …?
you **did not (didn't) work**	**Did** you **work** …?	you **did not (didn't) go**	**Did** you **go** …?
he/she/it **did not (didn't) work**	**Did** he/she/it **work** …?	he/she/it **did not (didn't) go**	**Did** he/she/it **go** …?
we **did not (didn't) work**	**Did** we **work** …?	we **did not (didn't) go**	**Did** we **go** …?
you **did not (didn't) work**	**Did** you **work** …?	you **did not (didn't) go**	**Did** you **go** …?
they **did not (didn't) work**	**Did** they **work** …?	they **did not (didn't) go**	**Did** they **go** …?

*Your mobile phone **was** on but you **didn't answer**.*
*Why **didn't** you **answer**?*

*Il tuo cellulare **era** acceso ma **non hai risposto**.*
*Perché **non hai risposto**?*

PRACTICE

1 Riscrivi le frasi alla forma negativa, utilizzando le parole fra parentesi.

1 I talked to Sam at the party. (*Tom*) .... I didn't talk to Tom at the party. ....

2 We drank coke with our pizzas. (*water*) ....

3 She studied French at school. (*English*) ....

4 John Lennon sang 'Imagine'. ('*Yesterday*') ....

5 I left my book at home. (*mobile*) ....

6 He had a shower this morning. (*bath*) ....

7 I enjoyed the book very much. (*film*) ....

8 We ate out yesterday evening. (*home*) ....

2 Scrivi cinque cose che **non hai fatto** ieri.

1 I didn't ....

3 Adesso chiedi a un tuo amico se ha fatto quelle cinque cose.

1 Did you…? ....

4 Guarda le immagini e usa i verbi nel riquadro per descrivere le differenze tra Alison **ora** e Alison **dieci anni fa**.

1

2

3

4

5

6

7

8

9

is	was	likes
liked	doesn't eat	didn't eat
goes	went	loves	loved	lives
lived	doesn't watch	didn't watch
can't	couldn't	rides	rode

1 Alison .....is...... tall and slim.   Alison ...was.... short and chubby.

2 She .... to college.   She .... to primary school.

3 She .... going for long walks.   She .... making sandcastles.

4 She .... junk food.   She .... vegetables.

5 She .... a scooter.   She .... a bike.

6 She .... with other students.   She .... with her parents.

7 She .... cook very well.   She .... cook at all.

8 She .... her boyfriend.   She .... her dog.

9 She .... cartoons.   She .... horror films.

5 Completa i seguenti mini-dialoghi.

1 **A** Do you like my new earrings? **B** They're lovely. ..*Where..did..you..buy..them*.. ? **A** At that new shop in the High Street.

2 **A** The journey was awful. **B** Really? .... ? **A** Four and a half hours!

3 **A** We went to Sardinia in August. **B** .... ? **A** In a campsite.

4 **A** John took his driving test yesterday. **B** .... ? **A** No, he didn't! He's really fed up.

5 **A** I had a long chat with Louise at the party. **B** Did you? .... ? **A** Her holiday, her new boyfriend… things like that.

6 **A** I'm afraid Nicky's not here. She's gone home. **B** .... ? **A** About half an hour ago.

2.4   IL *PAST SIMPLE*: QUANDO SI USA

Il *past simple* viene usato per parlare di:

■ **azioni ed eventi interamente conclusi**.

*We **had** an exam on Thursday.*   ***Abbiamo avuto/dato** un esame giovedì.*

■ **una sequenza** di azioni o di eventi.

*I **went** round the shops, then I **went** to the cinema.*   ***Ho fatto un giro** per i negozi, poi **sono andato** al cinema.*

■ situazioni **permanenti** o **di lungo termine** nel passato.

*I **spent** all my childhood in America.*   ***Ho trascorso** tutta l'infanzia in America.*

■ eventi **ripetuti** nel passato.

*My cousin Helen **fell in love** every summer.*   *Mia cugina Helen **si innamorava** ogni estate.*

PRACTICE

1 Leggi la cartolina e riempi gli spazi con il *past simple* dei verbi tra parentesi.

Hi Niki, We **(1)** *made* (*make*) a trip to Brighton last week. We **(2)** .... (*visit*) the Pavilion, and **(3)** .... (*see*) the nineteenth-century kitchen. I'm glad I **(4)** .... (*not work*) there in those days. The dining-room **(5)** .... (*be*) my favourite room. We **(6)** .... (*have*) coffee in the restaurant, then we **(7)** .... (*go*) for a walk by the sea and **(8)** .... (*eat*) some fish and chips for lunch. We **(9)** .... (*spend*) the afternoon shopping. We **(10)** .... (*find*) some funny little shops where we **(11)** .... (*buy*) some unusual clothes. **(12)** .... (*you/go*) anywhere interesting in the holidays? Love, Jenny.

2 Formula delle domande appropriate alle seguenti risposte. Utilizza le parole tra parentesi.

1 ....Where did you live when you were a child?.......... (*child*)
We lived in London until I was eight.

2 .... (*lottery*)
£500,000. He doesn't know what to do with it!

3 .... (*the weekend*)
Nothing special. I was really tired.

4 .... (*the film*)
I thought it was really exciting.

5 .... (*your leather jacket*)
In January in the sales.

6 .... (*his job interview*)
A suit and tie. He was very smart!

7 .... (*Milan*)
I went by train. It doesn't take long.

8 .... (*university*)
Because when I left school I wanted to start work straight away.

3 Leggi questo brano, poi formula domande appropriate alle risposte date.

> In March 1988 Helen Thayer, a 50-year-old nurse from New Zealand, set out from Resolute, in the N.W. Territories to ski to the North Pole – a distance of 582 km. Three days before her departure a local hunter gave her a black husky called Charlie to protect her on her difficult journey. The animal in fact saved her life on more than one occasion. Thayer fought polar bears, nearly drowned when she fell through the ice and survived terrible storms. Near the end of her journey a particularly bad storm blew away nearly all her food. During the last week all she had was a handful of walnuts and less than a litre of water a day. It took her 27 days to reach the Pole. On April 5th a plane picked her and Charlie up and took them back to civilisation.

1 When did Helen Thayer set out from Resolute?...... In March 1988.
2 .... She skied.
3 .... A black husky called Charlie.
4 .... Polar bears.
5 .... Because she fell through the ice.
6 .... A storm blew it away.
7 .... Less than a litre.
8 .... 27 days.

2.5   AVVERBI ED ESPRESSIONI DI TEMPO

Il *past simple* si usa spesso per indicare il momento o il periodo preciso in cui si sono verificati determinati eventi o azioni. In questi casi, il *past simple* è accompagnato da espressioni di tempo quali:

yesterday	*last night*	*10 minutes ago*	*in 2005*	*at 9 o'clock*	*in January*
	last month	*3 weeks ago*			*in September*
	last year				
	last summer				
	last Saturday				

Si usa il *past simple* nelle domande introdotte da **When**… *?* e **What time**… *?*

When **did** *Joe* **arrive**? (**Non** ~~When has Joe arrived?~~)   *Quando* **è arrivato** *Joe?*
He **arrived** *yesterday afternoon.*   **È arrivato** *ieri pomeriggio.*

PRACTICE

1 Completa le frasi seguenti con un'espressione di tempo appropriata nel riquadro.

> a few minutes ago   ~~in 1616~~   at 7.30   on Christmas Day   last August
> 50 years ago   yesterday evening   in February

1 Shakespeare died ....in 1616............ .

2 I went to Corsica ....

3 I woke up this morning ....

4 We went skiing for a week ....

5 Your wife phoned ....

6 There were no computers ....

7 Josh went out with Charlotte ....

8 We didn't eat turkey ....

2 Traduci.

1 Jenny non è andata a scuola la settimana scorsa perché aveva la febbre e il mal di gola.

2 **A** Quando sono partiti i tuoi amici?   **B** Sono partiti due ore fa.

3 **A** A che ora sei tornato ieri notte?   **B** Sono tornato a mezzanotte.

4 Ho incontrato Peter in palestra ieri. Mi ha detto che voleva chiamarti, ma poi se ne è dimenticato.

5 **A** Che cosa hai fatto domenica scorsa?   **B** Niente di speciale. Sono stata a casa e ho guardato la TV.

6 William Shakespeare scrisse *Romeo and Juliet* nel 1595. Fu il suo primo grande successo.

7 Non abbiamo giocato a tennis mercoledì scorso perché è piovuto tutto il giorno.

8 **A** Sono andato al cinema ieri sera.   **B** Che film hai visto?

2.6   IL *PAST CONTINUOUS*: FORMA AFFERMATIVA, NEGATIVA E INTERROGATIVA

Il *past continuous* si forma con l'ausiliare **was/were** e la forma **-ing** del verbo.

Affermativa	Negativa	Interrogativa
I **was** wait**ing**	I **was not** (**wasn't**) wait**ing**	**Was** I wait**ing** …?
you **were** wait**ing**	you **were not** (**weren't**) wait**ing**	**Were** you wait**ing** …?
he/she/it **was** wait**ing**	he/she/it **was not** (**wasn't**) wait**ing**	**Was** he/she/it wait**ing** …?
we **were** wait**ing**	we **were not** (**weren't**) wait**ing**	**Were** we wait**ing** …?
you **were** wait**ing**	you **were not** (**weren't**) wait**ing**	**Were** you wait**ing** …?
they **were** wait**ing**	they **were not** (**weren't**) wait**ing**	**Were** they wait**ing** …?

Il *past continuous* viene usato fondamentalmente per descrivere azioni che **erano in corso di svolgimento** nel momento o periodo del passato di cui si sta parlando. Corrisponde in genere all'**imperfetto** italiano, ma può anche essere tradotto con **stavo/stavi** … e il **gerundio**.

*At 3 o'clock in the morning Hermione **was** still **studying**.*
*Alle 3 di notte Hermione **studiava** ancora / **stava** ancora **studiando**.*

■ I verbi di stato, che come abbiamo visto non hanno la forma continua, **non** sono usati al *past continuous*.

*I **didn't know** him.* (**Non** ~~I wasn't knowing him.~~)   *Non lo **conoscevo**.*

PRACTICE

1 Ieri Tanya e suo fratello Tony hanno dato una festa. Leggi gli appunti e scrivi delle frasi con i verbi al *past continuous* per mostrare come si sono preparati per la festa.

	Tanya	Tony
10 am	make a shopping list	email their friends
1 pm	buy the drinks	choose the music
3 pm	tidy the house	prepare the food
6 pm	blow up the balloons	decorate the rooms
7 pm	iron her dress	have a shower

1 At ten o'clock ......Tanya was making a shopping list and Tony was emailing their friends........

2 At one o'clock ....

3 At three o'clock ....

4 At six o'clock ....

5 At seven o'clock ....

2 Descrivi quello che queste persone indossavano ieri all'Inaugurazione di una galleria di arte moderna, scegliendo tra le parole elencate nel riquadro.

boots   bow tie   dark glasses   dress   earrings   fur coat
gold watch   high heels   jeans   leather jacket   tie
mini-skirt   necklace   raincoat   silk scarf   suit   T-shirt

1 Lara *was wearing a mini-skirt.*
....

2 Sid ....
....

3 Paul ....
....

4 Helen ....
....

2.7   IL *PAST SIMPLE* vs IL *PAST CONTINUOUS*

Si usa il *past simple* per indicare:

■ un'azione **completamente finita** nel passato. L'azione può essere **di durata breve**

*At 8.30 I **sat down**.*
Alle 8.30 mi sono seduta.

oppure di **durata lunga**.

*I **studied** Medicine at University.*
Ho studiato medicina all'Università.

■ due o più azioni **in sequenza**.

*I **had** a quick breakfast, then I **went** to work.*
Ho fatto una colazione veloce, poi **sono andata** al lavoro.

■ **azioni ripetute** o **abituali** nel passato.

*I **phoned** you six times.*
*Ti **ho telefonato** sei volte.*
*We always **went** skiing in winter.*
Andavamo sempre a sciare d'inverno.

Si usa il *past continuous* per indicare:

■ un'attività **in corso** intorno **a un momento** del passato.

*At 9 o'clock I **was sitting** in the cinema.*
Alle 9 ero seduto al cinema.
*8.30 ... I was sitting in the cinema ... **9.45***

—

9 o'clock

■ due azioni **in corso allo stesso tempo** nel passato (spesso con **while** o **and**).

*I **was listening** to music **while** my brother was studying.*
Ascoltavo della musica **mentre** mio fratello **studiava**.
*I **was listening** to music.*
*My brother **was studying**.*

■ azioni **ripetute** nel passato, con un avverbio come **always** o **continually**, per esprimere critica o fastidio.

*Tim **was always playing** loud music.*
*Tim **suonava sempre** musica a volume altissimo.*

30

■ un'attività che **era in corso di svolgimento**, e che è **continuata**, quando si è verificato un **evento**. L'evento in questione è al *past simple.*

*When we **were queuing** for the cinema, we **saw** a really famous footballer.*
*Quando **eravamo** in coda davanti al cinema **abbiamo visto** un calciatore famosissimo.*
*We **were queuing**.*
*We **saw** a footballer.*

PRACTICE

1 Completa ogni frase con un verbo nel riquadro **A** al *past continuous* e un verbo nel riquadro **B** al *past simple.*

A

cook	dance	stay	study
	tidy	work	

B

burn	meet	fall	paint
	play	discover	

1 I ..was..dancing.. with my boyfriend when the disc jockey .....played..... our favourite song.

2 My parents .... in a restaurant when they ....

3 I .... grammar when I .... asleep.

4 The chef ...was..cooking........ spaghetti when he ...burned.... his hand.

5 The artist .... in the South of France when she .... her most famous picture.

6 The scientist .... his laboratory when he .... the new drug.

2 Leggi questa email e <u>sottolinea</u> l'alternativa corretta: *past simple* o *past continuous.*

Hi Bea

A funny thing **(1)** <u>*happened*</u> / *was happening* to me and my flatmates on Saturday.

On Friday night we **(2)** *went* / *were going* to the college party. There were some new students there and we **(3)** *met* / *were meeting* someone called Lucas. We **(4)** *invited* / *were inviting* him to Sunday lunch. It was a great party so we **(5)** *didn't go* / *weren't going* home until three o'clock.

Of course, we **(6)** *didn't get* / *weren't getting* up early on Saturday morning. At half past twelve I **(7)** *watched* / *was watching* TV in my pyjamas, Marie **(8)** *had* / *was having* a shower and Wendy **(9)** *read* / *was reading* a magazine. Suddenly someone **(10)** *rang* / *was ringing* the doorbell. I **(11)** *looked* / *was looking* out of the window to see who was there. Lucas **(12)** *stood* / *was standing* on the step. I **(13)** *went* / *was going* to the door but I **(14)** *didn't open* / *wasn't opening* it. I said 'Hello?' and he said 'Hello, I've come for lunch.' Oh no! He'd got the wrong day!

We **(15)** *got* / *were getting* dressed in three minutes! Luckily we **(16)** *had* / *were having* enough food, and he seemed to enjoy it. How was your weekend? Love Annette

3 Leggi questo articolo di giornale e coniuga i verbi tra parentesi al *past simple* o al *past continuous*.

An honest customer

Yesterday Jon Atkins **(1)** ......*went*........ (*go*) into Harpers' Art Gallery at the end of the afternoon. He **(2)** .... (*want*) to buy a present for his mother. It **(3)** .... (*be*) nearly closing time and owner Michael Harper **(4)** .... (*count*) the money. Quickly Jon **(5)** ....(*choose*) a small picture and Mr Harper **(6)** .... (*wrap*) it for him. While he **(7)** .... (*wait*) for his bus, Jon **(8)** .... (*decide*) to look at the picture again. In the parcel he **(9)** .... (*find*) £500 in cash as well as the picture. He **(10)** .... (*run*) back to the shop. It was closed so Jon **(11)** .... (*look*) through the window. Michael Harper **(12)** .... (*search*) under the counter, and his assistants **(13)** .... (*look*) in all the cupboards and drawers. 'I **(14)** .... (*knock*) on the window and **(15)** .... (*wave*) the money at them,' said Jon.

'I was so happy,' said Mr Harper. 'It's wonderful to know that there are honest people like Jon.'

ALL IN ONE REVISION

1 Guarda queste tre immagini di Donny. Dove si trova?

2 Ascolta la registrazione e verifica se avevi ragione.

1.4

What news does Donny tell his mother?

3 Ascolta di nuovo e rispondi alle seguenti domande.

1.5

1 What did Donny's mother do at eight o'clock? ....

2 Why didn't he answer his phone? ....

3 What did she do at nine o'clock? ....

4 Why wasn't his phone switched on? ....

5 What did she do at ten o'clock? ....

6 Why didn't he answer his phone at ten o'clock? ....

🎧
1.6

Adesso ascolta un'altra volta per controllare se le tue risposte erano giuste.

4 Rileggi le tue risposte nell'esercizio 3 e rispondi a queste domande.

1 Which sentences contain the past simple? ....

2 Which sentences contain the past continuous? ....

3 Which sentences tell you about a past activity which continued for some time? ....

4 Which sentences tell you about a single event? ....

5 Sottolinea l'alternativa corretta: *past simple* o *past continuous*.

BOY, 11, DRIVES DAD'S NEW CAR

Yesterday evening policemen **(1)** _stopped_ / *were stopping* a car in Banbury Road. The car **(2)** *went /
was going* at 50 mph in a 30 mph speed limit zone and **(3)** *did not have / was not having* its headlights
on. The driver of the car, who **(4)** *didn't wear / wasn't wearing* a seatbelt, was an 11-year-old local
schoolboy. When the police **(5)** *arrived / were arriving* at the boy's home his parents **(6)** *watched /
were watching* television. They **(7)** *thought / were thinking* that their son **(8)** *did / was doing* his
homework in his bedroom. 'My Dad **(9)** *bought / was buying* a new BMW and I just **(10)** *wanted / was
wanting* to try it out,' said the boy.

6 Completa gli spazi con il *past simple* o con il *past continuous* dei verbi fra parentesi.

1 My parents .... got .... (*get*) to know each other when they ...were studying... (*study*) at
university.

2 I .... (*see*) my brother and his girlfriend when I .... (*wait*) for the
bus, but they .... (*not see*) me.

3 Lily .... (*fill*) in the application form and .... (*give*) it to the
receptionist.

4 While I .... (*work*) in Rome, I .... (*meet*) a girl who
.... (*look*) just like your sister.

5 Simon .... (*finish*) with his girlfriend because she .... (*always
cancel*) dates at the last moment.

6 Anna's feeling depressed because she .... (*hope*) for a pay rise last week, but she
.... (*not get*) one.

7 Osserva l'immagine e completa il testo con verbi adeguati al *past continuous*.

When Emma arrived at her grandmother's 80th birthday party everybody else was already there. There were a lot of children at the party. Her niece Lucy **(1)** ...was showing... something to her grandmother, who **(2)** .... an amazing hat. Lucy's little brother Tom **(3)** .... under the table and **(4)** .... strawberries. Tom's cousin Josh **(5)** .... a hole in the flower bed and some other children **(6)** .... a tree. Most of the adults **(7)** .... large plates of food. Emma's brothers, Harry and George, **(8)** .... champagne and **(9)** .... rather angrily. They **(10)** .... about politics as usual. Emma's mother and aunt **(11)** .... on a bench in the shade. They **(12)** .... and Emma's mum **(13)** .... about something. Although everyone **(14)** .... a lot of noise, Emma's father **(15)** .... peacefully under a tree.

8 Inserisci nel testo i verbi elencati nel riquadro, coniugandoli al *past simple* o al *past continuous*.

feel	have to	fall	~~tie up~~	garden	ring	think	find	look up	try	arrive
		fish	dial	lose	be	answer				

LOCAL FISHERMAN FINDS WALLET

In July 1990 Alan Whitsitt lost his wallet while he **(1)** ...was tying up... his boat in Lychurch harbour. The wallet **(2)** .... out of his pocket into several metres of water and although Alan **(3)** .... to find it, a storm **(4)** .... and he **(5)** .... accept that his money was lost. Last week local fisherman Bob Goss **(6)** .... off Southby Point when he **(7)** .... a wallet in his nets. There was no money in it but the credit cards **(8)** .... still in good condition. Bob **(9)** .... Alan's number in the phone book. 'I **(10)** .... a bit worried while I **(11)** .... the number. I **(12)** .... maybe the owner of the wallet had died at sea, so I was very relieved when Alan **(13)** ....' Alan was of course delighted. 'I **(14)** .... when the phone **(15)** .... I couldn't believe the news! It was very kind of Bob to contact me. It's a pity about the money though. The day I **(16)** .... my wallet I had £200 in it which was quite a lot of money in those days!'

9 Traduci.

1 Tre studenti mangiavano un panino quando l'insegnante di francese è entrata in classe.
2 Ieri mattina la signora Chadwick ha fatto colazione e poi è andata al lavoro in macchina. Ha guidato con molta attenzione perché pioveva.
3 **A** Ti ho visto al supermercato, mentre facevi la spesa, ma tu non mi hai visto. **B** Perché non mi hai detto qualcosa? **A** Perché non avevo tempo. Il mio ragazzo mi stava aspettando fuori.
4 Mentre tornavo a casa ho visto un incidente. Una bambina è caduta mentre attraversava la strada e si è ferita alla testa.

I TEMPI DEL PASSATO (2)

3.1 Il *present perfect simple*

3.2 Il *present perfect simple* con *just, already, still, yet, ever, never*

3.3 *Have gone* e *have been*

3.4 Il *present perfect simple* vs il *past simple*

3.5 Il *present perfect continuous*

3.6 Il *present perfect simple/continuous* con *for* e *since*

3.1 IL *PRESENT PERFECT SIMPLE*

Il termine *present perfect* indica la caratteristica principale di questo tempo: mettere in relazione un'azione passata con il presente. **Il momento preciso** in cui l'azione è avvenuta non è rilevante, quindi non viene specificato. Il *present perfect simple* corrisponde al passato prossimo italiano.

Il *present perfect simple* si forma con l'ausiliare **have/has** e il **participio passato** del verbo.

■ Nei verbi **regolari**, il participio passato è uguale al *past simple*: si forma quindi aggiungendo il suffisso **-ed** alla forma base del verbo.

Forma base	*Past simple*	Participio passato	
work	worked	worked	lavorato
arrive	arrived	arrived	arrivato

■ Nei verbi **irregolari**, il participio passato corrisponde alla 3ª voce del paradigma. Può avere la stessa forma del *past simple*:

Forma base	*Past simple*	Participio passato	
have	had	had	avuto
make	made	made	fatto
buy	bought	bought	comprato

oppure può avere una forma completamente differente:

Forma base	*Past simple*	Participio passato	
break	broke	broken	rotto
be	was/were	been	stato
go	went	gone	andato

Affermativa	Negativa	Interrogativa
I **have** (**'ve**) arrived	I **have not** (**haven't**) arrived	**Have** I arrived …?
you **have** (**'ve**) arrived	you **have not** (**haven't**) arrived	**Have** you arrived …?
he/she/it **has** (**'s**) arrived	he/she/it **has not** (**hasn't**) arrived	**Has** he/she/it arrived …?
we **have** (**'ve**) arrived	we **have not** (**haven't**) arrived	**Have** we arrived …?
you **have** (**'ve**) arrived	you **have not** (**haven't**) arrived	**Have** you arrived …?
they **have** (**'ve**) arrived	they **have not** (**haven't**) arrived	**Have** they arrived …?

*Look! John **has bought** a new car!*

*The dog **has eaten** the birthday cake!*

■ È importante notare che, mentre in italiano alcuni verbi, come i verbi di moto e il verbo essere, hanno l'ausiliare **essere**, in inglese il *present perfect simple* ha sempre e solo l'ausiliare *have*.

*Peter **has gone** to the cinema.*   *Peter **è andato** al cinema.*
(**Non** ~~Peter is gone~~)
*The train **hasn't arrived**.*   *Il treno **non è arrivato**.*
(**Non** ~~The train isn't arrived~~.)

PRACTICE

1 Tom è stato via per una settimana. Al suo ritorno viene aggiornato su quello che è successo durante la sua assenza. Guarda le immagini e completa ogni frase con un verbo nel riquadro.

| has left   have ~~broken~~   has had   has stolen   have received |

1 Tom, the neighbours' children
..have..broken.. a window.

2 Your girlfriend .... you.

3 Someone .... your car.

4 Your sister .... a baby.

5 You .... 300 emails.

2 Completa le frasi con il *present perfect* dei verbi tra parentesi.

1 She 's ......*written*...... to me from New York. (*write*)

2 I .... my exam! (*pass*)

3 I .... my right arm. (*break*)

4 He .... his car keys. (*lose*)

5 I .... to do my homework. (*forget*)

6 We .... to go to Paris this summer. (*decide*)

7 Tom .... his old scooter. (*sell*)

8 I .... all the irregular verbs. (*learn*)

3 Formula delle domande con il verbo al *present perfect*, usando i prompt.

1 you / read / *War and Peace* / ? .... *Have you read War and Peace?* ....

2 everybody / arrive / ? ....

3 you / spend / all your money / ? ....

4 she / see / this film before / ? ....

5 you /meet / Gill's brother / ? ....

6 your mother / speak / to the teacher / ? ....

7 Sean / reply / to your email / ? ....

8 you / choose / what to wear / this evening / ? ....

4 Completa i seguenti mini-dialoghi con il *present perfect* dei verbi nel riquadro.

not finish   go   not arrive   not take   buy   leave   book   drive

1 **A** Can I speak to Jane please? **B** I'm sorry she's not here. She ......*'s gone*....... to the gym.

2 **A** I don't think Julia's coming to the concert. **B** Yes, she is. She .... her ticket.

3 **A** Are we all here now? **B** No, Susie ....

4 **A** The pizzeria is usually full on Saturday evening. **B** Don't worry. We .... a table.

5 **A** I need to use the computer. **B** Can you wait a minute? I .... downloading this track.

6 **A** Give her a call and tell her we're late. **B** I can't. I .... my mobile at home.

7 **A** Where's my iPod? **B** I don't know. I .... it!

8 **A** You're looking a bit nervous. **B** It's the first time I .... on the motorway.

5 Rhiannon sta facendo i preparativi per un viaggio all'estero con la sua amica Ellen. Leggi la lista che ha scritto ieri sera e poi completa la email che ha inviato ad Ellen, coniugando i verbi al *present perfect*.

To do

photocopy passport ✔

collect travellers' cheques ✔

buy money belt ✔

check camera ✗

choose clothes ✔

pack rucksack ✗

phone Granny ✔

see my cousins and say goodbye ✔

find my address book!! ✗ Ellen look?

buy coach ticket ✗

Hi Ellen

Are you ready? I am, almost!

Today I **(1)** 've photocopied my passport , I **(2)** .... my travellers' cheques and I **(3)** .... a money belt. I **(4)** .... my camera, but I **(5)** .... my clothes. I **(6)** .... my rucksack. I can do that tomorrow. I **(7)** .... Granny and I **(8)** .... my cousins and I **(9)** .... goodbye to them. One problem: I still **(10)** .... my address book. **(11)** .... (you) .... for it in your flat? Phone me if you find it. I'm going to the coach station now because I **(12)** .... my ticket to the airport. See you tomorrow evening at the check-in desk!

XX R

3.2   IL *PRESENT PERFECT SIMPLE* CON *JUST, ALREADY, STILL, YET, EVER, NEVER*

Il *present perfect* si usa spesso con i seguenti avverbi indeterminati.

■ *just* = **appena**, per parlare di un evento che è avvenuto poco tempo prima di adesso.

   I've just met her.   *L'ho appena incontrata.*

Just è posto immediatamente prima del participio passato.

■ *already* = **già**. *Already* suggerisce che un'azione si è verificata prima di quanto ci si aspettasse.

   A *When's your brother coming?* **B** *He has already arrived.*
   A *Quando viene tuo fratello?* **B** *È già arrivato.*

Already è posto immediatamente prima del participio passato.

■ *still, yet* = **(non) ancora**, in frase negativa, per indicare che un evento atteso non si è verificato fino a questo momento.

   I still haven't dried my hair. (= it's wet)   *Non mi sono ancora asciugato i capelli.*
   I haven't dried my hair yet.   ”   (= sono bagnati)

Still è posto immediatamente prima dell'ausiliare *have*, *yet* dopo il verbo.

■ *yet* si usa anche nelle frasi interrogative, con il significato di **già**.

   Have the guests arrived yet?   *Sono già arrivati gli ospiti?*

■ *ever, never* = **mai**, per parlare di un'esperienza che ha avuto luogo (o **non** ha avuto luogo) in un periodo di tempo fino ad ora: → *up to now*.

   Have you ever eaten snails?   *Hai mai mangiato le lumache?*
   My mother has never flown.   *Mia madre non ha mai preso l'aereo.*

PRACTICE

1 Sottolinea l'alternativa corretta.

1 It's nearly midday and Harry _still_ / yet hasn't woken up.

2 Karen's only 20 but she's _already_ / still got her degree.

3 I've _ever_ / just seen Johnny Depp! I'm sure it was him.

4 Has the post arrived _yet_ / just? I'm expecting a letter.

5 I've _ever_ / never been to New York but I'd love to go.

6 **A** Do you want a coffee? **B** I've _already_ / yet had one, thanks.

7 Have you _still_ / ever been to New Zealand?

8 Haven't you finished reading that book _already_ / yet?

2 Inserisci l'avverbio tra parentesi nella posizione corretta.

A Have you been to Jo's house in the mountains? (_ever_)

Have you ever been to Jo's house in the mountains?

B Yes, I've been a couple of times. (_already_)

....

A I've come back. It was really amazing! (_just_)

....

B Have they put in electricity? (_yet_)

....

A No! I've spent a weekend without TV before. (_never_)

....

B I bet they haven't put in a phone either. (_still_)

....

A No! No phone, no TV, no internet, no microwave... Amazing!

3 Traduci.

1 La mamma ha appena fatto una crostata di frutta.

2 **A** Hai mai letto un romanzo in inglese? **B** Sì, ho letto _A Christmas Carol_ di Dickens.

3 Ho appena finito i compiti. Adesso posso uscire!

4 **A** Scusi, è già arrivato il volo da Edimburgo? **B** Sì, è appena atterrato.

5 Grazie per la tua bella cartolina da Capo Nord, Jack. L'ho appena ricevuta.

6 **A** Sei pronta? **B** Non ancora. Ho fatto colazione, ma non mi sono ancora vestita.

3.3   *HAVE GONE* E *HAVE BEEN*

Il verbo *go* ha due forme al *present perfect*: *have gone* e *have been*.

He's been to the shops.
(= He went there and then returned home.)
È stato *a fare spese.*
(= C'è andato, poi è tornato a casa.)

She's gone to the city centre.
(= She went there and she's there now.)
È andata *in centro.*
(= C'è andata, ed è ancora là.)

Come si vede dall'esempio, *have been (to)* significa 'essere **stati** in un posto' ed essere ritornati, mentre *have gone (to)* significa 'essere **andati** in un posto' ed essere **ancora via**. Per questo motivo, *have/has gone* si usa solo con soggetti alla 3ª persona singolare e plurale.

PRACTICE

1 Sottolinea l'alternativa corretta.

1   **A** Can I speak to Louise, please? **B** I'm afraid she's just *gone* / *been* out.

2   **A** There's no milk! **B** I've already *gone* / *been* to the supermarket. I'm not going again.

3   He often has toothache but he hasn't *been* / *gone* to the dentist's for two years.

4   Mum's *gone* / *been* to pick up Luke from school. She'll be back soon.

5   Nick's having a shower because he's just *gone* / *been* jogging.

6   It's so quiet. The neighbours have *gone* / *been* on holiday.

7   Daisy's really brown. She's just *been* / *gone* to the Maldives.

8   You can't go to the cinema tonight. You've already *gone* / *been* twice this week.

2 Traduci.

1   **A** Sei mai stato all'estero? **B** Sì, sono andato a Madrid l'estate scorsa.

2   Jasmine è stata in vacanza. È appena tornata dai Caraibi.

3   **A** Non vedo Mike. Dov'è? **B** È andato all'ufficio postale e non è ancora tornato.

4   Ho ricevuto una cartolina da mia cugina. Adesso è a New York. È stata a San Francisco e a Los Angeles.

5   I miei genitori non sono a casa. Sono andati al supermercato.

3.4   IL *PRESENT PERFECT SIMPLE* vs IL *PAST SIMPLE*

A differenza dell'italiano, in cui si usa quasi sempre il passato prossimo per parlare di azioni concluse nel passato, in inglese il *present perfect* e il *past simple* sono usati in modo diverso.

Si usa il *present perfect*, **non** il *past simple*:

■ per eventi accaduti nel passato, quando non è importante il momento preciso, ma il **risultato nel presente**.

*They **have moved** to another town.*
***Si sono trasferiti** in un'altra città.*
*The bus **has arrived**.*
***È arrivato** l'autobus.*

■ con espressioni che indicano un **periodo di tempo non terminato**.

*The builders **have started** working on the kitchen **this week**.*
*I muratori **hanno cominciato** a lavorare alla cucina **questa settimana**.*
(= la settimana non è finita)

*I've **spent this morning** writing an essay.*
(= it's still morning)

***Ho passato la mattina** a scrivere una relazione.* (= è ancora mattina)

■ quando si riporta un **fatto nuovo**.

*I've **found** your glasses.*
***Ho trovato** i tuoi occhiali.*

*I've **read** The Lord of the Rings.*
***Ho letto** Il Signore degli Anelli.*

■ per azioni iniziate nel passato e che continuano nel presente, spesso con *for* e *since*. (Vedi **3.6**)

*I've **worked** there **for** two months.*
***Lavoro** là **da** due mesi.*

Si usa il *past simple*, **non** il *present perfect*:

■ per eventi accaduti in un **momento preciso** del passato.

*They **moved in July**.*
***Si sono trasferiti a luglio**.*
*The bus **arrived at 6**.*
*L'autobus **è arrivato alle 6**.*

■ con espressioni che indicano un **periodo di tempo terminato**.

*I **started** my essay **last week**.*

***Ho iniziato** la mia relazione **la settimana scorsa**.* (= la settimana scorsa è completamente finita)

*I **spent this morning** writing an essay.*
(= it's now afternoon, so this morning is in the past)
***Ho passato la mattina** a scrivere una relazione.* (= adesso è pomeriggio)

*I **lost** my new camera **in London**.*
***Ho perso** la macchina fotografica nuova **a Londra**.* (= il riferimento di luogo situa l'azione in un periodo finito)

■ quando si danno o si chiedono **ulteriori dettagli** sul fatto in questione.

*Great! **Where did you find** them?*
*Fantastico! **Dove li hai trovati**?*

*Did you **like** it?*
***Ti è piaciuto**?*

■ per azioni iniziate e terminate nel passato, spesso con *for*.

*She **worked** at the cinema **for** ten months.*
(= but she doesn't work there now)
***Ha lavorato** al cinema **per** dieci mesi.*
(= ma adesso non ci lavora più)

■ con domande introdotte da **How long** …?
quando l'azione continua nel presente.

*How long **have** you **lived** here?*
(= I know you still live here)
***Da quanto tempo abiti** qui?*
(= so che abiti ancora qui)

■ con domande introdotte da **What time** …?
e **When** …?

*When **did** you **move** here?*
(= the move is in the past)
***Quando ti sei trasferito** qui?*
(= ti sei trasferito nel passato)

Il *present perfect simple* si usa anche:

■ con **it's the first/second/third time**… per indicare quante volte una cosa si è ripetuta.

*This is **the first time** anyone **has complained**.*
***È la prima volta** che qualcuno **si lamenta**.*

Come si può vedere dall'esempio, in questo caso il *present perfect* si traduce in italiano con il presente.

■ dopo un superlativo.

*It's **the best** cup of coffee **I've had** here.*   ***È il miglior** caffè che **ho bevuto** qui.*

■ con gli avverbi **recently** e **lately**.

*I **haven't seen** Barbara **recently**.*   ***Non ho visto** Barbara **di recente**.*

PRACTICE

1 Decidi se le seguenti espressioni di tempo richiedono il *present perfect* (**PP**) o il *past simple* (**PS**).

1 last month ......(PS)......   **2** yesterday ....   **3** recently ....

4 when I was at University ....   **5** This is the second time ....

6 this year ....   **7** today ....   **8** ten minutes ago ....

9 yet ....   **10** in 1990 ....   **11** This morning (it's 5 pm) ....

2 Completa le frasi coniugando i verbi tra parentesi al *present perfect* o al *past simple*.

1 I ..ve been.. (*go*) to England three times. Last time I ...stayed... (*stay*) in Cambridge.

2 **A** .... you .... (*find*) your bag yet? **B** Yes, I .... (*leave*) it in the car.

3 **A** When .... you .... (*meet*) Dan? **B** I've .... (*know*) him for about a year now.

4 **A** .... you .... (*speak*) to Greta recently? **B** No, I .... (*not/see*) her for ages.

5 I never .... (*like*) Chinese food until I .... (*go*) to China.

6 This is the first time I .... (*fly*). I .... (*feel*) really nervous before we took off.

7 **A** How long .... you .... (*have*) that watch? **B** My parents .... (*give*) it to me for my birthday.

8 She .... (*change*) schools in September and she .... (*not/make*) many friends yet.

3 Un film ha appena vinto un premio. Ali, un giornalista, ha intervistato il regista, Mike, e la protagonista, per la sua rivista. Riempi gli spazi coniugando i verbi tra parentesi al *present perfect* o al *past simple*.

THE WINNING TEAM

Ali: How long **(1)** ...*have you known*... (*you/know*) each other?

Mike: We **(2)** .... (*meet*) two years ago.

Ali: And when **(3)** .... (*you/decide*) to make a film together?

Mike: Oh, very quickly.

Nika: We **(4)** .... (*begin*) filming immediately.

Mike: It was hard work, and seven months ago our money **(5)** .... (*run*) out.

Nika: That was frightening!

Mike: Yes. We **(6)** .... (*have*) to borrow a million pounds and of course, we **(7)** .... (*not pay*) it all back yet.

Ali: But now your film **(8)** .... (*win*) this prize, all your problems **(9)** .... (*disappear*).

Mike: I hope so.

Ali: And **(10)** .... (*you/plan*) your next film yet?

Nika: We want to make another film soon, but we still **(11)** .... (*not choose*) the story.

Ali: Well, congratulations on this one.

Mike: Thank you. Lots of people **(12)** .... (*help*) us last year and we want to thank everyone.

Nika: Because they're the best team in the world!

4 Riempi gli spazi con una parola o un'espressione del riquadro.

ever	for	~~just~~	how long	never	since	when	yet

1 I don't want to swim now because I've ....*just*........ had lunch.

2 My family has lived in this house .... thirty years.

3 Elena has .... played volleyball. She doesn't enjoy sport.

4 .... have you been a member of the swimming team?

5 I haven't seen my boyfriend .... last weekend.

6 .... did Zoe join the theatre company?

7 Have you .... worked in a shop before or is this your first job?

8 The boss hasn't arrived .... so we needn't start work.

5 Il tuo amico James è appena tornato da una vacanza. Scrivi un dialogo tra voi due seguendo le indicazioni date. Fai attenzione all'uso dei tempi: *present perfect* o *past simple*.

You
Saluta.
Di' che non l'hai visto recentemente.
Chiedi dove è stato.
Chiedi se si è divertito.
Chiedi che cosa ha fatto.
Chiedi se è stato a San Francisco.
Chiedi se ha fatto molte fotografie.

James
Risponde al saluto.
Risponde che è appena tornato da una vacanza.
Risponde che è stato in California.
Risponde che è stata una vacanza fantastica.
Risponde che ha fatto windsurf e ha preso il sole sulle spiagge di Carmel.
Risponde di sì: ha attraversato il Golden Gate Bridge e ha visitato il carcere di Alcatraz.
Risponde di sì e ti invita a casa sua a vederle.

3.5   IL *PRESENT PERFECT CONTINUOUS*

Come tutti i tempi inglesi, anche il *present perfect* ha due forme: *simple* e *continuous*.

Il *present perfect continuous* si forma con **have/has been** e la forma **-ing** del verbo.

Affermativa	Interrogativa	
I **have ('ve) been** driv**ing**	**Have** I **been** driv**ing** …?	+ *I **have been driving** all night.*
you **have ('ve) been** driv**ing**	**Have** you **been** driv**ing** …?	
he/she/it **has ('s) been** driv**ing**	**Has** he/she/it **been** driv**ing** …?	− *He **hasn't been working** hard.*
we **have ('ve) been** driv**ing**	**Have** we **been** driv**ing** …?	
you **have ('ve) been** driv**ing**	**Have** you **been** driv**ing** …?	? *How long **has she been dancing**?*
they **have ('ve) been** driv**ing**	**Have** they **been** driv**ing** …?	

Si usa di norma il *present perfect continuous* per parlare di azioni che sono cominciate nel passato e continuano fino al presente.

*I **have been studying** all morning. I need a break.*   *È tutta la mattina che **studio**. Ho bisogno di una pausa.*

A seconda del contesto, il *present perfect continuous* può significare che l'azione è ancora in corso di svolgimento, oppure che è terminata da poco tempo.

*The children **have been playing** happily all morning.*
*I bambini **hanno giocato** spensierati tutta la mattina.*
(= può voler dire che i bambini stanno ancora giocando oppure hanno smesso da poco)

■ Confronta: il *present perfect continuous* sottolinea **la durata dell'azione** nel tempo.

*I've been reading **all afternoon**.*	*Ho letto **per tutto il pomeriggio**. /* *È **tutto il pomeriggio** che leggo.*

Il *present perfect simple* sottolinea **il risultato dell'azione**.

*I've read **150 pages**.*	*Ho letto **150 pagine**.*

PRACTICE

1 Sottolinea l'alternativa corretta.

1 **A** How many foreign countries have you *been / been going* to?

   B About eight. I've *travelled / been travelling* all summer.

2 **A** Richard's *felt / been feeling* a bit depressed lately.

   B Not surprising. He's *failed / been failing* his exams and his girlfriend's *left / been leaving* him.

3 **A** Have you *finished / been finishing* your homework?

   B Nearly. I've *done / been doing* everything except the last exercise.

4 **A** Can you tell Matthew to get off the phone, Dad? He's *talked / been talking* for hours.

   B And he's *made / been making* about ten phone calls today!

5 **A** Your English has *improved / been improving* a lot recently.

   B My American cousin has *stayed / been staying* with us and he doesn't speak Italian.

6 **A** How long have you *learnt / been learning* English?

   B Five years. And I've *had / been having* five different teachers!

3.6   IL *PRESENT PERFECT SIMPLE/CONTINUOUS* CON *FOR* E *SINCE*

Sia il *present perfect simple* che il *present perfect continuous* si usano per esprimere **durata nel tempo**: azioni che sono iniziate nel passato e continuano nel presente.

I've been driving since 5 o'clock this morning.	**Sto guidando** *dalle 5 di mattina.*

Come si può vedere dall'esempio, quando esprime durata il *present perfect* si traduce in italiano con il presente.

La preposizione **da**, che si usa per esprimere durata in italiano, si traduce in inglese con *for* e *since*.

For indica un **periodo** di tempo.	*I've worked there **for two months**.* *Lavoro lì **da due mesi**.*

Since indica il **momento di inizio.**

*I've worked there **since April**.*
*Lavoro lì **da aprile**.*

Present perfect simple o **present perfect continuous**?

Alcuni verbi, come **live**, **study**, **learn**, **wait** e **work** possono essere usati indifferentemente nelle due forme: descrivono attività/azioni che di norma implicano un arco di tempo.

*Martin **has lived** / **has been living** in Australia for five years.*

*Martin **vive** in Australia da cinque anni.*

▦ Si usa il *present perfect simple*, **non** *continuous*:

con i **verbi di stato**, che si usano solo alla forma semplice.

I've known her since she was four years old.
*(**Non** I've been knowing)*

*La **conosco** da quando aveva quattro anni.*

nelle frasi negative.

*It **hasn't rained** for months.*
*I **haven't seen** Mark since last summer.*

***Non piove** da mesi. / Sono mesi che **non piove**.*
***Non vedo** Mark dall'estate scorsa.*

▦ La forma negativa del *present perfect continuous* si usa molto raramente, per negare/contraddire quello che è stato appena detto.

*I **haven't been watching** TV for hours. I only turned it on 10 minutes ago!*

*Non è molto che **guardo** la TV. (= non è vero che la guardo da molto tempo) L'ho accesa solo 10 minuti fa!*

▦ In tutti gli altri casi si tende a usare il *present perfect continuous*.

*How long **have you been watching** TV?*

*Da quanto tempo **guardi** la televisione?*

*Ann **has been playing** the piano since she was four.*

*Ann **suona** il pianoforte da quando aveva quattro anni.*

PRACTICE

1 Riempi gli spazi con **for** o **since**.

1 I've been waiting for Katie ......since....... nine o'clock.

2 I've had this doll .... I was three.

3 My aunt's been staying with us .... Christmas.

4 My elder sister's been living in Shanghai .... two years.

5 It's been snowing .... we got up this morning.

6 She hasn't stopped talking .... two hours!

7 I haven't seen Charlotte .... ages.

8 She hasn't been to school .... Monday.

2 Completa le frasi seguenti con il *present perfect simple* o *continuous* dei verbi nel riquadro e aggiungi *for* o *since*.

own   love   not see   stare

1 I ....haven't seen.... my aunt ......for....... years because she lives in Sweden.

2 That man .... at us .... we came in.

3 My family .... this house .... two hundred years.

4 I .... you .... the first day I met you!

3 Riscrivi le frasi seguenti usando il *present perfect simple* o *continuous* e le parole tra parentesi. A volte entrambe le forme sono possibili.

1 This is my car. I bought it six months ago. (*for*) ....I've had this car for six months.........

2 Rob is travelling in Asia. He left in July. (*since*) ....

3 I know Tim. I was six when I met him. (*since*) ....

4 I don't ride my scooter. I had an accident. (*since*) ....

5 I'm waiting for Anna. I arrived half an hour ago. (*for*) ....

6 I play the piano. I started five years ago. (*for*) ....

7 Maggie doesn't speak to me. I started going out with Jack. (*since*) ....

8 My parents are arguing. My father got home. (*since*) ....

4 Rispondi alle seguenti domande in modo personale.

1 How long have you known your best friend? ....

2 How long have you been learning English? ....

3 How long have you been studying at this school? ....

4 How long have you lived at your present address? ....

5 How long have you been awake today? ....

6 How long have you been doing these exercises? ....

5 *Present perfect* o *past simple*? Usa i prompt per formulare delle frasi al *present perfect* o al *past simple*. Aggiungi la preposizione corretta: *since*, *for*, *in* o *ago*.

1 My brother / be married / June. ....My brother has been married since June.........

2 My brother / get married / June. ....

3 I / have / this jacket / ages. ....

4 I / buy / this jacket / ages. ....

5 I / do hip hop / last year. ....

6 I / start hip hop / a year. ....

7 Robin / be in love with Julia / they were 13. ....

8 Robin / fall in love with Julia / 2006. ....

ALL IN ONE REVISION

1 James divide l'appartamento con sua sorella Annie. James sta dando una festa per il suo compleanno. Guarda le immagini e cerca di indovinare che cosa è successo.

2 Adesso ascolterai delle conversazioni durante la festa.

1.7

How does Garry know Annie? What happens at the end?

3 Ascolta di nuovo e completa le frasi seguenti.

1.8

1   I .... all the balloons up yet.

2   I still .... my hair.

3   I .... it this morning.

4   .... you two already .... ?

5   I .... there for two months.

6   I .... Annie last week at the cinema.

7   She .... there since April.

8   I .... in the cinema for you on Saturday.

9   But I .... just .... her!

10 She .... an hour ago.

4 Rileggi le tue risposte nell'esercizio 3 e rispondi a queste domande.

1   Which sentences are about an action or event in the past which is finished? Which tense is used?

2   Which sentences contain the words *yet, still, already* and *just*? Which tense is used?

3   Which sentences contain the words *for* and *since*? Which tense is used?

5 Leggi attentamente ogni coppia di frasi. Scrivi **S** se il significato è lo stesso e **D** se è differente.

1   Have you ever ridden a motorbike? / Have you ridden a motorbike recently? .....D.......

2   She's worked here since the summer. / She didn't work here after the summer. ....

3   I've been to London twice this year. / I've just come back from London. ....

4 This is the most expensive holiday I've ever had. /

I've never had such an expensive holiday before. ....

5 We've already seen this film. / We've seen this film before. ....

6 This is the second time I've visited Crete. / I've been to Crete once before. ....

6 Leggi il diagramma e completa il paragrafo su Joyce con la forma appropriata dei verbi tra parentesi: *past simple, present perfect simple* o *present perfect continuous*. Inserisci anche le preposizioni giuste: *for, since, in, from ... to, ago*. Poi, per analogia, completa i paragrafi su Emma e Sam.

					Joyce							
98	99	00	01	02	03	04	05	06	07	08	now	
											live in London	
											train to be a nurse	
											work at CC	
						X					get married	

Joyce, Emma and Sam all work at Charing Cross Hospital in London.

Joyce is a nurse. She **(1)** ...has been living... (*live*) in London **(2)** ....since...... 1999 when she **(3)** .... (*come*) to England from Ghana. She **(4)** .... (*had*) a job at Charing Cross Hospital **(5)** .... 2002. She **(6)** .... (*get*) married in 2005 and her son was born two years **(7)** ....

Emma's a surgeon. She **(8)** .... (*study*) Medicine at Bristol University **(9)** .... five years **(10)** ....1999 .... 2004. She **(11)** .... (*get*) her degree in 2004 and she **(12)** .... (*work)* at Charing Cross **(13)** .... then. She loves her work but she **(14)** .... (*not have*) a day off **(15)** .... six months!

Sam **(16)** .... (*do*) a degree in Art and design. When he **(17)** .... (*leave*) university he decided to become an art therapist. He **(18)** .... (*start*) his training course **(19)** .... September 2007. He **(20)** .... (*do*) work experience at Charing Cross **(21)** .... two months and has been working there full-time **(22)** .... then.

7 Abbina gli inizi delle frasi con le loro logiche conclusioni.

1 He's talked to her on the phone ..j..   **a** for years.

2 This summer the pool was only open .....   **b** on my way home from work yesterday.

3 The whole team felt exhausted .....   **c** since nine o'clock this morning.

4 The rent of my flat has gone up .....   **d** when the match finished.

5 She's had nothing to eat .....

6 I got very wet .....

7 I spent a month in Brazil .....

8 She's always enjoyed painting .....

9 I haven't had such a good time .....

10 The post arrived .....

e ever since she was very young.

f by 20 per cent this year.

g a few minutes ago.

h from April till September.

i in 1992.

j every night this week.

8 Completa le frasi con il *present perfect simple* o il *past simple* dei verbi tra parentesi.

1 This is only the second time I ....._'ve ever flown_...... (*ever fly*) in an aeroplane.

2 The child .... (*sleep*) from seven till seven without waking once.

3 Gabriella .... (*grow*) five centimetres since last month.

4 .... (*you learn*) to play chess when you were a child?

5 How long .... (*you have*) that bad cough?

6 The train .... (*just arrive*), so hurry and you might catch it.

7 I .... (*never see*) such a beautiful rainbow before.

8 I .... (*dream*) about a beautiful desert island last night.

9 On Sunday we .... (*meet*) outside the cinema as usual.

9 Riempi gli spazi con un verbo appropriato al *present perfect simple* o al *past simple*.

| Photos | Message board | Map |

Trip to Spain

I (1) ...._'ve been_................ here in Spain for two weeks now and I'm having a really good time.
When I (2) .... at the airport
I (3) .... very lonely.
But I (4) .... (*already*) some friends and I'm staying with a really nice family.
They (5) .... me to the seaside last weekend and we
(6) .... in the sea.
I really (7) .... it.
I (8) .... some Spanish but
I (9) .... (*not*) to any language classes yet – they start next week. It's now midnight and I need to go to bed as I (10) .... a very busy day.
I (11) .... shopping this morning and I (12) .... tennis this afternoon.
See you all in a month!
Richard

10 Leggi questa conversazione tra due persone in un centro sportivo. <u>Sottolinea</u> la forma più adatta del verbo.

Anna: Excuse me. **(1)** *We've waited* / <u>*We've been waiting*</u> to play tennis since 10.30. It must be our turn now. **(2)** How long *have you played* / *have you been playing*?

Tim: Since about 9.30. **(3)** *We've played* / *We've been playing* two sets so far this morning and **(4)** *we haven't finished* / *we haven't been finishing* the third yet. You'll have to wait or do something else.

Anna: But **(5)** *you've played* / *you've been playing* for more than two hours and it's our turn now.

Tim: I said you'll have to wait.

Anna: We're tired of waiting and we haven't got anything to do. **(6)** *We've read* / *We've been reading* the magazines we brought with us.

Tim: Why don't you do something else? **(7)** *Have you tried* / *Have you been trying* the swimming pool?

Anna: We don't want to swim, we want to play tennis.

Tim: Well, I always play on a Saturday morning. Anyway, **(8)** *we've already started* / *we've already been starting* the third set.

Anna: Oh well, it looks like we've got no choice, but **(9)** *we've booked* / *we've been booking* for next Saturday so you'll be unlucky then.

11 Traduci.

1   **A** Da quanto tempo suona il violino tua sorella? **B** Da quando aveva otto anni. Ha sempre amato la musica.

2   Mia nonna è in ospedale da lunedì scorso e io non sono ancora andata a farle visita.

3   **A** Da quanto tempo conosci Michael? **B** Lo conosco da circa dieci anni, da quando eravamo a scuola insieme.

4   I miei nonni si sono sposati subito dopo la guerra. Sono sposati da più di 60 anni.

5   **A** È mezz'ora che ti aspetto. Dove sei stata? **B** Scusa il ritardo. Sono appena tornata dalla palestra.

6   È tutto il giorno che lavori al computer. Non sei stanco?

I TEMPI DEL PASSATO (3)

4.1 Il *past perfect simple*
4.2 Il *past perfect simple* e il *past simple*
4.3 Il *past perfect continuous*
4.4 Il *past perfect continuous* vs il *past perfect simple*
4.5 *Used to* e *would*
4.6 *Used to* vs *be used to* vs *get used to*

4.1 IL *PAST PERFECT SIMPLE*

Il *past perfect* si usa quando stiamo già parlando del passato e vogliamo indicare un'azione avvenuta **prima** di un'altra anch'essa passata, quindi in un passato ancora anteriore.

Il *past perfect* si forma con l'ausiliare *had* e il **participio passato** del verbo.

Affermativa	Negativa	Interrogativa
I **had ('d)** painted	I **had not (hadn't)** painted	**Had** I **painted** …?
you **had ('d)** painted	you **had not (hadn't)** painted	**Had** you **painted** …?
he/she/it **had ('d)** painted	he/she/it **had not (hadn't)** painted	**Had** he/she/it **painted** …?
we **had ('d)** painted	we **had not (hadn't)** painted	**Had** we **painted** …?
you **had ('d)** painted	you **had not (hadn't)** painted	**Had** you **painted** …?
they **had ('d)** painted	they **had not (hadn't)** painted	**Had** they **painted** …?

Il *past perfect simple* corrisponde sia al **trapassato** italiano (prossimo e remoto) che al congiuntivo trapassato (per l'uso del congiuntivo, vedi *Units* **20** e **21**).

*When we arrived, the film **had** already **started**.*
*John was tired because he **had played** tennis for two hours.*

Quando siamo arrivati, il film **era** già **iniziato**.
John era stanco perché **aveva giocato** a tennis per due ore.

PRACTICE

1 Completa le frasi con il *past perfect simple* dei verbi tra parentesi.

1 When the bill arrived I realised I ...'d forgotten... (*forget*) my credit card.
2 I .... (*not/meet*) Paul before but we got on really well.
3 When I got to the shop they .... already .... (*sell*) the boots I wanted.
4 I .... never .... (*hear*) of the director before, but I really enjoyed the film.
5 I couldn't make a phone call because I .... (*not/charge*) my mobile.
6 **A** .... you ever .... (*see*) the man before? **B** No, never. He was a complete stranger.
7 The airline didn't tell us that they .... (*cancel*) the flight.
8 How long .... you .... (*have*) your car for when you sold it?

2 Completa questa email con i verbi tra parentesi, coniugandoli al *past perfect simple*.

Hi Billy

Well, I'm home from Africa. The late flight from Paris caused some problems at first but the holiday was great.

Because **(1)** ..we'd..never..visited.. *(never/visit)* that part of the world before,

(2) .... *(we/ask)* the holiday company to book us seats on the bus to the city centre to meet the tour manager. Our plane was an hour late and we ran through the airport to the car park but when we arrived the bus **(3)** .... *(just/leave)*. We got a taxi to the main square and found the company's local office, but the staff **(4)** .... *(already/go)* home for the day.

We **(5)** .... *(not/bring)* our mobiles, because they don't work in that country. At last we found a post office and luckily it **(6)** .... *(not/shut)* yet, so we called the company's head office in Canada. In ten minutes the tour manager was with us.

He **(7)** .... *(go)* to the airport to meet us, because he **(8)** .... *(realise)* our plane was late, but we **(9)** .... *(not/see)* him. Anyway, he took us to the hotel he **(10)** .... *(book)* for us and bought us dinner. So everything was fine in the end. And our trip to the jungle was amazing! I'll show you the photos when I see you.

XXXX Julie

3 Ieri è stata una serata no per Lucy. Le immagini mostrano che cosa è andato storto. Per ogni coppia di immagini, decidi in che ordine sono avvenuti i fatti, poi collegali usando **when**.

1

She arrived at the cinema.   The film started.

When Lucy arrived at the cinema
the film had already started

2

She came out of the cinema.   Someone stole her bike.

....
....

3

She got to the bus stop.   The last bus went.

....
....

4
 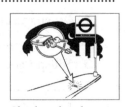

She finally arrived home.   She lost her keys.

....
....

4.2   IL *PAST PERFECT SIMPLE* E IL *PAST SIMPLE*

Si usa il *past perfect simple*:

■ quando stiamo già parlando del passato e vogliamo specificare che ci riferiamo a un periodo/evento **ancora precedente**.

*Last week I **visited** my home city.*	*La settimana scorsa **sono tornato** nella mia città*
*It **had changed** a lot.*	*natale. **Era cambiata** moltissimo.*

	The past	**The present**

←————————————————————————————→

earlier	*last week*	*now*
*It **had changed** a lot.*	*I **visited** my home city.*	*I am speaking now.*

■ con gli avverbi *just*, *already*, *ever* e *never*.

*I **had already decided** to become an engineer.* (**Non** *I already decided*)	***Avevo già deciso** di diventare ingegnere.*
*I'd **never seen** anything like it.* (**Non** *I never saw*)	*Non **avevo mai visto** niente del genere.*

 Just, *already*, *ever* e *never* vanno tra l'ausiliare e il verbo.

■ insieme a frasi **con when, after, by the time, as soon as** + *past simple*, per indicare che un evento è avvenuto **prima** dell'altro.

*When I **arrived**, Stefan **had finished** his work. = 1 He finished work; 2 (later) I arrived.*
***Quando** sono **arrivato**, Stefan **aveva finito** di lavorare.*

Le due azioni **sono indipendenti** l'una dall'altra.

Non si usa il *past perfect*, ma il *past simple* nei seguenti casi:

■ se due azioni accadono **allo stesso tempo**.

*When I **arrived**, Stefan **stopped** work. = I arrived and he stopped work at that time.*
***Quando** sono **arrivato**, Stefan **ha smesso** di lavorare.*

Le due azioni **sono** probabilmente **collegate**

■ se un'azione avviene immediatamente dopo l'altra ed è **collegata** all'altra.

*When Jill **heard** the baby cry, she **ran** to pick him up.* (**Non** *When Jill had heard*)
*Quando Jill **sentì** il bambino piangere **corse** a prenderlo in braccio.*

PRACTICE

1 Completa le frasi con il *past perfect simple* o il *past simple* dei verbi tra parentesi.

1 I ...'d... just ......*come*...... (*come*) home when the phone ......*rang*....... (*ring*).

2 He .... (*never/ski*) before so he .... (*fall over*) a lot.

3 When I .... (*get*) home my parents .... (*go*) to bed.

4 By the time he .... (*be*) 12 he .... already .... (*learn*) four languages.

5 As soon as he .... (*walk*) into the room, she .... (*know*) he was the man for her.

6 When I .... (*arrive*) at the airport I realised I .... (*not/bring*) my passport.

7 I .... (*read*) the book before seeing the film so I .... (*know*) who the murderer was.

8 When Lisa .... (*leave*) school she .... (*apply*) for a job in an advertising company.

2 In ognuna di queste frasi, uno dei verbi dovrebbe essere al *past perfect simple*. <u>Sottolinea</u> il verbo e scrivi la forma corretta in fondo.

1 I wanted to have a shower when I got home, but my sister <u>just had</u> a bath and there wasn't any hot water. *had..just..had..*

2 The concert started when we got to the theatre, so we missed the first two songs. ....

3 I couldn't tell my teacher about the film because I never saw it. ....

4 Freya didn't finish breakfast when I arrived, so I had a coffee while she ate her toast. ....

5 The children were very excited about flying because they were never in a plane. ....

6 Colin didn't know the poem but the other students already studied it. ....

7 We just visited Japan so we told our friends some good places to visit when they went there. ....

4.3 IL *PAST PERFECT CONTINUOUS*

Il *past perfect continuous* si forma con **had been** e la forma **-ing** del verbo.

Affermativa	Interrogativa	
I **had ('d) been** work**ing**	**Had** I **been** work**ing** ...?	+ *I'd been working hard.*
you **had ('d) been** work**ing**	**Had** you **been** work**ing** ...?	
he/she/it **had ('d) been** work**ing**	**Had** he/she/it **been** work**ing** ...?	− *She hadn't been working hard.*
we **had ('d) been** work**ing**	**Had** we **been** work**ing** ...?	
you **had ('d) been** work**ing**	**Had** you **been** work**ing** ...?	? *Had you been working hard?*
they **had ('d) been** work**ing**	**Had** they **been** work**ing** ...?	

Il *past perfect continuous* viene usato per parlare di azioni o situazioni prolungate nel tempo, che sono **continuate fino al momento del passato a cui ci riferiamo** o si sono concluse immediatamente prima.

When Jack found his sister, he could see that she **had been crying**.	*Quando Jack trovò sua sorella, vide che* **aveva pianto**.

PRACTICE

1 Riempi gli spazi con un verbo appropriato al *past perfect continuous*.

1 The phone .....*had been ringing*..... for several minutes before I heard it.

2 Katya .... (*not*) German with Mr Fauser for very long when he retired.

3 Liz didn't know about the surprise party which her parents .... for weeks.

4 I was very pleased when the bus finally arrived because I .... that I would be late for work.

5 When the doctor eventually called my name I .... for 40 minutes.

6 My brother lost his job because he .... jokes to everyone in the office by email.

7 The band .... (*not*) for long when the lights went out.

8 We .... our money to buy a car but we decided to go to Australia instead.

9 How long .... (*they*) for their keys when they found them in the boot of the car?

4.4   IL *PAST PERFECT CONTINUOUS* vs IL *PAST PERFECT SIMPLE*

Si usa il *past perfect* **continuous**:

■ per mettere in rilievo **l'azione precedente stessa** o **la sua durata**.

*He had a headache because he'**d been playing** computer games for hours.*
Aveva il mal di testa *perché* **aveva giocato** *al computer per ore.*

■ per indicare **per quanto tempo** è continuata un'azione fino al momento del passato di cui stiamo parlando.

***How long had** you **been driving** when the car broke down?*
Da quanto tempo guidavi *quando la macchina è rimasta in panne?*

*By the time she arrived I'**d been waiting** for two hours.*
Aspettavo *da due ore quando finalmente arrivò.*

Come si vede dagli esempi, in questo caso il *past perfect continuous* corrisponde generalmente all'imperfetto italiano.

Si usa il *past perfect* **simple**:

■ quando **non è necessario** mettere in rilievo **l'azione** o **la sua durata**.

*He'**d played** all of the computer games and wanted to do something different.*
Aveva fatto *tutti i giochi al computer e voleva fare qualcosa di diverso.*

■ per indicare **quante volte** si era verificata un'azione fino al momento del passato di cui stiamo parlando o con **quali risultati**.

*By the time I was 18 I'**d visited** Australia six times.*
A 18 anni **ero stata** *in Australia sei volte.*

*I'**d driven** six kilometres when the car broke down.*
Avevo percorso *sei chilometri quando la macchina è rimasta/rimase in panne.*

Molti verbi, come **live, study, learn, wait** e **work** possono essere usati nelle due forme, con una lieve differenza di significato.

*I **had been living** in London for six months when I decided to get a job in the United States.*

Vivevo *a Londra da sei mesi quando decisi di trovare un lavoro negli Stati Uniti.*
(= sottolinea una situazione temporanea)

*My parents **had lived** in London all their lives, but moved to the seaside when my father retired.*

I miei genitori avevano vissuto *a Londra tutta la vita, ma si trasferirono al mare quando mio padre andò in pensione.* (= sottolinea una situazione percepita come di lungo termine)

 I **verbi di stato** (vedi *Unit 1*) **non** si usano al *past perfect continuous*.

I'd known *her since she was four years old.*
(**Non** ~~I'd been knowing her~~)

La conoscevo *da quando aveva quattro anni.*

PRACTICE

1 Le frasi seguenti hanno tutte un verbo al *past perfect simple*. È possibile sostituirlo con il *past perfect continuous*?

1 I'd worked for the engineering company for three months before I realised my neighbour also worked there. ...Yes: I'd been working.....

2 As soon as George had finished the race, he drank three glasses of water. ....

3 Everything was white because it had snowed all night. ....

4 My parents were delighted when I qualified because they had always wanted me to be a doctor.
   ....

5 She was exhausted when she got out of the pool because she'd swum three kilometres.
   ....

6 We'd only just sat down when the waitress came to take our order. ....

7 I could tell from their faces that they had argued about something. ....

8 Our dinner wasn't cooked because I'd forgotten to switch the oven on. ....

2 Traduci.

1 L'insegnante mi rimproverò perché non avevo fatto i compiti.

2 I bambini giocavano nel giardino da un'ora quando iniziò a piovere.

3 Mary aveva lavorato tutto il giorno al computer, ecco perché aveva mal di schiena.

4 Vivevo in Inghilterra da due anni quando incontrai Tom.

5 Camminavamo da 20 minuti quando Martina inciampò e si slogò la caviglia.

6 Non giocavo a tennis da anni, così la prima partita è stata un disastro: ho perso 6-0.

4.5   USED TO E WOULD

Come abbiamo visto nella *Unit* **2**, quando si parla di azioni ripetute o abituali nel passato si usa generalmente il *past simple*.

*My father **went** to work by train.*   *Mio padre **andava** al lavoro in treno.*

Quando però si vuole sottolineare che una situazione o abitudine del passato **non è più vera** nel presente si usano ***used to*** e ***would***.

Used to (do)

Affermativa	Negativa	Interrogativa
I/you **used to** work	I/you **didn't use to** work	**Did** I/you **use to** work?
he/she/it **used to** work	he/she/it **didn't use to** work	**Did** he/she/it **use to** work?
we/you/they **used to** work	we/you/they **didn't use to** work	**Did** we/you/they **use to** work?

Would (do)

Affermativa	Negativa	Interrogativa
I/you **would** work	I/you **wouldn't** work	**Would** I/you work …?
he/she/it **would** work	he/she/it **wouldn't** work	**Would** he/she/it work …?
we/you/they **would** work	we/you/they **wouldn't** work	**Would** we/you/they work …?

*I **used to collect** all the autographs of film stars when I was a teenager.* (= I don't do this now)

*I **would go** up to town on my own.*
(= I don't do this now)

***Did** there **use to be** a field here?*
(= there isn't a field any more)

***Facevo collezione** di autografi di attori famosi quando ero una ragazzina.* (= ora non lo faccio più)

***Andavo** in città da sola.*
(= adesso non lo faccio più)

***C'era** un campo qui?* (= adesso non c'è più)

Used to e ***would*** vengono resi in italiano con l'imperfetto, per indicare che questa situazione è durata per mesi o per anni.

🔹 ***Used to*** si usa sia con i verbi di azione che con i verbi di stato, **mentre** *would* descrive **solo** azioni, quindi è meno comune.

*My grandmother **used to / would** often tell me stories about her childhood.*

Ma *I **used to love** the stories of Winnie the Pooh.* (**Non** ~~I would love~~)

*La nonna mi **raccontava** spesso storie della sua infanzia.*

*Mi **piacevano** tantissimo le storie di Winnie the Pooh.*

🔹 ***Used to*** **non** ha il presente: *I use to* **non** si può dire. Per parlare di abitudini nel presente si usa il *present simple* con un avverbio di frequenza o un'espressione di tempo.

I meet my friends on Saturday evenings.
(**Non** ~~I use to meet~~)

Vedo i miei amici il sabato sera.

PRACTICE

1 Riempi gli spazi in questa conversazione con la forma corretta di **used to** e un verbo del riquadro.

| be   not go   have   not have   ~~live~~   know   travel   walk |

Mina: There's Dahlia in her dad's sports car. Where do they get their money from?

Sara: Don't you know? Her family won the lottery.

Mina: Wow!

Sara: I knew her before that, though. Her family **(1)** ...used to live in our road... .

She **(2)** .... to school like all the other children in those days.

Mina: **(3)** .... (you) them very well?

Sara: Oh, yes. They **(4)** .... friendly people. And her father grew all their

vegetables because they **(5)** .... much money.

Mina: They go on holiday a lot now. **(6)** .... (they) abroad then?

Sara: No, they **(7)** .... away at all.

Mina: They're very lucky now.

Sara: Hmm, but they **(8)** .... more friends!

2 Completa ogni frase per indicare che cosa era differente nel passato. Usa la parola tra parentesi con **used to/didn't use to** + verbo, aggiungendo ogni altra parola necessaria.

1 Patrick .didn't use to take many photos. (*photos*) but he loves using his new camera.

2 You .... (*lazy*) but you're working very hard this term.

3 I .... (*slim*) but I've lost weight.

4 Bobby .... (*a bike*) but he drives a car now.

5 Bertie .... (*my brother*) but they've become friends recently.

6 Nora .... (*the cinema*) very often but she sees lots of films now.

7 My sister .... (*shy*) but she enjoys parties now.

8 We .... (*sport*) but we often play tennis these days.

9 Joanna .... (*a vegetarian*) but she had a sausage for breakfast.

10 They .... (*the city centre*) but their new house is in the country.

3 Scrivi cinque frasi vere su quando eri più giovane usando **used to/didn't use to** + verbo.

1 .I didn't use to do my homework on a computer...

4 Inserisci negli spazi *used to* o *would*, se necessario cambiando l'ordine delle parole. A volte entrambe le forme sono possibili. Usa *would* dove è possibile.

When I was a child I **(1)** ...used...to.. live in the country. Our house was about five miles from the village and I had to walk to school every morning. In summer I **(2)** .... enjoy the walk and I **(3)** .... often stop when I saw something interesting. But in winter I **(4)** .... like it at all. It was still dark when I set off and I **(5)** .... be frightened. I **(6)** .... always walk the long way round to avoid going through the dark woods. As a result I was often late for the first lesson. The teacher **(7)** .... always threaten to tell my mother, but she never did. I think she **(8)** .... feel a bit sorry for me. After school my father **(9)** .... give me a lift home on his bicycle. I **(10)** .... be so tired after my long day that I **(11)** .... sometimes fall asleep on the way. I never fell off though!

4.6 *USED TO* vs *BE USED TO* vs *GET USED TO*

Non bisogna confondere *used to*, che è un verbo del passato, con *be/get used to*, che possono indicare passato, presente o futuro. Quando *be/get used to* sono seguiti da un verbo, questo va alla forma *-ing*. In questo caso, infatti, *to* è una preposizione, **non** la particella dell'infinito.

I'm not used to getting up early.   ***Non sono abituato ad alzarmi*** *presto.*

Be used to (+ -ing) significa **essere abituato a**; *get used to (+ -ing)* esprime l'idea di **abituarsi a**.

Confronta le frasi seguenti:

*I **used to work** at weekends.* (= in the past I worked at weekends, but I don't now)

Lavoravo *tutti i fine settimana.* (= nel passato lavoravo durante il fine settimana, adesso non più)

*I'm **used to working** at weekends.* (= I often work at weekends, it doesn't worry me)

Sono abituato a lavorare *il fine settimana.* (= lavoro spesso il fine settimana, la cosa non mi preoccupa)

Be/get used to possono essere seguiti anche da un sostantivo.

*He **wasn't used to criticism** and found it hard to accept.*
(= people hadn't criticised him before so he didn't like it)
Non era abituato alle critiche *e trovava difficile accettarle.*
(= non era mai stato criticato prima e la cosa non gli piaceva)

PRACTICE

1 Riempi gli spazi con la forma appropriata di **be/get used to**.

1 Rita's very tired this morning. She ....isn't used to.............. (*not*) going to bed late.

2 Don't worry about the children, they .... going to school by bus.

3 My new boss .... giving orders, not receiving them.

4 She .... (*not*) drinking tea and it made her ill.

5 .... (*you*) our climate or do you miss the sunshine?

6 I had never stayed in such an expensive hotel before, but I soon .... it.

2 <u>Sottolinea</u> la forma corretta dei verbi.

MAKING CHANGES

<u>Ada Atkins, 93, explains why she has come to live in town</u>

Years ago, nobody in my village **(1)** *would lock / was locking* their front doors. We **(2)** *used to feel / would feel* safe in those days. Last month, I **(3)** *met / was meeting* my neighbour in the street when I **(4)** *was walking / would walk* home from the shops and she **(5)** *told / was telling* me some bad news. Thieves **(6)** *were breaking / used to break* into people's houses while they **(7)** *were sitting / would sit* in their back gardens.

I **(8)** *realised / was realising* that I **(9)** *wasn't wanting / didn't want* to live there any more. So last week I **(10)** *was moving / moved* to this little flat. I **(11)** *am not used / didn't use* to being in the town yet, but people are more friendly than I **(12)** *was thinking / thought* they might be, and I feel much happier and safer.

ALL IN ONE REVISION

1 Ascolterete Peter che parla alla radio di una città che ha visitato la settimana scorsa. Qui sotto ci sono due immagini della città. Quale delle due è della settimana scorsa? Quale è di sette anni fa?

2 Ascolta e verifica se avevi ragione.

1.9

1 Why did Peter go there?

2 What changes did he see?

3 Ascolta di nuovo e completa le frasi seguenti. Ferma la registrazione se è necessario.

1.10

1 Well, last week I ....visited............ my home city.

2 When I .... , Stefan .... his work for the day ...

3 When we .... lunch, we .... by the river.

4 The riverside .... the factory area ...

5 There didn't .... a sports centre in the city.

6 The engineers .... it the year I ....

7 I .... to become an engineer ...

8 I .... into the restaurant and I .... all my old friends.

4 Rileggi le tue risposte nell'esercizio 3 e rispondi a queste domande.

1 Look at sentences 4 and 5 and complete this statement.

We use .... to talk about things that were different in the past.

2 Look at the other sentences. Which contain two different verb forms? ....

In these sentences did one event happen before the other? ....

5 Ci sono due frasi sotto ogni immagine. Scegli la frase che descrive la situazione in modo corretto.

1 When we arrived, the concert started. ..✓...

When we arrived, the concert had started.

....

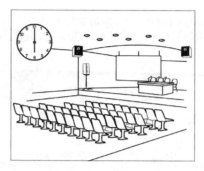

2 At 6 o'clock everyone went home. ....

At 6 o'clock everyone had gone home.

....

BYE DAN!

3 Dan left when Holly arrived. ....

Dan had left when Holly arrived.   ....

4 Miriam had never flown before the first time she went to London. ....

Miriam didn't fly before the first time she went to London. ....

Name:
Fiona Holmes
Address:
15 Pond Road, London SW18 4XY
Marital status:
divorced

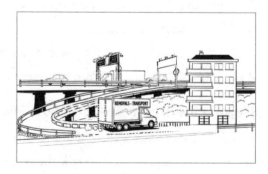

5 When I first met Fiona she was married. ....

When I first met Fiona she'd been married. ....

6 They built the motorway when we first moved here. ....

They'd built the motorway when we first moved here. ....

6 Completa la prima parte delle frasi nella colonna **A** con il verbo tra parentesi al *past perfect simple* o *past perfect continuous,* poi abbinale con le loro logiche conclusioni nella colonna **B**.

A	**B**
1 They ......'d sold........ (*sell*) all the tickets	so there was nothing to eat.
2 I knew she .... (*cry*)	but I didn't enjoy it.
3 I .... (*be*) awake for an hour	when we arrived at the stadium.
4 I .... (*look forward*) to the party for weeks	because her eyes were red.
5 He .... (*not/do*) the shopping	so the car didn't start.
6 He .... (*forget*) to turn off the headlights	when my alarm clock went off.

7 Riempi gli spazi con la forma corretta dei verbi tra parentesi. Usa il *present perfect* (*simple* o *continuous*), il *past simple* e il *past perfect* (*simple* o *continuous*).

Angelina Jolie's career started early. By the time she left school she **(1)** 'd already appeared. (*already/appear*) in a film with her father Jon Voight and **(2)** .... (*model*) for several years. But it wasn't until 'Lara Croft' in 2001 that she became a star.

She **(3)** .... (*already/win*) an Oscar as supporting actress two years earlier, but it was her role as the adventurous tomb raider that made her internationally famous.

Jolie **(4)** .... (*now/become*) one of the highest-paid actresses in Hollywood. She is also involved with humanitarian work. In 2001 she became Goodwill Ambassador for the United Nations and since then she **(5)** .... (*travel*) extensively throughout the developing world.

Jolie's private life **(6)** .... (*always/be*) front page news in the tabloids. Her self-destructive adolescence, her relationship with her father who she **(7)** .... (*not/speak*) to for several years and her stormy marriages have all attracted a lot of attention. When she met Brad Pitt in 2005 the gossip columns could speak of nothing else. At the time she **(8)** .... (*already/be*) married twice and Pitt was married to popular actress Jennifer Anniston. Since then the couple **(9)** .... (*be*) constantly in the news, although the latest reports claim that they **(10)** .... (*not/get on*) well recently.

Jolie's children are very important to her. She **(11)** .... (*adopt*) two children before she met Pitt. Since then they have adopted a third and **(12)** .... (*have*) a daughter, Shiloh Nouvel, who was born in Namibia in 2006.

8 Per ogni coppia di frasi, completa la seconda in modo che il significato non cambi. **Usa la parola data senza modificarla**. Usa tra **due** e **cinque** parole compresa la parola data.

(FCE)

1 I arrived at the station too late to catch the train. **already**

The train ......had already left...... when I arrived at the station.

2 I found it hard to share a room because I'd never done it before. **used**

I wasn't .... because I'd never done it before.

3 My grandmother's clothes were always black. **would**

My grandmother .... black clothes.

4 He stopped smoking when he had a heart attack. **smoke**

He .... before he had a heart attack.

5 They started the marathon at 7. I saw them at 10. **running**

They .... three hours when I saw them.

6 The film finished before they arrived. **time**

The film had finished .... arrived.

7 John's football team won for the first time last year. **before**

John's football team .... last year.

8 After a few weeks in London I didn't find it strange to speak English. **got**

After a few weeks in London I .... English.

9 Completa le frasi seguenti con una sola parola in ogni spazio.

1 I used to ......listen...... to heavy metal but now I prefer rap.

2 When I first arrived in Edinburgh I .... used to the Scottish accent.

3 At first I hated living alone but then I slowly .... used to it.

4 Did you .... to have an imaginary friend when you were a child?

5 My grandmother never complained because she .... used to a hard life.

6 I'm sure the traffic didn't use to .... so bad at this time of day.

7 When I started this job I had to get used to .... up early.

8 Siobhan .... to be such a sweet girl when she was younger.

9 We didn't sleep all night because we .... used to the noise.

10 Did you get used to .... spicy food when you lived in India?

10 Traduci.

1 Le strade erano bagnate perché era piovuto tutta la notte.

2 Ieri sera mio padre era molto stanco perché aveva lavorato per 10 ore.

3 Suonavo la chitarra abbastanza bene, ma sono anni che non mi esercito.

4 Sono abituata ad alzarmi presto adesso, ma è stato duro all'inizio.

5 Quando ero una ragazzina non mi piaceva la musica classica. Adesso la adoro.

6 Il traffico era terribile nel centro, ma la nuova zona pedonale ha migliorato le cose.

7 Jack era preoccupato perché non aveva studiato geografia.

8 Da bambina Jenny giocava con le bambole. Adesso è un maschiaccio (*tomboy*).

9 Jack lavorava come DJ al Roxy Club da qualche mese quando gli offrirono un nuovo lavoro alla radio.

10 L'estate scorsa i miei amici e io andavamo sempre alle spiagge bianche. Quest'anno ci incontriamo al Club della Vela.

I TEMPI DEL FUTURO

I TEMPI DEL FUTURO – INTRODUZIONE

Per parlare del futuro, in inglese si usano diverse forme verbali; le più comuni sono *will*, *be going to*, il *present continuous* e il *present simple*. Le differenze di significato e di uso tra le diverse strutture sono a volte minime; in alcuni casi, ma non sempre, è possibile usare forme diverse, con significati simili. Si tratta di un'area complessa della grammatica inglese, per la varietà di significati che può esprimere.

5.1 IL FUTURO SEMPLICE: *WILL*

Il futuro semplice si forma con l'ausiliare *will* e il verbo alla forma base, **infinito senza** *to*.

Affermativa	Negativa	Interrogativa	
I **will** (**'ll**) pay	I **will not** (**won't**) pay	**Will** I pay?	+ *I'll pay.*
you **will** (**'ll**) pay	you **will not** (**won't**) pay	**Will** you pay?	
he/she/it **will** (**'ll**) pay	he/she/it **will not** (**won't**) pay	**Will** he/she/it pay?	– *She* **won't** *pay.*
we **will** (**'ll**) pay	we **will not** (**won't**) pay	**Will** we pay?	
you **will** (**'ll**) pay	you **will not** (**won't**) pay	**Will** you pay?	? *Will you pay?*
they **will** (**'ll**) pay	they **will not** (**won't**) pay	**Will** they pay?	

Nell'inglese parlato si usa quasi sempre la forma contratta *'ll*; nella forma negativa, *will not* di norma si contrae in *won't*.

Do you think it'll rain?   Pensi che **pioverà**?

I missed the train, so I **won't get** *home*   Ho perso il treno, così **non arriverò** a casa fino a tardi.
until very late.

In contesti formali *shall* viene occasionalmente usato al posto di *will* alla 1ª persona singolare e plurale, *I* e *we*.

Il futuro con *will* viene usato per:

◼ fare delle **previsioni**, parlare di quello che pensiamo accadrà nel futuro, sulla base delle nostre convinzioni e/o conoscenze, specialmente con *probably*, *maybe*, *I think*, *I expect* e *I hope*.

*Everybody **will do shopping** by computer in a few years' time.* (= I believe this)	*Tra pochi anni tutti **faranno acquisti** con il computer.* (= ne sono convinto)
*I **probably won't be back** in time.*	***Probabilmente non ritornerò** in tempo.*

🔊 In italiano i verbi *think, believe, be sure* sono generalmente seguiti dall'infinito, in inglese **no**.

*Robin thinks **he'll get** a promotion.* (**Non** ~~Robin thinks to get~~)	*Robin pensa **di ottenere** una promozione.*

◼ **decisioni prese al momento** stesso in cui si parla.

*I**'ll have** a coffee with you.* (= she decides now)	***Prendo** un caffè con te.* (= decide sul momento)
*I**'ll ring** them now.*	*Li **chiamo** subito.*

◼ parlare di un evento futuro che **non dipende** dalla volontà o dalle intenzioni di chi parla.

*There**'ll be** a full moon tomorrow.*	*Ci **sarà** la luna piena domani.*
*Christmas Day **will be** on Saturday this year.*	*Natale **viene** di sabato quest'anno.*

PRACTICE

1 Completa le frasi seguenti con un verbo nel riquadro e con la forma corretta di *will*.

be   become   come   leave   need   ~~phone~~

1 I think ......I'll phone...... Rob because I haven't heard from him for a long time.

2 I (*not*) .... my bag here because it's got my camera in it.

3 My grandmother .... 65 on her next birthday.

4 No thanks, I (*not*) .... to the swimming pool with you because I've got a cold.

5 During the next hundred years the world .... warmer and warmer.

6 How much money (*you*) .... for the weekend?

2 Che cosa pensi che succederà? Fai delle previsioni, usando *I think* o *I don't think* e i verbi tra parentesi con *will*.

1 I'm taking a jacket because ....I think....... it ....will get........ cold later on. (*get*)

2 .... Italy .... a woman prime minister in the next ten years. (*have*)

3 In the future .... a lot of people .... to be a hundred. (*live*)

4 .... they .... a cure for cancer in my lifetime. (*find*)

5 .... I .... married before I'm thirty. (*get*)

6 .... you .... Charlie. He's really nice. (*get on with*)

7 .... Tasha .... her exam. She hasn't studied enough. (*pass*)

8 Dan's going out with Annie at the moment, but .... it .... (*last*)

3 Leggi attentamente queste situazioni, poi scrivi quello che credi succederà.

1 Anna has two cousins called Rebecca Smith and Rebecca Jones. Anna gets on very well with Rebecca Smith but she doesn't like Rebecca Jones. She has received letters from her cousins asking her if they can visit. She replies to them both. She wants to see Rebecca Smith but not Rebecca Jones. Unfortunately she puts the letters in the wrong envelopes.

How will her cousins feel when they receive her letters?

Rebecca Smith won't understand why Anna doesn't want her to visit. ....

What will happen? ....

How will Anna feel when she finds out? ....

2 A tour guide has just arrived in a foreign city with a group of 30 teenagers and their teachers at the end of a long journey. They don't know it yet but when they get to the hotel where they have booked rooms they will find that their rooms have been given to a group of elderly tourists who are already asleep in the rooms.

What will happen? ....

What will the hotel manager do? ....

How will the teenagers and their teachers feel? ....

5.2   IL FUTURO CON *BE GOING TO*

Il futuro con *be going to* è molto comune nell'inglese parlato. Si forma con l'ausiliare *be* seguito da *going to* e la forma base del verbo.

Affermativa	Negativa	Interrogativa
I **am going to** leave	I **am not going to** leave	**Am** I **going to** leave?
you **are going to** leave	you **are not going to** leave	**Are** you **going to** leave?
he/she/it **is going to** leave	he/she/it **is not going to** leave	**Is** he/she/it **going to** leave?
we **are going to** leave	we **are not going to** leave	**Are** we **going to** leave?
you **are going to** leave	you **are not going to** leave	**Are** you **going to** leave?
they **are going to** leave	they **are not going to** leave	**Are** they **going to** leave?

Going to si pronuncia spesso *gonna* in inglese colloquiale e si trova spesso scritto così nei fumetti e nelle canzoni.

*What **are** you **gonna do**?*	*Che cosa **farai / hai intenzione di fare**?*
(= What are you going to do?)	
*I'm **gonna go** home.* (= I'm going to go home.)	***Vado/Andrò** a casa.*

Il futuro con ***be going to*** viene usato per:

■ parlare di **progetti**, **intenzioni** e **decisioni** prese **prima del momento** in cui si parla.

*We're **going to see** the new James Bond film.*	***Andiamo a vedere** l'ultimo film di James Bond.*
(= we decided earlier)	(= lo abbiamo deciso prima)
*I've spoken to Eileen. She's **going to take** me to the airport.*	*Ho parlato con Eileen. Mi **porterà** lei all'aeroporto.*

■ **fare delle previsioni** sulla base di quello che possiamo vedere o sentire nel presente.

*Look at the clouds! It's **going to rain soon**.*	*Guarda che nuvoloni! **Sta per piovere. / Pioverà presto**.*
*Be careful! You're **going to break** that cup.*	*Stai attento o **romperai** quella tazzina.*

🔊 Ci sono tuttavia molte situazioni in cui si può usare sia ***be going to*** che ***will*** senza nessuna reale differenza di significato, ricordandosi che ***will*** tende a essere più comune nell'inglese formale e scritto, ***be going to*** nella conversazione.

*I'm **going to be** 17 next week. = I'**ll be** 17 next week.*	***Compirò** 17 anni la settimana prossima.*

PRACTICE

1   Scrivi una frase con ***be going to*** per ogni immagine. Usa i verbi nel riquadro.

be   join   play   rain   ~~wash~~   win

1   I 'm going to wash... the kitchen floor.

2   Number 5 (*not*) ....

3   They .... famous.

4   (*you*) .... the gym?

5   I .... football.

6   It (*not*) ....

2 Completa le frasi seguenti con la forma corretta di **be going to** e i verbi tra parentesi. Fai attenzione all'ordine delle parole.

1 Joe didn't say thank you so I *..I'm not going to help....* (*help*) him again.

2 When .... (*tell*) your mother that you've lost your mobile?

3 This traffic's terrible. We .... (*arrive*) on time.

4 When I'm 18 I .... (*live*) on my own.

5 **A** Jason's going to London. **B** How long .... (*stay*) there?

6 I've decided I .... (*stop*) eating chocolate and go jogging every morning!

7 How many people .... (*invite*) to the party?

8 Careful! That bag .... (*break*). It's too full.

3 Guarda le immagini e fai delle previsioni su quello che sta per succedere. Completa le frasi usando **be going to**.

1 She *...'s going to fall asleep.*

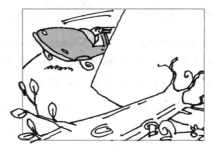

2 It ....

3 They ....

4 She ....

5 He ....

6 It ....

5.3   IL *PRESENT CONTINUOUS* CON VALORE DI FUTURO

Si usa il *present continuous* (vedi *Unit* **1**) per parlare di **progetti futuri** già definiti e prestabiliti. Quando ha valore di futuro, il *present continuous* è spesso accompagnato da un'espressione di tempo, come **this evening**, **tomorrow**, **next week**, **in September**.

next Friday
next month

***I'm meeting** a designer at 2.30.*	***Incontro/Vedo/Vedrò** un designer alle 2.30.*
(= we have an appointment)	(= abbiamo un appuntamento)

Si usa spesso il *present continuous* per fare domande sui progetti a breve termine delle persone, quando diamo per scontato che abbiano già dei programmi ben definiti.

*What **are you doing** tonight?*	*Che **fai** stasera?*
*Are you **coming** to Debbie's party on Saturday?*	***Vieni** alla festa di Debbie sabato?*

Come si vede dagli esempi, quando ha valore di futuro il *present continuous* si rende generalmente con il presente (semplice) italiano.

PRACTICE

1 Melissa vuole intervistare Liam O'Neill, un famoso DJ. Adesso sta parlando con Joe, l'assistente di Liam. Leggi l'agenda e riempi gli spazi usando il *present continuous*.

Melissa: I can meet Liam any time on Monday.
What **(1)** ...is he doing... during the day?

Joe: We **(2)** .... to new CDs all day.
He can't see you then.

Melissa: And what **(3)** .... in the evening?

Joe: He **(4)** .... to the *Daily Post* at 7.30.

Melissa: Oh. And where **(5)** .... on Tuesday?

Joe: He **(6)** .... to the TV studio early
and he **(7)** .... there all day.

Melissa: Oh, that's great. I **(8)** .... the day at
the TV studio.

Joe: But in the evening he's **(9)** .... his
TV show. He can't see you before that. But the
production team **(10)** .... a meal
together after that. Perhaps you can join them?

Melissa: Really? That's great! Thank you so much.

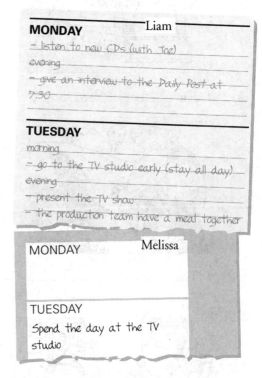

MONDAY   Liam
- listen to new CDs (with Joe)
evening
- give an interview to the Daily Post at
7.30

TUESDAY
morning
- go to the TV studio early (stay all day)
evening
- present the TV show
- the production team have a meal together

MONDAY   Melissa

TUESDAY
Spend the day at the TV
studio

2 Lucy sta parlando con la sua amica Kate di quello che farà nelle vacanze estive. Completa il dialogo con il *present continuous* dei verbi nel riquadro.

stay	~~leave~~	fly	spend	bring	hire	join	drive	come	have

Lucy: We've got the tickets! I'm so excited.

Kate: So when **(1)** ..a̲r̲e̲..y̲o̲u̲..l̲e̲a̲v̲i̲n̲g̲... ?

Lucy: July 25. The day after school finishes.

Kate: And **(2)** .... to Los Angeles?

Lucy: Yes, but we **(3)** .... much time there. We're going to San Francisco and then we
(4) .... a car and we **(5)** .... to the Grand Canyon and Death Valley.

Kate: What about Richard? **(6)** .... with you?

Lucy: He can't come until August so he **(7)** .... us in San Francisco. He **(8)** ....
his friend Luke too. You'd like Luke, he's really nice.

Kate: You're so lucky. I **(9)** .... here all summer. We **(10)** .... a holiday this
year except for ten days in Wales with my grandparents. It's going to be so boring!

5.4   IL *PRESENT SIMPLE* CON VALORE DI FUTURO

Si usa il *present simple* per parlare di **eventi programmati** nel futuro, come:

■ **orari** di arrivo e partenza (di treni, autobus, aerei).

*My flight **leaves** Rome at 11 pm on Saturday*   *Il mio volo **parte** da Roma sabato alle 11 di notte*
*and it **arrives** in London at 1 am.*   *e **arriva** a Londra all'una di mattina.*

■ **orari** di inizio e fine (di conferenze, lezioni, film, concerti, partite).

*The film **starts** at nine o'clock.*   *Il film **comincia/comincerà** alle nove.*
*What time **does** the conference **start**?*   *A che ora **inizia** la conferenza?*

■ **programmi** di persone che dipendono da orari prestabiliti.

*The main speaker **arrives** on Tuesday afternoon.*   *Il relatore principale **arriva/arriverà** martedì
pomeriggio.*

Are you free on Saturday evening?   ***Sei** libero sabato sera?*

PRACTICE

1 Leggi le risposte e scrivi le domande,
utilizzando le informazioni affisse nella
bacheca della *Abon Language School*.

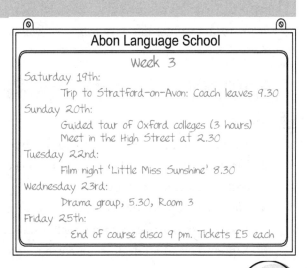

Abon Language School

Week 3

Saturday 19th:
    Trip to Stratford-on-Avon: Coach leaves 9.30
Sunday 20th:
    Guided tour of Oxford colleges (3 hours)
    Meet in the High Street at 2.30
Tuesday 22nd:
    Film night 'Little Miss Sunshine' 8.30
Wednesday 23rd:
    Drama group, 5.30, Room 3
Friday 25th:
    End of course disco 9 pm. Tickets £5 each

1 *What time does the coach leave for Stratford-on-Avon?* ....? At 9.30.

2 ....? In the High Street.

3 ....? 3 hours.

4 ....? At 8.30.

5 ....? In Room 3.

6 ....? On Friday 25th.

7 ....? At 9 pm.

2 Tu e il tuo amico Robert vi siete dati appuntamento per andare al cinema e lo stai aspettando alla fermata dell'autobus. Scrivi un dialogo tra voi due seguendo le indicazioni date.

You	Robert
Saluti Robert e gli dici che è in ritardo.	Ti saluta e si scusa.
Rispondi che non fa nulla. Chiedi a che ora comincia il film.	Risponde che comincia alle nove.
Chiedi a che ora finisce.	Risponde che finisce circa alle 10 e mezzo.
Chiedi se c'è un autobus dopo quell'ora.	Risponde che ce n'è uno alle 11 e avete tutto il tempo per prenderlo.

5.5   PREPOSIZIONI ED ESPRESSIONI DI TEMPO FUTURO

Quando si riferisce a un tempo futuro, la preposizione italiana **tra** corrisponde all'inglese *in*.

in a month = **tra** un mese; *in* two/three days' time = **tra** due/tre giorni; *in* ten years' time = **tra** dieci anni

La preposizione **entro** si traduce con:

by + momento preciso → *by* Friday = **entro** venerdì; *by* the end of the month = **entro** la fine del mese;

within + durata di tempo → *within* two weeks = entro due settimane; *within* a month = **entro** un mese.

PRACTICE

1 Traduci.

1 La traduzione sarà pronta entro la fine del mese.

2 Tra dieci anni tutte le famiglie avranno la connessione a Internet.

3 Sarò a casa entro le cinque.

4 Non preoccuparti, tra un paio di giorni starai bene.

5 I nostri ospiti arriveranno tra pochi minuti.

6 Sapremo i risultati degli esami entro un paio di settimane.

5.6   *WILL* vs *BE GOING TO*

Si usa *will*:

■ per esprimere **decisioni istantanee**, prese sul momento.

*Look, it's raining. I'**ll take** you in the car.*
*Guarda, sta piovendo. Ti **porto** in macchina.*

■ quando **ci si offre spontaneamente** di fare qualcosa.

A *This bag is very heavy.* **B** *I'**ll carry** it for you.*
A *Questa borsa è molto pesante.* **B** *Te la **porto io**.*

■ per fare previsioni su quello che **pensiamo** o **siamo convinti accadrà** nel futuro.

*Don't lend her your car. She's a very bad driver: she'**ll have an accident**.*
*Non prestarle la tua auto. Guida malissimo: **farà** (sicuramente) **un incidente**.*

*In 100 years the world **will be** a different place. There'**ll be** millions more people but there **won't be** as much oil available for energy.*
*Tra 100 anni il mondo **sarà** completamente differente. Ci **saranno** milioni di abitanti in più, ma **non** ci **sarà** altrettanto petrolio disponibile per l'energia.*

Si usa *be going to*:

■ per indicare **decisioni prese prima** del momento di parlare.

*I'**m going to do** a language course in Bristol. I've already paid the fees.*
***Farò** un corso di lingua a Bristol. Ho già pagato l'iscrizione.*

■ per fare previsioni basate su quello che **possiamo vedere** al momento.

*Look at those cars! They **are going to crash**.*
Guarda quelle macchine!
***Stanno per scontrarsi**.*

*How pale that girl looks. She'**s going to faint**.*
Quella ragazza è pallidissima.
***Sta per svenire**.*

Si usa *will* anche dopo verbi che indicano opinione, supposizione, certezza, speranza, come *think*, *expect*, *hope*, *be sure/afraid*.

*I **think I'll have** lunch in town.*   ***Penso di pranzare / che pranzerò** in città.*

Spesso è possibile usare entrambe le forme.

There are no oranges in the house.
*I'**ll get** some today.* (= decisione immediata)
*I'**m going to get** some today.* (= avevo già deciso)

PRACTICE

1 Leggi questa conversazione e riempi gli spazi con la forma corretta di *will* o *be going to*.

Colin: Hello Darius. **(1)** ..we're going to go.. (*we/go*) to a music festival this summer.

Darius: Are you? That sounds good.

Colin: Do you want to come? **(2)** .... (*we/buy*) tickets this afternoon.

Darius: **(3)** .... (*I/think*) about it.

Colin: **(4)** .... (*Paul and Ros/come*) too. It's quite cheap.

Darius: (5) .... (I/check) my diary. When is it?

Colin: 5–8 August.

Darius: OK, OK, (6) .... (I/buy) a ticket.

2 Completa le frasi seguenti con *will* o *be going to* e i verbi nel riquadro.

> enjoy   pay   do   ~~be~~   rise   be away   break   take

1 She's a really good pianist. I expect she ....'ll be........... famous one day.

2 The car's making a funny noise so I .... it to the garage tomorrow.

3 Don't worry. I'm sure you .... it when you get there.

4 A .... anything interesting this weekend? B Yes, I'm going away.

5 A Here's £10. B Thanks very much. I .... you back tomorrow.

6 Experts believe that water levels .... by 20cms in the next 50 years.

7 I can't see you on Thursday because I .... till Friday.

8 Stand up! The chair's ....

5.7   IL *PRESENT CONTINUOUS* vs *BE GOING TO*

Si usa il *present continuous*:

▥ per parlare di **programmi futuri già fissati**, con un'indicazione precisa di tempo.

I'm taking my History exam again tomorrow.
Do *l'esame di storia un'altra volta domani.*
(= la data dell'appello è stabilita)

Si usa *be going to*:

▥ per parlare di **progetti futuri** e **intenzioni** che possiamo non aver ancora definito in tutti i dettagli.

I'm going to take a History exam.
Ho intenzione di dare / Darò *un esame di storia.*

Spesso è possibile usare entrambe le forme per parlare di progetti futuri, senza una reale differenza di significato.

> *We're spending the weekend at the seaside.* = *We're going to spend the weekend at the seaside.*
> **Trascorreremo** *il fine settimana al mare.*

PRACTICE

1 Completa i seguenti mini-dialoghi usando il *present continuous* o *be going to*. In alcuni casi entrambe le forme sono possibili.

> ~~pay~~   come   wear   leave   do   wait   tell   play

1 A When ...*are you going to pay*..... this phone bill?

  B There's no hurry. It only arrived yesterday.

2 A I .... to school tomorrow.

  B Why not?   A I've got a doctor's appointment.

3 **A** I .... Susie she's failed. I don't want to upset her.

  B OK, I'll tell her then.

4 **A** It's my cousin's wedding tomorrow. I'm really looking forward to it.

  B Really? What .... ?

5 **A** Are you going on holiday soon?

  B Yes, we .... on Friday.

6 **A** Did you buy those boots then?

  B No, I'm .... until the sales.

7 **A** We've got an important match on Saturday.

  B Who .... against?

8 **A** Have you finished your homework?

  B Not yet. I .... it after supper.

5.8   IL *FUTURE CONTINUOUS*

Il *future continuous* si forma con **will be** e il verbo alla forma **-ing**.

Affermativa	Negativa	Interrogativa
I **will be** work**ing**	I **will not be** work**ing**	**Will** I **be** work**ing** …?
you **will be** work**ing**	you **will not be** work**ing**	**Will** you **be** work**ing** …?
he/she/it **will be** work**ing**	he/she/it **will not be** work**ing**	**Will** he/she/it **be** work**ing** …?
we **will be** work**ing**	we **will not be** work**ing**	**Will** we **be** work**ing** …?
you **will be** work**ing**	you **will not be** work**ing**	**Will** you **be** work**ing** …?
they **will be** work**ing**	they **will not be** work**ing**	**Will** they **be** work**ing** …?

Il *future continuous* viene usato per indicare un evento o un'attività che **sarà in corso di svolgimento** in un momento specifico del futuro o in un periodo di tempo del futuro.

*I'll **be working** at 7 o'clock.*
By the time you read this letter
*I'll **be sailing** towards Australia.*

*Alle 7 **starò lavorando**.*
*Quando leggerai questa lettera io **starò navigando** verso l'Australia.*

Nota la differenza:

  *I'll **be interviewing** him at 6.30.*

  (= l'intervista comincerà prima delle 6.30 e continuerà dopo)

  *I'm **interviewing** him at 6.30.*

  (= l'inizio dell'intervista è fissato per le 6.30)

PRACTICE

1 Immagina che cosa starai facendo:

  1 at 10 o'clock this evening ....

2 at midday tomorrow ....

3 at 11 pm on Saturday ....

4 this time next week ....

5 this time next year ....

5.9   IL FUTURO ESPRESSO CON *PRESENT SIMPLE* DOPO *WHEN, IF, UNLESS…*

A differenza dell'italiano, in inglese **non** si può usare il futuro in frasi subordinate introdotte da **when**, **as soon as**, **until**, **before**, **after**, **if**, **unless**.

Si usa il *present simple*, **non will**, al posto del futuro semplice italiano.

Frase principale		Frase subordinata
Everyone's going to be very surprised	**when**	*you* **arrive**. (**Non** ~~when you will arrive~~)
Saranno tutti molto sorpresi	**quando**	**arriverai**.
I won't go away	**until**	*the doctor* **comes**. (**Non** ~~until the doctor will come~~)
Non andrò via	**finché non**	**verrà** *il dottore*.
I'll give you a ring	**as soon as**	*I* **get** *to London*. (**Non** ~~I will get to London~~)
Ti telefonerò	**non appena**	**arriverò** *a Londra*.
We're going to have a picnic tomorrow	**unless**	*it* **rains**.
Faremo un picnic domani	**a meno che**	**piova**.

■ Allo stesso modo, si usa generalmente il *present perfect* nelle frasi subordinate in cui in italiano si usa il futuro anteriore, per indicare chiaramente che l'azione si è conclusa prima dell'altra.

We are not going to talk to any reporters **until we have had** *a long sleep.* .

Non parleremo con nessun giornalista **finché non avremo fatto** *una bella dormita.*

■ A volte si può usare sia il *present simple* che il *present perfect* con lo stesso significato.

We are going to eat a big hot meal **as soon as** *we* **find** *a restaurant.*

We are going to eat a big hot meal **as soon as** *we* **have found** *a restaurant.*

Mangeremo un bel pasto caldo **non appena troveremo / avremo trovato** *un buon ristorante.*

PRACTICE

1 Completa le frasi seguenti mettendo i verbi tra parentesi alla forma giusta: *present simple* o *will/won't*.

1 When she ....arrives........ (*arrive*), I ....'ll tell........ (*tell*) her.

2 She .... (*be*) furious when she .... (*find out*).

3 I .... (*not/invite*) him unless he .... (*apologize*) for being so rude.

4 I .... (*not/be able*) to sleep until you .... (*get*) home.

5 I .... (*wait*) with you until your bus .... (*arrive*).

6 As soon as I .... (*hear*) the results I promise I .... (*let*) you know.

7 He .... (*not/give back*) your CD unless you .... (*remind*) him.

8 Until the government .... (*take*) action nothing .... (*change*).

9 I .... (*go*) to bed as soon as the film .... (*finish*).

10 Unless you .... (*do*) more exercise you .... (*not/lose*) weight.

2 Scegli la frase corretta.

1 **a** I'm not going to pay you until you have cleaned up all this mess! ✔

   b I'm not going to pay you until you'll have cleaned up all this mess!

2 **a** Paul will probably arrive after all the others will have started work.

   b Paul will probably arrive after all the others have started work.

3 **a** When you'll see David, will you ask him if he wants to come to the cinema?

   b When you see David, will you ask him if he wants to come to the cinema?

4 **a** I'll collect your things from the cleaners when I go to the shops tomorrow.

   b I'll collect your things from the cleaners when I'll go to the shops tomorrow.

5 **a** Margaret's going to phone as soon as she'll have found out what the tickets will cost.

   b Margaret's going to phone as soon as she's found out what the tickets will cost.

5.10   IL *FUTURE PERFECT: SIMPLE AND CONTINUOUS*

Il *future perfect* corrisponde al futuro anteriore italiano e, come tutti i tempi inglesi, ha due forme: *simple* e *continuous*.

+	I/you/he/she/it/we/they **will have** wait**ed**	I/you/he/she/it/we/they **will have been** wait**ing**
–	I/you/he/she/it/we/they **won't have** wait**ed**	I/you/he/she/it/we/they **won't have been** wait**ing**
?	**Will** I/you/he/she/it/we/they **have** wait**ed**?	**Will** I/you/he/she/it/we/they **have been** wait**ing**?

■ Si usa il *future perfect simple* per indicare un'azione che sarà conclusa in un momento specifico del futuro. Di solito quel momento specifico viene indicato.

*By the end of the year I **will have saved** 1,500 euros.*   *Entro la fine dell'anno **avrò messo da parte** 1,500 euro.*

■ Si usa il *future perfect continuous* per mettere in evidenza quanto a lungo un'azione sarà durata fino a un momento specifico del futuro. Di solito è necessario specificare sia il momento specifico del futuro che la durata dell'azione.

*By the end of June I **will have been working** here for five years.*   *Alla fine di giugno **saranno cinque anni che lavoro** qui.*

🔊 I verbi di stato **non** possono essere usati al *future perfect continuous*.

PRACTICE

1 Questi sono appunti di un ricercatore, con le sue previsioni di come il mondo sarà cambiato entro l'anno 2100. Usa gli appunti per scrivere delle frasi complete al *future perfect simple*.

> **By the year 2100**
>
> 1 human beings / travel to Mars
> 2 the world's population / double
> 3 computers / replace / most manual workers
> 4 we / use / all the oil resources on Earth
> 5 doctors / discover / a cure for AIDS
> 6 scientists / invent / new sources of energy
> 7 sea temperatures / rise / by several degrees

1 Human beings will have travelled to Mars. ....

2 ....

3 ....

4 ....

5 ....

6 ....

7 ....

Adesso scrivi tre previsioni tue, usando il *future perfect simple*.

8 ....

9 ....

10 ....

2 Queste persone lavorano in un hotel. Adesso è mezzogiorno. Quanto a lungo ciascuno di loro avrà lavorato alle due? Scrivi una frase per ciascuno, usando il *future perfect continuous*.

1 chef / cook meals (started work at eight o'clock)

The chef will have been cooking meals for six hours. ....

2 secretary / type letters (started work at ten o'clock)

....

3 manager / interview new staff (started work at eight-thirty)

....

4 waitress / stand in the dining room (started work at eleven o'clock)

....

5 cleaner / vacuum floors (started work at seven o'clock)

....

5.11 *BE ABOUT TO*

Affermativa	Negativa	Interrogativa
I **am about to** go out	I **am not about to** go out	**Am** I **about to** go out?
you/we/they **are about to** go out	you/we/they **are not about to** go out	**Are** you/we/they **about to** go out?
he/she/it **is about to** go out	he/she/it **is not about to** go out	**Is** he/she/it **about to** go out?

Si usa **be about to** con il verbo alla forma base per parlare di un evento che sta per accadere, che è sul punto di accadere e per il quale ci stiamo già preparando.

Actually, we're about to leave.   *A dire la verità, stiamo per partire.*

Alla forma negativa, **be about to** spesso significa 'non abbiamo assolutamente intenzione di' fare una certa cosa.

We aren't about to change the rules just because you don't like them.
(= We refuse to change the rules just because you don't like them.)

***Non cambieremo certo** le regole solo perché non ti piacciono. (= ci rifiutiamo di farlo)*

PRACTICE

1 Leggi con attenzione le frasi seguenti, poi scrivi quello che le persone sono sul punto di fare in queste situazioni.

1 He's standing on the edge of the swimming pool. He ....'s about to jump.... in.

2 I'm in the kitchen putting on my apron. It's 8 pm. I .... the supper.

3 Sam is holding the dog's lead and the dog is very happy. They .... a walk.

4 The curtain is rising. The play ....

5 She set the alarm for seven. It's two minutes to seven. The alarm ....

6 Amy and Paul's wedding is this afternoon. They ....

7 The prime minister is standing on the podium. He's clearing his throat. He ....

8 Our plane is starting to move down the runway. We ....

9 There's heavy cloud and it's minus 2. It ....

10 Harry has blown up the balloon too much. The balloon ....

ALL IN ONE REVISION

1 Elliot sta parlando del prossimo fine settimana con la sua amica Kelly. Guarda le immagini. Quali sono i programmi di Elliot? Quali sono i programmi di Kelly?

2 Ascolta e verifica se avevi ragione.

1.11

Why is Kelly annoyed with Elliot?

3 Ascolta di nuovo e completa le frasi seguenti.

1.12

1 What does Kelly say about tonight? 'We ..*'re going to see*.... the new James Bond film.'

2 What does Elliot say about tonight? 'I .... for exams tonight.'

3 What does Kelly say about Saturday and Sunday? 'We .... the weekend at the seaside.'

4 What are Elliot's plans for Saturday? 'I .... a designer at 10.30 on Saturday.'

5 What does Elliot tell us about his journey from Rome? 'My flight .... Rome at 11 pm on Saturday and it .... in London at 1 am.'

6 What does Elliot say about Sunday? 'I expect I .... asleep all day on Sunday.'

7 What does Kelly agree to do? 'OK. I .... a coffee with you.'

8 What does Elliot say about the future? 'I .... really rich. I .... a fast car and I .... you all to the seaside…'

4 Adesso rileggi le tue risposte all'esercizio 3 e trova le frasi che contengono:

1 present simple ......   2 going to ......   3 present continuous ......   4 will future ......

5 a timetable ......   6 what someone believes about the future ......

7 plans someone has already made ......   8 what someone decides at that moment ......

5 <u>Sottolinea</u> la forma più appropriata dei verbi.

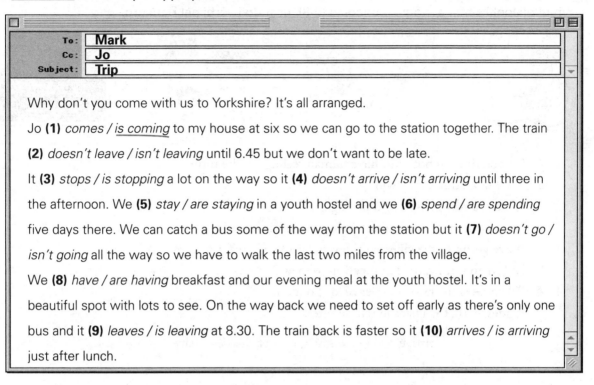

To: **Mark**
Cc: **Jo**
Subject: **Trip**

Why don't you come with us to Yorkshire? It's all arranged.

Jo **(1)** *comes / <u>is coming</u>* to my house at six so we can go to the station together. The train

(2) *doesn't leave / isn't leaving* until 6.45 but we don't want to be late.

It **(3)** *stops / is stopping* a lot on the way so it **(4)** *doesn't arrive / isn't arriving* until three in

the afternoon. We **(5)** *stay / are staying* in a youth hostel and we **(6)** *spend / are spending*

five days there. We can catch a bus some of the way from the station but it **(7)** *doesn't go /*

isn't going all the way so we have to walk the last two miles from the village.

We **(8)** *have / are having* breakfast and our evening meal at the youth hostel. It's in a

beautiful spot with lots to see. On the way back we need to set off early as there's only one

bus and it **(9)** *leaves / is leaving* at 8.30. The train back is faster so it **(10)** *arrives / is arriving*

just after lunch.

6 Riempi gli spazi usando *will* o il *present continuous* dei verbi tra parentesi.

1 Tim: Where are you going?

    Julie: To the cinema.

    Tim: Wait for me. I think I ....'ll come.......... (*come*) with you.

2 From next week all enquiries should be sent to Mary because Frances .... (*leave*)
    on Friday.

3 Rachel: I .... (*give*) Sophie a CD for her birthday. What ....
                (*you give*) her?

    Fiona: I .... (*probably get*) her a new purse. She keeps losing money from her
             old one.

4 John: I need to finish packing today because we .... (*move*) tomorrow and
             there's still lots to do.

    Peter: Don't worry. I .... (*come*) round tonight and help you.

7 Osserva le immagini (**1-4**) e leggi attentamente i dialoghi che le accompagnano. Poi scrivi dei mini-dialoghi simili per ogni immagine (**5-8**), usando i verbi nel riquadro.

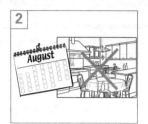

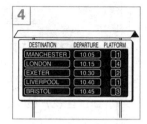

1 **A** Do you think robots **will have** human feelings in the future?

  B No, I don't think they **will**.

2 **A** What **are** you **going to do** in August?

  B I'm not sure yet. But I'**m not going to stay** at home.

3 **A** We'**re going** to the cinema this evening. Do you want to come?

  B I'd love to but I can't. I'**m meeting** John at 8.

4 **A** When **does** the next train **leave** for London?

  B It **goes** at 10.15. That's in ten minutes.

> arrive   do   ~~win~~   go   get   lose   have   study

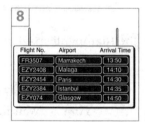

5 **A** Do you think Italy ......*will win*....... the next world cup?

  B No, I think they .... next time!

6 **A** What .... when you leave school?

  B I'm not sure yet. But I .... any more!

7 **A** We .... to the beach this weekend. Do you want to come?

  B I'd love to but I can't. It's my brother's eighteenth and we .... a party.

8 **A** When does the Paris flight .... ?

  B It .... in at 2.30. That's in half an hour.

8 Leggi questa conversazione tra il receptionist e un cliente dell'hotel. <u>Sottolinea</u> la forma più appropriata del verbo.

Guest: Excuse me. I **(1)** *i'm staying* / *stay* here till Friday. I'm **(2)** *going to look* / *looking* around the city now but I want to do some walking in the mountains while I'm here.

Receptionist: OK. There's a guided tour tomorrow. It **(3)** *is leaving* / *leaves* from outside the hotel at 10 am and it **(4)** *is returning* / *returns* at 5 pm.

Guest:	Oh good. I think I **(5)** *'m doing* / *'ll do* that.
Receptionist:	Would you like to order a packed lunch? Cheese or chicken sandwiches?
Guest:	I **(6)** *'ll have* / *have cheese* please. And are there any evening activities in the hotel?
Receptionist:	There's a concert tonight which **(7)** *is starting* / *starts* at 7.30.
Guest:	Oh I **(8)** *'m meeting* / *'ll meet* an old friend at 6 and I don't think I **(9)** *'m* / *'ll be* back in time.
Receptionist:	OK. **(10)** *Are you going to have* / *Do you have dinner* in the hotel tonight?
Guest:	No thanks.

9 Osserva le immagini e completa gli spazi con un verbo appropriato al *present continuous*, futuro con **will**, *present simple* o *future continuous*.

1 I expect my parents .will give me books. again for my birthday.

DOCTOR'S APPOINTMENT
Name: Sam Kelly
Date: 12 January
Time: 10.00

2 Sam .... tomorrow morning at ten o'clock.

HAPPY BIRTHDAY
80
today

3 My grandfather .... on his next birthday.

Concert
7pm

4 The concert .... at 7 pm.

English

5 I think I .... when I grow up.

6 At midday tomorrow I .... over the Atlantic.

SALE HERE
Mon-Fri

7 The sale .... on Friday.

8 This time next week we .... in Austria.

SHANNON FERRIES
Name: Mr & Mrs L. Murphy
Date of travel: 6 July
Depart: Holyhead
Destination: Dublin

9 We .... to Ireland by ferry this summer.

10 Maybe my father .... the money I need.

10 Completa i seguenti mini-dialoghi con le forme appropriate di futuro, usando le indicazioni tra parentesi.

1 A You must be looking forward to your holiday.

B You bet. This time tomorrow I *..'ll..be..lying..on..the..beach.* (*I / lie / beach*).

2 A Your car's absolutely filthy!

B Is it really that bad? I .... (*wash / tomorrow*), if I have time.

3 A What time can I phone this evening?

B Try about 9. I expect we .... (*finish / supper / by then*).

4 A Hurry up! I wouldn't mind seeing the beginning of the film, for once.

B It says in the paper that it .... (*start / 9*). We've got plenty of time.

5 A Have you decided who's coming to the party?

B Well, for a start I .... (*not / invite / Jack*).

6 A Sarah said she'd be here at 8. I hope nothing's happened.

B Don't worry. I'm sure .... (*be / soon*).

7 A Did you know that Steven .... (*leave / next week*)?

B No. Why?

A His father's got a new job in London.

8 A Just think, this Christmas we .... (*live / here*) for 10 years.

B Yes, and we still haven't put up those shelves in the sitting room.

11 Joely telefona alla sua amica Katrina per proporle di andare a vedere una mostra di arte pop (*Pop Art*). Completa la conversazione, tenendo presente che entrambe hanno molti impegni il weekend prossimo. Usa il *present continuous*, **be going to**, **will** e il *present simple*.

Katrina
Saturday 7th
10 hairdresser's
1.15 Alicia World Cafè
Sunday 8th

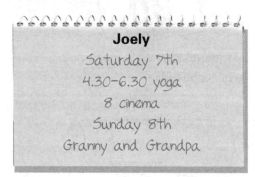

Joely
Saturday 7th
4.30–6.30 yoga
8 cinema
Sunday 8th
Granny and Grandpa

Joely: Hello, Katrina, it's Joely.

Katrina: Hi. How are you?

Joely: Fine, thanks. Listen, **(1)** *..are..you..doing..* anything interesting on Saturday?

Katrina: Nothing much. Why?

Joely: Do you feel like going to that Pop Art exhibition at the Tate Modern?

Katrina: Well, I'm busy in the morning. I **(2)** .... to the hairdresser's and then

(3) .... Alicia for lunch.

Joely: What time do you think you **(4)** .... free?

Katrina: Oh about 2.30 I expect. We could go after lunch.

Joely: But I've got my yoga class in the afternoon. It **(5)** .... at four-thirty so we

(6) .... much time.

Katrina: How about after yoga? When **(7)** .... ?

Joely: At 6.30. But I'm **(8)** .... at 8 so that's no good either.

Katrina: Maybe we could go on Sunday.

Joely: I can't go on Sunday because my grandparents **(9)** .... so I have to stay at

home.

Katrina: What about next week?

Joely: The trouble is the exhibition **(10)** .... on the tenth so this is our last chance.

Katrina: Hmm… look, I know, I **(11)** .... the hairdresser's and we can go tomorrow

morning. I don't want to miss it.

Joely: Are you sure?

Katrina: Of course. Shall we meet at about 9.30 at the entrance?

Joely: Great. 9.30 at the Tate Modern. See you tomorrow.

12 Riempi gli spazi con la forma corretta dei verbi tra parentesi. Usa **be going to**, *present simple*, **be about to**, *future perfect* o *future perfect continuous*.

A John: What are your plans for the weekend?

Sue: Well, we've just changed our plans, actually. We wanted to have a barbecue on Sunday.

But the weather forecast says it **(1)** *'s going to be* (be) cold and windy, so we

(2) .... (stay) indoors and watch a video.

B Beth: Is it all right for you to use the boss's office while he's on holiday?

Nick: Oh, I'm sure he won't mind when he **(3)** .... (find out) how many cars I've

sold this week.

C Terry: Are you very busy this afternoon?

Eddy: Well, that depends on why you're asking. I should really wash the car. Do you have a

better idea?

Terry: Yes. I **(4)** .... (look round) the new sports club.

Do you want to come? You can wash the car tomorrow.

Eddy: Sure. Let's go.

D Ben: Hurry up! We **(5)** .... (miss) the beginning of the concert.

Mary: Don't be silly. We've got plenty of time.

Ben: But it starts at nine. I want to arrive before the hall **(6)** .... (*get*) full, otherwise other people **(7)** .... (*take*) all the good seats by the time we get there.

E **Laura:** Do you have a moment to discuss this letter?

Bill: Well, I **(8)** .... (*have*) something to eat, and then I **(9)** .... (*write*) a report. Is it urgent?

Laura: We didn't talk about it yesterday in the end, because you were too busy. I must reply to it today and I need your opinion.

Bill: OK. I **(10)** .... (*finish*) my lunch by twenty past one. Can you come back then?

F **Chloe:** By next Friday I **(11)** .... (*work*) in this office for three years. Nobody has ever thanked me for anything I've done, so I **(12)** .... (*start*) looking for another job!

13 Traduci.

1 Vado in vacanza per alcuni giorni. Ti telefonerò non appena sarò di ritorno.

2 È una giornata bellissima. Staremo sulla spiaggia finché non farà buio.

3 Giocheremo a tennis domani a meno che non piova.

4 Non parlerò con Cameron finché non si scuserà per il suo comportamento.

5 Andremo a fare una passeggiata quando smetterà di piovere.

6 Se il tempo sarà bello faremo un picnic sulla spiaggia.

7 Mio padre ha promesso che mi comprerà un motorino se prenderò dei buoni voti a scuola.

8 Il prossimo treno parte tra 10 minuti. Non credo che arriverai alla stazione in tempo.

9 Ho intenzione di studiare biologia all'università.

10 Alla fine di quest'anno scolastico saranno 20 anni che insegno in questa scuola.

11 Alla fine di settembre saranno tre anni che abito a York.

12 Non darò la festa prima del 15 marzo. Entro allora mio fratello avrà dato l'esame di biologia, così avrà l'occasione di rilassarsi.

DOMANDE E RISPOSTE

6.1 Domande sì/no – *Yes/no questions*

6.2 Risposte sì/no – *Short answers*

6.3 Domande introdotte da *wh- words*

6.4 Domande in cui *wh- word* è soggetto

6.5 *Question tags*: vero? / non è vero?

6.6 Anch'io/neanch'io: *So do I / Neither do I*

6.7 Esprimere interesse: *Do you? / Is he?*

6.8 L'imperativo; *let's*

DOMANDE E RISPOSTE – INTRODUZIONE

I verbi ausiliari hanno grande importanza nella lingua inglese. Prima di tutto, sono necessari per formulare frasi interrogative e negative; inoltre svolgono molte funzioni comunicative ed esprimono una varietà di significati, per esempio **accordo**, **disaccordo**, **interesse e sorpresa**.

I verbi ausiliari si usano anche nelle risposte *yes/no*.

6.1   DOMANDE SÌ/NO – *YES/NO QUESTIONS*

▨ Le domande a cui si risponde **sì/no non** sono introdotte da una *wh- word*, ma direttamente da un verbo ausiliare; si mette il verbo ausiliare **davanti** al soggetto.

You're going on holiday soon.	→ *Are you going* on holiday soon?
Andrai in vacanza tra poco.	**Andrai** in vacanza tra poco?
He's packed his case.	→ *Has he packed* his case?
Ha fatto la valigia.	**Ha fatto** la valigia?

▨ Con il *present simple* e il *past simple* (vedi *Units* **1** e **2**) si usa l'ausiliare *do/does* e *did* per fare le domande.

You like Italy.	→ *Do you like* Italy?
Ti piace l'Italia. / A **te piace** l'Italia.	**Ti piace** l'Italia?
She prefers Greece.	→ *Does she prefer* Greece? (**Non** ~~*Does she prefers Greece?*~~)
Lei preferisce la Grecia.	**Lei preferisce** la Grecia?
They went to Corsica.	→ *Did they go* to Corsica?
Sono andati in Corsica.	**Sono andati** in Corsica?

▨ Nelle domande con il verbo *be*, il verbo *be* **precede** il soggetto.

They're in Madrid today.	→ *Are they* in Madrid today?
Sono a Madrid oggi.	**Sono** a Madrid oggi?

▨ Con i **verbi modali** (*can*, *could*, *may*, *might*, *must*, *ought to*, *shall*, *should*, *will* e *would*), che hanno funzione di ausiliare, si pone il verbo modale **davanti** al soggetto.

We can stay here.	→ *Can we* stay here?
Possiamo stare qui.	**Possiamo** stare qui?

Le domande negative si formulano allo stesso modo.

They like big cities.   → **Don't they like** big cities?
A loro piacciono le grandi città.   **A loro non piacciono** le grandi città?

Le domande negative spesso esprimono sorpresa.

Don't they like big cities?   (= I thought they liked big cities. Am I wrong?)
A loro non piacciono le grandi città?   (= Pensavo che a loro piacessero. Mi sbaglio?)
Can't she stay here?   (= I thought she could stay here. Is that impossible?)
Lei non può stare qui?   (= Pensavo che potesse stare qui. È impossibile?)

PRACTICE

1 Riordina queste parole in modo da formulare domande **sì/no**.

1 like / another / you / drink / would / ? .Would..you..like..another..drink?.................................

2 disturbing / am / you / I / ? ....

3 newspaper / buy / an / can / English / I / here / ? ....

4 remember / did / phone / Molly / to / you / ? ....

5 don't / music / you / like / to / listening / ? ....

6 Nicki / cousins / are / Sam / and / ? ....

7 your / basketball / like / friends / do / ? ....

8 Sophie's / isn't / ex-boyfriend / he / ? ....

9 seen / Psycho / you / have / ? ....

10 station / this / does / the / go / bus / to / ? ....

2 Trasforma queste frasi in domande **si/no**.

1 I live in Barcelona.   Do..you..live..in..Barcelona.............................. ?

2 Alex is a student.   Is..Alex..a..student.. ?

3 Sam and Emma are getting married.   .... ?

4 Bob drove to Malaga.   .... ?

5 Joanne's got lots of CDs.   .... ?

6 I can dive very well.   .... ?

7 Eddy watches football every Saturday. .... ?

8 Adam's seen that film.   .... ?

9 Mark had dropped his watch.   .... ?

10 I was late for school yesterday.   .... ?

6.2   RISPOSTE SÌ/NO – *SHORT ANSWERS*

Si risponde a una domanda **sì/no** aggiungendo lo stesso ausiliare o verbo modale della domanda.

Se la risposta è **sì**:

Are you going to Greece?	→ *Yes, I am.*
Vai in Grecia?	**Sì.**
Did you like the hotel?	→ *Yes, I did.*
Ti è piaciuto l'albergo?	**Sì.**

Se la risposta è **no**:

Are you going to Greece?	→ *No, I'm not.*
Vai in Grecia?	**No.**
Did you like the hotel?	→ *No, I didn't.*
Ti è piaciuto l'albergo?	**No.**

■ Il soggetto della risposta breve è **sempre** un pronome personale. Nelle risposte brevi affermative, l'ausiliare **non** può essere alla forma contratta.

Is Janet going to Molly's birthday party?　　　　→ *Yes, she is.*
Have your brothers done their homework yet?　　→ *Yes, they have.*

■ Le risposte brevi si possono usare anche dopo frasi dichiarative (non interrogative), per confermare o contraddire quello che è appena stato detto.

Concordare:	*That **was** surprising news!*	***Yes, it was.***
	affermativo →	**affermativo**
	*Manchester United **didn't** play very well.*	***No, they didn't.***
	negativo →	**negativo**
Contraddire:	*You **are** late.*	***No, I'm not.***
	affermativo →	**negativo**
	*Sarah **didn't sing** very well this evening.*	***Yes, she did.*** *She sang beautifully.*
	negativo →	**affermativo**

PRACTICE

1 Quali di queste risposte brevi puoi abbinare alle domande che hai formulato nell'esercizio 2 in **6.1** (pag. 90)?

a Yes, he did.	**b** No, I wasn't.	**c** Yes, they are.	**d** No, he doesn't.	**e** Yes, he had.
f Yes, I do.	**g** Yes, I can.	**h** No, he isn't.	**i** No, he hasn't.	**j** Yes, she has.

1 ..f... 　 2 ...... 　 3 ...... 　 4 ...... 　 5 ...... 　 6 ...... 　 7 ...... 　 8 ...... 　 9 ...... 　 10 ......

2 Scrivi risposte brevi a queste domande.

1 Do your parents know you're here?
   No, ...they don't................

2 Were you at school yesterday?
   Yes, ...

3 Have you got an iPod?
   No, ...

4 Are you going home now?
   No, ...

5 Did you have a good time last night?
   Yes, ...

6 Don't you know Simon's phone number?
   No, ...

7 Can you understand German?
   No, ...

8 Have you finished with the computer?
   Yes, ...

3 Formula domande appropriate.

1 .... Yes, I do.

2 .... No, we didn't.

3 .... No, I can't.

4 .... Yes, he does.

5 .... Yes, she did.

6 .... No, I wasn't.

7 .... Yes, it is.

8 .... Yes, they have.

4 Contraddici il contenuto delle frasi seguenti.

1 This pasta's delicious.   ....No, it isn't.......................

2 John can't play the guitar very well.   ....

3 We didn't have any homework.   ....

4 Jess has got blue eyes.   ....

5 The shops are closed on Sundays.   ....

6 Hannah hates horror films.   ....

7 You were rude to Aunt Helen.   ....

8 You haven't met Colin yet.   ....

6.3   DOMANDE INTRODOTTE DA *WH- WORDS*

Molto spesso le domande sono introdotte da pronomi o avverbi interrogativi, chiamati **wh- words**, che specificano il tipo di informazione richiesta. Quando l'informazione richiesta riguarda un complemento, o **oggetto**, l'ordine delle parole nella domanda è lo stesso che nelle domande **sì/no**.

Risposte	Domande				
	Wh- word	ausiliare	soggetto	verbo	complementi
*Denise will marry **Martin**.*	**Who**	will	Denise	marry?	
*Denise sposerà **Martin**.*	**Chi**				
*I wrote **a love song**.*	**What**	did	you	write?	
*Ho scritto **una canzone d'amore**.*	**Che cosa**				
*She can't sing **because she's tired**.*	**Why**	can't	she	sing?	
*Non può cantare **perché è stanca**.*	**Perché**				
*I've known Susan **for five years**.*	**How long**	have	you	known	Susan?
*Conosco Susan **da cinque anni**.*	**Da quanto tempo**				
*I trust **my sister's** advice.*	**Whose advice**	do	you	trust?	
*Mi fido dei consigli **di mia sorella**.*	**Dei consigli di chi**				
*I bought **four shirts** at Harrods.*	**How many shirts**	did	you	buy	at Harrods?
*Ho comprato **quattro camicie** da Harrods.*	**Quante camicie**				

◼ *What*, *which* e *whose* possono essere usati sia come pronomi che come aggettivi interrogativi.

Con funzione di **pronome** sono seguiti dal verbo ausiliare.

What are you doing?	*Che cosa stai* facendo?
Which is your waterproof jacket?	*Quale è* la tua giacca a vento?
Whose is that red car?	*Di chi è* quella macchina rossa?

Con funzione di **aggettivo** sono seguiti da un sostantivo.

What sort of books do you like?	*Che genere* di libri ti piacciono?
Which colour do you want, black or blue?	*Che colore* vuoi, nero o blu?
Whose coat is that?	*Di chi* è quel *cappotto*?

◼ *What* e *which* traducono entrambi **che/quale** nelle domande, con significati molto simili, e a volte entrambi sono possibili.

Which/What train did you catch?	*Che* treno hai preso?

Si usa generalmente *What* per indicare scelta tra un numero **illimitato** di risposte.

What's your favourite colour?	*Qual è* il tuo colore preferito?

Si usa generalmente *Which* per indicare scelta tra un numero **limitato**, **ristretto** di alternative.

Which pullover did you buy, the green one or the brown one?	*Che maglione* hai comprato, quello verde o quello marrone?

◼ *How* seguito da aggettivo o avverbio si usa in molte espressioni interrogative.

How much + sostantivo non numerabile

How much milk have we got?	*Quanto latte* abbiamo?

How many + sostantivo numerabile

How many foreign languages do you speak?	*Quante lingue straniere* parli?
How often do you go to the cinema?	*Quanto spesso* vai al cinema?
How tall is your brother?	*Quanto è alto* tuo fratello?
How high are the Rocky Mountains?	*Quanto* sono **alte** le Montagne Rocciose?
How far is Howe from here?	*Quanto* è **lontano** Howe da qui?

🔊 Fai attenzione alla differenza tra queste domande con *like*.

What does Jane *like*? (= What does Jane enjoy?)	She *likes* dancing.
Che cosa piace a Jane?	*Le piace ballare.*
What does Jane *look like*? (= describe her)	She's very tall.
Com'è Jane? (= descrivi il suo aspetto fisico)	*È molto alta.*
What's (is) Jane *like*? (= tell me about her)	She's clever and very tall.
Com'è Jane? (= parlami di lei)	*È intelligente e molto alta.*

PRACTICE

1 Leggi le domande e le risposte, poi completa le domande con la **wh- word** appropriata.

I called at your house yesterday, but you weren't in.

1	......*Where*.......... were you?	In Bristol.
2	.... did you go there?	Because I wanted to go shopping.
3	.... did you travel?	By car.
4	.... car did you go in?	My father's.
5	.... did you go with?	My sister and her friend.
6	.... were you there?	Five hours.
7	.... did you buy?	A new jacket and some boots.
8	.... did they cost?	£120.
9	.... did you have for lunch?	I didn't have any. I'd spent all my money!

2 Completa le seguenti domande con **what** o **which**.

1 ....*What*.......... sort of music do you like?

2 .... of these is yours?

3 .... colour was Kate's dress?

4 .... Coldplay song is your favourite?

5 .... of your friends lives closest to you?

6 .... are you talking about?

7 .... trainers are the most expensive?

8 .... did you do at the weekend?

3 Formula domande appropriate alle seguenti risposte. L'informazione richiesta è evidenziata.

1	................*Where's she living?*....................	She's living **in Miami**.
2	....	It's **3 kilometres**, so I come to school by scooter.
3	....	The dentist? Not more than **twice a year**.
4	....	I spend it on **CDs, clothes and going out**.
5	....	He didn't come **because he was ill**.
6	....	They got married **in 1960**.
7	....	It's **mine**. You can borrow it if you need to look up a word.
8	....	She's **1 metre 55**. I don't like tall girls.

4 Abbina le domande nella colonna **A** alle risposte nella colonna **B**.

A	B
1 What's Barcelona like?	a Everything apart from fish.
2 What does Harry look like?	b Most of them were very friendly.
3 What's your brother like?	c Very strict but interesting.
4 What does Emma like?	d It's great. It's my favourite city.
5 What were the people like?	e He's tall and dark.
6 What's the new teacher like?	f He's quite shy and funny.

6.4   DOMANDE IN CUI *WH- WORD* È SOGGETTO

Nelle domande in cui l'informazione richiesta riguarda il **soggetto**, in cui, cioè, *wh- word* e **soggetto coincidono**, l'ordine delle parole è quello della frase dichiarativa: **non** si usa l'ausiliare *do/does* al presente o l'ausiliare *did* al passato.

I pronomi interrogativi, che possono essere sia **soggetto** che **oggetto** delle domande, sono *who*, *what*, *which*, *whose*, *how much* e *how many*.

Confronta le domande seguenti:

<u>*Who*</u> invited you? (**Non** ~~*Who did invite you?*~~)   *Chi ti ha invitato?*
Risposta: <u>*Ted*</u> *(invited me).*   *Ted (mi ha invitato).*

Who did *you* invite?   *Chi **hai** invitato?*
Risposta: *I invited Ted.*   *Ho invitato Ted.*

<u>*Which CDs*</u> *cost £5?* (**Non** ~~*Which CDs do cost £5?*~~)   *Quali CD costano 5 sterline?*
Risposta: *These CDs.*   *Questi (costano £5).*

Which CDs did <u>*you*</u> buy?   *Quali CD **hai** comprato?*
Risposta: *I bought two Avril Lavigne CDs.*   *Ho comprato due CD di Avril Lavigne.*

Nelle domande soggetto, il pronome interrogativo *who* è sempre seguito da un verbo **singolare**

Who is coming to your party? (**Non** ~~*Who are coming?*~~)   *Chi viene alla tua festa?*

a meno che due o più persone siano specificate nella domanda.

*Who **are** your favourite **singers**?*   *Chi sono i tuoi **cantanti** preferiti?*

PRACTICE

1 <u>Sottolinea</u> l'alternativa corretta.

1 How many tourists <u>*visit*</u> / *do visit* London each year?

2 Who *uses* / *does use* the computer most in your family?

3 Who *spends* / *do you spend* most of your time with?

4 Which holiday *costs* / *does cost* more?

5 What *happens* / *does happen* if I press this button?

6 Who *won* / *did win* the MTV award for best group?

7 What *means 'scribble'?* / *does 'scribble' mean?*

8 How many people *told* / *did you tell* about the party?

95

2 Abbina gli inizi delle frasi con le loro logiche conclusioni.

1 Who broke this window? ..*e*..
2 How many people went to the lesson? .....
3 What happened to Dean last night? .....
4 Who do these CDs belong to? .....
5 Who wants the last biscuit? .....
6 How did the accident happen? .....
7 Who did you borrow that money from? .....
8 How many people phoned while I was out? .....

a He had an accident.
b I do, please.
c The road was icy.
d Only ten.
e Wayne did.
f Two: Mum and Rachel.
g They're mine.
h Nobody. It's mine.

3 Formula domande **soggetto** appropriate alle seguenti risposte.

1 **The number 21** goes to the centre. ....Which bus goes to the centre............... ?

2 **Picasso** painted *Guernica*. .... ?

3 **My sister** lent me some money. .... ?

4 There was **a fight** after the match. .... ?

5 **A strange noise** frightened her. .... ?

6 **David's** parents are bringing us home. .... ?

7 **Julie** gave Kamal your mobile number. .... ?

8 **19** Italians have won the Nobel Prize. .... ?

4 Leggi questo articolo e poi scrivi domande appropriate alle risposte date.

Top fashion model Charles Decker shocked his fans yesterday when he flew into London. He'd been on holiday in the Caribbean and he was wearing old shorts and a T-shirt. 'I was on the island of Grenada, but I had to come home suddenly because of a family emergency,' he explained. 'I was on the beach. My secretary phoned from London. I jumped onto my motorbike and went straight to the local airport. It took twenty minutes to get there. I'm going to visit my brother now. He's in hospital. I'll change my clothes after I've seen him.'

1 ....Who shocked his fans yesterday..........? Charles Decker.
2 ....? In the Caribbean.
3 ....? Old shorts and a T-shirt.
4 ....? Grenada.
5 ....? Because of a family emergency.
6 ....? His secretary.
7 ....? By motorbike.

8	....?	Twenty minutes.
9	....?	In hospital.
10	....?	After he's seen him.

6.5   *QUESTION TAGS:* VERO? / NON È VERO?

Nell'inglese parlato è molto comune aggiungere un *question tag* alla fine di una frase. Il *question tag* è una mini domanda che segue una frase affermativa o negativa, **mai** una frase interrogativa, per controllare se quello che abbiamo appena detto è vero o per sollecitare conferma da parte dell'interlocutore. Il *question tag* si può tradurre in italiano con 'vero?', 'non è vero?', 'no?'.

Il verbo del *tag* è l'**ausiliare** corrispondente a quello della frase. Nelle frasi al *present simple* si usa l'ausiliare del *present simple*, **do/does**; nelle frasi al *past simple* si usa l'ausiliare del *past simple*, **did**.

Se la **frase è affermativa**, il *tag* è **negativo**.

+   –

*They're going to Greece, **aren't** they?* (= il parlante si aspetta una risposta affermativa)

Se la **frase è negativa**, il *tag* è **affermativo**.

–   +

*You **aren't** going to Greece, **are** you?* (= il parlante si aspetta una risposta negativa)

■ Il soggetto del *tag* è sempre un pronome personale.

*Mary likes the seaside, **doesn't she?***	***A Mary piace** il mare, **no?***
*Your friends **haven't** arrived yet, **have they?***	***I tuoi amici non sono** ancora **arrivati**, **vero?***

■ Ricorda che i verbi modali hanno funzione di ausiliare.

*We **can** stay here, **can't we?***	***Possiamo** stare qui, **non è vero?***
*People **shouldn't** drop litter, **should they?***	***La gente non dovrebbe** buttare immondizia nelle strade, **vero?***

■ Il *question tag* di *let's* è *shall we?* (Vedi **6.8**)

*Let's go to France, **shall we?***	***Andiamo** in Francia, **che ne dite?***

■ Il *question tag* di *I am* (*I'm*) è *aren't I?*

*I am doing the right exercise, **aren't I?***	***Sto** facendo l'esercizio giusto, **vero?***
*I'm in the right place, **aren't I?***	***Sono** nel posto giusto, **vero?***

■ Nell'inglese parlato, il significato preciso del *question tag* è dato dall'intonazione.

Se il *question tag* è usato per confermare che quello che abbiamo detto è vero, non si tratta di una domanda vera, quindi l'intonazione **non sale** alla fine.

*They're going to Greece, **aren't they?*** (⤵)

Viceversa, se il *question tag* indica una domanda vera, se davvero vogliamo sapere qualcosa e non siamo sicuri, l'intonazione **sale** alla fine.

*They're going to Greece, **aren't they?*** (⤴)

PRACTICE

1 Aggiungi il *question tag* alle frasi seguenti.

1 He always forgets his homework, ...doesn't he................ ?

2 The teachers didn't see me, ... ?

3 You would like to come with us, ... ?

4 Let's have another coffee, ... ?

5 It couldn't possibly rain, ... ?

6 Molly will have to tell the truth, ... ?

7 We can't stop here, ... ?

8 You promise you'll never tell anyone, ... ?

2 Per ciascuna delle frasi seguenti scrivi una frase appropriata alla situazione con un *question tag*.

1 You're at a party with your friend Will. You think he's met Francesca before but you're not sure. Introduce her to him. (*met/before*)

You've met Francesca before, haven't you? ....

2 Carla's coming for supper. You don't think she's a vegetarian but you want to make sure. (*eat/meat*)

....

3 Your brother is coming to pick you up at the station. You don't want to wait. (*not/be/late*)

....

4 You're phoning Tessa to make sure she's coming to the cinema this evening.

....

5 Lucy is coming to your house. You've got a big dog. You don't think she's frightened but you want to make sure.

....

6 You and your friend are deciding what to do on Saturday. You'd like to go shopping and you think your friend would too.

....

3 Invitato a un party, Hercule Poirot fa sfoggio delle sue capacità deduttive. Completa le frasi con un *question tag*.

1 You weren't brought up in England, ...were you............ ?

2 You met your husband in India, ... ?

3 Your husband knows our hostess well, ... ?

4 Your husband is a handsome man, ... ?

5 You would like him to spend more time with you, ... ?

6 You don't get on well with our hostess, ... ?

7 She's been drinking a lot of champagne, ... ?

8 She shouldn't behave like that, ... ?

6.6   ANCH'IO/NEANCH'IO: *SO DO I / NEITHER DO I*

Le espressioni italiane 'anch'io' e 'neanch'io' sono rese in inglese rispettivamente con **so ... I** e **neither/nor ... I**.

Per concordare con una frase affermativa si usa **so** + **ausiliare** + **soggetto**;

per concordare con una frase negativa si usa **neither** o **nor** + **ausiliare** + **soggetto**.

+ *We went* to Spain last year. + *So did I.*	*Siamo andati* in Spagna l'anno scorso. **Anch'io.**
+ *She's been* to Manchester. + *So have I.*	*È stata* a Manchester. **Anch'io.**
– *I don't know* this song. – *Neither/Nor do I.*	*Non conosco* questa canzone. **Neanch'io.**
– *He can't* dance. – *Neither/Nor can I.*	*Lui non sa* ballare. **Neanch'io.**

Il soggetto che segue l'ausiliare può essere espresso anche da un sostantivo.

I didn't like the film.	*Non mi è piaciuto il film.*
*Neither did **my boyfriend**.*	*Neanche al **mio ragazzo**.*
Louise plays the violin beautifully.	*Louise suona il violino benissimo.*
*So does **her sister**.*	*Anche **sua sorella**.*

PRACTICE

1 Abbina gli inizi delle frasi con le loro logiche conclusioni.

1 I started learning English when I was ten. d...   **a** So am I.

2 I didn't find it very easy. .....   **b** Neither will I.

3 I was always trying to sing English songs. .....   **c** Neither did I.

4 But I couldn't understand the words at first. .....   **d** So did I.

5 I'm quite good at English now. .....   **e** So must I.

6 I've read a couple of novels in English. .....   **f** So have I.

7 I won't have many problems in England, I guess. .....   **g** Neither could I.

8 And I must do my homework now. .....   **h** So was I.

2 Hai appena incontrato Gemma a una festa e scoprite che avete molte cose in comune. Replica alle frasi della tua nuova amica.

1 I've been learning the guitar for five years. ....So have I...................

2 I used to like Italian music. ....

3 I can't stand heavy metal. ....

4 I messed up my exams this year. ....

5 I think maths should be optional. ....

6 I never have enough money. ....

7 My mother doesn't understand me. ....

8 I'll be going to Rimini in August. ....

6.7   ESPRIMERE INTERESSE: *DO YOU? / IS HE?*

Nella conversazione si usano spesso delle espressioni brevi per indicare che si sta ascoltando con attenzione e interesse. Un tipico indicatore di interesse è **Really?** = Davvero?, ma si può esprimere lo stesso significato con una struttura simile al *question tag*: **verbo ausiliare + pronome**.

A *John* **has won** *a scholarship to study Philosophy at Oxford.* **B** **Has he?** *That's great!*

A *We* **had** *a lovely holiday in Ireland.*
B **Did you?** *What did you do?*

A *John* **ha vinto** *una borsa di studio per studiare filosofia a Oxford.* **B** **Davvero?** *Fantastico!*

A *Abbiamo* **trascorso** *una bellissima vacanza in Irlanda.* **B** **Davvero?** *Che cosa avete fatto?*

Se la frase è negativa, anche il **tag** è negativo.

A *I* **don't** *understand.* **B** **Don't you?** *I'm sorry.*

A *Jenny* **isn't** *keen on pop music.*
B **Isn't she?** *I love it.*

A **Non** *capisco.* **B** **Sul serio?** *Mi dispiace.*

A *A Jenny* **non** *piace molto la musica pop.*
B **Davvero?** *Io la adoro.*

PRACTICE

1 Completa i seguenti mini-dialoghi con espressioni corrispondenti all'italiano 'Davvero?', per indicare che stai ascoltando con interesse.

1 A I never eat shellfish.   **B** ....*Don't you?*........ ? I love it.

2 A I've got a twin brother.   **B** .... ? Are you identical?

3 A My Dad's an astrophysicist.   **B** .... ? He must be very clever.

4 A I haven't been to the cinema for ages.   **B** .... ? Let's go on Saturday.

5 A I bought a new mobile phone yesterday.   **B** .... ? Let's have a look.

6 A I'm going to Dublin this summer.   **B** .... ? You'll love it.

7 A Max and Andy can't come this evening.   **B** .... ? What a pity!

8 A I'd hate to live in the country.   **B** .... ? I'd love to.

6.8   L'IMPERATIVO; *LET'S*

L'imperativo della 2ª persona singolare e plurale, **you**, si forma nel modo seguente:

Affermativa Forma base del verbo: infinito senza *to*		Negativa *Don't* + forma base del verbo	
Listen!	*Ascolta!/Ascoltate!*	*Don't listen!*	*Non ascoltare! / Non ascoltate!*
Go!	*Vai!/Andate!*	*Don't go!*	*Non andare/andate via!*
Be quiet!	*Stai buono! / State zitti!*	*Don't be late!*	*Non fare/fate tardi!*

Come si vede dagli esempi, nell'imperativo il soggetto viene omesso. La stessa struttura corrisponde anche alla forma italiana di cortesia, Lei.

Good morning, Mrs Branson.	*Buongiorno, Signora Branson.*
*Please **go in**. The doctor is waiting for you.*	***Entri pure**. Il dottore la sta aspettando.*

L'imperativo si usa per:

◼ **dare ordini e istruzioni**.

***Write** your answers on the answer sheet.*	***Scrivete** le risposte nel foglio apposito.*
***Don't use** tippex.*	***Non usate** la cancellina.*

◼ **fare raccomandazioni**.

***Sit down** and **have a rest**. You look exhausted.*	***Siediti e riposati un po'**. Sei sfinito.*
***Don't forget** to lock the door.*	***Non dimenticarti** di chiudere a chiave la porta.*

◼ **augurare qualcosa**.

***Have** a nice journey.*	***Fai** buon viaggio.*

◻ L'imperativo italiano **vieni a / vai a + infinito** si traduce generalmente con *go and… / come and…* .

***Come and see us** in the summer.*	***Vieni a trovarci** d'estate.*
(**Non** ~~Come to see us~~)	

◼ L'imperativo della 1ª persona plurale, *we*, o congiuntivo esortativo, si forma con *let us → let's* seguito dalla forma base del verbo e viene comunemente usato per fare delle proposte e dare suggerimenti.

***Let's go** to the cinema.*	***Andiamo** al cinema.*
***Let's take** Angela to the Junction.*	***Portiamo** Angela al Junction.*

La forma negativa è **let's not**.

*Please, **let's not quarrel**.*	*Per favore, **non litighiamo**.*

PRACTICE

1 Riempi gli spazi con la forma corretta dell'imperativo, usando i verbi nel riquadro. Usa ogni verbo una sola volta.

listen   walk   remember   have   ~~shout~~   lean out   leave   go

1 ....*Don't shout*............ , I'm not deaf!

2 .... to phone me later on. I'll be in all evening.

3 .... carefully to the instructions before you start.

4 .... and see your grandmother on the way home from school.

5 .... the window open. The mosquitoes will come in.

6 .... of the window when the train is moving.

7 .... home on your own late at night. It's dangerous.

8 .... a good trip and don't forget to send us a postcard.

2 Completa le frasi seguenti con **let's** o **let's not**.

1 ....*Let's not*......... go out this evening. I'm really tired.

2 .... meet outside the cinema at about 8.15.

3 .... argue about it. We'll do it the way you want.

4 .... wait a bit longer and see if she arrives.

5 .... try her number again. She might be home by now.

6 .... tell her yet. It'll be a nice surprise.

3 George sta scrivendo una mail al suo amico Ron, per invitarlo a casa sua il prossimo fine settimana. Riempi gli spazi con l'imperativo dei verbi nel riquadro.

get   walk   bring   not worry   come   cross   phone   not forget   let   get off

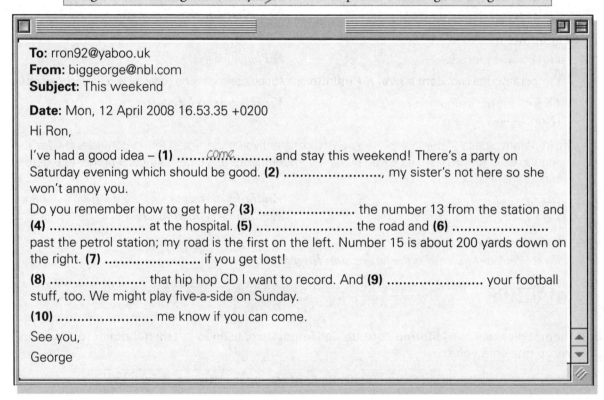

To: rron92@yaboo.uk
From: biggeorge@nbl.com
Subject: This weekend

Date: Mon, 12 April 2008 16.53.35 +0200

Hi Ron,

I've had a good idea – **(1)** ....come.......... and stay this weekend! There's a party on Saturday evening which should be good. **(2)** ...., my sister's not here so she won't annoy you.

Do you remember how to get here? **(3)** .... the number 13 from the station and **(4)** .... at the hospital. **(5)** .... the road and **(6)** .... past the petrol station; my road is the first on the left. Number 15 is about 200 yards down on the right. **(7)** .... if you get lost!

(8) .... that hip hop CD I want to record. And **(9)** .... your football stuff, too. We might play five-a-side on Sunday.

(10) .... me know if you can come.

See you,

George

ALL IN ONE REVISION

1 Della Dombey è una cantante americana. In questo momento è in una radio inglese per rispondere in diretta alle domande del pubblico.

I suoi fan le faranno alcune domande. Che domande vorresti fare tu al tuo cantante preferito?

Scrivi tre domande.

1 ....

2 ....

3 ....

2 Adesso ascolta l'intervista. Qualcuno dei fan di Della ha chiesto una delle domande a cui avevi pensato tu?

1.13

3 Ascolta di nuovo e completa le domande seguenti. Ferma la registrazione se è necessario.

1.14

1 .... *Do you like* .... Manchester?

2 .... stay here?

3 .... in public for the first time?

4 .... any clubs in Manchester?

5 .... your boyfriend now, Della?

6 .... best?

4 Leggi le domande che hai completato e abbinale a queste risposte.

a ....*6*.... My boyfriend Dean's.   d .... Dean Bradley.

b .... Yes, I do.   e .... Only four days.

c .... No, I haven't.   f .... At my high school concert.

5 Rileggi con attenzione gli esercizi 3 e 4.

1 Which of the questions in exercise 3 begin with question words? ....

2 Which of the questions in exercise 3 do not begin with question words? ....

3 What is different about the answers to these two groups of questions? ....

6 Replica alle frasi seguenti con *so...* oppure *neither...* come richiede il senso.

1 I like playing volleyball. ....*So do I*.......................................

2 I don't go out very often. ....*Nor do I or Neither do I*..................................

3 I've got a CD player. ....

4 I'm going to meet my friends this weekend. ....

5 I was at school last week. ....

6 I didn't go out last night. ....

7 I'd like to learn to fly a plane. ....

8 I couldn't speak English when I was five. ....

7 Scrivi sei domande che vuoi rivolgere a una persona che ammiri (ad esempio un attore o uno sportivo). Comincia le prime cinque con le *wh- words* date e aggiungi una domanda **sì/no**. Se vuoi, puoi anche rispondere!

1 Why .... ?   4 Who .... ?

2 How often .... ?   5 How long .... ?

3 Where .... ?   6 .... ?

8 Sono le 9 di sera e Peter telefona a Molly, la sua ragazza. Completa la loro conversazione con le espressioni nel riquadro.

Of course I do	Yes, I am	Have	shall we
So am I	Yes, I did	do	won't you

Molly: Hello?

Peter: Are you home at last?

Molly: **(1)** ....Yes, I am............ . Why?

Peter: You've been out all evening, haven't you?

Molly: What are you talking about?

Peter: I phoned three times and you didn't answer.

Molly: **(2)** .... you been checking up on me?

Peter: No, I haven't. I was just worried. You said you'd be in tonight, didn't you?

Molly: **(3)** .... But I had a change of plan, OK?

Peter: Of course. I'm sorry.

Molly: **(4)** .... I don't want to quarrel.

Peter: Neither do I. You know I love you, don't you?

Molly: **(5)** ....

Peter: And **(6)** .... you love me?

Molly: You know I do.

Peter: And you'll always love me, **(7)** .... ?

Molly: Of course I will. You can meet me tomorrow, can't you?

Peter: Sure. Let's meet by the college gate, **(8)** .... ?

Molly: Yes, let's. We'd better say goodnight, then.

Peter: OK. Good night. Love you.

Molly: Love you. Bye.

Peter: Bye.

9 Scegli la frase corretta.

1 **a** Who made the cake for the wedding? ✔

   b Who did make the cake for the wedding?

2 **a** We haven't got to do the washing-up, do we?

   b We haven't got to do the washing-up, have we?

3 **a** Does your sister live with your parents or she has got a flat of her own?

   b Does your sister live with your parents or has she got a flat of her own?

4 **a** Why can't you walk faster?

   b Why can't walk you faster?

5 **a** You went to school in Paris, haven't you?

   b You went to school in Paris, didn't you?

6 **a** What does Julie's brother look like?

   b What is Julie's brother look like?

10 Formula risposte adatte a queste domande, usando le parole tra parentesi e le tue idee.

1 *Where would you like to go on holiday?* .... (*go*)

The Caribbean.

2 *Did you finish all the ice cream?* .... (*finish*)

No, I didn't. There's some in the fridge.

3 .... (*spend*)

About an hour, usually.

4 .... (*try*)

No, I haven't. But I'd love to.

5 .... (*do*)

Sometimes I watch a film and other times I read.

6 .... (*see*)

About once a week. It depends how busy I am.

7 .... (*enjoy*)

Not really. The music wasn't good, and the people weren't very interesting.

8 .... (*be*)

Because I overslept.

11 Leggi questo articolo e scrivi domande adeguate alle risposte date.

LAST NIGHT BRIAN BAINES was celebrating his appointment as manager of Farley City Football Club. He says he is particularly happy to be going back to Farley, where he was born in 1968, after playing for a number of European teams. Baines telephoned his wife Shirley as soon as he had signed the contract. He said that she is really pleased that their three children will be able to settle at schools in the city. Their many old friends are looking forward to welcoming them back to Farley.

1 *What was Brian Baines celebrating last night?* ....

His appointment as manager of Farley City F.C.

2 .... In Farley.

3 .... His wife Shirley.

4 ....

As soon as he had signed the contract.

5 .... Three.

6 ....

Because their children will be able to settle at schools in Farley.

7 ....,........ . Their many old friends.

12 Formula tutte le domande possibili per le seguenti risposte, usando le **wh- words** indicate tra parentesi.

1 150,000 people demonstrated in London today against fox hunting.

(How many …? Where …? Why …?)

....

....

....

2 Tom Cruise met Nicole Kidman when they were working on *Days of Thunder* and they got married in 1990. (Who …? Which …? When …?)

....

....

....

3 Kevin has fallen in love with Alex's sister. (Who …? Whose …?)

....

....

4 There was a fire in the hotel because someone dropped a cigarette. (Where …? How …?)

....

....

5 The old lady who saw the thief leaving the flat described him as tall, dark and handsome.

(Who …? What … like?)

....

....

6 Jenny is clever and hard-working and she's never failed an exam.
(What … like? How often …?)

....

....

7 They travelled 300 miles to see the exhibition and when they got to the gallery it was closed
so they couldn't go in. (How far …? Why …?)

....

....

8 Fog held the flight up so they were two hours late. (What …? How late …?)

....

....

13 Traduci.

1 Che cosa è successo a Tom? Ha un aspetto terribile.

2 Chi hai visto alla festa di Debbie?

3 Quale autobus va alla stazione, il numero 23 o il numero 30?

4 **A** Che cosa sta succedendo laggiù? **B** Andiamo a dare un'occhiata.

5 **A** Chi ti ha detto che John è in ospedale? **B** Me l'ha detto suo padre.

6 **A** Ieri era il mio compleanno. **B** Perché non me lo hai detto?

7 Chi ha mangiato l'ultima fetta di torta?

8 **A** Che cosa hai mangiato per pranzo? **B** Ho mangiato un panino e un'insalata di pomodori.

9 Quante persone sono venute alla riunione?

10 Chi sta suonando il pianoforte?

UNIT 7

IL NOME

IL NOME – INTRODUZIONE

I nomi, o sostantivi, sono parole che indicano persone, animali, cose e altre entità. In inglese è necessario sapere se un nome è di persona, animale o cosa. Solo così si può sapere quali pronomi e quali aggettivi possessivi usare: *he* e *his* per uomini e ragazzi, *she*, *her* e *hers* per donne e ragazze, *it* e *its* per oggetti e animali, a eccezione di animali di cui conosciamo con certezza il sesso, ad esempio gli animali domestici, per i quali si usano comunemente *he* e *she*. Confronta le frasi seguenti:

The cheetah is the fastest animal in the world. *It can run at up to 100 kilometres per hour.* *I have a small dog.* **His** *name is Sammy:* *he loves playing with my slippers.*	*Il ghepardo è l'animale più veloce del mondo.* *Può correre fino a 100 chilometri all'ora.* *Ho un cagnolino. Si chiama Sammy: adora giocare con le mie pantofole.*

I nomi possono essere **numerabili**, se indicano entità che possono essere contate (si può dire *an apple*, **two apples**) o **non numerabili**, se si riferiscono a entità non definibili in termini di numero (**non** si può dire *a rice, two rices*).

PRACTICE

1 Come si chiamano queste cose? Abbina le parole del riquadro agli oggetti nelle immagini.

dogs family hair information love luggage money people trousers wine

1 .....luggage......... 2 .... 3 .... 4 .... 5 ....

6 .... 7 .... 8 .... 9 .... 10 ....

7.1   IL PLURALE

Il plurale dei nomi si forma di norma aggiungendo *-s* al singolare.

girl → girls   orange → oranges   book → books   spoon → spoons

IL PLURALE: VARIAZIONI DI SPELLING

I sostantivi che terminano in *-ch*, *-sh*, *-s*, *-ss*, *-x* e *-to* aggiungono *-es*:

sandwich → sandwiches   brush → brushes   bus → buses
class → classes   box → boxes   tomato → tomatoes

I sostantivi che terminano in *-y* **preceduta da consonante** trasformano *y* in *i* e aggiungono *-es*.

lady → ladies   party → parties

Ma i sostantivi che terminano in *-y* **preceduta da vocale** aggiungono regolarmente *-s*.

boy → boys   chimney → chimneys

I sostantivi che terminano in *-f/fe* hanno il plurale in *-ves*:

leaf → leaves   knife → knives   life → lives

Fanno eccezione alcune parole, tra cui

roof → roofs   belief → beliefs   cliff → cliffs   handkerchief → handkerchiefs

PLURALI IRREGOLARI

Alcuni sostantivi di uso comune hanno il plurale irregolare.

man → **men**	uomo, uomini	tooth → **teeth**	dente, denti
woman → **women**	donna, donne	foot → **feet**	piede, piedi
child → **children**	bambino, bambini	mouse → **mice**	topo, topi
person → **people**	persona, persone		

Alcuni sostantivi, che indicano **gruppi di persone**, sono sempre seguiti dal verbo al **plurale**.

*The **police are** looking for a tall man with a moustache.* — **La polizia sta** *cercando un uomo alto con i baffi.*

***People are** very interested in reality shows, and I can't understand why.* — **La gente è** *molto interessata ai reality, non riesco a capire perché.*

Altri sostantivi, come *family*, *team*, *government*, *public*, possono essere seguiti sia da verbi singolari che plurali.

*The team **is/are** playing very well.* — *La squadra **sta** giocando molto bene.*

La forma plurale è più comune quando il gruppo è visto come un insieme di persone che pensano e agiscono in modo personale, mentre la forma singolare è più comune quando il gruppo è considerato in modo impersonale.

Confronta le frasi seguenti:

*Her **family have** decided to move to the countryside. **They think** it's better for the children.*
La sua famiglia ha *deciso di trasferirsi in campagna.* **Pensa** *che sia meglio per i bambini.*

*The average Italian **family has** 1.2 children. **It is** much smaller than **it** used to be.*
La famiglia italiana media ha *1,2 figli.* **È** *molto meno numerosa di come era nel passato.*

NOMI SOLO PLURALI

Alcune cose che indossiamo o usiamo sono sempre plurali. Sono formate da due parti che non possono essere separate.

trousers = **pantaloni**   *pyjamas* = **pigiama**   *shorts* = **pantaloncini**   *jeans* = **jeans**   *tights* = **calze/collant**
pants = **mutande**   *sunglasses* = **occhiali da sole**   *glasses* = **occhiali**   *scissors* = **forbici**

Questi nomi hanno sempre il verbo **plurale**.

My trousers are new. (**Non** ~~My trousers is new.~~)   *I miei pantaloni sono nuovi.*
These shorts are dirty. (**Non** ~~These shorts is dirty.~~)   *Questi pantaloncini sono sporchi.*

Altre cose che portiamo possono essere singolari. Si compongono di due parti che possono essere separate.

shoe/shoes = **scarpa/scarpe**   *sock/socks* = **calzino/calzini**   *earring/earrings* = **orecchino/orecchini**

La parola *clothes* = abiti/vestiti non è mai singolare.

I bought some new clothes. (**Non** ~~I bought a new clothe.~~)   *Ho comprato degli abiti nuovi.*

PRACTICE

1 Scrivi il plurale dei seguenti nomi.

1 family ..*families*..   **2** school ....   **3** potato ....   **4** shelf ....

5 lady ....   **6** self ....   **7** monkey ....   **8** policeman ....

9 Euro ....   **10** belief ....   **11** beach ....   **12** church ....

13 holiday ....   **14** box ....   **15** secretary ....

2 Quali delle parole plurali nel riquadro possono essere usate anche al singolare?

boots	bracelets	clothes	earrings	gloves	jeans
	shorts	socks	shoes	tights	

7.2   L'ARTICOLO: *A(N), THE* E NESSUN ARTICOLO

▪ L'articolo indeterminativo italiano, **uno, una, un** e **un'**, corrisponde all'articolo inglese *a(n)* che è invariabile per genere: ha cioè la stessa forma per maschile, femminile e neutro.
L'articolo indeterminativo si scrive:

a davanti a parole che iniziano per **consonante, h aspirata** e suono /*ju*/

a bank   *a trolley*   *a house*   *a hint*   *a year*   *a university* /*ju*/   *a European country* /*ju*/

an davanti a parole che iniziano per **vocale** e **h grafica**, cioè muta.

an apple   *an umbrella*   *an idea*   *an honest person*   *an hour*   *an honour*

▪ L'articolo determinativo *the* è invariabile per genere e numero.

the girl = **la** *ragazza*   *the girls* = **le** *ragazze*   *the boy* = **il** *ragazzo*
the boys = **i** *ragazzi*   *the pond* = **lo** *stagno*   *the ponds* = **gli** *stagni*

	Significa:	**Si usa per:**	**Si usa con:**
A(n)	uno tra molti: *My sister works in **a cinema**.* *Mia sorella lavora in **un cinema**.*	informazioni nuove: *My friend was talking to **a girl**.* *Il mio amico stava parlando con **una ragazza**.*	nomi numerabili* *(cinema, girl)*
The	l'unico che c'è, o quello/quelli specifici: *The cinema opened last week.* ***Il cinema** è stato aperto la settimana scorsa.*	persone o cose già nominate: ***The girl** was very angry.* ***La ragazza** era molto arrabbiata.* indicare che sappiamo già di cosa stiamo parlando: *Where's **the money** I lent you?* *Dove sono **i soldi** che ti ho prestato?*	nomi numerabili* *(cinema, girl)* e nomi non numerabili* *(money)*
Nessun articolo	un'intera categoria o genere: *Cinemas show films.* ***I cinema** proiettano film.*	persone o cose in **senso generale**: ***Money** makes **people** happy.* ***I soldi** rendono felice **la gente**.* *I like **music**.* *Mi piace **la musica**.*	nomi numerabili* plurali *(cinemas)* e nomi non numerabili* *(money, music)*

* Vedi **7.4**

La differenza più significativa tra le due lingue riguarda **l'uso** o **l'omissione dell'articolo determinativo**: in inglese, a differenza che in italiano, **non** si usa l'articolo determinativo *the* quando si parla di qualcosa in senso generico, illimitato.

Confronta le seguenti coppie di frasi:

*I don't like **the music** my brother plays.* (= that particular music)
*Non mi piace **la musica** che suona mio fratello.* (= quella musica particolare)

***Music** helps me to concentrate when I'm working.* (= any music)
***La musica** mi aiuta a concentrarmi quando lavoro.* (= qualunque musica)

*We planted **the trees** in our garden five years ago.* (= the particular trees in our garden)
*Abbiamo piantato **gli alberi** nel nostro giardino cinque anni fa.* (= gli alberi specifici del nostro giardino)

***Trees** are easily damaged by **pollution**.* (= all trees; any pollution)
***Gli alberi** sono danneggiati dall'**inquinamento**.* (= tutti gli alberi; dall'inquinamento in generale)

***The cheese** is in **the fridge**.* (= the cheese you need; the only fridge here)
***Il formaggio** è **nel frigo**.* (= il formaggio che vuoi; l'unico frigo che c'è qui, dunque specifico)

*Help yourself to **cheese** and **biscuits**.* (= as much cheese and as many biscuits as you want)
*Prendi **il formaggio** e **i biscotti**: serviti pure.* (= tutto il formaggio e i biscotti che vuoi)

■ Adesso leggi attentamente questa frase, che evidenzia le tre possibilità: *a*, *the* e **nessun articolo**.

People used to believe that **the Moon** was **a goddess**.

(= people in general; the Moon that goes around this planet; one of many goddesses)

La gente credeva che ***la luna*** fosse ***una dea***.

(= la gente in generale; la luna che ruota intorno a questo pianeta; una di molte dee)

PRACTICE

1 Inserisci *a(n)* o *the* dove sono necessari. Se **nessun articolo** è necessario, lascia gli spazi vuoti.

1 In Japan ...—... thieves recently tried to rob ...a... bank by gaining access to ..the.. bank's password.

2 Have you phoned .... hotel to ask if they have .... room with .... balcony?

3 Can we come in? I'm afraid .... dogs are dirty because we've been for .... walk in .... park.

4 There's .... really good restaurant near .... station where you can eat .... Indonesian food.

5 I've lived in .... country all my life so I'm finding it hard to get used to .... traffic here in London.

6 Keith's very interested in .... modern art and he spends his free time visiting .... exhibitions.

7 Did you remember to lock .... front door? There have been several burglaries in .... neighbourhood since .... last time you were here.

8 My sister spends all her money on .... clothes so she never has enough money to pay .... rent.

2 Completa la conversazione con *a(n)* o *the* dove sono necessari. Se **nessun articolo** è necessario, lascia gli spazi vuoti.

Leo: What's the matter? You look really fed up.

Rachel: I am. I can't stand **(1)** ..the... weather.

Leo: It's not that bad.

Rachel: I'd like to live in **(2)** .... country which has **(3)** .... good weather for more than two weeks a year!

Leo: It sounds like **(4)** .... nice idea but I lived in Dubai for two years and after a while **(5)** .... sunshine got boring!

Rachel: But **(6)** .... days are so short at this time of year. It's really depressing.

Leo: Did you know that **(7)** .... scientists have recognised **(8)** .... illness called SAD – Seasonal Affective Disorder?

Rachel: What are **(9)** .... symptoms?

Leo: **(10)** .... depression and lack of energy.

Rachel: I think I've got it. What's **(11)** .... cure?

Leo: **(12)** .... holiday in Dubai! Otherwise you should get **(13)** .... light box.

Rachel: What's that?

Leo: **(14)** .... people with SAD need **(15)** .... light. If you can't sit in **(16)** .... sun, **(17)** .... artificial light works too.

Rachel: **(18)** .... artificial light? How depressing!

Leo: Hmm – I think you're **(19)** .... serious case. You definitely need **(20)** .... holiday!

7.3   OSSERVAZIONI SULL'USO DEGLI ARTICOLI

Tra le due lingue ci sono altre differenze sistematiche nell'uso degli articoli, ad esempio con nomi di luoghi, di professioni, nelle descrizioni fisiche e nelle esclamazioni.

NOMI DI LUOGHI

Non si usa l'articolo *the* davanti a

- nomi propri di continenti, nazioni, stati, città e paesi: *Europe, Italy, France, London, Florida.*

- **Ma** si usa l'articolo quando il nome proprio è **plurale** e/o contiene parole come *Republic* o *States*: **the** *Netherlands,* **the** *United Kingdom,* **the** *United States,* **the** *Czech Republic.*

- nomi di laghi: *Lake Garda, Lake Ontario.*

- edifici e luoghi che contengono il nome della loro città nella denominazione:

Manchester Airport = **l'Aeroporto di Manchester**	*Cardiff Station* = **la Stazione di Cardiff**
Edinburgh Castle = **il Castello di Edimburgo**	*Durham University* = **l'Università di Durham**

Si usa l'articolo *the* davanti a

- oceani, fiumi e mari: **the** *Pacific Ocean,* **the** *Black Sea,* **the** *Mediterranean,* **the** *Danube.*

- regioni: **the** *Far East,* **the** *Midlands.*

- gruppi di isole: **the** *Philippines,* **the** *Hebrides.*

- deserti, catene di montagne e montagne: **the** *Kalahari,* **the** *Alps,* **the** *Matterhorn* **eccetto**: *Mount Everest.*

- ambienti naturali: **the** *sea,* **the** *coast,* **the** *seaside,* **the** *beach,* **the** *country,* **the** *mountains,* **the** *hills,* **the** *sky,* **the** *Sun,* **the** *Moon.*

  My parents spend their holidays by **the coast***, but I prefer walking in* **the mountains***.*
  I miei genitori trascorrono le vacanze **sulla costa***, ma io preferisco camminare* **in montagna***.*

PROFESSIONI

A differenza dell'italiano, si usa l'articolo indeterminativo *a(n)* per dire che lavoro si fa.

I'm **a** *doctor.* (**Non** *I'm doctor.*)	*Sono (un) medico. / Faccio il medico.*
My sister works as **a** *teacher.*	*Mia sorella lavora come insegnante.*

DESCRIZIONI FISICHE

Nelle descrizioni delle persone, si usa l'articolo *a(n)* davanti a un nome singolare, **nessun articolo** davanti a nomi plurali e non numerabili*. (Vedi **7.4**)

John's got **a** *long nose.*	*John ha* **il** *naso lungo.*
My grandfather had **a** *beard.*	*Il mio nonno aveva* **la** *barba.*
Paula's got blue eyes.	*Paula ha* **gli** *occhi azzurri.*
My sister's got short hair.*	*Mia sorella ha* **i** *capelli corti.*

ESCLAMAZIONI

Nelle esclamazioni con **What ...!** si usa l'articolo indeterminativo **a(n)**.

What an exciting film! (**Non** ~~What exciting film!~~)   *Che film emozionante!*

Ma se l'esclamazione è plurale **non** si usa nessun articolo.

What lovely flowers!   *Che bei fiori!*

Non si usa nessun articolo nemmeno con i nomi non numerabili. (Vedi **7.4**)

What horrible weather!   *Che tempo terribile!*

DEFINIZIONI

Si usa **a(n)** per dare la definizione di qualcosa.

*A **department store** is a shop which sells a wide range of goods.*
***Il/Un grande magazzino** è un negozio che vende un'ampia varietà di merci.*

CASI PARTICOLARI: ARTICOLO SÌ, ARTICOLO NO

In alcune espressioni fisse si usa **the**, in altre **nessun articolo**.

*We travel **by train/bus/car**.* (**Non** ~~by the train~~)   *Si viaggia **in/con il treno**, **con l'autobus**, **in/con la macchina**.*

*We **have lunch/dinner** at one.* (**Non** ~~the lunch/dinner~~)   *Pranziamo/**Ceniamo** all'una.*

*We listen to **the radio**. **Ma** We watch **television**.*   *Ascoltiamo **la radio**. **Ma** Guardiamo **la televisione**.*

*We play **the guitar**. (a musical instrument) **Ma** We play **tennis**. (a sport)*
*Suoniamo **la chitarra**. (uno strumento musicale) **Ma** Giochiamo a **tennis**. (uno sport)*

*We go to **the cinema**, **the theatre**, **the gym**, **the disco**.*
*mentre in italiano: Andiamo **al cinema**, **a teatro**, **in palestra**, **in discoteca**.*

Confronta le espressioni seguenti:

*My mother is **at work**. Mia madre è **al lavoro**.*
Ma *My mother is **at the office**. Mia madre è **in ufficio**.*

Davanti ad alcuni nomi di luoghi si può usare l'articolo **the** o **nessun articolo**, con una differenza di significato.

*The children are **at school** now.* (= they are students there)
*I bambini sono **a scuola** ora.* (= studiano lì, frequentano la scuola)

*My father is **at the school** now.* (= he is visiting it)
*Mio padre è **a/alla scuola** ora.* (= sta visitando l'edificio scolastico, si trova lì)

*Peter spent a lot of time **in hospital** as a child.* (= he was a patient)
*Peter ha trascorso un sacco di tempo **in/all'ospedale** da bambino.* (= era ricoverato come paziente)

*Dr Dibble has an office **in the hospital** and another at home.* (= she works there)
*La Dottoressa Dibble ha un ufficio **in/all'ospedale** e un altro a casa.* (= lavora lì)

La stessa regola si applica anche ai termini **at church**, **in prison**, **at college** e **at university**.

PRACTICE

1 Leggi questi brevi articoli di giornale. Inserisci *the*, *a(n)* o **nessun articolo** negli spazi.

THAT WAS LUCKY!

Last weekend **(1)** ......a...... group of tourists had **(2)** .... lucky escape near **(3)** .... Mount Rushmore in **(4)** .... United States. Their car was hit by **(5)** .... small plane making an emergency landing. **(6)** .... pilot broke two toes. **(7)** .... tourists were not hurt, but their car and **(8)** .... plane were damaged.

NO MORE FOREIGN HOLIDAYS?

'We must do more to prevent pollution,' **(1)** .... professor at Exeter University in **(2)** .... South of England said yesterday. Professor Kirkwell said that pollution is increasing all over **(3)** .... world. 'Places like **(4)** .... Andes mountains and **(5)** .... Sahara desert will get warmer, and some small islands will disappear. Everyone wants to travel by **(6)** .... plane but this cannot continue. People must think more carefully about **(7)** .... environment when they choose **(8)** .... holiday.'

THE WRONG JOB

Janice Miller left her job at **(1)** .... cinema near **(2)** .... Bristol in **(3)** .... west of England yesterday after only one day because she didn't want to watch **(4)** .... horror film. 'I didn't know I'd see any films,' she explained. 'I saw **(5)** .... horror film once, and I was very frightened. I thought my job was just selling tickets.'

Stanley Greenham, **(6)** .... manager of **(7)** .... cinema, said that he was sorry.

'I didn't really explain **(8)** .... job to Janice at her interview,' he added. '**(9)** .... horror films we show aren't very frightening. **(10)** .... young people usually like them.'

2 Riempi gli spazi con le parole tra parentesi. Aggiungi *a* o *the* se necessario.

1   We've got some important visitors flying in from ...the..West..Indies... next week.
     Can you meet them at .... ? (*West Indies*, *Birmingham Airport*)

2 Ferdinand spent his holiday sailing across .... from .... to .... (*Mediterranean, Naples, Corsica*)

3 My brother's idea of a holiday is trekking across .... or exploring .... Personally, I'd rather explore .... and do some shopping! (*Sahara, Andes, Paris*)

4 Have you met Cora's new boyfriend? He's .... from .... (*ski instructor, Switzerland*)

5 What .... ! Our train broke down near Ely and we had to get a bus from there to .... and then wait hours for the next train. (*terrible journey, Peterborough Station*)

3 Osserva attentamente le immagini e completa le frasi, usando le parole nel riquadro e l'articolo *a(n)* quando è necessario.

glasses   lovely smile   ponytail   moustache   hooked nose   rather fierce expression
very white teeth   red curly hair   long hair   freckles   beard   contact lenses

1 She's got red curly hair and freckles . **2** She's got .... but she usually wears ....

3 He's got .... and .... **4** She's got .... and ....

5 He's got .... which he usually wears in ....

6 He's got .... but he hasn't got ....

4 Ora leggi la descrizione di una delle persone raffigurate nell'esercizio precedente. Inserisci *a(n)*, *the* o **nessun articolo** negli spazi.

Camilla is half Italian but you wouldn't think so, because she looks just like her mother who's Scottish. They've got **(1)** ..the.. same amazing hair: long, red and curly. I'd love to have **(2)** .... hair like that, but Cami hates it. She's got **(3)** .... pale skin and **(4)** .... freckles so in the summer she always wears **(5)** .... hat and she can't sit in **(6)** .... sun for long.

I think she's got **(7)** .... interesting face. She's got **(8)** .... high cheekbones, quite **(9)** .... long nose and **(10)** .... wide mouth. Her eyes are green and she's got **(11)** .... incredibly long eyelashes. She's tall and she's got **(12)** .... good figure, too.

You notice Camilla in **(13)** .... crowd because she's so different. She could definitely be **(14)** .... model if she wanted to, but she's not interested. It wouldn't suit her at all, actually, because she's quite **(15)** .... shy person, except when she's with **(16)** .... friends, and she hates being **(17)** .... centre of attention.

7.4   NOMI NUMERABILI E NON NUMERABILI

I nomi possono essere numerabili o non numerabili.

*I eat **an apple** every day.*
Io mangio **una mela** al giorno.

Apples are good for you.
Le mele fanno bene.

■ *Apple* è un nome numerabile.

*I eat **rice** once a week.*
Io mangio **il riso** una volta alla settimana.

Rice is good for you.
Il riso fa bene.

■ *Rice* è un nome **non** numerabile.

I nomi numerabili

■ possono essere **singolari** e **plurali**.

My brother has bought a new car.
Mio fratello ha comprato **una macchina** nuova.
I like sports cars.
Mi piacciono **le macchine** sportive.

■ al **singolare** possono essere preceduti da *a(n)* e *the*: **non possono** essere **senza** articolo.

*I've got a problem. (**Non** I've got problem.)*
Ho **un** problema.
The book I'm reading is very dull.
Il libro che sto leggendo è molto noioso.

■ hanno il verbo **singolare** o **plurale**.

*The car **is** new. The cars **are** new.*

■ con *some* hanno sempre la forma **plurale**.

*Would you like **some** biscuits?*
Vuoi **dei** biscotti?

I nomi **non** numerabili

■ **non** possono essere **plurali**.

*Money makes the world go round. (**Non** moneys)*
I soldi fanno girare il mondo.
*Cristina's got long hair. (**Non** hairs)*
Cristina ha **i capelli** lunghi.

■ **non** possono essere preceduti da *a(n)*. **Possono** essere **senza** articolo.

*What's **the** weather like today?*
Com'è **il** tempo oggi?
Petrol is expensive.
La benzina costa molto.

■ hanno **sempre** il verbo **singolare**.

*Exercise is good for you. (**Non** exercises are)*

■ con *some* mantengono la forma **singolare**.

*Would you like **some** bread and cheese?*
Vuoi **un po' di** pane e formaggio?

Molti sostantivi di uso comune sono **non numerabili** in **entrambe le lingue**, ad esempio:

air = **aria**, *pollution* = **inquinamento**, *bread* = **pane**, *meat* = **carne**, *flour* = **farina**, *butter* = **burro**, *water* = **acqua**, *milk* = **latte**, *wine* = **vino**.

Ma alcuni sostantivi numerabili in italiano non sono numerabili in inglese.

advice	**consiglio, consigli**
furniture	**mobili, mobilio**
hair	**capelli, capigliatura**
information	**informazione, informazioni**
work	**lavoro**, con i composti: *homework* = **compiti per casa** e *housework* = **lavori domestici** (**Ma** *job* = **lavoro** è numerabile)
luggage	**bagagli**
money	**soldi, denaro**
travel	**viaggio** (**Ma** *trip* e *journey* sono numerabili)

news   notizia, notizie (news *termina in* s *ma è non numerabile*)
business   affari (Ma business = impresa *è numerabile*)
accommodation alloggio

This **is good news!**	Questa **è una bella notizia!**
Business is bad this year.	**Gli affari vanno** male quest'anno.
My father always gives me **good advice.**	Mio padre mi dà sempre **dei buoni consigli.**
Have you done your **homework** yet?	Hai già fatto **i compiti?**
It's **hard work**, but I like it.	È **un lavoro duro**, ma mi piace.

■ I nomi non numerabili sono spesso usati con **some** e **any** che indicano una quantità indefinita.

I need **some information.** (**Non** ~~some informations~~)	Ho bisogno di **alcune informazioni.**
Can you lend me **some money?** (**Non** ~~some moneys~~)	Puoi prestarmi **un po' di soldi?**

■ Quando vogliamo specificare la quantità di cose che sono non numerabili, usiamo espressioni come

a bottle of = **una bottiglia di**   a glass of = **un bicchiere di**   a cup of = **una tazza di**
a piece of = **un pezzo di**   a packet of = **un pacchetto di**   a can of = **una lattina di**
an item of *(clothing, news)* = **un articolo di** *(vestiario, notizie)*

I need **a bottle of** water. (**Non** ~~I need a water.~~)	Ho bisogno di **una bottiglia d'**acqua.
I've bought **a loaf of** brown bread.	Ho comprato una **forma/pagnotta di** pane integrale.
I'll have **a glass of** milk.	Prendo **un bicchiere di** latte.
Anne has bought **some new pieces of furniture** for her flat.	Anne ha comprato **dei mobili nuovi** per il suo appartamento.

■ Molti nomi di bevande possono essere usati in modo numerabile e non numerabile.

Would you like **a coffee?** (= a cup of coffee)
Vuoi **un caffè?** (= una tazza di caffè)

I'd like **two coffees** and **a tea**, please. (= 2 cups of coffee + 1 cup of tea)
Vorrei **due caffè** e **un tè**, per favore. (= 2 tazze di caffè + 1 tazza di tè)

I bought **some coffee** in the market. (= a packet of coffee)
Ho comprato **del caffè** al mercato. (= un pacchetto di caffè)

📌 Molti sostantivi possono essere sia numerabili che non numerabili, ma con significati differenti. Confronta le seguenti coppie di frasi:

These grammar **exercises** are easy!	**Exercise** is good for you.
Questi **esercizi** di grammatica sono facili!	**L'attività fisica** ti fa bene.
The gallery was showing **works** by several artists. (= paintings, sculptures, etc.)	I don't enjoy hard **work**.
La galleria esponeva **opere** di diversi artisti.	Non mi piace **il lavoro** duro.
The French produce some wonderful **cheeses**. (= different types of cheese)	Do we have any **cheese** in the fridge? (= that type of food)
I francesi producono dei **formaggi** meravigliosi. (= tipi di formaggio)	Abbiamo del **formaggio** nel frigo? (= questo genere di cibo)

PRACTICE

1 Leggi questo avviso in una villetta per le vacanze. Accanto a ognuna delle parole in corsivo scrivi **s** se è plurale numerabile.

Rose Cottage, Hobbs Farm, Newton, near Norwich

Welcome!

To help you enjoy your stay, we offer some **(1)** *advice* ...... for **(2)** *visitor* ..s.. .

You can use **(3)** *euro* ...... in Norwich city centre but you need English **(4)** *money* ...... at the shop in Newton village. This shop sells good **(5)** *bread* ...... and you can buy fresh **(6)** *vegetable* ...... from the farmhouse. For other **(7)** *food* ...... use the **(8)** *shop* ...... in Ridby or Walcot.

If you want some **(9)** *information* ...... about **(10)** *travel* ...... and **(11)** *traffic* ...... in the Ridby area, try the local radio station.

Notes

If you want to listen to **(12)** *music* ...... please remember to keep the volume down.

Please use only garden **(13)** *chair* ...... in the garden. Do not take any sitting-room **(14)** *furniture* ...... outside.

Please be careful not to bring any **(15)** *sand* ...... or **(16)** *stone* ...... into the cottage from the beach.

Thank you – enjoy your stay!

---

2 **A** Completa ogni espressione con un nome nella lista dei numerabili e non numerabili. Usa il dizionario se necessario. È possibile che alcune delle espressioni vengano usate con più di uno dei sostantivi?

| **Uncountable:** | glass | luggage | meat | paper | rice |
| **Countable:** | books | cards | clothes | shoppers | tools |

1 an item of .....luggage........

2 a pack of ....

3 a sheet of ....

4 a crowd of ....

5 a pane of ....

6 a slice of ....

7 a set of ....

8 a bundle of ....

9 a grain of ....

10 a pile of ....

B Usa il dizionario per trovare parole che possono essere usate con questi sostantivi non numerabili. Ci può essere più di una possibilità per ogni sostantivo.

1 a .... of bread

2 a .... of ice

3 a .... of oil

4 a .... of wood

5 a .... of dust

3 Completa il diagramma con le parole che appartengono a ciascun gruppo. Se necessario usa il dizionario.

accommodation	advice	cheese	coffee	experience
experiment	glass	~~hair~~	hobby	homework
information	journey	leisure	luck	~~luggage~~
meat	scenery	time	traffic	~~vegetable~~

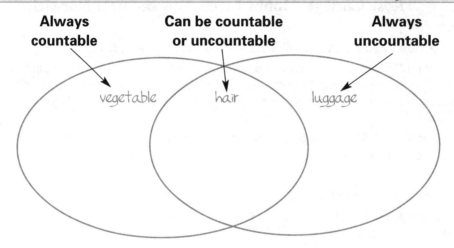

Always countable   **Can be countable or uncountable**   **Always uncountable**

vegetable   hair   luggage

4 In ciascuna di queste frasi c'è un errore. Trova gli errori e correggili.

1 I want to buy some trouser^s so I'll meet you by the new clothes shop.

2 Tom Cruise was wearing a black jacket, black jean and black shoes.

3 I'm happy with a furniture in my room, but I want to change the curtains.

4 I'm sending this card to wish you a good luck for your driving test.

5 My cousin's just been on a travel round France.

6 I listen to musics when I'm working so I feel more relaxed.

7 The weather was marvellous so we went to beach and swam in the sea.

8 I'll go to the swimming-pool for some informations about diving lessons.

9 If I send you a money, will you buy me some earrings like yours?

10 We saw some lovely old towns in Czech Republic on our last holiday.

7.5   IL POSSESSIVO DEL NOME: *SAXON GENITIVE / OF*

Il complemento di **possesso**, che in italiano viene espresso con la preposizione **di** (la macchina **di** Michael), viene generalmente tradotto in inglese con il *Saxon genitive*, che si forma così:

nome del possessore + **'s** + oggetto posseduto

*Michael**'s** car*

L'ordine delle parole è invertito rispetto all'italiano.

The boy's bedroom was very untidy.
                    (**Non** *the bedroom of the boy*)

*La camera **del** ragazzo era molto in disordine.*

Where are George's glasses? (**Non** *the glasses of George*)

*Dove sono gli occhiali **di** George?*

■ Si usa **'s** quando il possessore è un **essere animato**, **persona** o **animale**. Si usa invece **of** con i nomi di cose, perché gli oggetti inanimati **non possono possedere** qualcosa. Confronta le frasi seguenti:

The girl's clothes were very dirty.
(**Non** *the clothes of the girl*)

*Gli abiti **della** ragazza erano molto sporchi.*

The dog's teeth are very sharp.
(**Non** *the teeth of the dog*)

*Le zanne **del** cane sono molto aguzze.*

Ma *What's the price **of** that holiday?*
(**Non** *the holiday's price*)

*Qual è il prezzo **di** quella vacanza?*

*I don't know the title **of** the book.*
(**Non** *the book's title*)

*Non conosco il titolo **del** libro.*

Si usa **'s** anche con

■ le **espressioni di tempo**.

*I missed **last night's** programme.*
*That's **last year's** brochure.*
*I want to go on **a week's holiday**.*

*Ho perso il programma **della notte scorsa**.*
*Quello è il depliant **dell'anno scorso**.*
*Voglio farmi una vacanza **di una settimana**.*

■ i **nomi di nazioni**.

Britain's roads get more crowded every year.
*Le strade **della Gran Bretagna** diventano ogni anno più congestionate.*

POSIZIONE DELL'APOSTROFO: *'S, S'*

Con i nomi plurali che terminano già in **s**, l'apostrofo **'** **segue** la **s**: **s'**. Confronta le espressioni seguenti:

My cousin's friends. (= one cousin)
My cousins' friends. (= more than one cousin)

*Gli amici **di mio cugino**.*
*Gli amici **dei miei cugini**.*

■ Alcune parole rimangono spesso sottintese dopo **'s**, in genere quando ci si riferisce a un'abitazione o a un luogo di lavoro (**office**, **shop**).

I stayed at Sally's. (= Sally's **flat**)
He works in the newsagent's.
(= the newsagent's **shop**)
Let's go to White's! (= White's **restaurant**)

*Ho dormito **da Sally**.*
*Lavora all'**edicola**.*

*Andiamo **da White**!*

121

PRACTICE

1 Riempi gli spazi con le parole tra parentesi, collegandole tra loro con **'s** o con **of**.

1   We had to leave early so we didn't see .... *the end of the film* .... (*the end/the film*).

2   After the film we went to .... *Mark's house* .... (*the house/Mark*).

3   She's allergic so she can't drink .... (*milk/cow*).

4   Holly is .... (*daughter/Liz and Tom*).

5   We can stay in .... (*the flat/my grandparents*).

6   Look at the answers at .... (*the back/the book*).

7   Have you seen the headlines in .... (*the newspaper/today*)?

8   I didn't do it. It's .... (*fault/someone else*).

9   Some people disagree with .... (*the foreign policy/America*).

10   The climbers managed to reach .... (*the top/the mountain*).

11   Do you know about .... (*the meeting/tomorrow*)?

12   This summer I've only got .... (*holiday/two weeks*).

2 Martina sta spiegando alla sua amica Samira come è composta la sua famiglia. Guarda l'albero genealogico e completa la conversazione inserendo negli spazi una parola e **'s**.

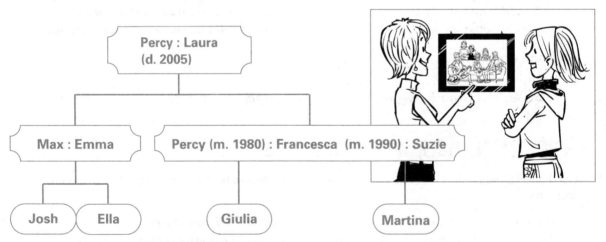

Martina: This is a photo of my family.

Samira: Let's have a look… What's your (**1**) ...*dad's?*....... name?

Martina: Percy! It was my (**2**) .... name too. Dad hates it!

Samira: Who's the girl on your dad's left?

Martina: That's my sister. Her name's Giulia.

Samira: She looks a lot older than you.

Martina: Well, my mum is my (**3**) .... second wife, so really I'm (**4**) ....

stepsister, but we're like sisters.

Samira: And is this your mum?

Martina: No, that's Emma, my aunt. And this is Max. He's **(5)** .... husband.

Samira: Have they got any children?

Martina: Yes. Two. My **(6)** .... names are Josh and Ella. Josh took the photo and this is Ella.

Samira: And is that **(7)** .... girlfriend?

Martina: No, Josh hasn't got a girlfriend. That's my friend Anya. I think Josh quite likes her!

3 Traduci.

1 C'è un parcheggio alla fine di questa strada.

2 Conosci l'indirizzo di Harry? Vorrei mandargli una cartolina.

3 Questi sono gli spogliatoi (*changing rooms*) dei ragazzi.

4 Io odio andare dal dentista.

5 I giocattoli dei bambini sono sul pavimento.

6 I genitori di Ellen trascorrono sempre le vacanze al mare.

7 L'appartamento di mia sorella è all'ultimo piano.

8 Gli studenti sono appena tornati da una gita di un giorno a Salisbury.

ALL IN ONE REVISION

1 Ascolterai alcuni annunci e messaggi pubblicitari su una radio locale. Guarda le immagini e abbinale a quello che ascolti.

1.15

A ......

B ......

C ......

2 Ascolta di nuovo il primo messaggio pubblicitario e completa queste frasi con i luoghi elencati nel riquadro. Qualche volta dovrai aggiungere *the*.

1.16

| Andes   Atlantic Ocean   Greece   Lake Garda   New York   Rome   Sahara Desert |

1 You can go climbing in the Alps or ....

2 We're not suggesting sailing across .... but you can sail around the coast of .... or on ....

3 You can watch the sun set over ....

4 Go on one of our city breaks to .... or ....

Do we use *the* before the names of:

countries? .... cities? .... mountain ranges? .... deserts? .... lakes? ....

oceans? ....

3 Ascolta di nuovo il secondo messaggio pubblicitario. Di che cosa parla?

1.17

jeans   pyjamas   shirts   shorts   shoes   socks   trousers

Quali delle parole elencate sopra possono essere usate solo al plurale?

4 Ascolta di nuovo l'annuncio, poi completa queste frasi.

1.18

1 The .... on 555FM is perfect for a Friday afternoon.

2 Are you sitting in your car in the .... ?

3 We bring you the latest .... every hour.

4 Then it's your chance to phone us and ask us a question about ....

5 Mark Sherlock, is here to give you ....

Rileggi i nomi che hai scritto. Puoi renderli plurali?

5 Riempi gli spazi con *a*, *an*, *the* o **nessun articolo**.

Pancake recipe

You need 100 grams of flour, **(1)** ....an.... egg, a little milk,
and a spoonful of butter.
Beat **(2)** .... egg with **(3)** .... flour. Add
(4) .... milk until the mixture is runny. Heat **(5)** ....
butter in **(6)** .... frying pan. Pour **(7)** ....
spoonful of **(8)** .... mixture into **(9)** .... pan.
Cook for one minute. Turn **(10)** .... pancake over and
cook a little longer. Serve hot, with **(11)** .... sugar
and **(12)** .... lemon juice.

6 <u>Sottolinea</u> l'alternativa corretta.

1 How much <u>*luggage*</u> / *bags* have you got?

2 Brunello is one of the most expensive Italian *wine* / *wines*.

3 I can't drink *coffee* / *coffees* because I get a headache.

4 If you don't do any *exercise* / *exercises* you'll put on weight.

5 **A** Anna's read the complete *work* / *works* of Charles Dickens. **B** I don't believe it.

6 I've been on two *trips / travels* to America this year.

7 A lot of new *business / businesses* have started up in the area this year.

8 It isn't easy to find a *work / job* nowadays.

7 Riempi gli spazi con le parole nel riquadro.

> jar   bar   tube   ~~cups~~   cans   slice   cartons   bottle

1 On average an English person drinks three ...~~cups~~.... of tea a day.

2 Would you like another .... of ham?

3 There's hardly any jam left. Can you get another .... when you go to the supermarket?

4 Everyone will be thirsty. You'd better put some more .... of coke in the fridge.

5 We've got two .... of milk. That should be enough until Monday.

6 The .... of shampoo that I had in my suitcase broke.

7 There was a .... of chocolate in the cupboard. Who's eaten it?

8 It really annoys me when people don't put the top on the .... of toothpaste.

8 È sabato sera. Jane e Bobby stanno passando in rassegna gli acquisti di un'intera giornata di shopping, per vedere se hanno comprato tutto quello di cui avevano bisogno. Riempi gli spazi con i nomi appropriati e **'s**.

> ~~Sally's~~   baker's   Harvey's   hairdresser's   Luigi's   newsagent's

Jane: I can't find the bag with my new shoes in. I'm sure I didn't leave it in the shop.

Bobby: Maybe you left it at **(1)** .....Sally's..... when we called in.

Jane: I'll give her a ring in a minute. It's a pity I didn't find a dress, isn't it?

Bobby: That one at **(2)** .... was quite nice. Why didn't you buy it?

Jane: Because it was far too expensive. We didn't really have enough time, did we?

Bobby: That's because you spent too long at the **(3)** ....

Jane: Me? *You* spent too long at the **(4)** .... looking for that computer magazine.

Bobby: Well, at least I found it in the end. Anyway, after all that we forgot to go to the

(5) .... We haven't got any bread.

Jane: Don't worry. Let's go out to eat.

Bobby: OK. Shall we go to **(6)** ....? They make the best pizza in London!

9 Correggi gli errori in questa email.

Dear Monique,

We had a great trip to the France last weekend. We went to little hotel that you recommended and it was very pleasant. Foods at the hotel weren't so good, as you warned us, but we strolled down to city centre on Saturday evening and had lovely meal there. In fact, we ate so much for the dinner that we didn't want a breakfast on Sunday!

Thanks again for the advice and informations. Now I must unpack and do the washings.

Here is photo of the hotel to remind you.

See you soon.

Love, Freda

10 Traduci.

1   Ho una notizia interessante per te.

2   Vorrei delle informazioni sui vostri corsi di musica.

3   Mi hai dato davvero un buon consiglio.

4   Devo comprare dei mobili nuovi per il mio appartamento: il divano e le poltrone sono vecchi e sporchi.

5   I tuoi bagagli sono molto pesanti. Te li porto io.

6   I miei capelli sono terribili. Devo lavarli ogni due giorni.

7   Sono appena tornata da un viaggio fantastico.

8   Abbiamo un sacco di compiti per domani.

9   **A** Ci sono notizie di Brad? **B** No, è partito da due settimane e non ha ancora chiamato.

10   Lavoro in un *call centre*. Non è un lavoro difficile, ma è noioso.

PRONOMI E DETERMINANTI (1)

8.1 Pronomi personali soggetto e complemento: *I* e *me*

8.2 Aggettivi e pronomi possessivi: *my* e *mine*

8.3 Pronomi riflessivi: *myself/yourself…*

8.4 Pronomi reciproci: *each other, one another*

8.5 Aggettivi e pronomi dimostrativi:
this, that, these e *those*;
this one, that one; the one, the ones

8.6 *There is / It is*

PRONOMI E DETERMINANTI (1) – INTRODUZIONE

Per determinanti si intendono parole come *a*, *the*, *this*, *that*, *some*, *much*, e *every*, che si trovano all'inizio del gruppo nominale, prima degli aggettivi.

those black clouds   *every* day   *some* interesting people   *a lot of* homework

I determinanti possono essere divisi in due grandi gruppi: uno che indica di **quali** cose si sta parlando, ad esempio **i possessivi** (le mie / le tue) e **i dimostrativi** (queste/quelle), e un altro che indica principalmente di **quante** cose si sta parlando: *some*, *a few*, *much*, e *many*.

Il primo gruppo viene trattato in questa sezione, insieme ai pronomi personali e riflessivi; il secondo gruppo, chiamato generalmente *quantifiers*, viene trattato nella *Unit* seguente.

8.1 PRONOMI PERSONALI SOGGETTO E COMPLEMENTO: *I* E *ME*

La struttura della frase affermativa inglese segue generalmente questo ordine:

Soggetto + verbo + complementi
My sister met *Sharon and Mel*. *She* invited *them* to dinner.

	Pronomi soggetto	Pronomi complemento	
S	I	**me**	*I saw Tom yesterday, but he didn't see **me**.*
	you	**you**	*You don't know Kate, but she has heard about **you**.*
	he/she/it	**him/her/it**	*George studies at Oxford. He is very clever. Do you know **him**?*
P	we	**us**	*We share a flat in Brighton. Come and see **us**.*
	you	**you**	*Boys! Are you listening? I'm talking to **you**.*
	they	**them**	*They're going to the cinema. I'll go with **them**.*

È importante notare che in inglese **il soggetto è sempre espresso**. Non può essere omesso.

It's very hot today.   *Fa molto caldo oggi.*
It seems to me that we don't have much choice.   *Mi sembra che non abbiamo molta scelta.*

PRACTICE

1 Leggi il dialogo e compila la tabella che segue.

Elizabeth: You look lovely, Jane. That dress really matches **your** eyes. What do you think of **mine**?

Jane: It's fabulous, Lizzy. The boys won't believe **their** eyes when they see you. They'll all want to dance with you and I will spend the evening in a corner on **my** own.

Elizabeth: Don't be silly. Anyway, I'm only interested in Jim. I want to see **his** face when he sees me dressed like this. Is that necklace you're wearing **Lydia's**?

Jane: It was, but it **belongs to me** now. I swapped the earrings that you gave me for **her** necklace.

Elizabeth: Oh, you didn't! They were a birthday present. How could you do such a thing?

Jane: Sorry, I didn't think you would mind. But they're **hers** now, and you'll see how well they go with **her** new haircut. Is that bracelet **yours**? It would go nicely with **my** necklace.

Elizabeth: Yes, it is **mine** and I'm wearing it tonight. Where on earth did you get that handbag? Does it **belong to you**? I've never seen it before.

Jane: No, it's **Mum's**. I borrowed it to put **our** money in.

Elizabeth: You can't take that! It looks like something from *Jurassic Park*!

That is my necklace.	That necklace is (1) ..mine... .	That necklace belongs to (2) ....
These are (3) .... earrings.	Are these earrings (4) .... ?	These earrings (5) .... to you.
This is (6) .... bracelet.	This bracelet is (7)	This bracelet (8) .... Lydia.
That is her handbag.	That handbag is (9)	That handbag belongs to (10) ....
Have you seen (11) .... new car?	That car is (12)	That car belongs to him.
Where can we keep (13) .... money?	That money is ours.	That money belongs to (14) ....
These are (15) .... clothes.	These clothes are theirs.	These clothes belong to (16) ....

2 Riempi gli spazi con un pronome personale soggetto o complemento.

1   How long does .....it..... take to get to school in the morning?

2   .... 'm so depressed! Bill says .... doesn't love .... any more.

3   Why don't .... invite Kate to your party? I know she's really fond of ....

4   When will .... stop raining?

5   Karen is my younger sister. .... spend a lot of time with ....

6   Karen and .... have a lot of interests in common. .... both listen to the same music and wear similar clothes. Our friends always invite .... both to parties.

7   Do you know that boy over there? .... 's very good-looking but I don't like .... much.

8   Mary and John are really nice. ....'m looking forward to seeing .... when .... come to Rome next week.

9   Don't .... think .... would be better to eat indoors?

10   Look at my new mobile phone! Isn't .... great? .... won .... in a competition.

3 Completa questa lettera con i pronomi personali corretti.

Dear Mandy,

How are **(1)** ...you...? **(2)** .... 'm writing to tell **(3)** .... something about **(4)** .... and my family.

My family consists of four people and two cats. My mother, Paola, is forty-two and works in a bank. I'm very close to **(5)** .... My father, Alessandro, is an engineer and I look very like **(6)** .... **(7)** .... works in Pomezia near Rome. My sister's name is Gianna. **(8)** .... is two years older than **(9)** .... (as you know, I'm fifteen) and **(10)** .... are very different. I'm much more interested in going out and having a good time than **(11)** ...., while **(12)** .... 's more serious than **(13)** ....

Our parents would like **(14)** .... to spend more time together as a family, but I actually prefer the cats, Pizzi and Fusa. I really enjoy playing with **(15)** .... ; **(16)** .... are great fun!

Write to **(17)** .... soon.

Valentina

8.2   AGGETTIVI E PRONOMI POSSESSIVI: *MY* E *MINE*

Pronomi soggetto	Aggettivi possessivi	Pronomi possessivi	
I	**my**	mine	*This isn't **my** mobile. **Mine** is a Nokia.* *Questo non è **il mio** cellulare. **Il mio** è un Nokia.*
you	**your**	yours	*This isn't **your** dictionary. **Yours** is on that desk.* *Questo non è **il tuo** vocabolario. **Il tuo** è su quel banco.*
he	**his**	his	*That's **his** house and the car in the garden is **his** too.* *Quella è **la sua** casa e anche la macchina nel giardino è **sua**.*
she	**her**	hers	*That's not **her** dog. That's a Dalmatian; **hers** is a poodle.* *Quello non è **il suo** cane. Quello è un Dalmata; **il suo** è un barboncino.*
it	**its**	–	*That house is very old. **Its** windows are all broken.* *Quella casa è molto vecchia. **Le sue** finestre sono tutte rotte.*
we	**our**	ours	*That's not **our** car over there. **Ours** is grey.* *Non è quella **la nostra** macchina. **La nostra** è grigia.*
you	**your**	yours	*I think these are **your** keys. Yes, I'm sure they're **yours**.* *Credo che queste siano **le vostre** chiavi. Sì, sono sicuro che sono **vostre**.*
they	**their**	theirs	***Their** flat is very big. **Ours** is much smaller than **theirs**.* ***Il loro** appartamento è molto grande. **Il nostro** è molto più piccolo del **loro**.*

Gli **aggettivi possessivi** sono sempre seguiti dal nome a cui si riferiscono.

*I went with **my friends**.*   *Sono andato con **i miei amici**.*
*How are **your children**?*   *Come stanno **i tuoi bambini**?*

Quando il possessivo **non** è seguito dal nome a cui si riferisce diventa un **pronome possessivo**.

*Give that key to her. It's not **yours**.*   *Dai a lei quella chiave. Non è **tua**.*

Confronta le frasi seguenti:

*This bicycle is **mine**.*
*Questa bicicletta è **mia**.*

*This is **my** bicycle.*
*Questa è **la mia** bicicletta.*

*This bicycle belongs to **me**.*
*Questa bicicletta appartiene a **me**.*

*This bicycle is **the boy's**.*
*Questa bicicletta è **del bambino**.*

*This is **the boy's** bicycle.*
*Questa è la bicicletta **del bambino**.*

*This bicycle belongs to **the boy**.*
*Questa bicicletta appartiene **al bambino**.*

■ A differenza che in italiano, in inglese gli aggettivi e i pronomi possessivi concordano con il possessore, non con la cosa posseduta. Questo è evidente con i possessivi della **3ª persona singolare**.

his significa **suo/sua/suoi/sue**, di un uomo o di un ragazzo;
her significa **suo/sua/suoi/sue**, di una donna o di una ragazza.

*He sees **his** girlfriend every night.*	*Lui vede **la sua** ragazza tutte le sere.*
*She shares a flat with **her** brother.*	*Lei divide un appartamento con **suo** fratello.*

Esiste anche l'aggettivo possessivo neutro, *its*, ma è usato raramente e principalmente per riferirsi alle **parti** che compongono qualcosa.

*I must mend my bike. **Its** tyres are both flat.*	*Devo aggiustare la mia bicicletta. **Le sue** ruote sono a terra.*
*This dictionary is very old. **Its** pages are all yellow.*	*Questo vocabolario è molto vecchio. **Le sue** pagine sono tutte ingiallite.*

■ È importante **non** confondere il pronome possessivo *its* con *it's* = *it is*.

■ Gli aggettivi e i pronomi possessivi in inglese **non** sono mai preceduti dall'articolo determinativo o indeterminativo o da un altro determinante. Confronta le frasi seguenti:

***My** friends are coming tomorrow.*	***Some** friends **of mine** are coming tomorrow.*
***I miei** amici arrivano domani.*	***Alcuni miei** amici arrivano domani.*
*George is **her** best friend.*	*George is **a** friend **of hers**.*
*George è **il suo** migliore amico.*	*George è **un suo** amico.*
*Miss Lafont is **our** French teacher.*	*Miss Lafont is **a** teacher **of ours**.*
*Miss Lafont è **la nostra** insegnante di francese.*	*Miss Lafont è **una nostra** insegnante.*
***Your** black trousers are very smart.*	***Those** black trousers **of yours** are very smart.*
***I tuoi** pantaloni neri sono molto eleganti.*	***Quei tuoi** pantaloni neri sono molto eleganti.*

■ Si usa sempre l'aggettivo possessivo, **non** l'articolo, con parti del corpo e abiti.

*My father broke **his** leg. (**Non** ~~My father broke the leg.~~)*	*Mio padre si è rotto **una gamba**.*
*Give me **your** hand. (**Non** ~~Give me the hand.~~)*	*Dammi **la mano**.*
*They changed **their** shoes when they came in.*	*Si cambiarono **le scarpe** quando entrarono.*

ESPRESSIONI CON *OWN*

Si usa l'aggettivo possessivo + *own* per sottolineare l'idea di possesso.

*He doesn't have **his own** flat. (= a flat just for him)*	*Lui non ha un appartamento **suo**. (= solo per sé)*
*I'd rather have **my own** car. (= just for me)*	*Preferirei avere una macchina **tutta mia**. (= solo mia)*

■ Lo stesso significato può essere reso con l'espressione *of (your) own*.

*He doesn't have a flat **of his own**.*	*Lui non ha un appartamento **per conto suo**.*
*I'd rather have a car **of my own**.*	*Preferirei avere una macchina **per conto mio**.*

■ L'espressione *on (your) own* significa 'da solo', 'per conto proprio', e può essere usata come sinonimo di *by (your) self*. (Vedi **8.3**)

*I'm going **on my own**. = I'm going **by myself**.*	*Vado **da sola**. = Vado **per conto mio**.*
*Sally wanted to be **on her own**.*	*Sally voleva stare **da sola**.*
*= Sally wanted to be **by herself**.*	*= Sally voleva stare **per conto suo**.*

PRACTICE

1 Riempi gli spazi con l'aggettivo possessivo corretto.

1 When you go into a Japanese house, you usually take ..your... shoes off.

2 Does Bill share a room with .... brother? Or does he have a room of .... own.

3 We live so close to the stadium that we can hear the crowd cheering from .... house.

4 At the age of fourteen, Tracy was already allowed to go out on .... own.

5 It's .... birthday next week and I'm going to have a party. Would you like to come?

6 Alice and Emily are identical twins. .... teachers are never sure which one they're talking to.

7 Robbers in a bank: Put .... hands up and don't move.

8 He usually keeps .... mobile in .... jeans pocket in case his girlfriend rings.

9 Have you seen .... school backpack anywhere? I can't find it.

10 Lindsay has just passed .... driving test and .... parents have promised to get her a car.

2 Trasforma le frasi seguenti. Usa sempre un pronome possessivo.

1 **A** Is that Bill's new scooter? **B** No, ...his...... is a Honda.

2 **A** I've known Sally since we were at primary school together. **B** Ah, so she's an old friend of ....

3 Give me back my sunglasses, you thief! Those sunglasses are ....

4 In a restaurant: **A** Is that the food we ordered? **B** No, it isn't. .... hasn't arrived yet.

5 **A** Greg used to go out with my sister. **B** Really, I didn't know he was an ex-boyfriend of ....

6 **A** Is this my drink? **B** No, ... is in the blue glass.

7 **A** Are these our seats, numbers three and four? **B** Yes, they're ....

8 **A** Is that the neighbours' car? **B** No, it isn't .... They've hired it for the weekend.

3 Completa questa tabella.

That is **(1)** ..my..bicycle.. .	That bicycle is mine.	That bicycle belongs to me.
That is my father's jacket.	That jacket is **(2)** my..father's .	That jacket belongs to **(3)** ....
These are our skis.	These skis **(4)**	These skis **(5)** ....
Is this your CD?	Is this CD **(6)** .... ?	Does this CD belong to **(7)** .... ?
This **(8)**	This **(9)**	This car belongs to my grandparents.
(10)	**(11)**	Those videos belong to them.

4 Riempi gli spazi con la parola corretta (**me/my/mine**, **you/your/yours** ecc.).

1   Sorry, I can't pay you because I've left ......my....... wallet at home.

2   My brother invited six of .... friends from school to stay the night.

3   My sister's hair is longer and thicker than ....

4   My uncle had grown a beard and I didn't recognise .... at first.

5   My parents have an old car. My car is new and it's more comfortable than ....

6   Our bags are almost the same. Where did you buy .... ?

7   My mother was really pleased when I told .... the news.

8   Maurice can't play tennis because he's hurt .... back.

9   Sarah told .... father a lie.

10   That woman is a neighbour of .... She lives in our road.

5 Completa le frasi usando un'espressione con **own**.

1   I always do my homework without any help from my parents. I do it on..my..own. .

2   Jim is so lucky. He's only ten years old and he already has a bedroom ....

3   Would you like to live .... or do you like living with other people?

4   When we were sixteen years old my friends and I went camping ....

5   Until you've passed your driving test, you can't go out in the car ....

6   Many eighteen-year-olds have a driving licence, but not many of them have a car ....

7   **A** Can I borrow your iPod?   **B** No, use .... !

8   My little brother could already walk .... when he was only ten months old.

6 Traduci.

1   Un mio cugino abita a Los Angeles.

2   Questa macchina non è mia. L'ho presa in prestito da mio padre.

3   Non abito per conto mio. Divido un appartamento con due mie amiche.

4   Quel tuo amico americano è molto simpatico.

5   John si è slogato una caviglia mentre giocava a tennis.

6   Togliti le scarpe. Sono tutte bagnate.

7   Selina ha un tatuaggio sulla spalla.

8   **A** Di chi sono questi fumetti? Sono tuoi?   **B** No, sono di mia sorella.

9   Mio fratello è in Irlanda con alcuni suoi compagni di scuola.

10   La prossima estate andrò a trovare dei parenti di mia madre in Australia.

8.3   PRONOMI RIFLESSIVI: *MYSELF/YOURSELF*...

Pronomi riflessivi		
I	→	myself
you	→	yourself
he	→	himself
she	→	herself
it	→	itself
we	→	ourselves
you	→	yourselves
they	→	themselves

Esiste anche il pronome riflessivo impersonale *oneself* anche se non è usato molto come *one*. Tuttavia, questa è la forma comunemente usata nei dizionari per indicare l'infinito di un verbo riflessivo: *to enjoy* **oneself** = *divertirsi*.

I pronomi riflessivi sono comunemente usati:

◼ quando il soggetto e l'oggetto del verbo coincidono.

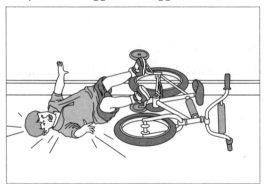

*Tim hurt **himself** when he fell off his bike.*
*Tim **si è fatto** male quando è caduto dalla bicicletta.*

Ma *Sam cried when Tim hurt **him**. (= Tim hurt Sam)*
*Sam ha pianto quando Tim **gli** ha fatto male.*
(= Tim ha fatto male a Sam)

*Amy blamed **herself** for what had happened.*

*Amy **si** rimproverò / dette la colpa a **se stessa** per quello che era successo.*

Ma *Amy blamed **her** for what had happened.*
(= Amy blamed another person, not herself)

*Amy **la** rimproverò / **le** dette la colpa per quello che era successo. (= Amy dette la colpa a un'altra persona, non a se stessa)*

◼ quando vogliamo esprimere enfasi.

*I went to this place **myself** to see what it was really like.*
*Sono andata in questo posto **di persona** per vedere come era davvero.*

*The house **itself** is small, but it is situated in an attractive residential neighbourhood.*
*La casa **in sé** è piccola, ma si trova in una bella zona residenziale.*

■ con verbi comunemente usati alla forma riflessiva, tra cui

enjoy oneself = *divertirsi*   *behave oneself* = *comportarsi bene*   *help oneself* = *servirsi*
make oneself at home = *mettersi comodi, fare come a casa propria*

■ A differenza che in italiano, in inglese di solito **non** si usa il pronome riflessivo dopo i verbi *wash*, *shave* e *dress*.

She **dressed** quickly.	**Si vestì** velocemente.
Go and **wash** your hands.	Vai a **lavarti** le mani.
You should **shave** every day.	Dovresti **raderti / farti la barba** tutti i giorni.

Ma si può usare il pronome riflessivo con questi verbi per esprimere enfasi.

*The little girl managed to **dress herself** quickly.* (= it was difficult for her)
*La bambina riuscì a **vestirsi** velocemente.* (= era una cosa difficile per lei)

■ L'espressione **by oneself** significa 'da solo', 'per conto proprio' o 'senza alcun aiuto' e ha lo stesso significato di **on one's own**.

*I did it all **by myself**.* (= I did it all on my own.)   *Ho fatto tutto **da sola / per conto mio**.*

PRACTICE

1 Completa ogni frase con il pronome riflessivo corretto.

1 Help .....*yourself*...... to a sandwich and a drink and then take it to the checkout.

2 Children, behave .... please.

3 The boys hurt .... when they fell out of the tree.

4 I went to the dentist with Jane because she doesn't like going by ....

5 I cut .... when I was making soup.

6 The actor looked at .... in the mirror before he went on stage.

2 Riempi gli spazi con un verbo nel riquadro e il pronome riflessivo corretto.

introduce	enjoy	not hurt	teach	help	cut	look after	blame

1 It was a good party, wasn't it? Did your friends ..*enjoy themselves*.. ?

2 Bill fell off his scooter the other day, but luckily he ....

3 .... to crisps and drinks, guys! It's all there on the table.

4 You mustn't .... for what happened. It really wasn't your fault.

5 At the age of eighteen most English kids leave home. This means that their mothers don't do all their washing and cooking – they have to know how to ....

6 Feeling a little embarrassed, Sally .... to her new headteacher and shook hands.

7 Be careful you don't .... with that knife. It really is very sharp.

8 I'm trying to .... Arabic, but I'm not making much progress.

8.4   PRONOMI RECIPROCI: *EACH OTHER, ONE ANOTHER*

I pronomi reciproci, *each other* e *one another*, traducono le particelle italiane **si/ci**, ma non devono essere confusi con i pronomi riflessivi, perché indicano un rapporto di reciprocità, di relazione **tra due o più di due entità** (l'un l'altro).

Nell'inglese moderno non c'è nessuna differenza reale tra le due forme, ma si tende a preferire *one another* quando ci si riferisce a **più di due**.

*Brad and Mel looked at **each other** / **one another**.*	*Brad e Mel **si** guardarono.*
*My students always help **one another**.*	*I miei studenti **si** aiutano sempre (l'un l'altro).*

Each other e **one another** possono essere usati anche alla forma possessiva.

*They borrow **each other's** / **one another's** shoes because they take the same size.*
*Si prestano le scarpe **l'uno dell'altro** perché hanno lo stesso numero.*

IL VERBO *MEET*

Il verbo *meet* ha tre significati di base = 'fare la conoscenza di', 'incontrare' e 'incontrar**si**'. Si tratta di un **verbo reciproco**, non riflessivo, ma **non** è mai seguito dal pronome reciproco *each other / one another*.

*Why don't we **meet** for lunch on Saturday?*	*Perché non **ci diamo appuntamento** per pranzo sabato?*
*We **met** at a party in Madrid.*	***Ci siamo incontrati** a una festa a Madrid.*

PRACTICE

1 Traduci.

1 Mary e Todd si sono conosciuti il primo anno di università e da allora sono sempre stati insieme.

2 Si riconobbero immediatamente, anche se non si vedevano da anni.

3 Incontriamoci alle sette davanti al cinema.

4 Frank e Bobby non si sopportano: non si parlano da mesi.

5 Kate e Tom si baciarono appassionatamente, anche se erano in mezzo alla gente.

6 Dopo quello che era successo, non avevano il coraggio di guardarsi l'un l'altro.

8.5   AGGETTIVI E PRONOMI DIMOSTRATIVI: *THIS, THAT, THESE* E *THOSE; THIS ONE, THAT ONE; THE ONE, THE ONES*

Si usa *this/these* per indicare cose e persone che sono **vicine a chi parla**;
si usa *that/those* per indicare cose e persone che sono **distanti da chi parla**.

Vicino a chi parla		Distante da chi parla	
Singolare: *this*	**Plurale:** *these*	**Singolare:** *that*	**Plurale:** *those*
this house	*these* houses	*that* house	*those* houses
questa casa	**queste** case	**quella** casa	**quelle** case
this child	*these* children	*that* child	*those* children
questo bambino	**questi** bambini	**quel** bambino	**quei** bambini
This is Liz.	*These* are Liz and Tom.	*that* day	*those* days
Questa è Liz.	**Questi** sono Liz e Tom.	**quel** giorno	**quei** giorni

■ Se sono seguiti da un nome, ***this/these*** e ***that/those*** hanno funzione di aggettivo.

This T-shirt suits me. (= I'm wearing it)

Questa *maglietta mi sta bene / mi dona.*
(= quella che indosso in questo momento)

That T-shirt suits you. (= you're wearing it, not me)

Quella *maglietta ti sta bene / ti dona.*
(= quella che indossi tu)

■ Se non sono seguiti da nome hanno funzione di pronome.

This is a good concert. (= I'm at the concert now)

Questo *è un bel concerto.*
(= sono al concerto adesso)

That was a good concert.
(= I'm not at the concert now)

Quello *fu un bel concerto.*
(= non sono al concerto adesso)

■ Quando ci riferiamo a un nome numerabile e non vogliamo ripeterlo, usiamo ***one/ones***.

Which picture do you like?	*This one. / That one.*	*The one of a sunset.*
Quale quadro ti piace?	**Questo./Quello.**	**Quello** *con il tramonto.*
Which pictures do you like?	*These ones. / Those ones.*	*The ones by Van Gogh.*
Che quadri ti piacciono?	**Questi./Quelli.**	**Quelli** *di Van Gogh.*

■ Quando **questo/questa/questi/queste** sono seguiti da un aggettivo o da un complemento si rendono con ***the one / the ones***.

Which chair do you want? **The** red **one.**
Which book are you looking for?
The one *I put on the top shelf.*

Che sedia vuoi? **Quella** *rossa.*
Che libro stai cercando?
Quello *che ho messo sulla mensola più alta.*

PRACTICE

1 <u>Sottolinea</u> le parole corrette in questo dialogo tra Nyree e Ian.

Nyree: Can we stop here a moment? I want to look in the window of **(1)** *this/that* shoe shop. I need to buy some new shoes.

Ian: OK. But **(2)** *these/those* ones you're wearing look really good. And they go with **(3)** *this/that* jacket.

Nyree: Yes, but **(4)** *these/those* aren't very comfortable now the summer is here. I'd like something lighter for **(5)** *this/that* warm weather.

Ian: What about **(6)** *these/those*, at the back of the window?

Nyree: Hmm, they look cool, but I don't like the colour. I prefer the **(7)** *one/ones* in front of them.

Ian: Let's go in and you can try them on.

2 Guarda le immagini e completa le frasi con **this**, **that**, **these** o **those**.

1   ......This...... is a really great party!

2   Do you remember .... rock concert we went to in Milan?

3   Wow! Look at .... heels!

4   Can I try .... shoes on, please?

5   .... photo of you is not very flattering!

6   You look so much better in .... photo instead.

3 Riempi gli spazi con **this**, **that**, **these** o **those**.

1   Have you seen .....that..... film in which Johnny Depp plays a pirate? I've forgotten its name.

2   Lying on the beach on a hot day, with good company and great music! What more could anyone want? .... is the life!

3   .... T-shirt you're wearing is really cool!

4 We had a good time with .... friends of yours last night, didn't we?

5 How do I look in .... jeans? Do they suit me?

6 Do you remember the Italy–Germany semi-final in the 2006 World Cup? .... was a great match.

7 Brrrrr! .... water is very cold. I'm getting out now.

8 .... girls over there are in the same class as me. Let's go over and talk to them.

9 Here's a good website! .... games look interesting. Shall we download them?

10 I'm bored with .... exercise. Let's do something else!

4 Traduci.

1 **A** Quale maglione hai comprato, quello blu o quello verde? **B** Quello blu.

2 Mi piacciono tutti i tuoi quadri eccetto questo. È troppo scuro.

3 Non metterti la giacca rossa. Quella nera ti sta meglio.

4 **A** Qual è il tuo ragazzo? **B** Quello con i capelli lunghi.

5 Queste magliette sono tutte carine, ma la mia preferita è quella con il colletto bianco.

6 Non mi piacciono i jeans larghi. Preferisco quelli attillati (*skinny*).

8.6 *THERE IS / IT IS*

La struttura **there** + verbo **be** = **c'è**, **ci sono**, **c'era** ecc., viene usata per dire che qualcuno o qualcosa **esiste**, soprattutto quando se ne parla per la prima volta.

There's a party in Angela's flat.   *C'è una festa a casa di Angela.*
There were a lot of people in the flat.   *C'era un sacco di gente nell'appartamento.*
Is there a newsagent's near here? No, there isn't.   *C'è un'edicola qui vicino? No, **non c'è**.*

Affermativa		Negativa		Interrogativa		Interrogativa/negativa	
There is	**C'è**	*There isn't*	**Non c'è**	*Is there ...?*	**C'è ...?**	*Isn't there ...?*	**Non c'è ...?**
There are	**Ci sono**	*There aren't*	**Non ci sono**	*Are there ...?*	**Ci sono ...?**	*Aren't there ...?*	**Non ci sono ...?**

Come si vede dalla tabella, il verbo dopo **there** concorda in numero con il soggetto che segue.

There are some lovely apartments.   *Ci sono degli appartamenti molto belli.*
There's a tour guide.   *C'è una guida turistica.*

There può essere usato con tutte le forme di **be**, anche quelle introdotte da un verbo modale.

There might be a night train to Norwich.   *Può darsi che ci sia un treno di notte per Norwich.*
There used to be a cinema here.   *C'era un cinema qui.*
Now there's a shopping centre.   *Ora c'è un centro commerciale.*
There must be somebody at home.   *Ci deve essere qualcuno a casa.*
The windows are all open.   *Le finestre sono tutte aperte.*

Si usa invece *it* + verbo *be (It's)* nei seguenti casi:

■ per riferirci ad una cosa, azione o situazione di cui abbiamo già parlato.

*There's a newsagent's in this street. **It's** on the corner.*   *C'è un'edicola in questa strada. **È** sull'angolo.*
*There's a hotel by the sea. **It's** quite old.*   *C'è un hotel sul mare. **È** piuttosto vecchio.*

■ per parlare dell'**ora**, della **distanza** e del **tempo**.

It's nine o'clock in the evening.   ***Sono** le nove di sera.*
It's ten kilometres from here to the city centre.   ***Ci sono** dieci chilometri da qui al centro.*
It's sunny here in New York.   ***C'è** il sole qui a New York.*

■ per evitare di usare un infinito o una forma *-ing* come soggetto della frase.

It's surprising to see you here.   ***È** sorprendente vederti qui.*

La frase ***To see you here is surprising***, anche se grammaticalmente corretta, suona antiquata in inglese moderno, e non viene più usata.

It's a waste of time coming here.   ***È** una perdita di tempo venire qui.*

La frase ***Coming here is a waste of time*** è possibile in inglese moderno, ma meno comune.

PRACTICE

1 **Riempi gli spazi in questa email con *it's* o *there is/are*.**

To:	Silva
Cc:	
Subject:	tomorrow

Hi Silva

I'm glad you can come tomorrow. You can walk to my house from the station as
(1) ....it's......... only about 500 metres. **(2)** .... some interesting shops on
the way. My favourite is the music shop. **(3)** .... the best one in town.

Anyway my house is easy to find. **(4)** .... on the corner and **(5)** ....
quite modern. Number 54. **(6)** .... a garage opposite.

I hope **(7)** .... sunny so we can have lunch in the garden. **(8)** .... a
tree we can sit under if **(9)** .... hot.

I can't wait to see you. **(10)** .... a train which arrives at 11.

Love

Alice

2 In sette di queste frasi c'è un errore. <u>Sottolinea</u> l'errore e correggilo.

1   This mobile phone is too complicated for me. <u>They are</u> hundreds of different functions.

   ...There are.....

2   **A** What's the weather like there in Corfu? **B** There's sunny, of course. ....

3   Help! It's a large spider in the bath. ....

4   How far is it to the nearest beach? ....

5   Is it a disco near here? ....

6   Is it enough time for a quick swim in the pool? ....

7   There is always a pleasure to go to the gym in the evening. ....

8   Susan hasn't spoken to me for a week. There must be a reason why she's ignoring me.

   ....

9   **A** What do you think of that new computer game? **B** I think there's a waste of time and money.

   ....

10 You look like you've been on a desert island for a few months. Isn't it time you had a haircut?

   ....

3 Riempi gli spazi con **it is**, **there is** o **there are**.

Sometimes I dream of a place where I'd like to live. **(1)** ....It is.......... at the top of a mountain and on the south-facing side **(2)** .... a little house. **(3)** .... very pretty and **(4)** .... flowers all around it. **(5)** .... no other houses nearby but **(6)** .... lots of sheep and goats and wonderful vegetables growing. **(7)** .... always sunny and warm and it only rains at night. **(8)** .... not far from a little village where **(9)** .... a restaurant which serves my favourite food. Unfortunately **(10)** .... just a dream!

ALL IN ONE REVISION

1 *Market Street* è una soap opera trasmessa in televisione tutte le sere. Ascolterai una ragazza che racconta a un'amica che cosa è successo nell'episodio di ieri sera. Guarda attentamente le immagini. La fine della storia manca. Riesci a indovinare che cosa è successo?

2 Ascolta e verifica se avevi ragione.

1.19

3 Queste sono alcune frasi tratte dalla registrazione. Riempi gli spazi con le parole nel riquadro, poi ascolta di nuovo e controlla le tue risposte.

1.20

| his | her own | herself | hers | their | ~~her~~ | his own | himself |

1 Sally lent ....*her*......... key to .... cousin Tony.

2 Tony doesn't have .... flat.

3 Tony broke .... leg.

4 Cara was looking forward to being in the flat on ....

5 Tony was sitting there by .... when he had an idea.

6 They were friends of ....

7 Cara really enjoyed ....

4 Sottolinea l'alternativa corretta.

A few years ago my brother, Alan, decided to travel round the world with a friend of

(1) *his* / *him* called Sam. They flew to Australia because a friend of our **(2)** *fathers'* / *father's* had said

they could stay with him. After a few weeks they found a flat because they preferred to be on

(3) *themselves* / *their own* so they could enjoy **(4)** *them* / *themselves.*

My brother met **(5)** *her* / *his* wife in Australia and stayed there. Now they live in a beautiful house.

(6) *It* / *There* is much bigger than **(7)** *my* / *mine* in London but they invite **(8)** *me* / *myself* there every year. **(9)** *There / It* is even a swimming pool and a tennis court. Alan and Sam are still friends although Sam now lives in Africa and his life is very different from **(10)** *Alans' / Alan's*!

5 Completa le frasi seguenti con una parola o un'espressione che abbia lo stesso significato delle parole in corsivo.

1   Sally is very strange. She spends a lot of time ..*on her own*... = *alone*

2   What was the party like? Did you all ....? = *have a good time*

3   I don't need to borrow your scooter. Bill has said he will lend me .... = *Bill's scooter*

4   Bill and Ben are going to Greece in August. My holidays won't be as good as ....
      = *their holidays*

5   Amy and Jim's birthdays are on the same day. They always .... a present. = *exchange presents*

6   Don't wear that dress to the party. Wear your .... = *the red dress*

6 Philip sta partendo per una vacanza negli Highlands scozzesi e chiede consigli a sua madre su che cosa portare. Completa il dialogo con **one**, **the one**, **the ones**, **it is**, **there are**, **these ones**, **which one** o **which ones**.

Philip: Where are my boots, Mum?

Mum: **(1)** ...*Which ones*....? Do you mean **(2)** .... you bought last year? I think they're in the cupboard under the stairs.

Philip: Ah yes, here they are. Which rucksack do you think I should take? My big **(3)** .... or this smaller **(4)** .... ?

Mum: I would take **(5)** .... with all the side pockets. They could be useful. What about a jacket? **(6)** .... are you going to take?

Philip: I can't decide. This blue **(7)** .... is warmer, but it isn't waterproof.

Mum: You must take something waterproof. **(8)** .... often wet and rainy in Scotland. And have you got any insect repellent? **(9)** .... a lot of insects in the Highlands.

Philip: I'll have to buy some there. Ok, I just need socks now.

Mum: I've already thought of that. Look at **(10)** .... I bought them specially. They're synthetic and so they dry more quickly.

Philip: Thanks. I'm beginning to really look forward to getting wet and eaten alive by insects!

7 Completa le frasi seguenti con un pronome riflessivo o reciproco. Se nessun pronome è necessario, lascia lo spazio vuoto.

1 In Great Britain it is common for friends to give ...*each other*... presents at Christmas.

2 **A** When can we next meet .... ? **B** How about on Friday after school?

3 Emily and Jessica were great friends at primary school, but they don't see .... much nowadays.

4 Italians often kiss .... when they meet .... , whereas the British are more likely to just say hello.

5 Did you make that song up .... ? It's really good.

6 I've had the same girlfriend for two years now. We really love ....

7 Revising is driving my sister mad. She walks round talking to .... about history and geography.

8 **A** Would you mind helping me tidy my bedroom? **B** Yes, I would. Do it .... !

9 I don't think Terry and Chris like .... very much. They rarely spend time together.

10 She's very selfish. She thinks of no one but ....

8 Riempi gli spazi in questa lettera con un aggettivo possessivo, un pronome possessivo, un pronome personale o un pronome riflessivo appropriato.

Dear Vicky,

How are you? Bill and I have just got back from a holiday in Australia. On the whole we enjoyed **(1)** _ourselves_ , but the first night was an adventure! We arrived at midnight at Sydney airport and Bill was stopped at customs control. I saw **(2)** .... arguing with two officials and then I saw **(3)** .... lead Bill away in handcuffs! I wanted to go back into the airport but they wouldn't let **(4)** .... , so I just had to wait. Eventually he was allowed through. They didn't like **(5)** .... passport because the cover had come off and Bill had stapled it back on **(6)** .... ! By then **(7)** .... hotel mini-bus had left so we had to get a taxi. **(8)** .... was a very old car, and as we were speeding down the road I suddenly saw smoke coming from **(9)** .... engine. The driver stopped and **(10)** .... all jumped out in a panic. Within seconds **(11)** .... were flames shooting from the car and all we could do was stand and watch until the fire brigade came and put it out. Luckily, another taxi took **(12)** .... to the hotel, but **(13)** .... was three in the morning before we got to bed. What a start!

How was **(14)** .... holiday in Ibiza? Was it as exciting as **(15)** .... ?

Love, Sally

9 Traduci.

1 Ci sarà molta gente alla festa di mio fratello.

2 C'è stato un terribile incidente sulla M24.

3 **A** Scusi, c'è una banca qui vicino? **B** Sì, ce n'è una in King Street.

4 Domani ci sarà la nebbia.

5 C'è un ristorante giapponese sul lungomare. È buono, ma è molto costoso.

6 Ci sono molti turisti qui d'estate. C'è sempre il sole.

7 Ci sono 30 miglia da qui a Brighton. Non è lontano.

8 C'è un sacco di rumore nella strada. Che cosa sta succedendo?

9 È difficile parlare bene un'altra lingua.

10 È una buona idea parlare delle cose che ti preoccupano.

PRONOMI E DETERMINANTI (2)

UNIT 9

9.1 *Some, any, no; any* in frase affermativa

9.2 *Somebody, anybody, nobody, everywhere, etc.*

9.3 *A lot of, lots of, much, many, a little, a few*

9.4 *All, most, some, no* e *none; all* e *whole*

9.5 *Both, either, neither, both ... and; either ... or, neither ... nor*

9.6 *Each* ed *every; every* e *all*

PRONOMI E DETERMINANTI (2) – INTRODUZIONE

Questo capitolo si occupa principalmente dei *quantifiers*, quei determinanti che si riferiscono alla **quantità** (*much, many, a few, a little*) di quello di cui si sta parlando. Talvolta la quantità può anche essere indefinita (*some, any*).

PRACTICE

1 Sarah sta organizzando un barbecue per il suo diciottesimo compleanno. Il suo ragazzo le telefona. Leggi il dialogo e decidi se le frasi che seguono sono vere o false.

Bill: Hello, Sarah. It's Bill. I'm just calling to know how the barbecue preparations are going. Is there anything I can do to help?

Sarah: Hi, Bill. Well, I still have a few things to do. Have you invited all your friends?

Bill: Yes, most of my class are coming, but neither of my brothers are here. They're both in London. How about you?

Sarah: Yes, I've invited everyone I can think of. There should be about fifty people.

Bill: That's a lot. Isn't that too many?

Sarah: There's lots of room in the garden, and I've told everybody to bring something to eat or drink.

Bill: Is there any furniture in the garden? Can people sit down?

Sarah: There are a few chairs, but people can sit on the grass. Could you bring some drinks?

Bill: Well, I've got absolutely no money. I spent every penny I had on my scooter last week.

Sarah: All right. Tell anybody else you invite to bring some soft drinks.

Bill: OK. I'll come over at five o'clock and give you a hand.

Sarah: Thanks. Bye.

True/False:

1 Sarah has already done everything. ...F...

2 Bill has two brothers. ....

3 There aren't any chairs in the garden. ....

4 Bill's got a lot of money. ....

5 Sarah needs some more drinks. ....

146

9.1   *SOME, ANY, NO*; *ANY* IN FRASE AFFERMATIVA

Some e *any* indicano una **quantità indefinita** e corrispondono agli aggettivi e pronomi indefiniti italiani **alcuni/e**, **qualche**, **un po' di**, ma anche alle preposizioni articolate **del/della**, **degli/dei/delle** con valore di partitivo.

		Nomi numerabili (*bag*)	Nomi non numerabili (*luggage*)
+	*a/some*	*He's got* **a** *bag /* **some** *bags.*	*He's got* **some** *luggage.*
–	*any*	*He has**n't** got* **a** *bag /* **any** *bags.*	*He has**n't** got* **any** *luggage.*
?	*any*	*Has he got* **a** *bag /* **any** *bags?*	*Has he got* **any** *luggage?*

Come si vede dalla tabella, *some* e *any* si usano sia con i nomi numerabili che non numerabili. Quando sono seguiti da un sostantivo **numerabile**, questo, a differenza dell'italiano, è sempre **plurale**.

There are **some** *mistakes in your translation.*   *C'è* **qualche** *errore / Ci sono* **degli** *errori nella tua traduzione.*

Are there **any** *letters for me?*   *Ci sono* **delle** *lettere / C'è* **qualche** *lettera per me?*

■ **No** significa **not any**.

He's got **no** *bags. = He has**n't** got* **any** *bags.*   *Lui non ha* **nessuna** *borsa.*
He's got **no** *luggage. = He has**n't** got* **any** *luggage.*   *Lui non ha* **nessun/alcun** *bagaglio.*

Ma **not any** non può essere mai usato all'inizio della frase.

No students can solve that problem.   **Nessuno studente** *può risolvere quel problema.*

■ In inglese, i partitivi sono sempre usati nelle frasi negative e interrogative, mentre in italiano possono essere omessi.

Have you got **any** *brothers or sisters?*   *Hai (dei) fratelli o (delle) sorelle?*
There aren't **any** */ are* **no** *classes on Saturday.*   *Non ci sono lezioni di sabato.*

CONTRASTO *SOME/ANY*

Some si usa:

■ nelle frasi **affermative**.

There's **some** *milk in the fridge.*
C'è **del / un po' di** *latte nel frigorifero.*
I've got **some** *friends in Barcelona.*
Ho **degli** *amici a Barcellona.*

■ nelle frasi **interrogative**, quando:
si **offre** qualcosa.

Would you like **some** *coffee?*
Vuoi **del / un po' di** *caffè?*
Shall I buy **some** *food?*
Devo comprare **qualcosa** *da mangiare?*

Any si usa:

■ nelle frasi **negative**.

There isn't **any** *milk in the fridge.*
Non *c'è latte nel frigorifero.*
He **never** *gives me* **any** *help.*
Non *mi dà* **mai** *(nessun) aiuto.*

■ nelle frasi **interrogative**.

Is there **any** *cheese left?*
C'è rimasto **del / un po' di** *formaggio?*
Have we got **any** *eggs?*
Abbiamo **delle** *uova?*

si fa una **richiesta**.

*Could I have **some** more cake?*
Potrei avere un altro po' di dolce?
*Can you buy **some** crisps?*
Puoi comprare delle patatine?

■ In generale, si usa **some** nelle domande quando ci si aspetta una **risposta affermativa**.

*(In a travel agency): Could I have **some** information about this cruise in the Mediterranean?*
(In un'agenzia di viaggi): Potrei avere delle informazioni su questa crociera nel Mediterraneo?

■ Si usa **any** quando si tratta di domande vere e proprie, a cui l'interlocutore può rispondere con un **sì** o con un **no**.

*Are there **any** other questions?*
Ci sono altre domande?
*Are **any** of these flats for sale?*
Qualcuno di questi appartamenti è in vendita?

■ Si usa **any** nelle frasi dubitative, spesso dopo **if** e **whether**.

*If you've got **any** photos of the baby, I'd like to see them.*
Se hai delle foto del bambino, mi piacerebbe vederle.

Nelle frasi affermative **any** significa **qualsiasi, qualunque**.

Any cardboard box will do.　　　**Qualsiasi scatola di cartone andrà bene.**
*You can phone me **any** time tomorrow.*　　**Puoi chiamarmi a qualunque ora domani.**

PRACTICE

1 Inserisci negli spazi **some** o **a/an**.

1 Here's ..*some*..... information about the concert next Saturday.

2 I've just heard .... interesting piece of gossip: Judy and Paul are going out together!

3 Would you buy me .... newspaper while you're out if you have time?

4 Let me give you .... good advice: never drive too fast and always wear .... helmet.

5 There's .... amazing dress in that shop window.

6 I really need .... iPod.

7 Waiter! There's .... fly in my soup!

8 I'd like .... bar of chocolate, please.

9 There's .... chocolate in the cupboard.

10 Don't worry, I've got .... money. I'll pay.

2 Completa le frasi con **some**, **any** o **no**.

1 **A** Which train should I take? **B** ....*Any*.... London train will be all right, but ...*some*... are faster than others.

2 Sausages and beans on pizza? .... Italian would eat such a strange combination.

3 If you've got .... questions, feel free to ask.

4 I'd prefer to get back before midnight. I don't want .... problems with my parents.

5 That house is occupied by .... young people with dogs.

6 Have you heard .... good music recently?

7 There is .... money at all in my bank account.

8 .... people enjoy going for a run before breakfast. It's a good way to start the day.

3 Leggi questa conversazione tra alcuni studenti di una scuola d'arte e il loro insegnante. Riempi gli spazi con *a*, *an*, *some*, *any* o *no*.

Rex: Hi, I'm Rex. Are you **(1)** .....*a*....... new student?

Jenny: Yes, I'm Jenny. I haven't been to **(2)** .... art class before.

Rex: The classes in this college are good. Have you brought **(3)** .... equipment?

Jenny: I've got **(4)** .... brushes and **(5)** .... pens, but I haven't got **(6)** ....
             paint. I didn't know what kind to buy.

Rex: That's OK. I can lend you **(7)** .... paint.

Jenny: Thanks very much.

Rex: Now we need **(8)** .... paper. Let's ask the teacher. Excuse me, is there **(9)** ....
             thick paper? There's **(10)** .... paper in the drawer because we used it all last week.

Teacher: Oh. Well, I'll fetch some from the store cupboard now.

4 È sabato e i signori Matthews sono usciti. I loro figli, Jane e Dan, hanno deciso di invitare degli amici a cena. Completa il loro dialogo con *some*, *any*, *no* o *a/an*.

Jane: What shall we make for dinner then? Have you got **(1)** ...*any*...... ideas?

Dan: No. Let's see what's in the fridge. Ah, look! There's **(2)** .... apple. That's **(3)** ....
         good start!

Jane: Yes, that reminds me, Luke's on **(4)** .... diet.

Dan: And Rebecca's **(5)** .... vegetarian. So let's see what's in the vegetable compartment.
         There are **(6)** .... courgettes. What could we make with those?

Jane: Risotto. Are there **(7)** .... onions?

Dan: I can't see **(8)** .... No, there are **(9)** .... onions.

Jane: OK, I'll make **(10)** .... shopping list. Look, there's **(11)** .... rice in the cupboard
         so we don't need to buy **(12)** .... But maybe we should buy **(13)** .... tomatoes
         and lettuce to make **(14)** .... salad. Is there **(15)** .... cheese in the fridge?

Dan: There's **(16)** .... parmesan and **(17)** .... old piece of cheddar. I think we'll have
         to buy **(18)** .... more.

Jane: Yes, and what about dessert? There's usually **(19)** .... ice cream in the freezer.

Dan: No, there's **(20)** .... ice cream here. Add that to the list.

5 Traduci.

1 **A** Hai degli animali domestici? **B** Sì, ho un cane. Si chiama Sammy.

2 **A** Tua sorella ha dei bambini? **B** Sì, ha due maschi ma nessuna femmina.

3 John mi ha regalato dei CD per il mio compleanno.

4 Puoi comprare del pane quando esci?

5 **A** Hai letto dei buoni libri recentemente? **B** Sì, ho letto una biografia di Nelson Mandela. Mi è piaciuta moltissimo.

6 Se ci sono delle parole che non conoscete, usate il vocabolario.

7 Ti dispiace se metto un po' di musica?

8 Puoi prendere qualsiasi autobus. Vanno tutti all'università.

9.2   *SOMEBODY, ANYBODY, NOBODY, EVERYWHERE, ETC.*

Some, *any*, *no* e *every* sono usati in molte parole composte.

	Persone	**Cose**	**Luoghi**
some	*somebody/someone* *qualcuno*	*something* *qualcosa*	*somewhere* *da qualche parte*
any	*anybody/anyone* *qualcuno, qualsiasi persona*	*anything* *qualcosa, qualsiasi cosa*	*anywhere* *da qualche/qualunque parte*
no	*nobody/no-one* *nessuno*	*nothing* *niente*	*nowhere* *da nessuna parte*
every	*everybody/everyone* *tutti, ognuno*	*everything* *tutto, ogni cosa*	*everywhere* *dovunque, dappertutto*

Le regole di uso di queste parole composte sono le stesse che valgono per *some*, *any*, *no* e *every*.

■ I composti di *some* si usano nelle frasi affermative.

*We'll find **somewhere** quiet.*   *Troveremo **qualche posto** tranquillo.*

■ I composti di *any* si usano nelle domande e nelle frasi negative.

*Have I forgotten **anything**?*   *Ho dimenticato **qualcosa**?*
*I haven't found **anything**.*   *Non ho trovato **niente**.*

■ I composti di *any* si usano anche nelle frasi affermative con il significato di **qualsiasi**, **non importa quale**.

***Anywhere** quiet will be fine.*   ***Qualunque posto** tranquillo andrà bene.*

■ I composti di *every* e *no* hanno un **significato plurale** ma sono seguiti da un **verbo singolare**.

*Where is **everybody**?*   *Dove sono **tutti**?*
***Nobody** wants to go to that hotel.*   ***Nessuno** vuole andare in quell'hotel.*
***Everything** is ready.*   ***Tutto** è pronto.*

A differenza dell'italiano, dopo questi composti l'aggettivo **non** può essere preceduto da *of*.
*Is there **anything interesting** on TV tonight?*   *C'è **niente di interessante** in TV stasera?*
*I want to go **somewhere sunny**.*   *Voglio andare **in qualche posto** dove c'è **il sole**.*

PRACTICE

1 Leggi questa storia e <u>sottolinea</u> l'alternativa corretta.

Last month my husband and I went to a wedding in the north of the country. We needed to stop for a night on the journey. We didn't have **(1)** <u>*anywhere*</u> / *nowhere* to stay, so I rang the tourist information office to find a bed and breakfast. I asked for **(2)** *somewhere* / *everywhere* near the main road and was given the address of a small inn.

When we arrived it was almost dark. The inn was an old-fashioned place with a garden that **(3)** *anyone* / *no-one* had tidied for a long time. The front door was locked. We soon began to feel that **(4)** *nobody* / *somebody* didn't want visitors. When we rang the bell **(5)** *anybody* / *nobody* answered, but we heard a noise inside the building. We called out but **(6)** *nothing* / *everything* happened. After several minutes we decided to look for **(7)** *anywhere* / *somewhere* else to stay. We found a modern hotel in the nearest village. When we asked about the old inn, **(8)** *everybody* / *somebody* in the hotel was really surprised. **(9)** *Anybody* / *Nobody* knew it.

'It's on the main road, just before this village,' we explained.

At last the hotel owner asked her father, a very old man. 'There was an inn many years ago, but it burned down,' he said. '**(10)** *No-one* / *Anyone* goes there now.'

After the wedding, we drove past the place again. There wasn't **(11)** *nothing* / *anything* there. It seemed like a dream. But we know we saw **(12)** *something* / *anything*. We just don't know what it was.

2 Leggi attentamente ogni coppia di frasi. Scrivi **S** se il significato è lo stesso e **D** se è differente.

1 I didn't bring my boots because I didn't have any space in my suitcase.
I didn't bring my boots because I had no space in my suitcase. ...*S*...

2 Is there anything in that box?
Does that box have anything in it? ....

3 Has everyone in the class read this book?
Has anyone in the class read this book? ....

4   There's nowhere to buy a coffee in the bus station.

There isn't anywhere to buy a coffee in the bus station. ....

5   I've got several jobs to do before I go out.

I don't have much work to do before I go out. ....

6   We're looking everywhere for our passports.

We don't know where our passports are. ....

7   Everything in that shop is expensive.

Nothing in that shop is cheap. ....

8   Did you eat anything at the barbecue?

Did you eat everything at the barbecue? ....

9.3   A LOT OF, LOTS OF, MUCH, MANY; A LITTLE, A FEW

A lot of / lots of = **molto/a**, **molti/e** è usato sia con nomi numerabili che non numerabili.

*I've got **a lot of / lots of** homework to do.*	*Ho **molti / un sacco di** compiti da fare.*
*Jane gets **a lot of / lots of** letters from her boyfriend.*	*Jane riceve **molte** lettere dal suo ragazzo.*

Much = **molto/a** si usa con i nomi non numerabili.

*I haven't got **much** time.*	*Non ho **molto** tempo.*
*Was there **much** traffic on the road to Cromer?*	*C'era **molto** traffico sulla strada per Cromer?*

Many = **molti/e** si usa con i nomi numerabili e plurali.

*Tom hasn't got **many** friends.*	*Tom non ha **molti** amici.*
*There aren't **many** seats in the new theatre.*	*Non ci sono **molti** posti a sedere nel nuovo teatro.*

Much non viene comunemente usato nelle frasi affermative. Confronta le frasi seguenti:

*My brother earns **a lot of** money.*	*Mio fratello guadagna **molti / un sacco di** soldi.*
(**Non** ~~My brother earns **much money**.~~)	
*My brother doesn't earn **much** money.*	*Mio fratello **non** guadagna **molti** soldi.*

MUCH E A LOT

Much e *a lot* possono anche avere funzione di avverbi.

*I like your sister **a lot**.*	*Tua sorella mi piace **molto**.*
*I don't go out **much** these days.*	*Non esco **molto** in questi giorni.*

A LITTLE E A FEW

A little significa **un po'**, **una piccola quantità** (= *not much*), e si usa con i nomi non numerabili.

A few significa **alcuni** (= più di due ma non molti) e si usa con i nomi numerabili e plurali.

*We've got **a little** cheese and **a few** eggs.*	*Abbiamo **un po' di** formaggio e **alcune/delle** uova.*
We can make an omelette.	*Possiamo fare una frittata.*

◼ Come *much* e *a lot*, anche *a little* può essere usato come avverbio.

*He has worked **a little** this morning.*	*Ha lavorato **un po'** questa mattina.*
*He walked **a little** down the road.*	*Ha camminato **un po'** per la strada.*

Con funzione di avverbio, *a little* può anche precedere gli aggettivi e gli avverbi comparativi.

*I'd like to stay **a little longer**.*	*Vorrei rimanere **un po' di più**.*
*The cream should be **a little thicker** than this.*	*La panna dovrebbe essere **un po' più densa** di così.*

◼ Con i sostantivi numerabili si possono usare anche le espressioni *a couple of* = **due** e *several* = **diversi**.

*He's got **a couple of** bags.*	*Ha **due / un paio di** borse.*
*I've read **several** English novels.*	*Ho letto **diversi** romanzi inglesi.*

PRACTICE

1 Riempi gli spazi con *much*, *a lot of*, *a little* e *a few*, come richiede il senso delle frasi.

1 Jim is very popular. He's got a lot of friends.

2 Harry is less popular. He's only got .... friends.

3 Hurry up and finish what you're doing. We haven't got .... time.

4 **A** Have you studied .... this week? **B** No, but I did .... work this morning.

5 **A** Do you have .... CDs? **B** No, I've only got ....

6 Donald spends .... time playing computer games – at least three hours a day.

7 Only .... of my friends live in the country.

8 **A** Has it rained .... in Italy this spring? **B** No, only ....

2 Leggi i nomi nel riquadro. Quali di essi sono numerabili e quali non numerabili?

CDs	homework	money	fruit	magazines	parties	jewellery	T-shirts

Quali di queste parole puoi usare con i nomi numerabili? Quali puoi usare con i nomi non numerabili?

Adesso scrivi delle frasi vere su di te o sui tuoi amici usando le parole nei due riquadri.

a couple of	a few	a little	lots of	many	much	several

1 I bought several CDs when I went shopping last week. ....

2 ....

3 ....

4 ....

5 ....

6 ....

9.4   ALL, MOST, SOME, NO E NONE; ALL E WHOLE

all	most	some	none
tutti	la maggior parte	alcuni	nessuno

Cose/Persone in generale

- **All** + nome:
  All teenagers watch TV.
  Tutti gli adolescenti guardano la TV.

- **Most/Some** + nome:
  Most people have a TV in their bedroom.
  (**Non** ~~Most of people have a TV in their bedroom.~~)
  La maggior parte delle persone ha una TV in camera.

- **No** + nome **senza** *the*:
  No bedroom has a fridge. = *No bedrooms* have fridges.
  Nessuna camera da letto ha il frigorifero.

Cose/Persone di un gruppo specifico

- **All (of)** + *the/my/this* ecc. + nome:
  All (of) the teenagers went home early. (the teenagers = a particular group of teenagers)
  Tutti gli adolescenti andarono a casa presto. (gli adolescenti = un gruppo specifico di adolescenti)

- **Most/Some of** + *the/my/this* ecc. + nome:
  Most of my friends like it.
  (**Non** ~~Most my friends~~)
  Alla maggior parte dei miei amici piace.

- **None of** + *the* + nome:
  None of the paintings is modern. = *None of the paintings are* modern.
  Nessuno dei quadri è moderno.

- **All/Most/Some/None** + *of* + pronome:
  All/Most/Some/None of them were very old.
  Tutti loro erano molto antichi.
  La maggior parte (di loro) era molto antica.
  Alcuni (di loro) erano molto antichi.
  Nessuno (di loro) era molto antico.

- ❗ *All of them* (**Non** ~~All them~~)
  Tutti loro

- **All**, **most** e **some** sono seguiti da un nome **senza** *the* quando il significato è generale.
  All hotels have bedrooms.   **Tutti gli alberghi** hanno camere da letto.
  (= hotels throughout the world)   (= gli alberghi in tutto il mondo)
  Most hotels have a restaurant.   **La maggior parte degli alberghi** ha un ristorante.
  Some hotels have a private beach.   **Alcuni alberghi** hanno una spiaggia privata.

■ Quando invece ci riferiamo a un gruppo specifico usiamo *all/most/some of the*.

All (of) the hotels (in this street) have a restaurant.	*Tutti gli alberghi* (in questa strada) hanno un ristorante.
Most of the hotels (in this town) are expensive.	*La maggior parte degli alberghi* (di questa città) è costosa.
Some of the hotels (in this brochure) have a swimming pool.	*Alcuni degli alberghi* (in questo depliant) hanno la piscina.

■ Come si vede dagli esempi, è possibile omettere *of* dopo *all* ma non dopo *some* o *most*.

■ Il pronome *none (of)* significa *'not any'*, ed esprime il significato di **nessuno (di)**. Di solito è seguito da un verbo singolare, ma a volte è possibile usare anche il plurale.

None of the apartments **has/have** a balcony.	*Nessuno degli* appartamenti **ha** un terrazzo.
None of them knew the answer.	*Nessuno di* loro conosceva la risposta.

All può essere usato

■ per dare enfasi

The hotels are **all** *near the airport.*	*Gli alberghi sono* **tutti** *vicino all'aeroporto.*
The children were **all** *tired after a whole day on the beach.*	*I bambini erano* **tutti** *stanchi dopo un'intera giornata sulla spiaggia.*

■ ma può essere anche usato da solo con il significato di **tutto ciò che**, **l'unica cosa che**.

All I want is somewhere quiet. (= the only thing)
Tutto ciò che voglio è un posto tranquillo. (= l'unica cosa)

Whole può essere usato al posto di *all* davanti a un nome singolare: in questo caso significa che ci riferiamo **all'intera/un'intera** esperienza.

The **whole trip** *was spoilt by the weather.*   *Tutta la gita / La gita intera* *fu rovinata dal maltempo.*

PRACTICE

1 Leggi questo prospetto che dà informazioni sui corsi di lingua a Upton, poi completa le frasi che seguono. Usa *all of*, *most of*, *some of* e *none of*.

	Courses for children	Qualified teachers	Library	Evening classes	Sports facilities	Weekend activities	City centre
Abbey Languages	✔	✔		✔		✔	
Brown's School		✔	✔	✔		✔	✔
Cottle's College	✔	✔		✔			✔
Drake's Academy	✔	✔	✔	✔			✔
Egmont Institute	✔	✔		✔			✔

Language Schools in Upton – a quick guide

1 .....Most..... of the schools in Upton offer courses for children.

2 .... the schools employ qualified teachers.

3 .... the schools have libraries.

4 .... them offer evening classes.

5 .... the schools have sports facilities for their students.

6 .... them organise weekend activities for their students.

7 .... the schools are in the city centre.

2 Completa le frasi seguenti con *some*, *most*, *all* e *none* e le parole tra parentesi. Aggiungi *of* quando è necessario.

1 The school team played badly and lost the game 5-0. None..of..the..players played well. (*the players*)

2 The government was divided over the electoral reform. As a result, ... resigned. (*the members of the cabinet*)

3 The amphitheatre museum is full of interesting artefacts found on the site. .... were found locally. (*the exhibits*)

4 A group of five young people have been kidnapped by local rebels. .... are European citizens. (*tourists*)

5 At the end of the meeting the boys and girls voted unanimously to occupy the school. .... were in favour of occupying the school. (*the students*)

6 Famous musicians usually have very irregular lives. .... have to travel a lot, and this can lead to all sorts of problems. (*pop stars*)

7 Travelling in Italy is much more expensive in August. .... cost double in high season. (*popular tourist destinations*)

8 There are twenty-eight students in my class, five of whom were born abroad. .... are foreign. (*my classmates*)

9 British children eat a lot of junk food. .... would happily eat nothing but chips. (*British teenagers*)

10 As a result of additional charges, the hotel was more expensive than anyone expected. .... thought it would cost so much. (*the guests*)

9.5   *BOTH, EITHER, NEITHER; BOTH ... AND; EITHER ... OR; NEITHER ... NOR*

both   *either*   *neither*

entrambi, tutti e due   l'uno o l'altro, uno dei due   nessuno dei due, né l'uno né l'altro

Both, **either** e **neither** si riferiscono a **due** cose o persone. Possono essere usati:

▪ con un nome o un pronome.

Both places are too noisy. o *Both (of) the places*... o *Both of them*... (verbo plurale)
Tutti e due / Entrambi i posti sono troppo rumorosi.
Either place suits me. (nome e verbo singolari)
L'uno o l'altro posto mi va/vanno bene.
Either/Neither of the places suit/suits me. (verbo singolare o plurale)

▪ da soli.

Which holiday would you prefer? Either./Neither.
Quale vacanza preferiresti? **O l'una o l'altra** (non fa differenza). / **Nessuna delle due.**
Which picture do you like? Both.
Quale quadro ti piace? **Tutti e due.**

▪ **All** e **both** possono essere posti **dopo** un verbo ausiliare.

They're all mad.   **Sono tutti** matti.
We've both finished.   **Abbiamo** finito **entrambi**.

▪ **Both ... and / Either ... or / Neither ... nor** sono anche usati come **congiunzioni**.

Both the Hotel Flora and the Hotel Princess have a good restaurant.
Sia l'Albergo Flora sia/che l'Albergo Princess **hanno** un buon ristorante.

I'd like to stay at either the Hotel Flora or the Hotel Princess.
Vorrei stare o all'Albergo Flora o all'Albergo Princess. (l'uno o l'altro non fa differenza)

Neither the Hotel Flora nor the Hotel Princess has a swimming pool.
Né l'Albergo Flora né l'Albergo Princess hanno una piscina.

▪ **Either ... or** sono anche usati per indicare una scelta tra due alternative: o l'una o l'altra.

You can have either tea or hot chocolate.   **Puoi avere tè o cioccolata calda.**

PRACTICE

1 In ognuna di queste frasi c'è un errore. <u>Sottolinea</u> l'errore e correggilo.

1   We had a drink but <u>none</u> food was available. ....*no*...........

2   Neither these jackets fits me. ....

3   We stopped for a meal because both of us was hungry. ....

4   I was surprised that most the people staying in the hotel were Italian. ....

5   He's tidied the garden and put away all chairs. ....

6   I liked both pairs of jeans, but I chose the black one for the party. ....

7   This was an awful meal we had yesterday. We won't go to that restaurant again. ....

8   We're having a party for my father and we're inviting all of old friends. ....

2 Le frasi seguenti descrivono tre fratelli, Peter, John e Rob. Completale usando le parole nel riquadro.

| bald   beard   earring   ~~fair hair~~   glasses   moustache   short hair |

Pete   John   Rob

1   Both .....*John*......... and .....*Rob have fair hair.*...

2   Both .... and ....

3   Neither .... nor ....

4   All of them ....

5   They all ....

6   None of them ....

Scrivi delle frasi simili sulla tua famiglia o su tre tuoi amici.

7   Both .... and ....

8   Neither my .... nor my ....

9   All my family/friends ....

10 None ....

9.6   *EACH* ED *EVERY*; *EVERY* E *ALL*

Each significa **ogni**, **ognuno**, **ciascuno**: è seguito da un sostantivo **singolare**, ma ha funzione sia di aggettivo che di pronome.

Every significa **ogni**: come *each* è seguito da un sostantivo **singolare**, ma ha valore plurale ed è comunemente tradotto in italiano con **tutti/tutte**.

*I see Elizabeth **every day**.* (**Non** ~~every days~~)	*Vedo Elizabeth **tutti i giorni**.*
***Every classroom** has a computer in it.*	***Tutte le classi** hanno un computer.*

Each e *every* possono essere usati con lo stesso significato.

Each/Every apartment has a balcony.	***Ogni appartamento** ha / **Tutti gli appartamenti** hanno un terrazzo.*

Ma a volte hanno un significato leggermente diverso.

◾ *Each* sottolinea l'individualità di ogni persona o cosa all'interno di un gruppo.

> *Each child drew a picture of her own parents.*
> **Ogni bambina** *ha fatto un disegno dei suoi genitori.*
> *The customs officer checked **each passport** in turn.*
> *Il funzionario della dogana controllò **ogni passaporto** a turno.*

◾ *Every* sottolinea che tutte le persone o le cose in un gruppo sono incluse.

> *Every student will receive a certificate of attendance at the end of the course.*
> **Tutti gli studenti** *riceveranno un certificato di frequenza alla fine del corso.*
> *Every theatre has a stage in it.*
> **Ogni teatro** *ha un palco.*

Quando ha funzione di pronome, *each* è comunemente seguito da *of* + **nome** o **pronome**.

Each of the people had a different job. (**Non** ~~Every of the people~~)
Ognuna di quelle persone *aveva un lavoro differente.*
Each of them had a different job. (**Non** ~~Every of them~~)
Ognuno di loro *aveva un lavoro differente.*

◾ *Every* viene anche usato con espressioni di tempo e luogo per indicare eventi o azioni che si ripetono a intervalli regolari.

> *The World Cup takes place **every** four years.*
> *La Coppa del Mondo viene giocata **ogni** quattro anni.*
> *Richard visits his grandmother **every** two weeks.*
> *Richard va a trovare sua nonna **ogni** due settimane.*

👣 *Every* e *all* possono spesso essere usati senza nessuna differenza di significato.

*Every wall **is** blue.* (verbo singolare)	***Ogni** parete è blu.*
*All the walls **are** blue.* (verbo plurale)	***Tutte** le pareti **sono** blu.*

Ma quando sono riferiti a espressioni di tempo, il significato è differente. Confronta le frasi seguenti:

> *He sat by the river **every morning**.* (= regularly)
> *Si sedeva sulla riva del fiume **tutte le mattine**.* (= regolarmente)

*He sat by the river **all morning**. (= one complete morning)*
***Rimase seduto sulla riva del fiume tutta la mattina.** (= una mattina intera)*
*They go to a different place **every week**.*   *Vanno in un posto differente **tutte le settimane**.*
*They spent **all week** decorating the house.*   *Hanno passato **tutta la settimana** a ridipingere la casa.*

PRACTICE

1 Leggi il depliant di questo albergo e <u>sottolinea</u> l'alternativa corretta.

The Regent Hotel

This attractive hotel offers accommodation for families and business visitors. **(1)** <u>*Both*</u> / *Every* groups can find everything they need.

The Main Building has ten luxury rooms and the Garden House has ten family rooms.
(2) *Each* / *Both* buildings have a dining-room. Adult guests and older children may use
(3) *either* / *every* of them at any time. **(4)** *All* / *Both* of them offer the same menu but in the evening children under six may only eat in the Garden House dining-room.

(5) *All* / *Every* bedroom has a DVD and CD player and **(6)** *all* / *every* of them have private bathrooms. The decoration is different in **(7)** *either* / *each* room, and is changed **(8)** *every* / *all* year.

There is a swimming-pool available for **(9)** *all* / *both* the guests. It is open on weekday evenings and **(10)** *both* / *all* day at weekends.

2 Riempi gli spazi con **each** o **every**. A volte ambedue sono possibili.

1   .Each/Every.... member of the winning team was awarded a medal.

2   Pete is a diabetic. He has to have insulin injections .... day.

3   There's a popular saying: .... cloud has a silver lining. It means that there is a positive side to all situations, even when they seem negative.

4   The band goes on tour .... year. This year they're coming to Europe.

5   Matthew goes to the gym .... two days.

6   The course is very challenging. .... day there is something new to learn.

7   There are three bedrooms in the house, ... of which has its own bathroom.

8   The witness looked at .... photo carefully, but he couldn't identify the man he'd seen.

ALL IN ONE REVISION

1 Guarda le quattro persone nelle immagini qui sotto. Hanno tutte lasciato un messaggio sulla segreteria telefonica di Mia. Dove si trova ognuna di loro? Perché credi che stiano chiamando?

2 Ascolta i quattro messaggi. Avevi ragione?

1.21

3 Ascolta di nuovo e rispondi a queste domande.

1.22

Tom   1 Why doesn't he need a taxi? *Because he hasn't got much luggage.* ....

2 What does he offer to buy? ....

Giorgio   3 Why is he surprised? ....

4 Who has he already rung? ....

Chloe   5 What has she found in the newspaper? ....

6 Why is she worried? ....

Roseanne 7 Who is coming to the picnic? ....

8 What should Mia bring? ....

9 What has Roseanne bought? ....

4 In ogni messaggio, gli amici di Mia dicono la stessa cosa in due modi diversi. Completa le frasi seguenti in modo che abbiano lo stesso significato. Se vuoi, ascolta di nuovo.

1.23

1 I haven't got ....*much*...... luggage. = I've only got a .... small bags.

2 There isn't .... here. = There's .... here.

3 I've found .... = I haven't found ....

4 I've got .... experience. = I haven't got .... experience.

5 .... of people are coming. = There'll be a .... people.

6 I bought a .... of cakes. = I got .... cakes.

5 Per ogni coppia di frasi, completa la seconda in modo che il significato non cambi. **Usa non più di tre parole**.

PET

1 In a European survey on happiness, ninety percent of Danes said that they were satisfied with their lives.

In a European survey on happiness, ...most..... Danes said that they were satisfied with their lives.

2 All the Italian interviewees said that they were unhappy with the justice system and the government.

.... the Italian interviewees were happy with the justice system and the government.

3 Jessica and Patricia are very attractive but they are not interested in boys.

Jessica and Patricia are very attractive but .... has a boyfriend.

4 When Gary's girlfriend first left him, he spent all morning on his own in his bedroom.

When Gary's girlfriend first left him, he spent the .... morning on his own in his bedroom.

5 Frank has decided to give up boxing because he doesn't have much time to train.

Frank has decided to give up boxing because he has .... time to train.

6 Everyone expected the team to win.

.... expected the team to lose.

6 <u>Sottolinea</u> l'alternativa corretta.

I'm going to tell you about a party game you might want to play. It's a game **(1)** <u>most</u> / most of people would enjoy and it's a good way to make sure that **(2)** anyone / any who is new to the group gets an opportunity to speak to the others. There is a pile of cards and **(3)** all / every card has the name of a famous person on it. **(4)** Every / Each of the famous people has a partner, for example, Romeo's partner is Juliet. It's important that they're people that **(5)** all / everyone has heard of. **(6)** Everyone / Someone has one of these cards pinned to their back and they have to find out who they are by questioning **(7)** every / all the other people in the room. The first pair to find one **(8)** another / the other gets a prize. **(9)** The whole / All the game takes about twenty minutes and by the end **(10)** nobody / anybody is feeling shy any longer.

7 Rispondi a queste domande in modo appropriato, usando le parole tra parentesi.

1 Have you made up your mind what you're going to do when you leave school? (*either … or*)
Either go to university or go abroad for a while.

2 Where do you want to go for your summer holidays this year? (*somewhere*)
....

3 How often do you go out with your friends? (*every*)
....

4 What job do you think you'll do when you've finished studying? (*either … or*)
....

5 What would you like for your birthday? (*something*)
....

6 In what ways are two members of your family similar to each other? (*both … and …*)
....

7 What do members of your family have in common? (*all*)

....

8 How old are your classmates? (*most*)

....

8 L'estate scorsa Kevin e James hanno conosciuto due ragazze a Santander, in Spagna. La settimana scorsa Kevin le ha incontrate di nuovo per caso a Londra, e adesso racconta a James le novità delle due amiche. Completa questa conversazione con **both**, **both … and**, **either**, **neither**, **either … or**.

Kevin: Do you remember those two French girls we met last summer in Spain? Sylvie and Jacqueline?

James: Of course. How could I forget? They were **(1)** ....*both*.... really good-looking. Why?

Kevin: Well, I bumped into them **(2)** .... in Oxford Street the other day.

James: You didn't! How are they?

Kevin: Fine. They're on an Erasmus exchange, but I can't remember which University they're at – **(3)** .... London .... Surrey.

James: What are they studying? Languages or Literature?

Kevin: **(4)** .... They're studying Art and drama.

James: Great! Are they still as good-looking as ever?

Kevin: Well, **(5)** .... of them has changed much, except they **(6)** .... have short hair now. It suits them.

James: Did they seem pleased to see you?

Kevin: Yes, and very surprised. **(7)** .... Sylvie .... Jacqueline seemed very interested in hearing about you. We should arrange to all meet up together one evening.

James: Yes, although I'm not sure what my girlfriend would think about that.

Kevin: No, I'm not sure what she'd think, **(8)** .... !

9 Traduci.

1 Dov'è Martin? Non riesco a vederlo da nessuna parte.

2 Non abbiamo fatto niente di interessante durante il fine settimana.

3 Devi lavarti i piedi dopo essere stato sulla spiaggia. Guarda! C'è sabbia dappertutto.

4 Ho suonato tre volte ma nessuno ha risposto. Non c'è nessuno in casa.

5 Sono molto stanca. Non voglio far nulla stasera.

6 **A** Ti preparo qualcosa da mangiare? **B** Sì, grazie, ho davvero fame. Non ho mangiato quasi niente da stamani.

7 Perché non andiamo da qualche parte per cena? Mi piacerebbe mangiare la pizza stasera.

8 Mia sorella ha viaggiato dappertutto in Europa.

9 C'è qualcuno alla porta.

10 Perché siete tutti imbarazzati? Ho detto qualcosa di sbagliato?

GLI AGGETTIVI

GLI AGGETTIVI – INTRODUZIONE

Diversamente che in italiano, in inglese l'aggettivo è **invariabile** per genere e numero.

*Jennifer has a **beautiful** voice.*	*Jennifer ha una **bella** voce.*
*I saw a **beautiful** film yesterday.*	*Ieri ho visto un **bel** film.*
*What **beautiful** flowers!*	*Che **bei** fiori!*
*There are a lot of **beautiful** photos in this book.*	*Ci sono tante **belle** foto in questo libro.*

PRACTICE

1 Ricorda che gli aggettivi si usano per descrivere. Usa gli aggettivi nel riquadro per descrivere le figure. Puoi usare alcuni degli aggettivi più volte.

beautiful	long	short	black	grey	white	cotton	leather	silk	wool

A ...long black... B .... C .... D .... E ....

10.1   POSIZIONE DEGLI AGGETTIVI

■ L'aggettivo usato in funzione di attributo, cioè quando accompagna un sostantivo, precede **sempre** il sostantivo.

*I bought a **white T-shirt**.*   Ho comprato una **maglietta bianca**.
(**Non** *a ~~T-shirt white~~*)

■ Quando invece ha la funzione di predicato nominale, l'aggettivo **segue** il verbo *to be*.

*My bike **is old** and **dirty**.*   La mia bici **è vecchia** e **sporca**.

■ Oltre al verbo *to be*, l'aggettivo **segue** anche altri verbi, come *get*, *become*, *look*, *seem*, *appear*, *sound*, *taste*, *smell*, *feel*.

*Grandfather **is getting old**.*   Il nonno **sta diventando vecchio**.
*The onion soup **tasted delicious**.*   La zuppa di cipolle **aveva un sapore squisito**.
*Mum **looks very tired**.*   La mamma **ha un aspetto molto stanco**.

! Alcuni aggettivi, come *afraid*, *alone*, *asleep*, *awake*, **non possono** precedere il sostantivo.

*The cat was **asleep** on the bed.*   Il gatto era **addormentato** sul letto.
(**Non** *~~The asleep cat was on the bed.~~*)

PRACTICE

1 Abbina gli inizi delle frasi con le loro logiche conclusioni.

1 My boyfriend sounded ..d..   *presto*
2 The school was ..g..   a tired because I got up too early.
   sembrare = TO SEEM   b bad so we didn't drink it.
3 My boss seemed ..e..   c wonderful because it was home-made.
   triste
4 We got ..f..   d sad on the phone.
5 The bread tasted ..c..   *fretto*
   sensazione   e angry but she was just in a hurry.
6 I was feeling ..a..   *bagneti*
7 The milk smelled ..b..   f wet because we didn't have our raincoats.
                                       g unusual because it had no rules.

2 Riordina queste parole in modo da formare frasi di senso compiuto.

1 jacket / wears / a / always / Jo / leather / . ...Jo always wears a leather jacket...........
2 sun / in / hot / the / it's / . ...It's hot in the sun..........
3 like / cold / would / a / drink / you / ? ....Would you like a cold drink?..........
4 when / home / mother / got / still / I / awake / my / was / . ...When I got awake my mother was still..........
   ancora   svegho
5 dress / great / your / silk / look / shoes / those / with / . ...Look your silk dress with those great shoes..........
   GRANDE   sete   home
6 sixteen / looks / for / grown-up / your / very / daughter / . ...Your daughter look grown-up very for sixteen..........
   CRESCERE
7 he's / actually / a / person / aggressive / seems / shy / but / James / .
   SEMBRA timido
   ....Actually James seems aggressive but he's a shy person..........
8 was / but / smelt / pasta / it / delicious / the / overcooked / .
   6   4   7   3   5   2   1   *scecotto*
                              8

10.2 ORDINE DEGLI AGGETTIVI

Quando un sostantivo è preceduto da due o più aggettivi, il loro ordine non è casuale: si comincia sempre con un aggettivo che esprime **opinione** o **impressione generale**.

A **strange** old wooden chair.   Una **strana**, vecchia sedia di legno.
(**Non** ~~A wooden old strange chair.~~)
A **dangerous** old car. (**Non** ~~An old dangerous car.~~)   Un'auto vecchia e **pericolosa**.

Gli aggettivi che danno informazioni sulle qualità del sostantivo **seguono** l'aggettivo di opinione, in questo ordine:

	Opinione/ impressione	Dimensione/età/ forma	Colore	Origine	Materiale	Sostantivo
a	lovely	short	black		wool	skirt
a		small oval		French		mirror
my	favourite	old	grey		leather	boots
an	expensive	new two-storey				flat

 Si usa **and**

■ fra due aggettivi di **colore**.

A **black and white** belt.   Una cintura **bianca e nera**.

■ quando un verbo è seguito da più di un aggettivo, si usa **and davanti all'ultimo**.

Lord Byron was described as **mad**, **bad and dangerous** to know.   Lord Byron fu descritto come **pazzo**, **malvagio e pericoloso** da conoscere.

PRACTICE

1 Riscrivi le frasi inserendo gli aggettivi tra parentesi nell'ordine giusto.

1 My friend gave me a ring for my birthday. (*silver / antique*)
My friend gave me an antique silver ring for my birthday.

2 I wore my jeans when I painted the ceiling. (*old / blue / dirty*)
....

3 I borrowed my sister's dress to wear to the party. (*silk / lovely / long*)
....

4 I was surprised that Mike wore that jacket. (*white / cotton*)
....

5 He bought some shoes yesterday. (*expensive / new*)
....

6 Jenny's father gave her a necklace for her 18th birthday. (*long / gold / beautiful*)
....

2 Scrivi l'ordine giusto degli aggettivi.

1 He told us about the *black / dangerous* snakes in the jungle.   ....*dangerous black*....

2 There was a *beautiful / old* tree in the middle of the field.   ....

3 We followed a *flat / pleasant* path beside the river.   ....

4 The model wore a *little / pretty* hat which matched her coat.   ....

5 The old couple employed two *active / young* students to tidy their garden.   ....

6 We went to a concert by a *new / popular* band.   ....

3 Osserva il bozzetto e completa gli appunti con gli aggettivi che descrivono le parti del costume.

1 an .....*enormous round blue*..... hat

2 a .... shirt

3 a .... ring

4 a pair of .... boots

5 a pair of .... trousers

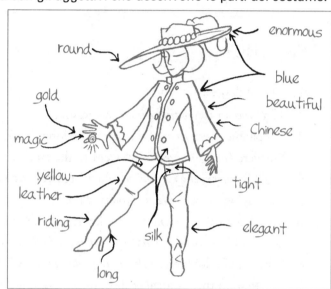

4 Riordina queste parole in modo da formare frasi di senso compiuto.

1 stone / on / sleep / floor / hard / had / I / the / to / . *I had to sleep on the hard stone floor.*

2 holiday / was / and / comfortable / our / flat / clean / . ...

3 white / bride / a / beautiful / wearing / silk / the / was / dress / .

....

4 room / paintings / modern / the / full / of / was / ugly / . ...

5 depressing / cold / the / grey / was / weather / and / . ...

6 first-floor / they've / flat / to / moved / an / expensive / modern / .

....

7 American / new / set / that / film / in / you / Greece / ancient / have / seen / ?

....

8 handmade / sells / expensive / shop / jewellery / the / silver / modern / .

....

10.3   AGGETTIVI IN -ING/-ED

Alcuni aggettivi comuni derivano da verbi e hanno **due forme**.

to surprise	→	surpris**ing**	sorprend**ente**
	→	surpris**ed**	sorpr**eso**
to bore	→	bor**ing**	noi**oso**
	→	bor**ed**	annoi**ato**

Si usa la forma **-ing** (*present participle*) per descrivere **cose**, **esperienze**, **eventi**;

si usa la forma **-ed** (*past participle*) per descrivere **sentimenti e sensazioni** che si provano.

That's **surprising** *news!*   **È una notizia sorprendente!**

I was **surprised** *to see Hannah at the party.*   **Fui sorpreso** *di vedere Hannah alla festa.*

PRACTICE

1   Sottolinea l'aggettivo corretto.

1   That was an *interesting* / *interested* lesson.

2   My parents were *tiring* / *tired* after the long flight.

3   We were *boring* / *bored* so we went to the cinema.

4   You'll be *surprising* / *surprised* when I tell you what happened.

5   I'm staying in an *amazing* / *amazed* hotel.

6   My friend was *annoying* / *annoyed* with me because I was late.

7   James told us some *fascinating* / *fascinated* stories about the music business.

8   Why are you looking so *depressing* / *depressed*? What's wrong?

9   The food in this canteen is absolutely *disgusting* / *disgusted*.

10   The astronaut gave a *relaxing* / *relaxed* wave and entered the space capsule.

2   Inserisci negli spazi un aggettivo in **-ing** o **-ed** usando i verbi nel riquadro.

interest	bore	frighten	depress	relax	surprise
confuse	disappoint	worry	annoy		

1   Anna looks very ......relaxed...... after her holiday.

2   I've always been .... of flying so I travel by train.

3   I found the film .... Everybody died at the end.

4   This map's very .... I've no idea where we are.

5   If I tell her I've lost her keys she'll be really ....

6   The beginning of the story was brilliant, but I was .... with the ending.

7   There's an .... exhibition on at the museum. You should go.

8   When John's sister was in hospital, it was a .... situation for everyone. Fortunately she's back home now.

9   I'm not .... you failed the exam if you didn't study.

10   I found the book long and .... and I didn't finish it.

3 Per ogni coppia di frasi, completa la seconda in modo che il significato non cambi. **Usa non più di tre parole**.

PET

Our weekend away didn't start well…

1   We were tired after the long journey. / Our journey was long ...*and tiring*........

2   And the atmosphere in the hotel wasn't at all relaxing. / And we didn't feel .... in our hotel.

3   At dinner my husband got very annoyed about the slow service.

At dinner my husband found the slow service ....

4   And I felt embarrassed because everyone stared at us!

And it .... because everyone stared at us!

But then the next day things got better.

5   We visited a fascinating science museum. / We .... by the science museum we visited.

6   And we were amazed by the modern architecture. / And the modern architecture ....

7   We weren't bored by anything. / Nothing was ....

8   The only thing I was a bit disappointed with was the food.

The only thing that was .... was the food.

4 Traduci.

1   Sarah fu molto delusa (*disappoint*) quando suo padre non la portò al cinema.

2   Penso che i reality show siano noiosi.   ◯ **shows** *in English!*

3   Jenny è molto interessata alla biologia.

4   Mia madre è sempre stanca quando torna dal lavoro.

5   Abbiamo trascorso una giornata rilassante sulla spiaggia.

6   Ieri ho guardato un programma interessante sulla foresta Amazzonica.

10.4   SOSTANTIVI USATI COME AGGETTIVI

In inglese è possibile mettere in sequenza due sostantivi, il primo dei quali descrive e specifica il secondo.

*a **birthday** party = una festa **di compleanno** (birthday specifica che tipo di party è)*
*a **computer** game, a **diamond** ring, a **student** card, a **library** book, **strawberry** jam, **rock** music*

PRACTICE

1 Abbina un sostantivo del riquadro **A** con un sostantivo del riquadro **B**, poi completa le frasi seguenti.

A

| address   alarm   bus   city   credit |
| football   evening   film   fire   police |
| traffic   wedding |

B

| book   boots   car   card   centre   clock |
| engine   invitation   jam   performance |
| star   stop |

.........*address book*........... ....*alarm clock*........... ....

....

....

....

1 I bought a new ....*alarm clock*......... because I couldn't wake up in the morning.

2 Everyone was looking at the .... as she came into the hotel.

3 The café wouldn't accept my .... so I paid cash.

4 I usally clean my .... when I get home from a match.

5 We couldn't get tickets for the .... so we went in the afternoon.

6 Our teacher was late because there was a big .... on the motorway.

2 Abbina a ogni immagine la sua definizione, poi scrivi il nome di ogni luogo.

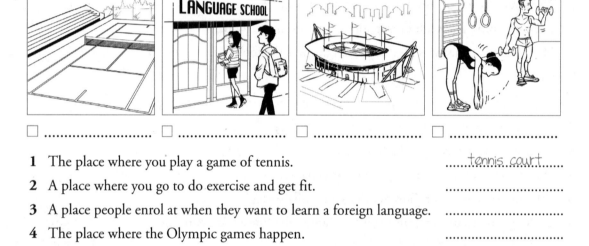

☐ .... ☐ .... ☐ .... ☐ ....

1 The place where you play a game of tennis.   ......*tennis court*......

2 A place where you go to do exercise and get fit.   ....

3 A place people enrol at when they want to learn a foreign language.   ....

4 The place where the Olympic games happen.   ....

10.5   AGGETTIVI DI NAZIONALITÀ

Gli aggettivi di nazionalità possono essere usati come sostantivi, per indicare la lingua e il popolo. Gli aggettivi terminanti in **-ish**, **-ese** e **-ch** rimangono invariabili.

Aggettivi in	Aggettivo	La lingua	Il popolo	
-ish	*English*	*English = l'inglese*	*English people*	*gli Inglesi*
-ese	*Japanese*	*Japanese = il giapponese*	*Japanese people*	*i Giapponesi*
-ch	*French*	*French = il francese*	*French people*	*i Francesi*

Per indicare la lingua si usa l'aggettivo **senza** articolo, mentre per indicare il popolo si usa l'aggettivo seguito dal sostantivo plurale **people**.

*Many people speak **Chinese**.*   *Molte persone parlano **cinese**.*
*My brother loves **Japanese** food and art.*   *Mio fratello ama il cibo e l'arte **giapponese**.*
*He has many **Japanese** friends.*   *Ha tanti amici **giapponesi**.*

Per indicare alcuni nomi di popoli, esistono anche i seguenti termini:

*i Finlandesi = **Finnish people** / **The Finns**;*   *gli Spagnoli = **Spanish people** / **The Spaniards**;*
*gli Scozzesi = **Scottish people** / **The Scots**;*   *i Polacchi = **Polish people** / **The Poles**;*
*gli Svedesi = **Swedish people** / **The Swedes**.*

■ Se preceduti dall'articolo **the**, gli aggettivi di nazionalità terminanti in **-ish**, **-ese** e **-ch** diventano plurali e indicano il popolo: questa forma, tuttavia, si usa sempre meno.

Gli aggettivi terminanti in **-an** aggiungono la **s** del plurale quando indicano il popolo.

Aggettivi in	Aggettivo	La lingua	Il popolo	
-an	*Italian*	*Italian = l'italiano*	*Italian people = the Italians*	*gli Italiani*
	German	*German = il tedesco*	*German people = the Germans*	*i Tedeschi*
	Russian	*Russian = il russo*	*Russian people = the Russians*	*i Russi*

Comunque è più frequente usare **Italian people** or semplicemente **Italians**.

Italian people / Italians / The Italians   **Gli Italiani**
celebrated all night when Italy   *hanno festeggiato tutta la notte quando l'Italia*
won the World Cup.   *ha vinto il Mondiale.*

*Bob studied **German** and **Italian** at university.*   *Bob ha studiato **tedesco** e **italiano** all'università.*

L'aggettivo di nazionalità ha sempre la lettera **maiuscola**.

*Can you speak **Spanish**?*   *Sai parlare (lo) **spagnolo**?*
*It took me many years to learn **Russian**.*   *Mi ci sono voluti molti anni per imparare il **russo**.*

PRACTICE

1 Completa le frasi con i sostantivi e gli aggettivi di nazionalità adeguati.

1   When Real Madrid won the match the ...Spanish... supporters were delighted.

2   .... is spoken by over 900 million people in China.

3   Most .... speak good English so you won't have to learn Swedish.

4   The .... are famous for their whisky.

5   When I lived in Berlin my .... got quite good.

6   His mother's from Helsinki so Andrew speaks fluent ....

7   There are a lot of .... on my course. Most of them come from Warsaw.

8   The Samurai is an important part of .... tradition.

2 Traduci.

1   José viene da Buenos Aires. È argentino e la sua lingua madre è lo spagnolo.

2   Dennis e Annie sono canadesi.

3   Razvan è italiano, i suoi genitori sono romeni e la sua fidanzata è francese.

4   Mia sorella abita a Canterbury e lavora in un'agenzia di viaggi. Lei parla inglese e ha molti amici là: dice che gli inglesi sono simpatici e amichevoli (*friendly*) e hanno un incredibile senso dell'umorismo (*sense of humour*).

5   **A** Di dove è Ayesha? **B** È di Edimburgo, ma i suoi genitori sono indiani.

171

10.6   AVVERBI CHE MODIFICANO GLI AGGETTIVI (IL SUPERLATIVO ASSOLUTO)

Il modo più comune per modificare l'aggettivo è con il superlativo assoluto, che si forma con **very +** **aggettivo**.

I'm **very tired** today.	Sono **molto stanca / stanchissima** oggi.
This book is **very interesting**.	Questo libro è **molto interessante / interessantissimo**.

Ci sono tuttavia altri avverbi che modificano il significato degli aggettivi e degli avverbi, con sfumature più o meno intense.

incredibly	extremely	really	very	rather	fairly	quite	slightly
incredibilmente	estremamente	davvero	molto	piuttosto	abbastanza	abbastanza	lievemente

←——→

più intenso   **meno intenso**

She'll be **really** pleased to see you.	Sarà **davvero** felice/felicissima di vederti.
The house was **quite** old.	La casa era **piuttosto/abbastanza** vecchia.
I cycle **very** quickly.	Io pedalo **molto** velocemente.

Alcuni aggettivi (ad esempio **perfect**, **impossible**, **freezing**) non possono essere modificati da **very**, ma solo da avverbi come **completely**, **absolutely**, **totally**, **entirely**. Possiamo dire:

This crossword puzzle is **completely impossible**. (**Non** ~~very impossible~~)	Questo cruciverba è **assolutamente impossibile**.

PRACTICE

1   Completa le frasi usando un avverbio nel riquadro e un aggettivo di tua scelta.

~~very~~   really   extremely   fairly   rather   quite

1   My town is .... *very crowded in summer.* ....

2   My best friend is ....

3   Some sports are ....

4   In my country the people are ....

5   When I come home from holiday I usually feel ....

6   In winter in Britain the weather is ....

2   Inserisci l'avverbio tra parentesi al posto giusto.

1   She plays the guitar well for her age. (*incredibly*) *She plays the guitar incredibly well for her age.*

2   The meal was delicious but expensive. (*rather, absolutely*) ....

3   My mother always insisted that good manners were important. (*terribly*)

    ....

4   We arrived late and the cinema was already full. (*slightly*) ....

5 It was cold on the beach and the water was freezing. (*quite, really*)

....

6 I thought the film was interesting but Sophie thought it was brilliant. (*fairly, totally*)

....

ALL IN ONE REVISION

1 Ascolterai una conversazione tra Callum ed Emily. Ascolta la prima parte della registrazione e rispondi alle domande.

1.24

1 Who is tired?   ....Callum.............   **5** Who is bored?   ....

2 Who is excited? ....   **6** What is interesting? ....

3 What is tiring? ....   **7** What is exciting?   ....

4 Who isn't really interested in clothes? ....

Qual è la differenza tra gli aggettivi terminanti in **-ed** e in **-ing**? Completa le frasi seguenti:

We use adjectives ending in .... to describe people.

We use adjectives ending in .... to describe things and people.

2 Adesso ascolta la seconda parte della registrazione e completa gli spazi vuoti.

1.25

1 a   ....lovely........   .... skirt

2 my   ....   boots

3 those ....   trainers

Rileggi gli aggettivi che hai scritto.

Which describe:

someone's opinion? ....   colour? ....

size or shape? ....   the material? ....

What kind of adjectives usually go first? ....

What kind of adjectives usually go last? ....

3 In questa email ci sono otto errori. Leggila con attenzione e correggi gli errori.

Hi Sally,

I can't see you next week because I'm going on holiday with my parents. We always stay near a ~~town very small~~ *very small town* on the coast. There is a lovely and sandy beach and the sea is clear and warm.

The town has lots of old beautiful buildings. My parents like going to the galleries art but I get boring so I go to the shops. You can buy cheaps clothes there.

I hope we go to my restaurant favourite.

Write back and tell me all your excited news.

Duncan

173

4 Traduci.

   1   La mia amica Cecilia si sposerà il mese prossimo con un giornalista spagnolo. Ho intenzione di regalarle una teiera d'argento antica per la sua nuova casa.

   2   Per il mio compleanno Peter mi ha regalato un maglione bianco e blu, poi abbiamo cenato in un piccolo ristorante cinese. Abbiamo mangiato degli involtini primavera deliziosi.

5 Inserisci gli aggettivi al posto giusto.

TEXT 1

> awake   busy   quiet   stimulating   violent   ~~worried~~   young

Many people are **(1)** ....*worried*.... about how much TV **(2)** .... children watch these days. **(3)** .... parents sometimes use TV to keep their children **(4)** .... instead of offering them more **(5)** .... activities. What's more, **(6)** .... films are often shown at times when children are still **(7)** ....

TEXT 2

> amazing   asleep   bored   confusing   dramatic   exhausting   impressed   tired

I went to see the film after an **(1)** .... day at work so I was feeling a bit **(2)** .... Maybe that's why I wasn't **(3)** .... The first scene wasn't bad. It was quite **(4)** .... with some **(5)** .... special effects. But after that the story got incredibly **(6)** .... and I was so **(7)** .... I fell **(8)** .... !

COMPARATIVI E SUPERLATIVI – INTRODUZIONE

I **comparativi** si usano per mettere a confronto **due cose**: due oggetti, due persone, due gruppi.

I **superlativi** si usano per mettere a confronto **più di due cose**: più di due oggetti, più di due persone, una persona all'interno di un gruppo.

Janet   Mischa

Janet   Mischa   Keira

*Janet is **taller than** Mischa.*
Janet è **più alta di** Mischa.

*Mischa is **younger than** Janet.*
Mischa è **più giovane di** Janet.

*Janet has got **longer** hair **than** Mischa.*
Janet ha i capelli **più lunghi di** Mischa.

*Janet is **the tallest** (**of** the three sisters).*
Janet è **la più alta** (**delle** tre sorelle).

*Mischa is **the youngest**.*
Mischa è **la più giovane**.

*Keira has got **the shortest** hair.*
Keira ha i capelli **più corti**.

PRACTICE

1 Completa le frasi su Mischa, Janet e Keira usando gli aggettivi tra parentesi alla forma corretta del comparativo o del superlativo.

1 Mischa is ....shorter........ than Janet. (*short*)

2 Janet has got .... hair. (*long*)   3 Keira is .... her sister. (*old*)

4 Keira is shorter than Janet but .... than Mischa. (*tall*)

5 Who is .... sister? (*young*)   6 Mischa's hair is .... than Keira's. (*long*)

10.7   COMPARATIVI E SUPERLATIVI DI MAGGIORANZA

Gli aggettivi formati da **una sola sillaba** formano il comparativo di maggioranza aggiungendo **-er** e il superlativo di maggioranza aggiungendo **-est**. Come in italiano, il superlativo di maggioranza è generalmente preceduto dall'articolo determinativo **the**.

Aggettivo	Comparativo	Superlativo
Una sillaba		
long	→ long**er**	→ **the** long**est**
great	→ great**er**	→ **the** great**est**
cheap	→ cheap**er**	→ **the** cheap**est**

Se terminano in **e** si aggiunge solo **-r** e **-st**.

Una sillaba terminante in **-e**		
nice	→ nice**r**	→ **the** nice**st**
large	→ large**r**	→ **the** large**st**

Se terminano in **c**onsonante-**v**ocale-**c**onsonante (**c v c**) si **raddoppia la consonante finale**.

Una sillaba terminante in c v c		
big	→ big**ger**	→ **the** big**gest**
fat	→ fat**ter**	→ **the** fat**test**
thin	→ thin**ner**	→ **the** thin**nest**

Si aggiunge -*er* ed -*est* anche agli aggettivi di **due sillabe** che terminano in -*y* (→ *ier/iest*), in -*ow* e -*er*.

Due sillabe terminanti in -*y, -ow* e -*er*		
dirty	→ dirtier	→ **the** dirtiest
tidy	→ tidier	→ **the** tidiest
easy	→ easier	→ **the** easiest
narrow	→ narrower	→ **the** narrowest
shallow	→ shallower	→ **the** shallowest
clever	→ cleverer	→ **the** cleverest

Gli altri aggettivi di due sillabe e **tutti gli aggettivi di tre o più sillabe** formano il comparativo di maggioranza premettendo *more* e il superlativo di maggioranza premettendo *the most*.

Due, tre o più sillabe		
famous	→ **more** famous	→ **the most** famous
boring	→ **more** boring	→ **the most** boring
useful	→ **more** useful	→ **the most** useful
popular	→ **more** popular	→ **the most** popular
expensive	→ **more** expensive	→ **the most** expensive
self-confident	→ **more** self-confident	→ **the most** self-confident

Alcuni aggettivi di due sillabe, come *common*, *quiet* e *pleasant*, possono avere **entrambe le forme**.

*This is one of **the most common / commonest** grammar mistakes in English.*
*Questo è uno degli errori di grammatica **più comuni** in inglese.*

■ Il secondo termine di paragone in un comparativo è introdotto da *than*.

*Your bedroom is tidier **than** mine.*   *La tua camera è più ordinata **della** mia.*
*Jeff is cleverer **than** me.*   *Jeff è più intelligente **di** me.*

■ Il superlativo è seguito da *in* se il riferimento è di luogo o di tipo geografico;
                                                          se il riferimento è a gruppi di persone.

*This is the cheapest hotel **in town**.*   *Questo è l'albergo più economico **della città**.*
The Principality of Monaco is the most   *Il Principato di Monaco è il paese più densamente*
*densely-populated country **in the world**.*   *popolato **del mondo**.*
*Patrick is the most talented musician **in the band**.*   *Patrick è il musicista più dotato **del gruppo**.*

■ Il superlativo è invece seguito da *of* se ci si riferisce a **uno tra molti** o a **un periodo di tempo**.

*Eileen is the youngest **of my friends**.*   *Eileen è la più giovane **dei miei amici**.*
*July is the hottest month **of the year**.*   *Luglio è il mese più caldo **dell'anno**.*

PRACTICE

1 Completa le frasi con un aggettivo alla forma comparativa.

1   My teacher is friendly but my sister's teacher is ....friendlier........ .

2 My bike is big but my brother's bike is ....

3 This biscuit tastes nice but those cakes taste ....

4 Geography is interesting but history is ....

5 I felt nervous but my friend felt ....

6 Tim is rich but John is ....

7 This exercise is easy but the next one is ....

8 Madrid is hot but Bangkok is ....

2 Inserisci negli spazi un comparativo di maggioranza usando gli aggettivi nel riquadro.

> exotic   noisy   ~~slim~~   popular   early   large   slow   boring

1 Mary's been on a diet. She's much ...~~slimmer~~.... than she used to be.

2 When the baby was born they moved into a .... flat.

3 I thought the second *Harry Potter* film was .... than the first.

4 You're always late for school. You must get up ....

5 Rimini's OK but I'd like to go somewhere .... , like the Caribbean, next year!

6 My internet connection is .... than yours.

7 The hotel rooms facing the road are .... than the rooms at the back.

8 There are lots of new Japanese restaurants but pizza is still .... than sushi.

3 Abbina gli aggettivi nel riquadro a sinistra con i loro contrari nel riquadro a destra.

> expensive   ~~near~~   old   small   tidy

> big   cheap   far   new   untidy

Osserva le immagini e leggi le inserzioni di tre case in vendita, poi completa il dialogo con il superlativo di maggioranza degli aggettivi.

A Fulbourn

B Cambridge

C Grantchester

BUILT 1887   £200,000
Two bedrooms,
one bathroom,
sitting room, kitchen,
5kms from city centre

BUILT 2004   £155,000
Three bedrooms,
two bathrooms,
sitting room, kitchen,
in city centre

BUILT 1934   £325,000
Five bedrooms,
three bathrooms, sitting
room, dining room, kitchen,
3kms from city centre

177

Sam: So which house are you interested in now you've seen them all?

Amy: Well, we're not really sure yet. I like the one in Cambridge because it's the **(1)** .nearest. to the city centre, and it's also the **(2)** .... – it was built in 2004 so everything's new.

Sam: It's the **(3)** .... too.

Amy: Yes, the price is really good.

Sam: So what's wrong with it?

Amy: Simon doesn't like the garden.

Sam: Why not?

Amy: It's small and very tidy. It's the **(4)** .... garden of the three. He wants a country garden.

Sam: So in that case Fulbourn is the best.

Amy: We like the village, but the house is the **(5)** .... : so it needs some repairs. It's also the **(6)** .... : it's only got two bedrooms.

Sam: Yes, that's a bit too small. The **(7)** .... house is the one in Grantchester.

Amy: But it's also the **(8)** .... of course. £325,000 is really too much for us.

Sam: It isn't an easy decision!

4 Completa le frasi con il superlativo o il comparativo di maggioranza degli aggettivi tra parentesi. Inserisci *in*, *of* o ***than***.

1 2000 was the ...hardest.. year ....of....... my life. (*hard*)

2 The tarantula's bite is actually no .... a bee sting. (*dangerous*)

3 Harry was looking slightly .... today .... when I last saw him. (*happy*)

4 The .... cause of death .... the UK is heart disease. (*common*)

5 My uncle James is the .... my relatives. (*broad-minded*)

6 The water near the beach is .... by the rocks. (*shallow*)

7 The village is a lot .... with tourists .... it used to be. (*popular*)

8 Jupiter is one of the .... planets .... the Solar System. (*inhospitable*)

10.8   COMPARATIVI E SUPERLATIVI IRREGOLARI

Alcuni aggettivi formano il comparativo e il superlativo in modo irregolare. Ecco i più importanti:

Aggettivo		Comparativo		Superlativo	
good	buono	**better**	migliore	**the best**	il migliore
bad	cattivo	**worse**	peggiore	**the worst**	il peggiore
far	lontano	**farther/further**	più lontano	**the farthest/** **the furthest**	il più lontano
much	molto/a	**more** {	più (uncountable)	**the most** {	il più
many	molti/e		più (countable)		i più
little	poco/a	**less**	meno	**the least**	il meno
old	vecchio	**older** {	più vecchio	**the oldest** {	il più vecchio
		elder {	maggiore	**the eldest** {	il maggiore

The apple pie is **better than** *the cream cake.*	*La crostata di mele è* **migliore del** *dolce alla crema.*
It's **the best** *cake I have ever eaten.*	*È il dolce* **migliore** *che ho mai mangiato.*
The situation is **worse than** *I thought.*	*La situazione è* **peggiore di** *quanto pensassi.*
Keith is **the worst** *player in the team.*	*Keith è il giocatore* **peggiore** *della squadra.*
My brother is **older than** *me.*	*Mio fratello è* **più vecchio di** *me.*
My **elder** *brother lives in Paris.*	*Il mio fratello* **maggiore** *vive a Parigi.*

PRACTICE

1 Scegli l'alternativa corretta. A volte entrambe sono possibili.

1 I think this is the *best* / *better* film I've ever seen.

2 Could I have a bit *less* / *least* pasta, please?

3 My *older* / *elder* brother is ten years *older* / *elder* than me.

4 What's the *farthest* / *furthest* you've been by bike?

5 Things can't get much *worst* / *worse* than this.

6 The *oldest* / *eldest* man in the world is 142.

7 I've never had a *better* / *best* holiday in my life.

8 Who took the *least* / *less* time to finish the exam?

2 Completa le frasi con il comparativo o il superlativo degli aggettivi tra parentesi.

1 I earn the .....least..... money out of all my friends. (*little*)

2 My headache's getting .... (*bad*)

3 Their latest CD is much .... than the last one. (*good*)

4 This year Memphis is the .... team in the NBA. (*bad*)

5 Who scored the .... goals in the match? (*many*)

6 I've got three sisters. The .... is married with two children. (*old*)

7 A trip to the nearest town was the .... my grandfather ever travelled. (*far*)

8 Travelling by train causes .... damage to the environment than flying. (*little*)

10.9   COMPARATIVI DI UGUAGLIANZA

Il comparativo di uguaglianza si esprime così:

Frase affermativa	
as* + aggettivo + *as	*Laura is* **as clever as** *her brother Tom.* *Laura è* **intelligente quanto** *suo fratello Tom.*
	Classical music is **as popular as** *rock music with our customers.* *La musica classica è* **popolare come** *la musica rock tra i nostri clienti.*
	My son is **as tall as** *me.* *Mio figlio è* **alto come** *me.*

179

Frase negativa	
not as/so + aggettivo + as	*The weather in France is **not as/so wet as** in Wales.* Il tempo in Francia **non è umido come** in Galles. *Cassettes usually **aren't as/so expensive as** CDs.* Le cassette di solito **non sono costose come** i CD. *My suitcase **isn't as/so heavy as** yours.* La mia valigia **non è pesante come** la tua.

PRACTICE

1 Riscrivi le frasi inserendo **as … as** o **than** a seconda del significato.

1 The film is good the book. .... The film is as good as the book. ....

2 Yesterday was colder today. ....

3 Swimming isn't tiring jogging. ....

4 He's never been ambitious his brother. ....

5 Sharing a flat is cheaper living alone. ....

6 This exercise isn't difficult the last one. ....

2 Leggi attentamente le informazioni contenute nella tabella e completa le frasi con **as … as** o **(not) as/so … as** su Liz e Mandy, usando le indicazioni date.

	Liz	Mandy
Height at 5:	1.15 m	1.15 m
Height now:	1.68 m	1.72 m
Grades in GCSEs:	Maths: A Art: A French: B	Maths: A Art: B French: C
Hobbies at 15:	reading, listening to music, computer games, cinema	playing the guitar, listening to music, singing, dancing
University:	Medicine: 5 years	Business Studies: 3 years
Present salary:	£ 25,000 p.a.	£ 25,000 p.a.
Sports:	skiing	tennis, swimming, aerobics

Height: **1** When she was five Liz was .... as tall as .... Mandy.

                     2 But now she isn't .... Mandy.

GCSEs: **3** Mandy's results weren't .... Liz's.

                     4 But she was .... Liz at Maths.

Hobbies at 15:   **5** Liz was .... in music as Mandy.

University: **6** Mandy's university course wasn't .... Liz's.

Present salary: **7** Mandy's salary is as .... Liz's.

Sports: **8** Liz isn't .... Mandy.

10.10   COMPARATIVI E SUPERLATIVI DI MINORANZA

Il comparativo di minoranza si forma premettendo *less* all'aggettivo, di qualunque lunghezza questo sia. Il secondo termine di paragone è introdotto da *than*.

*The CDs in the sale are **less expensive than** usual.*	*I CD in saldo sono **meno costosi del** solito.*
*Kevin is **less fit than** last year.*	*Kevin è **meno in forma dell'**anno scorso.*
*High-heeled shoes are **less comfortable than** trainers.*	*Le scarpe con il tacco alto sono **meno comode di** quelle da ginnastica.*

Analogamente, il superlativo di minoranza si forma premettendo *the least* all'aggettivo.

*I'm **the least fit** in my team.*	*Sono **la meno in forma** della mia squadra.*
*I bought **the least expensive** flat.*	*Ho comprato l'appartamento **meno costoso**.*

PRACTICE

1 Usa i prompt per mettere a confronto questi sport.

1   Football / exciting / volleyball.   *Football is more exciting than volleyball*

2   Golf / safe / horse-riding. ....

3   Water-skiing / difficult / swimming. ....

4   Motorcycling / noisy / cycling. ....

5   Rugby balls / heavy / tennis balls. ....

Riscrivi ogni frase in due modi diversi, senza cambiare il significato.

6   *Volleyball isn't as exciting as football.   /   Volleyball is less exciting than football.*

7   ....

8   ....

9   ....

10 ....

10.11   COMPARATIVI: ALCUNI CASI PARTICOLARI

■ Il doppio comparativo

Le espressioni italiane '**sempre più** caldo/costoso/bello…', che indicano un processo di cambiamento in corso, si esprimono in inglese con un doppio comparativo, così:

-er and -er	*Kate is becoming **prettier and prettier**.* *Kate si sta facendo **sempre più graziosa**.*
more and more	*Petrol is getting **more and more expensive**.* *La benzina sta diventando **sempre più costosa**.*

■ Il comparativo correlato

Quando due cambiamenti sono l'uno il prodotto dell'altro, l'espressione italiana '**più … più**' si traduce in inglese con **due comparativi**, preceduti dall'articolo *the*.

***The sooner** we get this job done, **the better** (it is).*	**Prima** finiamo questo lavoro **meglio** è.
***The older** you are, **the more difficult** it is to learn.*	**Più vecchio** sei, **più difficile** è imparare.

181

PRACTICE

1 Completa i dialoghi inserendo le espressioni nel riquadro.

> more and more bored   the sooner the better   worse and worse
> the more the merrier   heavier and heavier   the bigger the better

1 A I promise I'll tidy up my room this afternoon, Mum.

B The sooner the better !

2 A Do you mind if I bring my cousin to the party?

B Of course not. .... !

3 A The garden's enormous. It'll be difficult to look after!

B I wouldn't worry. .... !

4 A Can you manage with those cases or shall I give you a hand?

B Would you? They seem to be getting ....

5 A Are you any better today?

B No. I'm feeling .... Those pills are absolutely useless.

6 A Have you finished studying for tomorrow's test?

B I can't concentrate. I'm just getting ....

ALL IN ONE REVISION

1 Ascolterai un ragazzo e una ragazza che parlano di tre riviste. Ascolta la prima parte della registrazione e completa le frasi seguenti.

1.26

1 *Hits!* seems more ....colourful..... than *Buzz*.   **4** *Hits!* is .... than *Buzz* too.

2 *Buzz* is as .... as *Hits!*   **5** *Buzz* isn't as .... as *Hits!*

3 *Hits!* is less .... than *Buzz*.

2 Ascolta la seconda parte della registrazione e indica le riviste giuste.

1.27

Which magazine	Hits!	Buzz	Smash
is the newest?			
has got the most reviews?			
is the most expensive?			
has the most adverts?			

3 Considera gli esercizi 1 e 2. Quale dei due mette in relazione due cose? Quale esercizio mette in relazione più di due cose?

4 In sette di queste frasi c'è un errore nell'uso delle forme comparative e superlative. Sottolinea l'errore e scrivi la forma corretta.

1   That was the *worse* film I've ever seen! ....worst................

2 If you need a suitcase, I've got a leather old lovely one that you can borrow. ....

3 He should catch a more earlier train if he wants to get to London by five. ....

4 This is one of the commonest mistakes made by new students. ....

5 Clothes aren't cheap here; in fact, these jeans are so expensive as the ones you bought back home. ....

6 Our last holiday wasn't so enjoyable than this one. ....

7 My home town is small pretty peaceful. ....

8 I'm really boring with this exercise. Let's go and have a coffee. ....

5 Completa questo articolo inserendo gli aggettivi tra parentesi alla forma corretta del comparativo o del superlativo.

SHOPPING IN THE LANES

If shopping is your favourite pastime then you won't find anywhere **(1)** ....better.... (*good*) than The Lanes. It has the **(2)** .... (*big*) variety of shops in the city centre and some of **(3)** .... (+ *reasonable*) prices too.

As you walk down the street each window is **(4)** .... (+ *interesting*) than the last. You'll find everything you need from the **(5)** .... (*late*) fashions to antiques, from **(6)** .... (+ *exclusive*) designer labels to second-hand stores. You'll be able to admire local artists' work as well as produce from the **(7)**................. (*far*) corners of the world. And it's all pedestrianised so it's **(8)** .... (– *stressful*) shopping you could wish for. If you do start feeling tired, you can have a rest at some of the **(9)** .... (*trendy*) cafés in town or stop to watch **(10)** ....(+ *talented*) street artists.

So come to The Lanes for a great shopping experience. The **(11)** .... (*bad*) thing that can happen is that your wallet will be slightly **(12)** .... (*light*) at the end of the day than when you arrived!

6 Completa questa lettera con le forme comparative e superlative degli aggettivi tra parentesi, aggiungendo tutte le parole necessarie (***more***, ***as***, ***than*** ecc.).

Dear Lily,

Well, we've moved at last! When we got here, the flat seemed **(1)** ....larger...... (*large*) than we remembered, because it was empty, but now it's got our furniture in it, it doesn't feel **(2)** .... (*spacious*) before. We've got to do some decorating, and that will be **(3)** .... (*expensive*) we expected because the walls are in a **(4)** .... (*bad*) condition than we thought. But we'll manage somehow, and soon we'll have **(5)** .... (*smart*) house in the town. And if your Uncle Bob has his way, we'll have **(6)** .... (*lovely*) garden as well. We'll also be **(7)** .... (*poor*) and **(8)** .... (*exhausted*) householders in the country, but never mind. We still think moving here is **(9)** .... (*good*) thing we've done for years. We can't imagine now why we didn't do it when we were **(10)** .... (*young*). Come and see us soon. Catch a train if you can, because it's almost **(11)**..................... (*cheap*) the bus, and the railway station is **(12)**..................... (*near*) our end of town.

Love from us both,

Auntie Rosie

7 Per ogni coppia di frasi, completa la seconda in modo che il significato non cambi. **Usa la parola data senza modificarla.** Usa tra **due** e **cinque** parole compresa la parola data.

(FCE)

1 We'd expected to have better weather. **as**

The weather wasn't .... *as good as we'd* .... expected.

2 My husband's more stubborn than I am. **less**

I'm .... my husband.

3 Their new flat isn't as near the centre. **from**

Their new flat is .... the centre.

4 The composition wasn't as difficult as the other exercises. **the**

The composition was .... other exercises.

5 Tom and Nick are both good-looking. **as**

Tom is .... Nick.

6 I don't have as much free time as you. **than**

I have .... you.

7 The ozone layer is getting thinner every year. **as**

The ozone layer isn't .... was.

8 I've got two younger brothers. **than**

I'm .... brothers.

8 Per le domande **1-12**, leggi attentamente il brano seguente e scegli l'opzione corretta (**A, B, C** o **D**).

(FCE)

PUBLIC SCHOOLS

British public schools are some of the **(1)** ...D.... and selective schools in Europe. They are usually boarding schools, which means that pupils spend **(2)** .... of their time at school and only go home for holidays and weekends. Pupils at boarding schools therefore see **(3)** .... of their families than pupils attending day schools. Public schools tend to be **(4)** .... than state schools. For example boys at Eton (one of the **(5)** .... public schools in the country) have to wear a uniform which has remained **(6)** .... unchanged since the 19th century. This consists of a tailcoat, with silver buttons for **(7)** .... boys, and a white tie. Discipline is strict. Until it was finally banned in the nineties, corporal punishment was **(8)** .... in public schools than in state schools.

You might think that this type of school is becoming **(9)** .... popular but, although the class system isn't **(10)**......... it used to be, many people believe you are still **(11)** .... to be offered a place at Oxford and Cambridge and a job in the **(12)** .... companies, if you went to a public school.

1	**A** best	**B** less costly	**C** more famous	**D** most expensive
2	**A** most	**B** more	**C** the worst	**D** fewer
3	**A** less than	**B** less	**C** little	**D** more than
4	**A** more traditional	**B** moderner	**C** as popular	**D** so cheap
5	**A** more well-known	**B** most famous	**C** narrowest	**D** less crowded

6	**A** more and more	**B** rather	**C** more or less	**D** much more
7	**A** older	**B** elder	**C** cleverer	**D** higher
8	**A** quite widespread	**B** commoner	**C** as hard	**D** frequent
9	**A** less and less	**B** the least	**C** much more	**D** more than
10	**A** so good as	**B** as rigid as	**C** surprised as	**D** worse than
11	**A** more possibly	**B** as easy	**C** more likely	**D** as usual
12	**A** more wealthy	**B** most prestigious	**C** international	**D** less competitive

9 Traduci.

1 Ero molto stanco ieri sera, così sono andato a letto prima del solito.

2 Questo è il vestito più elegante che ho.

3 Alton Towers è il parco dei divertimenti (*amusement park*) più eccitante che ho mai visitato.

4 La signora Chadwick ha quattro figli: il maggiore è già all'università, il più piccolo ha solo due anni.

5 Se continui a mangiare dolci, diventerai sempre più grasso.

6 Beth è la persona più testarda (*obstinate*) che conosco. Più cerchi di convincerla meno ti ascolta.

7 Il libro è molto noioso, ma il film è anche peggiore.

8 Sabato sera c'era molta gente al Maliki. La discoteca (*nightclub*) era più affollata del solito.

9 Vorrei raggiungere le rovine dell'abbazia, all'estremità più lontana dell'isola.

UNIT
11

GLI AVVERBI

11.1 Significato e formazione degli avverbi
11.2 Avverbi irregolari
11.3 Avverbi di grado: *quite, very, fairly*
11.4 Posizione degli avverbi e dei complementi
11.5 Avverbi: comparativi e superlativi

GLI AVVERBI – INTRODUZIONE

L'avverbio è una parte del discorso che comunica informazioni di vario tipo. Può indicare:

◼ il **modo** in cui si svolge l'azione.

*The students listened **carefully** to the examiner's instructions.*
*Gli studenti ascoltarono **attentamente** le istruzioni dell'esaminatore.*

◼ chiarire **dove** e **quando**.

*He left **here** at 7 o'clock this morning.*	*È partito **da qui** alle 7 di stamani.*
***Tomorrow** I've got a meeting in Bristol.*	***Domani** ho una riunione a Bristol.*

◼ sottolineare l'**intensità** del significato di un aggettivo.

*Don't lift that box: it's **very** heavy.*	*Non sollevare quella scatola: è **molto** pesante.*
*The English test was **fairly** easy.*	*Il compito di inglese era **abbastanza** facile.*

11.1   SIGNIFICATO E FORMAZIONE DEGLI AVVERBI

Gli aggettivi si riferiscono ai nomi e ai pronomi. Gli avverbi si riferiscono ai verbi, agli aggettivi o ad altri avverbi.

*He's a **careful** cyclist. He cycles **carefully**.*	*È un ciclista **prudente**. Lui va in bicicletta **con prudenza**.*
*Today I feel **happy** because the weather is **beautiful**.*	*Oggi mi sento **felice** perché il tempo è **magnifico**.*
*Some children are playing **happily** in the street and a blackbird is singing **beautifully** in a tree outside.*	*Dei bambini giocano **allegramente** nella strada e un merlo canta **in modo magnifico** su un albero là fuori.*

Gli avverbi specificano la frequenza (*how often*), il luogo (*where*), la quantità (*how much*), il modo (*how*) e il tempo (*when*).

	How often?	Verb	How?	Where?	When?
I	*often*	*come*		*here*	*on Friday lunchtimes.*
Io	*spesso*	*vengo*		*qui*	*il venerdì all'ora di pranzo.*
She		*is waiting*	*patiently*	*at her friend's house.*	
Lei		*sta aspettando*	*pazientemente*	*a casa della sua amica.*	

186

Come si vede dalla tabella, gli avverbi possono essere costituiti da una o più parole. Quelli costituiti da più parole corrispondono sostanzialmente ai complementi italiani di tempo e di luogo.

*He's arriving **on Tuesday**, so we're meeting him **at the station**.*
*Arriva **martedì**, così andiamo a prenderlo **alla stazione**.*

■ Molti avverbi, in particolare gli avverbi di modo, si formano aggiungendo il suffisso *-ly* all'aggettivo corrispondente.

Aggettivo		Avverbio
perfect	→	perfect**ly**
usual	→	usual**ly**
sad	→	sad**ly**

FORMAZIONE DEGLI AVVERBI: REGOLE DI SPELLING

Gli aggettivi terminanti in *-y* trasformano la *-y* in *i* e aggiungono *-ly*.

Aggettivo terminante in *-y*		Avverbio
noisy	→	nois**ily**
angry	→	angr**ily**

Gli aggettivi terminanti in *-le* fanno cadere la *-e* e aggiungono *-y*.

Aggettivo terminante in *-le*		Avverbio
comfortab**le**	→	comfortab**ly**
simp**le**	→	simp**ly**

Gli aggettivi terminanti in *-e* generalmente mantengono la *-e* e aggiungono *-ly*.

Aggettivo terminante in *-e*			Avverbio
	saf**e**	→	saf**ely**
	extreme	→	extreme**ly**
MA	true	→	tru**ly**
	whole	→	whol**ly**

🔊 Alcune parole possono essere scambiate per avverbi perché terminano in *-ly*, ma in realtà sono aggettivi.

*friendly = **amichevole***   *likely = **probabile***   *lively = **vivace***   *lonely = **solo/solitario***
*lovely = **bello/incantevole***   *silly = **sciocco***   *ugly = **brutto***

*He was a **friendly** man. He told me a **silly** story.*
*Era un uomo **amichevole**. Mi ha raccontato una storiella **sciocca**.*

Questi aggettivi non possono essere trasformati in avverbi: per formare l'avverbio si ricorre a espressioni con *way* o *manner*.

*She started the interview **in a friendly manner**.*   *Iniziò l'intervista **in modo amichevole**.*
*He laughed **in a silly way**.*   *Rise **in modo sciocco/scioccamente**.*

187

Come abbiamo visto nella *Unit* **10** alcuni verbi inglesi sono seguiti da aggettivi e non da avverbi.

You **look miserable**.	Hai **un aspetto orribile**.
I **feel good**.	Mi **sento proprio bene/felice**.

PRACTICE

1 Riempi gli spazi con l'aggettivo o l'avverbio tra parentesi.

1 I ...*seriously*..... think that you should have a haircut. (*serious / seriously*)

2 Jackie is too .... for my liking. She hardly ever smiles and she never laughs at jokes. (*serious / seriously*)

3 It has been raining .... for the past week here in Scotland. (*heavy / heavily*)

4 Peter is a very .... sleeper; nothing wakes him up. (*heavy / heavily*)

5 The newsreader's voice was .... when she announced the national team's victory. (*triumphant / triumphantly*)

6 The winning team picked up their captain and the cup and ran .... round the pitch. (*triumphant / triumphantly*)

7 Jim can't see .... without his glasses. (*clear / clearly*)

8 There's no need for you to repeat yourself. It is perfectly .... what you mean. (*clear / clearly*)

9 Your version of Messenger is .... from mine. (*different / differently*)

10 Sometimes teenagers and their parents speak very .... (*different / differently*)

2 Riscrivi queste frasi sostituendo le parole <u>sottolineate</u> con un avverbio o un'espressione avverbiale.

1 Ralph <u>had an angry reaction</u> to his teachers' criticisms.

Ralph reacted .....*angrily*..... to his teachers' criticisms.

2 The class <u>were very kind to him</u> when he was new to the school.

The class treated him .... when he was new to the school.

3 Why were you so careless with your best friend's bicycle? <u>Your behaviour was really silly</u>.

Why were you so careless with your best friend's bicycle? You behaved ....

4 Bill can be very embarrassing. <u>His voice is always too loud when he's</u> in public places.

Bill can be very embarrassing. He always speaks .... in public places.

5 Piotr's Italian is not very good yet, but he <u>seems friendly</u>.

Piotr's Italian is not very good yet, but he behaves ....

6 The fans <u>showed great patience</u> as they waited for their hero to come out of his hotel.

The fans waited .... for their hero to come out of his hotel.

7   The dog looked at me <u>with a guilty expression</u> and I immediately understood where the sausages had gone!

The dog looked at me .... and I immediately understood where the sausages had gone!

8   Although the musicians were on stage for the first time, they <u>showed confidence during their performance</u>.

Although the musicians were on stage for the first time, they performed ....

3 Usa gli aggettivi tra parentesi per formare degli avverbi e completa le frasi seguenti.

1   She picked up the sleeping baby .....*gently*...... . (*gentle*)

2   When she handed him his lost wallet, he smiled at her .... (*grateful*)

3   She couldn't see her son anywhere and called his name .... (*anxious*)

4   They followed the directions to the hotel .... (*easy*)

5   He admitted his mistake and apologised .... (*sincere*)

6   When Susie finished singing, the audience clapped .... (*enthusiastic*)

7   If you are all sitting .... , we can start. (*comfortable*)

8   I would .... give you a hand, but I'm afraid that I don't understand the exercise myself. (*happy*)

9   Sally felt very self-conscious when she first met her boyfriend's parents, but they treated her .... (*warm*)

10   If you want to have good skin, you should eat .... (*healthy*)

4 Leggi questo brano. Per ogni spazio, decidi se trasformare l'aggettivo in avverbio o se lasciare l'aggettivo.

Teenagers like to dress **(1)** ..*fashionably*. (*fashionable*) but their parents don't always think their clothes are **(2)** .... (*suitable*). They look **(3)** .... (*unhappy*) at their children as they leave the house. Some parents are **(4)** .... (*honest*) and say **(5)** .... (*polite*) what they think; others get **(6)** .... (*angry*) and shout that they don't like the clothes. But the best idea is for parents to sit **(7)** .... (*calm*) in their chairs and say nothing. They forget that when they were teenagers they didn't like to dress **(8)** .... (*different*) from their friends and they didn't always choose their clothes **(9)** .... (*sensible*). But their opinions changed **(10)** .... (*slow*) and by the time they were 30, they had started to dress like their own parents!

11.2   AVVERBI IRREGOLARI

Per avverbi irregolari si intendono quegli avverbi che **non** si formano aggiungendo **-ly** all'aggettivo corrispondente.

■ Alcuni aggettivi e avverbi hanno la stessa forma. Quelli più comuni sono: **fast**, **early**, **hard**, **late**, **daily**, **weekly**, **monthly**.

Aggettivo	Avverbio
*He caught the **fast** train.*	*He ran **fast** to catch the train.*
*Prese il treno **veloce**.*	*Corse **velocemente** per prendere il treno.*
*He caught an **early** train.*	*He always arrives **early**.*
*Prese un treno **mattutino / di prima mattina**.*	*Arriva sempre **presto**.*
*She's a **hard** worker.*	*She works **hard**. (**Non** ~~She works hardly~~.)*
*È una lavoratrice **instancabile**.*	*Lavora **sodo/duramente**.*
*We made a **late** booking.*	*We couldn't find any tickets in the first row because we booked too **late**. (**Non** ~~too lately~~)*
*Abbiamo fatto una prenotazione **all'ultimo momento**.*	*Non abbiamo trovato biglietti in prima fila perché abbiamo prenotato troppo **tardi**.*
*My **daily** newspaper costs 50p.*	*I swim **daily**.*
*Il mio giornale **quotidiano** costa 50p.*	*Io nuoto **quotidianamente**.*

■ *Hard* e *hardly* sono entrambi avverbi, ma hanno un significato diverso: *hard* significa 'sodo', 'con impegno'; *hardly* significa 'quasi non', 'a malapena'. Può occupare diverse posizioni nella frase.

*She **hardly** noticed when he came into the room.* (= she almost didn't notice)
*Si accorse **a malapena** che entrò nella stanza.* (= quasi non lo notò)

*I had **hardly** finished my breakfast when they arrived.* (= only just)
*Avevo **appena** finito la colazione quando arrivarono.* (= proprio in quel momento)

*They **hardly ever** go on holiday.* (= almost never)
Non *vanno **quasi mai** in vacanza.*

Poiché ha significato negativo, *hardly* si usa spesso insieme a **any**.

*There was **hardly anyone** in the cinema.* (= almost nobody)
*Non c'era **quasi nessuno** al cinema.*

***Hardly any** of the children could read.* (= almost none of them)
***Quasi nessuno** dei bambini sapeva leggere.*

■ *Late* e *lately* sono entrambi avverbi, ma hanno un significato diverso: *late* significa 'tardi', 'in ritardo'; *lately* significa 'recentemente'.

*I haven't read any good books **lately**.*	*Non ho letto nessun libro buono **ultimamente**.*

■ L'avverbio di **good** è **well**, mentre l'avverbio di **bad** segue la regola generale = **badly**.

*He's a **good** boss. He treats us **well**.*	*È un **buon** capo. Ci tratta **bene**.*
*He had a **bad** cold. He sang **badly**.*	*Aveva un **brutto** raffreddore. Cantò **male**.*

PRACTICE

1 Leggi le parole in corsivo e decidi se sono corrette. Se no, scrivi la parola corretta.

1 They listened *careful* when the instructor told them what to do. ...*carefully*...

2 The weather today is *well*. ....

3 We trained *hardly* because we had an important match. ....

4 We have a *weekly* spelling test in English. ....

5 I slept *bad* because there was a thunderstorm. ....

6 He answered the question *correctly*. ....

7 I arrived at school *lately* and missed the beginning of the lesson. ....

8 Cara's cousin gave her a *friendly* wave as he left. ....

9 I could understand quite *good* because the teacher spoke *clear*. ....

10 We worked *fast* and finished *early*. ....

2 Completa le frasi seguenti con un avverbio nel riquadro.

| ~~hard~~   early   hardly   fast   well   high   late   daily |

1 John is exhausted. He has been studying very .....*hard*........ over the last few months.

2 It's dangerous to drive .... in a built-up area.

3 Most teenagers like to sleep in. They hate getting up ....

4 Urzula is Russian, but she seems like a native speaker. She has learnt to speak and write Italian very ....

5 Lenny tries to look after himself. He goes jogging ....

6 My mother learnt to drive very .... She was forty years old at the time.

7 He kicked the ball .... over the goal.

8 John twisted his ankle playing football and now he can .... walk.

11.3   AVVERBI DI GRADO: *QUITE, VERY, FAIRLY*

Alcuni avverbi sono usati per attenuare o rafforzare il significato degli aggettivi e degli avverbi.

incredibly	*extremely*	*really*	*very*	*rather*	*fairly*	*quite*	*slightly*
incredibilmente	estremamente	davvero	molto	piuttosto	abbastanza	abbastanza	lievemente

← ── →

più intenso   **meno intenso**

He dances **extremely** *well.*   *Lui balla* **estremamente** *bene.*
The weather was **very** *hot.*   *Il tempo era* **molto** *caldo / caldissimo.*
He spoke to her **rather** *fiercely.*   *Le si rivolse in modo* **piuttosto** *violento.*
The house was **quite** *old.*   *La casa era* **abbastanza** *vecchia.*

PRACTICE

1 Riempi gli spazi con un avverbio di grado e un aggettivo appropriato.

1 So far this year the weather has been

............*extremely dry / absolutely beautiful / rather pleasant*............ . (*possible answers*)

2 Lately my school results have been ....

3 Italian boys tend to be ....

4 Politics can be ....

5 Living in the country must be/is ....

6 English grammar is ....

7 My parents are usually ....

8 The game of cricket must be ....

11.4 POSIZIONE DEGLI AVVERBI E DEI COMPLEMENTI

La maggior parte degli avverbi normalmente **segue** il verbo. Si trova cioè **in posizione finale**.

*The meeting took place **suddenly**.* (how?)   *La riunione si è svolta **improvvisamente**.* (come?)
*The meeting took place **in the Town Hall**.* (where?)   *La riunione si è svolta **nel Palazzo Comunale**.* (dove?)
*The meeting took place **last Tuesday**.* (when?)   *La riunione si è svolta **martedì scorso**.* (quando?)

Se ci sono più avverbi, seguono in genere questo ordine:

Come?	Dove?	Quando?
*The meeting took place **suddenly***	*in the Town Hall*	*last Tuesday.*
*Josh cycled **quickly***	*to the station*	*at one o'clock.*

■ Gli avverbi di **frequenza** si trovano in posizione **intermedia**: **prima** del verbo principale, ma **dopo** il verbo **essere**.

*I **usually** travel by train.*   *Di solito viaggio in treno.*
Ma *I am **often** late.*   *Sono **spesso** in ritardo.*

Nei verbi composti, l'avverbio di frequenza va **dopo il primo ausiliare**.

*I've **never** forgotten you.*   *Non ti ho **mai** dimenticato.*
*He had **often** been praised by the teachers.*   *Era stato elogiato **spesso** dagli insegnanti.*

■ Gli avverbi di **luogo** possono essere posti anche **all'inizio della frase**, per dare enfasi.

***Yesterday** he painted the kitchen.*   ***Ieri** ha dipinto la cucina.*

■ Anche gli avverbi **di modo** possono andare **all'inizio della frase** per dare enfasi: in questo caso sono seguiti da una virgola.

Suddenly, she burst into tears.   *Improvvisamente* scoppiò in lacrime.
Angrily, she stormed out of the room.   **Con rabbia** si precipitò fuori della stanza. /
                                                                          Furibonda, si precipitò fuori dalla stanza.

Come si vede dal secondo esempio, gli avverbi di modo spesso si rendono in italiano con un aggettivo.

■ Gli avverbi di **modo** possono talvolta occupare tutte e tre le posizioni.

Carefully, he packed his suitcase.
He *carefully* packed his suitcase.
He packed his suitcase *carefully*.

👣 L'avverbio non può **mai** essere posto tra il verbo e il complemento oggetto.

*He speaks Spanish **very well**.* (**Non** ~~He speaks very well Spanish.~~)
*Lui parla **benissimo** lo spagnolo. / Lui parla spagnolo **benissimo**.*

*I wrapped the present **carefully**.* (**Non** ~~I wrapped carefully the present.~~)
*Incartai il regalo **accuratamente**. / Incartai **accuratamente** il regalo.*

PRACTICE

1 Gli avverbi nelle frasi seguenti sono in posizione corretta? Correggi gli errori.

1 You will learn quickly English. ....*You will learn English quickly.*..........................

2 I missed yesterday the train. ....

3 I enjoyed very much that television programme. ....

4 I usually go to college by bus. ....

5 I never have been to Spain. ....

6 We have just finished painting the room. ....

7 They still were waiting when we arrived. ....

8 This shop always is open on Sundays. ....

9 Taeko and I have already become friends. ....

10 My friends and I went last night to a nightclub. ....

2 Metti gli avverbi sulla destra nella posizione corretta in ogni riga.

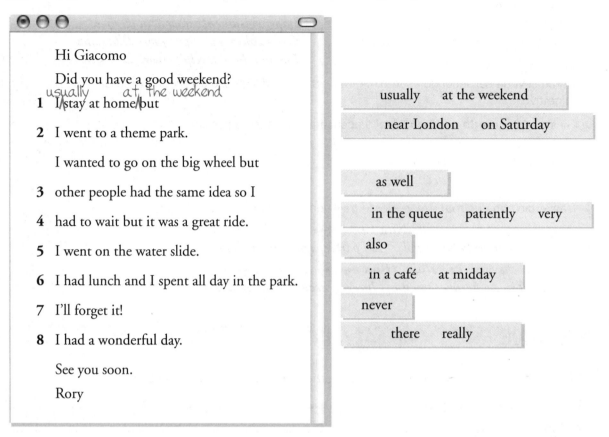

Hi Giacomo

Did you have a good weekend?

1 I ~~usually~~ stay at home ~~at the weekend~~ but

2 I went to a theme park.

I wanted to go on the big wheel but

3 other people had the same idea so I

4 had to wait but it was a great ride.

5 I went on the water slide.

6 I had lunch and I spent all day in the park.

7 I'll forget it!

8 I had a wonderful day.

See you soon.

Rory

> usually   at the weekend
>
> near London   on Saturday
>
> as well
>
> in the queue   patiently   very
>
> also
>
> in a café   at midday
>
> never
>
> there   really

3 Inserisci gli avverbi tra parentesi nella posizione più comune.

1 Yesterday I did my homework (*very quickly, on the school bus*).
Yesterday I did my homework very quickly on the school bus..................

2 As soon as they were alone, she kissed him (*passionately, on the lips*).
....

3 After my fourteenth birthday I started to spend more time (*suddenly, in front of the mirror*).
....

4 Basketball was invented in 1911 (*originally, in America*).
....

5 Mr Golddigger opened a new bank account (*secretly, in Switzerland*).
....

6 The band is on its third tour (*currently, in Scandinavia*).
....

7 Rugby is an aggressive game played with an oval ball (*highly, on a grass pitch*).
....

8   Brian likes dancing (*very much, at parties*).

   ....

9   He drove the hired car (*carefully, back to the airport*).

   ....

10   Jake defended his beliefs (*passionately, in the school debating society*).

   ....

11.5   AVVERBI: COMPARATIVI E SUPERLATIVI

Gli avverbi **regolari** che terminano in **-ly** formano il comparativo con **more** e **less** e il superlativo con **the most** o **the least**.

Avverbio	Comparativo	Superlativo
slowly	**more** slowly	**the most** slowly
beautifully	**more** beautifully	**the most** beautifully
easily	**more** easily	**the most** easily

*My brother speaks English **more fluently than** I do.*
Mio fratello parla inglese più fluentemente di me.

*I speak English **less fluently than** my brother does.*
Io parlo inglese meno fluentemente di mio fratello.

*Out of all the students, Maria speaks English **the most fluently**.*
Di tutti gli studenti, Maria è quella che parla inglese più fluentemente.

Gli avverbi che **non** terminano in **-ly** (ma anche *early*) formano il comparativo e il superlativo seguendo le stesse regole che valgono per gli aggettivi **brevi**. (Vedi *Unit* **10**)

Avverbio	Comparativo	Superlativo
hard	hard**er**	the hard**est**
high	high**er**	the high**est**
late	lat**er**	the lat**est**

*My brother runs **faster than** I do but Alex runs **the fastest**.*
Mio fratello corre più velocemente di me ma Alex corre **più velocemente di tutti**.

Alcuni avverbi formano il comparativo e il superlativo in modo **irregolare**.

Avverbio		Comparativo		Superlativo	
well	*bene*	*better*	*meglio*	*the best*	*il meglio*
badly	*male*	*worse*	*peggio*	*the worst*	*il peggio*
far	*lontano*	*farther*	*più lontano*	*the farthest*	*il più lontano*

*I did **better** than him in the test.*
None of the students lives very near the school,
*but Darren lives **farthest** away.*

*Ho fatto **meglio** di lui nel test.*
Nessuno degli studenti vive molto vicino alla scuola,
*ma Darren vive **più lontano** di tutti.*

■ Le regole d'uso del comparativo sono le stesse per aggettivi e avverbi.

*He shouted **as loudly as** she did.*
*I can't add up **as quickly as** you can.*
*They arrived **later than** we did.*

*Lui gridava **forte quanto** lei.*
*Io non riesco a contare **velocemente come** te.*
*Arrivarono **più tardi di** noi.*

PRACTICE

1 Completa le frasi seguenti con la forma comparativa dell'avverbio derivante dagli aggettivi tra parentesi.

1 I really must take an aspirin and go to bed. My headache is getting ....*worse*........ . (*bad*)

2 Nowadays young people live .... than in the past. (*dangerous*)

3 His scooter goes .... than mine. (*fast*)

4 My mother sings as .... as a bird. (*sweet*)

5 Jack is working .... than I expected. (*hard*)

6 Most teenagers help their parents .... if a reward is offered. (*willing*)

7 The average young Italian expresses himself .... (*articulate*) than his British peer.

8 You should eat .... (*healthy*) or you'll get ill.

2 Per ogni coppia di frasi, completa la seconda in modo che il significato non cambi. **Usa non più di tre parole.**

(PET)

1 I find swimming easier than running. I can swim *more easily than* I can run.

2 The increase in global warming is more rapid than most people think.

Global warming is increasing .... people think.

3 Sandra didn't throw the discus as far as Mandy.

Mandy threw the discus .... Sandra.

4 Tom is the fastest sprinter in the team.

Nobody in the team can sprint .... Tom.

5 No-one rides a motorbike as well as Valentino.

Valentino rides his motorbike .... anyone.

6 Mary doesn't train as hard as Janet.

Janet trains .... Mary.

7 David bends the ball more skilfully than anyone else.

No-one bends the ball .... David.

8 No-one ice skates as elegantly as Jane.

Jane ice skates .... anyone else.

ALL IN ONE REVISION

1 Josh abita a Manchester, il resto della sua famiglia abita a Londra. Che cosa stanno facendo tutti loro questo venerdì mattina?

2 Ascolterai tre conversazioni che Josh ha avuto venerdì, più tardi.

1.28

Conversation 1: Where is Josh? .... Why is he going home? ....

Conversation 2: Where is Josh? .... Why is his sister unhappy? ....

Conversation 3: Where is Josh? .... Where is his sister? .... Why? ....

3 Ascolta di nuovo la conversazione 1 e riempi gli spazi con un avverbio.

1.29

1   I cycle very   3   I know I'm .... late for everything.

2   Oh, but ride .... won't you?   4   You've arranged everything ....

Come si forma di solito un avverbio da un aggettivo? Quali sono gli aggettivi di questi quattro avverbi?

4 Ascolta di nuovo la conversazione 2 e riempi gli spazi.

1.30

1   It's going to be .... boring.   3   I wrapped it .... well.

2   We have to work .... hard.   4   It's .... noisy here.

Le parole che hai scritto sono avverbi. In che modo cambiano il significato delle parole che seguono?

5 Ascolta di nuovo la conversazione 3. Metti gli avverbi e i complementi sulla destra negli spazi giusti delle frasi. Ferma la registrazione se è necessario.

1.31

1   Well I can't come ....

2   They .... stop ....

3   The traffic's moving ....

4   She's waiting ....

5   She .... goes ....

| outside our house   there |
| round the corner   patiently |
| now   always   after school |
| very slowly |
| at her friend's house   often |
| to the station |

Guarda gli avverbi e i complementi che hai scritto. Per ciascuno di essi, decidi se specificano *how often?*, *how?*, *where?* o *when?*

197

6 Che cosa potresti dire in queste situazioni? Completa ogni frase con un avverbio appropriato tra quelli dati nel riquadro.

on time   frequently   ~~very hard~~   fluently   extremely   absolutely

1 You're going to have to practise ..very..hard.. if you want to become a professional!

2 Mark's exam started at 9 am. He didn't get to school ....

3 My father was .... furious when I told him I had crashed his car.

4 My mother is .... fat.

ICH BIN ALICE

5 Alice speaks German ....

6 Mandy and her boyfriend .... have arguments.

7 In cinque di queste frasi c'è un errore nell'uso dell'avverbio. <u>Sottolinea</u> gli errori e correggili.

1 I tried <u>hardly</u> to remember where I had seen him before, but I couldn't. ....hard........

2 Bill always arrives lately for football practice. ....

3 Mark is my cousin, but I hardly know him. ....

4 Gerald can jump extremely highly. I think he'll be a champion one day. ....

5 I'm a very nervous passenger, and Michael drives too fastly for my liking. ....

6 I would happily drive you to the gym, but I don't have the car today. ....

7 This computer is so slow. It works badlier than mine. ....

8 Natalie's teachers think very highly of her. ....

8 Completa le frasi seguenti con la forma comparativa corretta degli avverbi derivati dagli aggettivi nel riquadro.

| efficient | early | fast | eccentric | bad |
| passionate | clear | high | good (x2) | |

1   Gianni works quickly and doesn't waste any time. He studies .more. efficiently. than everyone else in the class.

2   You sing so beautifully. I wish I could sing as .... as you.

3   I'm very jealous of my brother's English. I wish I could speak English .... than him.

4   Neil kissed his girlfriend .... than he ever had before.

5   Phoebe has always worn some very strange clothes, but yesterday she came to school dressed .... than ever.

6   If you got up as .... as your sister, you wouldn't always be late for school.

7   The new maths teacher explains things .... than the previous one.

8   Sam can kick the ball .... than anyone else in the team.

9   Both sisters are great athletes, but Gill can run .... than her sister.

10   I've never seen Gary play as .... as he did yesterday. What's wrong with him?

1.32

9 Ascolterai l'inizio della radiocronaca di una partita di calcio. Ascolta e riempi gli spazi. Ferma la registrazione se è necessario.

1   And ....finally........ the players are coming onto the pitch.

2   There were such terrible traffic jams .... that the match is starting ....

3   … the spectators have been waiting .... since two o'clock …

4   … they're cheering ....

5   Rossi … is running .... down the pitch …

6   … he's fallen ....

7   He's so experienced in these kinds of conditions that he .... falls.

8   Now Parker is running .... towards the goal …

9   Parker is playing incredibly ....

10   .... he scored the winning goal …

11   It's .... Parker who shoots that important goal.

199

Tutte le parole che hai inserito negli spazi sono avverbi e complementi. Ci danno informazioni su quando, dove, come o quanto spesso si è verificato qualcosa. Adesso inserisci nella colonna giusta le risposte che hai dato nell'esercizio precedente.

When?	Where?	How?	How often?
finally	in the city	patiently	rarely

10 Sottolinea l'alternativa corretta.

1 She stepped *confident* / *confidently* onto the stage to begin her talk.

2 The meeting at lunchtime was a *complete* / *completely* waste of time.

3 She did *good* / *well* in the exam and she won a prize.

4 Max tried *hard* / *hardly* to make the hotel receptionist understand him, but his Spanish wasn't *fluent* / *fluently* enough.

5 After looking at the computer screen all day I had an *awful* / *awfully* headache.

6 Even though Deborah did the job *efficient* / *efficiently*, they sacked her after two months.

7 The doctor couldn't understand why Carol felt so hot because her temperature was *normal* / *normally*.

8 The boy behaved *bad* / *badly* on a school trip so the school refused to take him on any more.

11 Riscrivi queste frasi mettendo gli avverbi tra parentesi nella posizione appropriata.

1 She plays volleyball well for her age. (*incredibly*)
She plays volleyball incredibly well for her age.

2 They eat steak because it is so expensive. (*rarely, nowadays*)
....

3 My grandfather used to take us swimming. (*in the summer holidays, in the lake*)
....

4 There is a good film on TV. (*usually, on Sunday evenings*)
....

5 My father insisted that saying 'please' and 'thank you' was important. (*terribly, always*)
....

12 Riempi gli spazi con le parole nel riquadro.

always	earlier	hardly	now	rather	silently
	skilfully	stiffly	very	warmly	

She shut the door **(1)** ...silently... after her. Her father wasn't expecting her — she had arrived **(2)** .... than she had said. He was sitting where he **(3)** .... sat, in his favourite armchair by the window. It was **(4)** .... old but had been repaired **(5)** .... so that he could continue using it. The room had been redecorated since her last visit and was looking **(6)**.............. elegant. On the shelves were all the books which her father **(7)** .... ever looked at any more. She called her father's name. He stood up and she noticed that he moved very **(8)**.............. . He smiled and held out his arms to her. She hadn't been in touch with him for five years but **(9)** .... he welcomed her as **(10)** .... as he always had.

13 In otto di queste frasi c'è un errore. <u>Sottolinea</u> gli errori e correggili.

1 The child spread <u>thickly the jam</u> on the piece of bread. ....the jam thickly...................

2 I used to see Sharon at the gym every week but I haven't seen her lately. ....

3 My grandmother drives less careful than she used to. ....

4 I never have bought anything from that expensive shop over there. ....

5 Paul is extremely careless – he loses something nearly every day. ....

6 At Tony's garage I always have my car repaired. ....

7 You must return the book by next Friday to the library. ....

8 My uncle speaks very well Spanish because he lived in Peru for a while. ....

9 My sister doesn't make friends as easily than I do. ....

10 Jon can't go out much at the moment as he has to study hardly for his degree. ....

14 Traduci.

1 L'esame fu sorprendentemente facile e tutti gli studenti lo superarono.

2 Siamo arrivati alla stazione sabato mattina alle nove.

3 Gary non ha giocato bene come al solito e la sua squadra ha perso.

4 Bess gioca a scacchi molto meglio di suo padre.

5 Da giovani si impara più velocemente.

6 Se non guidi in modo più prudente, prima o poi farai un incidente.

7 Puoi venire più tardi, per favore? Adesso sono molto occupato.

8 Non è giusto! Matt studia meno di tutti ma ottiene sempre i voti migliori della classe.

9 Lucy va in palestra più spesso di te. Ecco perché è più in forma.

10 Di solito mi vesto in modo sportivo.

I RELATIVI

I RELATIVI – INTRODUZIONE

I pronomi relativi collegano due frasi, trasformando la seconda in una frase subordinata relativa.

*This evening there's a film on TV. I've never seen **that** film.*
Stasera c'è un film in televisione. Non ho mai visto **quel film.**

*This evening there's a film on TV **which** I've never seen.*
Stasera c'è un film in televisione **che non ho mai visto.**

*I get on well with Greg. **Greg** works with me.*
*I get on well with Greg, **who** works with me.*

Vado d'accordo con Greg. **Greg** lavora con me.
Vado d'accordo con Greg, **che** lavora con me.

I pronomi relativi, quindi, non solo sostituiscono i nomi a cui si riferiscono, ma hanno anche la funzione di **mettere in relazione**, cioè di unire, due frasi separate.

I pronomi relativi sono *who, which, that, whose, where* e *why*.

12.1   I PRONOMI RELATIVI: *WHICH, WHO* E *THAT*

Il pronome relativo *which* si riferisce a **cose** o **animali**;
il pronome relativo *who* si riferisce a **persone**;
that può essere riferito sia a **cose** che a **persone**.

Persone	Cose o animali
who/that	*which/that*
che, il quale / la quale, i quali / le quali	*che, il quale / la quale, i quali / le quali*

*Here's **a photo. It** shows Harry and Jane on their wedding day.*
Ecco **una foto. Mostra Harry e Jane il giorno del loro matrimonio.**

*Here's a photo **which** shows Harry and Jane on their wedding day.* (**Non *which it shows***)
Ecco una foto **che mostra Harry e Jane il giorno del loro matrimonio.**

*I know **the people. They** gave Tom a lift to the station.*
Conosco **le persone. Hanno dato a Tom un passaggio fino alla stazione.**

*I know the people **who** gave Tom a lift to the station.* (**Non *who they gave***)
Conosco le persone **che hanno dato a Tom un passaggio fino alla stazione.**

That può sostituire sia **who** che **which**.

*Here's a photo **that** shows Harry and Jane on their wedding day.*
*I know the people **that** gave Tom a lift to the station.*

■ Quando ha funzione di complemento, **who** può essere sostituito da **whom**, ma solo in contesti formali. L'uso di **whom** sta diventando sempre più raro nell'inglese moderno.

*This is the girl (**who/whom**) I met in Majorca.*	*Questa è la ragazza **che** ho conosciuto a Maiorca.*
*His girlfriend, **who/whom** he neglected, became very depressed.*	*La sua ragazza, **che** lui trascurava, diventò molto depressa.*

PRACTICE

1 Inserisci **who** o **which** nelle frasi seguenti.

1 This is the house ....which.... Jack built.

2 The tall man .... was sitting next to me was my father.

3 *The Lord of the Rings* is the most famous of the books .... J.R.R. Tolkien wrote.

4 Bob Marley was the person .... made reggae music famous.

5 Andy Warhol is the name .... we first think of when we hear the term 'Pop Art'.

6 We have an old television .... doesn't work.

7 I have a friend in America .... plays basketball for the national team.

8 The people .... live in the flat above us are Bolivians.

2 Collega queste frasi usando **who** o **which**.

1 I've got a ring. It belonged to my grandmother. / I've got a ring which belonged to my grandmother.

2 My sister has a beautiful leather jacket. It cost £200.

My sister has a beautiful leather jacket ....

3 I have a penfriend. He lives in Australia. / I have a penfriend ....

4 This is the computer. It doesn't work. / This is the computer ....

5 Those are the singers. They won a music competition on television last night.

Those are the singers ....

6 My brother told me about his friend. She worked for a film company.

My brother told me about his friend ....

3 Completa le frasi seguenti. Scegli il finale più appropriato tra quelli nel riquadro e trasformalo in una frase relativa.

> members of the anti-globalisation movement appreciate **him** /
>
> both children and adults enjoy **it** / **it** has taken place since 1980 / my sister always chooses **it** /
>
> we visited **it** last year / young women read **it** / I went on holiday with **them** / the fans all admire **him**

1   *Northern Lights* is a book .... which both children and adults enjoy ....

2   Manu Chao is a pop star ....

3   Pistoia Blues is a festival ....

4   *Marie Claire* is a monthly magazine ....

5   These are the friends ....

6   This is the ice cream ....

7   Neil is the striker ....

8   Here is a photo of the castle ....

12.2   OMISSIONE DEL PRONOME RELATIVO

In italiano il pronome relativo **deve sempre essere espresso**, qualunque sia la sua funzione nella frase. In inglese, invece, il pronome relativo può essere **omesso** quando ha funzione di **oggetto**.

*That's the restaurant which **Simon** runs.*	*Quello è il ristorante che **Simon** gestisce.*

Simon è il soggetto della frase relativa, mentre **which** ha funzione di oggetto. In questa frase non è necessario usare **which** o **that**.

That's the restaurant Simon runs.

■ **Who**, **which** o **that** **non** possono essere omessi quando hanno funzione di soggetto. Confronta le frasi seguenti:

*This is the T-shirt (which/that) **I** bought for my boyfriend.*	*Questa è la maglietta che ho comprato per il mio ragazzo.*

Il soggetto della frase relativa è **I**, quindi **which/that** può essere omesso.

*This is the colour **which/that** suits you best.*	*Questo è il colore **che** ti sta meglio.*

Il pronome relativo è soggetto, quindi **non** può essere omesso.

*Here's a footballer (who/that) **you**'ll recognise.*	*Ecco un calciatore che riconoscerete.*

Il soggetto della frase relativa è **you**, quindi **who/that** può essere omesso.

*Here's a footballer **who/that** played for England.*	*Ecco un calciatore **che** ha giocato per l'Inghilterra.*

Il pronome relativo è soggetto, quindi **non** può essere omesso.

PRACTICE

1 Leggi attentamente le frasi seguenti. Decidi in quali di esse **who**, **which** o **that** possono essere omessi e cancellali.

1   Sandra is the teacher who we invited to tea.

2   Here's the book which I promised to lend you.

3   Why did you change the plan that we made?

4   That's the hotel which has a swimming pool on the roof.

5   Where's the bunch of flowers that you bought yesterday?

6   Elaine wrote to the university that had offered her a place.

7   This is the letter that caused all our problems.

8   I emailed all the people who my boss wanted to see.

9   Andrew is the man who won the science prize.

10   When will you finish the work which I asked you to do?

2   Collega le frasi seguenti usando un pronome relativo, come nell'esempio. Scrivi il pronome tra parentesi quando è possibile ometterlo.

1   Have you seen the ring? My parents gave it to me on my 18th birthday.

.......Have you seen the ring (which/that) my parents gave me on my 18th birthday?......

2   These are the jeans. I bought them in last winter's sales.

....

3   Ernest Hemingway was an American writer. He wrote *A Farewell to Arms*.

....

4   Johnny Depp is an actor. Women love him.

....

5   This is a picture of the tourist resort. We are going to visit it next month.

....

6   A soft drink is a cold drink. It is often fizzy.

....

7   Peter is a person. He has qualities that I really admire.

....

8   Have you seen the new iPod? Harry was talking about it last week.

....

9   This is the secret. I've wanted to tell you it for days.

....

10   Mika is the pop singer. I saw him in concert last week.

....

3   Riempi gli spazi in questa lettera usando **who** o **which** dove sono necessari. Se il pronome può essere omesso, scrivi –.

Dear Mr Trotter,

I have a number of complaints about the work **(1)** .... your company did in my house last week. You promised that the men **(2)** .... carried out the work would arrive by 8.00. As you know, I have to catch the bus **(3)** .... leaves at 8.15. On three days the men arrived after eight, so I missed my bus and my boss, **(4)** .... is very strict, was extremely annoyed. The foreman lost the written instructions **(5)** .... I gave him. The paint **(6)** .... he used for the hall was the one **(7)** .... should have been used in the kitchen. The sitting-room wallpaper, **(8)** .... I had chosen with great care, was the wrong way up. My bathroom, **(9)** .... you and I agreed did not need redecorating, has been painted. If you do not promise to put right the mistakes **(10)** .... your men have made within two weeks, I will go to my lawyer.

Yours sincerely,

Cecil J. Trubshaw

12.3   WHERE, WHEN, WHOSE E WHY

Le frasi relative possono essere introdotte anche da **where**, **when**, **whose** e **why**.

where (= at / in which) ***dove, in cui***	*when* (= on / in which) ***quando, in cui***	*whose* ***di cui, il cui, dei quali / delle quali***	*why* (= for which) ***perché, per cui***

■ **Where** si usa per introdurre una frase relativa collegata a un nome di **luogo**.

*Do you know a shop **where** I can buy flip flops for the beach?* (= a shop at **which**)
*Conosci un negozio **dove*** (= in cui) *posso comprare delle infradito per la spiaggia?*

*Brighton is the place **where** I spend my summer holidays.* (= the place in **which**)
*Brighton è il posto **dove** trascorro le vacanze estive.* (= il posto in cui)

■ **When** si usa per introdurre una frase relativa dopo un riferimento di **tempo**.

*I'll never forget the day **when** I first met Mark.* (= the day on **which**)
*Non mi scorderò mai il giorno **in cui** ho incontrato Mark per la prima volta.*

*That was the year **when** I went to England for the first time.* (= the year in **which**)
*Quello è l'anno **in cui** sono andato in Inghilterra per la prima volta.*

■ **Whose**, oltre a essere una **wh- word**, ha anche la funzione di pronome relativo possessivo; viene usato **davanti** a un nome per indicare possesso e sostituisce **his**, **her**, **their**, **its**.

*Jack's the boy **whose** bike was stolen.* (= Jack's the boy. + **His** bike was stolen.)
*Jack è il ragazzo **la cui** bicicletta è stata rubata.* (= Jack è il ragazzo. + **La sua** bicicletta è stata rubata.)

*There's a girl in my class **whose** name I can never remember.*
(= There's a girl in my class. + I can't remember **her** name.)
*C'è una ragazza nella mia classe **di cui** non mi ricordo mai il nome / **il cui nome** non mi ricordo mai.*
(= C'è una ragazza nella mia classe. + Non mi ricordo mai **il suo** nome.)

■ **Why** si usa per introdurre una frase relativa, specialmente dopo parole come **the reason**.

*A hot climate is the reason **why** people in some countries have a siesta.*
*Il clima caldo è il motivo **per cui** in alcuni paesi si fa la siesta.*

*Do you know the reason **why** he quit his job?*
*Conosci il motivo **per cui** ha lasciato il suo lavoro?*

PRACTICE

1 Completa queste frasi con **who**, **which**, **whose** o **where**.

1 I met a man .....who...... plays football for Germany.

2 This is the library .... I usually study.

3 That's the woman .... daughter won the chess prize.

4 That's the girl .... my brother is going to marry.

5 We lost the map .... you drew for us.

6 Please show me the cupboard .... you keep your cleaning materials.

7 Mungo opened the present .... his friends gave him.

8 Can you tell me the name of the man .... car you borrowed?

9 Gabrielle painted the picture .... hangs in our sitting-room.

10 I have a friend .... lives in Barcelona.

Leggi di nuovo le frasi 1-10. In quali frasi puoi omettere il pronome relativo?

2 Leggi con attenzione le situazioni descritte sotto e collega le frasi seguenti con **when**, **where** o **why**.

1 I used to spend my summer holidays in a small fishing village. I went back there last week.
   Last week I went back to the small fishing village where I used to spend my summer holidays.

2 I like thinking about holidays in the past. My parents were still together in these memories.
   ....

3 My best friend isn't speaking to me. I don't know the reason for this.
   ....

4 Sardinia is a beautiful island. The sea is always clean, and there are long white sandy beaches there.
   ....

5 The food and wine in Italy are delicious. That is one of the reasons tourists go there.
   ....

6 Vicky and I met on a school trip to Sicily. At the time we were only thirteen years old.
   ....

7 I'm looking for a photo booth or a photography shop. I need some photos for my new passport and I can get them there.
   ....

8 People are fascinated by military things. I can't understand the reason for this.
   ....

9 Scarperia is a small town in Tuscany. They make knives there.
   ....

10 I want to go to university and study medicine. There are a lot of reasons for this.
   ....

3 Leggi questa conversazione tra Emily e suo padre. Riempi gli spazi nella conversazione con frasi relative, usando le informazioni nel riquadro.

1 May plays in Emily's volleyball team.
2 Alec lived next door when Emily was small.
3 Bernard gave Emily guitar lessons last year.
4 Emily met Ailsa at Spanish lessons.
5 They are staying at a guesthouse called Sunny Villa.
6 The party will be at a club called the Beach House.
7 Emily has bought a present for Herman.
8 They're going to Herman's party.

Emily: Dad, I want to go away with some friends for Herman's birthday party.

Dad: Who are these friends?

Emily: May, Alec, Bernard, Ailsa and Herman. The party's at the Beach House.

Dad: But I don't know these people. Who's May?

Emily: She's a girl **(1)** ...who plays in my volleyball team... .

Dad: And who's Alec?

Emily: Dad, you know Alec. He's the boy **(2)** ....

Dad: Oh, yes. Well, who's Bernard? I don't know him.

Emily: No, but Mum knows him. He's the boy **(3)** ....

Dad: I see. And Ailsa, who's Ailsa?

Emily: She's the girl **(4)** .... We're sharing a room at Sunny Villa.

Sunny Villa's the guesthouse **(5)** ....

Dad: And what's this Beach House?

Emily: The Beach House is the club **(6)** ....

Dad: What's that parcel?

Emily: It's the present **(7)** ....

Dad: And who's Herman?

Emily: Oh Dad! He's the boy **(8)** ....

Dad: Oh, I see. I suppose it's all right if your mother agrees.

12.4   FRASI RELATIVE DETERMINATIVE E NON DETERMINATIVE (*DEFINING* E *NON-DEFINING RELATIVE CLAUSES*)

Le frasi relative si dividono in determinative e non determinative.

Defining relative clauses	*Non-defining relative clauses*
Frasi relative determinative	**Frasi relative non determinative**

Le frasi relative determinative forniscono informazioni **essenziali** sulle persone e le cose a cui si riferiscono.

*Janet Curtis is the woman **who** has moved into the flat next door.*
*Janet Curtis è la donna **che** si è trasferita nell'appartamento accanto.*

Se togliamo la frase *who has moved into the flat next door* non sappiamo perché si sta parlando di Janet Curtis e il senso del discorso è incompleto.

Le frasi relative non determinative forniscono informazioni **accessorie** sulle persone e le cose a cui si riferiscono.

*Janet Curtis, **who** lives in the flat next door, is a journalist.*
*Janet Curtis, **che** vive nell'appartamento accanto, è una giornalista.*

Se togliamo la frase *who lives in the flat next door* conosciamo comunque **l'informazione essenziale**, che Janet Curtis è una giornalista.

Le frasi relative determinative:

■ possono iniziare con i pronomi relativi *who* (per le persone), *which* (per le cose) e *that* (per le persone e le cose).

*The building **which/that** we have just visited dates back to the Tudor period.*
L'edificio *che* abbiamo appena visitato risale al periodo Tudor.

*Gabriel is the student **who/that** has won a prize in a literary competition.*
Gabriel è lo studente *che* ha vinto un premio in un concorso letterario.

■ generalmente **omettono** il pronome relativo quando questo ha funzione di complemento.

*Have you returned the book (**which/that**) you borrowed from the library last week?*
Hai restituito il libro *che* hai preso in prestito dalla biblioteca la settimana scorsa?

■ **non** sono mai separate con una **virgola** dal resto del periodo.

*The lady **who** lives on the first floor teaches English at the university.*
La signora *che* abita al primo piano insegna inglese all'università.

■ possono **iniziare** con *why*, dopo l'espressione *the reason*.

*Do you know **the reason why** she won't talk to me?*
Conosci *il motivo per cui* non vuole parlarmi?

■ possono **omettere** *why* e *when*.

I'll tell you the reason he wasn't invited.
*= I'll tell you the reason **why** he wasn't invited.*
Ti dirò il motivo *per cui* non è stato invitato.

That was the year my sister was born.
*= That was the year **when** my sister was born.*
È l'anno *in cui* è nata mia sorella.

Le frasi relative non determinative:

■ iniziano sempre con *who* (per le persone) e *which* (per le cose); **non** possono iniziare con *that*.

*The building, **which** is very old, costs a lot of money to repair. (**Non** ~~that is very old~~)*
L'edificio, *che* è molto vecchio, costa un sacco di soldi in riparazioni.

*Gabriel, **who** has just walked in, is my sister's boyfriend. (**Non** ~~that has just walked in~~)*
Gabriel, *che* è appena entrato, è il ragazzo di mia sorella.

■ **non** omettono **mai** il pronome relativo.

*I've read the seventh Harry Potter book, **which** I found absolutely brilliant.*
Ho letto il settimo libro di Harry Potter, *che* mi è sembrato fantastico.

■ devono essere separate con una **virgola** dal resto del periodo.

*My sister Paola, **who** lives in Germany, teaches Italian at the university.*
Mia sorella Paola, *che* vive in Germania, insegna italiano all'università.

■ Il pronome relativo *whose* **non** può mai essere omesso, né nelle frasi determinative né in quelle non determinative.

*That's the teacher **whose** pupils have won the first prize.*
Quello è l'insegnante *i cui* allievi hanno vinto il primo premio.

*My great-grandfather, **whose** wife was a great beauty, had 10 children.*
Il mio bisnonno, *la cui* moglie era una grande bellezza, ebbe 10 figli.

PRACTICE

1 Leggi attentamente queste frasi e decidi se le relative che contengono sono **determinative** o **non determinative**. Indicale con **D** o **ND**.

1 Our mother always speaks to us in French, which is her native language. ......ND............

2 Bob Marley, who made reggae music famous, died in 1981. ....

3 Bob Marley was the artist who made reggae music famous. ....

4 I was born in 1990, which was the year of the Horse in the Chinese Zodiac. ....

5 Cricket is a game which is played mainly in Great Britain and its former colonies. ....

6 The secondary school that my mother went to no longer exists. ....

7 My mother, who never had the opportunity to go to university, is trying to persuade me to study engineering. ....

8 The sister that Hilary is closest to lives in New York. ....

2 Collega le frasi seguenti in modo che la seconda diventi una frase relativa non determinativa.

1 My brother loves chocolate ice cream. He is rather fat. My brother, who is rather fat, loves chocolate ice cream...........................

2 My uncle's cottage has been damaged by floods. We usually spend our holidays there.

....

3 My bicycle has been stolen. I only got it last week.

....

4 The chemistry exam was actually quite easy. We had been worrying about it.

....

5 The young man caused a fight in a bar. His girlfriend had left him.

....

6 During the summer there are dreadful traffic jams. Everyone goes on holiday then.

....

7 My parents enjoyed that film very much. They don't often go to the cinema.

....

3 Collega le frasi seguenti usando **who**, **which**, **where** o **when**. Talvolta ci sono due possibilità. Ricorda di usare la punteggiatura corretta.

1 Mrs Weber teaches German. She's very kind.

...Mrs Weber, who teaches German, is very kind. Or: Mrs Weber, who is very kind, teaches German....

2 The River Thames flows through central London. It is the main geographical feature of the city.

....

3 Marilyn Monroe was a famous actress and model. She died at the age of thirty-six.

....

4 Hip-hop music started in the Afro-American ghettoes of New York. Many rappers lived there.

....

5 In Great Britain education is compulsory between the ages of five and sixteen. Most schools are state schools.

....

6 Laptop computers can be very useful. They are becoming increasingly light and easy to carry.

....

7 Emily told me the good news last week. I was on holiday.

....

8 Martin Luther King was a civil rights activist. He was assassinated in 1968.

....

12.5   PRONOMI RELATIVI CON PREPOSIZIONI

Il pronome relativo può essere preceduto da una preposizione, come nelle frasi seguenti:

*Lo studente **con cui** divido l'appartamento è canadese.*
*Dov'è il ristorante **di cui** mi hai parlato?*

A differenza che in italiano, in cui l'ordine **preposizione + relativo non** può essere cambiato, in inglese di solito si **sposta** la preposizione alla fine della frase, dopo il verbo da cui dipende. Questa è la forma più comune nella lingua parlata:

*The student **with whom** I share a flat is Canadian.* (formale) → *The student (**who/whom**) I share a flat **with** is Canadian.* (forma più frequente)
*Where is the restaurant **about which** you told me?* → *Where is the restaurant (**which/that**) you told me **about**?*

Anche in questo caso, il pronome relativo **si può omettere** nelle frasi non determinative. Confronta le frasi seguenti:

Relativa determinativa:

*The girl **with whom** he fell in love was very tall.* → *The girl he fell in love **with** was very tall.*
*La ragazza **di cui** si innamorò era molto alta.*

Relativa non determinativa:

Peter, **with whom** *my father used to work, has become a government minister.* → *Peter,* **who** *my father used to work* **with***, has become a government minister.*

Peter, *con cui mio padre lavorava, è diventato ministro.*

Nelle frasi relative **non** si può mai usare preposizione + *that*.

The Conference Room, **in which** *the meeting was held, was not really big enough.*
(**Non** ~~in that the meeting was held~~)
La sala delle Conferenze, **in cui** *fu tenuto l'incontro, non era abbastanza grande.*

PRACTICE

1 Completa le frasi seguenti con una delle espressioni nel riquadro, come richiede il senso.

the police are looking for.	I ever went out with.
my father works for.	you told me about?
I share a flat with.	you can rely on.
does he listen to?	I just can't agree with.

1 Rob is the American student ....I share a flat with.............................

2 Is this the film ....

3 That is the company ....

4 What kind of music ....

5 Martin was the first boy ....

6 Ilse is a person ....

7 He must be the man ....

8 My father has some views ....

2 Scegli la frase corretta.

1 **a** Have you ever been back to the town, that you were born in?

   b Have you ever been back to the town that you were born in? ✔

2 **a** My left ankle which I broke last winter is still giving me trouble.

   b My left ankle, which I broke last winter, is still giving me trouble.

3 **a** Is that the man you were talking about?

   b Is that the man you were talking about him?

4 **a** I'm looking for the book you lent me last week.

   b I'm looking for the book what you lent me last week.

5 **a** The region, where we go for our holidays, is becoming increasingly popular.

   b The region where we go for our holidays is becoming increasingly popular.

6 **a** The friend that I want to introduce you to her is away this weekend.

   b The friend I want to introduce you to is away this weekend.

7 **a** Do you remember the name of the place in that the crime was committed?

   b Do you remember the name of the place where the crime was committed?

12.6 FRASI RELATIVE ESPRESSE CON IL PARTICIPIO: *A MESSAGE SAYING…, THE PEOPLE INVITED…*

Le frasi relative possono a volte essere espresse con un participio presente, *-ing*, o con un participio passato, *-ed*, al posto di un pronome relativo e di un verbo di modo finito.

Participio presente: *-ing*	Participio passato: *-ed*
*Dad has left a message **saying** that he will be late for dinner.* (= **which** says)	*All the people **invited** to the party had a great time.* (= **who** had been invited)
*Il babbo ha lasciato un messaggio **che dice** che farà tardi per cena.*	*Tutte le persone **invitate** alla festa si sono divertite moltissimo.* (= **che** erano state invitate)
*Who's the girl **talking** to your brother?* (= **who** is talking)	*The painting **stolen** from the museum was by Munch.* (= **which** was stolen)
*Chi è la ragazza **che sta parlando** con tuo fratello?*	*Il quadro **rubato** al museo era di Munch.* (= **che** è stato rubato)
Il participio presente indica di norma che l'azione della frase principale e della relativa sono contemporanee.	Il participio passato indica che la frase relativa ha significato passivo.

PRACTICE

1 Unisci le frasi seguenti tramite una frase relativa con la forma *-ing*, come nell'esempio.

1 A man was sitting next to me on the train. I didn't take much notice of him.

I didn't take much notice of the man sitting next to me on the train.

2 The United Kingdom is a constitutional monarchy. It comprises England, Scotland, Wales and Northern Ireland.

....

3 My friend wrote me a long email. She explained why I should go to university.

....

4 Other people are coming on the skiing holiday. I don't know them.

....

5 A train is standing on platform ten. It is leaving in five minutes for Milan.

....

6 We live in a large second-floor flat. It overlooks the river.

....

2 Riscrivi le frasi relative <u>sottolineate</u> con la forma *-ing* o il participio passato. Qualche volta la trasformazione non è possibile.

1 Who's that man <u>who is standing outside the front door</u>? I mean the one <u>who's wearing a scarf</u>.

…Who's that man standing outside the front door? I mean the one wearing a scarf.

2   The people <u>who were rescued by the lifeguards</u> were taken to hospital for shock treatment.

....

3   Do you see that tower <u>that is standing on the top of the hill</u>? It was built in the seventeenth century.

....

4   The group of hikers <u>who were caught in the blizzard</u> on their way back had to spend the night on the mountain.

....

5   The text message <u>that I sent him</u> was an invitation to a party.

....

6   Can you see that person <u>who is waving at us</u>? Is he trying to tell us something?

....

7   The music <u>that I was listening</u> to last night was jazz.

....

8   Many of the British children <u>who were evacuated during the Second World War</u> were sent to Canada.

....

ALL IN ONE REVISION

1   Leggi i nomi dei programmi televisivi nel riquadro. Abbina tre di essi alle immagini.

| documentary   news   sports programme   quiz   soap opera   cookery programme |

2   Ascolterai una guida che accompagna alcuni studenti in una visita a degli studi televisivi.

1   Which studio do they visit first, second and third? ....

2   Who do the students meet on their tour? ....

2.2

3   Ascolta di nuovo e completa le frasi seguenti.

1   We may meet some other people ....who.......... you can talk to.

2   The news team choose the stories .... will be in the news.

2.3

3 Here's a man .... face you'll recognise.

4 That's the soap opera .... you can see every evening at seven on TBC.

5 This is the room .... Mark asked Jill to marry him.

6 We report on all the sports events .... take place around the world.

7 For instance, people .... were stars like Sally Ravenna.

8 Jack's the man .... old boots were sold recently for £10,000.

4 Rileggi le parole che hai scritto.

1 Can you take out any of the words and keep the same meaning? ....

2 Which of the words can you replace with *that*? ....

5 Abbina gli inizi delle frasi con le loro logiche conclusioni, collegandoli con il pronome relativo *who*, *which* o *where*.

1 A werewolf is a person ..c..   **a** which you use for work and play.

2 A desert island is a place .....   **b** who looks after you.

3 A boat is a form of transport .....   **c** who turns into a wolf when there's a full moon.

4 A school is an institution .....   **d** where you go to be on your own.

5 A computer is a tool .....   **e** where you go to get an education.

6 A mum is a person .....   **f** which doesn't have wheels or wings.

6 Riscrivi le frasi sostituendo le parole in corsivo con *where*, *when* e *why*.

1 There are moments *in which* everything seems to go wrong.

There are moments when everything seems to go wrong.

2 There are reasons *for which* I decided to buy the new Macintosh computer.

....

3 There are restaurants *in which* you can never get a table without booking.

....

4 The Victorian Age was the period *during which* Oscar Wilde was writing.

....

5 *Time Out* is a magazine *in which* you can see all the current events and performances.

....

6 The nineties was the decade *during which* Brit Pop was the musical trend.

....

7 Queste frasi sono molto formali. Riscrivile in modo che suonino più spontanee, omettendo il pronome relativo e spostando la preposizione.

1 The company *for which* he works makes computer games.

The company he works for makes computer games.

2 Who was that boy with whom you went to the cinema?

....

3 *The Catcher in the Rye* is the book about which the teacher spoke.

....

4 My cousin, Andy, of whom I am very fond, is going to university next September.

....

5 The computer for which you paid 1,000 euros last year now costs a great deal less.

....

6 My friends are all people on whom you can rely.

....

7 The sister to whom I am closest is Sally.

....

8 The airline with which I flew to Moscow was Aeroflot.

....

9 The teachers for whom I have the most respect are always friendly.

....

10 The issue about which I care most is education.

....

8 Per ogni coppia di frasi, completa la seconda in modo che il significato non cambi.

1 Martin works for a company which is opening new branches in North America.

The company .... Martin works for is opening new branches in North America ....

2 My sister shares a flat with students who study the same subject as her.

The students ....

3 I'm going out with a girl who is Italian but has Polish parents.

The girl ....

4 Peter is responsible for a group of children who live in the same village as him.

The group of children ....

5 Michael lives in a suburb of the city that not many tourists know.

Not many tourists know ....

6 My brother writes for a newspaper that tries to avoid scandal and gossip.

The newspaper ....

7 Mandy has fallen in love with a boy who is crazy about football.

The boy ....

8 My parents have invested their money in a bank that is based in Switzerland.

The bank ....

9 Yesterday my sister bumped into an old friend who has become a fantastic musician.

The old friend ....

10 I don't agree with my father's political views.

My father has ....

9 Ascolterai un uomo che accompagna alcuni visitatori in una visita guidata del castello dove vive. Prima di ascoltare, guarda attentamente le immagini.

Riesci a indovinare in che periodo queste persone vivevano? ....

Pensi che siano membri della stessa famiglia? ....

10 Ascolta e verifica se avevi ragione. Mentre ascolti, abbina i nomi alle immagini.

2.4

1 Margaret .... **2** Edmund .... **3** Henry .... **4** William .... **5** Jane ....

11 Ascolta di nuovo e completa le risposte a queste domande. Ferma la registrazione se è necessario.

2.5

1 What do we learn about the ship in the picture of Edmund?

It's the one .... _which he was captain of during a famous naval victory._ ....

2 Which is the picture of Henry and William?

It's the picture ....

3 How do we know who William is?

He's the one ....

4 Which side did Henry support in the Civil War?

It was the side ....

5 Which year was the picture of Jane and her children painted?

It was the year ....

12 Sottolinea la prima parola in ognuna delle risposte che hai dato nell'esercizio precedente. Sono tutte parole che possono introdurre una frase relativa. A che cosa si riferisce ciascuna di esse?

1 .... **2** .... **3** .... **4** .... **5** ....

13 Completa queste frasi con le tue idee, usando i pronomi relativi nel riquadro.

| where   when   which   which   which   who   whose   why |

1   I don't really enjoy films ....

2   I don't often go to parties ....

3   My teacher usually explains things ....

4   I can remember several occasions ....

5   I cannot understand the reason ....

6   Have you ever met anyone ....

7   I envy people ....

8   I would hate to have a job ....

14 Inserisci le virgole dove sono necessarie.

(1) Yorkshire which is the county where I was born is the largest county in England. **(2)** The North York moors where farmers keep sheep and you can see many other animals and birds are famous. **(3)** The moors are particularly striking in the summer when the purple heather is in flower. **(4)** The city that gives its name to the county is York itself which attracts a large number of tourists every year. **(5)** York Minster which is the largest Gothic cathedral in northern Europe is particularly impressive. **(6)** But one of the most pleasant memories that I have of York is the smell of chocolate that used to come from its chocolate factory. **(7)** Other happy memories are of our trips to Whitby from where Captain Cook set off on his voyages in the 18th century. **(8)** I love going back to Yorkshire to visit the places I knew as a child which is not surprising as it was a lovely place to grow up.

15 Traduci.

1   Il ristorante indiano che ha aperto due mesi fa è già molto popolare.

2   Hai ricevuto la cartolina che ti ho spedito dal Messico?

3   Il ragazzo che ho conosciuto in vacanza mi ha mandato un sms ieri sera.

4   Come si chiama la banca per cui lavora tua sorella?

5   Ho un amico la cui sorella studia matematica a Oxford.

6   Non capisco il motivo per cui ha rifiutato il mio invito.

7   Qual è il nome del ristorante in cui avete cenato sabato sera?

8   Bettina, che è in Inghilterra da poche settimane, parla già inglese molto bene.

9   La mia amica Gemma, con cui sono andata in Brasile l'estate scorsa, adesso lavora là per un'organizzazione umanitaria.

10   Mary, i cui bambini sono molto piccoli, sta cercando un lavoro part-time.

I VERBI MODALI (1)

I VERBI MODALI (1) – INTRODUZIONE

I verbi modali sono un gruppo di verbi ausiliari che presentano caratteristiche particolari.

Si chiamano anche difettivi, perché difettano, cioè **mancano**, di alcuni modi e tempi verbali: l'infinito, il gerundio, il participio presente e passato. Non possono quindi formare i tempi composti, il futuro e, nella maggioranza dei casi, il *past simple*. Per questo devono essere sostituiti da altri verbi nei modi e nei tempi mancanti.

I verbi modali sono *can, could, may, might, must, shall, should, ought to, will* e *would*. Sono usati per esprimere significati fondamentali come **possibilità**, **capacità**, **permesso**, **obbligo**, **certezza**.

In questa *Unit* sono illustrate le caratteristiche grammaticali generali dei verbi modali e le principali funzioni comunicative che essi esprimono.

Nella *Unit* seguente sono trattati gli aspetti più specificamente grammaticali dell'uso dei modali, con particolare riferimento ai verbi che sostituiscono le forme mancanti come *be able to* e *have to*.

13.1 I VERBI MODALI: CARATTERISTICHE PRINCIPALI

I verbi modali sono una categoria specifica di verbi ausiliari che seguono regole differenti da quelle degli altri verbi.

■ I verbi modali sono **invariabili: non** aggiungono *-s* alla terza persona singolare del *present simple*, o *-ed* o *-ing*.

*Angela **can** borrow my camera whenever she wants.* (**Non** *Angela cans borrow*)
*John **must** study harder.*
*He **might** help.*

■ Sono seguiti dalla forma base, infinito **senza** *to* (a eccezione di *ought to*).

*I **can** help.* (**Non** ~~I can to help.~~)

*You **should** get up earlier.* (**Non** ~~You should to get up earlier.~~)   *Dovresti alzarti prima.*

■ Sono immediatamente seguiti da *not* nelle frasi negative.

*That **will not** (= **won't**) be necessary.*

■ Precedono il soggetto nelle frasi interrogative.

***Could** you wake me up?*   ***Potresti** svegliarmi?*

👆 Il verbo *ought* che, come *should*, corrisponde al condizionale di 'dovere', differisce dagli altri verbi modali perché è seguito da *to* + **infinito**.

*You **should not** (**shouldn't**) be late for college.*   *Non **dovresti** fare tardi a scuola.*
*= You **ought not to** be late for college.*

PRACTICE

1 <u>Sottolinea</u> l'alternativa corretta.

1 The teacher spoke very quickly and I couldn't <u>*take*</u> / *to take* notes.

2 Would you like *go* / *to go* to the cinema tonight?

3 My printer isn't working. I must *buy* / *to buy* a new one.

4 Sam wants *learn* / *to learn* to play the guitar.

5 Sheila hasn't got anything to wear to her sister's eighteenth birthday party. She ought *get* / *to get* some new clothes.

6 Melanie is saving up for a new scooter. She hopes *find* / *to find* a holiday job.

7 It may *rain* / *to rain* later. We'd better take an umbrella.

8 Are you going to the shopping centre? Could you *get* / *to get* me a cartridge for my printer?

2 Claire e Tim stanno organizzando una festa.
Forma delle frasi usando i verbi modali tra parentesi.

1 we / tidy the flat before the party. (*must*) ....We must tidy the flat before the party........

2 Peter / help us. (*ought*) ....

3 we / decorate the flat. (*will*) ....

4 we / (not) invite too many people. (*should*) ....

5 you / bring your CDs? (*can*) ....

6 your mother / lend us some plates? (*could*) ....

7 we (not) / make too much noise. (*must*) ....

8 the neighbours / complain. (*might*) ....

13.2   I VERBI MODALI: POTERE, DOVERE E VOLONTÀ

I verbi modali esprimono una varietà di significati connessi ai concetti di **potere**, **dovere** e **volontà**.

	Affermativa	Negativa	Contratta
differenti significati di **potere**	can could may might	cannot could not may not might not	can't couldn't – mightn't
differenti significati di **dovere**	must shall ('ll) should ought to	must not shall not should not ought not to	mustn't shan't shouldn't oughtn't to
differenti significati di **volontà**	will ('ll) would ('d)	will not would not	won't wouldn't

I significati fondamentali di **potere** espressi dai verbi modali sono riassunti nella seguente tabella:

	Significato	Esempi
can/could *can't/couldn't*	capacità/abilità	*Laura **can** speak six foreign languages fluently.* *Laura **sa** parlare sei lingue straniere con scioltezza.* *Janet **could** play the violin from the age of six.* *Janet **sapeva** suonare il violino quando aveva sei anni.* *My brother **can't** swim.* *Mio fratello **non sa** nuotare.*
can/could	possibilità	*You **can** swim in this lake, but the water's very cold.* ***Si può** nuotare in questo lago, ma l'acqua è molto fredda.*
can't/couldn't	impossibilità	*Thomas **can't** come today as he is busy.* *Thomas **non può** venire oggi perché è impegnato.* *I **couldn't** go to school yesterday because I had a temperature.* ***Non sono potuta** andare a scuola ieri perché avevo la febbre.*
can/could/may	permesso	*Can/Could/May I borrow your French dictionary?* ***Posso/Potrei** prendere in prestito il tuo vocabolario di francese?* *You **can** use my laptop.* ***Puoi** usare il mio portatile.* *Customers **may** use the car park.* *I clienti **possono** usare il parcheggio.*
can/could	richiesta	*Can/Could you lend me 10 euros until tomorrow?* ***Puoi/Potresti** prestarmi 10 euro fino a domani?*
may/might	probabilità	*I **may** go to Norwich next week.* (= about a 50% chance) ***Può darsi** che io vada a Norwich la settimana prossima.* *My sister **might** come with me.* (= about a 30% chance) *Mia sorella **potrebbe** venire con me.*

Nella seguente tabella sono riassunti i significati fondamentali di **dovere**:

	Significato	Esempi
must / have to	obbligo	*You **must** stop teasing your sister.* **Devi** smettere di prendere in giro tua sorella. *We **have to** wear uniforms at school.* **Dobbiamo** indossare l'uniforme a scuola.
mustn't	proibizione	*You **mustn't** break the rules.* **Non devi** infrangere le regole.
need to / have to / must	necessità	*You **need to / have to** get some sleep.* **Devi** assolutamente dormire un po'. *The children **must** rest.* I bambini **devono** riposarsi.
don't have to / *needn't /* *don't need to*	mancanza di necessità	*We **don't have to** leave so early.* *We **needn't** leave so early.* *We **don't need to** leave so early.* **Non dobbiamo / Non è necessario** partire così presto.
must / had better	ordine/consiglio	*You **must** type your essay: your handwriting is illegible.* **Devi** scrivere il tema al computer: la tua grafia è illeggibile. *You'**d better** ask him first.* **Faresti meglio a** chiederlo a lui per primo.
should / ought to	consiglio/ raccomandazione	*You **should / ought to** join a sports club.* **Dovresti** iscriverti a un circolo sportivo.

Questi significati sono trattati in modo dettagliato nei prossimi paragrafi, **13.3**, **13.4**, **13.5** e **13.6**.

PRACTICE

1 Scrivi risposte brevi a queste domande.

1 Can Bill play the saxophone? Yes, ...he can.....

2 Could Loida speak Italian when she first came to Italy? No, ...

3 Might you go on holiday with Graham? Yes, ...

4 Must we go home so soon? Yes, ...

5 Should I leave the modem on? No, ...

6 Shouldn't you ask your brother before you use his scooter? Yes, ...

7 Need we do all the exercises in this unit? No, ...

8 Hadn't we better set the alarm if we want to catch the early train? Yes, ...

2 Abbina gli inizi delle frasi con le loro logiche conclusioni.

1 Do people in Britain have to carry an identification card with them? ..f..

2 I've got a headache. What should I do? .....

3 My bike's been stolen. Do you think I ought to report it to the police? .....

4 I'd love to try cross-country skiing. Can you ski? .....

5 Could I have a glass of water, please? .....

6 I couldn't go to school yesterday because there was a bus strike. .....

7 It's a public holiday tomorrow. We'd better check we have everything before the shops close. .....

8 I must lose some weight. I can't get into my jeans any more. .....

9 Can you take food onto the plane? .....

10 Do children need to eat meat and fish to develop? .....

a Good idea. We may need to get some more milk.

b Yes, you never know! They might find it.

c You'd better lie down for a while until it passes.

d You ought to take up a sport. You don't do enough exercise.

e Of course. Do you prefer still or fizzy?

f No they don't, although that may change in the future.

g Well, vegetarians say that it isn't absolutely necessary. But you have to make sure they're getting a well-balanced diet.

h No, you can't. You have to buy it when you're on board.

i You're so lucky! We all had to do a test.

j I could when I was a child, but I haven't done it for years.

13.3   FUNZIONI COMUNICATIVE CON I MODALI: RICHIESTE – *CAN, COULD, WILL, WOULD*

I verbi modali *can*, *could*, *will* e *would* sono usati per **chiedere a qualcuno di fare qualcosa**.

Richieste		Risposte	
Informali	**Formali / Più cortesi**	**Acconsentire**	**Rifiutare**
Can/Will you help me?	*Could/Would* you help me?	*Yes, of course. / Of course (I can/will).*	*I'm afraid not. / I'm sorry (I can't).*
Puoi *aiutarmi?*	***Potresti/Vorresti*** *aiutarmi?*	*Sì, certo.*	*Ho paura di no. / Mi dispiace (non posso).*
Vuoi *aiutarmi? /* ***Mi*** *aiuti?*	***Mi*** *aiuteresti?*	*Certainly. / Yes, sure.* *Certamente./Sicuro.*	*I'm sorry but + reason* *Mi dispiace ma + motivo* **Non** ~~*No, I won't.*~~ *(= molto scortese)*

■ *Can you?* e *Will you?* si usano in situazioni **informali**.

Can you pass me the bread?   **Puoi** passarmi il pane?
Will you get me some stamps from the post office?   *Mi prendi dei francobolli all'ufficio postale?*

■ Per essere più cortesi si usano *Could you?* e *Would you?*

Could you tell me where the station is?   **Potrebbe** dirmi dov'è la stazione?
Would you lend me your camera?   *Mi presteresti la tua macchina fotografica?*

■ **Non** si può usare *May you?* per fare richieste.

Non ~~May you give me a lift?~~

PRACTICE

1 Sam si è rotto il polso e sta partendo per un viaggio in pullman, così chiede agli altri passeggeri di aiutarlo. Che cosa dice? Usa ognuna delle espressioni seguenti almeno una volta.

He asks someone to:

| Can you ...?   Will you ...?   Could you ...?   Would you ...? |

1 carry his bags to the coach ....Would you carry my bags, please?........

2 hold the door ....

3 fasten his seat belt ....

4 open his bottle of water ....

5 help him put his coat on ....

6 close the window ....

2 Riempi gli spazi in queste frasi.

1 A ....Can......... I change traveller's cheques here? **B** ..I'm afraid not.... (–)

2 A I'm sorry to bother you. .... I look at your timetable, please?

   B .... (+)

3 A .... you get that tin down from the shelf for me, Dad? I can't quite reach.

   B .... (+)

4 A .... you post this parcel for me on your way to work, please? **B** .... (+)

5 A Excuse me, ... you tell me where the nearest tube station is?

   B .... (–)

6 A .... you turn that television down? I need to use the phone. **B** .... (+)

3 Gemma ha una brutta influenza ed è assente da scuola da una settimana. Adesso telefona alla sua amica Mel per chiederle di aiutarla a mettersi in pari. Scrivi il dialogo tra le due amiche seguendo le indicazioni date:

Gemma	Mel
Puoi dirmi che compiti abbiamo per la settimana prossima?	Sì, certo. Abbiamo biologia per lunedì. Il professor Davies ha spiegato un nuovo capitolo.
Oh, no! Puoi prestarmi i tuoi appunti?	Ma certo. Spero che tu riesca a capirli. E la signorina Lagrange ha fissato il compito di francese per venerdì.
È un disastro. Io ho perso tutte le ultime spiegazioni. Puoi venire a studiare con me questo pomeriggio?	Mi dispiace ma oggi pomeriggio non posso. Ho un allenamento di pallavolo dalle 5 alle 7. Possiamo studiare insieme domani.
Domani va benissimo, grazie. Ci vediamo domani allora, Mel.	

13.4   FUNZIONI COMUNICATIVE CON I MODALI: PROPOSTE E SUGGERIMENTI – *SHALL I/WE, WHY DON'T YOU/WE, COULD, LET'S, HOW ABOUT + -ING, WHAT ABOUT + -ING*

Il verbo modale *shall*, seguito da un soggetto di prima persona singolare o plurale, *I/we*, viene usato per dare suggerimenti, fare proposte o offrirsi di fare qualcosa per qualcuno.

Shall we go to the cinema this evening?   **Andiamo** al cinema stasera? (= proposta, suggerimento)
Shall I carry this bag for you?   **Ti porto** questa borsa?   (= offrirsi di fare qualcosa)

Come si vede dagli esempi, *shall* può essere usato solo alla forma interrogativa.

*What **shall** we **do** this evening?*   *Che cosa **facciamo** stasera?*   (= invito a fare una proposta)
*What time **shall** we **meet**?*   *A che ora **ci vediamo**?*   (= invito a fare una proposta)

■ Per fare una proposta o offrirsi di fare qualcosa per qualcuno si usa anche *can*.

*I **can** make you one of my special recipes.*   ***Posso** cucinarti una delle mie ricette speciali.*
***Can** we help you to cook dinner?*   ***Possiamo** aiutarti a preparare la cena?*

■ Se non siamo completamente convinti di quello che stiamo suggerendo si usa *could*.

*We **could** go to a Chinese restaurant tomorrow.*   ***Potremmo** andare a un ristorante cinese domani.*
*We **could** go by bicycle today.*   ***Potremmo** andare in bicicletta oggi.*

■ Per dare suggerimenti o fare proposte possiamo anche usare le seguenti espressioni:

Shall I/we	*go by bicycle today?*	***Vado/Andiamo** in bicicletta oggi?*
Why don't I/we	*go by bicycle today?*	***Perché non vado/andiamo** in bicicletta oggi?*
Let's	*go by bicycle today!*	***Andiamo** in bicicletta oggi!*
How about / What about	*going by bicycle today?*	***Che ne dici/dite** di andare in bicicletta oggi?*

Queste sono alcune espressioni comunemente usate per **accettare** o **rifiutare** una proposta.

Accettare	Rifiutare	Fare un'altra proposta
That's a great idea!	*I'm not so sure about that.*	*Why don't we …, instead? /* *What /How about + **-ing** instead?*
Ottima idea! *Yes, OK.* *Yes, let's (do that). / Right, we'll do that.* *Sì, dài. Facciamolo.*	*Non sono proprio convinto.* *Well, + reason why not.* *Beh, + motivo per cui si rifiuta.*	*Perché non …, invece?*

PRACTICE

1 Sam ha ancora il braccio ingessato, dopo essersi rotto il polso. Il suo amico Jamie è andato a trovarlo. Completa la loro conversazione con le espressioni nel riquadro.

> shall I get   I could do   Shall I show   What about having   I can cook   I could give

Jamie: I'm sorry you've broken your wrist, Sam. **(1)** ...I..could..do... some shopping for you.

Sam: It's OK. I've got lots of food. I just can't cook at the moment.

Jamie: Oh. Well, **(2)** .... something for you.

Sam: That would be good. **(3)** .... a pizza and some salad?

Jamie: Fine. And **(4)** .... you a drink? What would you like?

Sam: Can you open that orange juice in the fridge? I can't do it with one hand.

Jamie: OK. Look, I've brought some work from college. **(5)** .... you?

Sam: Actually, I'm coming into college this afternoon.

Jamie: I'm going too. **(6)** .... you a lift. I've got my motorbike outside.

2 <u>Sottolinea</u> l'alternativa corretta.

1 I know you want to learn to sail. I *could* / *may* teach you.

2 Why don't we *eat* / *eating* in the new Chinese restaurant?

3 *Could* / *Would* I speak to Silvana, please?

4 *Can* / *May* you drive me to school today?

5 *Shall* / *Will* I carry that for you? It looks very heavy.

6 *Shall* / *Will* you give me Maria's phone number, please?

7 I enjoyed playing tennis with you. *Shall* / *Would* we play again next week?

8 How about *inviting* / *invite* my sister too?

9 A *Would* / *May* you help me to write this letter? B I'm sorry. I'm busy.

10 Let's *meet* / *meeting* in the café at 7.

3 Usa **shall** per fare proposte o chiedere consigli nelle seguenti situazioni.

1   You and Ellen are going out for the evening. You don't know what to do.

You: What ....shall we do this evening.. ?

Ellen suggests going to that jazz concert in the local park.

Ellen: .... ?

You agree, and suggest going for a pizza first.

You: Good idea! .... ?

Ellen agrees and suggests going on her scooter.

Ellen: All right. .... ?

2   You can't decide where to go on holiday this summer. You ask your friend Katie if she has any ideas.

You: Where .... ?

Katie suggests going camping by the sea.

Katie: I've got a new tent. .... ?

You agree and ask her if she can suggest which campsite to go to.

You: Brilliant! Which .... ?

Katie says she doesn't know and suggests looking for one on the internet.

Katie: I don't know. .... ?

3   You and Donald want to do something to cheer up a friend, Gary, who's depressed.

You: What .... ?

Donald suggests taking him out for the evening.

Donald: .... ?

You agree and suggest phoning him first to make sure he's free.

You: OK, let's do that. .... ?

Donald disagrees and suggests just going to his house and giving him a surprise.

Donald: No, he might make an excuse. .... ?

4   You want to know where to go to buy a digital camera.

You: Where .... ?

Your brother suggests going to the new shopping centre in Via Roma together.

Your brother: .... ?

You suggest going tomorrow.

You: All right, but it'll be crowded this afternoon. .... ?

4 Mentre tornano a casa da scuola, Bob, Jennifer e Kate discutono di che cosa regalare a un amico per il suo compleanno. Ciascuno dei tre amici fa una proposta e alla fine giungono a una decisione comune. Completa il loro dialogo.

Bob: It's David's birthday on Saturday. **(1)** ...Let's get/buy him... a present together this year.

Jennifer: Yes, **(2)** .... That way we can get him something really good. Have you got any ideas?

Kate: I have. Why (3) .... a ticket for the Arsenal versus Manchester United match? You know he's crazy about football.

Bob: No, he's already got a season ticket. (4) .... something for his computer? A new video game, for example.

Jennifer: Well, I think he spends too much time playing those games. (5) .... something more outdoor?

Kate: He plays five-a-side football twice a week. (6) .... an Arsenal shirt?

Bob: (7) .... I'm a Liverpool supporter! (8) .... a new video phone? That way he can call his girlfriend in London and see her while they speak. He'd really like that.

Jennifer: (9) .... then.

Kate: (10) ....

13.5   FUNZIONI COMUNICATIVE CON I MODALI: PERMESSO – *CAN, COULD, MAY*; *BE ALLOWED TO*

Quando si chiede il permesso per fare qualcosa si usano generalmente i modali *can*, *could* e *may*.

Un permesso può essere **accordato** o **rifiutato**.

Richieste di permesso		Risposte	
Informali	**Formali / Più cortesi**	**Concedere il permesso**	**Rifiutare il permesso**
Can I sit here?	*Could/May I sit here?*	*Yes, of course. / Of course (you can).*	*I'm afraid not + reason.* (= cortese)
Posso *sedermi qui?*	**Potrei** *sedermi qui?*	*Yes, certainly. / OK.*	*Sorry, but + reason. / No, you can't.* (= non molto cortese)

Can I leave my bag here while I look around the museum? (= una richiesta di permesso semplice, alla quale ci aspettiamo risposta affermativa)

Posso *lasciare la borsa qui mentre faccio un giro del museo?*

Could I borrow your car for a few days? (= forma più cortese; una richiesta più impegnativa, alla quale non siamo sicuri sarà data risposta affermativa)

Potrei *prendere a prestito la tua macchina per qualche giorno?*

May I sit here? (= richiesta di permesso più formale, rivolta a una persona che non si conosce)

Potrei *sedermi qui?*

■ *Can* e *can't* si usano per dire che si ha o non si ha il permesso di fare qualcosa, oppure per parlare di ciò che è permesso o non è permesso in generale.

*We **can** finish work early tomorrow.*   **Possiamo** *finire di lavorare presto domani.*
*You **can't** use the phone.*   **Non puoi** *usare il telefono.*
*You **can't** join this club until you are 16.*   **Non puoi** *iscriverti a questo club finché non hai 16 anni.*

■ **May** è invece spesso usato nei cartelli o negli avvisi scritti per indicare quello che è o non è consentito.

*You **may** borrow six books from the library.*	**È consentito/permesso** *prendere a prestito sei libri dalla biblioteca.*
*You **may not** keep any book for longer than three weeks.*	**Non è consentito/permesso** *tenere alcun libro per più di tre settimane.*

Per parlare di permessi o divieti si può usare anche la forma passiva **be allowed to**, che significa **essere consentito/permesso**. **Be allowed to** non è un verbo modale. A differenza dell'italiano, questo verbo ha sempre una costruzione personale: **non** può avere il soggetto impersonale *it*.

*We **weren't allowed to** camp in the pine wood.*	**Non ci fu permesso di / Non potevamo** *campeggiare nella pineta.*
*Are you **allowed to** take your mobiles into the classroom?*	**Potete / Vi è permesso di** *portare i cellulari in classe?*
*I **wasn't allowed to** visit my friend when he was ill.*	**Non mi fu permesso** *di vedere il mio amico quando era malato.*

Be allowed to è spesso usato per indicare divieti negli avvisi scritti.

*Dogs **are not allowed**.*	**Non è consentito** *l'ingresso ai cani.*

PRACTICE

1 Chiedi ai tuoi genitori il permesso di fare cinque cose che per te sono importanti.

2 Gabriella è ospite presso una famiglia inglese. Usa le indicazioni tra parentesi per formulare le richieste che fa alla sua *landlady*, poi completa ogni mini-dialogo scegliendo la risposta più adatta tra quelle date nel riquadro. Ricordati di usare espressioni appropriate al contesto.

> OK. I'll make up the spare bed.
> Sorry, but it belongs to my daughter and she doesn't like other people using it.
> ~~Yes, certainly. I'll put the kettle on immediately.~~
> No, I'm afraid not. We've just redecorated the room.   Of course. I love Italian food.
> Certainly, but you need to buy a phone card at the newsagent's.

1 Gabriella: ....May/Can/Could I have a cup of tea, please.............. ? (*have a cup of tea*)

   Landlady: ....Yes, certainly. I'll put the kettle on immediately...........................

2 Gabriella: .... ? A friend from Italy would like to come and visit.

   (*have guests*)

   Landlady: ....

3 Gabriella: .... ? I'd like to make us all an Italian meal one evening.

   (*use the kitchen*)

   Landlady: ....

4 Gabriella: ....? I've just bought a poster of my favourite pop star.

   (*put up posters on the wall*)

Landlady: ....

5 **Gabriella:** ....? I'd like to phone my family in Italy occasionally.
(*use the phone*)

Landlady: ....

6 **Gabriella:** ....? (*use the bicycle that's in the garden*)

Landlady: ....

3 Leggi con attenzione le seguenti situazioni e completa le frasi con un modale e un verbo appropriato. In alcuni casi possono esserci più possibilità.

1 You have done all your homework. You ask your mother: ' ..*Can/May I watch*.. TV now?'

2 It's your fourteenth birthday. You ask your parents: '........................... a scooter now?'

3 You're staying in a youth hostel in Britain and you're not sure of the rules.
You ask a member of staff: '........................... until midnight?'

4 You're at school and you're not feeling very well. You ask your teacher: '........................... home?'

5 You've been invited to go on holiday by your best friend's family.
You ask your parents: '........................... with Gianni's family?'

6 You're doing an English exam.
You ask your English teacher: '........................... monolingual dictionaries?'

7 You want to have a stud in your nose. You ask your mother: '........................... my nose?'

8 You're learning how to play tennis.
You ask the instructor: '........................... the ball outside this line?'

4 Spiega il significato di questi cartelli, usando le espressioni *you can/can't*, *you may/may not*, *you are/aren't allowed to*.

1 ....
....
....

2 ....
....
....

3 ....
....
....

4 ....
....
....

5 ....
....
....

6 ....
....
....

13.6   FUNZIONI COMUNICATIVE CON I MODALI: ORDINI, CONSIGLI E RACCOMANDAZIONI – *MUST, HAD BETTER, SHOULD / OUGHT TO, COULD*

Per chiedere e dare consigli si usano i verbi modali **must**, **had better**, **should / ought to** e **could**.

Questi modali esprimono vari gradi di intensità.

| *must* | *had better* | *should / ought to* | *could* |

← →

consiglio forte   **consiglio meno forte**

must	Si usa per dare un **ordine**, per esprimere un'opinione che ci sta particolarmente a cuore.	*You really **must*** **Devi** *proprio* *You **must*** **Devi**	*start looking for a job.* *cominciare a cercare un lavoro.* *check the details.* *controllare i dettagli.*
had ('d) better *had better not*	Si usa per dare un **consiglio forte**, che si riferisce generalmente all'immediato futuro ed è più urgente di *should / ought to*.	*You'd better* **Faresti meglio** *a* *I'd better not* **Farei meglio a non**	*start looking for a job.* *cominciare a cercare un lavoro.* *upset her today.* *farla arrabbiare oggi.*
should / ought to *shouldn't / ought not to*	Traducono il **condizionale presente di 'dovere'** e hanno lo stesso significato. *Ought to* è più formale e meno comune.	*You **should / ought to*** **Dovresti** *They **shouldn't*** *Non **dovrebbero*** *I **ought not to*** *Non **dovrei***	*start looking for a job.* *cominciare a cercare un lavoro.* *talk so much.* *parlare così tanto.* *eat that cake.* *mangiare quel dolce.*
could	Viene usato per esprimere un **suggerimento**.	*You **could*** **Potresti** *You **could*** **Potresti**	*start looking for a job.* *cominciare a cercare un lavoro.* *take some books.* *prendere dei libri.*

Non si usa la forma negativa di *must* e *could* per dare un consiglio. *Mustn't* ha significato di **proibizione** e *couldn't* esprime **impossibilità**.

231

PRACTICE

1 Immagina di avere un lavoro part-time in un negozio. Un tuo amico inizierà a lavorare nello stesso negozio la settimana prossima. Dai dei consigli al tuo amico. Usa ciascuna delle espressioni nel riquadro.

| You must ...   You ought to ...   You could ...   You should ...   You shouldn't ...   You mustn't ... |

1 be polite to the customers .... *You should be polite to the customers*.......................

2 offer to work extra hours ....

3 arrive at work on time ....

4 look tidy ....

5 look bored ....

6 lose the key to the safe ....

2 Daniel gestisce la sua attività, ma non è molto ordinato. Domani un cliente importante andrà a trovarlo in ufficio. Dagli dei consigli, usando almeno quattro strutture differenti e le parole nel riquadro.

| coat   cups   desk   filing cabinet   lampshade   telephone   wastepaper bin   window |

1 *You'd better tidy the desk*.......................................

2 ....

3 ....

4 ....

5 ....

6 ....

7 ....

8 ....

3 Leggi con attenzione le situazioni presentate sotto e dai a ciascuna di queste persone dei consigli adeguati. Usa *should*, *shouldn't*, *had better*, *had better not*, *must* e *could*.

1 Carol is overweight and she would like to lose weight, but she misses breakfast and lunch. In the evening she has a small meal, but then she gets hungry and eats cakes and crisps.

....

2 Harry's girlfriend has left him for another boy and he's feeling very depressed. It's June and he was looking forward to spending the summer with her. He doesn't know what to do to feel better.

....

3 Alessandro really likes a girl in his class and would like to ask her out, but she's very unpopular. His friends make fun of her. He feels embarrassed about telling his friends about his feelings as he knows they would laugh at him.

....

ALL IN ONE REVISION

1 Mr Kent, Maria e Alex lavorano insieme.
Dove pensi che lavorino?
Qual è il loro mestiere?

2 Ascolterai tre conversazioni. In quale conversazione:

2.6

1   Alex dà dei suggerimenti o si offre di fare delle cose? ....

2   Maria chiede ad Alex di fare delle cose? ....

3   Alex chiede il permesso di fare delle cose? ....

3 Ascolta di nuovo e completa queste frasi.

2.7

1   .... *Can* .... I sit here for a minute?

2   .... I get a drink of water?

3   .... I use the phone?

4   .... you do those tables over there?

5   .... you help me put out today's menus?

6   And .... you check the salt and pepper?

7   Then .... you sweep the floor?

8   But .... we move some tables outside?

9   And we .... serve more interesting food perhaps.

10   I .... make one of my special recipes if you like.

4 Che cosa hanno detto queste persone in queste situazioni? Completa ogni domanda con un'espressione differente.

1   Anan suggested meeting outside the supermarket.

Anan said: '*Shall we meet outside* the supermarket?'

2   Mirsad asked for permission to leave work early.

Mirsad said: '...................... work early?'

3   Fernando asked me to buy some stamps.

Fernando said: '...................... some stamps?'

4   Jasmina offered to paint her grandmother's kitchen.

Jasmina said: '...................... your kitchen?'

5   Martina suggested leaving a message for Luca.

Martina said: '...................... a message for Luca?'

6 Michael offered to do the washing up.

Michael said: '... washing up.'

7 The teacher gave the boy permission to use the computer.

The teacher said: '... the computer.'

8 Katharine asked the shop assistant to find a bigger size.

Katharine said: '... a bigger size?'

9 Ellie suggested buying a CD for Tom's birthday.

Ellie said: '... a CD for Tom's birthday?'

10 Sanja asked for permission to put a poster on the wall.

Sanja said: '... a poster on the wall?'

5 In ognuna delle frasi seguenti c'è un errore. Talvolta si tratta di un errore grammaticale, talvolta il significato non corrisponde all'indicazione tra parentesi. <u>Sottolinea</u> l'errore e scrivi la correzione.

1 Why don't we <u>going</u> dancing this evening? (*suggestion*) ......go........

2 Motorists mustn't pay to use the motorway in Great Britain. (*absence of necessity*) ....

3 You may start studying now if you want to pass your exams. (*advice, recommendation*) ....

4 Are eighteen-year-olds can hire a car? (*permission*) ....

5 Which is the quickest way to the city centre? You may take a bus from here. (*possibility*) ....

6 It shall rain tomorrow. (*possibility*) ....

7 You'd better to set the alarm if you want to get up early. (*advice, recommendation*) ....

8 Dogs had better not enter the supermarket. (*absence of prohibition*) ....

9 May you give me a lift to the station? (*request*) ....

10 How about go for a romantic walk along the river? (*suggestion*) ....

6 Completa questo dialogo con le espressioni nel riquadro.

Can I do
~~Can I help~~
Could I see
I'm afraid
Shall I ask
Would you exchange
You can't have
You could give
You'd better not
You should ask

Assistant: (1) .....*Can I help*................. you?

Laura: I'd like to have a refund on a CD which I was given as a present. (2) .... that here?

Assistant: Yes you can. I'll do it for you. (3) .... the receipt, please?

Laura: (4) .... not. I haven't got one, you see, because it was a present.

Assistant: (5) .... a refund without the receipt. Those are the rules, I'm afraid.

Laura: (6) .... it for something else then?

Assistant: What CD is it? Oh, but you've taken it out of its wrapping. You shouldn't have done that if you want to return it.

Laura: Christabel did it before she gave it to me.

Assistant: Did you say Christabel? Does she work here at weekends?

Laura: I don't know. She's got dark hair and glasses.

Assistant: (7) .... her where she got this. She was probably given it free because it has no wrapping. (8) .... the manager what he thinks?

Laura: (9) .... do that. I don't want to get her into trouble.

Assistant: (10) .... it to someone else for their birthday, I suppose.

7 Che cosa diresti nelle situazioni seguenti? Scrivi le frasi.

1 You have just started work in a new office and you want to know how the coffee machine works. Ask someone.

Excuse me, could you tell me how the coffee machine works, please? ....

2 Your sister has just moved into a new flat and you offer to help her clean it.

....

3 Your brother puts lots of salt onto his food. You don't think this is a good idea because too much salt is bad for you. What do you say?

....

4 You want a book which you can't find in the bookshop. Ask the assistant to order it.

....

5 You are buying something in a shop and you want to pay by credit card. Ask the assistant if this is possible.

....

6 Your friend is always late because he doesn't have a watch although he can afford to buy one. What advice do you give him?

....

7 You have been at a party at a friend's house and the kitchen is in a terrible mess. Offer to help clear up.

....

8 You need a lift home. Your friend has a car but lives in the other direction. Ask him politely for a lift.

....

235

8 Chelsea e un'amica hanno deciso di fare un breve viaggio a Madrid, una città in cui non sono mai state prima. La madre di Chelsea ha viaggiato molto, così le dà consigli utili. Completa il loro dialogo usando i verbi modali corretti. A volte c'è più di una possibilità.

Mother: Listen Chelsea, you **(1)** ..should.. book somewhere to stay before you leave because the Easter period is very busy in Spain.

Chelsea: All right. **(2)** .... you help me find something? **(3)** .... we do a search on the internet together?

Mother: Yes, turn the computer on then. Now you **(4)** .... put your money and documents in various different places, not all in the same wallet. You **(5)** .... be robbed, so it's better to avoid losing everything at once. **(6)** .... get one of those money pouches that you wear around your waist?

Chelsea: Good idea. And if I am robbed?

Mother: First of all, you **(7)** .... cancel your credit cards, and then you **(8)** .... report it to the police.

Chelsea: **(9)** .... I take my mobile with me?

Mother: Yes, you can, but remember it costs more, so avoid using it too much. Now, you **(10)** .... buy ten-trip tickets for getting around on the underground and the buses. They cost half the price of ten single-trip tickets.

Chelsea: And what do you think we **(11)** .... see?

Mother: Well, you absolutely **(12)** .... see the Prado Museum, and the Royal Palace, and the Plaza Mayor for a start. **(13)** .... downloading an itinerary from the internet? We **(14)** .... look at it together.

9 Traduci.

1 È tardi. Non faremmo meglio a tornare a casa?

2 **A** Che cosa facciamo stasera? **B** Perché non andiamo al ristorante cinese? Poi potremmo andare al *Likuid*, il nuovo locale vicino al porto.

3 Se vuoi davvero migliorare il tuo inglese, dovresti fare un corso di lingua.

4 Sei molto stanco. Dovresti andare a letto presto stasera.

5 **A** Posso usare il tuo computer portatile? **B** Certo che puoi.

6 Potrei dare un'occhiata alla sua rivista?

7 Dovresti telefonare ai tuoi genitori più spesso.

8 Non so se Josh è stato avvertito. Farei meglio a chiamarlo.

9 **A** Dovremmo invitare Maggie alla nostra festa? **B** Sì, penso che dovremmo.

10 **A** Ti aiuto a sparecchiare? **B** No, grazie, lo faccio io più tardi.

I VERBI MODALI (2)

14.1	Capacità/abilità/possibilità: *can, could, be able to*
14.2	Obbligo o necessità: *must / have to*; *mustn't* e *don't have to*
14.3	Necessità e mancanza di necessità: *need, needn't, don't have to*; mancanza di necessità al passato: *didn't need to do* e *needn't have done*
14.4	Deduzione, certezza, possibilità, probabilità: *must, can't, may, might* e *could*
14.5	Forme composte dei verbi modali: *should have known, could have been*

I VERBI MODALI (2) – INTRODUZIONE

Nella *Unit* precedente abbiamo introdotto lo studio dei verbi modali dal punto di vista delle funzioni comunicative che esprimono.

Questa *Unit* affronta gli aspetti più specificamente grammaticali dell'uso dei modali, con particolare attenzione alle **forme sostitutive** e alle **forme composte**.

14.1 CAPACITÀ/ABILITÀ/POSSIBILITÀ: *CAN, COULD, BE ABLE TO*

I can esprime diverse sfumature di **capacità** e **possibilità**: io so fare qualcosa, sono capace di farlo, sono in grado di farlo, riesco a farlo, posso farlo.

Per esprimere questa varietà di significati **al presente** si usano *can*, un verbo modale, e *be able to*, un verbo non modale.

	Can		**Be able to**
+	*I can swim.*	*Io so nuotare.*	*I'm able to swim.*
–	*She can't swim.*	*Lei non sa nuotare.*	*He's not able to swim.*
?	*Can you swim?*	*Sai nuotare?*	*Are you able to swim?*

I due verbi possono essere usati al presente senza una particolare differenza di significato.

James can / is able to play chess but he can't / isn't able to ride a bicycle.
James sa / è capace di giocare a scacchi ma non sa / non è capace di andare in bicicletta.

■ *Can* è però più comune di *be able to*.

The children can swim but they can't dive yet.   *I bambini sanno nuotare ma non sanno ancora tuffarsi.*
I can't make up my mind.   *Non riesco a decidermi.*
Can you play badminton?   *Sai giocare a badminton?*

■ **Be able to** è meno comune ed è usato quando si vuole sottolineare l'essere in grado o il non essere in grado di fare qualcosa.

*My grandfather **is able to** cook his own meals but he **isn't able to** walk to the shops.*
Il mio nonno è in grado di / riesce a *cucinarsi i pasti ma* **non è in grado di** *andare a fare la spesa.*

*I'm **not able to** answer that question.*   **Non sono in grado di / Non so** *rispondere a quella domanda.*

PASSATO: *COULD* E *WAS/WERE ABLE TO*

Per parlare di azioni che eravamo capaci di fare nel passato o che erano possibili nel passato si usano **could** (*past simple* di **can**) e **was/were able to** (*past simple* di **be able to**).

*He **could/was able to** read when he was three.*   **Sapeva / Era capace di** *leggere a tre anni.*

🔊 Nelle frasi affermative c'è una differenza di significato tra le due forme.

Si usa **could** per indicare che si aveva l'abilità **in generale** di fare qualcosa nel passato, mentre si usa **was/were able to** per riferirsi all'abilità dimostrata in un'**occasione specifica** del passato.

Confronta le frasi seguenti:

*When I was younger I **could** swim up to twenty laps at a time.*
Quando ero più giovane potevo / ero capace di *nuotare fino a venti vasche consecutive.*
                                                    (= abilità in generale nel passato)

*They **were able to** see the match because they had a day off.* (**Non** ~~They could see the match~~)
Poterono *assistere alla partita perché avevano il giorno libero.* (= circostanza particolare)

Come si può vedere dagli esempi, **could** è generalmente usato per rendere l'**imperfetto** italiano, mentre **was/were able to** corrisponde al passato remoto o al passato prossimo italiano: riuscii / sono riuscito, fui in grado di, potei.

■ Alla forma **negativa**, tuttavia, i due verbi possono essere usati senza particolari differenze di significato.

*The athletes **couldn't / weren't able to** train because the weather was bad.*
Gli atleti **non poterono / non hanno potuto** *allenarsi perché il tempo era brutto.*
*She **was able to** come to the meeting but she **couldn't / wasn't able to** stay for lunch.*
Riuscì a *venire alla riunione ma* **non poté** *rimanere per il pranzo.*

TEMPI MANCANTI: *BE ABLE TO*

Per tutti i tempi mancanti di **can/could** si ricorre ai tempi corrispondenti di **be able to**.

Futuro con *will*	*I **will** never **be able to speak** German as well as you do.*
	Non riuscirò mai **a parlare** tedesco bene come te.
	*If it rains, we **won't be able to eat** in the garden.*
	*Se piove **non potremo mangiare** in giardino.*
Present perfect	*Harry **hasn't been able to solve** the problem yet.*
	*Harry **non è** ancora **riuscito a risolvere** il problema.*
	*They **haven't been able to contact** Mary because of the storms.*
	***Non sono riusciti a contattare** Mary a causa dei temporali.*
Condizionale	*If you saved enough money, you **would be able to visit me** in New Zealand.*
	*Se risparmiassi abbastanza, **potresti venire a trovarmi** in Nuova Zelanda.*
Infinito	*My friends hope **to be able to come back** next week.*
	*I miei amici sperano **di poter ritornare** la settimana prossima.*
Forma base	*I may not **be able to log on** to my computer tomorrow.*
	*Può darsi che non **riesca a collegarmi** al mio computer domani.*
Forma *-ing*	*She had to calm down a bit before **being able to speak**.*
	*Dovette calmarsi un attimo prima di **riuscire a parlare**.*

PRACTICE

1 Queste immagini ci fanno vedere quello che Robin è capace o non è capace di fare. Completa le frasi seguenti con **can** o **can't** e un verbo appropriato.

1 He ....*can play*.. the guitar but he *can't play*. the trumpet.

2 He .... a scooter but he .... a car.

3 He .... but he ....

4 He .... Spanish but he .... Chinese.

5 He .... but he ....

6 He .... but he ....

2 Completa le frasi seguenti con **can**, **can't**, **could** o **couldn't**.

1   I'm sorry I ....can't........ come to your party. I'm busy on Saturday.

2   You .... sing much better than that when you were younger.

3   Rachel's son .... count to 20 and he's only two!

4   We didn't speak the language so we .... understand what the woman said.

5   .... you read that notice from here? I haven't got my glasses with me.

6   Anne-Marie likes to sit close to the stage so she .... see the actors' faces clearly.

7   I'm afraid of going on a boat because I .... swim.

8   When I was a teenager I walked everywhere because I .... drive.

9   He looked everywhere for the ring but he .... find it.

10   .... you open this window? I've tried, but it's too heavy.

3 Riempi gli spazi con le parole nel riquadro.

are	be	to be	haven't been	isn't	will	weren't	wasn't	won't be	were

1   None of the students ....were........ able to read the teacher's writing.

2   Your sister speaks very good Spanish. .... you able to speak any foreign languages?

3   .... you be able to finish that homework by tomorrow?

4   They .... able to see anything from the plane because it was cloudy.

5   I'm sorry, I .... able to come to your wedding next month because I've got exams.

6   If you want to do the diving course, you have .... able to swim.

7   I looked everywhere but I .... able to find the photograph because Laura had it.

8   Let's phone the theatre. We may .... able to get seats for tonight.

9   I wanted to invite James but I .... able to contact him.

10   The manager .... able to see you now. Can you come back tomorrow?

4 Commenta con delle domande appropriate quello che viene detto. Usa la forma corretta di **be able to** e un verbo nel riquadro.

sleep	find	recognise	come	go for a swim	see

1 A   The concert was great. It's a pity that our seats were so far back.

 B   ...Were.... you ..able to see. the stage from where you were?

2 A   I'll be 18 next Tuesday and I'm inviting all my friends to my birthday party in the evening.

 B   .... your friends .... on a Tuesday evening?

3 A   I'd like my American girlfriend to come and live in Italy when she finishes her studies.

 B   But isn't she studying to be a lawyer? If she came here .... she .... a good job?

4 A My brother is very worried about his exams.

B He looks very tired. .... he .... recently?

5 A Let's go to the beach.

B We've only just had lunch. Won't we have to wait before .... ?

6 A I saw a man behaving very suspiciously last night.

B .... you .... him if you saw him again?

5 Completa l'articolo seguente con **can**, **can't**, **could**, **couldn't** o la forma corretta di **be able to**. A volte sono possibili due risposte.

The maths genius

Ryan Kennedy speaks to Nick Evans about his amazing talent.

One day when I was four years old, my father was telling my mother how much money he'd spent and while he was talking I added it all up. They didn't believe that I **(1)** could/was able to do that because I **(2)** .... read or write. I'm now at university and I **(3)** .... still add up complicated sums in my head. I did a maths exam once which I finished so quickly I **(4)** .... eat a meal in the canteen before the others had finished. Next year we have to write essays and I'm not sure whether I **(5)** .... do that because I **(6)** ....

(*never*) spell very well. I would like **(7)** .... use my mathematical skill in a job but I haven't decided what yet. I **(8)** .... be a maths teacher – I'd enjoy the maths but I'm not sure about the children! I entered a maths quiz show on TV once but when they asked me the questions I **(9)** .... think of the answers because I was just too nervous. So I **(10)** .... imagine myself as a TV star. I **(11)** .... always get work in the supermarket when the tills break down, I suppose!

6 Traduci.

1 Puoi aiutarmi a finire questo esercizio?

2 Non siamo riusciti a trovare i biglietti per il concerto di Wembley.

3 Rebecca spera di poter andare in America la prossima estate.

4 Il compito era lungo e difficile. Non sono riuscita a rispondere a tutte le domande.

5 Ho cercato il libro dappertutto, ma non sono riuscito a trovarlo.

6 Deve essere molto bello saper parlare diverse lingue straniere correntemente.

7 Potrò comprarmi un'auto nuova l'anno prossimo.

8 Hai potuto parlare con tuo fratello?

14.2   OBBLIGO O NECESSITÀ: *MUST / HAVE TO; MUSTN'T* E *DON'T HAVE TO*

Il significato fondamentale di **dovere** indica che qualcosa è **obbligatorio**, **è essenziale** o **necessario**.

Per esprimere questo significato di **dovere** al presente si usano *must* e *have to*.

Have to è un verbo non modale, quindi richiede l'ausiliare *do/does* nelle frasi interrogative e negative.

	Must (verbo modale)		Have to (verbo non modale)	
+	*I must go.*	**Devo** andare.	*I have to go.*	**Devo** andare.
+	*She must go.*	Lei **deve** andare.	*She has to go.*	Lei **deve** andare.
?	*Must you go?*	**Devi** andare?	*Do you have to go?*	**Devi** andare?
?	*Must he go?*	**Deve** andare?	*Does he have to go?*	**Deve** andare?

Nella forma **affermativa** e **interrogativa** i due verbi hanno significati simili e possono spesso essere usati indifferentemente.

*I **must go** now or I'll miss the bus.*   **Devo andare** adesso o perderò l'autobus.
(= I **have to** go now or I'll miss the bus.)
Must she leave now? (= **Does** she **have to** leave now?)   **Deve** partire adesso?

◾ *Must* esprime un obbligo più forte rispetto a *have to* ed è usato per dare un ordine o una forte raccomandazione, anche a noi stessi.

*You **must** tell me everything.* (= I feel strongly about this)
Devi dirmi tutto. (= mi sta a cuore, te lo ordino io)

*She **must** be home by midnight.* (= these are my instructions)
Deve essere a casa entro mezzanotte. (= queste sono le mie istruzioni; deve farlo perché lo dico io)

*You **must** come to the hotel one day.* (= I strongly advise you to)
Devi venire all'albergo un giorno. (= te lo consiglio caldamente)

*I **must** phone my friends.* (= I have decided to do this)
Devo telefonare ai miei amici. (= ho deciso di farlo, è un obbligo che sento io)

◾ In genere, si usa *must* quando l'obbligo è sentito come **interno** a sé e dipende da colui che parla.

*I really **must** stop spending so much money on clothes.*
Devo proprio smettere di spendere così tanto in vestiti.

◾ Viceversa, *have to* è più comune quando l'obbligo dipende da **regole** e **circostanze esterne**.

*You **have to pay** to park your car here.* (= this is a rule)
Devi pagare / Si deve pagare per parcheggiare la macchina qui. (= questa è una regola)
*I **have to stay** until all the children have gone.* (= this is part of my job)
Devo rimanere finché tutti i bambini non se ne sono andati. (= fa parte del mio lavoro)

◾ *Have to* è più comune anche quando si parla di **azioni abituali**.

*I **have to** get up early to get to work on time.*
Devo alzarmi presto per arrivare puntuale al lavoro.
*My sister **has to** practise the piano for twenty minutes a day.*
*Mia sorella **deve** esercitarsi al pianoforte per venti minuti al giorno.*

Alla forma negativa i due verbi hanno significati diversi: *mustn't* esprime **proibizione**, mentre *don't have to* indica **mancanza di necessità**.

■ *mustn't* esprime **proibizione, divieto** = *don't do it*

You *mustn't* drive so fast: there's a speed limit here.
Non devi guidare così velocemente: c'è un limite di velocità qui.

You *mustn't* take those tablets: they have dangerous side effects.
Non devi prendere quelle pillole: hanno controindicazioni pericolose.

I *mustn't* wear jeans at work.
(= it isn't allowed)
Non devo indossare i jeans al lavoro.
(= non è permesso)

■ *don't have to* esprime **mancanza di necessità** = *it's not necessary to do it*

You *don't have to* drive so fast: we've got plenty of time.
Non devi guidare così velocemente: / **Non è necessario** che tu guidi così velocemente: abbiamo un sacco di tempo.

You *don't have to* take those tablets any more: your rash has gone.
Non è necessario che continui a prendere quelle pillole: la tua infiammazione è guarita.

You *don't have to* stay at school until you're 18. (= you are not obliged but you can if you want)
Non devi stare a scuola fino a 18 anni.
(= non sei obbligato, ma puoi farlo se vuoi)

TEMPI MANCANTI: *HAVE TO*

Must si usa solo al presente. Per tutti i tempi mancanti si ricorre al verbo sostitutivo *have to*.

Past simple	I **had to** go to work by car because there was a train strike. **Sono dovuto** andare al lavoro in macchina perché c'era lo sciopero dei treni. Did you **have to** wait long? **Hai dovuto** aspettare a lungo? I **didn't have to** write my essay on the computer. **Non ho dovuto** scrivere la mia relazione al computer.
Futuro con *will*	You'll (**will**) **have to** tell him the truth. **Dovrai** dirgli la verità.
Present perfect	I've **had to** take the dog to the vet. **Ho dovuto** portare il cane dal veterinario. Has she **had to** go home yet? **È già dovuta** andare a casa?
Condizionale	If I got the job, I'd (**would**) **have to** buy a car. Se ottenessi il lavoro, **dovrei** comprare una macchina.
Infinito	I hate **to have to** tell you, but your joke was in bad taste. Odio **dovertelo** dire, ma la tua battuta era di cattivo gusto.
Forma base	I may **have to** stay overnight. Può darsi che **debba** rimanere per la notte.
Forma -*ing*	I avoided **having to** speak to him by crossing the street. Ho evitato di **dovergli** rivolgere la parola attraversando la strada.

PRACTICE

1 Completa queste frasi usando la forma corretta di **must** o **have to**. Pensa bene a quale tempo di **have to** devi usare.

1 I .....didn't have to..... (*not*) get up early yesterday because it was Saturday. (*have to*)

2 You .... always tell the truth. (*must*)

3 I .... buy a new computer next year. (*have to*)

4 .... (*we*) wash up now? (*have to*)

5 When he was in the school team, Simon .... train every Saturday. (*have to*)

6 Children .... (*not*) go in the pool without an adult. (*must*)

7 I .... (*not*) pay to use the health club because I'm a member. (*have to*)

8 How long .... (*you*) wait for the bus last night? (*have to*)

2 In ogni frase, <u>sottolinea</u> la forma corretta: **mustn't** o **don't have to**.

1 Tell John he *mustn't / <u>doesn't have to</u>* drive me to the station because Martha can.

2 The students *mustn't / don't have to* eat in the library.

3 He can stay at home. He *doesn't have to / mustn't* come with us.

4 You *mustn't / don't have to* tell Chloe because it's a surprise.

5 I *mustn't / don't have to* forget to phone Jan tonight – I promised her.

6 You *mustn't / don't have to* bring any football boots because you can borrow mine.

7 We *mustn't / don't have to* clean this room because it's not dirty.

8 We *mustn't / don't have to* be late because we don't want to miss the beginning of the film.

3 Riscrivi ogni frase in modo che il significato non cambi. Usa **mustn't** o **don't/doesn't have to**.

1 It's not necessary to pay to go into the British Museum. It's free.
You ....don't have to pay to go into the British Museum. It's free...............

2 This meeting is very important. I really don't want to be late.
I ....

3 Passengers are forbidden to use their mobile phones during the flight. They interfere with the plane's electronic equipment.
Passengers ....

4 Motorists are usually not required to pay to drive on motorways in England.
Motorists ....

5 Passengers are not allowed to pack dangerous articles such as compressed gases, weapons, explosives, or fireworks in their luggage.
Passengers ....

6 It isn't necessary for Peter to do this homework for tomorrow. It's for Friday.
Peter ....

4 Completa le frasi con il tempo di *have to* indicato tra parentesi. Decidi se il verbo è alla forma affermativa o negativa, a seconda del senso della frase.

1 I'm sorry ...to.have..to... tell you this, but that dress really doesn't suit you. (infinito)

2 The flight leaves at six o'clock in the morning. That means that we .... get up at about three o'clock. (*going to*)

3 I'd like to lose a couple of kilos without .... go on a drastic diet. (forma *-ing*)

4 If I came on holiday with you, I .... join you at the beginning of July. I've got exams until the end of June. (condizionale)

5 I saw a man lying unconscious in the street and called an ambulance. I .... never .... do that before. (*past perfect*)

6 Ben is so lucky. His parents have offered to pay for his holiday in Cuba, so he .... get a weekend job. (futuro con *will*)

7 Before the nineties people .... wear a helmet to ride a scooter. (*past simple*)

8 I think you should get to the airport very early. You .... queue for a long time because there are a lot of new security checks. (forma base)

5 Riempi gli spazi con la forma corretta di *have to* o *must*.

1 Most students in Britain .....have..to...... pay at least part of their university fees.

2 Joe .... get up early on Fridays as he has no lectures in the morning.

3 You .... talk during the film because other people will get annoyed.

4 Jeremy .... drive to work because the bus gets there too late.

5 You .... borrow this DVD – you'll enjoy watching it.

6 .... (*you*) work every Saturday in your new job?

7 You .... come to the rehearsal tomorrow if you want to be in the play.

8 When I was a child, I .... change schools seven times because my parents moved house a lot.

9 I .... stop eating so much chocolate or none of my clothes will fit.

10 They've promised to lend me a tennis racket so I .... take mine.

14.3   NECESSITÀ E MANCANZA DI NECESSITÀ: *NEED, NEEDN'T, DON'T HAVE TO*; MANCANZA DI NECESSITÀ AL PASSATO: *DIDN'T NEED TO DO* E *NEEDN'T HAVE DONE*

Il verbo *need* significa **avere bisogno di, dovere, essere necessario**. Si comporta generalmente come un verbo normale in tutti i tempi verbali ma può assumere le caratteristiche di un verbo modale nelle **domande** e nelle **frasi negative al presente**.

Need (verbo modale)	*Need* (verbo non modale)
Need I come with you? ***Devo venire*** con te? / ***C'è bisogno che venga*** con te? *I needn't tell you.* ***Non c'è bisogno che te lo dica.***	*Do I need to come* with you? ***Devo venire*** con te? / ***C'è bisogno che venga*** con te? *I don't need to tell you.* ***Non c'è bisogno che te lo dica.***

■ Nelle frasi affermative, *need* si costruisce sempre come un verbo normale.

■ È seguito da un verbo all'infinito con *to*.

   I need to buy some bread.   ***Ho bisogno di*** comprare del pane.

■ Può essere seguito dal complemento oggetto.

   Do you need help?   ***Hai bisogno di aiuto?***

Come si capisce dagli esempi, la forma negativa di *need* indica **assenza di obbligo**, **mancanza di necessità** e ha lo stesso significato di *don't have to*.

   *You **needn't** worry. = You **don't need to** worry. = You **don't have to** worry.*
   ***Non ti devi** preoccupare. / **Non c'è bisogno che** tu ti preoccupi.*

Nelle frasi affermative al passato, *need* si comporta come un verbo normale.

*He **needed to** buy some food.*   ***Aveva bisogno** di comprare del cibo.*

Tuttavia, la forma **negativa** di *need* al passato può avere due costruzioni e due significati diversi.

Soggetto + *didn't need* + infinito	Soggetto + *needn't have* + participio passato
*He **didn't need to** buy any food.* ***Non dovette** comprare del cibo.* ***Non ci fu bisogno** che comprasse del cibo.*	*He **needn't have** bought any food.* ***Non doveva** comprare del cibo.* ***Non c'era bisogno** che comprasse del cibo.*

L'azione non era necessaria, quindi non fu compiuta.   L'azione fu compiuta ma non era necessaria.

PRACTICE

1 Completa queste conversazioni con **need to** o **needn't**.

1 **A** I'm going walking in the mountains.

   B You .....*need to*...... take some suncream because the sun's very strong.

   A Yes, you're right, but at least I .... carry my raincoat.

2 **A** Can I get ready for the party at your flat? I .... have a shower after work.

   B Of course and you .... bring a hair-dryer because you can use mine.

3 **A** I'm going to town now. **B** Why? **A** I .... buy a birthday present. **B** Have you got some cash? **A** No, I .... take cash because I've got my credit card. **B** What about the bus fare? **A** I've got a bus pass so I .... pay.

2 Leggi questa conversazione tra due amici che parlano di vacanze al campeggio. Riempi gli spazi con la forma corretta di **need**.

Rena: I'm going to that campsite by the beach next week. When you went,

              (1) .*did you need*. *(you)* to take a sleeping bag?

Dominic: Of course. It was very cold. And we **(2)** .... to take plenty of food too as there were no restaurants.

Rena: So **(3)** .... *(you)* to make a fire to cook your food on?

Dominic: No, because we took a small cooker with us. We had one small frying pan so we cooked everything in that. We **(4)** .... *(not)* to use any saucepans.

Rena: Maybe I could borrow that frying pan and cooker.

Dominic: Sure.

3 Leggi questo articolo su una pop star.

The diary column

Popstar Lee Divine travelled from London to New York yesterday by plane. Lee had visited his hairdresser before he went to the airport and wore his latest designer clothes, as he likes to look his best in photos. Press photographers usually follow him wherever he goes but the weather was very bad yesterday and, to Lee's obvious disappointment, there were no photographers at the airport. Because he is famous, he didn't stand in the queue and his bodyguard carried his luggage for him. Although most people have to walk from the car park, Lee has a driver who drove him right to the door. Even this did not seem to make him happy. Lee got angry with his driver on the way because he said she wasn't driving fast enough. Of course, they arrived at the airport in plenty of time.

Adesso scrivi sei frasi su Lee Divine.

1 He needn't have ......*visited his hairdresser*..

2 He needn't have ....

3 He didn't need to ....

4 He didn't need to ....

5 He didn't need to ....

6 He needn't have ....

14.4   DEDUZIONE, CERTEZZA, POSSIBILITÀ, PROBABILITÀ: *MUST, CAN'T, MAY, MIGHT* E *COULD*

I modali *must*, *can't*, *might*, *may* e *could* sono usati per esprimere deduzioni e vari gradi di certezza logica e possibilità.

> It must be from Steven because he's in Australia

Certezza che una cosa è vera: *must* + forma base	Possibilità/probabilità che una cosa sia vera: *might/may/could* + forma base	Certezza che una cosa non è vera: *can't* + forma base
*She **must** be English.* **Deve** essere inglese. Sono sicuro: legge sempre il *Sunday Times*.	*She **might/may/could** be English.* **Potrebbe** essere inglese. Non ne sono sicuro.	*She **can't** be English.* **Non può** essere inglese. È impossibile: parla italiano perfettamente.

■ *Might*, *might not*, *may*, *may not* e *could* si usano anche quando non siamo sicuri di qualcosa riguardo al futuro.

> *I **may go** to Greece next month.* (= it's possible but I'm not certain)
> **Può darsi che io vada** in Grecia il mese prossimo. / **Potrei andare** in Grecia il mese prossimo.
>
> *My football team **might win** the cup.*   La mia squadra **potrebbe vincere** la coppa.

■ Quando facciamo delle deduzioni o supposizioni in riferimento a eventi passati si usano queste forme:

Passato	Vero	Non vero
Certezza	***must have*** + participio passato *I can't contact Tom. He **must have** **switched off** his mobile.* Non riesco a contattare Tom. **Deve aver spento** il telefonino.	***can't have*** + participio passato ***couldn't have*** + participio passato *He **can't have switched** it **off**. He never does. Perhaps the battery is dead.* **Non può averlo spento**. Non lo fa mai. Forse la batteria è scarica.
Possibilità	***might have / may have / could have*** + participio passato	***might not have / may not have*** + participio passato

PRACTICE

1 <u>Sottolinea</u> l'alternativa corretta.

Carlotta: I can't find my keys and I'm late. There **(1)** <u>*might*</u> / *must* be a lot of traffic in town so I need to hurry. They're not in my bag so they **(2)** *must* / *can't* be in the flat somewhere.

George: Have you looked in the kitchen?

Carlotta: They **(3)** *can't* / *could* be there because I haven't been in the kitchen. They **(4)** *might* / *must* be in the bedroom because I changed my clothes there or they **(5)** *could* / *must* be on the table in the hall. I'll go and look. No, they're not there.

George: Did you leave them in the car?

Carlotta: They **(6)** *could* / *can't* be in the car because I opened the door with them. They **(7)** *can't* / *must* be here somewhere.

George: I can't see them. Let's think. They **(8)** *might* / *can't* be in your coat pocket because you weren't wearing one but they **(9)** *can't* / *might* be in your jeans pocket. Have you looked there?

Carlotta: Oh, thanks. I've found them. I **(10)** *can* / *may* be home a bit late tonight. Bye.

2 Guarda queste fotografie. Dove sono? Scrivi tre frasi per ogni fotografia, iniziando con **It might be … , It could be … , It can't be …** o **It must be …** . Fai riferimento ai posti elencati nel riquadro.

| Sweden   Nepal   Australia   India   Brazil   South Africa |

It can't be Australia....
It might be Nepal..........   ....
It must be..............   ....
....

3 Riempi gli spazi con un verbo modale che esprime certezza o possibilità e la forma corretta del verbo tra parentesi.

1 Jenny's brother ....*can't be*............... (*be*) a doctor because he's only 18.

2 I don't seem to have my wallet. I .... (*leave*) it at home because I paid for my train ticket.

249

3 **A** I left Camilla a message on her answerphone but she hasn't rung yet.

B She .... (*not listen*) to it yet. She usually has a shower as soon as she gets home from work.

4 **A** I found this watch in the changing rooms.

B It .... (*be*) Peter's. I think he's got one like that.

5 I can't make the DVD player work. I .... (*do*) something wrong. Where are the instructions?

6 I can't think what's happened to Annie. She left home hours ago so she

.... (*be*) here by now.

7 These football boots don't fit me any more. My feet .... (*grow*).

8 He remembers when there were fields here instead of houses so he ....

(*be*) very old.

4 Leggi attentamente questo rapporto di polizia riguardo al furto di un quadro.

> A very small but valuable painting has been stolen from Sidcombe Art Gallery.
> We know it was stolen between 6.00 and 7.30 on Friday evening.
> There are several suspects. They all have keys to the art gallery:

The caretaker, Sam Willis
Sam, who has worked at the gallery for 32 years, locked up at 6.30 as usual after the cleaners had left.

A student, Daniel Foreman
When the gallery shut at 5.30 Daniel begged the caretaker to let him stay a bit longer to finish his work. The caretaker saw him coming out of the toilets at 6.30 and told him to leave. He bought an expensive car on Saturday.

A cleaner, Sandra Thompson
Sandra cleaned the offices and the galleries with two other cleaners. They finished at 6.00 and had a chat in the cloakroom before leaving together at 6.15. She says the picture was still there at 6.00.

The shop manager, Sophie Christie
Sophie closed the museum shop at 5.30 but had to stay and wait for a delivery. The driver got delayed in the traffic and arrived at 6.05. He left straight away and Sophie said she left at about 6.15 but nobody saw her leave the building.

The director, William Rees
William was on the phone in his office between 6.00 and 7.00. He says he left the gallery at 7.15 but nobody saw him leave.

The cloakroom attendant, Josie McCartney
The cloakroom closed at 5.30 and Josie tidied up. She was just leaving when the cleaners arrived and she stopped to have a chat with them. They all left together at 6.15.

Chi ha avuto l'opportunità di rubare il quadro? Completa queste frasi con **must have**, **can't have**, **couldn't have**, **might have**, **may have** e **could have**. Usa ogni forma una volta.

1   Sam Willis ......*might have stolen*....... the painting because ......*he was there until 6.30.*........

2   Sandra Thompson .... the painting because ....

3   William Rees .... the painting because ....

4   Daniel Foreman .... the painting because ....

5   Sophie Christie .... the painting because ....

6   Josie McCartney .... the painting because ....

5 Per ogni coppia di frasi, completa la seconda in modo che il significato non cambi. **Usa la parola data senza modificarla.** Usa tra **due** e **cinque** parole compresa la parola data.

(FCE)

1   The streets are wet. I assume it rained during the night. **must**
   It .*must have rained*. during the night.

2   Bill has lost his wallet. It's possible that he left it in the school bar. **might**
   He .... in the school bar.

3   It's four o'clock and John's plane was due to arrive at half past three. John is certain to have arrived by now. **must**
   He .... by now.

4   That house was built in the mid-sixteenth century when Leonardo da Vinci had already died. It isn't possible that Leonardo da Vinci lived in that house. **can't**
   Leonardo da Vinci .... in that house.

5   The car battery is flat. I'm certain that you left the lights on all night. **must**
   You .... the lights on all night.

6   Susan and Jill still haven't returned from their walk in the hills. It's possible that they have got lost. **may**
   They .... lost.

7   Someone rang the doorbell at ten o'clock. It's possible that it was the postman. **could**
   It .... the postman.

8   Somebody has taken my Ligabue CD. It isn't possible that it was my brother because he's away on holiday. **can't**
   It .... because he's away on holiday.

9   Don't be so negative about this morning's exam. You never know, it's just possible that you passed it. **might**
   You .... passed it.

10 Mary is terrified of dogs. It's possible that she was bitten by one as a child. **may**
   A dog .... her when she was a child.

14.5   FORME COMPOSTE DEI VERBI MODALI: *SHOULD HAVE KNOWN, COULD HAVE BEEN*

Come abbiamo visto, una delle caratteristiche fondamentali dei verbi modali è che non hanno la forma del participio passato; non hanno, cioè, l'equivalente di **potuto** e **dovuto**. I tempi mancanti sono quindi espressi da verbi sostitutivi, in particolare *be able to* per *can* e *have to* per *must*.

Tuttavia, molti significati relativi al passato possono essere espressi con la seguente struttura.

Verbo modale + *have* + participio passato
letteralmente: *You **should have known**.*   *Dovresti averlo saputo.*   ↓   ***Avresti dovuto saperlo.***
letteralmente: *I **could have helped** you.*   *Potrei averti aiutato.*   ↓   ***Avrei potuto aiutarti.***
*They **shouldn't / ought not to have talked** so much.*   letteralmente: *Non dovrebbero aver parlato così tanto.*   ***Non avrebbero dovuto parlare*** *così tanto.*
*You **might have been** kinder to her.*   letteralmente: *Potresti essere stato più gentile con lei.*   ↓   ***Avresti potuto essere*** *più gentile con lei.*

Queste forme hanno generalmente un valore condizionale. Confronta le frasi seguenti:

***Could** you give me a lift to the station?*   ***Potresti** darmi un passaggio alla stazione?*

*I **could have given you** a lift to the station.*   ***Avrei potuto darti** un passaggio alla stazione.*

*You **should** accept that job. It is well paid.*   ***Dovresti** accettare quel lavoro. È ben retribuito.*

*You **should have accepted** that job.*   ***Avresti dovuto accettare** quel lavoro.*

PRACTICE

1 Riempi gli spazi con **should, shouldn't, should have** o **shouldn't have**, come richiede il senso, e con un verbo nel riquadro alla forma corretta.

use   come   ~~leave~~   comb   cycle   go   join   eat

1 It was freezing cold last night and now you've got a bad cough. You ......*shouldn't have left*...... your coat at home.

2 Your hair is looking very messy. You ....

3 Get some lights for your bicycle. You .... around town at night without lights.

4 Dawn missed the bus to school this morning. She .... to bed so late last night.

5 Hey, Frank! The concert was great. You .... !

6 I feel really sick after eating all those chocolates. I .... so many.

7 Look at that man! He .... his mobile phone in the car like that. It's dangerous!

8 Peter needs to lose weight. He .... a gym and do some exercise.

2 Sottolinea la forma verbale corretta.

1 You *didn't have to throw away* / <u>*shouldn't have thrown away*</u> that glass bottle. There's a recycling bank round the corner.

2 We knew that the concert would start late and that we *didn't need to hurry* / *needn't have hurried*.

3 Gary was in London last week. He *could have visited* / *may have visited* us.

4 David desperately needed the money and he knew that he would never get a better offer. He *had to accept* / *should have accepted* the contract.

5 The police *were able to keep* / *could have kept* a low profile at the demonstration, and this was appreciated by the demonstrators.

6 Darren *shouldn't have been* / *didn't need to be* so rude to the teacher. He's in real trouble now.

7 The concert was much too short. The musicians *should have played* / *must have played* for longer.

8 Erika *could have helped* / *had to help* her mother, but instead she went shopping with her friends.

3 Completa le frasi seguenti usando **could**, **couldn't**, **could have** o **couldn't have** e i verbi tra parentesi alla forma corretta.

1 **A** I didn't call you last night, because it was eleven o'clock by the time I got home.
B Oh, you ....could have called..... me at eleven. I usually go to bed much later than that. (*call*)

2 Mark .... the maths exam last June because he was ill so he's taking it next week. (*take*)

3 My little sister .... by the time she was four. (*swim*)

4 That .... Bill you saw. He doesn't live in Italy any more. (*be*)

5 You .... me while you were in Rome. Why didn't you? (*visit*)

6 Sally didn't send me an email last night because she .... (*log on*)

7 I .... to buy my flat without my parents' help. (*afford*)

8 Melanie .... very well at school if she worked harder. (*do*)

4 Abbina gli inizi delle frasi con le loro logiche conclusioni.

1 Ted will have to get out of work early if he wants to get to the station on time. ..c..

2 You should have booked the tickets by phone. It may be too late now. .....

3 Sam ought to look after his appearance more. He could be really attractive. .....

4 We might not be able to come to your sister's wedding. Our aunt's very ill. .....

5 I must get Carmen Consoli's new CD. It's great. .....

6 You needn't have come to get me. I could have walked home. .....

a Yes, I can't understand why he always wears those horrible T-shirts.

b Maybe you could just pop into the reception for half an hour. You don't need to dress up.

c He can't do that. They have to meet a deadline and so no one is allowed to leave before five.

d You don't need to buy it. You can download it. It's cheaper.

e You can only do that if you have a credit card.

f I thought you might be tired. Anyway, you oughtn't to walk around at night on your own.

ALL IN ONE REVISION

1 Riempi gli spazi in questa email con le parole e le espressioni elencate nel riquadro.

had   'll have   ~~must~~   should   needn't   didn't have   shouldn't

Dear Sarah

I **(1)** ......must.......... tell you about my weekend with my friend Erica who lives in Leeds. The journey wasn't easy because I **(2)** .... to change trains three times. But Erica lives near the station so I **(3)** .... to take a taxi or the bus to her flat. We spent all weekend chatting and shopping. You **(4)** .... come with me next time. You **(5)** .... spend every weekend studying. I need to study hard this week. If I don't pass my maths exam, I **(6)** .... to take it again. I want to visit Erica again next weekend. Why don't you come with me? You **(7)** .... decide yet. You can tell me on Friday.

2 Ascolterai due studentesse, Clare e Fiona, che parlano di un ragazzo di nome Danny. Prima di ascoltare, osserva l'immagine. Pensi che Danny sia seduto con sua sorella, la sua ragazza o sua madre?

....

3 Ascolta e verifica se avevi ragione.

2.8

4 Ascolta di nuovo e rispondi a queste domande.

2.9

1 Who does Clare think Danny is with at first? ....

2 Fiona doesn't agree. Why not? ....

3 What do the two girls decide to do? ....

4 Why doesn't Fiona want to say hello? ....

5 What do you think Fiona really feels about Danny? ....

5 Ascolta di nuovo e riempi gli spazi.

2.10

1 **Clare:** It ....*might be*.......... Danny.

2 **Clare:** She .... his mother.

3 **Fiona:** She .... his mother.

4 **Fiona:** He .... me.

5 **Fiona:** She .... his new girlfriend.

6 Rileggi le frasi dell'esercizio 5. In quali frasi la ragazza che parla:

1 sembra sicura che qualcosa sia vero? ....

2 pensa che qualcosa sia possibile, ma non è sicura? ....

7 Riscrivi queste frasi usando la forma corretta di *must*, *need*, *should* o *have to*.

1 I don't expect you to phone me before you come.
   You ....*needn't/don't need to/don't have to phone me before you come.*...............

2 It is essential for students to buy a good dictionary.
   Students ....

3 It was wrong of you to take money from my purse without asking.
   You ....

4 It's not fair that I do the washing-up on my own.
   You ....

5 Students aren't allowed to make too much noise in the canteen.
   Students ....

6 She turned the music down to avoid disturbing her neighbours but they'd gone out.
   She ....

7 I think she's wrong to make promises which she doesn't keep.
   She ....

8 You can give the tour guide a tip but it is not necessary.
   You ....

8 Abbina gli inizi delle frasi con le loro logiche conclusioni.

1	I shouldn't ..g..	**a**	wear a helmet when he's cycling on a busy road.
2	Need I	**b**	to take any money or is it free?
3	We don't need	**c**	to ask his boss before he leaves the office.
4	They needn't	**d**	take sandwiches with them because Jenny's cooking lunch.
5	He should	**e**	to send them our new address because they already have it.
6	Should you	**f**	fill in my application form now? I'm busy at the moment.
7	He needs	**g**	spend so much time playing computer games.
8	Do they need	**h**	carry that suitcase with your bad back?

9 Completa le frasi seguenti riguardo all'uomo nella figura usando alcune delle parole e delle espressioni elencate nel riquadro.

can't   could   couldn't   may   might   must   must

1 He ....may.............. be famous.
2 He .... be fit.
3 He .... be married.
4 He .... be disappointed.
5 He .... be Spanish.
6 He .... be an excellent tennis player.
7 He .... be a grandfather.

10 Leggi che cosa è successo durante una vacanza in campeggio.

> Two boys are camping with their families near a lake. One day they find an old boat and decide to row out to an uninhabited island. They explore the island until suddenly they realise it's getting dark. They run to find the boat, but it's gone.

Queste sono alcune delle cose che i genitori dicono quando i due ragazzi non tornano.

1 There can't be much to eat on the island.
2 Someone may have noticed them rowing across the lake.
3 They could be stuck there for days.
4 A fishing boat might see them.
5 They must have forgotten how late it was.
6 They must be getting scared.
7 There may be a cave or hut they can shelter in.
8 The boat could have sunk.
9 Someone may have taken the boat.
10 They can't have tied the boat up properly.

Scrivi il numero delle frasi accanto al loro significato, **a** o **b**.

a I feel certain about this. ...1...
b I think this is possible. ....

11 Per ogni coppia di frasi, completa la seconda in modo che il significato non cambi. **Usa la parola data senza modificarla**. Usa tra **due** e **cinque** parole compresa la parola data.

1   She was capable of running really fast when she was a child. **could**
    She ....*could run*.... really fast when she was a child.

2   Fortunately, Mum and Dad didn't make me go to my cousin's wedding. I don't enjoy that kind of occasion. **have**
    Fortunately, I .... to my cousin's wedding.

3   Henry told me that I was the best-looking girl that he knew, but perhaps he was joking. **may**
    Henry told me that I was the best-looking girl that he knew, but I think that he ....
    joking.

4   Did the man you saw have a red beard? If so, I'm certain it was Hamish. **must**
    Did the man you saw have a red beard? If so, it .... Hamish.

5   Everyone has their umbrellas up, so I assume that it is raining. **must**
    Everyone has their umbrellas up, so .... raining.

6   Copying CDs from the internet is illegal. **allowed**
    You .... copy CDs from the internet.

7   It was a sunny day and so it wasn't necessary to put up the marquee. **need**
    It was a sunny day and so they .... put up the marquee.

8   My library card has been missing for a week now. I think that it's been stolen. **may**
    My library card has been missing for a week now. It .... stolen.

9   I'm afraid that I probably can't come to your party on Friday. I've got my driving test the next morning. **able**
    I'm afraid that I am unlikely .... to your party on Friday.
    I've got my driving test the next morning.

10 It's a pity we didn't go to the concert. I've heard it was brilliant. **should**
    We .... to the concert. I've heard it was brilliant.

12 Traduci.

1   È molto tardi. Faremmo meglio a sbrigarci.

2   Peter lavora di sabato, ma potrebbe raggiungerci la domenica mattina.

3   Una collana di ambra! Grazie, nonna, ma davvero non avresti dovuto farmi un regalo così costoso!

4   Avresti dovuto aiutare tuo fratello a fare i compiti.

5   Non avresti dovuto dimenticare di spedire quella lettera. Sapevi che era urgente.

6   Avresti potuto dirmi che Alan e Kate si sono lasciati.

7   A Non riesco a trovare i miei occhiali. B Può darsi che tu li abbia messi nella borsa marrone.

8   Saresti dovuto venire con noi. Ci siamo divertiti tantissimo.

9   A Non avresti dovuto parlare in quel modo a tuo padre. B Lo so e mi dispiace. Mi sono scusato.
    Che altro posso fare?

10 Bob avrebbe potuto far domanda per quel lavoro. L'avrebbe ottenuto di sicuro.

IL PASSIVO

IL PASSIVO – INTRODUZIONE

Per trasformare una frase attiva in passiva sono necessari tre elementi.

Soggetto	**Verbo transitivo**	**Complemento oggetto**
Fleming	*discovered*	*penicillin.*

Soggetto	**Verbo passivo**	**Complemento d'agente**
Penicillin	**was** *discover***ed**	**by** *Fleming.*

Il complemento d'agente non viene espresso quando non è rilevante per la comprensione della frase oppure quando è indeterminato.

Soggetto	**Verbo transitivo**	**Complemento oggetto**
They	*cancelled*	*my flight.*

Soggetto	**Verbo passivo**	**Complemento d'agente**
My flight	**was** *cancel***led**	– .

15.1 IL PASSIVO: COME SI FORMA, QUANDO SI USA

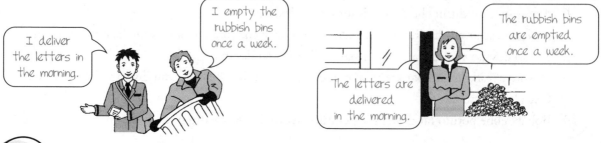

Il passivo si forma con l'ausiliare *to be* seguito dal **participio passato** del verbo.

L'ausiliare *to be* è coniugato allo stesso modo e allo stesso tempo del verbo della frase attiva.

	Forma attiva	Forma passiva	
Infinito presente	to catch	to be	
Infinito passato	to have caught	to have been	
Forma *-ing* presente	catching	being	
Forma *-ing* passata	having caught	having been	
Present continuous	am/are/is catching	am/are/is being	
Present simple	catch/catches	am/are/is	
Futuro con *will*	will catch	will be	
Futuro anteriore	will have caught	will have been	
Be going to	am/are/is going to catch	am/are/is going to be	**caught**
Present perfect	has/have caught	has/have been	
Past simple	caught	was/were	
Past continuous	was/were catching	was/were being	
Past perfect	had caught	had been	
Condizionale presente	would catch	would be	
Condizionale passato	would have caught	would have been	
Verbi modali	can/must/may… catch	can/must/may be	

Forma attiva

*The police officer **saw** the robber at the airport.*
*L'ufficiale di polizia **vide** il rapinatore all'aeroporto.*

*She's **following** him.*
*Lo **sta seguendo**.*

*She'll **catch** him soon.*
*Lo **catturerà** presto.*

Forma passiva

*The robber **was seen** at the airport.*
*Il rapinatore **fu visto** all'aeroporto.*

*He's **being followed**.*
*È **seguito** / **viene seguito**.*

*He'll **be caught** soon.*
***Sarà**/**Verrà catturato** presto.*

259

USI DEL PASSIVO

Il passivo viene usato spesso in inglese, sia nel parlato che nello scritto.

Si usa il passivo:

■ quando non sappiamo chi o che cosa ha compiuto l'azione.

*My bicycle's **been stolen**.* (= Someone has stolen my bicycle.)
*La mia bicicletta **è stata rubata**.* (= Qualcuno ha rubato la mia bicicletta.)
*The first tools **were made** in Africa two million years ago.*
*I primi utensili **furono fabbricati** in Africa due milioni di anni fa.*

■ quando si vuole mettere in risalto l'azione stessa piuttosto che chi l'ha compiuta.

*Income tax **was introduced** in England in 1798.*
*L'imposta sul reddito **fu introdotta** in Inghilterra nel 1798.*

■ quando l'autore dell'azione è ovvio oppure non è importante specificarlo.

*My train **was cancelled**.*	*Il mio treno **fu / è stato cancellato**.*
*The bridge **is being repaired**.*	*Il ponte **è in corso di riparazione**.*
*Letters **aren't delivered** on bank holidays.*	*La posta **non è consegnata** nei giorni di festa nazionale.*
*The thief's **been arrested**.*	*Il ladro **è stato arrestato**.*

IL PASSIVO DEI VERBI CON PREPOSIZIONE: *I WAS SENT FOR; THE BABY WAS LOOKED AFTER*

In inglese, a differenza che in italiano, la forma passiva è usata anche con i verbi che reggono una preposizione.

*They **sent for** the doctor immediately.*	→ *The doctor **was sent for** immediately.*
***Mandarono** a chiamare immediatamente il dottore.*	*Il dottore **fu mandato** a chiamare immediatamente.*
*Somebody has **to look after** the dog.*	→ *The dog has **to be looked after**.*
*Qualcuno deve **occuparsi** del cane.*	
*We must **write to** her.*	→ *She must **be written to**.*
*Dobbiamo **scriverle**.*	

Come si vede dagli esempi, la preposizione segue immediatamente il verbo da cui dipende.

IL COMPLEMENTO D'AGENTE: *BY*

Se è importante specificare **da chi** è stata compiuta l'azione, si usa la preposizione **by** + l'agente.

*The robber was seen **by the police officer**.*   *Il rapinatore fu visto **dall'ufficiale di polizia**.*

Nelle frasi interrogative la preposizione **by** è di norma collocata in fondo alla frase, dopo il verbo.

***Who** was A Christmas Carol written **by**?*	***Da chi** è stato scritto A Christmas Carol?*
***Who** were you invited **by**?*	***Da chi** sei stato invitato?*

260

IL 'SI' PASSIVANTE: *WHAT IS THIS CALLED?*

È importante notare che la costruzione passiva è comunemente usata in inglese per tradurre il 'si' passivante italiano.

*English **is spoken** in this hotel.*	*In questo albergo **si parla** inglese.*
*Sea urchins **are eaten** in this part of the country.*	*In questa zona **si mangiano** i ricci di mare.*
*What **is** this place **called**?*	*Come **si chiama** questo posto?*

PRACTICE

1 Abbina le azioni rappresentate in ciascuna figura con i nomi dei tempi dei verbi.

1 The house is being built.		**a** past simple passive
2 The house has been built.		**b** future perfect passive
3 The house was built in 1870.		**c** present continuous passive
4 The house is going to be built.		**d** 'going to' future passive
5 The house was being built in July 2008.		**e** past continuous passive
6 The house will have been built by 2014.		**f** present perfect simple passive

2 Osserva attentamente i verbi sottolineati in queste frasi. Indicali con **A** se sono attivi e con **P** se sono passivi.

1 I'm not allowed to drive my parents' car.

2 Our test was marked by the headteacher but our class teacher told us the results.

3 My brother is having a party tonight and you're invited.

4 The letters were sent to the wrong address and we never saw them.

261

5 This painting <u>will be finished</u> at the weekend and I <u>think</u> it'<u>ll be</u> good.

6 I <u>paid</u> the taxi driver before I <u>opened</u> the door.

7 Important visitors <u>expect</u> <u>to be met</u> at the airport.

8 If the house needs <u>to be cleaned</u>, I'<u>ll help</u> you.

3 Che cosa succede quando un cantante fa una tournée? Ci sono un sacco di cose da fare. Leggi questi appunti e scrivi delle frasi usando la forma passiva del *present simple*.

1	plan the tour	.The..tour..is..planned............................
2	book the plane tickets	....
3	send contracts to concert hall managers	....
4	reserve hotel rooms	....
5	design posters	....
6	hire musicians	....

4 Riempi gli spazi in questo articolo usando la forma passiva del *past simple*.

The singer Hywel Evans **(1)** ...was..educated.... (*educate*) in Wales. He **(2)** .... (*give*) the main part in a school play when he was ten. He **(3)** .... (*see*) by a theatre director and he and another boy **(4)** .... (*ask*) to sing in a TV advert. They **(5)** .... (*not pay*) much but they **(6)** .... (*hear*) by a record producer. Hywel's friend **(7)** .... (*ask*) to be in a musical. Hywel **(8)** .... (*not give*) a part in the musical, but he **(9)** .... (*invite*) to star in a film.

5 Per ogni coppia di frasi, completa la seconda in modo che il significato non cambi. **Usa non più di tre parole.**

(PET)

1 This shop is owned by my uncle. My uncle ....owns................. this shop.

2 Charles Dickens wrote this letter. This letter .... by Charles Dickens.

3 Teenagers don't visit the museum. The museum .... by teenagers.

4 Those emails were read by my boss! My boss .... those emails!

5 That text wasn't received by my mother. My mother .... that text.

6 This match will be watched by five million football fans. Five million football fans .... this match.

7 Bono wore these jeans. These jeans .... by Bono.

8 This music won't be played by disc jockeys. Disc jockeys .... this music.

6 Riempi gli spazi con la forma passiva corretta dei verbi tra parentesi.

1 Breakfast ....is..served.... (*serve*) at 7.30 every day except on Sundays.

2 Harry's scooter .... (*repair*) at the moment. It's at the mechanic's.

3 Our house .... (*build*) in the 1930s.

4 Norman had to share a room with his little brother while his bedroom .... (*redecorate*).

5 Jack .... (*offer*) a lot of money for his vintage motorbike, but he doesn't want to sell.

6 When our neighbours got back from their holidays they discovered that their house .... (*burgle*).

7 Acne has always been a problem for teenagers but there's a hope that a cure .... (*find*).

8 Seatbelts must .... (*fasten*) before take-off.

7 Trasforma queste frasi da attive a passive. Ometti il complemento d'agente se non è rilevante.

1 People of all ages can play this game. This game ...... *can be played by people of all ages.* ......

2 They are choosing the student representatives for the school year.

The student representatives for the school year ....

3 Do people speak English in Malta? .... in Malta?

4 The headteacher gave a warm welcome to the new English teacher.

The new English teacher ....

5 The festival organisers held the show in a tent because it was raining.

The show .... because it was raining.

6 The Swedish Academy of Arts and Sciences has awarded the Nobel Prize for Literature to six different Italian writers in the last 106 years.

Six different Italian writers .... in the last 106 years.

7 Hydrogen will power cars in the future. In the future cars ....

8 You must test dogs for rabies before customs officials allow them to enter the United Kingdom.

Dogs .... for rabies before they .... the United Kingdom.

8 Le frasi seguenti hanno tutte come soggetto un pronome personale o indefinito. Riscrivile alla forma passiva corretta.

1 They are serving dinner now. ...... *Dinner is being served now.* ......

2 They are opening a new nightclub in the city centre.

....

3 They don't accept credit cards in this restaurant.

....

4 Someone has stolen my MP3 player. ....

5 People will never accept those conditions. ....

6 Where do they make those DVD players? ....

7 They store the information in a database. ....

8 They are going to cut the cake at the end of the ceremony.

....

9 Tutte queste frasi contengono verbi seguiti da preposizione, che in italiano non possono essere resi passivi. In inglese sì! Riscrivile al passivo come nell'esempio.

1 My friend has already paid for the drinks. *The drinks have already been paid for by my friend.*

2 You can always rely on my brother for moral support.

....

3 Someone broke into John's car during the night. ....

4 A Polish woman looks after my grandmother. ....

5 They have shut down the best disco in town. ....

6 You must fill in the application form first. ....

7 They carried on their struggle for civil rights after their leader's death.

....

8 They will have cut down all the trees by next year. ....

15.2 IL PASSIVO DEI VERBI CON DUE OGGETTI: *I WAS TOLD; THEY WERE GIVEN*

Alcuni verbi attivi di uso comune, come *give*, *tell*, *ask*, *answer*, *send*, *show*, *teach*, *lend* e *offer*, possono essere seguiti da due oggetti, generalmente in questo ordine: il primo oggetto si riferisce a una persona e corrisponde al complemento di termine italiano, il secondo oggetto è il complemento oggetto vero e proprio.

Struttura A	Soggetto	Verbo attivo	1° oggetto/persona	2° oggetto/cosa
	The students	*gave*	*the teacher*	*a bunch of flowers.*
	Gli studenti	*regalarono*	***all'***insegnante	*un mazzo di fiori.*
	A witness	*gave*	*the police*	*some information.*
	Un testimone	*dette*	***alla*** *polizia*	*delle informazioni.*
	Mrs Walsh	*taught*	***me***	*English.*
	Mrs Walsh	***mi*** *ha insegnato*		*l'inglese.*

Tuttavia è possibile anche l'ordine seguente, che corrisponde alla struttura italiana.

Struttura B	Soggetto	Verbo attivo	1° oggetto/cosa	2° oggetto/persona
	The students	*gave*	*a bunch of flowers*	***to*** *the teacher.*
	A witness	*gave*	*some information*	***to*** *the police.*
	Mrs Walsh	*taught*	*English*	***to*** *me.*

Entrambe queste strutture possono essere rese passive.

Struttura A	Soggetto	Verbo passivo		
	The teacher	*was given*	*a bunch of flowers*	***by*** *the students.*
	The police	*were given*	*some information*	***by*** *a witness.*
	I	*was taught*	*English*	***by*** *Mrs Walsh.*

Struttura B	Soggetto	Verbo passivo		
	A bunch of flowers	*was given*	***to*** *the teacher*	***by*** *the students.*
	Some information	*was given*	***to*** *the police*	***by*** *a witness.*
	English	*was taught*	*(****to****) me*	***by*** *Mrs Walsh.*

PRACTICE

1 Riscrivi le frasi seguenti alla forma passiva, iniziando con la parola data.

   1 They asked him some difficult questions in the exam.

   He .... *was asked some difficult questions in the exam* ....

   2 They will pay us €50 to empty the garage.

   We ....

   3 Mr Brown teaches my brother English.

   My brother ....

   4 Museum officials give tourists information about the area.

   Information about the area ....

   5 Their trainer has shown the team a video of the opposition.

   A video of the opposition ....

   6 Children sometimes tell their parents lies.

   Parents ....

2 Volgi le frasi seguenti alla forma passiva più comunemente usata.

   1 The class gave Hilary some flowers. .... *Hilary was given some flowers by the class* ....

   2 Somebody sent Trevor an anonymous letter.

   ....

   3 Lenny's parents have promised him a scooter.

   ....

   4 The university has offered Paula a scholarship. ....

   5 Politicians never tell us the truth. ....

   6 They will give all the children a Christmas present.

   ....

   7 The examiners will explain the rules to the students.

   ....

   8 They will show the staff the latest technology.

   ....

15.3 *TO HAVE/GET SOMETHING DONE*

Quando chiediamo a qualcuno di **fare qualcosa per noi**, spesso usiamo la struttura: *to have +* *something* **+ participio passato**.

Di solito **non** è necessario indicare chi ha compiuto l'azione.

> *I **had** my hair **cut**.* (= the hairdresser cut my hair)
> *Mi **sono tagliata** i capelli.* (= me li ha tagliati il parrucchiere)

I'm having my kitchen painted. (= The decorator is painting my kitchen.)
Sto facendo ridipingere la cucina. (= L'imbianchino sta ridipingendo la cucina.)
They want to have their car fixed. (= They want the garage to fix their car.)
*Vogliono **farsi riparare** l'auto.* (= Vogliono che il meccanico ripari la loro auto.)
*The president **had** the car **taken** to the airport* (= by his driver).
*Il presidente **si fece portare** l'auto all'aeroporto* (= dal suo autista).

In contesti informali, talvolta si usa **get** al posto di **have**.

*I **got** my hair **cut**.* = *I **had** my hair **cut**.*

PRACTICE

1 Indica qual è il significato giusto, **a** o **b**, di ogni immagine.

a Angela is taking a photograph. ....
b Angela is having her photograph taken. ✓.

a Bill is shaving his head. ....
b Bill is having his head shaved. ....

a Jim is mending his scooter. ....
b Jim is having his scooter mended. ....

a Kevin is decorating his room. ....
b Kevin is having his room decorated. ....

a Silvia is piercing her ears. ....
b Silvia is having her ears pierced. ....

a Lucy is plaiting her hair. ....
b Lucy is having her hair plaited. ....

2 Formula delle frasi appropriate a queste situazioni usando la struttura **to have something done**, come nell'esempio.

1 The windows of my flat were dirty, but I didn't have time to clean them myself.

Yesterday, I .... had my windows cleaned ....

2 Tom has lost three bicycles this year. Each time someone has stolen them.

Tom ....

3 Jean can't see the board well at school. She should go to the optician's to see if she needs glasses.

Jean ....

4 My brother is getting married next week, but his suit is dirty. Now it's at the cleaner's.

My brother ....

5 Sometimes footballers get cramp in their legs and you see their trainers massaging them.

Sometimes you see footballers ....

6 Bob broke his right arm last week. Now his mother cuts his food up for him.

Bob ....

7 My computer got a virus last month. I took it back to the shop where the technician reformatted the hard disk.

I ....

8 Nancy took a lot of photographs on holiday, but she still hasn't taken them to be printed.

Nancy ....

3 Abbina le due metà della conversazione e riempi gli spazi con la forma corretta dei verbi tra parentesi.

1 I thought those chairs were broken.   ..*e*..

a I .... (*have/colour*).

2 Your bike's got a flat tyre!   ......

b Yes, you need .... (*have/take in*).

3 This carpet's filthy.   ......

c I can .... (*get/fix*) at the cycle shop.

4 What's happened to your hair?   ......

d I agree – we should .... (*get/redecorate*).

5 I don't like this room. It's too dark.   ......

e I've ..*had them mended*.......... (*have/mend*).

6 These jeans are much too loose.   ......

f At the garage. We .... (*have/service*) before we go away.

7 What a beautiful garden!   ......

g We must .... (*get/clean*).

8 Where's the car?   ......

h Thank you. We .... (*have/design*) by an expert.

4 Leggi la web page di questa cantante pop, in cui parla di come si prepara per un concerto. Riempi gli spazi con la forma corretta di **to have something done** e le parole tra parentesi.

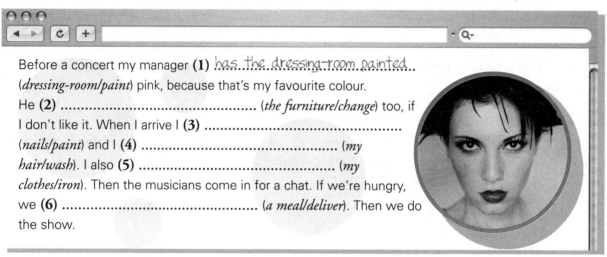

Before a concert my manager **(1)** <u>has the dressing-room painted</u> (*dressing-room/paint*) pink, because that's my favourite colour.

He **(2)** .... (*the furniture/change*) too, if I don't like it. When I arrive I **(3)** .... (*nails/paint*) and I **(4)** .... (*my hair/wash*). I also **(5)** .... (*my clothes/iron*). Then the musicians come in for a chat. If we're hungry, we **(6)** .... (*a meal/deliver*). Then we do the show.

5 Traduci.

1 Mia sorella si fa tagliare i capelli due volte all'anno.

2 Ho perso la chiave della porta d'ingresso. Dovrò farmi fare una chiave nuova.

3 Ogni quanto tempo ti fai revisionare l'auto?

4 Ho versato del caffè sulla mia camicia bianca. Devo farla lavare.

5 Quando hai intenzione di far ridipingere il tuo appartamento?

6 **A** Mi piacerebbe vedere le foto che hai fatto quando eri in vacanza. **B** Mi dispiace, ma non le ho ancora fatte stampare.

7 Devo far controllare i pneumatici della mia auto.

8 Jennifer si è fatta fare il piercing al naso.

ALL IN ONE REVISION

1 Alan sta parlando con la sua amica Maria di una serie di film di fantascienza. <u>Sottolinea</u> le parole che pensi sentirai.

alien	army	earth	experiment
flower	garage	human	planet
	scientist	spaceship	

NORMAN STARMAN III

2 Ascolta e controlla se avevi ragione. Metti un segno a fianco delle parole che senti.

2.11

Does Maria decide to see the film?

3 Ascolta di nuovo e completa le frasi seguenti.

2.12

1 The first two Starman films ....were made......... about three years ago.

2 The main part .... to a different actor.

3 He .... to their planet.

4 But the spaceship .... when they land although they .... , luckily.

5 Norman .... by the army.

6 The aliens .... , I guess, and then they'll go back their planet again.

4 Rileggi le risposte che hai dato nell'esercizio 3. Sono tutti verbi passivi.

How do we make the passive in the present? ....
the past? ....
the future? ....

5 Formula domande relative alle parole in **neretto** usando una forma passiva.

1 My **grandmother** painted that picture.
Pardon? ....Who was that picture painted by................................. ?

2 **Gary** sent that text message.
What did you say? Who .... ?

3 The teacher told us to write about ***Pride and Prejudice***.
Sorry? What .... ?

4 **Sammy** organised that holiday.
What did you say? Who .... ?

5 A witch turned her into **a mouse**.
Pardon? What .... ?

6 **Nick Hornby** wrote the original book.
Sorry? Who .... ?

7 A courier is delivering **the contract** this afternoon.
Pardon? What .... ?

8 They've blamed Bob **for the accident**.
Sorry? What .... ?

9 **A shark** attacked Christine's brother while he was surfing in Australia.
What was that? What .... ?

10 Thieves had planned to break into **the castle**.
Pardon? Where .... ?

269

6 Scegli la frase corretta.

1 **a** The children wanted to be allowed to stay up late and see the fireworks. ✔

   b The children wanted to been allowed to stay up late and see the fireworks.

2 **a** Our flight was delaying by fog and we missed our connection.

   b Our flight was delayed by fog and we missed our connection.

3 **a** Lauren was sulking because she hadn't been invited to Ralph's party.

   b Lauren was sulking because she wasn't been invited to Ralph's party.

4 **a** By the time we arrived at the market, the best fruit had be sold.

   b By the time we arrived at the market, the best fruit had been sold.

5 **a** While the meal was being prepared we had a drink on the terrace.

   b While the meal was been prepared we had a drink on the terrace.

6 **a** The new library will be opened by the Mayor next Saturday.

   b The new library will be open by the Mayor next Saturday.

7 **a** The rock star was sent a chocolate cake by one of his fans.

   b The rock star was sent a chocolate cake to one of his fans.

7 Riempi gli spazi con la forma passiva corretta dei verbi tra parentesi.

1 A government minister ....was found........ (*find*) guilty of fraud yesterday.

2 It was a lovely surprise to find all the washing-up .... (*do*) while I was asleep.

3 These souvenirs .... (*make*) by children from the local school.

4 I didn't come here in order .... (*make*) a fool of!

5 The votes .... (*count*) right now and we should know the result before midnight.

6 This parcel appears .... (*open*) before it .... (*delivered*).

7 As he .... (*sack*) from his previous job, he found it hard to get another.

8 The judges still have to decide which design .... (*award*) the top prize.

8 Questo articolo descrive come viene fatto un cartone animato. Riempi gli spazi con il passivo dei verbi tra parentesi.

Animation is a way of making a moving picture from many unmoving images. The images
(1) .....are put...... (*put*) together one after another, and then **(2)** .... (*play*) at a fast speed to give the appearance of movement. Animations **(3)** .... (*create*) by an animator. The following steps can **(4)** .... (*follow*). First the idea for a story has to
(5) .... (*find*). A simple example might be a piece of meat **(6)** .... (*leave*) on the table and while the owner is doing something else, it **(7)** .... (*steal*) by the cat or the dog. The characters **(8)** .... (*design*) either first on paper and then **(9)** ....
(*scan*) on to the computer, or they can be designed directly onto the computer using a programme like

Photoshop. Then they **(10)** .... (*colour in*). Many animations are created using Flash, a computer programme. The main positions of the characters and objects in the story **(11)** .... (*programme*) and the intermediary positions can **(12)** .... (*produce*) by the computer programme. In this way time **(13)** .... (*save*). The time for the movements must **(14)** .... (*set*) and if there is dialogue or music, it must **(15)** .... (*integrate*) into the cartoon timeline. Time and patience **(16)** .... (*require*) for the creation of a cartoon, even with the help of the latest technology, but it is well worth it for the satisfaction that **(17)** .... (*feel*) by the animator once it **(18)** .... (*complete*).

9 Leggi questo articolo pubblicato sul *Cybernian News*.

CYBERNIAN NEWS

22 October 3004

| Home | News | Entertainment | Sport | Business | Video Report | Weather | Going Out | TV Guide |

Victory for Cybernia

The victorious Cybernian Inter-galactic Forces report:

Yesterday we invaded Planet Upstart with a large force. We have completely crushed the year-old rebellion there. Our space ships have destroyed ninety per cent of the Upstart space fleet. A special Cybernian task force landed near the central communications building and captured it without difficulty. We immediately broadcast a message to the population announcing that we had liberated them from the illegal Upstart government and we called on them to cooperate with the new government of their planet. We have arrested the rebel leaders and we are taking them back to Cybernia where the government will put them on trial.

Riempi gli spazi con la forma passiva dei verbi usati nell'articolo precedente.

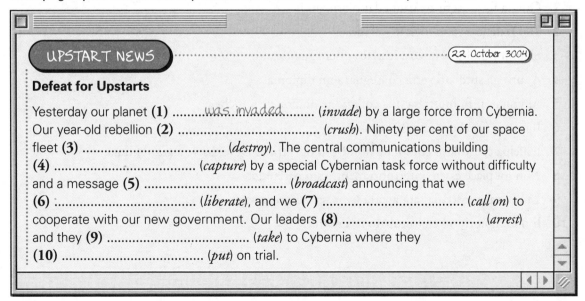

UPSTART NEWS .... 22 October 3004

Defeat for Upstarts

Yesterday our planet **(1)** ....was invaded......... (*invade*) by a large force from Cybernia. Our year-old rebellion **(2)** .... (*crush*). Ninety per cent of our space fleet **(3)** .... (*destroy*). The central communications building **(4)** .... (*capture*) by a special Cybernian task force without difficulty and a message **(5)** .... (*broadcast*) announcing that we **(6)** .... (*liberate*), and we **(7)** .... (*call on*) to cooperate with our new government. Our leaders **(8)** .... (*arrest*) and they **(9)** .... (*take*) to Cybernia where they **(10)** .... (*put*) on trial.

10 Leggi questo articolo di giornale e riempi gli spazi con la forma passiva corretta dei verbi tra parentesi.

The following story appeared in British newspapers the day after the famous 'Great Train Robbery' in 1963.

1963: TRAIN ROBBERS MAKE OFF WITH MILLIONS

The Glasgow to Euston mail train **(1)** has been ambushed (*ambush*) by thieves, and thousands of pounds **(2)** .... (*steal*). Banks estimate over £2m **(3)** .... (*lose*) in used, untraceable banknotes in the biggest ever raid on a British train.

The Post Office train had run every night for 125 years until last night when it **(4)** .... (*bring*) to a halt by a red light at 3.15 in Buckinghamshire. Driver Jack Mills, 58, **(5)** .... (*detain*) in hospital with head injuries after **(6)** .... (*knock*) unconscious. It **(7)** .... (*think*) that the raiders were masked and armed with sticks and iron bars. But most of the 75 mail sorters working on the train were unaware of the 20-minute incident as the engine and front two carriages of the train **(8)** ....

(*detach*) and **(9)** .... (*drive*) to Bridego Bridge a mile away. There the carriages **(10)** .... (*break into*), the four postal workers inside having **(11)** .... (*tie up*), and 120 mail and money bags **(12)** .... (*load*) into a lorry waiting on the road nearby.

Investigators arrived on the scene, near Cheddington, in the early hours of the morning and found that signals **(13)** .... (*interfere with*) and telephone wires **(14)** .... (*cut*). The Detective Superintendent of Buckinghamshire CID said: 'This was obviously a brilliantly planned operation.' Rewards totalling a record £260,000 **(15)** .... already .... (*offer*) by insurers, banks and the Post Office for information leading to the arrest and conviction of the gang.

11 Traduci.

1 Questa fortezza fu costruita dai Normanni.

2 Tuo fratello è stato invitato alla festa?

3 Sharon è molto vanitosa: le piace essere guardata.

4 A tutti gli studenti verrà consegnato un diploma.

5 Ai visitatori fu mostrata una collezione di monete antiche.

6 Il museo fu inaugurato 20 anni fa.

7 La felpa che volevo comprare non è più in vetrina. Deve essere stata venduta.

8 Non mi piace essere interrotto mentre sto parlando.

9 La nuova autostrada sarà aperta la prossima primavera.

10 Il mio motorino è stato rubato ieri notte.

IL DISCORSO INDIRETTO

16.1 Verbo introduttivo al passato

16.2 Futuro con *will* e frasi condizionali nel discorso indiretto

16.3 Verbo introduttivo al presente

16.4 Elementi della frase che cambiano:
pronomi ed espressioni di tempo e di luogo

16.5 *Say* e *tell*

16.6 Altri verbi usati per introdurre il discorso indiretto:
answer, remind, invite, order…; suggest

16.7 Domande indirette

IL DISCORSO INDIRETTO – INTRODUZIONE

Nella vita di tutti i giorni capita continuamente di riferire conversazioni, messaggi, opinioni, ecc. senza ripetere parola per parola quello che è stato detto, ma mantenendo inalterato il significato globale. Per fare questo, sono necessarie alcune trasformazioni morfosintattiche che riguardano i pronomi personali, i tempi verbali e i riferimenti di spazio e di tempo.

Discorso diretto: parole originali	*I'll call you tomorrow.*	***Ti chiamo domani.***
Discorso indiretto: parole riferite	*Will said that he'd call me the next day.* ***Will disse che mi avrebbe chiamato il giorno dopo/seguente.***	

La congiunzione dichiarativa ***that*** può essere omessa:

*The sun **is shining**.* → *He said (that) the sun **was shining**.*

16.1 VERBO INTRODUTTIVO AL PASSATO

Una conversazione viene di solito riferita in un momento successivo rispetto a quando è avvenuta: il tempo che introduce il discorso indiretto è quindi generalmente al **passato**, per esempio *said*.

La madre di Nick torna a casa inaspettatamente e si trova nel bel mezzo di una festicciola che Nick ha organizzato tra amici in sua assenza. Secondo te, che cosa sta dicendo la madre di Nick?

Più tardi, Nick riferisce all'amico Will quello che è successo. Nella colonna a sinistra ci sono le parole precise che Nick e sua madre hanno detto; nella colonna a destra le frasi che Nick usa per riferire la conversazione al suo amico Will.

I **tempi verbali cambiano** in questo modo:

Present simple → **Past simple**

*The house **is** dirty.*
La casa **è** sporca.

*My mother said (that) the house **was** dirty.*
Mia madre ha detto che la casa **era** sporca.

Present continuous → **Past continuous**

*I'm **expecting** visitors.*
Sto aspettando visite.

*She said (that) she **was expecting** visitors.*
Ha detto che **stava aspettando** visite.

Past simple → **Past perfect**

*I **washed** the car.*
Ho lavato la macchina.

*I said (that) I'd/I **had washed** the car.*
Io ho detto che **avevo lavato** la macchina.

Present perfect → **Past perfect**

*You **haven't tidied** the house.*
Non **hai messo in ordine** la casa.

*She said (that) I **hadn't tidied** the house.*
Ha detto che non **avevo riordinato** la casa.

am going to → **was going to**

*I'm **going to** keep your pocket money.*
Ti tratterrò la paghetta. / **Ho intenzione di trattenerti** la paghetta.

*She said (that) she **was going to** keep my pocket money.*
Ha detto che **mi avrebbe trattenuto** la paghetta. / Ha detto che **aveva intenzione di trattenermi** la paghetta.

will → **would**

*I'll/I **will** wash up.*
Laverò i piatti.

*I said (that) I'd/I **would** wash up.*
Ho detto che **avrei lavato** i piatti.

can → **could**

*You **can't** go out.*
Non puoi uscire.

*She said (that) I **couldn't** go out.*
Ha detto che **non potevo** uscire.

FORME VERBALI CHE NON CAMBIANO

▨ Come in italiano, il *past perfect,* o trapassato indicativo, e il **condizionale passato** rimangono **invariati** nel passaggio tra discorso diretto e discorso indiretto.

*I **hadn't expected** her to come home early.* →

Non mi aspettavo / **Non avevo previsto** che tornasse a casa presto.

*He said he **hadn't expected** her to come home early.*

Ha detto che **non si aspettava** / **non aveva previsto** che tornasse a casa presto.

*I'd/I **would have helped** you clean up if I had known.* →
Ti avrei aiutato a ripulire se avessi saputo.

*He said he'd/he **would have helped** me clean up if he had known.*
Ha detto che mi **avrebbe aiutato** a ripulire se avesse saputo.

▨ **Rimangono** inoltre **invariati** i seguenti verbi, anche se il verbo dichiarativo che introduce il discorso indiretto è al passato: *could, should, might, ought to* e *used to*.

*I **couldn't** understand.* → *He said that he **couldn't** understand.*
Non riuscivo a capire. Ha detto che **non riusciva** a capire.

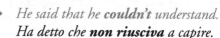

*You **should** clean the whole house.* → *She said I **should** clean the whole house.*
***Dovresti** pulire tutta la casa.*   *Ha detto che **dovrei** pulire tutta la casa.*
*Your friends **should** help.* → *She said my friends **should** help.*
*I tuoi amici **dovrebbero** aiutarti.*   *Ha detto che i miei amici **dovrebbero** aiutarmi.*

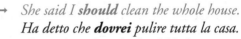
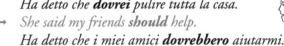

*Your mother **might** change her mind.* → *He said my mother **might** change her mind.*
*Tua madre **potrebbe** cambiare idea.*   *Ha detto che mia madre **potrebbe** cambiare idea.*

*You **ought to** apologise.* → *He said that I **ought to** apologise.*
***Dovresti** chiederle scusa.*   *Ha detto che **dovrei** chiederle scusa.*

*You **used to be** so thoughtful.* → *She said I **used to be** so thoughtful.*
***Eri** così premuroso.*   *Ha detto che **ero** così premuroso, nel passato.*

■ Il verbo *must* può rimanere invariato o essere sostituito da ***had to***. La forma ***had to*** è più comune.

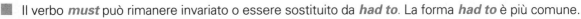

*You **must** stay at home.* → *She said I **must/had to** stay at home.*
***Devi** rimanere a casa.*   *Ha detto che **dovevo** rimanere a casa.*

🔊 Tuttavia si usa **sempre** *must*, **non** *had to*, quando il discorso indiretto è:

■ una **proibizione**.

*You **mustn't** do that again.* → *She said I **mustn't** do that again.*
***Non devi** farlo di nuovo.*   *Ha detto che **non devo/non dovevo** farlo di nuovo.*

■ una **deduzione**.

*Your mother **must** be furious to react like this.* → *He said my mother **must** be furious to react like that.*
*Tua madre **deve** essere furibonda   *Ha detto che mia madre **doveva** essere*
per reagire in questo modo.   *furibonda per reagire in quel modo.*

PRACTICE

1 Abbina le frasi usate da Nick mentre riferisce quello che è successo all'amico (discorso indiretto) con le parole precise che Nick e sua madre hanno detto (discorso diretto).

1 She said I couldn't go out. ..*e*..
2 She said she was expecting visitors. .....
3 She said the house was dirty and untidy. .....
4 I said I would wash up. .....
5 She said that I should clean the whole house! .....
6 I said that I had washed the car the week before. .....
7 She said that I had to stay at home last night. .....
8 She said that she was going to keep my pocket money this week. .....
9 She said I hadn't tidied the house and I hadn't washed up. .....

a The house is dirty and untidy.
b I washed the car last week.
c You should clean the whole house!
d You haven't tidied the house and you haven't washed up.
e You can't go out!
f You must stay at home tonight.
g I'll wash up.
h I'm expecting visitors.
i I'm going to keep your pocket money this week.

275

2 Completa la seconda frase in modo che abbia lo stesso significato della prima.

1 He said he was hungry. (I ....'m.......... hungry.

2 They said they were going to be late. (We .... late.

3 She said she had never flown in a helicopter before. (I .... in a helicopter before.

4 They said they'd bought a new computer. (We .... a new computer.

5 He said she should try harder. (You .... try harder.

6 She said she was waiting for her friend. (I .... for my friend.

7 He said he loved cheese. (I .... cheese.

8 She said she would send me an email. (I .... you an email.

3 Una fila di persone è in attesa davanti a un nuovo ristorante. Riferisci che cosa hanno detto.

1 'I'll come back later.' He said he ......would....... come back later.

2 'We can't get a table.' They said they .... a table.

3 'We're going to wait.' They said they ....

4 'I've never eaten Thai food before.' He said he .... Thai food before.

5 'The restaurant is too small.' She said the restaurant .... too small.

6 'There won't be a free table for at least an hour.' They said there .... a free table for at least an hour.

7 'We'd expected to get a table.' They said they .... to get a table.

8 'We're going home.' They said they .... home.

4 Stai parlando al telefono con Luke, un amico. Ecco quello che ti dice.

1 'I've given up my job.'

2 'I can easily find another one.'

3 'I'm going to travel round Africa.'

4 'I lived there as a child.'

5 'I might get a part-time job there.'

6 'I'm packing my bag.'

7 'I'm really excited.'

8 'I'll be away for a year.'

9 'I may stay longer.'

10 'You could come too.'

Quando la telefonata è finita, racconti a un altro amico quello che Luke ha detto.

1 He said he ....had given up his job..

2 He said he ....

3 He said he ....

4 He said he ....

5 He said he ....

6 He said he ....

7   He said he ....

8   He said he ....

9   He said he ....

10   He said I ....

16.2   FUTURO CON *WILL* E FRASI CONDIZIONALI NEL DISCORSO INDIRETTO

Come si può vedere dalle regole enunciate in **16.1** (pag. 274), i cambiamenti verbali nel passaggio da discorso diretto a discorso indiretto corrispondono generalmente a quanto avviene in italiano, a eccezione del **futuro con** *will* e del **condizionale presente**.

■ In italiano un futuro semplice del discorso diretto si trasforma in un condizionale passato. In inglese, invece, si trasforma in un condizionale presente, così:

will → *would*

I'll (will) help you. →	*He said he would help me.*
Ti aiuterò.	*Disse che mi avrebbe aiutato.*
Sue will be in London on Sunday. →	*He said Sue would be in London on Sunday.*
Sue sarà a Londra domenica.	*Disse che Sue sarebbe stata a Londra domenica.*

Il condizionale presente nel discorso indiretto indica che l'azione non era ancora avvenuta nel momento in cui si stava parlando ed era ancora possibile: si tratta quindi di un'azione **futura** rispetto a quel momento del passato.

■ Per lo stesso motivo, **il condizionale presente rimane invariato in inglese**, mentre in italiano si trasforma in un condizionale passato.

I would like to learn another language. →	*He said he would like to learn another language.*
Mi piacerebbe imparare un'altra lingua.	*Ha detto che gli sarebbe piaciuto imparare un'altra lingua.*
I would buy a new car if I had enough money. →	*He said he would buy a new car if he had enough money.*
Comprerei un'auto nuova se avessi abbastanza denaro.	*Disse che avrebbe comprato un'auto nuova se avesse avuto abbastanza denaro.*

PRACTICE

1 Tutte queste frasi si riferiscono a un'azione futura o condizionale. Trasformale in discorso indiretto.

1 'I'll give you £10 if you wash the car.'

She said ....*(that) she would give me £10 if I washed the car*.................

2 'I'll be sixteen next birthday.'

He said ....

3 My brother said: 'I'll give you back your DVD soon.'

My brother said ....

4 'I would leave home if I could find a job.'

She said ....

5 'We'll be in Spain in two days.'

She said we ....

6 'I'd ask Susan out if I thought she'd accept.'

He said ....

7 'I'd like to go swimming later.'

I said ....'

8 'You'll be late if you don't hurry up.'

She said ....

2 Traduci.

1 Il mio amico disse che sarebbero sicuramente venuti a prendermi all'aeroporto.

2 Jack promise che sarebbe venuto alla mia festa.

3 Mio cugino era sicuro che gli avrebbero dato un aumento di stipendio.

4 Kate disse che le sarebbe piaciuto venire con noi al cinema.

5 Christy era stanca di aspettare. Non avrebbe aspettato un minuto di più.

6 Mia sorella disse che avrebbe incontrato i suoi amici alle sette.

7 Laura disse che sarebbe tornata subito.

8 Ero sicura che mi avresti chiamato.

9 I miei genitori dissero che mi avrebbero comprato il motorino se avessi preso dei buoni voti.

10 Gary disse che mi avrebbe dato un passaggio.

11 Mary disse che sarebbe partita tra un paio d'ore.

12 Pensavo che mi sarei divertita in vacanza, ma sfortunatamente mi sono ammalata e ho trascorso tutto il tempo a letto.

16.3 VERBO INTRODUTTIVO AL PRESENTE

Quando il verbo che introduce il discorso indiretto è al presente, i tempi della frase originale **non cambiano**.

Amy: *'I've missed the bus so I'll be a bit late.'* → Amy **says** she**'s missed** the bus so she**'ll be** late.
Amy: *'**Ho perso** l'autobus così **farò** un po' tardi.'*   Amy **dice** che **ha perso** l'autobus così **farà** un po' tardi.

■ A volte, tuttavia, si possono mantenere gli stessi tempi della frase originale anche se il verbo dichiarativo è al passato. Come in italiano, questo avviene se la situazione di cui si è parlato **è ancora vera**.

Bob: *'I **have** three sisters.'* → Bob **said** he **has** three sisters. = Bob **said** he **had** three sisters.
Galileo discovered that the Earth   *Galileo scoprì che la Terra **gira/girava***
goes/went around the Sun.   *intorno al Sole.*

278

Carlo: *'I'm getting married in June.'*   Carlo: *'**Mi sposo** a giugno.'*

Se riferiamo a qualcuno **prima di giugno** quello che Carlo ha detto possiamo usare ambedue i tempi.

*Carlo said he **is getting** married in June.*   Or   *Carlo said he **was getting** married in June.*

PRACTICE

1 La zia Petunia è anziana e parla a voce bassissima. Il dottore non riesce a capire quello che gli sta dicendo, così tu devi ripetere a voce alta ogni sua frase.

1 Aunt Petunia: 'I've got a bad sore throat.'

Aunt Petunia says ......*she's got a bad sore throat.*....................................

2 Aunt Petunia: 'I went out in the rain.'

Aunt Petunia says ....

3 Aunt Petunia: 'I'm going dancing.'

Aunt Petunia says ....

4 Aunt Petunia: 'I want something that will make me feel better quickly.'

Aunt Petunia says ....

5 Aunt Petunia: 'My eyesight isn't as good as it was.'

Aunt Petunia says ....

6 Aunt Petunia: 'I'm going to get some really trendy new glasses.'

Aunt Petunia says ....

7 Aunt Petunia: 'I'd like to join a walking club to stay fit and healthy.'

Aunt Petunia says ....

8 Aunt Petunia: 'Soon I'll need a doctor's certificate saying that I'm still fit to drive.'

Aunt Petunia says ....

2 Traduci.

1 John dice che l'Irlanda è meno costosa dell'Inghilterra.

2 Di' a tua sorella che passerò a prenderla alle otto.

3 Stella dice che non ha visto Robert ieri sera.

4 Mio fratello dice che quel ristorante è molto buono.

5 Debbie dice che c'è un programma interessante in TV stasera.

6 Kevin dice che non può uscire perché ha un esame importante domani.

16.4   ELEMENTI DELLA FRASE CHE CAMBIANO: PRONOMI ED ESPRESSIONI DI TEMPO E DI LUOGO

Come in italiano, anche in inglese di solito è necessario cambiare i **pronomi personali** e gli **aggettivi possessivi** quando riferiamo quello che qualcuno ha detto.

Discorso diretto	Discorso indiretto
I	he – she
you	them – us
my	his – her
we	they
our	their

*'I can't go out with **you** because **my** mother's taken **my** money.'* → *He said **he** couldn't go out with **them** because **his** mother had taken **his** money.*

*'Non posso uscire con **voi** perché **mia** madre ha confiscato **i miei** soldi.'* → ***Ha** detto che non poteva uscire con **loro** perché **sua** madre aveva confiscato **i suoi** soldi.*

Anche i **riferimenti di tempo e di luogo** cambiano.

Discorso diretto	Discorso indiretto
now	then
today	that day
tomorrow	the next/following day
next week	the following week
tonight	that night
yesterday	the day before
last week	the week before
here	there
this	that

*'I often buy bread **here** in **this** shop.'* → *She said she often bought bread **there** in **that** shop.*
*'Compro spesso il pane **qui** in **questo** negozio.'* → *Disse che comprava spesso il pane **là** in **quel** negozio.*

*'I saw him **here** yesterday.'* → *She said that she had seen him **there** the day before.*
*'L'ho visto **qui** ieri.'* → *Disse che l'aveva visto **lì** il giorno prima.*

PRACTICE

1 Leggi questo rapporto scritto da un poliziotto e poi riempi gli spazi nella conversazione sotto.

◆ POLICE

A woman called the police station about a car parked near her flat. I went to the street to talk to her.

She told me that she had seen the car several times before. She said <u>she</u>'d seen it <u>there the week before</u> for the first time. But <u>the day before</u> two men had got out. They'd looked at all the houses in <u>that</u> street. I asked her if I could phone <u>her</u> <u>that evening</u> or <u>the next day</u> to ask some more questions. She agreed.

Policeman: Can (**1**) ....you......... tell me about the car please?

Woman: (**2**) .... 've seen it several times before. (**3**) .... saw it
(**4**) .... (**5**) .... for the first time. But (**6**) .... two
men got out. They looked at all the houses in (**7**) .... street.

Policeman: Can I phone (**8**) .... (**9**) .... or (**10**) .... to ask some
more questions?

Woman: Of course.

2 Leggi quello che Sally ha detto al telefono ad Anne-Marie, poi completa
la email che Anne-Marie ha scritto a suo fratello più tardi.

'I was at a Coldplay concert yesterday. I climbed onto the stage at the end.
Chris Martin kissed my hand so I'll never wash it again! I'm going to get
their new CD tomorrow. I can't think about anything except their music! I've
read everything on their website. Perhaps I might write them a letter.'

Hi

Sally phoned me last weekend and said (**1**) ....she'd been... at a Coldplay concert
(**2**) .... She said that (**3**) .... onto the stage at the end and Chris
Martin (**4**) .... hand so (**5**) .... it again. She said (**6**) ....
their new CD (**7**) .... because (**8**) .... about anything except their
music!
She said (**9**) .... everything on their website, and perhaps (**10**) ....
them a letter. Isn't she crazy?!

CU

Anne-Marie

16.5   *SAY* E *TELL*

I verbi più comunemente usati per introdurre il discorso indiretto sono *say* e *tell*. Entrambi significano
dire, ma presentano delle importanti differenze grammaticali.

Say	*Tell*
■ **non** è necessariamente seguito dal complemento di termine.	■ è **sempre** seguito dal complemento di termine; il complemento di termine **non** è mai introdotto da *to*.
*He **said** (that) they would win.* ***Disse** che avrebbero vinto.*	*He **told me** (that) they would win.* (**Non** ~~He told that~~; **Non** ~~He told to me~~) ***Mi disse** che avrebbero vinto.*
■ se il complemento di termine è espresso, *say* è immediatamente seguito da *to*.	■ *tell* significa anche **raccontare**.
*He **said to me** (that) they would win.* (**Non** ~~He said me~~) ***Mi disse** che avrebbero vinto.*	*When I was a child, my mother used to **tell me** the stories of Winnie the Pooh.* *Quando ero piccolo, mia madre **mi raccontava** sempre le storie di Winnie the Pooh.*

CASI PARTICOLARI CON *TELL*

Nelle espressioni seguenti si usa **tell** anche in mancanza del complemento di termine.

tell the time	*dire l'ora*
tell the truth	*dire la verità*
tell a lie	*dire una bugia*
tell a joke/story	*raccontare una barzelletta/storia*

*I don't think he's **telling the truth**.*   *Non penso che **stia dicendo la verità**.*

PRACTICE

1 Sottolinea il verbo corretto, **said** o **told**.

1 My cousin <u>said</u> / *told* he'd like to come and stay with us.

2 Sarah *said* / *told* us she'd enjoyed her holiday.

3 Craig *said* / *told* goodbye to us and left the room.

4 When I invited them they *said* / *told* they were busy.

5 I *said* / *told* Frances that I was going to watch television all evening.

6 The shop assistant *said* / *told* that the shop was closed on Wednesdays.

7 She *said* / *told* she hated cooking.

8 The bus driver *said* / *told* the passengers the bus had broken down.

2 Completa le frasi seguenti con **said** o **told**.

1 Mandy ......said...... she wanted to go on holiday with me.

2 Walter .... us a very funny joke yesterday.

3 Lucy .... her boyfriend that she didn't want to go out with him any longer.

4 The children loved it when you .... them stories.

5 My mother .... us to always do our best in everything.

6 Melanie .... she was going to England for the summer.

7 Giuliano .... to me that he'd like to invite me to dinner.

8 I .... Giuliano that his cooking was excellent.

3 Traduci.

1 Thea mi disse che era stanca.

2 Gary disse che abitava in un piccolo appartamento vicino a Regents Park.

3 Gli dissi che non potevo aiutarlo.

4 Chi ti ha detto che sarei arrivato stasera?

5 Jenny mi ha detto che non le piace la carne.

6 Non puoi fidarti di Fred. Dice un sacco di bugie.

16.6   ALTRI VERBI USATI PER INTRODURRE IL DISCORSO INDIRETTO: *ANSWER, REMIND, INVITE, ORDER...; SUGGEST*

Say e *tell* non sono gli unici verbi che si possono usare per riferire quello che qualcuno ha detto. I verbi che introducono il discorso indiretto possono avere costruzioni diverse.

Alcuni verbi si comportano come *tell*. Sono immediatamente seguiti dal complemento indiretto senza *to* e dalla congiunzione *that*.

remind + *someone* + *that*
rammentare/ricordare a qualcuno che

persuade + *someone* + *that*
persuadere qualcuno che

inform + *someone* + *that*
informare qualcuno che

'Don't forget to collect that parcel at the post office.'
'Non dimenticarti di andare a ritirare quel pacchetto all'ufficio postale.'
→   *She* **reminded me (that)** *I had to collect a parcel at the post office.*
    Mi **ha ricordato che** *dovevo andare a ritirare un pacchetto all'ufficio postale.*

'I'm taking a day off next week.'   *'Prenderò un giorno di permesso la settimana prossima.'*
→   *I* **informed my colleagues (that)** *I was taking a day off the following week.*
    Ho **informato i miei colleghi che** *avrei preso un giorno di permesso la settimana successiva.*

■   Alcuni di verbi, come *answer* e *reply*, sono di norma seguiti da *that* e tendono a non esprimere il complemento di termine.

I asked him if he wanted a lift but he **answered that** *he'd rather walk.*
Gli chiesi se voleva un passaggio ma mi **rispose che** *preferiva camminare.*

■   Altri verbi, come *agree*, *explain* e *mention*, sono di norma seguiti da *that* e di solito specificano il complemento indiretto.

'You're right, that's the best thing to do.'   *'Hai ragione, è la cosa migliore da fare.'*
→   *He* **agreed** *(with me)* **that** *that was the best thing to do.*
    Fu **d'accordo** *con me* **che** *era la cosa migliore da fare.*

'You have to use Lagrange's theorem.'   *'Devi usare il teorema di Lagrange.'*
→   *He* **explained** *(to me)* **that** *I had to use Lagrange's theorem.*
    Mi **spiegò che** *dovevo usare il teorema di Lagrange.*

■   **Ordini**, **richieste**, **offerte**, **consigli** e **promesse** sono generalmente introdotti da verbi seguiti da *to* + **infinito**. Questi verbi includono *tell*, *ask*, *invite*, *order*, *remind*, *promise*, *advise* e *offer*.

'Be careful.'	→	*I* **told** *him* **to be** *careful.*
'Sii prudente.'		*Gli* **dissi di essere** *prudente.*
'Would you like to have lunch with me?'	→	*I* **invited** *him* **to have** *lunch with me.*
'Vuoi pranzare con me?'		*Lo* **invitai a pranzare** *con me.*
'Write a new article!'	→	*He* **ordered** *me* **to write** *a new article.*
'Scrivi un nuovo articolo!'		*Mi* **ordinò di scrivere** *un nuovo articolo.*

283

'I'll be a good leader.'	→	*He **promised to be** a good leader.*
'Sarò un buon leader.'		***Promise di essere** un buon capo.*
'You should put on warmer clothes.'	→	*He **advised us to put on** warmer clothes.*
'Dovreste mettervi dei vestiti più pesanti.'		***Ci consigliò di metterci** vestiti più pesanti.*
'We could help you.'	→	*They **offered to help** me.*
'Potremmo aiutarti.'		***Si offrirono** di aiutarmi.*

Quando la frase riportata è **negativa**, gli stessi verbi sono seguiti da **not to** + **infinito**.

'Please don't smoke.'	→	*I **asked** her **not to** smoke.*
'Non fumare, per favore.'		*Le **chiesi di non** fumare.*
'Please don't take any photographs.'	→	*He **told** us **not to** take any photographs.*
'Per favore non fate fotografie.'		*Ci **disse di non** fare fotografie.*

Il verbo **suggest non** può essere seguito da **to** + infinito, ma si costruisce in due modi diversi.

suggest that	*'**You** look tired. Why don't **you** rest for a while?'* *I **suggested that he** rested for a while.* *I **suggested that he (should)** rest for a while.*	Il suggerimento/consiglio riguarda **una persona diversa** da colui che parla.
suggest + -ing	*'Shall **we** / Why don't **we** go to the cinema?'* *He **suggested going** to the cinema.*	Il suggerimento/consiglio riguarda **anche colui che parla**.

PRACTICE

1 Alcuni studenti stanno per fare una gita in barca a vela. L'insegnante dice loro di fare queste cose. Completa le frasi seguenti.

1 'Get up early.'   He told them ....to get up early.....

2 'Have breakfast.'   He advised them ....

3 'Don't be late.'   He ordered them ....

4 'Wear a hat.'   He told them ....

5 'Don't wear leather shoes.'   He told them ....

6 'Bring a packed lunch.'   He reminded them ....

7 'Don't bring expensive cameras.'   He warned them ....

8 'Don't fall in!'   He told them ....

2 Leggi nella colonna a sinistra quello che alcune persone hanno detto, poi completa le frasi sulla destra con un verbo nel riquadro. Puoi usare alcuni verbi due volte.

asked   advised   invited   ordered   reminded

1 'Could you fill in a form please?'   He .....asked....... me to fill in a form.

2 'Remember to take your keys.'   She .... them to take their keys.

3 'Tidy your room immediately!'   She .... them to tidy their room.

4 'Would you like to watch a DVD with me?'   She .... him to watch a DVD with her.

5 'Don't forget to phone Jim.'   She .... him to phone Jim.

6 'Would you walk more slowly please?'   He .... her to walk more slowly.

7 'Don't move.'   He .... them not to move.

3 Completa le frasi seguenti al discorso indiretto.

1 'Can you be quiet after ten o'clock?'
Our next-door neighbour has asked .... *us to be quiet after ten o'clock* ....

2 'Don't forget to take some suncream.'
Their mother reminded ....

3 'I think you should spend less time on the computer.'
Bill's father suggested ....

4 'You're right. We can't spend the whole holiday sunbathing.'
Judy agreed ....

5 'Would you like to come out with us, Janet?'
Cora invited ....

6 'You'd better ask your parents first.'
Nick advised ....

7 'Tidy up your room immediately!'
Mum ordered ....

8 'I'll study hard and I'll help at home.'
Andrew promised ....

16.7   DOMANDE INDIRETTE

Le domande indirette hanno una struttura diversa da quella delle domande dirette e generalmente

■ non hanno il punto interrogativo alla fine;

■ **non** hanno l'ausiliare *do/does* e *did*;

■ spostano il verbo principale **dopo** il soggetto. Presentano quindi lo stesso *word order* delle frasi dichiarative.

Domanda diretta	Domanda indiretta
A *How do you feel?*	**A** Verbo introduttivo + *wh- word* + soggetto + verbo *I asked her how she felt.* *Le chiesi come si sentiva.*
B *Are you tired?*	**B** Verbo introduttivo + *if/whether* + soggetto + verbo *I asked her if/whether she felt tired.* *Le chiesi se era stanca.*

285

Come si vede dalla tabella, ci sono due tipi di domande:

A domande che iniziano con **wh- word**: **which**, **when**, **what**, **who**, **why**, **where**, **how**, **how long**;

B domande **yes/no**.

Le domande che iniziano con **wh- word** mantengono la **wh- word** anche nella forma indiretta.

> '*What's* the weather like?' → *I asked her **what** the weather **was** like.*
> (**Non** ~~I asked her **what was** the weather like.~~)
>
> '*Com'è il tempo?*' *Le chiesi **come era** il tempo.*

Le domande **yes/no** nella forma indiretta sono introdotte da **if/whether**.

> '*Is the weather good?*' → *I asked her **if/whether** the weather **was** good.*
> '*Il tempo **è** buono?*' *Le chiesi **se** il tempo **era** buono.*
> '***Do** you know my sister?*' → *I asked him **if/whether** he knew my sister.*
> (**Non** ~~if/whether did he know~~)
>
> '*Conosci mia sorella?*' *Gli chiesi **se** conosceva mia sorella.*

DOMANDE INDIRETTE: FORMA DI CORTESIA

Si usa generalmente la forma interrogativa indiretta quando si vuole chiedere un'informazione in modo cortese.

***Can you tell me** when the match starts?* (**Non** ~~Can you tell me when does the match start?~~)
***Può dirmi** quando inizia la partita?*

***I'd like to know** if there's a flight to Australia next week.*
***Vorrei sapere** se c'è un volo per l'Australia la settimana prossima.*

***Could you tell me** where you live?* (**Non** ~~Could you tell me where do you live?~~)
***Potrebbe dirmi** dove abita?*

Nella forma di cortesia **non si cambia** il tempo del verbo. La forma di cortesia può essere a sua volta introdotta da una domanda: in questo caso mantiene il punto interrogativo alla fine.

***Can you tell me** what time the next train leaves?*
***Può dirmi** a che ora parte il prossimo treno?*

PRACTICE

1 In un programma televisivo, il pubblico fa delle domande a una cantante di nome Dina. Ecco come le domande sono riportate sul sito web del programma. Scrivi le domande originali fatte dal pubblico.

> ► Kim asked Dina when she would record her next CD.
> ► Miguel asked Dina if she could play any instruments.
> ► Louisa asked Dina if she was going to make a film.
> ► Thomas asked Dina which countries she'd visited.
> ► Olga asked Dina if she sang with other people.
>
> ► George asked Dina why she had become a singer.
> ► Lauren asked Dina how many CDs she had recorded.
> ► Ned asked Dina if she was planning any trips.
> ► Cristina asked Dina what her favourite CD was.
> ► Olivia asked Dina if she felt nervous on stage.

1 Kim: '........*When will you record your next CD*............ ?'

2 Miguel: '.. ?'

3 Louisa: '.. ?'

4 Thomas: '.. ?'

5 Olga: '.. ?'

6 George: '.. ?'

7 Lauren: '.. ?'

8 Ned: '.. ?'

9 Cristina: '.. ?'

10 Olivia: '.. ?'

2 Alcuni turisti stanno facendo delle domande a una guida turistica. Non sono molto cortesi. Riscrivi le loro domande in forma cortese.

1 'What will we eat tonight?'   I'd like to know ....*what we'll eat tonight*........

2 'Is there a swimming pool?'   Can you tell me ....

3 'Does this city have underground trains?' Can you tell me ....

4 'How long are we staying here?'   I'd like to know ....

5 'Are we going on a river trip?'   I'd like to know ....

6 'Where is the nearest bank?'   Can you tell me ....

7 'Can the hotel change my room?'   I'd like to know ....

8 'When does it get dark?'   Can you tell me ....

3 Hai fatto domanda per lavorare in un campo estivo per bambini. Quando incontri l'organizzatore, lui ti fa queste domande:

1 Are you married?

2 How old are you?

3 Which university are you studying at?

4 Where do you come from?

5 Have you worked with children before?

6 What sports do you play?

7 Will you work for at least two months?

8 Can you start immediately?

9 Do you need accommodation?

10 Would you like any more information?

> **Work abroad**
> We are looking for enthusiastic and lively young people to work in a children's holiday camp over the summer.

Un tuo amico di nome Miguel ha intenzione di fare domanda per lavorare nello stesso campo estivo. Completa la lettera seguente, dicendogli quali domande ti sono state fatte nel colloquio.

Dear Miguel

  Good luck with the job application! These are the things the organiser asked me about – he'll probably ask you the same sorts of questions.

  He asked me **(1)** ....if I was married.................. . He wanted to know **(2)** ...., which university **(3)** .... at and where **(4)** .... Then he asked **(5)** .... with children before and what sports **(6)** ....

  He wanted to know **(7)** .... for at least two months and **(8)** .... immediately. He asked **(9)** .... accommodation and wondered **(10)** .... any more information.

ALL IN ONE REVISION

1 Un giornalista di nome Tim ha scritto un servizio giornalistico su un campione di calcio, Joe Chapman. Il capo di Tim ha scritto il titolo. Secondo te, l'articolo corrisponde al titolo?

CHAPMAN: THE GIRLFRIENDS, THE TV CAREER, THE MONEY

Tim Donnelly finds out about Joe Chapman's life away from the football field.

Last season Joe Chapman scored more goals than any other player and he's become one of our star players. But where were the goals on Saturday in the away match? There weren't any. This is because he hurt his knee in training and isn't fully fit. So what plans does Joe have? He's had offers to join other teams but isn't interested. He wants to see United win the cup this year for the third time.

2 Ascolterai Tim parlare dell'articolo che ha scritto. Perché il suo capo è arrabbiato?

2.13

3 Ascolta di nuovo e metti un segno accanto alle domande che Tim ha effettivamente chiesto.

2.14

1 Have you got a new girlfriend?

2 Why didn't you score any goals on Saturday? ✔

3 Who were you with at that nightclub?

4 Does your mother always watch your games?

5 Did you argue with the new manager?

6 How long are you going to stay with the team?

7 What do you do in your free time?

8 When will we see your TV programme?

9 How much do you earn from adverts?

10 Will your team win the cup?

4 Riferisci quello che queste persone hanno detto, usando il verbo fra parentesi al *past simple.*

1 Leah said: 'Let's go out for a pizza.'

Leah suggested going out for a pizza... (*suggest*)

2 Bill said to Tracy: 'Would you give me a lift to the station?'

.... (*ask*)

3 Susan said to Sam: 'We're going to eat in this restaurant tomorrow evening.'

.... (*tell*)

4 Hilary said to John: 'You ought to take a holiday because it might do you good.'

.... (*tell*)

5 The doctor said to Peter: 'How do you feel today?'

.... (*ask*)

6 The teacher said to the class: 'Do you understand this grammar point?'

.... (*ask*)

7 Mandy said to her boyfriend: 'Come to the seaside with me and my family.'

.... (*invite*)

8 Mandy's boyfriend said: 'I don't think I would enjoy a week by the sea with your family.'

.... (*reply*)

5 Il tuo aereo è appena atterrato all'aeroporto di Stansted. Una signorina che lavora per un'agenzia di ricerche di mercato ti chiede gentilmente se può farti alcune domande. Le informazioni che vuol sapere sono riassunte nel seguente questionario. In che modo la signorina ti chiede quelle informazioni?

1 Could you tell me what your full name is, please?

2 ....

3 ....

4 ....

5 ....

6 ....

7 ....

8 ....

9 ....

10 ....

Customer satisfaction Questionnaire

1. Full name

2. Nationality

3. Date of birth

4. Occupation

5. Do you often fly to Stansted?

6. What company do you fly with?

7. Reason for travelling:

☐ tourism ☐ work ☐ study

8. Opinion of safety standards

9. Are you satisfied with the service?

10. Any criticisms of the airline?

289

6 Abbina gli inizi delle frasi con le loro logiche conclusioni.

1 She told ..c..   a I could help my neighbour mend his car.

2 My sister asked ......   b whether my sister could give me a lift.

3 I said ......   c me she couldn't afford to come to the theatre.

4 My parents said ......   d to me, 'You shouldn't watch so much TV.'

5 I wanted to know ......   e if I wanted to go on holiday with her.

6 I told ......   f the dentist that Thursday was the only day I was free.

7 Un insegnante sta parlando con Andy, uno studente. Più tardi, Andy racconta a un amico quello che l'insegnante gli ha detto. Completa le sue frasi.

You need to work harder.

You could do well.

Do you study every evening?

What time do you go to bed?

You won't get good marks.

You spend too much time with your friends.

Have you decided on a career yet?

1 He said ....*I needed to work harder.*...........................

2 He told ....

3 He wanted to know ....

4 He wondered ....

5 He warned ....

6 He complained ....

7 He asked ....

8 Leggi che cosa è successo a Suzie l'altro giorno, poi scrivi la conversazione che ha effettivamente avuto con la signora seduta accanto a lei in autobus.

I travel to college on the same bus every day. The other day when I got on the bus I realised that I had left my purse at home and didn't have the money for the bus fare. But the woman sitting behind me told me not to worry because she would lend me some money. She said the same thing had happened to her the day before. I asked her what she had done. She said someone had lent her the fare and she was going to give it back that day on the bus, so she was happy to do the same for me. She told me I could give the money back to her the following day. I thanked her very much and told her I was very glad she was there.

Woman: ....*Don't worry. I'll lend you some money*..............................

....

Suzie: ....

Woman: ....

....

....

Suzie: ....

9 Traduci.

1 La mia insegnante mi ha consigliato di fare un corso di inglese in Inghilterra.

2 I miei genitori mi hanno detto di tornare a casa prima di mezzanotte.

3 Jenny chiese alla sua amica dove aveva comprato quel maglione bianco.

4 Alan chiese a suo padre se poteva passare a prenderlo a scuola.

5 Bob mi chiese se volevo uscire con lui il sabato successivo.

6 Jack vuole sapere se sei pronto.

7 Scusi, può dirmi dov'è la stazione?

8 Non so se mia sorella ha finito di leggere il libro che le hai prestato.

9 Chiesi a Kate se abitava ancora a Bristol.

10 Michael chiese a Jen perché non lo aveva chiamato la sera prima.

INFINITO E FORMA -*ING*

17.1	Infinito come soggetto: -*ing*
17.2	La forma -*ing* e l'infinito italiano; Verbo + preposizione + -*ing*: *Thank you for coming*
17.3	*Go/come* + -*ing*
17.4	Infinito di scopo: *I'm studying to be a doctor*
17.5	Verbi + *to* infinito: *I decided to go*
17.6	Verbi + -*ing*: *I enjoy drawing*
17.7	Verbi + *to*/-*ing*
17.8	*Make* e *let*
17.9	Verbi + -*ing* o infinito senza *to*: *I watched them playing/play*
17.10	Aggettivi + *to* infinito: *difficult to say*
17.11	Costruzione oggettiva: *want / would like someone to do*

INFINITO E FORMA -*ING* – INTRODUZIONE

L'infinito italiano può essere tradotto in inglese in tre modi diversi: infinito **con** *to*, infinito **senza** *to* e forma -*ing*. Quest'ultima corrisponde anche al gerundio e al participio presente.

*I want **to dance**.*	*Voglio **ballare**.*
*Can you **dance**?*	*Sai **ballare**?*
*I like **dancing**.*	*Mi piace **ballare**.*

Quale forma verbale si usa per rendere l'infinito italiano dipende da vari fattori: il tipo di verbo che lo regge, se l'infinito è preceduto da una preposizione e se l'infinito ha funzione di soggetto oppure no.

17.1   INFINITO COME SOGGETTO: -*ING*

Quando l'infinito è il **soggetto della frase**, e ha quindi funzione di sostantivo, si usa generalmente la forma -*ing*.

***Running** is good exercise.*	***Correre** (= **la corsa**) è un buon esercizio fisico.*

La forma -*ing* può essere seguita da un nome.

***Running a marathon** is good exercise.*	***Correre la maratona** è un buon esercizio fisico.*
***Playing tennis** is one of my favourite activities.*	***Giocare a tennis** è una delle mie attività preferite.*

La forma -*ing* e *no* -*ing* si legge spesso su cartelli stradali e avvisi scritti per segnalare un divieto.

***Parking** is not allowed.*	***Parcheggiare** (= **il parcheggio**) non è consentito.*
***No talking** except on business.*	***Divieto di parlare** eccetto per motivi di lavoro.*

PRACTICE

1 Completa i cartelli in modo che abbiano lo stesso significato di queste frasi. Usa la forma -*ing* e aggiungi tutte le parole necessarie.

1 Only employees can park here.

No parking.
EXCEPT FOR EMPLOYEES

2 You aren't allowed to smoke.

NO ....

3 You are forbidden to eat or drink in the library.

....
in the library

4 You must not cycle on this path.

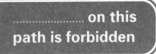

.... on this path is forbidden

5 Do not talk to the driver when the bus is moving.

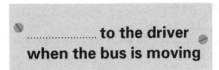

.... to the driver when the bus is moving

6 Do not play games on school computers.

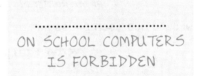

....
ON SCHOOL COMPUTERS IS FORBIDDEN

2 Riscrivi le frasi seguenti in modo che il significato non cambi. Inizia ogni frase con la forma -*ing*.

1 I feel more cheerful when I wear bright colours.
Wearing bright colours makes me feel more cheerful.....................................

2 We are not allowed to send text messages during lessons.
....

3 It is dangerous to walk around the city alone at night.
....

4 I am frightened when I fly. ....

5 All he wants to do is play his guitar. ....

6 It is wrong to cheat in exams. ....

3 Traduci.

1 Ascoltare musica classica è davvero rilassante.

2 Noleggiare un DVD è meno costoso che andare al cinema.

3 Fare errori è normale quando si impara una lingua straniera.

4 Dividere un appartamento con altre persone può essere difficile.

5 Il nuoto è il mio sport preferito.

17.2   LA FORMA -*ING* E L'INFINITO ITALIANO; VERBO + PREPOSIZIONE + -*ING*: *THANK YOU FOR COMING*

Quando il verbo all'infinito è immediatamente preceduto da una preposizione si usa la forma -*ing*.

*She can work for hours at the computer **without taking** a break.*
*Riesce a lavorare al computer per ore **senza fare** un'interruzione.*

*I use my computer **for downloading** music.*
*Uso il computer **per scaricare** musica.*

*Instead **of walking**, you could go by bicycle.*
*Invece **di camminare**, potresti andare in bicicletta.*

BY + -ING

Anche la preposizione **by** è seguita dalla forma -*ing*. Tuttavia, a differenza delle altre preposizioni, in italiano questa struttura corrisponde a un gerundio con valore strumentale e non a un infinito.

*We can book the hotel **by filling** in this form online.*
*Possiamo prenotare l'albergo **riempiendo** questo modulo online.*

*You can improve your pronunciation **by listening** to pop songs.*
*Puoi migliorare la tua pronuncia **ascoltando** canzoni pop.*

Alcuni verbi sono quasi sempre seguiti da una preposizione specifica.

verbo + preposizione + complemento

We enquired   about   our reservation.
Ci informammo   sulla   nostra prenotazione.

Se, invece che da un sostantivo, la preposizione è seguita da un verbo, questo si coniuga alla forma -*ing*. Anche in questo caso, la forma -*ing* corrisponde di norma all'**infinito italiano**.

Verbo		+ preposizione	+ -ing
apologise for	*They **apologised***	*for*	*start**ing** without me.*
scusarsi per/di	*Si **scusarono***	**per**	**aver iniziato** senza di me.
approve of	*She doesn't **approve***	*of*	*arriv**ing** late.*
approvare / essere a favore di	*Lei è **contraria***	**ad**	**arrivare** in ritardo.
enquire about	*We **enquired***	*about*	*book**ing** a room.*
informarsi su	*Ci **informammo***	**su come**	**prenotare** una stanza.
insist on	*My boss **insists***	*on*	*not hav**ing** plants in the office.*
insistere, ostinarsi a	*Il mio capo **insiste***	**a**	*non **volere** piante in ufficio.*
look forward to	*I'm really **looking forward***	*to*	*meet**ing** him.*
non vedere l'ora di / aspettare con impazienza	*Non vedo l'ora*	**di**	**conoscerlo.**
succeed in	*Did you **succeed***	*in*	*find**ing** accommodation?*
riuscire a	*Sei **riuscito***	**a**	**trovare** un alloggio?
think of	*I'm **thinking***	*of*	*buy**ing** a new computer.*
pensare di	*Sto **pensando***	**di**	**comprare** un nuovo computer.

Altri verbi hanno la seguente costruzione: **verbo** + *someone* + **preposizione** + *-ing*. Tra i più comuni ci sono:

Verbo		+ *someone*	preposizione	+ *-ing*
accuse of	*They* ***accused***	*the girl*	*of*	*taking the parcel.*
accusare di	**Accusarono**	**la ragazza**	**di**	**aver preso** *il pacchetto.*
congratulate on	*He* ***congratulated***	*me*	*on*	*passing the exam.*
congratularsi per	*Si è* **congratulato** *con*	**me**	**per**	**aver passato** *l'esame.*
forgive for	*She can't* ***forgive***	*that man*	*for*	*telling all those lies.*
perdonare per	*Non può* **perdonare**	**quell'uomo**	**per**	**aver detto** *tutte quelle bugie.*
prevent from	*I tried to* ***prevent***	*the boy*	*from*	*falling down the stairs.*
impedire di/che	*Cercai di* **impedire che**	**il ragazzo**	**–**	**cadesse** *giù dalle scale.*
suspect of	*I* ***suspect***	*her*	*of*	*being dishonest.*
sospettare di/che	**La sospetto**	**–**	**di**	**essere** *disonesta.*
thank for	*I* ***thanked***	*Brad*	*for*	*bringing me the books.*
ringraziare di/per	*Ho* **ringraziato**	**Brad**	**per**	**avermi** *portato i libri.*

Come si vede dagli esempi, in alcuni casi la forma *-ing* può corrispondere

■ all'**infinito passato** italiano.

*She thanked me **for helping** her.*   *Mi ringraziò di **averla aiutata**.*
*They apologised **for starting** without me.*   *Si scusarono per **aver iniziato** senza di me.*

■ al **congiuntivo imperfetto**.

*I tried to **prevent** the boy **from falling**.*   *Cercai di **impedire che** il ragazzo **cadesse**.*

BEFORE, AFTER, WHEN, WHILE, SINCE + -ING

Le congiunzioni *before* = prima / prima di / prima che; *after* = dopo / dopo di / dopo che; *when* = quando; *while* = mentre e *since* = da quando introducono una subordinata temporale. Sono seguite dalla forma *-ing* quando il soggetto delle due frasi è lo stesso.

***Before** leaving the room, I turned the computer off.* (= **I** turned the computer off. **I** left the room.)
***Prima di lasciare** la stanza spensi il computer.* (= **Io** spensi il computer. **Io** lasciai la stanza.)

*I dropped my passport **when getting** off the train.*
(= **I** got off the train and **I** dropped the passport at the same time.)
*Ho fatto cadere il passaporto **quando sono sceso** dal treno.*
(= Sono sceso dal treno e ho fatto cadere il passaporto allo stesso tempo.)

*I found this website **while looking** for photographs for my history project.*
*Ho trovato questo sito web **mentre cercavo** delle fotografie per il mio progetto di storia.*

*I haven't had a pleasant day **since joining** that company.*
*Non ho più avuto un giorno piacevole **da quando ho cominciato a lavorare** per quella ditta.*

Per una trattazione completa delle subordinate temporali, vedi *Unit* **23.6**.

PRACTICE

1 Completa le frasi seguenti usando le preposizioni nel riquadro.
Alcune preposizioni possono essere usate più di una volta. | of   on   in   from   to   for |

1 He insisted ....*on*........ paying for the drinks.

2 She was accused .... cheating during the maths exam.

3 The fine did not stop Bruno .... speeding again.

4 She'd like to go travelling for a year instead .... looking for a job straight away.

5 Henry succeeded .... passing his driving test the first time he took it.

6 My parents insist .... me being home by midnight.

7 The man thanked me .... finding his wallet.

8 Gill is looking forward .... going to New Zealand next year.

2 Abbina gli inizi delle frasi con le loro logiche conclusioni.

1 The footballer succeeded ..*f*..

2 Bill thanked his godmother .....

3 The headteacher congratulated me .....

4 Faisal never apologised .....

5 Harry is thinking .....

6 The teachers prevented the students .....

7 Helen suspected her friend .....

8 My mother doesn't approve .....

a on winning a scholarship to university.

b for forgetting my birthday.

c from copying during the exam.

d of lying about her family.

e of teenagers having tattoos.

f in heading the ball into the goal.

g for paying for his trip around the world.

h of working on a conservation project.

3 Completa le frasi che descrivono quello che è accaduto in ogni vignetta, usando i verbi tra parentesi.

1 She congratulated Eric ......*on winning the cup*.......... . (*win*)

2 He prevented .... (*come in*)

3 She insisted .... (*help*)

4 He thanked .... (*help*)

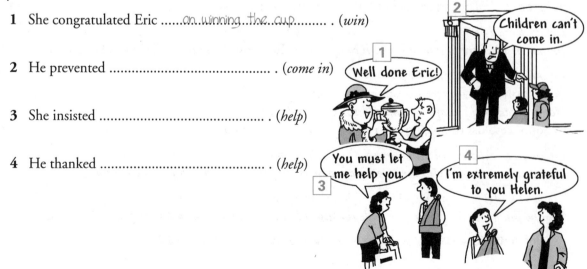

5 Sue apologised .... (*break*)

6 He forgave .... (*break*)

7 They succeeded .... (*pass*)

8 She asked .... (*help*)

5 Oh, I'm sorry.

6 It doesn't matter Sue.

7 We've passed!

8 Please help me!

---

4 Collega ogni coppia di frasi usando la parola tra parentesi + **-ing**.

1 Use the kitchen. Clear the table. (*after*) .... Clear the table after using the kitchen ....

2 Check the address. Post the parcel. (*before*) ....

3 Read the instructions. Connect the mouse to the keyboard. (*before*)

....

4 Ask the price. Book seats for the concert. (*when*)

....

5 Pass your exam. Take a holiday. (*after*) ....

17.3 GO/COME + -ING

Si usa il verbo **go** seguito dalla forma **-ing** per parlare di alcuni sport e attività del tempo libero, come:

	walking	**andare a camminare**
	camping	**fare campeggio / andare in tenda**
	swimming	**andare a nuotare**
go	*shopping*	**andare a fare compere**
	sailing	**andare in barca a vela**
	dancing	**andare a ballare**

*Can we **go walking** there?*   *Possiamo **andare a camminare** là?*

Quando invitiamo qualcuno a unirsi a noi in queste attività, si usa il verbo **come** + **-ing**:

*Would you like to **come swimming** with us?*   *Vuoi **venire a nuotare** con noi?*

297

PRACTICE

1 Completa questa email con le parole e le espressioni nel riquadro.

after eating	before going	being	by emailing	for texting	shopping	since starting
	studying	swimming	without dieting			

Dear Parissa

How are you? I'm fine now the school holiday has started.

(1) ...*Being*......... at home is great because **(2)** .... is horrible when the weather is hot.
Could we meet some time soon? We can go **(3)** .... and have lunch together.
And then, **(4)** .... , we can see a film or something. Perhaps you'd like to come
(5) .... with me at the new pool. I go there almost every day.

(6) .... to that pool, I didn't really like swimming, but it's really great, with slides and
waves and so on. And the really good news is that I've lost two kilos **(7)** .... to swim
regularly. And I've done it **(8)** .... !

Let me know which day is best for you **(9)** .... me. Or you can text me. I've got a new
mobile and I can use it **(10)** ....

I look forward to getting your email. Love Abby

17.4   INFINITO DI SCOPO: *I'M STUDYING TO BE A DOCTOR*

Per tradurre una frase finale, che indica **lo scopo** di un'azione, si usa di norma **to** + **infinito**.

*I'm going to France **to learn French**.*   *Vado in Francia **per imparare** il francese.*
(**Non** ~~for to learn~~ **Non** ~~for learning~~)

*He stopped the car **to look** at the view.*   *Fermò la macchina **per guardare** il panorama.*

***To switch off**, press the blue button.*   ***Per spegnere**, premi il pulsante blu.*

■ Per esprimere scopo, si può usare anche **in order to** e **so as to**. Queste due forme sono più
comuni quando la frase finale è negativa: **in order not to** e **so as not to**.

*Bob turned down the music **in order not**   *Bob abbassò la musica **per non disturbare** i vicini.*
to disturb his neighbours.*

*They spoke quietly **so as not to wake** the baby.*   *Parlarono a bassa voce **per non svegliare** il bambino.*

PRACTICE

1 Completa le frasi seguenti scegliendo il verbo adatto dal riquadro.

remind	put on	forget	warn	book	make	write	celebrate

1 Jen graduated with a first class degree. She is throwing a party ....*to celebrate*...

2 Renata went into the changing room .... her bikini.

3 Bill and Darren logged on .... some tickets for the theatre.

4 Vivian phoned her psychotherapist in order .... an appointment.

5 Gary phoned his mother .... her he was going to be late.

6 Sally sat down at the computer .... an email.

7 Ronald sent his girlfriend a message .... her where they were meeting.

8 I often watch films in the original language so as .... my English.

2 Riordina queste parole in modo da formare frasi di senso compiuto.

1 post / my / stamps / buy / I / sister / to / some / to / office / sent / the / .

I sent my sister to the post office to buy some stamps. ....

2 is / Harry / his / please / to / hard / parents / studying / .

....

3 money / petrol / father / gave / some / some / to / him / John's / buy / .

....

4 early / not / train / so / got / as / up / miss / Lorraine / to / the / .

....

5 order / have / way / eat / in / to / the / let's / on / something / to / stop / .

....

6 to / you / your / book / buy / improve / this / English / should / .

....

17.5   VERBI + *TO* INFINITO: *I DECIDED TO GO*

Alcuni verbi di uso comune sono seguiti da *to* + **infinito**.

(can't) afford agree* aim appear arrange* attempt choose decide* demand* deserve fail hope* learn manage neglect offer omit plan prepare pretend* promise* refuse seem tend threaten* (can't) wait wish	***to* + infinito**

*I **can't afford to** buy an amber necklace.*

***Non posso permettermi** di comprare una collana d'ambra.*

*If you **decide to** come, just give me a ring.*
***Do you hope to** sell your old car?*

*Se **decidi di** venire, chiamami.*
***Speri di** vendere la tua vecchia auto?*

Ricorda che l'infinito negativo si forma con *not to* + la forma base del verbo.

*They decided **not to come**.*
*They agreed **not to tell him**.*

*Hanno deciso **di non venire**.*
*Furono d'accordo **di non dirglielo**.*

299

■ I verbi contrassegnati da * nella tabella precedente possono anche essere seguiti da **that** e frase dichiarativa, con lo stesso significato.

They **promised to** come. = They **promised that** they would come.
Promisero di venire. = **Promisero che** sarebbero venuti.

■ I verbi seguenti, che richiedono **to** + **infinito**, sono **sempre** seguiti da un complemento diretto.

advise	encourage	force	invite	order		
persuade	remind	teach	tell	warn	someone	*to* + infinito

Her father **taught her to play** tennis.   Suo padre **le insegnò a giocare** a tennis.
I **advise students to buy** a monolingual dictionary.   **Consiglio agli studenti di comprare** un dizionario monolingue.

The teacher **reminded the children to bring**   L'insegnante **ricordò ai bambini di portare** la
their swimming things.   roba da nuoto.

■ Infine, i verbi seguenti, che reggono sempre **to** + **infinito**, **possono** essere seguiti da un complemento diretto. (Per una spiegazione più esauriente, vedi **17.10**).

want	help	beg	would prefer		
expect	ask	intend	would like	(someone)	*to* + infinito

Confronta le frasi seguenti:

We **expect to be** late.   **Prevediamo di arrivare** in ritardo.
We **expect** Tom **to be** late.   **Prevediamo** che Tom **arrivi** in ritardo.
We **wanted to stay** longer.   **Volevamo rimanere** più a lungo.
We **wanted** them **to stay** longer. **Volevamo** che loro **rimanessero** più a lungo.

■ È importante ricordare **la differenza tra** *would like* e *like*.

Would you **like to play** tennis?   *Do* you **like playing** tennis?
Vuoi giocare a tennis? (= un invito a giocare) **Ti piace giocare** a tennis? (= mi informo sulle tue preferenze)

I **would like to go** to the cinema.   I **like going** to the cinema.
Vorrei andare al cinema (= condizionale di   **Mi piace andare** al cinema. (= parlo di ciò che
want, forma più cortese)   mi piace fare)

PRACTICE

1 Completa la seconda frase in modo che abbia lo stesso significato della prima. Usa i verbi nel riquadro e aggiungi tutte le parole necessarie.

~~advised~~   agreed   asked   intended   invited   promised   refused   ~~warned~~

1 'Don't touch the wire, Claire,' said the teacher. The teacher .....warned..Claire..not..to..touch. the wire.

2 'You should eat more fruit, Jane,' said the nurse. The nurse ...advised Jane to eat.. more fruit.

3 'OK, I'll help you, Amina,' said Nat. Nat .... Amina.

4 'I won't tell you anything, Sally,' said Lorna. Lorna .... anything.

5 'Can you open the box for me, Zena?' asked Paul. Paul .... the box for him.

6 'I won't forget the tickets,' said Mel. Mel .... the tickets.

7 'I'm going to read ten books in one week,' said Brian. Brian .... in one week.

8 'Would you like to stay at my house, Aziza?' said Helen. Helen .... at her house.

2 Traduci.

1 Tom mi insegnerà a suonare la chitarra.

2 Eileen merita di vincere il primo premio.

3 Non posso permettermi di andare al ristorante tutte le sere.

4 Ho deciso di iscrivermi a un club di scacchi.

5 Mary si è offerta di prestarmi i suoi appunti di storia.

6 I miei genitori mi hanno sempre incoraggiato a imparare le lingue straniere.

17.6   VERBI + *-ING: I ENJOY DRAWING*

Alcuni verbi di uso comune sono seguiti dalla forma *-ing*.

admit*	appreciate*	avoid	can't face	can't help	can't stand	
carry on	confess*	consider*	delay	deny*	detest	
dislike	enjoy	fancy	feel like	finish	give up	imagine*	*-ing*
involve	keep/keep on	mention*	(not) mind	miss		
postpone	practise	put off	risk	resist	suggest*	

Avoid putting on heavy make-up.
Keep reading.
Imagine living in a loft in Manhattan!

My job **involves travelling** abroad a lot.

Evita di metterti un trucco pesante.
Continua a leggere.
Immagina di vivere in un attico a Manhattan!
(= immagina che cosa significherebbe!)

Il mio lavoro **comporta viaggiare** molto all'estero.

La forma negativa di *-ing* è *not -ing*.

If you don't leave immediately, you **risk** **not** *catching your plane.*

Can you **imagine not having** *a car nowadays?*

Se non parti immediatamente, **rischi di non prendere** l'aereo.

Riesci a **immaginare di non avere** la macchina al giorno d'oggi?

I verbi contrassegnati da * possono anche essere seguiti da *that* e frase dichiarativa, senza differenza di significato.

He admitted **taking** *bribes.* = *He admitted* **that he had taken** *bribes.*

Ammise **di aver preso** *tangenti.* = *Ammise* **che aveva preso** *tangenti.*

301

PRACTICE

1 Riempi gli spazi in questa conversazione con la forma corretta del verbo tra parentesi: **to** + infinito o **-ing**.

Mum: Hi Ben, you're home early. I didn't expect **(1)** ....to see...... (*see*) you before midnight. Are you hungry?

Ben: No, you carry on **(2)** ....eating........ (*eat*). I don't feel hungry.

Mum: What's the matter?

Ben: Oh, I planned **(3)** .... (*go*) to the city centre with Maria, but she didn't manage **(4)** .... (*get*) to the station in time. I didn't feel like **(5)** .... (*go*) alone, so I decided **(6)** .... (*come*) home. I'm going to give up **(7)** .... (*see*) her.

Mum: I suggest **(8)** .... (*talk*) to her. She seems **(9)** .... (*be*) a nice girl.

Ben: I don't mind **(10)** .... (*wait*) for a good reason, but she never even phones.

Mum: You'll miss **(11)** .... (*spend*) time with her if you break up.

Ben: Perhaps. But I don't like **(12)** .... (*waste*) my evenings.

2 Traduci.

1   Non mi dispiace lavare i piatti, ma detesto stirare.

2   Jonathan ha ammesso di avere una cotta per Angela.

3   Hai voglia di fare una passeggiata?

4   Mio fratello ha rischiato di non passare l'esame di guida.

5   Sarah si esercita a suonare il piano due ore al giorno.

6   Stiamo prendendo in considerazione di trasferirci in un appartamento più grande.

17.7 VERBI + *TO/-ING*

Alcuni verbi possono essere seguiti sia dalla forma **-ing** sia da **to** + infinito, **senza differenza di significato**: *begin*, *can't bear*, *continue*, *hate*, *like*, *love*, *prefer*, *start*.

He **continued talking** loudly.
= He **continued to talk** loudly.

Continuò a parlare ad alta voce.

I **prefer using** a dictionary.
= I **prefer to use** a dictionary.

Preferisco usare il dizionario.

Tuttavia, non si possono di norma avere due forme **-ing** di seguito.

I was **starting to make** a cake when the phone rang. (**Non** ~~I was starting making a cake~~)
Stavo **cominciando a fare** una torta quando squillò il telefono.

I LIKE TO DO / I LIKE DOING

Quando è seguito da *to* + infinito, il verbo *like* ha un significato lievemente diverso rispetto a *like* + -*ing*.

I *like to catch* the early bus on Monday mornings.
Mi piace prendere il primo autobus il lunedì mattina.
(= È un'abitudine o una scelta di convenienza, non necessariamente qualcosa che mi piace in sé.)

I *like dancing*.
Mi piace ballare.
(= Mi piace davvero farlo.)

VERBI + TO/-ING CON DIFFERENZA DI SIGNIFICATO

I verbi seguenti hanno un significato diverso a seconda che siano seguiti da *to* + **infinito** o dalla forma -*ing*.

verbo + *to* infinito	verbo + -*ing*
remember to	**remember -ing**
Remember **to lock** the door.	I remember **checking** that I had my keys when I left the house.
Ricordati **di chiudere** la porta a chiave.	Mi ricordo **di aver controllato** che avevo le chiavi quando sono uscito di casa.
(= un'azione che sarà necessario fare)	(= la memoria di un'azione passata)
forget to	**forget -ing**
Don't forget **to phone me**.	I'll never forget **meeting her**.
Non dimenticarti **di telefonarmi**.	Non dimenticherò mai **di averla / quando l'ho incontrata**. (= ricordo di un evento passato)
(= un'azione che sarà necessario fare)	
try to	**try -ing**
Try **to walk** quickly.	Try **taking** more exercise.
Cerca **di camminare** velocemente.	Cerca **di fare** più attività fisica.
(= se ci riesci)	(= un esperimento, vediamo se funziona)
stop to	**stop -ing**
She **stopped to have** a rest.	He **stopped shouting** at us.
Si **fermò per riposarsi**.	**Smise di urlare** contro di noi.
mean to	**mean -ing**
They don't **mean to upset you**.	If you go by train that **means taking** a taxi to the station.
Non **intendono farti preoccupare**.	Se vai in treno, questo **vuol dire prendere** un taxi per andare alla stazione.
(= non è loro intenzione)	(= comporta questo)
go on to	**go on -ing**
He **went on to tell** them how many medals he had won.	They **went on cycling** until they reached the farm.
Andò avanti a raccontare quante medaglie aveva vinto. (= quello che fece poi fu dir loro)	**Continuarono a pedalare** finché raggiunsero la fattoria. (= non smisero di pedalare)

■ **regret to**

*I **regret to inform you** that your application was unsuccessful.*
Mi dispiace doverla informare *che la sua domanda non è stata accettata.*

■ **regret -ing**

*We **regret sending** our daughter to that school.*
Ci dispiace / Rimpiangiamo di aver mandato *nostra figlia a quella scuola.*
(= vorremmo non averlo fatto)

PRACTICE

1 Completa le frasi seguenti con la forma corretta dei verbi nel riquadro.

| change   check   contact   look   phone   send   spend   travel |

1 Remember ......*to send*........ your grandmother a card on her birthday next week.

2 She stopped .... at a poster and missed the train.

3 Do you remember .... alone for the first time?

4 I'll never forget .... three weeks in the rainforest.

5 Don't forget .... your email before you leave home.

6 He tried .... his hair colour, but he still looked awful.

7 Please stop .... me at work. My boss doesn't allow personal calls.

8 I tried .... my boss, but he was on a climbing holiday.

2 Sottolinea la forma corretta di ogni verbo. In un caso entrambe sono corrette.

Hi Pete

How are you? I'm on holiday by the sea. I'd hoped **(1)** *to go / going* abroad but I couldn't afford **(2)** *fly / to fly* anywhere because I started **(3)** *to save / saving* too late. But I don't mind **(4)** *not to travel / not travelling* abroad because this is a great place.

My brother encouraged me **(5)** *to come / coming*. I'd love you **(6)** *seeing / to see* it. You should try **(7)** *to get / getting* a few days holiday so you can come here. My landlady will let you **(8)** *share / to share* my room. I hope **(9)** *hear / to hear* from you soon.

Love Eric

PS Don't forget **(10)** *to book / booking* a seat on the coach if you travel at the weekend!

3 Riempi gli spazi con un verbo appropriato alla forma corretta.

1 If I go to the wedding it will mean ....buying......... a new dress.

2 Please try .... to the airport in good time – I'll be nervous waiting for you.

3 Will you stop .... that noise? I'm trying .... this book.

4 I forgot .... a table at the restaurant and it was full when we got there.

5 The two children went on .... their ball against the wall although they had been told several times to stop.

6 We regret .... you that the course you applied for is now full.

7 Tommy says he didn't come to the party because he didn't know about it but I remember .... him.

8 When you go out, remember .... the key with your neighbour because I haven't got one.

9 Why don't you try .... glasses? Then you might not get so many headaches.

10 I saw Philip when I was in the park so I stopped .... to him.

11 I meant .... you a postcard but I didn't have time.

12 I regret not .... to Egypt with my sister because she says it was a really great trip.

13 After getting a degree in biology, my son went on .... a book about monkeys.

14 I shall never forget .... the sun come up over the mountains when I was in the Himalayas.

17.8   *MAKE* E *LET*

L'espressione italiana 'far fare qualcosa a qualcuno' si rende in inglese nei modi seguenti:

make + oggetto + infinito senza **to**

She **made**   *me*   **carry** *two heavy bags.*
     Mi fece   **portare** *due borse pesanti.*

let + oggetto + infinito senza **to**

Let   *me*   **get** *my umbrella.*
Fammi   **prendere** *l'ombrello.*

Il verbo *let* esprime il significato di **lasciare**, **consentire**, mentre *make* ha una sfumatura di significato più forte.

*I'll **let** you decide.*	*Ti **lascerò** decidere.*
*He **made** me cry.*	*Mi **ha fatto** piangere.*

Alla forma passiva, *make* è seguito da *to* + **infinito**.
I was made to do *my homework.*

In italiano, tuttavia, questa struttura viene comunemente tradotta con la forma attiva.
Mi fecero fare *i compiti.*

PRACTICE

1   Abbina gli inizi delle frasi con le loro logiche conclusioni.

1	The official demanded ..*e*...	**a**	people to forget my birthday.
2	My maths teacher pretended	**b**	me to check my email.
3	My music teacher made	**c**	the children watch a video.
4	My boss reminded	**d**	not to see me at the disco.
5	I'd hate	**e**	to see my passport.
6	I let	**f**	me take the exam.

2   Riscrivi le frasi seguenti usando *make* o *let*.

1   My parents usually give us permission to stay up late on Saturday evenings.

My parents .... *usually let us stay up late on Saturday evenings* ....

2   I had to weed the garden as a punishment.

I ....

3   I feel very self-conscious when I speak English.

Speaking English ....

4   My elder brother has promised to allow me to drive his car.

....

5   I can't stand tripe. I feel sick when I smell it.

The smell of tripe ....

6   My parents would never force me to practise the piano if I didn't want to.

My parents ....

17.9   VERBI + -*ING* O INFINITO SENZA *TO*: *I WATCHED THEM PLAYING/PLAY*

I verbi *feel*, *hear*, *notice*, *see*, *watch*, che indicano principalmente **percezione**, possono essere seguiti da:

▪ complemento oggetto + **infinito senza *to***.
Si usa questa costruzione quando l'azione viene percepita **dall'inizio alla fine**.

*I **watched** the boy **save** a penalty kick.*
Ho guardato il bambino **parare** un calcio di rigore. (= azione intera, dall'inizio alla fine)
*She **heard** the doorbell **ring**.*
Sentì suonare il campanello. (= azione completata)

▪ complemento oggetto + -*ing*.
Si usa questa costruzione quando l'azione viene percepita per un breve periodo **durante il suo svolgimento**.

*I **watched** the boys **playing** football.*
Ho guardato i bambini **giocare / che giocavano** a calcio. (= mentre giocavano a calcio)
*She **heard** her mother **singing** as she came downstairs.*
Sentì sua madre **cantare / che cantava** mentre scendeva le scale. (= azione che continua)

PRACTICE

1 Riempi gli spazi con i verbi nel riquadro alla forma corretta: -*ing* o infinito senza *to*.

| play   knock   ~~sing~~   get off   behave   snore   land   touch   talk |

1 Listen! Can you hear the birds ....singing...... ?

2 I saw the plane .... and the passengers ....

3 Jim never misses an Arsenal match. Last Saturday he went to watch them .... in Manchester.

4 The witness saw the suspect .... to another man. They seemed to be arguing.

5 I saw you .... that vase over. You'd better offer to pay for it.

6 The walls are so thin I can hear the neighbours .... during the night.

7 During dinner she suddenly felt something wet .... her leg. It was the dog's nose.

8 The teacher noticed the boy .... suspiciously during the test. He was trying to cheat.

2 Il tuo *penfriend* inglese ti ha scritto una lettera in cui ti racconta di un'esperienza paurosa che ha avuto, ma che fortunatamente è finita bene. Riempi gli spazi nella lettera con il verbo tra parentesi alla forma corretta: *-ing* o infinito senza *to*.

Dear Gianni,

How are you? I wanted to tell you about a frightening experience I had the other day. I was in the local post office and it was very hot and crowded. I noticed two men (1) ...standing... (*stand*) in a corner and I thought they were behaving strangely. They seemed nervous; twice I saw them (2) .... (*speak*) into a mobile phone in low voices. Then suddenly I saw two more men (3) .... (*run*) into the post office and I heard a woman (4) .... (*scream*). The men were armed and wore masks and they ordered everyone to lie on the floor face down. It was terrifying. As I lay on the floor I could hear children (5) .... (*cry*) around me and I heard the robbers (6) .... (*give*) an order to one of the clerks. The whole episode probably only lasted ten minutes but it seemed much longer. When I next raised my head and looked, I was just in time to see the men (7) .... (*run*) towards the door. The two men I had watched earlier were with them. Of course, this meant that I was able to give the police a really detailed description as I had watched them (8) .... (*act*) suspiciously earlier.

Speak to you soon.

Love, Henry

17.10 AGGETTIVI + *TO* INFINITO: *DIFFICULT TO SAY*

Molti aggettivi sono di norma seguiti da *to* + infinito.

Soggetto + verbo *be*	afraid cheap dangerous* delighted difficult* easy* expensive happy impossible interesting nice* pleased possible safe sorry surprised	*to* infinito

*I'm **surprised to see you** here.*   *Sono **sorpresa di vederti** qui.*
*I'm **sorry to hear** that.*   *Mi **dispiace di sentire** ciò.*
*Modern poetry is **difficult to understand.***   *La poesia moderna è **difficile da capire.***

■ Gli aggettivi contrassegnati da asterisco * possono anche essere seguiti da *-ing* senza che il significato cambi.

*It's **nice meeting** friends after school.* = *It's **nice to meet** friends after school.*
*È **bello incontrare** gli amici dopo la scuola.*

PRACTICE

1 Riscrivi le frasi seguenti iniziando con le parole date.

1   Playing the guitar is very difficult. The guitar .... *is very difficult to play* ....

2   Reading foreign newspapers is interesting. It is interesting ....

3   Travelling abroad can be fascinating. It is fascinating ....

4   Seeing you so happy makes me feel good. It is good ....

5   Breaking a promise is wrong. It is wrong ....

6   Using the underground in London is easy. The underground in London is easy ....

7   Understanding the lyrics of songs can be hard. It can be hard ....

8   Knowing that you've been selected for the final makes me very happy.

I am very happy ....

17.11   COSTRUZIONE OGGETTIVA: *WANT / WOULD LIKE SOMEONE TO DO*

I verbi che significano **volere**, come *want*, *would like* e *would prefer*, sono sempre seguiti da *to* + **infinito**.

I would like to help you.	*Vorrei aiutarti.*
I don't want to know.	*Non voglio saperlo.*

Questa costruzione corrisponde sostanzialmente a quella italiana. Tuttavia, mentre in italiano i verbi di volere reggono anche la frase oggettiva esplicita, per esempio 'Voglio **che tu mi aiuti**', i verbi *want* e *would like* **non** possono essere seguiti da *that*. Si costruiscono invece nel modo seguente:

Want, would ('d) like	+ oggetto	*to* infinito
I'd like ***Vorrei che***	*you* **tu**	*to understand.* ***capissi.***
*Mr Johnson **doesn't want*** *Il signor Johnson **non vuole che***	*his daughter* ***sua figlia***	*to go out with that boy.* ***esca** con quel ragazzo.*
Would you like ***Vuoi che***	*me* –	*to help you?* ***ti aiuti?***
I don't want ***Non voglio che***	*her* **lei**	*to know that I'm here.* ***sappia** che sono qui.*

Come si vede, questa costruzione è molto diversa da quella italiana e mostra che in inglese c'è un uso limitato del congiuntivo.

*I'd like Grandma **to come** and live with us.* (**Non** ~~*I'd like that Grandma to come*~~)
***Vorrei che** la nonna **venisse** a vivere con noi.*

PRACTICE

1 Riscrivi le frasi seguenti iniziando con le parole date.

1 I get angry when my mother reads my emails. I don't want ....my..mother..to..read..my..emails....

2 My parents would be happy if I went to university.

My parents would like ....

3 You wouldn't be happy if people teased you about your appearance.

You wouldn't like ....

4 Sam is reluctant to do his homework. Sam doesn't want ....

5 Please could you give me some advice. I'd like ....

6 I phone my girlfriend every day because it's what she wants.

My girlfriend wants ....

7 I'd be happy if my mother dressed more fashionably.

I'd like ....

8 Tracy's parents are against her going on holiday with her boyfriend.

Tracy's parents don't want ....

2 Completa queste domande, usando **Do you want me to ...?** o **Would you like me to ...?** e un verbo appropriato. Aggiungi le parole necessarie. Ricorda che le due espressioni hanno lo stesso significato, ma **Would you like me to ...?** viene preferito in situazioni più formali.

1 Do you know how to use this software, Mrs Jones, or would..you..like..me..to..show..you. ?

2 Are you hot, Grandad? .... the air conditioning?

3 So your train gets in at 9 pm, Bill. .... station?

4 Are you having problems with maths at school, darling? .... ?

5 Is the music too loud for you, Mr Brown? .... ?

6 It's time for lunch, Mum. .... ?

7 I know you really like my brother. .... your party?

8 You have to get up at 6 am tomorrow morning. .... ?

ALL IN ONE REVISION

1 Leggi questa lista di attività che possono essere fatte con il computer. Tu usi il computer per fare queste cose? Conosci altre persone che usano il computer per farle?

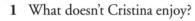

booking accommodation   buying tickets   doing homework
downloading music   finding out information   having online conversations
paying bills   planning holidays   playing games   writing emails

2 Ascolterai una conversazione tra Mickey e Cristina.

2.15

1 What doesn't Cristina enjoy?

2 What has Mickey used the computer for this afternoon?

3 Ascolta di nuovo e abbina le domande con le loro risposte. Ferma la registrazione se è necessario.

2.16

1   What does the manager's new notice say? ......
2   How long has Mickey been on the internet? ......
3   When do Mickey and Cristina need to get plenty of information? ......
4   When did Mickey find the website about Doubtful Sound? ......
5   What did Mickey promise Cristina? ......
6   What is one of the main attractions of the trip? ......
7   What is a possibility on the trip? ......
8   When should people tell the company if they are vegetarians? ......
9   When does Cristina need a good coffee? ......

a   While looking for ideas about the South Island.
b   To go walking with her on holiday.
c   After working in that office all day.
d   No talking except on business.
e   Before planning their holiday.
f   Since finishing his essay.
g   Taking photographs.
h   Seeing penguins.
i   When booking.

4 Rileggi le risposte che hai dato nell'esercizio 3.

Che tipo di parola segue *since, before, while, when* e *after*?

5 Scrivi delle frasi complete usando le espressioni suggerite. Fai attenzione a usare il tempo giusto.

1   I was getting too fat, so Joey / persuade me / join a gym.
   I was getting too fat, so Joey persuaded me to join a gym.

2   I've got no money. I can't afford / buy a present for Daniel.
   ....

3   Your bedroom is a mess. Please don't forget / tidy it before / leave the house.
   ....

4   If you don't know where to stay, you could try / phone the tourist information office.
   ....

5   Barbara hates / book holidays on the internet. She'd prefer / speak to someone on the phone.
   ....

6   Sandra's lost her purse. She remembers / see it in the bar because she got it out / pay for the drinks.
   ....

6 Rhiannon sta raccontando alle sue amiche di come lei e il suo ragazzo, Sean, si sono conosciuti. Completa quello che dice usando la forma corretta dei verbi nel riquadro.

| try imitate meet go talk get pay laugh see take have |

I'll never forget **(1)** ...*meeting*... my boyfriend Sean for the first time. I was with my friend Janet one evening and we went for a walk along the pier. We met some boys she knew from school and she introduced me to Sean. We noticed each other straight away and he suggested **(2)** .... for an ice cream. We decided to **(3)** .... Tony's Ice creams and we really enjoyed **(4)** .... to each other. He really made me **(5)** .... when he tried **(6)** .... Mika. He offered **(7)** .... for my ice cream and he wanted **(8)** .... me out the following evening. I accepted, of course. We started **(9)** .... each other about three times a week, and we've never stopped **(10)** .... fun together. We'd like **(11)** .... married one day.

7 Completa questa conversazione usando i verbi tra parentesi.

Andy: I've decided **(1)** ...*to leave*... (*leave*) my job next month.

Sally: But I thought you enjoyed **(2)** .... (*work*) in an architect's office.

Andy: Oh, I do. But I feel like **(3)** .... (*do*) something different for a while.

Sally: Didn't you promise **(4)** .... (*stay*) there at least two years?

Andy: Yes, I did but I just can't stand **(5)** .... (*work*) with those people. One of them refuses **(6)** .... (*stop*) talking while she works, another one keeps **(7)** .... (*sing*) to himself. And then there's a man who attempts **(8)** .... (*tell*) awful jokes all the time which he always gets wrong. I detest **(9)** .... (*work*) with all that noise around me.

Sally: It sounds quite a cheerful place to me. Can't you manage **(10)** .... (*ignore*) them and get on with your work?

Andy: No, I can't. I just can't carry on **(11)** .... (*go*) there every day. I'm hoping **(12)** .... (*go*) abroad for a bit.

Sally: Well, good luck.

8 <u>Sottolinea</u> la forma corretta del verbo.

1 I noticed the man *drop* / *dropping* / *to drop* his ticket so I picked it up for him.

2 The tour guide advised the tourists not *take* / *taking* / *to take* too much money out with them.

3 The old man said he would love *have* / *having* / *to have* the chance to fly in an aeroplane again.

4 I saw the boy *jump* / *jumping* / *to jump* into the lake before anyone could stop him.

5 I recommend *phone* / *phoning* / *to phone* the hotel before you set off.

6 My father used to forbid us *play* / *playing* / *to play* in those woods.

7 The college doesn't allow *eat* / *eating* / *to eat* in the classrooms.

8 It was my drama teacher who encouraged me *become* / *becoming* / *to become* an actor.

9 Tony sta per andare in gita nella tua città natale. Lui non sa niente del tuo paese.
Completa queste frasi con dei consigli appropriati.

1 I advise you ....to visit the market in Green Street.............. (*visit*)

2 You'll enjoy .... (*see*)

3 Don't miss .... (*go*)

4 Before you go, don't forget .... (*buy*)

5 While you're there, try .... (*eat*)

6 You must promise .... (*send*)

7 Avoid .... (*swim*)

8 Remember .... (*take*)

10 Completa questi mini-dialoghi con la forma corretta del verbo: *-ing* o *to* infinito.

1 **A** Will you remember ..to get.. me two blank CDs while you're out? (*get*)

   B I'll try ..to remember.... , but you know what my memory's like! (*remember*)

2 **A** How do you fancy .... to the cinema this evening? (*go*)

   B Great idea! I'd love .... the new Matt Damon film. (*see*)

3 **A** Listen, I'm sorry. I really didn't mean .... you. (*upset*)

   B Well, if you stopped .... my spots all the time, it would help! (*mention*)

4 **A** Would you mind .... on the way? I'm dying of thirst. (*stop*)

   B I'd rather not stop if it means .... half an hour in a service station. We'll be late. (*waste*)

11 In sei delle frasi seguenti c'è un errore. <u>Sottolinea</u> l'errore e correggilo.

1 Kevin found his passport while <u>to tidy</u> his room.   ...tidying...

2 I'd be delighted be your bridesmaid when you get married next month.   ....

3 My brother is thinking to leave his girlfriend.   ....

4 Our English teacher has encouraged us to go and study in England.   ....

5 I use my MP3 player for listen to music when I go jogging.   ....

6 Mandy is going to the hairdresser's for to have some streaks put into her hair.   ....

7 You can improve your social life by taking up a hobby and joining a club.   ....

8 To make telephone calls during dinner is very rude.   ....

12 Traduci.

1 **A** C'è un sushi bar in città? **B** Non lo so. Hai provato a guardare nell'elenco telefonico?

2 Ho cercato di perdere qualche chilo, ma è molto difficile.

3 Janet ha smesso di parlarmi e non riesco a capire perché.

4 Smettetela di chiacchierare!

5 Ho pedalato per un'ora, poi mi sono fermata per riposarmi.

6 Vorrei che i miei genitori mi facessero uscire il sabato sera.

7 I miei genitori vogliono che rimanga a casa stasera.

8 Vuoi davvero che te lo dica?

LE PREPOSIZIONI

LE PREPOSIZIONI – INTRODUZIONE

Le **preposizioni** sono parti del discorso che collegano e mettono in relazione due elementi della frase; sono generalmente seguite da un nome o da un pronome e introducono i diversi complementi.

Le preposizioni sono una parte importante e complessa della lingua: alcune hanno più di un significato, e la stessa preposizione inglese può essere tradotta in diversi modi in italiano.

Claire is going	*to the cinema.* *to the gym.* *to the dentist's.*	*Claire sta andando*	*al cinema.* *in palestra.* *dal dentista.*

Questa *Unit* non introduce singolarmente tutte le preposizioni che esistono in inglese, molte delle quali sono già state presentate all'interno delle *Unit* precedenti, ma si concentra su alcune di esse, scelte sulla base della varietà dei loro usi e dei loro significati.

18.1 PREPOSIZIONI DI LUOGO: *IN, ON* E *AT; ONTO/OFF* E *OUT OF / INTO*

In, on e *at* corrispondono sostanzialmente alle preposizioni italiane **in**, **su** e **a**.

In si usa per indicare che una persona o una cosa **si trovano**:

■ **in** un continente, una nazione, una città, un parco, un giardino, una stanza.

*Uruguay is **in** South America.*	*L'Uruguay è **in** America Latina.*
*The Prime Minister is **in** Washington.*	*Il primo ministro è **a** Washington.*
*You can cycle anywhere **in** the park.*	*Puoi andare in bicicletta dappertutto **nel** parco.*
*There are some lovely trees **in** the garden.*	*Ci sono degli alberi bellissimi **nel** giardino.*

■ **dentro** qualunque tipo di contenitore: **in** a cupboard, **in** a box, **in** a bag, **in** a wallet, **in** a file.

*There's a lot of money **in** this bag.*	*C'è molto denaro **in** questa borsa.*
*Do you keep all your credit cards **in** this wallet?*	*Tieni tutte le tue carte di credito **in** questo portafoglio?*
*We found a picture of the castle **in** our guide book.*	*Abbiamo trovato una fotografia del castello **nella** nostra guida.*

■ **in** un'automobile, un taxi, un elicottero.

*They arrived **in** their father's car.*   *Sono arrivati **con** la macchina del padre.*
*He came home **in** a taxi.*   *È venuto a casa **in/col** taxi.*

On corrisponde all'italiano **su** e indica che due oggetti sono uno sopra l'altro, con contatto.

*The dictionary is **on** the teacher's desk.*   *Il vocabolario è **sulla** cattedra.*

On si usa inoltre per indicare:

■ un punto **su una linea precisa**: **on** a road, **on** the coast.

*Seattle is **on** the Pacific coast.*   *Seattle è **sulla** costa del Pacifico.*
*There's heavy traffic **on** the road.*   *C'è traffico pesante **sulla** strada.*

■ che ci troviamo **su un'isola**.

*There is a barbecue **on** the island twice a week.*   *C'è un barbecue **sull'**isola due volte alla settimana.*
*The Statue of Liberty is located **on** a 12-acre island.*   *La Statua della Libertà si trova **su** un'isola di 12 acri.*

■ che **un oggetto si trova** on a wall, **on** the floor, **on** the ceiling.

*I put the picture **on** the wall.*   *Ho messo il quadro **sulla** parete.*
*The baby's toys are scattered **on** the floor.*   *I giocattoli del bambino sono sparsi **sul** pavimento.*
*My flat is **on** the second floor.*   *Il mio appartamento è **al** secondo piano.*
*There's a spider **on** the ceiling.*   *C'è un ragno **sul** soffitto.*

■ che ci si trova su un **mezzo di trasporto pubblico**: **on** a bus, **on** a train, **on** a plane.

*I do my homework **on** the bus.*   *Faccio i compiti **sull'**autobus.*
*They met **on** a plane.*   *Si sono conosciuti **su** un aeroplano.*

At si usa in modo analogo alla preposizione italiana **a**. Si usa **at**:

■ per indicare un posto **in termini della sua funzione** o come **luogo di incontro**.

*The President of the US lives **at** the White House.*   *Il presidente degli Stati Uniti vive **alla** Casa Bianca.*
*I'll see you **at** the station.*   *Ci vediamo **alla** stazione.*

■ per indicare un luogo dove accade **un evento**.

*There were a lot of strangers **at the party**.*   *C'erano un sacco di persone che non conoscevo **alla festa**.*

*Did you have a good time **at Alex's house**?*   *Vi siete divertiti **a casa di Alex**?*
*My favourite band played **at the concert**.*   *Il mio gruppo preferito ha suonato **al concerto**.*
*There were lots of students **at the conference**.*   *C'erano un sacco di studenti **alla conferenza**.*
*I saw that film **at the** local **cinema**.*   *Ho visto quel film **al cinema** locale.*

■ nelle espressioni **at the top** = in alto, in cima; **at the bottom** = in basso, in fondo; **at the side** = di lato, di fianco.

*Please sign this form **at the bottom** of the first page.*   *Per favore firmi questo modulo **in fondo** alla prima pagina.*

■ quando si danno **indicazioni stradali**.

*Go left **at the traffic lights**.*   *Svolti a sinistra **al semaforo**.*

■ dopo il verbo **arrive**, quando la destinazione è **un luogo/edificio**.

*We arrived **at the airport** very early.*   *Siamo arrivati **all'aeroporto** molto in anticipo.*
*When you arrive **at your cottage** you'll find a hot meal.*   *Quando arriverete **alla villetta** troverete un pasto caldo.*

315

Attenzione: con nomi di **città** e **nazioni**, **arrive** è seguito da *in*.

*When do we arrive **in** Brussels?*   *Quando arriviamo **a** Bruxelles?*
*We arrived **in** Greece three days ago.*   *Siamo arrivati **in** Grecia tre giorni fa.*

Le preposizioni **onto/off** e **into/out of** indicano **movimento di entrata e di uscita**.

Si usa **onto/off** con mezzi di trasporto pubblici, quindi di dimensioni grandi.

*We got **onto/off** the bus.*   *Siamo **saliti sull'** / **scesi dall'**autobus.*
*Get **off** the Tube at Covent Garden.*   *Scendi alla fermata di Covent Garden.*

Si usa **into / out of** con **luoghi chiusi** o **automobili**.

*He walked **into / out of** the shop.*   *Entrò nel / Uscì dal negozio.*
*She got **into** a car parked outside the hotel.*   *Salì su un'auto parcheggiata davanti all'albergo.*

PRACTICE

1   Inserisci *in, on* o *at*.

1 The poster is ..on.. the wall.

2 You'll find a knife ...... the drawer.

3 Barbara is ...... the bath.

4 Please sign ...... the bottom of the page.

5 Whitby is ...... the coast.

6 Bill dreams of living ...... a desert island.

7 The Prime Minister arrived ...... a helicopter.

8 My identity card is ...... my wallet.

9 They're showing *Harry Potter* ...... the Odeon.

10 Turn right ...... the crossroads.

2 Abbina gli inizi delle frasi con le loro logiche conclusioni.

1 The Prado is in .h...   a the coast of the Pacific Ocean.
2 Part of New York is on ...... b North Africa.
3 Tunisia is in ......   c the top of the page.
4 Chile is on ......   d art college before he was famous.
5 Michelangelo painted on ...... e the River Nile.
6 The exercise is at ......   f the Tower of London.
7 John Lennon was at ......   g the island of Manhattan.
8 Trains from Cardiff arrive at ...... h Madrid.
9 Cairo is on ......   i Paddington Station in London.
10 The British Crown jewels are in ...... j the ceiling of the Sistine Chapel.

18.2 PREPOSIZIONI DI LUOGO: *UNDER* E *ON TOP OF; ABOVE/OVER* E *BELOW/UNDER; ALONG, THROUGH* E *ROUND; ACROSS* E *OVER*

under	*on top of*	*above/over*	*below/under*

Queste preposizioni indicano vari modi di tradurre **sotto** = *under* e *below*, e **sopra** = *on top of*, *above* e *over*.

Under e *on top of* si usano per descrivere oggetti **che sono a contatto**:

The DVD player is **under** the television.   Il lettore DVD è **sotto** il televisore.
The magazine is **on top of** the television.   La rivista è **sopra** la televisione.

Per indicare oggetti che **non sono a contatto** si possono usare *below* e *under*, *above* e *over*.

The books are **below/under** the DVD player.   I libri sono **sotto** il lettore DVD.
The picture is **above/over** the television.   Il quadro è **sopra** il televisore.

along	*through*	*round*
lungo	**attraverso**	**intorno a**
across		*over*
attraverso		**attraverso / di là da**

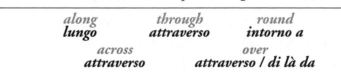

*I followed the man **along** the river, **round** the car park and **through** the wood.*
*Seguii l'uomo **lungo** il fiume, **intorno** al parcheggio e **attraverso** il bosco.*

Across e *over* hanno un significato simile e talvolta possono essere usati indifferentemente.
*The cottages are **across/over** the lake.*   *Le villette sono **al di là** del lago.*

Tuttavia, la preposizione italiana **attraverso** si rende di norma con *across*.
*Their eyes met **across** the table.*   *I loro occhi si incontrarono **attraverso** il tavolo.*

317

PRACTICE

1 Completa le frasi seguenti usando le preposizioni nel riquadro.

above	~~at~~	at	below	in	in	into	off	on top of	onto

1 What time will Ali arrive ......a.t...... the restaurant?

2 There are lots of examples .... a good dictionary.

3 I climbed .... a wall to see what was happening.

4 From the top of the hill, we had a good view of the village .... us.

5 There are lots of shoe shops .... the city centre.

6 I saw Terry get .... a taxi, but I don't know where it took him.

7 You can leave your bike .... the side of the house.

8 I couldn't find my book because someone had put the newspaper .... it.

9 We keep medicines in the cupboard .... the basin so the children can't reach them.

10 Harry got .... the bus at the wrong stop because he was dreaming about his girlfriend.

2 Sottolinea la preposizione corretta.

1 We can walk to the shops more quickly if we go *along / across* the sports field.

2 I was really annoyed when I found our cat asleep *on top of / above* my clean jumper.

3 We drove *round / along* the market square several times but we didn't see Simon.

4 There's a small shelf for your books *on top of / over* the bed.

5 Joseph ran quickly *along / through* the corridor to the office.

6 Nicky found her mobile *under / below* a cushion on the sofa.

7 To get to the lifts, walk *over / through* the perfume department.

8 Please write your name clearly *on top of / above* your signature.

9 You can see *through / across* the harbour from our balcony.

10 The ball flew *over / along* the goal and landed in the crowd.

18.3 PREPOSIZIONI DI LUOGO: *IN FRONT OF, BEHIND, OPPOSITE, BETWEEN; BY, BESIDE* E *NEXT TO*

in front of	*behind*	*opposite*	*between*
davanti a	**dietro (a)**	**di fronte a**	**tra**
by		*beside*	*next to*
presso / vicino a		**accanto a**	**accanto a**

*The woman is **in front of** the television.*
*The television is **behind** the woman.*
*The mother is **between** her two sons.*
*The girl is **by / beside / next to** her father.*

*La donna è **davanti** al televisore.*
*Il televisore è **dietro** la donna.*
*La madre è **tra** i (due) figli maschi.*
*La ragazzina è **accanto** al padre.*

Opposite non ha lo stesso significato di **in front of**, ma indica che due cose sono di fronte l'una all'altra.

*The girl is **opposite** her mother.* (= The girl is on the other side of the table from her mother.)
*La ragazzina è **di fronte** a sua madre.* (= dall'altro lato del tavolo)

La preposizione italiana **tra** può tradursi in inglese con **between** o **among**.

*The dictionary is **between** the grammar book and the atlas.*

*Il vocabolario è **tra** il libro di grammatica e l'atlante.*

*Is there a dictionary somewhere **among** these books?*

*C'è un vocabolario da qualche parte **tra** questi libri?*

Between si usa quando ci si riferisce a **due** cose o persone.

Among si usa per identificare qualcosa all'interno di un gruppo.

beyond	*behind*
oltre / al di là	**dietro**

Beyond si usa per indicare una cosa che è più lontana da noi rispetto a un'altra, sia che riusciamo a vederla oppure no.

*There's a traffic jam stretching **beyond** the beginning of the motorway.*
*C'è un ingorgo che si estende **oltre** l'inizio dell'autostrada.*
*You can't see the lake. It's **beyond** the forest.*
*Non puoi vedere il lago. È **oltre / al di là** della foresta.*

Behind si usa per riferirci a qualcosa che è parzialmente o completamente coperto da un oggetto situato davanti.

*The robber stood **behind** the door, hoping he wouldn't be seen.*
*Il ladro rimase in piedi **dietro** la porta, sperando di non essere visto.*

319

PRACTICE

1 Guarda attentamente il quadro e completa le frasi con delle preposizioni.

The bed is **(1)** ..between.... the door and the window. There are
four pictures **(2)** .... the wall **(3)** .... the bed.
There are some clothes hanging **(4)** .... the head of the
bed. In the corner is a table with a mirror **(5)** .... it
and a jug and other things **(6)** .... it.
There's a chair **(7)** .... the head of the bed and another
chair **(8)** .... the foot of the bed **(9)** .... a door.
There's a towel hanging **(10)** .... this door.

2 Scrivi una descrizione della stanza in cui ti trovi o di un'altra stanza che conosci bene. Usa le
espressioni dell'esercizio precedente per aiutarti.

3 In ognuna di queste frasi c'è una preposizione sbagliata. <u>Sottolinea</u> gli errori e correggili.

1   There are lots of art galleries <u>at</u> Amsterdam. ....in.........

2   She watched the children run onto the park to play. ....

3   Timmy saw Mel in the party but he didn't speak to her. ....

4   Andy ran through the beach to the next village and came back by bus. ....

5   I took the ticket out from my bag and gave it to the man by the door. ....

6   Please don't park behind my window – I can't see anything. ....

7   We were very tired when we arrived at Paris after a long flight. ....

8   Jacky hid between a car when she saw Lewis because she didn't want to speak to him. ....

9   I called in Rebecca's house, but she wasn't at home. ....

10   The guide held a small flag on top of her head so that the tourists could follow her easily. ....

18.4   PREPOSIZIONI DI TEMPO: *AT, ON* E *IN*

Quando hanno significato di tempo, le preposizioni **at**, **on** e **in** presentano notevoli differenze rispetto
all'uso italiano.

Si usa **at** per indicare:

■ **l'ora**.	*at six o'clock* = **alle sei**
■ **il momento del giorno**.	*at dawn* = **all'alba**; *at lunchtime* = **all'ora di pranzo**
■ **le feste**.	*at Christmas* = **a/per Natale**; *at Easter* = **a/per Pasqua**
■ **nelle seguenti espressioni**:	*at the weekend* = **nel/durante** *il fine settimana*
	at first / the beginning = **all'inizio**
	at last = **finalmente**
	at present / the moment = **al momento, ora**
	at times = **a volte**
	at once = **immediatamente**

Si usa **on** con:

▨ **le date, i giorni della settimana, giorni particolari**.

> **on** *Monday*
> **on** *3rd December* (**Ma** si dice **on** *the third of December*)
> **on** *New Year's Eve*
> **on** *Christmas Day*
> **on** *my birthday*
> **on** *the day of the race*

Si usa **in** con:

▨ **le parti del giorno, i mesi, le stagioni, gli anni, i secoli, i periodi storici**.

> **in** *the morning/afternoon/evening* (**Ma** *at* *night*)
> **in** *July*
> **in** *(the) winter*
> **in** *1953*
> **in** *the 90s*
> **in** *the twenty-first century*
> **in** *the Middle Ages*

ALCUNE ESPRESSIONI DA NON CONFONDERE

Confronta le espressioni seguenti:

in *the end* (= the final result)
I looked everywhere for my shoe.
In the end *I found it under my bed.*
Cercai la mia scarpa dappertutto.
Alla fine *la trovai sotto il mio letto.*

on *time* (= punctual)
The train's **on time**. *I'll be home at six.*
Il treno è **in orario**. *Sarò a casa alle sei.*

at *the end* (= the last thing to happen)
The film was very exciting with a long car chase **at the end**.
Il film era molto emozionante, con un lungo inseguimento in auto **alla fine**.

in *time* (= at or before the correct time)
If we leave now, we'll be home **in time** *for the news.*
Se partiamo ora, saremo a casa **in tempo** *per il telegiornale.*

PRACTICE

1 Riempi gli spazi con **at**, **on** o **in**.

1 You'll have to get up ....a.t.... dawn if you want to catch the early coach.

2 Paul was born .... New Year's Eve.

3 Their flight arrived .... the morning.

4 Would you like to go out .... lunchtime?

5 Jane has to train for several hours a day. .... times she finds it very hard.

6 A lot of snow falls in the mountains .... the winter.

7 House prices went up considerably .... the nineties.

8 Only twenty-five percent of all trains arrive .... time.

9 We are now .... the twenty-first century.

10 My brother is going to get married .... my birthday.

11 Francis bought the car .... once. He knew it was a bargain.

12 Dan couldn't decide whether to study architecture or engineering. .... the end he chose engineering.

2 Completa le frasi seguenti usando le parole o le espressioni nel riquadro.

> last   the moment   Monday   14th June   the 1950s   New Year   the evening
> the end of this lesson   the nineteenth century   their wedding anniversary

1 I'll meet you on .... Monday ....

2 Did you visit your cousins at .... ?

3 The exam took place on ....

4 Ian looked everywhere for his camera and at .... he found it in his bag.

5 Women first came to this university in ....

6 We took my parents to a restaurant on ....

7 Where is Michael living at .... ?

8 My grandparents went to Australia in ....

9 We don't often go shopping in .... because we're too tired.

10 Let's go to the café at ....

18.5   PREPOSIZIONI DI TEMPO: *BY* E *UNTIL/TILL*; *IN*, *DURING* E *FOR*

by = **entro**

*Can you clean the car **by** four o'clock?*   *Puoi pulire la macchina **entro** le quattro?*
*I intend to finish my dissertation **by** December.*   *Intendo finire la mia tesi **entro** dicembre.*

until/till = **fino a**

*They played **until** dark.*   *Giocarono **fino a** buio.*
Part of the motorway will remain closed   *Parte dell'autostrada rimarrà chiusa*
until *this afternoon.*   **fino a** *questo pomeriggio.*

Until è spesso usato in frasi negative.

*Don't wait **until/till** July to get your tickets.*   *Non aspettare **fino a** luglio per prendere i biglietti.*

In e **during** possono essere usati con lo stesso significato.

In/During *the summer we often go for long walks.*   **In/Durante l'estate** *facciamo spesso lunghe passeggiate.*

*It rained **during** the match.*   *È piovuto **durante** la partita.*

Ma during mette in rilievo un evento particolare sullo sfondo di un periodo di tempo.

*Some houses got burgled **during** the night.*   *Alcune case sono state svaligiate **durante** la notte.*

For corrisponde alle preposizioni italiane **per** e **da**. In entrambi i casi, si riferisce a una durata di tempo.

In italiano la preposizione **per** può talvolta essere omessa, in inglese di norma no, eccetto che in espressioni come *(for) a long time*.

*We went to Spain **for** the summer.*	*Siamo andati in Spagna **per** l'estate.*
*I run every day **for** one or two hours.*	*Tutti i giorni corro (**per**) una o due ore.*
*I've known Ron (**for**) a long time.*	*Conosco Ron **da** un sacco di tempo.*

In traduce anche la preposizione italiana **tra**.

*One of my favourite events is **in** ten days' time.*	*Uno dei miei eventi preferiti sarà **tra** dieci giorni.*
*I'll meet you **in** ten minutes.*	*Ci vediamo **tra** dieci minuti.*

PRACTICE

1 Riempi gli spazi in questo messaggio con *at*, *on*, *in*, *by* o *until*. Se nessuna preposizione è necessaria, lascia lo spazio vuoto.

> Hi Tabitha
>
> I hope you're all ready for our trip to Stockholm. Remember to bring a jacket because Sweden can be very rainy, even (**1**) ....in.......... summer and it may be cold (**2**) .... night. But I'm sure we'll have a good time. My brother was there (**3**) .... 2004. I spoke to him (**4**) .... last week and he says it's a great place. Our plane arrives there (**5**) .... lunchtime so we'll have plenty of time to find somewhere to stay. Then we can go out (**6**) .... the evening and go to some art galleries (**7**) .... Friday. I've booked tickets for a guided tour (**8**) .... the weekend. But we'll have time for shopping, don't worry. You can phone me (**9**) .... tomorrow if you want to ask me anything. I'll be at home (**10**) .... about two, but I have to go out after that. That's it, really. I'll meet you at the airport (**11**) .... quarter past eleven (**12**) .... Thursday. I know the flight's not (**13**) .... 12.30 but we have to check in (**14**) .... 11.30 at the latest so please make sure you're there (**15**) .... time!
>
> Love
> Francine

2 <u>Sottolinea</u> le preposizioni corrette in questo articolo di una rivista di gossip.

New Year Romance

The singer Petunia is getting married again! She told our reporter the news:

I've known Carlo (**1**) *in / <u>for</u>* six months. He's a wonderful person and I'm so happy. I met him (**2**) *during / at* my European tour last autumn. He asked me to marry him and of course I said 'Yes' immediately. But we didn't want to make an announcement (**3**) *for / until* we'd told our families. We're having a house built near Milan. The architect promises it'll be ready (**4**) *by / till* the summer so we can move in straight away. I'm so excited. (**5**) *On / In* three weeks I'll be Mrs Bianchi! And I'm going to be Mrs Bianchi (**6**) *in / for* the rest of my life. Isn't that wonderful?

3 Chuck sta progettando di andare a trovare il suo cugino inglese, Rick. Riempi gli spazi della loro chat online con la preposizione corretta.

Hi Rick. A few questions, if you have time?

Hi Chuck. Ask anything.

I'll be in classes **(1)** ......on....... weekdays. Will I have time for shopping?

Of course! You can go shopping **(2)** .... weekends. Most shops are open all day **(3)** .... Saturdays, but they don't open **(4)** .... ten or eleven o'clock **(5)** .... Sundays.

What about getting home if I stay out late **(6)** .... the evening?
Do buses run **(7)** .... the night in your town?

There are some buses **(8)** .... the middle of the evening, but not after that, so if you're not home **(9)** .... ten, you'll have to get a taxi. Or cycle.

I don't really want to cycle in England **(10)** .... winter. Perhaps I could hire a car.

I don't think you can hire a car **(11)** .... your twenty-first birthday actually! But don't worry. You'll be here **(12)** .... six weeks and you'll soon get used to everything. Anyway, I'll make sure you have a good time.

That's great. Thanks for the help. See you.
Bye.

18.6   *BY, WITH* E *FOR*

La preposizione *by* ha diversi significati e può essere tradotta in italiano in modi diversi. Abbiamo già visto che corrisponde all'italiano **presso** quando ha valore di luogo e a **entro** quando ha valore di tempo. Ma *by* ha molti altri usi.

■ Si usa *by* per introdurre il **complemento di agente** nelle frasi passive.

*The window was smashed **by** Andy.*   *La finestra fu frantumata **da** Andy.*
*The fire was started **by** an electrical fault.*   *L'incendio fu causato **da** un guasto elettrico.*

■ *By* + *-ing* indica **come** viene compiuta un'azione e corrisponde al **gerundio** italiano.

*He smashed the window **by hitting** it with a hammer.*
*Frantumò la finestra **colpendola** con un martello.*
*He got in **by breaking** a window.*
*Riuscì ad entrare **spaccando** una finestra.*

By viene inoltre usato in molte espressioni di uso comune, che indicano:

■ **modi di viaggiare**.

324

by air/plane *in aereo*	by car *in macchina*	by bus *in/con l'autobus*	by rail/train *in/con il treno*	**Ma** *on foot* *a piedi*

My father usually goes to work by bus.   *Mio padre di solito va al lavoro con l'autobus.*
Do you prefer to travel by air or by train?   *Preferisci viaggiare in aereo o in treno?*

■ **modi di mettersi in contatto.**

by post	by email	by phone	**Ma** *to be on the phone* = *essere al telefono*

■ **modi in cui possono capitare le cose.**

by chance *per caso*	by accident *accidentalmente / per caso*	by mistake *per errore/sbaglio*	**Ma** *on purpose* *apposta / di proposito*

I got this job almost by chance.   *Ho avuto questo lavoro quasi per caso.*
I'm sorry, I dialled your number by mistake.   *Mi dispiace, ho fatto il suo numero per errore.*

■ Si usa *with* + **sostantivo** per indicare lo **strumento** con cui un'azione è stata compiuta.

He smashed the window with a hammer.   *Spaccò la finestra con un martello.*
He covered his face with his handkerchief.   *Si coprì la faccia con un fazzoletto.*
The butler was killed with a knife.   *Il maggiordomo fu ucciso con un coltello.*

■ Si usa *for* seguito da *-ing* o da **sostantivo** per spiegare **la funzione di un oggetto**.

Hammers are normally used for knocking in nails, not for smashing windows!
I martelli di solito si usano per conficcare i chiodi, non per spaccare le finestre!

■ Si usa *for* seguito da *-ing* o da **sostantivo** anche per **spiegare il motivo di un'azione**.

They thanked me for listening to them.   *Mi ringraziarono per averli ascoltati.*
The man received an award for bravery.   *L'uomo ricevette un premio per il suo coraggio.*

PRACTICE

1 Riempi gli spazi con *by*, *with* o *for*.

1 Many people prefer to travel ...by... train. It's more relaxing.

2 Harry's hands were full so he opened the door .... his foot.

3 The forest fire was started .... an arsonist.

4 This means that someone started the fire .... a match or a lighter.

5 Mary met her ex-boyfriend in a bookshop .... chance. She hadn't seen him for years.

6 I use my iPod .... listening to music when I travel.

7 The underground system in Paris is quite complicated. It's easy to get off the train at the wrong station .... mistake.

8 Ben was sent confirmation of his booking .... email.

9 My father was given a fine .... speeding.

10 Emily lost the key to her bicycle. Her father had to cut the chain .... a saw.

11 Some people react very badly when they are stung .... a bee.

12 Emails are very useful .... keeping in touch with friends.

325

2 Completa le frasi seguenti usando **by** e una delle parole nel riquadro.

> ear   Florence University   ~~accident~~   ferry   post   global warming

1   I didn't mean to take your English book. I took it .....by accident........ .

2   You can go to Ireland ....

3   Roberto Benigni was given an honorary degree ....

4   Many scientists believe that extreme meteorological conditions are caused ....

5   The contract will be sent ....

6   She is very musical. She can pick out any tune on the piano ....

18.7   ESPRESSIONI COMUNI CON PREPOSIZIONI: *ON HOLIDAY, IN A HURRY*

Molte espressioni di uso comune sono introdotte da preposizioni. Ecco qualche esempio:

on holiday	*in vacanza*
on/off duty	*in/fuori servizio*
on business	*per affari*
to be in love	*essere innamorato*
to fall in love	*innamorarsi*

John is in love with Mischa. He fell in love with her during the school trip.
John è innamorato di Mischa. Si è innamorato di lei durante la gita scolastica.

in secret	*in segreto*
in danger	*in pericolo*
in bed	*a letto*
in a hurry	*in/di fretta*
in/out of stock	*disponibile/esaurito*
in/out of danger	*in/fuori pericolo*
at lunch	*a pranzo*
at peace	*in pace*
at war	*in guerra*

ALCUNE ESPRESSIONI DA NON CONFONDERE

Confronta le espressioni seguenti:

at least	**at last**
*That bike must have cost **at least** five hundred pounds.*	*The work took a long time but **at last** it was finished.*
*Quella bicicletta deve essere costata **almeno** cinquecento sterline.*	*Il lavoro ha richiesto un sacco di tempo, ma **finalmente / alla fine** è stato completato.*

on the way	in the way
*I'm going to my office so I'll call and see you **on the way**.*	*I can't move the table because that chair's **in the way**.*
Sto andando in ufficio così passerò a trovarti mentre sono per strada.	*Non riesco a muovere il tavolo perché quella sedia è **d'ostacolo / nel mezzo**.*
to be the matter with	to be about
*What **was the matter with** Lesley? Why was she upset?*	*What's the book **about**?*
Cosa era successo a *Lesley? Perché era turbata?*	**Di che cosa parla** *quel libro?*

PRACTICE

1 Riempi gli spazi con una preposizione.

1   I didn't buy any new boots because the shop didn't have my size ....in..... stock.

2   Most of our guests arrived .... car but my brother came .... foot.

3   You shouldn't be .... work with that awful cough. You should be .... home, ... bed.

4   I deleted your email .... mistake. I didn't do it .... purpose.

5   I usually travel .... train when I go to Scotland .... business.

6   The movie star met her lover .... secret because they didn't want to be seen together .... public.

7   Every time I try to see the manager he's either .... lunch or .... the phone.

8   They met .... chance on a train and they've been .... love ever since.

9   If you're not .... a hurry, we could go to the city centre .... bike.

2 Completa le frasi seguenti con le espressioni nel riquadro. Usa ogni espressione una sola volta.

on business	out of stock	in the way	at least	in love
the matter with	at lunch	in bed	in a hurry	on the way

1   Sally's mother is frequently away from home ...on business.... .

2   Did you say you need help with your computer? I'll drop in .... home.

3   **A** What's .... Peter? **B** He's met a girl. He's ....

4   Could you move your scooter, please? It's .... and I can't get mine out.

5   The journey will take .... an hour, so you're unlikely to be home by lunchtime.

6   I wanted to buy the latest *Harry Potter* book for my little brother, but at the bookshop they said it was ....

7   Bill tried to phone his father in his office at 12.30, but the secretary said that he was ....

8   My sister is very lazy. She sometimes stays .... until lunchtime.

9   Would you mind giving me a lift to school? I'm late and so I'm ....

18.8   *TO BE* + AGGETTIVO + PREPOSIZIONE

Alcuni aggettivi sono seguiti da preposizioni particolari. Ecco alcuni esempi di uso comune:

To be + aggettivo + preposizione + complementi			
He *was good*	*at*	football.	**Era bravo** *a calcio.*
We *were angry*	*with*	our friends.	**Eravamo arrabbiati con** *i nostri amici.*
She *will be angry*	*about*	losing the match.	**Sarà arrabbiata per** *aver perso la partita.*
Were they *happy/excited/ worried*	*about*	their exam results?	**Erano felici/eccitati/preoccupati per** *il risultato degli esami?*
I *was pleased*	*with*	the present.	**Fui contento del** *regalo.*
We mustn't *be unkind*	*to*	our cousins.	Non dobbiamo **essere scortesi con** *i nostri cugini.*
Don't *be rude*	*to*	anyone at the party.	Non **essere maleducato con** *nessuno alla festa.*
Please *be polite*	*to*	my parents.	Per favore **sii cortese con** *i miei genitori.*
Are you *interested*	*in*	football?	**Sei interessato al** *calcio?*

PRACTICE

1   Abbina gli inizi delle frasi con le loro logiche conclusioni.

1   The taxi driver was angry ....*e*...
2   My brother is very good ....
3   Peter was worried ....
4   David was pleased ....
5   The postman was rude ....
6   We're not interested ....

a   in football.
b   with the present.
c   to my neighbour.
d   about losing his job.
e   with the cyclist.
f   at doing word puzzles.

2   In ognuna di queste frasi c'è una preposizione sbagliata. <u>Sottolinea</u> gli errori e correggili.

1   We saw that the house was <u>in</u> fire, but luckily no one was in danger. ....*on*...........
2   The nurses have been very kind to you so you mustn't be rude with them. ....
3   There are boats at hire here, or we can go for a swim. ....
4   Are you in this country for holiday or are you working? ....
5   My mother's in work at the moment, but she can phone you this evening. ....

ALL IN ONE REVISION

1 Ascolterai un notiziario. Prima di ascoltare, guarda attentamente le immagini sullo schermo e cerca di indovinare di che notizie si tratta.

a ....   **b** ....

c ....   **d** ....

2 Ascolta e verifica se avevi ragione. Mentre ascolti, metti le immagini sullo schermo nell'ordine in cui vengono date le notizie.

1 ....   2 ....   3 ....   4 ....

2.17

3 Ascolta di nuovo e rispondi a queste domande. Ferma la registrazione se è necessario.

2.18

1 Where will the Prime Minister be for the next two days? ..At..a..conference..in..Washington........

2 When will he fly to Mexico? ....

3 Where did Moira MacNab's plane hit bad weather? ....

4 When does she say she will be quite well? ....

5 How far do the traffic jams stretch? ....

6 How long will the motorway remain closed? ....

7 Where was the security man? ....

8 When was the manager released? ....

4 Rileggi le risposte che hai dato nell'esercizio 3.

1 Which prepositions are used in answers about time? ....

2 Which prepositions are used in answers about place? ....

5 Sara è in treno e sta parlando al telefonino con la sua amica Rebecca. Completa la conversazione con le preposizioni nel riquadro.

| at | at | by | by | during | for | in | in | ~~on~~ | over | until |

In Rebecca's office, 11.30 am.

Rebecca: Rebecca White.

Sara: Hi, it's Sara. I'm **(1)** ......on....... the train. Can you meet me **(2)** .... the station?

Rebecca: What time?

Sara: Three.

Rebecca: I think so. The car's got a puncture. If I can arrange to get it fixed **(3)** .... my break, I'll be there.

Sara: Thanks, that's great.

At the garage, 1.40 pm.

Rebecca: Can you fix this puncture for me?

Mechanic: Yes, probably. But my assistant won't be back from lunch **(4)** .... half an hour and I'll be working on this other job **(5)** .... then.

Rebecca: Well, I've got to collect someone from the station **(6)** .... three.

Mechanic: Oh, that's no problem. We'll have it done **(7)** .... half past two easily.

Rebecca: Thanks. I'll be back **(8)** .... an hour, OK?

Mechanic: Fine. See you then.

On the train, 2.10 pm.

Sara: Hello?

Rebecca: The car's being fixed now. I'll wait for you **(9)** .... the main door of the station, so I can help carry your stuff.

Sara: Don't worry. I haven't got anything heavy. I'll see you **(10)** .... the car park. It's just **(11)** .... the footbridge, isn't it?

Rebecca: Yes, that's right. See you there.

Sara: Bye.

6 Riempi gli spazi in questa email con le preposizioni appropriate.

Hi everyone!

How are you? We're having a great time in Thailand. **(1)** .... the moment we're still **(2)** .... the north of the country. This evening we're flying to Bangkok where we'll visit the amazing palaces **(3)** .... the morning and then go shopping **(4)** .... a few hours. **(5)** .... the weekend we'll head south to Phuket. We're going to book a morning flight so we'll be there **(6)** .... midday at the latest. We'll go to Phi Phi island from there **(7)** .... Monday. We've booked a bungalow. The tourist office says it's **(8)** .... the end of a long beach, **(9)** .... gardens which lie **(10)** .... the beach and the hillside. We're going to go snorkelling and we can't wait to go swimming **(11)** .... the tropical fish! We'll stay there **(12)** .... about a week and then we'll come home.

See you all then,

love Emmy and Sam

7 Il proprietario di un albergo sta mostrando ad alcuni visitatori il suo albergo completamente ristrutturato. Riempi gli spazi con le preposizioni corrette.

We're now standing **(1)** ....in........... the lounge, a beautiful room, with paintings **(2)** .... the ceiling and a wonderful view **(3)** .... the park to the hills **(4)** .... it. The cellar is being decorated **(5)** .... present, but we will open it as a restaurant **(6)** .... a few months' time. **(7)** .... then we are serving meals **(8)** .... the dining room only.

Do you see the trees planted all **(9)** .... the sides of the road up to the front door? They are going to be hung with coloured lights **(10)** .... special occasions. If we go **(11)** .... that gate, we'll reach the rose garden, where you can see a number of interesting sculptures on display **(12)** .... the bushes.

8 Traduci.

1   Siamo arrivati a Buckingham Palace alle 11 e mezzo, in tempo per vedere il Cambio della Guardia.

2   Se vuoi un biglietto per il concerto, fammelo sapere entro martedì.

3   Abbiamo pianto tutti alla fine del film.

4   Partiamo domani mattina, ma saremo di ritorno tra due settimane.

5   All'inizio non mi piaceva, ma alla fine siamo diventati buoni amici.

6   Nella mia scuola le lezioni iniziano sempre in perfetto orario.

7   A che ora sei arrivato al lavoro ieri mattina?

8   Non c'è nessuno a casa. Devono essere in vacanza.

9   Questa chiesa fu costruita nel XV secolo.

10   Ho trovato una lettera sul pavimento sotto il divano.

I *PHRASAL VERBS*

I *PHRASAL VERBS* – INTRODUZIONE

Per *phrasal verbs* si intende un gruppo di verbi tipici della lingua inglese, chiamati in italiano verbi frasali o fraseologici. Sono formati da **due parti**: la prima è un verbo, breve e di uso comune, come *look*, *get*, *make*; la seconda consiste di una o due parole (una preposizione, un avverbio, oppure avverbio + preposizione).

Uno stesso verbo può formare *phrasal verbs* differenti.

look after	*Ted **looks after** his little brother.*
	***Ted si occupa del / bada al** fratellino.*
look out	***Look out!** There's a car coming.*
	***Stai attento!** Sta arrivando una macchina.*
look up	*They **looked up** the word in the dictionary.*
	***Cercarono** la parola nel vocabolario.*
look forward to	*I'm **looking forward to** meeting them.*
	***Non vedo l'ora di** incontrarli.*

Talvolta il significato dei *phrasal verbs* è chiaro: la preposizione o l'avverbio che ne fanno parte sono collegati intuitivamente al verbo.

put down	*Please **put down** your pencils. (**put + down**)*
	*Per favore **posate** (= mettete giù) le matite.*

Spesso, però, il significato del *phrasal verb* non è così evidente e nemmeno il contesto lo chiarisce in modo definitivo. Bisogna quindi impararne il significato.

make up	*Bill is very good at **making up** stories.*
	*Bill è bravissimo a **inventare** storie.*

L'impiego dei *phrasal verbs* segnala che colui che parla sa usare la lingua inglese in modo spontaneo e naturale.

19.1 SIGNIFICATO E FORMA

Come abbiamo visto, a volte il significato dei *phrasal verbs* è intuibile.

pick up	*I **picked up** the phone.*
	***Sollevai** il ricevitore.*

In questo caso *picked* e *up* mantengono il loro significato normale.

Tuttavia, molti *phrasal verbs* sono **idiomatici**, perché il loro significato è diverso da quello delle parole separate che li compongono, e l'unica soluzione è imparare il loro significato. Possono essere formati dallo stesso verbo ma avere significati completamente differenti, a seconda della preposizione o dell'avverbio che segue.

turn back	*He **turned back** because he had left something at home.*
	***Tornò indietro** perché aveva lasciato qualcosa a casa.*
turn down	*He **turned down** the invitation because he was feeling tired.*
	***Rifiutò** l'invito perché si sentiva stanco.*
turn up	*They **turned up** unexpectedly.*
	***Arrivarono** inaspettatamente.*

Lo stesso *phrasal verb* può avere diversi significati.

*She **put on** her clothes.*	***Si mise** i vestiti.*
*She **put on** weight.*	***Ha messo su** peso. / È ingrassata.*
*She **put on** the light.*	***Accese** la luce.*
*The students **put on** a play.*	*Gli studenti **misero in scena** una commedia.*

La forma dei *phrasal verbs* può variare.

Alcuni verbi sono formati da **due parole**: un **verbo** e un'altra parola, talvolta chiamata particella, che può essere una **preposizione** (*at, from* ecc.) oppure un **avverbio** (*back, out* ecc.).

*Let's **get off** the bus.*	***Scendiamo** dall'autobus.*
*You can't **go on** like that.*	*Non puoi **continuare** così.*

Alcuni verbi sono formati da **tre parole**: un **verbo** (es. *come*) + **un avverbio** (es. *up*) + una **preposizione** (es. *against*).

*We have **come up against** a lot of difficulties.*	***Abbiamo incontrato** molte difficoltà.*

I *phrasal verbs* si comportano diversamente a seconda che siano costituiti da:

- ■ verbo + preposizione
- ■ verbo + avverbio
- ■ verbo + avverbio + preposizione

PRACTICE

1 Riempi gli spazi con un *phrasal verb* nel riquadro. Fai attenzione a usare il tempo giusto.

turn down	put on (x2)	not go on	turn up	get off	turn back	come up against

1 Jake ..*has put on*.. a lot of weight recently. He's looking quite plump.

2 Sally only invited fifteen friends to her party, but another twelve people .... on the day.

3 Did you really .... Riccardo's invitation to dinner?

4 My drama club .... *Macbeth* next month.

5 Jim and Barry almost got to the top of the mountain, but then it started snowing and they had to ....

6 Sandra managed to pass her final exams, but she .... a lot of difficulties because there were various problems in her family at the time.

7 I know this isn't our stop, but would you mind .... the bus here? I feel sick.

8 Karen .... with her studies after her exams because she was fed up with school.

2 Ci sono otto *phrasal verbs* in questa storia. <u>Sottolineali</u>, poi abbinali al verbo nel riquadro che ha lo stesso significato. Usa il dizionario se ne hai bisogno, oppure consulta **Appendice 3 –** *Phrasal verbs*, pag. 433.

1 arrived	**2** became	**3** connected	**4** delayed ....
5 entered	**6** refused	**7** removed	**8** started ....

Last night I had dinner with some friends and set off around eleven o'clock to walk home. Passing an office block, I saw a moving light through a window so I phoned the police station. I was put through to a detective and told him what I'd seen. He promised to come immediately, but he was held up for three-quarters of an hour by a traffic jam. All the city centre roads were blocked by an accident. While I was waiting for him, a man turned up in a car. He asked me why I was there. I explained I'd seen a light, and he told me he was a policeman on his way home. We went to the back of the building and found a broken window. The man got into the building through the window. I said I could help him but he turned down my offer, so I waited for the detective. At last he arrived with a colleague and I told him about the man in the car. He made a note of the number and phoned the police station. Some more police came. One took away the car and the others watched the building. When the man and his friend tried to leave, the detectives arrested them. I'd planned a quiet walk, but it turned into an adventure!

19.2 DIFFERENZA TRA PREPOSIZIONI E AVVERBI

In inglese, la differenza tra preposizioni e avverbi non è così netta come in italiano. Alcune particelle possono avere valore sia di preposizione che di avverbio.
Confronta le frasi seguenti:

Preposizione	Avverbio
down	*down*
*I **ran down** the stairs.*	*Please **sit down**.*
Corsi giù *per le scale.*	**Sedetevi**, *per favore.*
in	*in*
*We tried all the doors but we couldn't **get in**.*	*They didn't **let** me **in**.*
*Abbiamo provato tutte le porte ma non siamo riusciti a **entrare**.*	*Non mi fecero **entrare**.*

up
*We **climbed up** the hill.*
*Ci **arrampicammo su** per la collina.*

round
*I don't know how the news **got round** the office,*
but everyone seems to know!
*Non so come la notizia **si sia diffusa** in ufficio,*
ma sembra che tutti lo sappiano!

up
*She **picked** the book **up**. / She **picked up** the book.*
Raccolse il libro.

round
Come round one of these evenings.
Vieni a trovarmi una di queste sere.

Solo preposizione	Solo avverbio
from during into at for of with after	back away out

La maggioranza di queste particelle, tuttavia, può avere entrambe le funzioni. Queste sono le più importanti:

Preposizione/avverbio
above   about   across   along   before   behind   by   down   in   off   on   over   past   round   through   under   up

Quando non siamo sicuri, è opportuno controllare in un buon dizionario se un *phrasal verb* è formato da **verbo** + **preposizione** oppure da **verbo** + **avverbio**.

PRACTICE

1 Per ogni coppia di *phrasal verbs*, indica se la particella che compone il *phrasal verb* ha funzione di preposizione o di avverbio. Scrivi **P** per preposizione e **A** per avverbio.

1 a George got **on** his motorbike and went to work. ..P...

b Bill has a terrible relationship with his dad. They don't get **on** at all. ......

2 a If you get **off** the train at Camden Town, you can walk to the market from there. ......

b It took them all morning to get ready. They didn't set **off** until lunchtime. ......

3 a Sam was so tired after the football match that he went to lie **down** for an hour. ......

b He was driving so fast he nearly ran **down** a pedestrian on the corner. ......

4 a Mandy went **up** the hill to see the view from the top. ......

b Jim was injured last month. He's had to give **up** football. ......

5 a Teenagers usually care **about** their appearance. ......

b Religious conflict can bring **about** war. ......

19.3 VERBO + PREPOSIZIONE: *LOOK AFTER, COUNT ON* – POSIZIONE DELL'OGGETTO

Verbo + preposizione + oggetto		
get over	*Sally has got over*	*her illness.*
	Sally ha superato	*la sua malattia.*

Quando un ***phrasal verb*** è formato da un verbo e una preposizione:

▪ è transitivo, quindi ha sempre un **oggetto**. L'oggetto può essere implicito.

*We couldn't **get in** (the house).*　　　　　*Non siamo riusciti a **entrare** (in casa).*

▪ l'**oggetto** (nome o pronome) va sempre **dopo la preposizione**: il verbo e la sua preposizione **non possono essere separati**.

look after	*My husband **is looking after** the kids today.* (**Non** ~~is looking the kids after~~)
	*Mio marito **si occupa dei** bambini oggi.*
count on	*I **counted on** them.* (**Non** ~~counted them on~~)
	***Contavo su** di loro.*
care about	*I really **cared about** him.* (**Non** ~~I cared him about~~)
	***Tenevo molto a** lui. / Gli **volevo davvero bene**.*
look for	*I'm **looking for** my keys.* (**Non** ~~I'm looking my keys for~~)
	*Sto **cercando** le mie chiavi.*
look into	*The police **are looking into** the disappearance of an ancient manuscript.*
	*La polizia **sta indagando** sulla scomparsa di un antico manoscritto.*
look at	*I'll get the doctor **to look at** your knee.*
	*Chiederò al dottore **di guardarti** il ginocchio.*

PRACTICE

1 Riempi gli spazi con le preposizioni nel riquadro.

for	over	after	on	off	about	into	at	in	across

1 It's important to be able to count ....on.......... your friends.

2 Kylie's boyfriend left her six months ago, but she still hasn't got .... it.

3 Kylie was very upset when her boyfriend left her. She really cared .... him.

4 The burglar tried to climb through the bathroom window, but it was too small and he couldn't get ....

5 Susie doesn't mind looking .... her little sister because she's such good company.

6 A woman was robbed by a gang of teenagers yesterday. The police are looking .... it.

7 Joe got .... the underground at Marble Arch and walked across Hyde Park to Speakers' Corner.

8 Alice has lost her iPod charger. She's been looking .... it for two hours.

9 Escher's drawings often look possible at first, but when you look .... them more carefully you realise that they are an optical illusion.

19.4 VERBO + AVVERBIO: *CALL OFF, BACK UP* – POSIZIONE DELL'OGGETTO

I *phrasal verbs* formati da un verbo e un avverbio possono essere sia **transitivi** che **intransitivi**. Questo significa che:

■ non sempre hanno l'oggetto.

get together	*They **got together** every Monday morning.*
	Si riunivano/incontravano *tutti i lunedì mattina.*
carry on	*They **carried on** without me.*
	Continuarono *senza di me.*

■ quando sono **transitivi** hanno sempre un **oggetto**. L'oggetto può essere sia un **nome** che un **pronome**.

Quando è un nome, l'oggetto può essere posto **sia prima che dopo l'avverbio**: verbo e avverbio possono essere separati.

Quando è un pronome, l'oggetto **deve andare tra il verbo e l'avverbio**.

Confronta le frasi seguenti:

*They **called** the concert **off**.*	*They **called** it **off**.*
*They **called off** the concert.*	(**Non** ~~called off it~~)
Cancellarono *il concerto.*	*Lo* **cancellarono**.
*They **didn't back** Britney **up**.*	*They **didn't back** her **up**.*
*They **didn't back up** Britney.*	(**Non** ~~didn't back up her~~)
Non appoggiarono *Britney.*	*Non la* **appoggiarono**.
*They **threw out** the trouble-makers.*	*They **threw** them **out**.*
*They **threw** the trouble-makers **out**.*	(**Non** ~~threw out them~~)
Buttarono fuori *gli esagitati.*	*Li* **buttarono fuori**.

Quando l'oggetto è molto lungo, di solito è posto **dopo l'avverbio**.

*They **called off** the concert, which had already been postponed twice.*
(**Non** ~~called the concert, which had already been postponed twice, off~~)
Cancellarono *il concerto, che era già stato rinviato due volte.*

📝 Alcuni *phrasal verbs* hanno due significati differenti: in un caso sono transitivi e nell'altro sono intransitivi. Confronta le frasi seguenti:

Give in

Transitivo: verbo + avverbio + oggetto	Intransitivo: verbo + avverbio
*I **gave in** my homework on time.*	*I won't **give in** until they pay me what they owe.*
Consegnai *i compiti con puntualità.*	*Non* **mi arrenderò** *finché non mi pagheranno quello che mi devono.*

PRACTICE

1 Riscrivi le frasi seguenti due volte, cambiando l'ordine delle parole. Usa il dizionario se ne hai bisogno, oppure consulta **Appendice 3 – *Phrasal verbs***, pag. 433.

1 She put on the television. .... *She put the television on. / She put it on.* ....

2 It isn't easy to bring children up these days. ....

3 Luca put away his football scarf at the end of the season. ....

4 The organisers decided to put off the celebrations until the weather improved.

....

5 Could you pick Michael up after the concert? ....

6 My mother made me take down the poster. ....

7 Anita has thrown her old dolls away. ....

8 I couldn't take in the information. ....

9 The dog frequently knocks over their little boy. ....

10 He brought his library books back on time. ....

2 Completa questi mini-dialoghi con un ***phrasal verb*** alla forma giusta e con il pronome tra parentesi. Fai attenzione a mettere il pronome nella posizione corretta. Usa il dizionario se ne hai bisogno, oppure consulta **Appendice 3 – *Phrasal verbs***, pag. 433.

1 **A** Do you think you'll ever give up playing football? (*it*)

   B Probably. My father .... last year at the age of forty-five.

2 **A** Don't forget to take your sunglasses off before you jump in. (*them*)

   B Thanks for reminding me. I've often dived in before .... in the past.

3 **A** Have you handed in your English essay yet? (*it*)

   B Yes, I .... yesterday.

4 **A** Do you think your friend in Amsterdam would put up my brother and his girlfriend for a few days? (*them*)

   B I'm sure he wouldn't mind ....

5 **A** Would you turn the music down a little? I can't concentrate. (*it*)

   B OK. I .... in a minute.

6 **A** I know it's my turn to pick the children up after school, but I've got a staff meeting at 4 o'clock. (*them*)

   B Don't worry, I'll .... I'm free this afternoon.

7 **A** When you finish filling in this form, please sign on the dotted line. (*it*)

   B Right. I've just finished .... and I've signed it.

8 **A** When did Lucy give out the leaflets about the competition? (*them*)

   B She .... on Saturday morning.

19.5 VERBO + AVVERBIO + PREPOSIZIONE: *GET ON WITH, COME UP AGAINST*

Quando un *phrasal verb* consiste di **tre parti**:

- è sempre **transitivo**, quindi **ha un oggetto**;
- l'oggetto, **sia nome che pronome**, va sempre **dopo** il *phrasal verb*: **le tre parti non possono essere separate**.

get on with	*I always **get on with** the other members of the group.* Io **vado** sempre **d'accordo con** gli altri membri del gruppo.
come up against	*We **came up against** some problems.* **Abbiamo incontrato** alcuni problemi.
put up with	*I can't **put up with** his rudeness any longer.* Non riesco più a **tollerare** la sua maleducazione.
	*I will have to **put up with** her for two more days.* Dovrò **sopportarla** altri due giorni.
get away with	*He **got away with** being late because the teacher didn't see him.* Arrivò in ritardo e **la passò liscia / la fece franca** perché l'insegnante non lo vide. *You are not going to **get away with** it.* Non **te la caverai.** / Non **la passerai liscia.**

PRACTICE

1 Inserisci accanto ai seguenti *phrasal verbs* le espressioni nel riquadro, a seconda del loro significato. Alcune espressioni sono comunemente associate con più di un verbo.

his parents   murder   my parents' rules   being rude   boring teachers   opposition
people at school   speeding   breaking the rules   resistance   his bad manners
my brothers   difficulties   terrible conditions   the school uniform   doing the minimum
pain   my teachers   a problem   the other members of the team   obstacles
my sister's horrible boyfriend   tax evasion

Phrasal verb collocations	
get on with	his parents, my brothers,
come up against	
put up with	
get away with	

2 **A** Cerca nel dizionario i **phrasal verbs** seguenti e decidi se sono formati da verbo + preposizione, verbo + avverbio o verbo + avverbio + preposizione. Poi decidi se il nome sottolineato può andare in un'altra posizione e riscrivi le frasi quando questo è possibile.

1 I can't *give up* chocolate however hard I try.
.....Verb + adverb. I can't give chocolate up however hard I try.....

2 He was so angry he *broke up* the sculpture into small pieces.
....

3 The girl *went over* her work several times before she was satisfied.
....

4 We've *run out of* biscuits – could you fetch some more?
....

5 I could tell from his expression that he'd *made up* the excuse.
....

6 I can't *put up with* that noise any longer.
....

7 I *looked after* the children while their mother was busy.
....

8 Don't forget to *put out* the lights when you leave.
....

9 With her dark eyes and hair, she *takes after* her father.
....

10 That shop *puts up* its prices every month.
....

B Sostituisci i nomi tra parentesi con un pronome e riscrivi le frasi mettendo il pronome nella posizione corretta.

1 I can't give up (*chocolate*) however hard I try.
.....I can't give it up however hard I try.....

2 He was so angry he broke up (*the sculpture*) into small pieces.
....

3 The girl went over (*her work*) several times before she was satisfied.
....

4 We've run out of (*biscuits*) – could you fetch some more?
....

5 I could tell from his expression that he'd made up (*the excuse*).
....

6 I can't put up with (*that noise*) any longer.
....

7   I looked after (*the children*) while their mother was busy.

....

8   Don't forget to put out (*the lights*) when you leave.

....

9   With her dark eyes and hair, she takes after (*her father*).

....

10   That shop puts up (*its prices*) every month.

....

19.6   ALCUNI *PHRASAL VERBS* CON *TAKE*

Quelli che seguono sono solo alcuni esempi di **phrasal verbs** con **take**, con i loro significati di uso più comune.

Phrasal verbs	Significati	Esempi
take after	**assomigliare** (a un membro della famiglia)	*You* **take after** *your mother.* **Assomigli** *a tua madre.*
take down	**prendere nota**, scrivere	***Take down*** *my email address.* **Segnati** *il mio indirizzo email.*
take off	**decollare**	*The flight to London Stansted* **has** *just* **taken off**. *Il volo per Londra Stansted* **è** *appena* **decollato**.
take (sb) off	**imitare**, fare il verso a qualcuno	*James can* **take off** *the Headteacher's voice perfectly.* *James sa* **imitare** *perfettamente la voce del Preside.*
take (sthg) off	**togliersi** i vestiti, spogliarsi	***Take off*** *your coat.* **Togliti** *il cappotto.*
take (sb) on	**assumere, impiegare**	*They are* **taking on** *extra staff for the summer.* **Stanno assumendo** *altro personale per l'estate.*
take (sthg) on	**assumersi, accettare** (es. una responsabilità)	*You can't* **take on** *any more responsibility.* *Non puoi* **assumerti** *altre responsabilità.*
take to	**prendere in simpatia**, affezionarsi a	*I* **took to** *her at once.* **Mi affezionai** *subito a lei.*
take up	**occupare spazio** (spesso eccessivo)	*This table* **takes up** *too much room.* *Questo tavolo* **occupa** *troppo spazio.*

PRACTICE

1 Abbina i *phrasal verbs* nelle frasi seguenti con i significati elencati sotto.

1 I've given all my old videos to a charity shop. They *took up* too much room on my shelves. ...f...

a left the ground

2 You really *take after* your dad. You've got exactly the same way of speaking. ....

b liked

3 We *took off* half an hour late, but we regained time during the flight. ....

c imitates/mimics

4 During security checks at airports passengers have to *take off* their coats and jackets and put them in a tray to be scanned. ....

d remove

5 Sophie really makes me laugh when she *takes off* Britney Spears. ....

e are similar to

6 I liked Maria immediately, but I've never *taken to* her twin sister. ....

f occupied/filled

2 Riempi gli spazi con un *phrasal verb* formato da *take*. Fai attenzione a usare il tempo giusto.

1 Pamela is a really nice girl. I'm sure you 'll take to her. at once when you meet her.

2 Would you work in a restaurant as a waiter if they .... ?

3 In order to really appreciate a comedian imitating someone, you have to know who s/he ....

4 I can't remember what we have to do for homework. I should have ....

5 My mother is very tired. She .... too much responsibility at work recently.

6 My elder sister, Clara, is so pretty and popular. I wish I ....

7 Don't forget .... your wet boots before you come into the house.

8 The plane caught fire while it ....

3 Traduci. I verbi in **neretto** sono tutti *phrasal verbs* con *take*.

1 Jemima **assomiglia** tutta a suo padre. Ha gli stessi occhi e lo stesso carattere.

2 **Mi sono trovata bene con** Julia dal momento in cui è venuta in classe nostra.

3 Come fai a muoverti qui? Il letto **occupa** mezza stanza.

4 Il poliziotto **prese nota dei** nomi dei testimoni.

5 Sto cominciando a pentirmi di **aver accettato** quel lavoro: faccio gli straordinari tutti i giorni.

6 **Togliti** le scarpe e i calzini e asciugati i piedi o prenderai un brutto raffreddore.

ALL IN ONE REVISION

Usa il dizionario per fare questi esercizi se ne hai bisogno, oppure consulta **Appendice 3 –** *Phrasal verbs*, pag. 433.

1 Ascolterai una ragazza di nome Donna parlare di un gruppo pop di cui ha fatto parte. Guarda le immagini, che fanno vedere quello che è successo. Leggi le frasi che seguono e mettile nell'ordine corretto.

a Bella, Jo and Zoe made plans without telling Donna. ☐

b Donna had some problems. ☐

c Donna left the group. ☐

d Donna was in a pop group with Bella, Jo and Zoe. ☐

e Donna had a row with the other girls. ☐

f One night the group didn't perform. ☐

2 Ascolta e verifica se avevi ragione.

2.19

3 Leggi le definizioni 1-11. Si riferiscono tutte ai *phrasal verbs* che Donna usa. Ascolta di nuovo e completa i *phrasal verbs*. Ferma la registrazione se è necessario.

2.20

1 separate = ...*break*........ up

2 have a good relationship = ... on with

3 rely on = ... on

4 support = ... up

5 take care of = ... after

6 continue = ... on

7 cancel = ... off

8 meet = ... together

9 discuss = ... over

10 make someone leave = ... out

11 surrender = ... in

343

4 In ciascuna di queste situazioni, il verbo in **neretto** suona molto formale. Sostituiscilo con un verbo dallo stesso significato scelto tra quelli nel riquadro, in modo che la frase suoni più naturale.

put out	take off	put off	put up

1 We've missed the last train. Can you **accommodate** us for the night? ....put us up.............

2 It's no good **postponing** it. That English essay is for tomorrow. ....

3 Tom forgot to **remove** his expensive new watch before going for a swim. ....

4 It took the firemen five hours to **extinguish** the fire. ....

5 Completa queste frasi con le preposizioni e gli avverbi nel riquadro in modo da formare *phrasal verbs* appropriati con *get*.

at	away with	by	down	on	out of	over	round	round to	through

1 Simon always manages to (get ...out of.....) doing the washing-up because he says he has a lot of homework.

2 My grandfather (got ....) the flu very quickly because he's such a fit man.

3 Maria's daughters must be on the phone all the time because I can never (get ....) when I try to ring her.

4 I tried to take a message but I didn't (get ....) everything Paula said.

5 Peter hasn't had much success with jobs so far but I'm sure he'll (get ....) in his new one.

6 I finally (got ....) watching the video of a film I recorded two months ago.

7 People think they need lots of money but you can (get ....) with very little.

8 We don't keep things on the top shelf because we can't (get ....) them without standing on the table.

9 The news of Billy and Jane's engagement (got ....) the office very quickly.

10 I can never (get ....) telling a lie because my face always goes bright red.

6 Riempi gli spazi con i **phrasal verbs** nel riquadro che hanno lo stesso significato dei verbi tra parentesi.

care for carry on cut down fill in put off ring up set off take in turn down turn up

I had been doing the same job for years and I didn't really **(1)** ...care for.... (*like*) it

any more but it was extremely well paid. Then one day I decided to look for another job, realising

I would need to **(2)** .... (*reduce*) what I spent on luxuries.

I **(3)** .... (*completed*) lots of forms but all my applications were **(4)** .... (*rejected*).

I **(5)** .... (*continued*) looking for a job but nothing suitable **(6)** .... (*appeared*) so

I booked a holiday. The day before I was due to **(7)** .... (*leave*) I was **(8)** ....

(*telephoned*) by a TV company who asked me to go for an interview the next day. I **(9)** ....

(*postponed*) my holiday immediately. It was the job of my dreams.

I could hardly **(10)** .... (*absorb*) the news when they offered it to me. And I never went

on that holiday!

7 Riempi gli spazi con la forma corretta dei verbi nel riquadro, in modo da formare i **phrasal verbs** appropriati.

break come do fall get give go hand look make turn work

On the Run

The film *On the Run* tells the story of three prisoners who manage to **(1)** ....break..... out of a jail on an island. One of the prison guards is not very honest. The prisoners **(2)** .... round him by offering him money and he **(3)** .... over some keys. They **(4)** .... for a nearby forest and decide to wait there for a bit because they haven't had time to **(5)** .... out a plan. While they **(6)** .... over the possibilities, a woman who is walking through the forest **(7)** .... across them and promises to bring them food each day if they help her to **(8)** .... for wood. They are hungry and are not very good at **(9)** .... without their dinner. She is also very beautiful so they **(10)** .... in with her idea. But on the third day the woman **(11)** .... up with a policeman. She **(12)** .... away their secret in order to get the reward offered.

★★★

345

8 Traduci queste frasi, usando in ognuna un ***phrasal verb***.

1 Devo telefonare al dentista per **rinviare** l'appuntamento alla settimana prossima.

2 **Non vedo l'ora di** festeggiare il mio diciottesimo compleanno. Tutti i miei amici verranno alla mia festa.

3 Non **vado d'accordo con** Bill. Lo trovo presuntuoso e arrogante.

4 Tutti gli studenti **hanno consegnato** il compito prima che finisse l'ora.

5 Non siamo riusciti a trovare una camera d'albergo. Puoi **ospitarci** per la notte?

6 Jeff dice un sacco di bugie, ma **riesce sempre a cavarsela**.

7 Può **compilare** questo modulo, per favore?

8 Dovettero **annullare** il concerto a causa del maltempo.

9 Non so come fai a **sopportare** il suo cattivo carattere.

10 Non preoccuparti per Angela: sa **badare a** se stessa.

FRASI CONDIZIONALI (1)

FRASI CONDIZIONALI (1) – INTRODUZIONE

Le frasi condizionali o ipotetiche indicano la **condizione necessaria** (*if* = **se**) affinché si verifichi il **risultato** espresso nella frase principale. In inglese la condizione si definisce *if- clause*.

Condizione: *if- clause*	Risultato: frase principale = *main clause*
If I **didn't have** *a lot of work,*	*my evenings* **would be** *free.*
Se non avessi *così tanto lavoro,*	*le mie serate* **sarebbero** *libere.*

Non tutte le frasi condizionali richiedono il modo condizionale. L'uso dei modi e dei tempi nelle frasi condizionali dipende dal tipo di condizione e di risultato.

La condizione e il suo risultato possono essere:

■ **reali**;

■ **possibili** oppure riferirsi **a un'ipotesi immaginaria**;

■ **non più realizzabili**;

■ **veri** in generale, oppure **collegati a un evento particolare**.

Spesso la *if- clause* precede la frase principale, ma talvolta la principale viene prima. Quando la frase principale viene prima **non** si usa la virgola.

If- clause	frase principale
If *you work here,*	*your evenings will be free.*
Se *lavorerai qui,*	*avrai le serate libere.*

Frase principale	*if- clause*
Your evenings will be free	*if* *you work here.*
Avrai le serate libere	*se* *lavorerai qui.*

In inglese esistono quattro tipi diversi di frasi condizionali, o **periodo ipotetico**: tipo zero, primo tipo, secondo tipo e terzo tipo.

Per prima cosa, questa *Unit* introduce il periodo ipotetico di tipo zero e di primo tipo, che enunciano rispettivamente verità generali o ipotesi realistiche e vengono espressi con il modo indicativo.

Vengono presentati poi i tempi del condizionale e i significati che essi esprimono. Infine, si passa a trattare il periodo ipotetico di secondo e terzo tipo, che richiedono l'uso dei tempi del condizionale, *would* e *would have*.

20.1 PERIODO IPOTETICO DI TIPO ZERO

Il periodo ipotetico detto di tipo zero è usato per enunciare **verità generali**, leggi naturali sempre valide. Nel periodo ipotetico di tipo zero i tempi della frase principale e della *if- clause* sono uguali.

If- clause If + present simple,	frase principale present simple	Frase principale Present simple	if- clause if + present simple
*If you're in love, nothing else **matters**.* **Se sei** innamorato, nient'altro **conta**.		*Nothing else **matters** if you're in love.* Nient'altro **conta** se sei innamorato.	
*If you're in love, all the world **seems** wonderful.* **Se sei** innamorato, tutto il mondo **sembra** meraviglioso.		*All the world **seems** wonderful if you're in love.* Tutto il mondo **sembra** meraviglioso **se sei** innamorato.	
*If customers **have** to wait, they **get** annoyed.* **Se** i clienti devono aspettare, **si irritano**.		*Customers **get** annoyed if they **have** to wait.* I clienti **si irritano** se **devono** aspettare.	
*If we **heat** ice, it **melts**.* **Se si riscalda** il ghiaccio, **si scioglie**.		*Ice **melts** if we **heat** it.* Il ghiaccio **si scioglie** se si riscalda.	

Nel tipo zero *if* può essere generalmente sostituito da **when**, senza differenza di significato.

*If/When we **heat** ice, it **melts**.*   **Se/Quando** si **riscalda** il ghiaccio, si **scioglie**.

PRACTICE

1 Completa le frasi seguenti in modo personale.

1 Coffee tastes good .... *if you put sugar in it* ....

2 Parties are fun if ....

3 Children are naughty if ....

4 People steal things if ....

5 I always phone my friends if ....

6 Politicians lose elections if ....

2 Completa le frasi seguenti coniugando i verbi tra parentesi al tempo richiesto dal periodo ipotetico di tipo zero.

1 If your mobile phone *doesn't work*, the battery probably *needs* recharging. (*not work, need*)

2 If a cat .... ginger fur, it .... probably male. (*have, be*)

3 When Italians .... to Great Britain, they .... an adaptor for their electrical appliances. (*go, need*)

4 If children .... their vegetables, they .... fewer defences against illness. (*not eat, have*)

5 If a lizard .... its tail, it .... again. (*lose, grow*)

6 When the temperature .... below zero, country roads .... often icy. (*fall, be*)

7 If you .... plants, they .... (*not water, die*)

8 When rain .... , it .... as hail. (*freeze, fall*)

9 When someone .... as famous as Julia Roberts, everyone .... them in the street. (*be, recognise*)

20.2 PERIODO IPOTETICO DI PRIMO TIPO

Il periodo ipotetico di primo tipo viene usato per parlare di un'ipotesi che riteniamo **realistica** o **possibile**. È importante notare che nella frase introdotta da *if* si usa **sempre** il **presente**, mentre in italiano si può usare anche il futuro.

If I save £2000, I'll go to South America.
Se metto/metterò da parte £2000, andrò in Sudamerica.

Anche nel periodo ipotetico di primo tipo la **if-clause** può precedere o seguire la frase principale, a seconda del rilievo che vogliamo darle.

If-clause If + present simple,	frase principale will future	Frase principale will future	if-clause if + present simple
*If you **leave** me, I'll **die** of a broken heart.* (**Non** *If you'll leave*) **Se mi lasci morirò** con il cuore spezzato. *If you **buy** me a diamond ring, I'll **love** you forever.* (**Non** *If you'll buy*) **Se mi compri/comprerai** un anello di diamanti ti **amerò** per sempre.		*I'll **die** of a broken heart **if** you **leave** me.* **Morirò** con il cuore spezzato **se mi lasci**. *I'll **love** you forever **if** you **buy** me a diamond ring.* **Ti amerò** per sempre **se mi compri/comprerai** un anello di diamanti.	

Talvolta è possibile usare l'imperativo per esprimere questa idea. L'**imperativo precede sempre**.

Imperativo + *and* + *will future*
*Leave me **and** I'll **die** of a broken heart.* **Lasciami e morirò** con il cuore spezzato. *Buy me a diamond ring **and** I'll **love** you forever.* **Comprami** un anello **e ti amerò** per sempre.

Anche nel periodo ipotetico di primo tipo *if* può essere sostituito da **when**, ma con una differenza di significato.

When I have £2000, I'll go to South America.
Quando avrò £2000 andrò in Sudamerica.
(= **sono sicuro** che avrò £2000 un giorno e allora andrò sicuramente in Sudamerica)

If I have £2000, I'll go to South America.
Se avrò £2000 andrò in Sudamerica.
(= **forse** riuscirò a mettere da parte £2000 un giorno e allora andrò in Sudamerica)

PRACTICE

1   Abbina gli inizi delle frasi con le loro logiche conclusioni.

1 If you never smile ..h..	**a** I won't invite her again.
2 Give him the opportunity	**b** he'll go somewhere exciting in the summer.
3 If you leave your bedroom door open	**c** I'll call you and we can meet up.
4 If Lizzie doesn't come to my party	**d** global warming will get worse.
5 If I'm ever in the area	**e** and he'll do well.
6 If Joe manages to save some money	**f** she'll never pass her school exams.
7 Do what your mother tells you	**g** they'll find it more difficult to do later.
8 If governments don't change their energy policies	**h** people will think you're unfriendly.
9 If people don't look after themselves when they're young	**i** or she won't let you go out this evening.
10 If Jill doesn't start doing some work	**j** the cat will sleep on the bed.

2   Completa le frasi seguenti con la forma corretta dei verbi nel riquadro.

> become   buy   die   eat   not enjoy   give   learn   ~~make~~   take   tell

1   If you're tired, I ......'ll make..... some coffee for you.

2   These flowers .... if you forget to water them.

3   Many students .... faster if they work with a friend.

4   We .... some fruit if we go to the market this afternoon.

5   If you don't want that sausage, the cat .... it.

6   The bus driver .... us when we reach our stop if we ask him.

7   Children .... school if the lessons are boring.

8   My boyfriend's parents .... him a car if he passes all his exams.

9   If people don't get enough sleep, they .... ill.

10   I .... you to the cinema if you help me finish this exercise.

3   Leggi questa conversazione e <u>sottolinea</u> **if** o **when** a seconda del significato della frase.

Liz: I'm going to walk to the station to catch the London train.

Dan: But it may rain. Why not get a taxi?

Liz: Don't worry, I'll use my umbrella **(1)** *if* / *when* it rains.

Dan: Well, hurry up! **(2)** *If* / *When* you don't leave now, the train will go without you.

Liz: OK, I'm going. Goodbye.

Dan: Will you phone me **(3)** *if / when* you arrive in London?

Liz: I'll try to phone from the hotel **(4)** *if / when* I have time before
my first meeting.

Dan: Leave a message **(5)** *if / when* I'm not in. I might be at the shops. Bye.

Liz: Bye.

20.3   IL CONDIZIONALE PRESENTE: *WOULD*

Il condizionale presente si forma con l'ausiliare *would* seguito dalla **forma base** del verbo, **infinito senza** *to*.

Affermativo	Negativo	Interrogativo		
I **would** (**'d**) go	I **wouldn't** go	**Would** I go?	**+**	*I'd go*
you **would** (**'d**) go	you **wouldn't** go	**Would** you go?		
he/she/it **would** (**'d**) go	he/she/it **wouldn't** go	**Would** he/she/it go?	**−**	*She **wouldn't** go.*
we **would** (**'d**) go	we **wouldn't** go	**Would** we go?		
you **would** (**'d**) go	you **wouldn't** go	**Would** you go?	**?**	*Would you go?*
they **would** (**'d**) go	they **wouldn't** go	**Would** they go?		

Il condizionale presente viene usato di norma:

■ per esprimere un **desiderio**. (Vedi *Unit* **21**)

I'd like to go to New York next year.　　*Vorrei andare a New York l'anno prossimo.*
*She **would be** really happy to meet you.*　　*Sarebbe molto felice di conoscerti.*

■ per **chiedere** o per **offrire** qualcosa in modo cortese.

*Would you **lend** me your car this afternoon, please?*　　*Mi **presteresti** la tua macchina questo pomeriggio, per favore?*
*Would you **like** something to eat?*　　*Vorresti qualcosa da mangiare?*
*Would you **like** me to stand in for you?*　　*Vuoi che ti sostituisca?*

■ nel periodo ipotetico di secondo tipo.

*If you studied harder, you'**d have** better results.*　　*Se studiassi di più **avresti** risultati migliori.*

■ per esprimere l'idea di **futuro nel passato** (= *future in the past*), che si trova di solito nel discorso indiretto introdotto da un verbo al passato nella frase principale e indica un avvenimento futuro rispetto al momento del passato a cui si fa riferimento.

*He said (that) he **would be back** before six.*　　*Disse che **sarebbe tornato** prima delle sei.*
*At the party he met the girl who **would** later **become** his wife.*　　*Alla festa conobbe la ragazza che **sarebbe diventata** sua moglie.*

■ Come si vede dall'esempio, in italiano l'idea di **futuro nel passato** si esprime generalmente con il condizionale passato. (Vedi *Unit* **16.2**) È importante sottolineare che, dal punto di vista della descrizione grammaticale, in questo caso l'ausiliare *would* non esprime una forma condizionale, bensì il passato di *will*.

PRACTICE

1 Che cosa diresti in queste situazioni? Ricordati di usare sempre **would**.

1   Brad has come round to your flat. He looks thirsty. You offer him something to drink.

   You: .....Would you like something to drink..... ? Brad: Yes, please. I'd love some fruit juice.

2   You've just finished dinner and you see that your mother's very tired. You offer to do the washing-

   up. You: .... ? Mother: Oh, that would be lovely. Thank you.

3   Your father wants you to take the dog for a walk. Father: .... ?

   He needs some exercise.

4   You see an old lady fall over in the street. She's hurt her knee and she seems very shaken.

   You offer to call an ambulance. You: .... ? Old lady: No,

   thank you. I'll be all right in a minute.

2 Traduci.

1   Vorrei provarmi questo maglione, per favore.

2   Sarei molto felice di aiutarti.

3   Pensi che sarebbe difficile per me imparare il tedesco alla mia età?

4   Mi faresti un favore?

5   Sei sicura che tua sorella non vorrebbe rimanere un po' più a lungo?

6   Vorrei andare a letto presto stasera. Devo alzarmi presto domani.

7   Non credevo che l'avrebbe fatto.

8   Lo so, ti ho promesso che avrei lavato la macchina, ma non ho detto che l'avrei fatto oggi.

20.4   PERIODO IPOTETICO DI SECONDO TIPO

Il periodo ipotetico di secondo tipo è usato per esprimere ipotesi immaginarie, che riteniamo impossibili o difficilmente realizzabili.

*If you **left** me, I'd (**would**) **die** of a broken heart.*
Se mi **lasciassi morirei** con il cuore spezzato. (= Ma non credo che mi lascerai, così il mio cuore è salvo.)

*I'd (**would**) **love** you forever **if** you **bought** me a diamond ring.*
Ti **amerei** per sempre **se** mi **comprassi** un anello di diamanti.
(= Ma non mi aspetto che tu me lo compri, quindi potrei non amarti per sempre!)

La struttura base del periodo ipotetico è la seguente:

If- clause: *if + past simple*,	frase principale: *would* + forma base
If she **liked** me,	she **would** phone me.
Se le **piacessi**,	mi **telefonerebbe**.
If I **didn't have** an exam next week,	I **would go** clubbing at the weekend.
Se non avessi un esame la settimana prossima,	**andrei** in discoteca il fine settimana.
If I **had** a car,	I **wouldn't be** late for work.
Se avessi la macchina,	**non arriverei** tardi al lavoro.
If you **were** in love,	nothing else **would matter** to you.
Se tu **fossi** innamorato,	nient'altro **conterebbe** per te.

Frase principale: *would* + forma base	if- clause: *if + past simple*
She **would phone** me	*if* she **liked** me.
Mi **telefonerebbe**	**se** le **piacessi**.
I **would go** clubbing at the weekend	*if* I **didn't have** an exam next week.
Andrei in discoteca il fine settimana	**se non avessi** un esame la settimana prossima.
I **wouldn't be** late for work	*if* I **had** a car.
Non arriverei tardi al lavoro	**se avessi** la macchina.
Nothing else **would matter** to you	*if* you **were** in love.
Nient'altro **conterebbe** per te	**se** tu **fossi** innamorato.

Come si vede dagli esempi, il **congiuntivo imperfetto** italiano della frase subordinata corrisponde al *past simple* inglese. L'unica parziale eccezione è il congiuntivo imperfetto del verbo **to be**, che è **were** per tutte le persone, specialmente nello stile formale.

If I **were** *you, I would apply for that job.*   **Se fossi** *in te farei domanda per quel lavoro.*

Tuttavia, nel linguaggio informale si tende sempre più spesso a usare il *past simple* di **to be** al posto del congiuntivo.

If I **was/were** *you, I wouldn't phone him.*   *Se* **fossi** *in te non gli telefonerei.*
If she **was/were** *here, we'd have a lot of fun.*   *Se lei* **fosse** *qui ci divertiremmo un sacco.*

■ Possibili alternative

Altri verbi modali con valore condizionale, come **might** o **could**, possono essere usati nella frase principale al posto di **would**.

I **might** *love you if you bought me a diamond ring.*
Potrei *innamorarmi di te se mi comprassi un anello di diamanti.*

If I had a pay rise, I **could** *buy a new car.*
Se avessi un aumento di stipendio **potrei** *comprare una macchina nuova.*

PRACTICE

1 Leggi la prima frase, poi completa il consiglio nella seconda.

1 You don't talk to people at parties.

You would enjoy parties if you ......talked...... to people.

2 You should practise dancing.

You'd be a good dancer if you ....

3 You eat too much cheese.

You wouldn't have spots if you .... too much cheese.

4 You wear your school shirt at weekends.

If you .... your school shirt at weekends, you'd look better.

5 You never give presents to your friends.

You would be more popular if you .... presents to your friends.

6 You make jokes about your classmates.

If you .... jokes about your classmates, they would like you better.

2 Di nuovo, leggi la prima frase, poi completa il consiglio nella seconda.

1 You don't revise before exams so you don't get good marks.

You ......'d get...... good marks if you revised before exams.

2 You drink coffee after supper and then you can't sleep well.

You .... well if you didn't drink coffee after supper.

3 You don't wear a warm coat and you often catch colds.

If you wore a warm coat, you .... colds so often.

4 You spend all your money on clothes so you don't have any for books.

You .... enough money for books if you didn't spend it all on clothes.

5 You lose things because you never tidy your room.

You .... things if you tidied your room.

6 You're late every morning because you spend hours in the shower.

If you didn't spend hours in the shower, you .... late every morning.

3 Completa le frasi seguenti con la forma corretta dei verbi tra parentesi.

1 There ..wouldn't be.. (*not be*) so many accidents if people drove more carefully.

2 If he .... (*win*) the lottery, he would travel around the world.

3 If I .... (*be*) a songwriter, I'd write you a song.

4 If I .... (*not have*) any friends, I'd feel lonely.

5 If Jack .... (*listen*) to his grandmother, he'd learn all sorts of interesting things about the past.

6 I'd go to the cinema tomorrow if there .... (*be*) any good films on.

4 Riscrivi le frasi seguenti usando il periodo ipotetico di secondo tipo, in modo che il significato non cambi.

1 That computer is too expensive; that's why I can't buy it.

..If that computer wasn't/weren't so expensive, I would/could buy it..................

2 Carlo has a cold so we've decided not to go out. ....

3   Reception isn't good here so I won't phone you. ....

4   Giuliano lives a long way away, so Maggie can't see him often. ....

5   The dog's got fleas so I won't let it go into the sitting room. ....

6   Bob can't sing well; that's why he hasn't joined a choir. ....

7   Pete gets up very late and so he often doesn't have time for breakfast. ....

8   Barbara has a foreign accent, so everyone knows she isn't Italian. ....

9   I have too much work and so I can't go to the beach. ....

10 My scooter is too old so we can't use it to go on holiday. ....

20.5   IL CONDIZIONALE PASSATO: *WOULD HAVE*

Il condizionale passato si forma con il condizionale del verbo *have*, *would have*, seguito dal **participio passato** del verbo.

Soggetto + *would have* + participio passato		
I	*would have*	*liked* to see him.
Mi	**sarebbe**	**piaciuto** vederlo.
She	*would have*	**been** happy to be of help.
	Sarebbe	**stata** felice di essere di aiuto.

Il valore fondamentale del condizionale passato è quello di indicare eventi, desideri, possibilità **irrealizzabili**. Il condizionale passato si usa quindi per esprimere ipotesi riferite al passato, che non possono più verificarsi.

*What **would** you **have done** in my shoes?*   *Che cosa **avresti fatto** al mio posto?*
*If we had left earlier, we **wouldn't have**   *Se fossimo partiti prima **non avremmo perso** l'aereo.*
missed our flight.*

PRACTICE

1 Coniuga i verbi tra parentesi alla forma corretta del condizionale passato.

1   It's a pity you didn't take part in the competition. I'm sure you .would.have.won. . (*win*)

2   It's a good thing Robert didn't come to the concert. He .... (*not enjoy*) it.

3   It's a pity Pete didn't continue playing in that band. He .... (*become*) rich and famous, like the other members of the group.

4   I don't know whether I made the right decision there. What .... you .... ? (*do*)

5   If Nora hadn't gone to that party, she .... (*not meet*) Frank.

6   If I had known there would be no food on the plane, I .... (*eat*) before.

355

7   If your mother hadn't got married, ... she .... (*have*) so many children?

8   Did you really jump into that muddy water? I .... (*not swim*) in that lake.

9   If she hadn't fallen down the stairs, my grandmother .... (*go*) skiing.

10   .... you .... (*like*) to be in the school football team when you were a child?

2 Riempi gli spazi con *would* o *would have* e un verbo appropriato.

1   If we had a webcam, we ...could/would..see.. each other when we chat.

2   If only it hadn't rained, the holiday .... great.

3   I couldn't believe the way you behaved last night. I .... to my mother like that.

4   Antonio .... more confident if he didn't have a complex about his nose.

5   Carol .... to the party, but her mother's ill at the moment.

6   James .... such a careless mistake if he hadn't been so tired.

7   Pity you didn't come shopping with us. We saw Riccardo Scamarcio in the street. You .... thrilled!

8   If you really loved me, you .... my text messages.

9   .... these shoes? They were very expensive but I really like them.

10   If you had given me a hand instead of reading your book, you .... me a lot of trouble.

3 Traduci.

1   Queste scarpe erano in svendita, altrimenti non le avrei comprate.

2   Hai fatto la cosa giusta. Io avrei fatto la stessa cosa.

3   Perché non mi hai detto che avevi bisogno del mio vecchio libro di latino? Non l'avrei buttato via.

4   Perché non sei venuta? Una passeggiata in campagna ti avrebbe fatto bene.

5   Mi sarebbe piaciuto venire alla festa di Ron, ma non mi sentivo bene.

6   Non mi sono divertito molto. Avrei preferito rimanere a casa.

20.6   PERIODO IPOTETICO DI TERZO TIPO

Il periodo ipotetico di terzo tipo si riferisce a eventi passati che **non possono essere più cambiati**: eventi che avrebbero potuto realizzarsi se si fossero verificate certe condizioni nel passato. Per questo il periodo ipotetico di terzo tipo è anche detto dell'**irrealtà**.

If you'd (had) left me, I'd (would) have died of a broken heart.
Se tu mi avessi lasciato sarei morta con il cuore spezzato.
(= Ma non mi hai lasciato, così il mio cuore è intatto.)

If- clause: *if + past perfect*,	principale: *would have* + participio passato
If you **had been** in love, **Se** tu **fossi stato** innamorato, If you **had bought** me a diamond ring, **Se** mi **avessi comprato** un anello di diamanti, If I **hadn't seen** it with my own eyes, **Se** non **l'avessi visto** con i miei occhi,	nothing else **would have mattered**. nient'altro **avrebbe avuto importanza**. I **would have loved** you forever. ti **avrei amato** per sempre. I **wouldn't have believed** it. **non** ci **avrei creduto**.

Principale: *would have* + participio passato	if- clause: *if + past perfect*
Nothing else **would have mattered** Nient'altro **avrebbe avuto importanza** I **would have loved** you forever Ti **avrei amato** per sempre I **wouldn't have believed** it **Non** ci **avrei creduto**	if you **had been** in love. **se** tu **fossi stato** innamorato. if you **had bought** me a diamond ring. **se** mi **avessi comprato** un anello di diamanti. if I **hadn't seen** it with my own eyes. **se** non **l'avessi visto** con i miei occhi.

Come si vede dagli esempi, il congiuntivo trapassato italiano corrisponde al *past perfect* inglese: il rapporto tra i tempi della frase principale e della **if- clause** è lo stesso nelle due lingue.

■ Possibili alternative

Altri verbi modali composti con valore di condizionale passato, come **might have** e **could have** + **participio passato**, possono essere usati nella frase principale al posto di **would have** + **participio passato**.

I **could have helped you** if you had told me that you were in trouble.
Avrei potuto aiutarti se mi avessi detto che eri nei guai.

You **might have passed** the exam **if** you **hadn't gone** clubbing at the weekend.
Avresti potuto passare l'esame **se non fossi andato** in discoteca il fine settimana.

PRACTICE

1 Completa le frasi che si riferiscono alle immagini usando il periodo ipotetico di terzo tipo, per mostrare come il fatto di aver perso l'autobus un giorno abbia avuto per Zoe una conseguenza inaspettata: trovare un altro lavoro.

357

1   If she hadn't missed her bus, she wouldn't .... *have gone into the café* ....

2   If there had been a free table, she ....

3   .... , she wouldn't have had to wait for her coffee.

4   .... , she wouldn't have read the back of the
    man's paper.

5   If she hadn't noticed the advertisement, ...

2 Le frasi seguenti sono tutte periodi ipotetici di terzo tipo. Riempi gli spazi coniugando i verbi tra parentesi alla forma corretta.

1   If I ..... *hadn't gone* ..... (*not go*) to the seaside, I could have studied.

2   If there hadn't been a large hole in the road, Sam .... (*not have*) that accident.

3   Bob might have answered the phone if he .... (*know*) that it was me phoning.

4   If the postman hadn't kicked the dog, the dog .... (*not bite*) him.

5   If my mum .... (*not help*) me write that essay, I would never have finished it.

6   She .... never .... (*have*) so much success if she hadn't been the daughter of a famous actor.

7   If I .... (*not open*) that email attachment, the computer wouldn't have got a virus.

8   I wouldn't have kissed him if he .... (*not give*) me some flowers.

3 Per ogni coppia di frasi, completa la seconda in modo che il significato non cambi.

1   I meant to go and visit my grandmother but I didn't have time.
    If I .... *had had time, I would have visited my grandmother* ....

2   Luke wanted to go to the United States last summer but he didn't have enough money.
    If Luke ....

3   Dan ate too much at lunch and had to go to bed for an hour.
    If Dan ....

4   I went to Lake Como for a holiday and met George Clooney at a party.
    If I ....

5   It rained non-stop for three weeks in England and many towns were flooded.
    If it ....

6   The burglar didn't wear gloves so he left his fingerprints everywhere.
    If the burglar ....

7   Fred wanted to be a poet but he had a family to support.
    If Fred ....

8   Derek intended to go to Stansted Airport by train, but there was a rail strike.
    If there ....

9   Federico went to London on his own for six months and learnt to speak English fluently.
    If Federico ....

10 Kevin didn't take a map with him and so he got lost.

If Kevin ....

4 Completa il seguente dialogo coniugando i verbi tra parentesi alla forma corretta. In alcuni casi è più appropriato usare il modale **could** al posto di **would**.

Ugo: So how did your camping weekend go?

Piero: It was great. Pity you didn't come. You **(1)** _would have enjoyed_ (*enjoy*) it.

Ugo: I **(2)** .... (*come*) if my brother **(3)** .... (*not get married*) on Saturday. Obviously, I couldn't miss my brother's wedding.

Piero: You **(4)** .... (*meet*) my cousin, Lavinia. She's really good fun.

Ugo: Is she? But there **(5)** .... (*not be*) room in the tent for me as well.

Piero: Yes, there would. Anyway, we **(6)** .... (*sleep*) out in the open. The weather was beautiful. You **(7)** .... (*bring*) your guitar, and we all **(8)** .... (*sing*) together.

Ugo: So what did you do in the evenings?

Piero: We made a fire and watched for shooting stars. One evening we had a story-telling competition for the best ghost story. You probably **(9)** .... (*win*) that!

Ugo: Yes, I **(10)** .... (*frighten*) you all to death with my story about the headless duchess.

Piero: Yes, although I don't know whether you **(11)** .... (*sleep*) after Lavinia's story about the legless duke. That was very scary!

5 Completa le frasi seguenti con **could have** o **might have** e le espressioni nel riquadro, in modo da formare periodi ipotetici di terzo tipo. A volte entrambe le alternative sono possibili.

come	marry	win	become	not fall over	learn

1 I _might have married_ him if he'd found a job. I didn't want to marry someone who was unemployed.

2 Did you say you were in Florence last week? You .... to see me.

3 Ned .... famous if he'd continued to play in the band.

4 France .... the World Cup in 2006 if they hadn't missed two penalties.

5 I .... if the road hadn't been wet.

6 Harry .... to fly if he hadn't been colour blind.

20.7 PERIODO IPOTETICO MISTO

Talvolta un'ipotesi riferita al passato può essere rapportata alle sue conseguenze nel presente. Per esprimere questo significato si usa una combinazione di periodo ipotetico di secondo e terzo tipo: spesso il verbo nella **if- clause** rimane al *past perfect,* mentre nella frase principale si può trovare il **condizionale presente** al posto del condizionale passato.

If- clause: if + past perfect,	principale: *would* + forma base
*If the weather **had been** fine last week,* **Se** il tempo **fosse stato** bello la settimana scorsa,	there **would be** roses in my garden. ci **sarebbero** delle rose nel mio giardino.
*If you **had listened** to me,* **Se** mi **avessi ascoltato**	you **wouldn't be** in trouble now. adesso **non saresti** nei guai.

Tuttavia, è anche possibile trovare un *past simple* nella **if- clause** al posto del *past perfect,* mentre il verbo nella frase principale rimane al condizionale passato.

If- clause: if + past simple,	principale: *would have* + participio passato
*If my boyfriend **gave** me diamonds like that,* **Se** il mio ragazzo mi **regalasse** dei diamanti così,	I **would have married** him by now. l'**avrei** già **sposato**.
*If Leslie **was** better organised,* **Se** Leslie **fosse** più organizzato,	he **wouldn't have missed** the bus. **non avrebbe perso** l'autobus.

PRACTICE

1 Le frasi seguenti sono esempi di periodo ipotetico misto. Riempi gli spazi coniugando i verbi tra parentesi alla forma corretta.

1 If Piotr ..hadn't spent.. (*not spend*) a year in New York, he ..wouldn't speak.. (*not speak*) English so well now.

2 Carol .... (*not be*) so fit and healthy now that she's eighty if she .... (*not do*) yoga all her life.

3 If Iris .... (*not get married*) and .... (*have*) children so young, she .... (*have*) a more senior position in the company now.

4 If I .... (*be*) you, I .... (*accept*) that job offer that you turned down.

5 If Hilary .... (*not have*) such a traumatic childhood, she .... (*have*) fewer problems now.

6 If you really .... (*love*) me, you .... (*not forget*) my birthday last week.

7 If Teresa .... (*be*) more intelligent, she .... (*not fail*) her exams last June.

8 Nigel .... (*be*) world champion by now if he .... (*not have*) a road accident five years ago.

2 Trasforma queste frasi in modo che il significato non cambi.

1 You went to bed too late last night. That's why you are so tired now.

.... *If you had gone to bed earlier last night /* ....

.... *If you hadn't gone to bed so late last night, you wouldn't be so tired now.* ....

2 Tracy is very disorganised. That's why she missed the boat.

....

3 Leonardo da Vinci painted the *Mona Lisa*; thousands of tourists go to the Louvre to see it.

....

4 I bought this grammar book in 2007. As a result I know a lot of English grammar.

....

5 Daniel is a brilliant musician. He has practised very hard over the years.

....

6 The British encouraged people from Commonwealth countries to go and work in Britain in the fifties. That's why Britain is so multi-cultural now.

....

7 When I was a child my father taught me to play the trumpet. Now I play in a big band.

....

8 I ate too much over Christmas. My jeans are too tight now.

....

9 Mandy is very pretty. That's why she won the beauty contest.

....

10 Barbara's father was born in Great Britain. This means that Barbara has a British passport.

....

ALL IN ONE REVISION

1 Ascolterai un agente segreto, conosciuta/o come Double X, parlare con il suo capo, Mr Seymour, di una fotografia che Mr Seymour gli mostra. Mr Seymour chiede a Double X di fare qualcosa. Prima di ascoltare, cerca di indovinare che cosa le/gli chiede.

....

....

....

361

2 Ascolta l'inizio della conversazione e verifica se avevi ragione.

2.21

3 Ascolta tutta la conversazione e rispondi a queste domande. Ascolta la registrazione due volte se necessario.

2.22

1 What does Mr Seymour want Double X to do? *To follow a man and find out all about him.*

2 Why doesn't Mr Seymour give Double X a better photo? ....

3 Who sent the photo to Mr Seymour? ....

4 Why is the photo fuzzy? ....

5 How is it possible to make the picture clearer? ....

6 Who is in the photo? ....

7 Can you guess who sent the photo to Mr Seymour, and why? ....

4 Ascolta di nuovo e riempi gli spazi.

2.23

1 If you .... him, I .... extremely pleased.

2 If we .... a better picture, we .... it to you.

3 If she .... us that, I .... to ask for your help.

4 It .... me somewhere to start if I .... where she'd phoned from.

5 It .... a bit clearer if you .... at it with your eyes half closed.

5 Rileggi le frasi nell'esercizio 4 e rispondi a queste domande.

1 Look at sentence 5. Which tense is used after *if*? ....

2 Look at sentence 1. Which tense is used after *if*? ....

3 Look at sentences 2 and 4. Which tense is used after *if*? ....

4 Look at sentence 3. Which tense is used after *if*? ....

6 Abbina gli inizi delle frasi con le loro logiche conclusioni.

1	The house wouldn't have been such a mess ...j...	**a**	if she wasn't such a jealous type.
2	If Mike had listened to his father, ...	**b**	I'd probably have lots of boyfriends.
3	I would quite like Juno	**c**	they usually wait until their parents go out.
4	If Dave didn't work so much, ...	**d**	and you'll never forget his face.
5	We would have arrived early	**e**	he wouldn't have got into trouble.
6	If I was as lovely as Nancy, ...	**f**	I still wouldn't love you!
7	If teenagers want to have a party, ...	**g**	she'll get a nasty surprise.
8	If Sally opens that door, ...	**h**	if the roads had been less busy.
9	Take one look at Alan	**i**	he wouldn't get so tired.
10	If you were as handsome as a film star, ...	**j**	if the guests hadn't been careless.

7 Coniuga i verbi tra parentesi alla forma corretta.

1 I won't help you with your homework if you ....don't tidy.... (*not tidy*) your bedroom.

2 You'll need a visa if you .... (*want*) to travel to China.

3 If he .... (*care*) about other people's feelings, he wouldn't behave that way.

4 She .... (*not be*) successful if she doesn't learn to control her temper.

5 If I'd known you were such a gossip, I .... (*not tell*) you my secret.

6 They would work harder if they .... (*not be*) so tired.

7 The boss .... (*be*) furious if he'd found out what you were up to.

8 If the temperature .... (*fall*) below freezing, water turns to ice.

9 If they .... (*not expect*) delays, they wouldn't have set off so early.

10 Open the envelope and we .... (*discover*) what John has been doing.

8 Che cosa diresti ai tuoi amici nelle seguenti situazioni? Scegli un commento appropriato tra quelli riportati nel riquadro.

A You should have known better. If you hadn't answered the phone, you wouldn't have been so distracted.

B I wouldn't swim after lunch if I were you. It's dangerous.

C She probably would have left you even if you had stayed at home.

D What about accommodation? If they give you a place, will you live on the campus?

E Will you send me a postcard if you go to India?

F If I had enough money in the bank, I'd buy a better computer.

---

1 Tom has just had a big lunch but can't wait to swim in the ocean.

You: ....I wouldn't swim after lunch if I were you. It's dangerous...................

2 Sarah has applied to go to York University, three hundred kilometres from home.

You: ....

3 Your computer is too slow and not powerful enough for many of the things you want to do. You can't afford a new one.

You: ....

4 Jan is thinking of going on a world tour. Her brother, Tony, is fascinated by India.

Tony: ....

5 John's girlfriend has left him. He thinks it's because he went on holiday with the friends he plays football with.

You: ....

6 Patrick had an accident this morning on the way to school. He was talking on his mobile phone and went into the back of a car.

You: ....

9 Completa le frasi seguenti in modo personale.

1 If I was incredibly good-looking .... *my friends would be jealous of me* ....

2 I wouldn't have to study English if ....

3 If I pass First Certificate ....

4 I won't pass my exam if ....

5 If my teacher didn't ....

6 If I hadn't ....

7 If English grammar ....

8 You have to .... if ....

9 If you listen to English pop songs ....

10 If I complete this sentence quickly ....

10 In otto di queste frasi c'è un errore. <u>Sottolinea</u> gli errori e scrivi le correzioni.

1 Jessica would have made fewer mistakes if <u>she read</u> the instructions carefully. ..*she had read*....

2 If Brad weren't so slow he didn't take so long to do his homework. ....

3 Harry would have enjoyed the party if he would have gone. ....

4 I would have copied the CD for you if you'd asked me to. ....

5 I'll scream if I would have to do any more grammar exercises! ....

6 Molly might help you with your maths homework if you had asked her nicely. ....

7 If I believed in ghosts, I might be frightened to sleep in this old castle. ....

8 That dog would be much happier if he wouldn't live in a tiny flat. ....

9 If you really wanted one, I'd have given you a new iPod for your birthday. ....

10 You'll definitely pass the exam if you continued to study so hard. ....

11 Per ognuna delle situazioni descritte, scrivi un periodo ipotetico di secondo o terzo tipo, in modo che il significato non cambi.

1 I didn't have enough money; that's why I couldn't take a taxi.

If I had had enough money, I could/would have taken a taxi.

2 You're always unfriendly to him; it's no wonder he avoids you.

....

3 Jane spent all her birthday money. Now she hasn't got enough to buy a new pair of trainers.

....

4 Franca doesn't get on with her parents; that's why she's decided to leave home.

....

5 Mark loves the water; that's why he's so good at water sports.

....

6 Sylvia doesn't look after her teeth; that's why she needs to see a dentist now.

....

7 Lucia has got a lovely voice; that's why she was asked to sing at Terry's wedding.

....

8 Valentino got into trouble because he didn't pay his taxes.

....

9 Dave is very cheeky. That's why his mother tells him off so often.

....

10 I love listening to music. That's why I have such a huge collection of CDs.

....

12 Traduci.

1 Se non mangiassi troppo la tua salute migliorerebbe.

2 Che cosa faresti se vincessi 10 000 sterline?

3 Se non fossi così stanca uscirei con te.

4 Se non avessi speso così tanto, tua madre non sarebbe così arrabbiata.

5 Se mi avessi detto che sei vegetariana non avrei preparato la carne arrosto.

6 Avremmo comprato quell'appartamento se non fosse stato così costoso.

7 Se non avessi avuto una mappa mi sarei persa.

8 Non sarei andata al cinema se avessi saputo che il film era così noioso.

9 Se avessi saputo che era sola sarei andata a trovarla.

10 Che cosa avresti fatto se lo avessi saputo?

UNIT 21 — FRASI CONDIZIONALI (2)

21.1 *I wish* e *if only*

21.2 *Unless*

21.3 *In case*

21.4 *Provided/Providing that, as/so long as*

21.5 *It's time* e *I'd rather; otherwise* e *or else*

FRASI CONDIZIONALI (2) – INTRODUZIONE

Il condizionale e il congiuntivo sono modi strettamente collegati: a differenza dell'indicativo, che è il modo della realtà, dell'oggettività, i tempi del **condizionale** e del **congiuntivo** esprimono **possibilità, ipotesi, aspirazioni, desideri, rimpianti**.

Nella *Unit* precedente abbiamo trattato i quattro tipi fondamentali di periodo ipotetico e le loro possibili varianti. In questa *Unit* vengono presentate altre strutture con valore condizionale e congiuntivo che esprimono questa gamma di significati.

21.1   *I WISH* E *IF ONLY*

I wish = **vorrei / come vorrei** e *if only* = **se solo / se soltanto** hanno lo stesso significato. *If only* è meno comune e di solito indica una sfumatura più forte di sentimento.

I wish / If only + past simple
I wish / If only you were here.
Vorrei che / Se solo tu fossi qui.

Le espressioni *I wish / If only* + *past simple* vengono usate per esprimere un **desiderio riferito al presente** e ritenuto molto difficile, se non impossibile da realizzare.

I wish you loved me. (= but you don't love me)   ***Vorrei** che mi **amassi**.* (= ma non mi ami)

I wish / If only I had more free time.   ***Vorrei avere / Se soltanto avessi** più tempo libero.*
  (= but I don't)   (= ma non ce l'ho)

I wish I could speak Spanish. (= but I can't)   ***Vorrei saper** parlare spagnolo.* (= ma non lo parlo)

If only he could drive. (= but he can't)   ***Se soltanto sapesse** guidare.* (= ma non sa guidare)

If only there were a solution.   ***Se soltanto ci fosse** una soluzione!*
(= we haven't found one so far)   (= finora non l'abbiamo trovata)

Come si vede dagli esempi, il *past simple* retto da **wish** / **if only** corrisponde sostanzialmente al congiuntivo italiano, come nella frase subordinata del periodo ipotetico di secondo tipo. Allo stesso modo, quindi, è possibile usare **were** anche con i soggetti di prima e terza persona singolare, *I* e **he/she/it**.

*I wish **I was/were** clever like you.* (= but I'm not)
Vorrei essere *in gamba come te.* (= ma non lo sono)

*I wish the weather **wasn't/weren't** so wet here.* (= but it is wet)
Vorrei *che il tempo **non fosse** così umido qui.* (= ma è umido)

I wish / If only + past perfect
*I wish / **If only** you **had been** here.* **Vorrei che / Se solo** *tu **fossi stato** qui.*

Le espressioni ***I wish / If only*** + *past perfect* vengono usate per esprimere un **rimpianto**, un **desiderio riferito al passato**, dunque non più realizzabile. Hanno lo stesso significato del periodo ipotetico di terzo tipo: l'evento non può più essere cambiato.

*I **wish** / **If only** I **had had** more free time.* (= but I didn't)
Vorrei *che / **Se soltanto avessi avuto** più tempo libero.* (= ma non l'ho avuto)

*She **wishes** she'd (had) never **met** him.* (= but she did meet him)
Vorrebbe non averlo *mai **incontrato**.* (= ma lo ha incontrato)

*I wish we **had come** a few weeks ago.* (= but we didn't come)
Vorrei *che **fossimo venuti** alcune settimane fa.* (= ma non siamo venuti)

*If only I **hadn't broken** his heart.* (= but I did break it)
Se soltanto non *gli **avessi spezzato** il cuore.* (= ma gliel'ho spezzato)

I wish / If only + would
*I **wish** you **would go** home.* **Vorrei che** *tu **andassi** a casa.* *If only the rain **would stop**.* **Se solo smettesse** *di piovere.*

Le espressioni ***I wish / If only*** + *would* sono usate per esprimere **un desiderio riferito al presente o al futuro**.

▓ Il desiderio che una **determinata cosa si verifichi**.

*I **wish** the train **would arrive**.*   **Vorrei** *che il treno **arrivasse**. / **Magari arrivasse** il treno.*
*If only he **would call** me.*   **Se solo** *mi **chiamasse**.*

▓ Il desiderio che **qualcuno faccia qualcosa**, o **smetta di fare qualcosa che ci irrita**.

*I **wish** / **If only** you **would listen**.*   **Vorrei** *che / **Se solo** tu **ascoltassi**.*
*I **wish** the waiter **would hurry up**.*   **Vorrei** *che il cameriere **si muovesse**.*
*I **wish** you **wouldn't leave** your*   **Vorrei** *che **non lasciassi** la borsa nell'ingresso.*
bag in the doorway.

▓ **Differenza tra** *I hope* + *will* e *I wish* + *would*

Sia *I hope* + *will* che *I wish* + *would* sono usati per esprimere un desiderio riferito al futuro, ma con una differenza di significato.

*I **hope** he **will phone**.* (= there's a good chance he will phone)
Spero *che **telefoni**.* (= c'è una buona probabilità che telefoni)

*I **wish** he **would phone**.* (= it's unlikely he will phone)
Vorrei *che **telefonasse**.* (= è poco probabile che telefoni)

PRACTICE

1 Abbina le figure alle frasi con **wish** e **if only**.

1 I wish my eyes were bigger. ..E...

2 I wish my boyfriend would tell me the truth. ......

3 Doug wishes he had paid his taxes. ......

4 Bill wishes he had a sports car. ......

5 Daria wishes she had paid more attention during English lessons. ......

6 If only he would look my way. ......

7 I wish I had gone on holiday somewhere else! ......

8 If only I didn't have such an embarrassing dad. ......

2 Noel è il fratello maggiore di Danny. Danny è geloso di Noel. Leggi che cosa dice Danny e poi completa le frasi che seguono.

Noel is handsome, but I'm not. He has straight dark hair, but mine is light brown and curly. He works in a sports club. He earns lots of money and owns a motorbike. He lives in the city centre, but I live in a village with our parents. He's twenty-two and I'm only thirteen and a half. When I'm twenty-two I want to be like Noel.

1 I wish I ......was....... handsome.

2 I wish I .... curly hair.

3 I wish I .... in a sports club.

4 I wish I .... lots of money.

5 I wish I .... a motorbike.

6 I wish I .... in a village.

7 I wish I .... thirteen and a half.

3 Completa questa email con la forma corretta dei verbi tra parentesi.

Hi Suzanne

How are you? It's very boring here. I wish there **(1)** ....._were_...... (*be*) some clubs and good shops.
We spend every holiday in the Highlands because my father likes it here. If my father
(2) .... (*not want*) to go climbing we **(3)** .... (*stay*) in Edinburgh with my uncle's
family. I wish we **(4)** .... (*not come*) to the same place every year.
I don't think my mother likes it here either. She **(5)** .... (*enjoy*) going to museums if we
(6) .... (*go*) to Edinburgh. And I **(7)** .... (*meet*) new people if I **(8)** .... (*go*)
clubbing with my cousins.
I wish I **(9)** .... (*have*) more money. I wish I **(10)** .... (*not have to go*) on holiday
with my parents.

Email me soon.

LOL Victoria

4 Chloe è in vacanza in una città straniera. Era così occupata ad ammirare i luoghi di interesse
che si è persa. Che cosa vorrebbe adesso? Scrivi delle frasi appropriate con **wish**.

1 I haven't got a map.

....._I wish I had a map._........

2 The streets all look the same.

....

3 I didn't bring my mobile phone.

....

4 I can't speak the language.

....

5 I didn't buy a phrase book.

....

6 I'm hot and thirsty.

....

7 I came here alone.

....

8 I need someone to help me.

....

9 I'm sorry I came here.

....

10 I want to be back in my hotel.

....

369

5 Completa queste frasi con le tue idee.

1 If I won the lottery, ...*I'd travel round the world*....................................

2 If only I were a fashion model, ...

3 If everyone liked pop music, ...

4 If exams were always easy, ...

5 If only I lived in Hawaii, ...

6 If I spoke perfect English, ...

7 I wish politicians ....

8 I wish I had ....

21.2 *UNLESS*

Unless significa **a meno che non / se non** e si riferisce al futuro, ma è seguito dal presente: *present simple* o, più raramente, *present continuous*. Non è mai seguito dal futuro.

Unless può essere di norma sostituito da *if not* nel senso di **a meno che non, eccetto, se**.

> *We are going **unless** the weather **gets** much worse.* (= **if** the weather **doesn't get** much worse)
> ***Partiremo a meno che** il tempo **non peggiori**. (= se il tempo **non peggiora**)*

*We won't have time to reach the top of the mountain **unless** we **set out** early.* (= **if** we **don't set out** early)
*Non avremo il tempo di raggiungere la cima della montagna **a meno che non ci mettiamo in cammino** presto.*
(= se non ci mettiamo in cammino presto)

> *Unless you **drive** more slowly, I'll be sick.* (= If you **don't drive** more slowly, I'll be sick.)
> ***Se non guidi** più piano mi verrà la nausea.*

PRACTICE

1 Riempi gli spazi in modo che la seconda frase abbia lo stesso significato della prima.

1 I'll give you a lift unless you want to walk. / I'll give you a lift if *you don't* want to walk.

2 I get up early if I'm not ill. / I get up early .... I'm ill.

3 No-one will see us if we don't put the light on. / No-one will see us .... we put the light on.

4 I'll go to the disco unless I have a headache. / I .... to the disco if I have a headache.

5 I don't sleep well if I'm worried about something. / I sleep well .... I'm worried about something.

6 I'll go clubbing unless I'm tired. / I'll go clubbing if .... tired.

2 Riscrivi le frasi seguenti usando *unless* al posto di *if not*.

1 Sam will pass his driving test if he doesn't drive too fast.
Sam will pass his driving test unless he drives too fast...

2 They'll be here soon if their plane isn't delayed.

....

3 If you're not in a hurry, you could take the bus.

....

4 I won't be able to come to see you tomorrow if my brother can't give me a lift.

....

5 If the factory doesn't increase its production, it will close down.

....

6 If you don't write your address down for me, I'll forget it.

....

7 I won't stay in that hotel if it doesn't have a good restaurant.

....

8 If I don't hear from you, I'll meet you at six.

....

21.3   *IN CASE*

L'espressione *in case* significa **in caso / nel caso che**. Si usa per indicare che un'azione viene compiuta per prudenza, **nell'eventualità** che se ne verifichi un'altra.

In case può essere seguito dal *present simple* o dal *past simple*.

▪ *In case* + *present simple* si riferisce a un evento che potrebbe verificarsi nel futuro.

*Take my phone number **in case** you **miss** the bus.*
*Prendi il mio numero di telefono **in caso** tu **perda** l'autobus.*
*Take a whistle **in case** you **get separated**.*
*Prendi un fischietto **in caso** vi **perdiate di vista**.*

▪ *In case* + *past simple* chiarisce il motivo per cui un'azione è stata compiuta.

*He took his surfboard **in case** they **went** to the beach.*
*Prese la tavola da surf **nell'eventualità che andassero** in spiaggia.*

▪ *In case* può anche essere seguito dal *present perfect*.

*I'll buy some extra food **in case** the visitors **have** already **arrived**.*
*Comprerò del cibo in più **in caso / nel caso** che gli ospiti **siano** già **arrivati**.*

▪ **Differenza tra** *in case* **e** *if*

In case **non** ha lo stesso significato di *if*.

In case	*If*
*I'll cook a meal **in case** Sarah **comes** overnight.* *Preparerò un pasto **in caso** Sarah **venga** per la notte.* (= Lo cucinerò adesso nell'eventualità che Sarah venga a trovarmi più tardi.)	*I'll cook a meal **if** Sarah **comes** overnight.* *Preparerò un pasto **se** Sarah **verrà** per la notte.* (= Non cucinerò adesso perché può anche darsi che Sarah non venga a trovarmi.)

PRACTICE

1 Riempi gli spazi con **in case** o **if**.

1 Elaine will post the letters ....*if*.......... she goes out.

2 I'll go for a swim .... my lesson at college finishes early.

3 I'll teach you to windsurf .... you teach me to play golf.

4 I always leave the answerphone on when I go out .... I miss an important phone call.

5 I'll take Tim's address with me .... I have time to visit him while I'm in London.

6 Our team will win the match .... our goalkeeper plays like he did last week.

7 It's a good idea to have two address books .... you lose one of them.

8 I'll leave these DVDs here .... you have time to watch them.

2 Il tuo fratello più piccolo sta partendo per la prima volta per una vacanza in campeggio in montagna. Tu ci sei già stato e lo aiuti a preparare i bagagli in modo da essere ben attrezzato per ogni eventualità. Formula i tuoi consigli con **in case**.

Me: Are you ready to leave then?

Harry: I hope so! Can you think of anything I might have forgotten?

Me: Well, it's a good idea to take a penknife in case you **(1)** ...*need to cut something*... . Take your Swiss penknife.

Harry: Yes, I've already packed that. Do you think I need something waterproof in case it **(2)** .... ?

Me: Definitely. The weather in the mountains can be very unpredictable. Take plenty of synthetic clothes in case you **(3)** .... They dry much more quickly than cotton or wool.

Harry: That's good advice. Thanks.

Me: Oh, and you'd better take a torch in case the tent **(4)** .... during the night. It's also useful inside the tent once it's dark.

Harry: OK, I'll buy one later. What about warm clothes for the evening?

Me: Take a couple of fleece jumpers in case it **(5)** .... Have you got a camera, by the way? If not I'll lend you mine in case you **(6)** .... some photos. They'll be great to show your friends later.

Harry: All right. Has it got a flash in case I **(7)** .... it when it's dark?

Me: Yes, it's automatic. Oh, and one last thing. When I went camping I took some extra tent pegs in case I **(8)** .... some. They're important if you want your tent to stay up.

Harry: Right!

21.4   *PROVIDED/PROVIDING THAT, AS/SO LONG AS*

Provided/providing that, *as/so long as* = **a patto che, a condizione che, purché**: queste congiunzioni sono seguite dal presente ma esprimono un'ipotesi riferita al futuro. Hanno lo stesso significato di *if*.

As long as we **stay** together, we'll have a great time.
Purché/Se stiamo insieme ci divertiremo tantissimo.
Provided that it **doesn't snow** too heavily, I'll see you here at six o'clock.
A condizione che / Purché non nevichi troppo forte, ci vediamo qui alle sei.

È importante ricordare che, a differenza che in italiano, in inglese **non** si può usare il futuro in frasi subordinate introdotte da *when*, *as soon as*, *until*, *before*, *after*, *if*, *unless*. Si usa il *present simple*, **non** *will*, al posto del futuro semplice italiano. (Vedi *Unit* **5.9**) La stessa regola si applica a tutte le frasi subordinate che esprimono ipotesi riferite al futuro.

We are having dinner in the garden **provided that** it **doesn't rain**. (**Non** ~~provided that it won't rain~~)
Ceneremo in giardino **purché non piova**.

PRACTICE

1 <u>Sottolinea</u> l'alternativa corretta.

1 I'll lend you my scooter <u>*so long as*</u> / *unless* you promise to bring it back by tomorrow evening.

2 You can bring the dog *provided that* / *until* he stays on the lead.

3 Dan doesn't mind taking his little brother *unless* / *as long as* he doesn't complain.

4 I'll stand by you *as soon as* / *as long as* I live.

5 *Providing that* / *Unless* the weather gets worse, we can eat outside.

6 *As long as* / *Until* there's enough light, we can play football outside.

7 Frank should get here on time *provided that* / *unless* the train's late.

8 Travelling on public transport in the city is convenient *providing that* / *as soon as* there isn't a strike.

2 Per ogni coppia di frasi, completa la seconda in modo che il significato non cambi. **Usa la parola data senza modificarla**. Usa tra **due** e **cinque** parole compresa la parola data.

1 Bring a swimming costume because we may go to the beach.   **case**

Bring a swimming costume 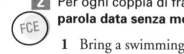 the beach.

2 You must have a rest, then you'll feel better.   **provided**

I'm sure you'll feel better, ... a rest.

3 Give me your MP3 the minute you arrive and I'll get it repaired in a couple of days.   **soon**

If you give me your MP3 .... , I'll get it repaired in a couple of days.

4 In case of fire, leave the building by the fire escape.   **if**

Leave the building by the fire escape .... fire.

5 I don't want to speak to Bill again unless he apologises for his bad behaviour.   **provided**

I will .... he apologises for his bad behaviour.

6 This book is Valerie's. Can you take it to school with you because you might see her.   **case**

This book is Valerie's. Can you take it to school with you .... her.

7 My mum's old car is fine for short trips providing that it works.   **long**

My mum's old car is fine for short trips .... works.

8 You'll never learn to use your computer if you don't make more effort.   **unless**

You'll never learn to use your computer .... more effort.

21.5   IT'S TIME E I'D RATHER; OTHERWISE E OR ELSE

Le strutture verbali *it's time* = **è l'ora** e *I'd (would) rather* = **preferirei** sono seguite dal *past simple* con valore di congiuntivo ma hanno un significato presente.

■ *It's time* + *past simple* implica che non è il momento giusto, è un po' tardi.

It's time we ate dinner now. It's eight o'clock.
È ora di cenare / che andiamo a cena. *Sono le otto.*

*The children are getting tired. **It's time they went** to bed.*
*I bambini si stanno stancando. **È l'ora che vadano** a letto.*

■ *I'd (would) rather* + *past simple* è usato per indicare una preferenza, spesso in alternativa a quanto è stato proposto.

A *Shall I cook something for you?*   B ***I'd rather you made** me a cup of tea.*
A *Ti cucino qualcosa?*   B ***Preferirei che tu** mi **facessi** una tazza di tè.*

***I'd rather you didn't bring** large cameras.*
***Preferirei che non portaste** delle macchine fotografiche grandi. (= piccole sono più maneggevoli)*

■ *Otherwise* e *or else* significano **altrimenti**, **oppure**, **se non** e sono sempre usati nel mezzo di una frase. Queste espressioni vengono impiegate per far capire che il fatto indicato nella frase precedente avrà sicuramente una determinata conseguenza.

*I have to go to bed early, **otherwise** I get too tired.* (= **If** I **don't go** to bed early, I get too tired.)
*Devo andare a letto presto, **altrimenti** mi stanco troppo.* (= **Se non vado** a letto presto mi stanco troppo.)

*Carry that tray with both hands **or else** you'll drop it.*
(= **If** you **don't carry** it with both hands, you'll drop it.)
*Reggi quel vassoio con tutte e due le mani **oppure/altrimenti** lo farai cadere.*
(= **Se non reggi** quel vassoio con tutte e due le mani lo farai cadere.)

Come si può vedere dagli esempi, *otherwise* e *or else* rappresentano una possibile variante del periodo ipotetico di tipo zero o di primo tipo.

PRACTICE

1 Che cosa diresti in queste situazioni? Formula delle frasi usando **it's time** o **'d rather** e un verbo appropriato nel riquadro.

talk	leave	tell	cut	give	pierce

1 You've had dinner with some friends but now it's midnight. Your hosts are starting to yawn.

You say: It's time .... I /we left ....

2 Your mother wants to choose a birthday present for you, but you'd prefer to have some money.

You say: I'd rather ....

3 Your friend Abigail's hair is getting long and untidy. You think she should have it cut.

You say: It's time ....

4 You want to have a stud in your nose, but your mother doesn't agree.

Your mother says: I'd rather ....

5 You've argued with your best friend and you haven't spoken to each other for a week. You want to get things out in the open.

You say: It's time ....

6 You've told a friend that you'd like to go out with his sister, but now you're afraid he might say something to her.

You say: I'd rather ....

2 Riscrivi i seguenti periodi ipotetici di primo tipo usando **otherwise** o **or else**.

1 Kevin can't study in silence. He has to have background music. (*otherwise*)

Kevin has to have background music, otherwise he can't study. ....

2 Your scooter doesn't have any lights; Jill tells you they are very important because without them motorists can't see you. (*or else*)

Jill says: ....

3 It's midnight and you know that you'd better go home straight away if you don't want your parents to be angry. (*otherwise*)

You say: ....

4 You and Dave want to go to a concert at Wembley Stadium. Dave thinks that it'd be better to book the tickets in advance to avoid making the trip for nothing. (*or else*)

Dave says: ....

5 Your father thinks you should see a dentist as soon as possible because if you don't your toothache will get worse. (*otherwise*)

Your father says: ....

6 You tell your brother to give you back your iPod. If he doesn't you'll make him cry. (*or else*)

You say: ....

ALL IN ONE REVISION

1 Ascolterai un uomo che parla a un gruppo di persone di quello che faranno domani. Queste sono alcune delle cose che porteranno con sé. Che cosa pensi che faranno?

2 Ascolta e verifica se avevi ragione.

2.24

3 Ascolta di nuovo e riempi gli spazi. Ferma la registrazione se necessario.

2.25

1 We're going .... *unless* .... the weather gets much worse.

2 .... that it doesn't snow too heavily tonight, I'll see you back here at six o'clock.

3 We won't reach the top of the mountain .... we set out early.

4 You need a whistle .... you get separated from the rest of the group.

5 .... you didn't bring large cameras.

6 .... we all stay together, we'll have a great time.

7 I .... you'd come a few weeks ago.

8 .... we had dinner now.

4 Rileggi le frasi 1, 2, 3, 4 e 6 dell'esercizio 3. Con quale tempo sono coniugati i verbi che seguono le parole negli spazi?

....

5 Che cosa diresti in queste situazioni? Che cosa vorrebbero le persone che si trovano nelle situazioni raffigurate in ciascuna vignetta? Esprimi un desiderio usando **wish** + **would** o **wish** + *past perfect* e scegliendo un verbo dal riquadro.

| come home | dress | hurry up | turn down | not break down | go off | not drive | ~~stop~~ |

1 I wish it ....*would stop raining.*..

2 I wish the car ....

3 I wish he ....

4 I wish he ....

5 I wish they ....

6 I wish he ....

7 I wish she ....

8 I wish the bell ....

6 Joe ha fatto delle scelte sbagliate in passato e adesso è pieno di rimpianti. Esprimi i suoi pensieri usando **wish** o **if only** + *past perfect*.

1 Lucy was such a sweet girl. I was a fool to leave her. I wish I ....*hadn't left Lucy*.. .

2 I wasted all my savings. Now I really need some money. I wish I ....

3 I went into the town centre by scooter instead of by bus. The police clamped my wheels and gave me a parking fine. If only I ....

4 I argued with my two best friends. Now they don't want to see me. I wish I ....

5 I gave up the guitar when I was fifteen. I could have become a musician. I wish I ....

6 My father always gave me good advice but I never followed it. If only ....

7 I went to a party last week. I didn't know my ex-girlfriend, Liz, was going to be there. It was very embarrassing. I wish I ....

8 I confided in Harry. He told his girlfriend what I said and now everyone knows. If only I ....

377

7 In sette di queste frasi c'è un errore nell'uso del verbo. <u>Sottolinea</u> gli errori e scrivi accanto la forma corretta.

1   I wish I <u>wouldn't have</u> such a big nose.   ...didn't have....

2   Ray wishes he would have studied more when he was at school.   ....

3   Unless you help me, I'll be grateful to you for the rest of my life.   ....

4   Barry wouldn't behave so strangely unless there was a good reason for it.   ....

5   Many more people would give money to charity if they had believed it would really help.
    ....

6   I wish you didn't be late all the time.   ....

7   If Parvin had come to Italy when she was younger, she'd speak Italian more fluently now.
    ....

8   I'm perfectly happy to go walking as long as it doesn't rain.   ....

9   John drew me a map in case I get lost.   ....

10   I wish you had lived nearer to me. I miss you.   ....

8 Collega le frasi seguenti usando *unless*.

1   Jane is very shy. She'll speak to you only if you ask her something.
    Jane won't speak to you unless you ask her something.

2   Your sister wants to borrow your new jacket. You want to borrow her curling tongs in return.
    ....

3   Your grandmother is deaf. You have to shout if you want her to hear you.
    ....

4   I can't afford a car. If my parents help me I'll be able to get one.
    ....

5   Tom wants a rise. If he doesn't get one he's going to look for a new job.
    ....

6   I'm going home now. But if you want me to, I'll stay.
    ....

7   You are allowed to use the swimming pool. However, you have to be a member of the leisure centre.
    ....

8   Laura rarely does any work. She only does some if it's absolutely necessary.
    ....

9 Leggi attentamente questa email e completa gli spazi con la forma corretta del verbo nel riquadro. Alcuni dei verbi sono negativi.

| be | be | behave | bring | can | change | finish | ~~have~~ | learn | know |

To: **JOE**
From: **ROBIN**
Subject: **PARTY!**

Hi Joe

I'm having a birthday party on Saturday in my uncle's flat. I wish I **(1)** .... had .... a bigger flat but I haven't. Anyway, my uncle has offered me his flat so long as there **(2)** .... no more than thirty people and provided that the party **(3)** .... by midnight. So please come and bring a friend, but I'd rather you **(4)** .... Matthew with you because he always causes trouble. I wish he **(5)** .... to behave better. I had to work hard to persuade my uncle and unless everyone **(6)** .... well, he won't let me do it again. I'll send you a map in case you **(7)** .... the street where my uncle lives. If you **(8)** .... find it, just ring me on my mobile. So I'll see you on Saturday unless my uncle **(9)** .... his mind! By the way, has Sally changed her phone number? I can't get hold of her. I wish I **(10)** .... rude to her last week, as she's not speaking to me now.

Bye for now.

Robin

10 Per ogni coppia di frasi, completa la seconda in modo che il significato non cambi. **Usa la parola data senza modificarla.** Usa tra **due** e **cinque** parole compresa la parola data.

(FCE)

1 John will look for a place of his own when he finds a job. **soon**

 John will look for a place of his own ... as soon as he finds ..... a job.

2 You can't use the underground unless you have a valid ticket. **providing**

 You can use the underground .... valid.

3 Take this money because you might need it. **case**

 Take this money .... it.

4 Regular exercise would make you feel much better. **if**

 You'd feel much better .... regular exercise.

5 I met you on that skiing holiday. **if**

 I wouldn't have met you .... on that skiing holiday.

6 I wish she wouldn't wear those horrible glasses because she'd be so attractive without. **only**

 She'd be so attractive .... wear those horrible glasses.

379

7 You need a balanced diet in order to grow. **unless**

You won't grow .... a balanced diet.

8 My mum says that she sometimes regrets not having had more children! **wishes**

My mum says that she sometimes .... more children!

9 You're not a child any more. You should be more responsible with money. **time**

You're not a child any more. .... more responsible with money.

10 I'd really like to look like my best friend. He's much better-looking than me. **wish**

I .... my best friend. He's much better-looking than me.

11 Traduci.

1 Vorrei che smettessi di interrompermi.

2 Se solo avessi imparato a suonare il pianoforte! Ma adesso è troppo tardi per imparare.

3 Vorrei che Eileen fosse qui. Lei saprebbe che cosa fare.

4 Sarebbe bello rimanere ancora un po'. Vorrei non dover andar via subito.

5 Vorrei che il nostro appartamento fosse più grande.

6 Vorrei aver studiato di più. Adesso non avrei paura di essere bocciato all'esame.

7 Mettiti un maglione pesante altrimenti avrai freddo.

8 Scrivi il tuo nome e indirizzo sulla valigia in caso sia smarrita.

9 Mi hanno consigliato di fare un'assicurazione in caso avessi bisogno di cure mediche mentre sono all'estero.

10 Puoi uscire con i tuoi amici a condizione che torni a casa entro mezzanotte.

UNIT 22

I CONNETTIVI (1)

22.1 *Because, as* e *since; because of*

22.2 *So* e *therefore*

22.3 *To, in order to* e *so (that)*

22.4 *So* e *such*

22.5 *Enough* e *too*

I CONNETTIVI (1) – INTRODUZIONE

Il termine **connettivo**, o *linking word*, si riferisce a tutte quelle parole ed espressioni che servono per creare legami tra frasi e per strutturare le parti di un discorso. Si tratta di **congiunzioni**, **avverbi** e **locuzioni** di vario tipo.

In questa *Unit* vengono introdotti i connettivi che hanno valore:

▪ causale: *because, as, since; because of*

▪ conclusivo: *so, therefore*

▪ finale o di scopo: *(in order) to, so (that)*

▪ di causa ed effetto: *so* e *such; enough* e *too*

22.1   BECAUSE, AS E SINCE; BECAUSE OF

Because, as e *since* corrispondono alle congiunzioni italiane **perché**, **poiché**, **dal momento che** e introducono le frasi subordinate causali, che indicano la causa di ciò che è espresso nella frase principale. *Because* è più comune di *as* o *since* e mette in maggiore rilievo la motivazione, ma spesso può essere usato con lo stesso significato.

Azione	Linking word	Causa/motivo
She said nothing	*because/as/since*	*she didn't recognise him.*
Non disse niente	**perché**	non lo riconobbe.
I didn't understand the lesson	*because/as/since*	*I hadn't done my homework.*
Non ho capito la lezione	**perché**	non avevo fatto i compiti per casa.

Quando *because, as* e *since* si trovano all'inizio del periodo, di solito c'è una virgola prima della frase principale.

> *Because/As/Since I hadn't done my homework, I didn't understand the lesson.*
> **Poiché / Dal momento che** *non avevo fatto i compiti per casa non capii la lezione.*

▪ **Solo** *because* può essere usato per rispondere alle domande che iniziano con **why**.

Why?	Because
Why was he there?	*Because he was waiting for his brother.*
Perché era là?	**Perché** stava aspettando suo fratello.
Why didn't you understand the lesson?	*Because I hadn't done my homework.*
Perché non hai capito la lezione?	**Perché** non avevo fatto i compiti per casa.

Because of significa **a causa di** ed è **sempre** seguito da un nome, non da una frase.

*I knew him **because of** my job.*
*We were late **because of** the traffic.*

Lo conoscevo **a causa del** / **grazie al** mio lavoro.
Siamo arrivati in ritardo **a causa del** traffico.

PRACTICE

1   Riempi gli spazi con **because** o **because of**.

We chose this flat **(1)** ...because..of......... the balcony.

We had to move **(2)** .... our old flat was

too small. The rent is quite high **(3)** ....

this block is in the city centre, but we like it

(4) .... the view over the park. And it's

good **(5)** .... we can get to work in only

ten minutes.

2   Traduci.

1   Hanno scelto Cecilia per quel lavoro perché parla perfettamente il russo.

2   **A** Perché non mi hai mandato un sms? (*to text someone*) **B** Perché avevo lasciato il cellulare a casa.

3   Abbiamo dovuto rimandare la gita a causa del brutto tempo.

4   **A** Perché stai piangendo? **B** Perché ho litigato con il mio ragazzo.

5   Poiché hanno giocato male, hanno perso la partita.

6   Sono arrivata tardi perché ho perso l'autobus.

22.2   *SO E THEREFORE*

So = **così/quindi** e *therefore* = **perciò** indicano il risultato, la conseguenza di un'azione o di un evento. **So** si trova di solito nel mezzo di una frase, mentre **therefore** si trova all'inizio di una frase nuova ed è usato principalmente in contesti formali e nell'inglese scritto.

Azione	*Linking word*	Risultato
The students were misbehaving	*so*	*the teacher gave them extra homework.*
Gli studenti erano indisciplinati,	**così**	l'insegnante dette loro dei compiti in più.
The students were misbehaving.	*Therefore*	*the teacher gave them extra homework.*
Gli studenti erano indisciplinati.	**Perciò**	l'insegnante dette loro dei compiti in più.
We missed the last bus	*so*	*we had to take a taxi.*
Abbiamo perso l'ultimo autobus,	**così**	abbiamo dovuto prendere un taxi.
We missed the last bus.	*Therefore*	*we had to take a taxi.*
Abbiamo perso l'ultimo autobus.	**Perciò**	abbiamo dovuto prendere un taxi.

Possiamo però esprimere lo stesso significato usando *because*, *as* o *since* e invertendo l'ordine delle frasi.

*We had to take a taxi **because/as/since** we missed the last bus.*

Abbiamo dovuto prendere un taxi *perché* avevamo perso l'ultimo autobus.

Confronta le frasi seguenti:

*It was late **so** James walked Sadie home. = James walked Sadie home **because/as/since** it was late.*

Era tardi, *così* James accompagnò Sadie a casa. = James accompagnò Sadie a casa *perché/poiché* era tardi.

*The teachers were on strike. **Therefore** the school was closed.*

*= The school was closed **because/as/since** the teachers were on strike.*

Gli insegnanti erano in sciopero. *Perciò* la scuola era chiusa.

= La scuola era chiusa *perché/poiché* gli insegnanti erano in sciopero.

Come si nota dagli esempi, in questo tipo di frasi la punteggiatura inglese è spesso differente da quella italiana.

PRACTICE

1 Abbina gli inizi delle frasi con le loro logiche conclusioni.

1	I finished my lunch quickly since ..d..	**a**	a traffic jam.
2	I bought a new umbrella as	**b**	I didn't hear my phone.
3	I gave my friend a present because	**c**	I couldn't contact her.
4	I lost my friend's phone number so	**d**	I had to go out.
5	I got home very late because of	**e**	I'd lost my old one.
6	I was listening to music so	**f**	it was her birthday.

2 Completa la seconda frase in modo che il significato non cambi.

1 Peter missed his station because he fell asleep on the train.

Peter fell asleep on the train ....so he missed his station................................

2 Hannah goes to lots of concerts because she likes music.

Hannah likes music ....

3 Thieves steal from parked cars. Therefore it is important to lock your vehicle.

It is important to lock your vehicle ....

4 Parissa was feeling sick so she didn't eat her ice cream.

Parissa didn't eat her ice cream ....

5 Sam got a job because he needed money.

Sam needed money ....

6 Theresa enjoyed sport so she joined the tennis club.

Theresa joined the tennis club ....

7 Sheila went for a walk as she had a headache.

Sheila had a headache ....

8 Philip opened the parcel since he believed it was for him.

Philip believed the parcel was for him ....

383

22.3   TO, IN ORDER TO E SO (THAT)

Abbiamo già visto che, per tradurre una frase finale, che indica il fine o lo scopo di un'azione, si usa generalmente **to** + **infinito**. (Vedi *Unit* **17.5**)

Lo stesso significato può essere espresso dalle seguenti locuzioni: *in order to* + **infinito** e *so (that)*.

I've been training every day	*to be* really fit.
	in order to be really fit.
	so (that) I'm really fit.
Mi sono allenato tutti i giorni	*per essere* in forma perfetta.
	per essere / in modo da essere in forma perfetta.
	così da essere / così sono / cosicché sono in forma perfetta.

In order to e *so that* sottolineano lo scopo dell'azione.

*Robin goes to evening classes **in order to** learn Greek.*
*Robin frequenta una scuola serale **per** imparare il greco.*

*I'm doing a computer course **so that** I can get a better job.*
*Sto facendo un corso di informatica **in modo da** trovare un lavoro migliore.*

Le frasi finali negative si formano nel modo seguente:

so as not to + **infinito**
in order not to + **infinito**
so that + **frase negativa**
per non + **infinito**

Tom always drives carefully	*so as not to* have an accident.
	in order not to have an accident.
	so that he doesn't have an accident.
Tom guida sempre con prudenza	*per non* avere incidenti.

Le frasi con *so* possono avere due significati differenti, come la seguente:
*I've been training every day **so** I'm really fit.*

Questa frase può significare:

*I've been training every day **in order to** be really fit.*
*Mi sono allenato tutti i giorni **per essere** in forma perfetta.*

*I've been training every day. **Therefore** I'm really fit.*
*Mi sono allenato tutti i giorni. **Perciò** sono in forma perfetta.*

PRACTICE

1 Completa queste frasi con **to** + infinito e un verbo nel riquadro.

check	lose	make	mend	tour	use

1 We phoned the cinema ....to check......... the time of the film.

2 They hired a car .... the mountains.

3 We joined the swimming club .... the pool.

4 He went on a diet .... weight.

5 She went into the kitchen .... some coffee.

6 Did you come here .... my computer?

2 <u>Sottolinea</u> le parole corrette in questa email.

Hi Lizzie – I need your help, quickly.

I went to the airport this morning **(1)** *because* / <u>*in order to*</u> meet my friend Adam. I wanted to drive him to his house **(2)** *so* / *as* I borrowed my father's car. I usually go to the airport by bus **(3)** *because* / *so* the airport car park is so expensive. However, I knew he'd be tired **(4)** *so* / *since it was* a long flight.

The traffic was very heavy **(5)** *as* / *so* I was nearly late. I went to the machine for a ticket when I parked. I pressed the button **(6)** *so* / *to get* a ticket but it didn't give me one, but I pressed it again and this time it gave me a ticket. I put it in my purse without looking at it and ran into the airport.

When we came out, I went to the kiosk **(7)** *to* / *because of* pay. The car park man said I had to pay three hundred pounds **(8)** *so* / *because* the car had been there for two weeks! The ticket machine had printed the wrong date. He didn't believe there was anything wrong with the ticket **(9)** *since* / *so* we had to leave the car and come home on the bus. I don't know what I'm going to tell my father **(10)** *therefore* / *as* I borrowed the car without asking him. What am I going to do??? — Lisa

---

3 Per ogni coppia di frasi, scrivi **S** se il significato è lo stesso e **D** se è differente.

1 I've bought a computer as I work at home.

I've bought a computer since I work at home. ...S....

2 I chose it because of the low price.

I chose it as it was cheap. ....

3 A friend helped me to set up my email as I don't know much about it.

A friend helped me to set up my email. Therefore I don't know much about it. ....

4 I'm working at home in order to save money on train fares.

I'm working at home to save money on train fares. ....

5 I've sold my car because I don't drive to work.

I've sold my car so I don't drive to work. ....

6 I wear old clothes since I stay at home all day.

I stay at home all day as I wear old clothes. ....

22.4   SO E SUCH

So e *such* corrispondono all'italiano **così/talmente** e sono usati davanti a un aggettivo o a un avverbio per metterne in rilievo l'intensità.

so + aggettivo o avverbio	*such* + (a) + (aggettivo) + nome
*You're **so lazy**.* (aggettivo) *Sei **così pigro**.* *You're **so lucky**.* (aggettivo) *Sei **così fortunato**.* *You lose weight **so easily**.* (avverbio) *Riesci a perdere peso **così facilmente**.*	*You're **such a lazy person**.* (nome numerabile) *Sei **una persona così pigra**.* *You say **such unkind things**.* (nome numerabile plurale) *Dici **cose così scortesi**.* *You talk **such nonsense**.* (nome non numerabile) *Dici **tali sciocchezze**.*
so + many/few + nome numerabile	*such* + a lot of + nome numerabile o non numerabile
*You make **so many excuses**.* *Trovi **così tante scuse**.* *I've got **so few** nice **clothes**.* *Ho **così pochi abiti** belli.*	*You make **such a lot of excuses**.* *Trovi **così tante scuse**.*
so + much/little + nome non numerabile	
*They cost **so much money**.* *Costano **così tanto / così tanti soldi**.* *I have **so little time**.* *Ho **così poco tempo**.*	*They cost **such a lot of money**.* *Costano **così tanto / così tanti soldi**.*

■ *So* e *such* + *that*

  So e *such* possono anche essere usati con funzione di congiunzione subordinante per indicare una relazione di **causa** ed **effetto**.

   *He walked **so slowly that** we arrived late.* = *He was **such a slow walker that** we arrived late.*
               *Camminava **così lentamente che** arrivammo in ritardo.*

La congiunzione *that* può essere omessa, soprattutto nel parlato.

           *It was **such an untidy office** we couldn't find our books.*
        = *It was **such an untidy office that** we couldn't find our books.*
    *Era **un ufficio così disordinato che** non riuscivamo a trovare i nostri libri.*

Azione/evento	so/such	+ (that) conseguenza
I'm	*so busy*	*(that) I can't think about keeping fit.*
Sono	**così impegnato**	**che** non posso pensare a tenermi in forma.
He spoke to her	*so rudely*	*(that) she walked out of the room.*
Le parlò	**in modo così scortese**	**che** lei uscì dalla stanza.
Her father is	*such a rich man*	*(that) he's never travelled by bus.*
Suo padre è	**un uomo così ricco**	**che** non ha mai viaggiato in autobus.
The concert was	*such a success*	*(that) they decided to give another.*
Il concerto fu	**un tale successo**	**che** decisero di darne un altro.
He's invited	*so many / such a lot of people*	*to the party (that) there's nowhere to sit down.*
Ha invitato	**così tante persone**	alla festa **che** non c'è nemmeno un posto per sedersi.
Max lost	*so much weight*	*(that) he had to buy new clothes.*
Max ha perso	**così tanto peso**	**che** ha dovuto comprarsi degli abiti nuovi.
You complain	*so much*	*(that) everyone gets bored.*
Ti lamenti	**così tanto**	**che** vieni a noia a tutti.

PRACTICE

1 Riempi gli spazi con **so** o **such**.

1 Everyone likes her because she's ......so....... funny.

2 That was .... an unkind thing to say.

3 He has .... few good friends.

4 Our team lost because they played .... badly.

5 My brother's .... handsome all my friends want to go out with him.

6 We had .... fun at the seaside.

7 I saw .... many wonderful places when I was on holiday.

8 It was .... a lovely surprise to see my cousin at the meeting.

9 I'm sorry I have .... little time for sightseeing on my business trips.

10 It's .... a pity you can't come with us to the theatre.

2 Completa questa email con le frasi **a-g** nel riquadro.

> **a** they had no time for a break
> **b** I got there in ten minutes
> **c** they were selling very quickly
> **d** I could hardly get in the door
> **e** I had to come home in a taxi
> **f** everyone wants them
> **g** nobody believes him

Delete	Reply	Reply All	Forward	Print

Hi Suzi

How are you?

Yesterday I bought so many new clothes **(1)** ..📍.. ! My brother Ricky told me there was a half-price sale on at Gabrielle's, you know, that expensive shop in town. It sells such beautiful clothes that **(2)** ....

Well, at first, I wasn't sure because Ricky usually talks such nonsense **(3)** .... Anyway, Mum said it was true. I ran so fast **(4)** .... The shop already had so many customers **(5)** .... The clothes were so cheap **(6)** .... I did find some good things. I felt sorry for the staff, though. They were working so hard all day that **(7)** .... When can you come and see what I bought?

Love

Frances

22.5   ENOUGH E TOO

Enough e *too* sono indicatori di quantità.

Enough significa **abbastanza** e indica **una quantità giusta, sufficiente**; *too* significa **troppo, più che abbastanza**, e indica una quantità eccessiva.

■ *enough* + **nome**

*We've got **enough sandwiches**.*
Abbiamo **abbastanza sandwich/tramezzini**.

*We haven't got **enough sandwiches**.*
Non abbiamo **abbastanza sandwich/tramezzini**.

■ **aggettivo/avverbio** + *enough*

*This room is **warm enough**.*
Questa stanza è **abbastanza calda**.

*This room isn't **warm enough**.*
Questa stanza non è **abbastanza calda**.

*Am I speaking **loudly enough**?*
Sto parlando **abbastanza forte**?

■ *too much/many* + **nome**

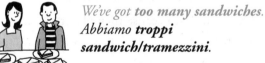
*We've got **too many sandwiches**.*
Abbiamo **troppi sandwich/tramezzini**.

*We've got **too much food**.*
Abbiamo **troppo cibo**.

■ *too* + **aggettivo/avverbio**

*This room is **too warm**.*
Questa stanza è **troppo calda**.

*This room is **too cold**.*
Questa stanza è **troppo fredda**.

*Am I speaking **too loudly**?*
Sto parlando **a voce troppo alta**?

Come si vede dagli esempi, *enough* **precede i nomi**, ma **segue gli aggettivi e gli avverbi**.

We haven't got **enough time**.	*Non abbiamo* **abbastanza tempo**.
Have you got **enough money** *for the car park?*	*Hai* **abbastanza soldi** *per il parcheggio?*
Is it **warm enough** *for you?* (**Non** ~~*enough warm*~~)	*È* **abbastanza caldo** *per te?*
Am I speaking **slowly enough** *for you?* (**Non** ~~*enough slowly*~~)	*Sto parlando* **abbastanza lentamente** *per te?*

ENOUGH/TOO + TO INFINITO

Enough e *too* possono essere seguiti da *to* + **infinito**.

It's **too far to walk**. = *It's* **not near enough to walk**.
È **troppo lontano per arrivarci a piedi**. = *Non è* **abbastanza vicino per arrivarci a piedi**.
You are **too young to go** *clubbing.* = *You are* **not old enough to go** *clubbing.*
Sei **troppo giovane per andare** *per discoteche.* = *Non sei* **abbastanza grande per andare** *per discoteche.*

This bag is **too heavy to carry**.	*Questa borsa è* **troppo pesante da portare**.
I'm not **strong enough to carry** *this bag.*	*Non sono* **abbastanza forte da portare** *questa borsa.*
He wasn't running **quickly enough to catch us**.	*Non correva* **abbastanza velocemente da prenderci**.

La frase infinitiva può essere preceduta da *for* + **nome/pronome**, mentre in italiano **per** + **nome/pronome** segue la costruzione infinitiva.

This bag is **too heavy for me to carry**.	*Questa borsa è* **troppo pesante da portare per me**.
It was **too icy for the plane to take off**.	*C'era* **troppo ghiaccio perché l'aeroplano decollasse**.
Am I speaking **slowly enough for the students to understand?**	*Sto parlando* **abbastanza lentamente perché gli studenti capiscano?**

PRACTICE

1 Completa la seconda frase in modo che abbia lo stesso significato della prima. Usa la parola tra parentesi.

1 This coffee is very sweet. I can't drink it.

This coffee ....is too sweet to drink.......................... (*too*)

2 You can't put all your clothes in your leather suitcase.

Your leather suitcase .... (*enough*)

3 I've got a lot of work to do. I can't finish it all.

I've got .... (*too*)

4 The weather's cold and this jacket is too light.

This jacket .... (*enough*)

5 You don't need any more CDs.

You've got .... (*enough*)

6 You should eat more slowly.

You eat .... (*too*)

389

7   I need to have my hair cut.

My hair .... (too)

8   We've got lots of extra glasses. We don't need them all.

We've got .... (too)

9   I don't play games on my computer because it has very little memory.

I don't play games on my computer because it .... (enough)

10   She got up late so she missed the bus.

She missed the bus because she .... (enough)

2   Leggi questa conversazione e <u>sottolinea</u> la parola corretta, **to** o **for**.

Landlady: This is your bedroom. I hope it's big enough **(1)** *to / for* you and this cupboard is for
clothes. Is there enough room **(2)** *to / for* all your things?

Student: Yes, I think so.

Landlady: We can put your big suitcase in the basement if it's too big **(3)** *to / for* go on top of the
cupboard.

Student: Thank you.

Landlady: The bathroom is next door. Switch the water heater on in the morning so there's enough
hot water **(4)** *to / for* have a shower. Can you understand everything? Do I speak slowly
enough **(5)** *to / for* you?

Student: Yes, I can understand you. But my English isn't good enough **(6)** *to / for* say everything I
want to.

Landlady: Oh, don't worry. I'm sure you'll soon learn.

3   Unisci le frasi seguenti usando **too** o **enough**.

1   We couldn't swim in the sea. It was too cold.

The sea was too cold to swim in.

2   Tom couldn't buy a new scooter. He didn't have enough money.

....

3   Helen didn't get a place in the athletics team. She wasn't a fast enough runner.

....

4   Dora would like to see all her friends. She doesn't have enough time.

....

5   We can't cycle to the school. It's too far away.

....

6   We'd like to eat outdoors. It isn't warm enough.

....

7   Frank has too much homework. He can't go out after school.

....

8   Don't lie in that hammock. It isn't strong enough for two people.

....

ALL IN ONE REVISION

1   Nancy sta parlando con Steve di un programma televisivo che ha guardato la sera precedente. Prima di ascoltare, guarda le immagini e cerca di metterle nell'ordine giusto per raccontare la storia del programma.

2   Ascolta e verifica se avevi ragione.

What happened to Orville?

2.26

3   Ascolta di nuovo e completa le frasi seguenti.

2.27

1   Claudia went to an evening class ....to.......... learn Greek.

2   He put on a false beard .... he didn't want her to recognise him.

3   Damian was there .... he was waiting for his girlfriend.

4   Claudia knew Damian .... her job.

5   Orville was making a terrible noise .... the college receptionist called the police.

6   No-one helped him .... he was taken to the police station.

4   Rileggi l'esercizio 3. Le frasi seguenti hanno lo stesso significato di quelle nell'esercizio 3? Fai un segno accanto a quelle che hanno lo stesso significato.

1   Claudia wanted to learn Greek so she went to an evening class. ..✓..

2   Orville put on a false beard because he didn't want Claudia to recognise him. .....

3   Damian was waiting in the entrance hall to meet his girlfriend. .....

4   Claudia knew Damian because she'd met him when she was working. .....

5   Orville was making a terrible noise because the college receptionist called the police. .....

6   Orville was taken to the police station because no-one helped him. .....

391

5 Questo testo è stato diviso in sequenze, che sono state tagliate e mescolate. Metti le sequenze nell'ordine corretto, in modo da ricostruire il testo originale. Fai particolare attenzione alle parole in **neretto**, i **connettivi** o *linking words*, che servono a dare coesione logica al discorso.

1   Emma Watson, an English actress, was born on 15th April 1990. She is world famous **because**

2   her parents divorced. Already at the age of three she had told her grandmother that she wanted to be a 'mattress' (she meant actress), **so**

3   she need never work for money again. However, she recently agreed to act in the final two *Harry Potter* films.

4   she has co-starred in five movie adaptations of the bestselling books *Harry Potter* in the role of Hermione Granger. She was born in Paris to English parents, but she moved to Oxford in England with her mother and brother when she was five **as**

5   her schooling would not be interrupted. However, her exam results have been excellent and she wants to go to university **since**

6   compete for the role of Hermione. She was cast **because of**

7   she really has fulfilled her childhood dreams. At the age of nine she auditioned eight times **in order to**

8   'learning keeps [her] motivated'. She has made **so** much money in her acting career (ten million pounds by 2007) **that**

9   her similarity to the literary character, 'self-confident and bossy'. During filming over the last six years, she has often had to have private teachers **so that**

6 Leggi questa intervista con Colin Grant, vincitore di tre medaglie alle Olimpiadi, e completa le frasi inserendo **una sola** parola in ogni spazio.

Interviewer: Congratulations, Mr Grant, on yet another gold medal for the United States. Could you give young athletes some advice on what they can do **(1)** ....in.......... order to get to the Olympics?

CG: Sure. Well, first of all, you have to train every day or you'll never be fit **(2)** .... to compete.

Interviewer: How many hours a day do you recommend?

CG: I do two hours a day of workouts in **(3)** .... to keep my muscles elastic, and I get up early **(4)** .... go for a 10-mile run before breakfast. **(5)** .... I have to be at work by nine, that means getting up at six in the morning.

Interviewer: **(6)** .... how many hours a night do you sleep?

CG: Eight. Sleep is very important **(7)** .... you can't work well if you don't get **(8)** .... , but it's not a good thing to sleep **(9)** .... much either.

Interviewer: I see. And what about diet? Do you follow any diet in particular?

CG: Yes, I eat lots of meat and fish **(10)** .... I need plenty of protein, but it's better to eat six small meals rather than three heavy ones. I frequently eat high-protein snacks **(11)** .... as not to get hungry during the day. I also eat a lot of fruit and drink plenty of water.

Interviewer: And what do you do in the evenings?

CG: I do yoga **(12)** .... I find it relaxing and it keeps me awake mentally. Television makes me **(13)** .... sleepy so I avoid that. I believe in the old saying: 'healthy body, healthy mind'.

Interviewer: Don't you find it difficult to keep up **(14)** .... a rigorous routine?

CG: Well, I don't mind it, but I have so little spare time my family complains that they don't see **(15)** .... of me. **(16)** .... I try to make time for them, too.

---

7 Leggi il rapporto in cui il detective Thomas Pitt descrive come ha smascherato il responsabile di un crimine. Riempi gli spazi con **because of**, **as**, **so**, **therefore**, **in order to**, **so that**, **enough** e **too**.

I was called in to investigate the fire at Pill's Pharmaceutical factory and the death in the fire of Mr Knowall, the night watchman. The fire brigade managed to save most of the buildings, and the fire was apparently an accident. **(1)** ......As....... an empty bottle of vodka was found in the night watchman's office next to his body, it was assumed that the victim had drunk **(2)** .... much that he had fallen asleep with a cigarette in his hand. I discovered, however, that Mr Knowall had recently deposited enormous amounts of money in his bank account. **(3)** .... I began to suspect that the case was not as simple as it seemed. We searched Knowall's house, and certain files found on his computer were **(4)** .... to convince me that he was probably blackmailing the factory owner, Sir William Pill. Knowall had discovered and could prove that the factory was secretly producing illegal drugs and selling them on the black market, and Sir Pill was probably paying Knowall **(5)** .... stop him from reporting it to the police. **(6)** .... at this point we searched Sir Pill's mansion **(7)** .... see what further evidence we could find. Clothes that smelt of petrol and a gun were hidden in the cellar. I deduced that Pill had shot Knowall **(8)** .... he wouldn't talk, set fire to his office **(9)** .... get rid of the body, and planted an empty bottle of vodka **(10)** .... make it seem like an accident. It was only **(11)** .... the anonymous phone call to the fire brigade that we had suspected anything. Of course, it was made **(12)** .... late to save Knowall, but early **(13)** .... to save the rest of the factory. Sir Pill later pleaded guilty of murder.

8 Riempi gli spazi, usando le parole e le espressioni nel riquadro.

| as | because | enough | in order to | so | so | so that | too |

1

Why are you staring at me like that?

.....Because..... you've got a large black mark on the end of your nose!

2

It's only eleven o'clock. Why aren't you still at school?

We've been sent home early .... revise for our exam tomorrow.

3

How was the trip to the museum?

.... several galleries were closed for repairs, it was rather disappointing.

Gallery Closed

4

What are all those students doing in the park?

The university term has ended .... they're having a picnic to celebrate.

5

Why are you working late today?

I want to finish this essay .... I'll be free to go out tomorrow.

6

Come on! If we run fast ...., we'll catch the early train.

7

Sorry, I've got .... many bags I can't run.

8

Oh, never mind. If we're .... late for that train, we can have a drink while we wait for the next one.

9 In sei di queste frasi c'è un errore. <u>Sottolinea</u> gli errori e scrivi accanto la correzione.

1 We're packing our cases tonight <u>so</u> we're leaving very early tomorrow. ...._as_................

2 Have you got money enough for your journey? ....

3 My father says I'm too young for have a motorbike but I don't agree. ....

4 I've lost weight so I can wear a tight skirt at my party. ....

5 Since that I've never been to New York, I can't tell you much about it. ....

6 She's been given too much advice that she doesn't know what to do. ....

7 I've booked a table at the restaurant so we won't have to wait. ....

8 It was a such sad film I couldn't stop crying at the end. ....

10 Abbina gli inizi delle frasi con le loro logiche conclusioni.

1 Tessa's got so much homework ..h...   a he should be in bed.

2 Stephen's so vain ....   b to make sandwiches for us all.

3 Jessie has so many hobbies ....   c he can buy any clothes he wants.

4 This music isn't too loud ....   d she neglects her schoolwork.

5 Saskia hasn't got enough money ....   e for us.

6 Keith earns so much money ....   f to come on holiday with us.

7 I think there's enough bread ....   g he thinks every girl fancies him.

8 Peter has such a bad cold ....   h she can't come out with us.

11 Completa queste frasi usando le tue idee.

1 The bus company offers cheaper fares at weekends in order to ......attract more passengers......

2 The hotel dining-room is closed this week. Therefore guests ....

3 We'd better phone a qualified electrician, as we ....

4 Because my brother uses a wheelchair, he often ....

5 I don't have a mobile phone so my friends ....

6 She has such beautiful clothes she ....

7 We enjoyed the party so much we ....

8 Is this box big enough to ....

12 Riscrivi le frasi seguenti usando le parole tra parentesi in modo che il significato non cambi.

1 I set the alarm because I was afraid of oversleeping the next morning. (*in order*)
   I set the alarm in order not to oversleep the next morning....................................

2 The motorway staff were on strike so we didn't have to pay the toll. (*as*)
   ....

3 Harry is too short to play basketball. (*enough*)
   ....

4 Sophie hid her iPod to stop her sister from using it. (*so that*)
   ....

5 The music was so great that we couldn't help dancing. (*such*)
   ....

6 Since Barbara hadn't studied, she didn't pass the exam. (*therefore*)

....

7 Jimmy tells such incredible stories that you never know whether to believe them or not. (*so*)

....

8 The play wasn't interesting enough for us to stay to the end. (*too*)

....

13 Traduci.

1   Il film era così noioso che mi sono addormentato mentre lo guardavo.

2   Il libro che mi hai regalato era così interessante che l'ho letto in un giorno.

3   Fred è un ragazzo così dolce. Io lo adoro.

4   Non ho mai conosciuto una persona così simpatica.

5   Abbiamo così tante cose da fare, e così poco tempo.

6   Sono troppo stanca per uscire.

7   **A** Andiamo al cinema? **B** No, è troppo tardi per andare al cinema ormai.

8   Vorrei comprare un computer nuovo, ma non ho abbastanza soldi al momento.

9   Il tavolo era troppo pesante da sollevare.

10   Questi fichi non sono abbastanza maturi da mangiare.

I CONNETTIVI (2)

I CONNETTIVI (2) – INTRODUZIONE

In questa *Unit* vengono presentati altri connettivi, o *linking words*, utilizzati per strutturare un discorso. Questi connettivi sono usati per esprimere:

▉ concessione o contrasto: *but*, *although* e *though*; *in spite of* e *despite*; *even though* e *even if*

▉ inclusione o alternativa: *both ... and*; *either ... or*

▉ relazione di tempo: *when*, *until*, *before*, *after*, *as soon as*, *while* e *since*

Nella seconda parte della *Unit* vengono inoltre introdotte le frasi subordinate costituite dal participio presente, o forma *-ing*, e dal participio passato. Queste frasi hanno di norma valore causale e temporale.

23.1   *BUT, ALTHOUGH* E *THOUGH*

But, *although* e *though* introducono un fatto o un'idea in contrapposizione a quanto è indicato nella frase principale.

Although e *though* significano propriamente **sebbene / per quanto / anche se** ed esprimono un contrasto più forte rispetto a *but*. *Though* è più comune di *although* nell'inglese parlato.

Frase A	Linking word	Frase B
The hotel was excellent	***but***	*the food was boring.*
L'albergo era eccellente	**ma**	*il cibo era banale.*
I like making films	***but***	*I'm really a stage actor.*
Mi piace fare film	**ma**	*in realtà sono un attore di teatro.*
The hotel was excellent	***although/though***	*the food was boring.*
L'albergo era eccellente	**anche se /**	*il cibo era banale.*
	sebbene / nonostante	*il cibo fosse banale.*

Linking word	Frase A	Frase B
Although/Though	*the food was boring,*	*the hotel was excellent.*
Sebbene/Nonostante	*il cibo fosse banale,*	*l'albergo era eccellente.*

But è sempre posto nel mezzo della frase.

Although e *though* possono essere posti sia all'inizio che nel mezzo della frase. Quando si trovano all'inizio, di solito c'è una virgola prima della frase principale.

> *I like making films **although/though** I'm really a stage actor.*
> = ***Although/Though** I'm really a stage actor, I like making films.*
> ***Sebbene / Per quanto** io sia in realtà un attore di teatro, mi piace fare film.*

Although/Though e *but* **non possono** essere usati nella stessa frase.
(**Non** ~~Although/Though I'm really a stage actor, **but** I like making films.~~)

PRACTICE

1 Riscrivi queste frasi usando *although/though*.

1 I don't often eat ice cream but I really like it.
Although .... I really like ice cream, I don't often eat it. ....

2 Elena speaks Polish but she's never been to Poland.
.... though ....

3 Zach didn't want to go to the disco but he enjoyed it when he got there.
Although ....

4 No-one eats fruit but Mum still buys it.
.... though ....

5 Dennis didn't get good marks in his exams but he went to university.
Though ....

6 Mahmoud is the shop manager but he's only nineteen.
.... although ....

2 Abbina gli inizi delle frasi con le loro logiche conclusioni.

1 Although the weather was cold, ..f...
2 Jack was absolutely exhausted ......
3 Though Luciano Pavarotti was already very ill ......
4 I have cleaned the DVD drive ......
5 Jill's bedroom is always a terrible mess ......
6 Danny passed the exam first time ......
7 Though I love music, ...
8 Carlo's English is not very good ......

a he sang at the opening of the Winter Olympics in 2006.
b but it still hasn't solved the problem.
c though her mother is always telling her to tidy it up.
d I've never learnt to play an instrument.
e although he hadn't done any work for it.
f we enjoyed our trip.
g although he usually gets his message across.
h but he managed to complete the marathon.

23.2   IN SPITE OF / DESPITE

In spite of e *despite* significano **nonostante** e mettono in contrasto due eventi o idee: sono usati per collegare un evento a una situazione che sembrerebbe rendere l'evento stesso improbabile. A differenza di *although/though* sono seguiti da un nome o dalla forma *-ing*, **non** da una proposizione esplicita (soggetto + verbo). *In spite of* è più comune di *despite* in contesti informali.

In spite of / Despite

▧ sono seguiti da un **nome** o dalla forma *-ing*.

*The hotel was excellent **in spite of / despite the boring food**.*
*L'albergo era eccellente **nonostante il cibo noioso**.*

*He continued to work **in spite of / despite his illness**.*
*Continuò a lavorare **nonostante la sua malattia**.*

*He continued to work **in spite of / despite being** ill.*
*Continuò a lavorare **nonostante fosse** malato.*

▧ possono essere posti all'inizio o in mezzo alla frase.

***In spite of / Despite having** little money, we were very happy.*
***Nonostante avessimo** pochi soldi eravamo molto felici.*

*We were very happy **in spite of / despite having** little money.*
*Eravamo molto felici **nonostante avessimo** pochi soldi.*

▧ si trovano spesso nella costruzione *in spite of the fact that* + **soggetto** + **verbo**.

*I got the part **in spite of the fact that** I had no experience.*
*Ottenni la parte **nonostante il fatto che** non avessi esperienza.*

***Despite the fact that** he was feeling unwell, he played very well.*
***Nonostante (il fatto) che** si sentisse male, giocò molto bene.*

🔊 È importante ricordare che *in spite of / despite* **non** possono essere seguiti da una proposizione esplicita, soggetto + verbo.

(**Non** ~~The hotel was excellent in spite of the food was boring~~.)

PRACTICE

1 Riempi gli spazi con *although/though* o *in spite of / despite*.

1   <u>In spite of / Despite</u>... the fact that I don't have any experience with children, I've been offered a job on a children's summer camp.

2   .... Judy wasn't feeling well, she didn't want to miss the concert.

3   John often feels lonely .... having plenty of friends.

4   .... Pavarotti's origins were humble, he became the richest opera singer in the history of music.

5   .... playing with only ten men, Manchester United still won the match 3-0.

6   Frank decided to walk home .... the fact that it was late.

7 .... the collapse in profits for recording companies, more people are going to live concerts than ever.

8 .... it's never too late to start taking exercise, it's a good idea to build up your routine gradually.

9 .... Harry is a very talented actor, he finds it difficult to get good parts in plays.

2 Unisci le frasi seguenti usando la parola tra parentesi.

1 I enjoyed the film. The story was a bit soppy. (*in spite of*)
   In spite of the story being a bit soppy, I enjoyed the film.

2 I invited my parents to my eighteenth birthday party. They decided not to come. (*although*)
   ....

3 There was a lot of media coverage. The stolen painting wasn't found. (*despite*)
   ....

4 Max Money is only seventeen years old. He already makes $100,000 a year. (*in spite of*)
   ....

5 Alessia speaks English fluently. She has never been to England. (*although*)
   ....

6 The local residents didn't complain. The concert went on until one o'clock in the morning. (*though*)
   ....

3 Traduci.

1 Nonostante la pioggia, i bambini si sono divertiti moltissimo.

2 Non riuscivo ad addormentarmi, nonostante fossi molto stanco.

3 Nonostante il raffreddore, Joyce ha cantato molto bene.

4 Nonostante che non studi molto, mio fratello ottiene risultati migliori di me.

5 Nonostante il traffico, siamo arrivati puntuali.

6 Silke ha superato il test, nonostante che non avesse mai studiato inglese prima.

23.3   *EVEN THOUGH* E *EVEN IF*

Even though e *even if* significano **anche se** e mettono in particolare rilievo l'idea di concessione e contrasto. Hanno un significato lievemente differente.

Even though

■ viene usato quando si sta parlando di un fatto di cui si è certi.
*She was given the part **even though** she had no experience.*
*Le fu data la parte **anche se** non aveva esperienza.* (= colui che parla sa per certo che la ragazza non aveva esperienza.)

Even if

■ è usato per riferirsi a un'ipotesi aperta, qualcosa di cui non si è certi.
*I'll support my team **even if** they don't win the Cup.*
*Farò il tifo per la mia squadra **anche se** non vinceranno la Coppa.* (= non so se vinceranno la Coppa, ma farò comunque il tifo per loro.)

PRACTICE

1 Completa le frasi seguenti con **even if** o **even though**.

1 Alan's parents have bought him a new scooter, ...even though... he didn't pass his exams.

2 .... we enjoyed the holiday, we were still glad to get home.

3 We're going to go to Mexico .... you decide not to come.

4 .... we don't win the match, we can still have lots of fun.

5 Maria got the job .... she doesn't speak English very fluently.

6 I'll finish this exercise .... I am feeling exhausted.

7 You'll be late for school .... you leave immediately.

8 .... you go down on your knees, she won't forgive you.

23.4   BOTH … AND; EITHER … OR

Both … and

- sono usati per **includere** due persone o due cose: **sia** l'uno **che** l'altro.

  Both Steven and his wife work very hard.
  Sia Steven **che** sua moglie lavorano sodo.

- sono spesso usati nella seguente costruzione: nome **and** nome + **both** + **verbo**.

  Jane and Will both work very hard.
  Jane e Will lavorano entrambi duramente.

🔸 *Both* **segue** il verbo *to be* e i verbi ausiliari.

  My wife and I were both looking forward to a holiday.
  Sia io **che** mia moglie non vedevamo l'ora di andare in vacanza.

  We were both very tired.
  Eravamo entrambi molto stanchi.

Either … or

- sono usati per indicare un'**alternativa**: **o** l'uno **o** l'altro.

  Either the bookings manager or the secretary made a mistake.
  O il responsabile delle prenotazioni **o** la segretaria ha fatto un errore.

- sono spesso usati per **collegare due verbi**.

  Either phone me or send me an email.
  Chiamami **oppure** scrivimi un'email.

  You can either eat out or have dinner in your hotel.
  Potete mangiare fuori **o/oppure** cenare in albergo.

🔸 Per la forma negativa *Neither … nor* vedi *Unit* **9.5**.

PRACTICE

1 Unisci le frasi seguenti usando le parole tra parentesi.

1 I travelled to New York. There was a strike. (*in spite of*)
I travelled to New York in spite of the strike.

2 Nigel bought some CDs. Anthony bought some CDs. (*both ... and*)
Both Nigel and Anthony bought some CDs. or Nigel and Anthony both bought some CDs.

3 Tom sent that email. Martin sent that email. (*either ... or*)
....

4 Dolores was working in the garden. The sun was hot. (*despite*)
....

5 Her dress is new. Her jacket is new. (*both ... and*)
....

6 Michael wasn't late. There was a traffic jam. (*in spite of*)
....

7 My father gave me some money. My mother gave me some money. (*both ... and*)
....

8 Do your homework now. Get up early and do it tomorrow. (*either ... or*)
....

9 You can go on your bike. You can come with me in the car. (*either ... or*)
....

2 Traduci.

1 Sia Carlos che sua sorella parlano inglese perfettamente.

2 Sto cercando un lavoro sia qui che all'estero.

3 Sia Eileen che Dave hanno promesso di venire, ma non so se ce la faranno. Sono entrambi molto occupati in questo periodo.

4 O mangi la verdura o rinunci (*go without*) al dolce: scegli tu.

5 I miei amici arriveranno o stasera o domani mattina.

6 Steven è fatto così: o lo ami o lo detesti.

23.5   WHEN, UNTIL, BEFORE, AFTER, AS SOON AS, WHILE

When, **until**, **before**, **after**, **as soon as** e **while** indicano una relazione temporale.

When we arrived in Florida, we hired a car.

Quando *siamo arrivati in Florida abbiamo noleggiato una macchina.*

*We waited with our friends **until** their bus arrived.*

*Aspettammo insieme ai nostri amici **finché** arrivò il loro autobus.*

È importante ricordare che in inglese **non** si può usare il futuro nelle frasi subordinate introdotte da una congiunzione temporale. (Vedi *Unit* **5.9**)

*We'll hire a car, **when** we **arrive** in Florida. (**Non** when we'll arrive)*

*Noleggeremo una macchina **quando arriveremo** in Florida.*

PRACTICE

1 Greta sta parlando di quando ha finito la scuola. <u>Sottolinea</u> le parole corrette.

Although we sometimes enjoyed school, because we were with our friends, we were happy **(1)** <u>*when*</u> / *while* we left. We all walked out of the gate together **(2)** *after* / *before* we took the final exam. We wanted to go on holiday **(3)** *while* / *as soon as* the school term finished, but we had to wait **(4)** *after* / *until* we had our marks. I got a job **(5)** *while* / *before* I waited to get my exam results. I needed to earn some money **(6)** *before* / *when* I went away. We all phoned our friends **(7)** *until* / *when* the results arrived. Everyone had passed! I was so happy **(8)** *after* / *when* I knew that. We could all enjoy our holiday.

2 Leggi questa email e coniuga i verbi tra parentesi al tempo corretto: *present simple* o futuro con **will**.

Hi Andreas

You asked about my plans for this summer. You'll be jealous when I **(1)** ....tell.......... (*tell*) you!

I'm going to fly to Argentina as soon as my holiday **(2)** .... (*begin*). My uncle will meet me when I **(3)** .... (*arrive*) and take me to his house.

I expect I **(4)** .... (*stay*) with his family for about a month. My cousins will show me around the city before we **(5)** .... (*go*) to their holiday house. After I **(6)** .... (*leave*) Buenos Aires, I'm going to fly to Ecuador. I **(7)** .... (*tour*) around until my money **(8)** .... (*run*) out. I don't have fixed plans, but I'm definitely going to take a river trip while I **(9)** .... (*be*) in Ecuador. I'm really excited.

What about you? What are you going to do after your exams **(10)** .... (*be*) over?

All the best

Euan

3 In cinque di queste frasi c'è un errore. Individua gli errori e correggili.

1 Although the film was quite exciting at the beginning, ~~but~~ the last part was so boring I fell asleep.
Although the film was quite exciting at the beginning, the last part was so boring I fell asleep.

2 Both university students and school teachers can use this library. ....

3 We had a good time at the beach in spite of the weather was windy. ....

4 Maggie isn't really friendly though she is very polite. ....

5 We'll leave the restaurant as soon as the waiter will bring our bill. ....
....

6 This room is terribly untidy! Or help me to tidy it or go away. ....

7 In spite of our hard work, we didn't win the prize. ....

8 I don't play an instrument although my father and my mother both are musicians. ....
....

9 We're going to change our car before we start our tour of Scandinavia. ....
....

23.6   *BEFORE, AFTER, WHEN, WHILE* E *SINCE* + *-ING*

Le congiunzioni temporali *before* = **prima / prima di / prima che**; *after* = **dopo / dopo di / dopo che**; *when* = **quando**; *while* = **mentre** e *since* = **da quando**, possono essere seguite dalla forma -*ing* quando il soggetto della frase principale e della subordinata è lo stesso. (Vedi *Unit* **17.3**)

Questa costruzione è più comune nell'inglese scritto piuttosto che nel parlato: *before* e *after* + *-ing*.

Primo evento:

*I **had** a long talk with my parents.*   ***Feci** una lunga chiacchierata con i miei genitori.*

Secondo evento:

*I **accepted** the job abroad.*   ***Accettai** il lavoro all'estero.*

→   *I **had** a long talk with my parents **before accepting** the job abroad.*
    ***Feci** una lunga chiacchierata con i miei genitori **prima di accettare** il lavoro all'estero.*

→   *After **having** a long talk with my parents, I **accepted** the job abroad.*
    ***Dopo aver fatto** una lunga chiacchierata con i miei genitori **accettai** il lavoro all'estero.*

When + *-ing*

Due eventi accadono allo stesso tempo.

    *When **leaving** the train, passengers should ensure that they have all their possessions with them.*
***Quando scendono** dal treno, i passeggeri dovrebbero assicurarsi di avere tutti i loro oggetti personali con sé.*

    *It's important to make a good impression **when starting** a new job.*
    *È importante fare una buona impressione **quando si inizia** un nuovo lavoro.*

While + -ing

Un'azione accade mentre un'altra è in corso di svolgimento.

> *I was offered two more jobs **while working** abroad.*
> **Mi furono offerti altri due lavori *mentre lavoravo* all'estero.**
>
> ***While playing** tennis last week I slipped and sprained my ankle.*
> ***Mentre giocavo** a tennis la settimana scorsa sono scivolato e mi sono slogato la caviglia.*

Since + -ing

Collega un'azione o situazione in corso al momento in cui è iniziata.

> *Since leaving school, he has made a number of trips abroad.*
> ***Da quando ha finito** la scuola ha fatto un sacco di viaggi all'estero.*
>
> *She hasn't been in touch **since moving** to New York.*
> *Non si è tenuta in contatto **da quando si è trasferita** a New York.*

PRACTICE

1 Collega ogni coppia di frasi usando la parola tra parentesi + **-ing**.

1 I came across a lot of new groups. I followed the rock contest on the radio. (*while*)

I came across a lot of new groups while following the rock contest on the radio............

2 Wait for the tone. Leave your message. (*before*) ....

3 Vivian isn't happy. She goes to an all-girls' school. (*since*) ....

4 Take your contact lenses out. Leave them in a saline solution. (*after*) ....

5 Stick to the bicycle lanes. Cycle around the ring road. (*when*) ....

6 Remember to look to your right. Cross the road in Great Britain. (*before*) ....

2 Riempi gli spazi in questa conversazione al cellulare. Usa **before**, **after**, **when**, **while** o **since**.

Tom: Hello?

Kai: Tom, I know it's late, but I need to tell you something.

Tom: It's OK. I'm not home yet. I'm back at the taxi office.

Kai: But I thought you got a taxi immediately **(1)** ..after... leaving the club.

Tom: I did. But **(2)** .... getting into the taxi, I haven't been able to find my wallet.
I can't pay the taxi driver.

Kai: I know where your wallet is. But it's empty.

Tom: What?

Kai: Well, I left the club soon after you, and **(3)** .... waiting for my bus, I
noticed a wallet on the pavement. I looked round **(4)** .... picking it up, but
there wasn't anyone near. **(5)** .... looking in it for a name or address,

I thought about taking it to the police station. But then I noticed the initials on it and guessed it might be yours. Someone probably dropped the wallet **(6)** .... taking the money.

Tom: Oh no. I guess I was robbed **(7)** .... leaving the club. Can you come to the taxi office and explain?

Kai: Yeah, I suppose someone's got to rescue you. But next time, check your wallet **(8)** .... taking a taxi, OK?

23.7   COSTRUZIONI CON IL PARTICIPIO

Una frase subordinata può essere costituita dal participio presente (= forma **-ing**) o dal participio passato quando si verificano le seguenti condizioni:

> la frase principale e la subordinata hanno lo stesso soggetto;
>
> il participio può sostituire la sequenza **soggetto** + **verbo** della prima frase.

Considera le frasi seguenti:

I work far from home. + *I sometimes feel lonely.*

→ *Working far from home, I sometimes feel lonely.*
  Lavorando lontano da casa, qualche volta mi sento solo.

Gemma was asked about the play. + *Gemma said it was great.*

→ *Asked about the play, Gemma said it was great.*
  Richiesta di parlare della commedia, Gemma disse che era fantastica.

Il participio presente (forma *-ing*)

■ può sostituire un verbo **attivo**.

We were short of time. + *We had to run for the bus.*

→ *Being short of time, we had to run for the bus.*
  Avendo poco tempo, abbiamo dovuto correre per prendere l'autobus.

■ collega due azioni che **accadono** più o meno **allo stesso tempo**, sia nel presente che nel passato.

The girl used all her strength. + *The girl pushed open the heavy doors.*

→ *Using all her strength, the girl pushed open the heavy doors.*
Usando tutta la sua forza, la ragazzina riuscì ad aprire le porte pesanti.

Il participio passato

■ può sostituire un verbo **passivo**.

The girls were refused entry to the club. + *The girls walked slowly home.*

→ *Refused entry to the club, the girls walked slowly home.*
  (Essendo stato) rifiutato loro l'ingresso al club, le ragazze tornarono lentamente a casa.

■ collega due eventi o situazioni che hanno un rapporto tra sé.

'Greensleeves' was written in the sixteenth century. + *'Greensleeves' is still a famous song.*

→ *Written in the sixteenth century, 'Greensleeves' is still a famous song.*
  Scritta nel XVI secolo, 'Greensleeves' è ancora una canzone famosa.

Le costruzioni con il participio si trovano più spesso nello scritto che nel parlato.

PRACTICE

1 Collega le frasi seguenti usando la forma *-ing* o il participio passato.

1 Romeo believed that Juliet was dead. Romeo killed himself.
   Believing that Juliet was dead, Romeo killed himself.

2 Miranda was rejected by her best friend. Miranda walked home from school on her own. ....

3 Jim suspected something terrible had happened. Jim phoned his girlfriend.

4 Pavarotti had one of the most beautiful voices that have ever existed. It is not surprising that Pavarotti became so rich and famous. ....

5 The Eiffel Tower was originally intended to stand for a maximum of twenty years. It has become France's national symbol. ....

6 Tom's mother didn't know where Tom was. She was worried to death.

7 I'm rather short of money. I can't really afford a new digital camera.

8 *A Clockwork Orange* was originally written in 1962. It was later adapted for the screen by Stanley Kubrick. ....

2 Riscrivi la storia seguente sostituendo i verbi in **neretto** con la forma *-ing*.

Little Red Riding Hood set off through the woods for her grandmother's house. **(1)** She **disobeyed** her mother's warning and **strayed** from the path and soon she met a hungry-looking wolf. **(2)** The wolf **saw** her basket of food and asked her where she was going. **(3)** Little Red Riding Hood **didn't suspect** that the wolf had evil intentions and told him the truth. When she arrived at her grandmother's she knocked on the door and went in. **(4)** The wolf was waiting for her in her grandmother's bed, but Little Red Riding Hood **was** very short-sighted, so she didn't immediately notice anything unusual.
(5) When she **sat** next to the bed, however, she **saw** the wolf's big ears and said, 'What big ears you have, Grandmama!' **(6)** The wolf **answered** in a gruff voice, 'All the better to hear you with, my dear!'
(7) Little Red Riding Hood **didn't realise** that she could have killed time by commenting on the wolf's deep voice, hairy hands, very full stomach, and greedy eyes, so she went straight to the heart of the matter: 'What big teeth you have, Grandmama!' **(8)** The wolf **didn't even bother** to answer, but jumped out of the bed and pounced on Little Red Riding Hood. **(9)** But he **wasn't used to** wearing a nightdress and he had already eaten Grandmama so he was too slow, and Little Red Riding Hood ran out of the cottage. **(10)** Luckily, a hunter heard her screams and when he **saw** the wolf running after her, he shot the wolf. **(11)** He **noticed** the wolf's bulging stomach and he cut the wolf open to see what was inside. Out stepped Grandmama, and would you believe it? She was fine!

(1) *Disobeying her mother's warning and straying from the path, she soon met a hungry-looking wolf.*

ALL IN ONE REVISION

1 Ascolterai un'intervista a una giovane donna. Prima di ascoltare, leggi i titoli dei giornali di due anni prima. Solo uno dei titoli indica i fatti correttamente. Gli altri sono sbagliati.

a **New star signs contract to make three films in a year**

b **15-YEAR-OLD GIVEN LEADING ROLE IN NEW FILM**

c **Teenage film actor wins starring part**

d **GIRL WITH NO ACTING EXPERIENCE IS NEW FILM STAR**

2.28

Ascolta l'intervista e indica il titolo giusto.

2.29

2 Ascolta di nuovo e riempi gli spazi. Ferma la registrazione se necessario.

1 …you've been world famous ..... *since making* ..... the film *Starshine* two years ago…

2 I got the part .... no film experience.

3 The director chose me to play the part .... several schools.

4 I had a long talk with my parents .... it.

5 I was offered two more films .... *Starshine*…

6 …but .... far from home, I sometimes felt very lonely.

7 I'd be happy to do another film later, ... booked up for the next few months.

8 It's actually a comedy, ... called *Dark Days*.

3 Quale forma hanno i verbi che seguono *since*, *in spite of*, *despite*, *after*, *before* e *while* nell'esercizio 2?

....

4 Abbina gli inizi delle frasi con le loro logiche conclusioni.

1 I know Shanghai quite well, ..g....   a you should read it carefully.

2 In spite of injuring his foot, ...   b he was a very wealthy man.

3 He doesn't earn very much, ...   c he won the race.

4 Although he's not keen on computers, ...   d in spite of being so talented.

5 Smiling and holding hands, ...   e this book is still very useful.

6 When changing the torch battery, ...   f they announced their engagement.

7 Before signing that document, ...   g but I've never been to Beijing.

8 After winning the lottery, ...   h Dad emails us when he's away.

9 Despite the fact that it is very old, ...   i be careful not to damage the bulb.

5 In otto di queste frasi c'è un errore. <u>Sottolinea</u> gli errori e scrivi accanto la correzione.

1 <u>While</u> paying in cash, you should always ask for a receipt. ....When....................

2 Although Sharon quite enjoys musicals, but she really prefers more serious drama. ....

3 Smiling broadly, Sue announced she had won the lottery. ....

4 Chloe's father has promised her a car, even though she doesn't pass her exam. ....

5 Working for an international company, they often send me abroad on business. ....

6 Brian continued to work long hours, in spite of his doctor told him to take it easy. ....

7 Asked to explain his behaviour, Sam admitted that he had lost his temper. ....

8 Warning of storms ahead, the climbers reluctantly returned to their hostel. ....

9 Despite that I searched everywhere, I didn't find the money. ....

10 After driving the new car home, our garage was too small for it. ....

6 Selina, un'impiegata della Bestways Tours Holiday Company, ha telefonato a Mr Smart per avere la sua opinione sulla vacanza organizzata dalla sua agenzia. Guarda attentamente il dépliant e poi la foto scattata da Mr Smart. Quale pensi che sia stato il problema di Mr Smart?

7 Adesso leggi un estratto della conversazione tra lui e Selina. Le parole **in neretto** sono **connettivi**, o *linking words*. Inseriscile nella tabella a seconda del significato che esprimono.

Selina: Hello, Mr Smart. This is Selina from Bestways Tours Holiday Company. Could you tell me about the holiday we sold you?

Mr Smart: Well, I enjoyed most of the holiday, **but** I didn't enjoy the first night.

Selina: Oh, why was that?

Mr Smart: Because of the noise. **Although** I asked for a quiet hotel, your company put me in the *Concordia*, on the main road along the beach. My wife and I both work very hard and we need to relax **when** we're on holiday. The first night we couldn't sleep **until** the clubs and the restaurants closed at four o'clock in the morning!

Selina: Oh, dear. I hope our local staff were able to help you.

Mr Smart: Not at first. I phoned your local office in the morning, **but** unfortunately **both** the manager **and** his assistant were out.

Selina: I'm sure the manager phoned you **as soon as** he could.

Mr Smart: **Although** I left several messages, he didn't phone me back until the second day. I couldn't change my hotel **until** then.

Selina: But was the second hotel all right?

Mr Smart: Oh yes, he offered us **either** the *San Francisco* **or** the *Cristina* and we moved to the *San Francisco* **after** I spoke to him, and that was lovely. Well, the hotel was excellent **but** the food was boring. Anyway we didn't mind that very much as we ate out most nights. **In spite of** the bad start, we had a good holiday.

Selina: I'm so pleased. Thank you very much for your help, Mr Smart. Goodbye.

Mr Smart: Goodbye.

concessione o contrasto	but
inclusione o alternativa	
relazione di tempo	

8 Collega le frasi seguenti, usando la forma *-ing* o il participio passato.

1 Arnold was faced with a difficult decision. Arnold decided to consult his boss.
  Faced with a difficult decision, Arnold decided to consult his boss.

2 The singer waved to her fans. The singer got into her car.
  Waving to her fans, the singer got into her car.

3 Simon grumbled about the amount of homework he had. Simon took out his grammar book.
  ....

4   The scientist felt very excited about her latest discovery. The scientist invited the journalists into the laboratory.

....

5   The children were puzzled by what they had heard. The children asked their teacher what it meant.

....

6   Wendy was a sensible girl. Wendy didn't panic when she cut her hand.

....

7   Paul heard cries for help. Paul dived into the water.

....

8   This CD was released only last week. This CD is already at the top of the charts.

....

9   Completa queste frasi usando le tue idee personali.

1   I quite enjoy playing tennis, in spite of the fact that .... *I usually lose* ....

2   Although Agnes is only thirteen, she ....

3   While painting my room, ...

4   .... before attempting to run a marathon.

5   Dressed only in his underwear, ...

6   I hardly ever receive any letters even though ....

7   Waving .... the football fans cheered their team loudly.

8   They insist they'll have a barbecue even if ....

9   My grandfather swims in the lake every day despite ....

10   Since arriving in this country, ...

10   Completa questa conversazione tra Victoria e Jill usando la forma *-ing* o il participio passato dei verbi tra parentesi.

Victoria: Why didn't you come to Mel's party? We had such fun!

Jill: Well, George had told me he couldn't go. So, **(1)** ..... *knowing* ..... that he wouldn't be there, I just didn't feel like going. (*know*)

Victoria: Honestly, you must stop fantasising about George. **(2)** .... in this world of dreams is not doing you any good. (*live*)

Jill: You might be right. It wasn't much fun **(3)** .... at home on my own. (*stay*)

Victoria: I can imagine. And anyway, George did come, but he came late after his football match. **(4)** .... completely obsessed with sport, he's just not interested in girls. (*be*)

Jill: Oh, now I feel really stupid. How was Mel?

Victoria: She was on excellent form. **(5)** .... on a good day, she's really funny. (*catch*)

But as you know, she has her bad moments. **(6)** .... her only brother like that was such a tragedy. (*lose*)

Jill: Yes, **(7)** .... how she is, she always says she's fine, but sometimes you can see she's not. (*ask*)

Victoria: Poor Mel! **(8)** .... of brothers, that reminds me. It's my brother's eighteenth next week and he's having a party. Why don't you come, too? (*talk*)

Jill: OK. Will George be there?

11 Traduci.

1 Rendendosi conto che aveva lasciato il portafoglio nella borsa marrone, Jane tornò di corsa a casa.

2 Vedendo che Harry era stanco, sua madre gli preparò una cena leggera e gli disse di andare a dormire.

3 Conoscendolo bene, mi resi conto che qualcosa non andava.

4 Sapendo che la nonna stava poco bene, andai a farle un po' di compagnia.

5 Non rendendosi conto che aveva lasciato il computer acceso, John uscì di casa e andò al lavoro.

6 Scritta da Oscar Wilde nel 1895, *The Importance of Being Earnest* è ancora una commedia di grande successo.

7 Cresciuta in campagna, non mi sono mai abituata a vivere a Londra.

8 Sconfitto nella battaglia di Trafalgar, Napoleone dovette abbandonare il piano di invadere l'Inghilterra.

9 Incitato da migliaia di tifosi, Beckham segnò il goal decisivo.

10 Rubata nel 1911, la Gioconda (*the 'Mona Lisa'*) fu ritrovata in Italia due anni dopo.

STRUTTURE VERBALI PARTICOLARI

24.1 Verbi con costruzione personale e impersonale:
I won't take long; It won't take me long

24.2 Verbi con costruzione passiva personale e impersonale:
They say she is very rich; she is said to be very rich

24.3 Inversione soggetto/verbo ausiliare:
Should you need more information, please ...;
Never had I been more surprised

24.4 Verbi da non confondere: *do* e *make*; *remember* e *remind*;
lend e *borrow*

STRUTTURE VERBALI PARTICOLARI – INTRODUZIONE

In questa *Unit* finale vengono illustrati alcuni verbi e strutture verbali che, per la loro complessità sintattica o per il loro significato, presentano una certa difficoltà nell'apprendimento della lingua inglese. Si tratta di strutture avanzate, il cui uso indica che colui che parla ha interiorizzato una conoscenza profonda dell'inglese, sia a livello parlato sia in contesti formali/letterari.

24.1 VERBI CON COSTRUZIONE PERSONALE E IMPERSONALE: *I WON'T TAKE LONG; IT WON'T TAKE ME LONG*

Alcuni verbi inglesi di uso comune, come *happen*, *seem*, *appear* e *take*, possono essere costruiti sia in modo personale che impersonale. Poiché la costruzione impersonale corrisponde in genere all'uso italiano, ci soffermeremo maggiormente su quella **personale**.

Il verbo *take* è uno dei verbi più comuni della lingua inglese: esprime diversi significati e si trova in molte espressioni idiomatiche e in molti *phrasal verbs*. (Vedi *Unit* **19.6**)

Quando significa **impiegarci/volerci (riferito al tempo)**, il verbo *take* può avere sia costruzione personale che impersonale. Confronta le frasi seguenti.

Costruzione personale A: la persona è soggetto

I won't take long.	***Non ci metterò*** *molto.*
I took two hours to get to work this morning.	***Mi ci sono volute*** *due ore per arrivare al lavoro stamani.*

Costruzione personale B: l'attività è soggetto

Writing the letter *won't take me long.*	*Non ci metterò molto **a scrivere la lettera**.*
The journey *to work took me two hours.*	*Mi ci sono volute due ore **per arrivare** al lavoro.*

Costruzione impersonale: *it* è soggetto

It won't take me long.	***Non ci metterò*** *molto.*
It took me two hours to get to work.	***Mi ci sono volute*** *due ore per arrivare al lavoro.*

La costruzione con soggetto impersonale *it* è comunque più comune e viene di solito usata nelle domande.

*How long **will it take you** to do your homework?*   *Quanto tempo **ci metterai** a fare i compiti?*

Come si vede dagli esempi, il verbo ***take*** può essere seguito da un pronome personale complemento (***me***, ***you***, ...) o da un nome di persona sia nella **Costruzione personale B** che nella **Costruzione impersonale**. Il pronome personale indica che ci riferiamo all'esperienza specifica di qualcuno. Confronta le frasi seguenti:

*How long **does it take** to get to Southwold?*   *Quanto tempo **ci vuole** per andare a Southwold?*
*How long does it take **you** get to Southwold?*   *Quanto tempo **ti** ci vuole per andare a Southwold?*

Il verbo ***happen*** significa **accadere/succedere**. La costruzione personale viene usata per enfatizzare il significato di 'per caso' / 'darsi il caso che' / 'capitare di'.

*You may not like Peter, but **he happens** to be a friend of mine.*
*Peter può anche non piacerti, ma **si dà il caso che** sia mio amico.*

***I happened** to meet an old friend from University on the train to Cambridge.*
***Mi è capitato** di incontrare un vecchio compagno di università sul treno per Cambridge.*

I verbi ***seem*** e ***appear*** significano **sembrare** e, come ***to be***, sono verbi copulativi: questo significa che sono seguiti da un aggettivo, **non** da un avverbio.

*The boss **seems/appears** (to be) **angry** today.*   *Il capo **sembra arrabbiato** oggi.*
(**Non** ~~he seems/appears angrily~~)

Con entrambi i verbi, la costruzione personale tende a essere usata per esprimere un'impressione soggettiva, mentre la costruzione impersonale indica un'opinione generalmente condivisa.

Costruzione personale **Soggetto + *seem/appear* + *to* infinito**	**Costruzione impersonale** **A *It seems/appears that* + frase**
They do not seem to be at ease. *Non sembra che si trovino a proprio agio.*	*It seems that our flight will be delayed.* *Sembra che il nostro volo subirà un ritardo.*
Your brother seems to know Alice very well. *Sembra che tuo fratello conosca Alice molto bene.* (= questa è la mia impressione)	*It seems that your brother knows Alice very well.* *Sembra che tuo fratello conosca Alice molto bene.* (= lo dicono tutti)
	B *It seems/appears as if* + frase
	It seemed as if everything was going wrong. *Sembrava che tutto andasse per il verso sbagliato.*

Il verbo ***seem*** è molto più comune di ***appear***. Quest'ultimo viene in genere usato in contesti formali.

PRACTICE

1 Completa le frasi seguenti con la forma appropriata del verbo **take**. A seconda della struttura della frase, usa la costruzione personale o quella impersonale. Aggiungi un pronome personale complemento se necessario.

1 How long does *it take you* to get to school in the morning? I mean from the moment you shut your house door to when you walk into the school building.

2 Hilary is one of the vainest people I know. Just putting on her make-up and fixing her hair .... at least an hour in the morning. It's infuriating when she gets into the bathroom before you!

3 Getting to the scene of the fire .... the fire brigade twenty minutes. By that time the fire had spread to the woods.

4 How long do you think it .... to finish that painting? It looks likes you still have a lot to do.

5 The band .... a whole year to release their first CD, but it was worth waiting for.

6 Making a cartoon .... time and patience. It's quite a long process.

2 Riscrivi le frasi seguenti usando la forma appropriata del verbo **happen** al posto delle espressioni in **neretto**.

1 What would you tell him **if, by chance, you met him**? ...... *if you happened to meet him?* ......

2 **By pure chance I was** by the river when the fireworks began, so I had a great view.
....

3 **Just by chance Tom noticed** his girlfriend wink at Harry. ....

4 You might not have realised it, but **by pure chance** your boss plays golf with my father.
....

5 If, **by any chance, you know** the answer, please tell me what it is. ....

6 I met Bill at a party and within five minutes we discovered that, **by some strange coincidence**, **we had** a friend in common. ....

3 Commenta le frasi seguenti usando il verbo **seem**.

1 A Debbie's son has been at home with flu for a week now. Is he getting better?
B He seems ..... *to be getting better* .... He isn't in bed any longer.

2 A Have you heard? John's father has been arrested for embezzling the company's money.
B Yes, it seems .... for years!

3 A Do you know why Jessica was so late? Was there an accident on the motorway?
B Yes, it seems ....

4 A How's your little sister getting on at primary school? Does she like it?
B Yes, she seems .... She's already made some friends.

5 **A** What's happened to Michael? I haven't seen him at the club for ages. Has he given up boxing?

   B Yes, it seems .... Perhaps he didn't have enough time for it.

6 **A** Look at this photo of my mum when she was young. Don't you think she looks really happy?

   B Yes, she seems ....

24.2   VERBI CON COSTRUZIONE PASSIVA PERSONALE E IMPERSONALE: *THEY SAY SHE IS VERY RICH; SHE IS SAID TO BE VERY RICH*

Quando si riferisce quello che viene generalmente detto o pensato, con verbi come **say, think, know, believe, suppose, expect** e **report**, si possono usare due diverse costruzioni passive.

Mrs Jones always wears expensive jewellery.   ***People say*** *she is enormously rich.*

   A →   ***She is said*** *to be enormously rich.*

   B →   ***It is said that*** *she is enormously rich.*

*People **expect that** the Government will make education their first priority.*
*La gente **si aspetta che** il governo dia all'educazione la priorità assoluta.*

*Art historians **believe that** that landscape was painted by Constable.*
*Gli storici dell'arte **ritengono che** quel paesaggio sia stato dipinto da Constable.*

A Costruzione personale	
Soggetto + verbo passivo + infinito	**presente:** se l'evento è contemporaneo a quando viene riferito.
The Government is expected	***to make*** *education their first priority.*
Soggetto + verbo passivo + infinito	**passato:** se l'evento è precedente a quando viene riferito.
That landscape is believed	***to have been painted*** *by Constable.*

La costruzione passiva personale è una struttura tipica della lingua inglese, di cui non esiste un equivalente in italiano.

B Costruzione impersonale
It **+ verbo passivo +** ***that***
It is expected that the Government will make education their first priority.   **Si prevede / Ci si aspetta che** *il governo dia all'educazione la priorità assoluta.*   *It is believed that that landscape was painted by Constable.*   **Si ritiene che** *quel paesaggio sia stato dipinto da Constable.*

Come si vede dagli esempi, la costruzione impersonale corrisponde al 'si' passivante italiano.

Entrambe le costruzioni sono usate frequentemente nei notiziari e negli articoli di giornale.

*The police **believe that** the robbers had an accomplice in the bank.*
*La polizia **ritiene che** i rapinatori avessero un complice all'interno della banca.*

→ *The robbers **are believed** to have had an accomplice in the bank.*
→ ***It is believed that*** *the robbers had an accomplice in the bank.*

PRACTICE

1 Riscrivi le frasi seguenti al passivo in due modi diversi.

1 They say that the latest Dan Brown book is very good.

The latest Dan Brown book is said to be very good. / It is said that the latest Dan Brown book is very good.

2 It is believed that Madonna is intending to adopt another child.

People .... to adopt another child.

Madonna .... to adopt another child.

3 Police suspect that famous criminals were involved in the shootings.

It .... were involved in the shootings.

Famous criminals .... in the shootings.

4 10,000 people are thought to have attended the festival.

People .... have attended the festival.

It .... have attended the festival.

5 People expect that the government will call a general election in the autumn.

It .... will call a general election in the autumn.

The government .... a general election in the autumn.

6 The organisers say that several celebrities have agreed to appear at the charity concert.

Several celebrities .... to appear at the charity concert.

It .... to appear at the charity concert.

7 People expect that a champion footballer will be absent from Premier League football for six weeks due to an operation.

It .... from Premier League football for six weeks due to an operation.

A champion footballer .... from Premier League football for six weeks due to an operation.

8 It is reported that two thousand families have been affected by the floods.

Two thousand families .... affected by the floods.

Authorities .... affected by the floods.

2 Bruce sta facendo uno stage come reporter presso l'*East Anglian Press* ma ha ancora molto da imparare. Riscrivi il suo articolo in stile più giornalistico, sostituendo i verbi in **neretto** con una forma passiva appropriata.

Authorities **(1) have reported** that at least sixty-four people were made homeless in the fires that swept across the country this summer. People **(2) believe** that most of them were families with young children. The government **(3) believes** that arsonists and political extremists are responsible for the fires and people **(4) say** that the police will catch some of the culprits. The public **(5) think** that the government was incompetent in its handling of the crisis and there have been protests in the streets. We **(6) know** that a lot of money has already been spent on immediate relief, but people **(7) expect** that the final bill will be much higher.

417

24.3   INVERSIONE SOGGETTO/VERBO AUSILIARE: *SHOULD YOU NEED MORE INFORMATION, PLEASE ... ; NEVER HAD I BEEN MORE SURPRISED*

Si definisce **inversione** un cambiamento del *word order* consueto della frase.

Il *word order* della frase dichiarativa inglese, come abbiamo visto, è di norma il seguente:

Soggetto + verbo + complementi

Ci sono tuttavia alcuni casi in cui la struttura della frase dichiarativa può cambiare e assumere il *word order* della frase interrogativa, in cui **il verbo ausiliare precede il soggetto**.

Ci sono diversi tipi di inversione nella lingua inglese. In questa sezione tratteremo i seguenti casi:

inversione soggetto/ausiliare nel periodo ipotetico di secondo e terzo tipo;
inversione soggetto/ausiliare con espressioni di significato negativo.

Inversione soggetto/ausiliare nel periodo ipotetico di secondo e terzo tipo

I periodi ipotetici di secondo e terzo tipo sono entrambi usati per esprimere ipotesi immaginarie, che si esprimono con il congiuntivo: nel secondo tipo queste ipotesi si riferiscono al presente, nel terzo tipo si riferiscono al passato e sono quindi, per definizione, non più realizzabili. (Vedi *Unit* **20.4** e **20.6**)

In contesti di tipo formale, oppure nella corrispondenza commerciale, *if* può essere omesso **solo** quando è seguito dagli ausiliari *should*, *had* e *were*. In questo caso, la struttura del periodo ipotetico diventa la seguente:

Should *Had* + soggetto + verbo *Were*	frase principale: invariata
Should you need more information, (If you should need more information), *Se aveste bisogno di altre informazioni,*	*please don't hesitate to contact us.* *non esitate a contattarci.*
Had I known about his problem, (If I had known about his problem), *Se avessi saputo del suo problema,*	*I wouldn't have insisted on his coming.* *non avrei insistito che venisse.*
Were you to apply before the 30th October, (If you were to apply before the 30th October), *Se doveste presentare domanda entro il 30 ottobre,*	*you would still be eligible for our discount.* *avreste ancora diritto al nostro sconto.*

Come si vede dallo schema, l'inversione soggetto/ausiliare si verifica nella *if- clause*, mentre la frase principale rimane invariata.

Inversione soggetto/ausiliare con espressioni di significato negativo

Quando si vuole dare **particolare enfasi** a quello che si sta dicendo, è possibile porre all'inizio della frase un avverbio o un'espressione avverbiale **di significato negativo o restrittivo**, come:

never = **mai**; *seldom* = **raramente**; *on no account / under no circumstances* = **per nessun motivo**; *nowhere* = **in nessun luogo / da nessuna parte**; *only when* = **solo quando**; *only by* = **solo (facendo)**; *not only* = **non soltanto**.

Si tratta di un uso molto formale: la struttura della frase cambia e assume il *word order* della frase interrogativa.

Avverbio negativo + ausiliare + soggetto + verbo

> *Never **had I seen** anything like that!*
> ***Mai avevo visto** una cosa del genere!*

> ***Under no circumstances will I tolerate** such behaviour.*
> ***Per nessun motivo tollererò** un tale comportamento.*

> ***Not only did he borrow** my mobile without asking, he even dropped it and now it's not working.*
> ***Non soltanto ha preso** il mio cellulare senza permesso, l'ha anche fatto cadere e ora non funziona.*

> ***Only** three days later **did the rescuers** finally **reach** the hikers.*
> ***Solo** dopo tre giorni **i soccorritori** finalmente **riuscirono a raggiungere** gli escursionisti.*

Alcuni di questi avverbi di significato restrittivo introducono una correlazione.

Hardly ..., when A malapena / quasi non ... quando

> ***Hardly** had the meeting begun, **when** the protesters arrived.*
> ***A malapena** era iniziata la riunione, **quando** arrivarono i dimostranti.*

È importante ricordare che *hardly* ha valore negativo, quindi **non** è mai seguito da una negazione. (Vedi *Unit* **11.2**)

No sooner ... than Appena / A malapena ... che/quando

> ***No sooner** had I got into the bath **than** the telephone rang.*
> *Ero **appena** entrata nella vasca **quando** squillò il telefono.*

Se, tuttavia, l'avverbio negativo non è posto all'inizio della frase, si usa il *word order* normale della frase dichiarativa.

> *I had **never** seen anything like that.*
> *Non avevo **mai** visto una cosa del genere.*

> *I won't **tolerate** such behaviour **under any circumstances**.*
> ***Non tollererò** un tale comportamento **per nessun motivo**.*

> *He **not only borrowed** my mobile without asking, he even dropped it and now it's not working.*
> ***Non soltanto ha preso** il mio cellulare senza permesso, l'ha anche fatto cadere e ora non funziona.*

> *The hikers were found **only** three days later, exhausted but unhurt.*
> *Gli escursionisti furono ritrovati **solo** tre giorni dopo, esausti ma sani e salvi.*

> *The meeting had **hardly** begun **when** the protesters arrived.*
> *La riunione era iniziato **a malapena quando** arrivarono i dimostranti.*

> *I had **no sooner** got into the bath **than** the telephone rang.*
> *Ero **appena** entrata nella vasca **quando** squillò il telefono.*

PRACTICE

1 Le frasi seguenti sono periodi ipotetici di secondo e terzo tipo. Per ognuno di essi, riscrivi la *if- clause* omettendo *if* e facendo tutti i cambiamenti necessari.

1 If I had known that the tickets were so expensive, I would never have agreed to come.

.Had..I..known..that..the..tickets..were..so..expensive,..I..would..never..have..agreed..to..come....

2 If you should see the headteacher before the meeting, please tell him that I will be absent.

....

3 If you were to enrol for the exam, you would have to start working straight away.

....

4 If the teacher had been informed in advance, this difficult situation could have been avoided.

....

5 If you should decide to attend the course, the books can be bought directly from the school.

....

6 If the customers were to complain, management would look into the matter.

....

7 If Barry had felt well enough, he would have gone on the walk.

....

8 If the telephone should not be up to standard, the guarantee is valid for six months.

....

2 Riempi gli spazi con un avverbio o con un'espressione nel riquadro. In alcuni casi c'è più di una possibilità.

on no account	seldom	only by	only	never	hardly ... when
not only	only when	little	nowhere		

1 ......Only....... once in my life have I come close to having a motorbike accident.

2 .... will you find a greater variety of migratory birds.

3 .... must you leave the building without informing a member of staff first.

4 .... he eventually arrived at the top did John realise that he had forgotten to bring the flag.

5 .... have temperatures been so high in Alaska. They are the highest on record.

6 .... had I let myself into the house, ... the telephone started to ring.

7 This has been one of the most disastrous years of my life. .... have so many things gone wrong at the same time.

8 .... did you ignore me when I arrived, you didn't say a word to me all day!

9 .... did Luke realise that he was walking into a trap.

10 .... training daily will you be up to standard in time for the race.

3 Riscrivi le frasi seguenti iniziando con le parole in **neretto**. In alcuni casi le parole in **neretto** devono essere lievemente modificate.

1 I **only** understand **now** what she must have felt.

   Only now do I understand what she must have felt.

2 Eric had **no sooner** started work at his computer than there was a power cut.

   ....

3 I have **never** heard anyone talk such rubbish in my life.

   ....

4 The conference had **hardly** started when all the lights went out.

   ....

5 Visitors must not feed the animals **under any circumstances**.

   ....

6 He **only** looked up when I screamed.

   ....

7 You are not to go into the water **on any account**.

   ....

8 You can access the site **only by** inserting the correct password.

   ....

24.4   VERBI DA NON CONFONDERE: *DO* E *MAKE*; *REMEMBER* E *REMIND*; *LEND* E *BORROW*

Alcuni verbi hanno significati simili ed è possibile confonderli.

Do **e** *make*

Il verbo *do* esprime il significato generale di **fare** ed è usato per parlare di attività indefinite: fare un lavoro, uno sport, svolgere un'attività; *make* significa invece 'fare' nel senso di **costruire**, **creare**, **produrre**.

Confronta le frasi seguenti:

   A *What are you **doing**?*
   B *I'm **making** a cake for Mum's birthday.*

   A *What does your father **do**?*
   B *He works for a factory that **makes** mechanical components.*

   A *I like **making** my own clothes.*
   B *Oh, I'm terribly lazy. I prefer **doing** nothing.*

Tuttavia, la differenza tra *do* e *make* non è sempre così chiara, e i due verbi sono usati in alcune collocazioni di uso molto comune.

421

Do e make

Usi di *do*:

do a job	*fare un lavoro / una professione*
do some work	*fare un lavoro*
do one's homework / an exercise	*fare i compiti / un esercizio*
do one's duty	*fare il proprio dovere*
do one's best	*fare del proprio meglio*
do one's hair	*fare i capelli*
do someone a favour	*fare un favore a qualcuno*
do sport/exercise	*fare sport / attività fisica*
do the shopping	*fare la spesa*
do the housework	*fare le faccende / i lavori di casa*
do the cleaning/washing up/ironing	*fare le pulizie / lavare i piatti / stirare*

Usi di *make*:

make a decision	*prendere una decisione*
make a suggestion	*dare un suggerimento*
make an excuse	*addurre una scusa / un pretesto*
make an appointment	*fissare/prendere un appuntamento*
make a plan	*fare un progetto*
make a journey	*fare un viaggio*
make a mistake	*fare un errore*
make a phone call	*fare una telefonata*
make friends	*fare amicizia*
make money / a fortune	*fare soldi / (una) fortuna*
make love/peace/war	*fare l'amore / la pace / la guerra*

 Fai attenzione a queste espressioni:

> **fare** *una fotografia =* **take** *a picture*
> **fare** *un'esperienza interessante =* **have** *an interesting experience*

Remember e remind

Remember significa **ricordare** nel senso di **tenere presente nella memoria**;
remind significa **ricordare** nel senso di **ricordare qualcosa a qualcuno, rammentare, far venire in mente**.

■ **remember**

I must **remember** *to pay the telephone bill.*
Devo ricordarmi *di pagare la bolletta del telefono.*

I **remember** *Jane's father well.*
Ricordo *bene il padre di Jane.*

Remember *that you promised to wash my car.*
Ricordati *che hai promesso di lavarmi la macchina.*

■ **remind**

Please **remind** *me to pay the telephone bill.*
Per favore **ricordami** *di pagare la bolletta del telefono.*

Jane **reminds** *me of her father.*
Jane **mi ricorda** *suo padre.* (= è come lui)

I **reminded** *him that he had promised to wash my car.*
Gli **ricordai** *che aveva promesso di lavarmi la macchina.*

Lend e borrow

Lend e **borrow** sono opposti.

Lend significa **prestare** qualcosa **a** qualcuno; **borrow** significa **prendere in prestito** qualcosa **da** qualcuno.

■ **lend**

*Can **you lend me** your umbrella?*
Puoi prestarmi *il tuo ombrello?*
*I **have lent** Julia my new CD.*
Ho prestato *a Julia il mio nuovo CD.*

■ **borrow**

*Can **I borrow** your umbrella?*
*Posso **prendere** il tuo ombrello?*
*I **have borrowed** a very interesting book **from** the school library.*
Ho preso a prestito *un libro molto interessante **dalla** biblioteca della scuola.*

PRACTICE

1 Completa le frasi seguenti con la forma appropriata di **do** o **make**.

1 I 've been doing. these exercises for an hour now.

2 I think you should .... a decision. Do you want to go to university, or are you going to get a job?

3 Would you mind .... me a favour? I need help with my English.

4 It's important .... warm-up exercises before every game.

5 Frank is obsessed with .... money.

6 If I might .... a suggestion, I think you should get your hair cut before the interview.

7 Since the first year of primary school John .... always .... his best at school, but he's decided that he's had enough of studying now.

8 Kate usually .... most of the food shopping at the local supermarket. It's near home and so very convenient for her.

9 Are you intending .... any work before you go to bed?

10 Stop .... excuses! You don't want to go out because you're feeling lazy.

2 Sofia sta parlando alla sua *host family* inglese delle abitudini della sua famiglia. Riempi gli spazi con la forma corretta di **do** o **make**.

Mrs Brown: (1) .....Does... your mother ....do... all the housework at home, Sofia? Or do you all help?

Sofia: My mother (2) .... most of the cleaning, but we all (3) .... our own beds in the morning. And my father (4) .... quite a lot of the cooking.

Mrs Brown: Really? What does he like making?

Sofia: Well, he loves barbecues, cooking meat on the grill, that sort of thing. And actually, he's very good at (5) .... cakes, too.

Mrs Brown: That's great. So who **(6)** .... the shopping?

Sofia: They share that. They quite like going to the supermarket together.

Mrs Brown: And what's your role? Do you do anything to help?

Sofia: I have to admit that I **(7)** .... the minimum. The excuse I usually **(8)** ....
is that I have too much homework **(9)** .... And anyway, I generally try not
(10) .... a mess. I'm not like my brother, who's incredibly untidy.

Mrs Brown: I see. Well, it would be nice if you **(11)** .... a big effort to be as tidy as possible
here, too.

3 Traduci.

1 Quando eravamo in vacanza abbiamo fatto amicizia con due ragazzi di Madrid.

2 Qualche volta aiuto mia madre a fare i lavori di casa, ma odio stirare.

3 Puoi farmi un favore, Sally? Puoi prestarmi il tuo cellulare? Devo fare una chiamata urgente e il
mio è scarico.

4 Il motto del movimento hippy era 'Fate l'amore, non la guerra'.

5 Quanti errori hai fatto nel compito di inglese?

6 Non puoi guardare la televisione finché non hai fatto i compiti.

4 Completa le frasi seguenti con la forma appropriata di **remember** o **remind**.

1 .Will..you..remind... me to get a new cartridge for my printer when we're out, please?

2 Gary .... that he had promised his mother that he would babysit that evening.

3 You're right, it's Kevin's birthday tomorrow. Thank you for .... me.

4 Hello. .... me? We met at a student demonstration last month.

5 The new boy really .... me of someone but I can't .... who.

6 Although Mick was only five when his grandfather died, he .... him vividly.

7 **A** Did Jane phone? **B** Yes. Oh, that .... me. She's invited us to dinner tomorrow
evening.

8 You must .... to shake hands when you meet someone new.

9 How .... all those dates and historical facts? You've got such an incredible memory!

10 If I didn't have such a terrible memory myself, I .... you to move your car for
street cleaning every Monday evening.

5 Hilary dimentica spesso di fare qualcosa. Usa **remember** o **remind** per farle queste
raccomandazioni.

1 Spegnere il computer prima di uscire.

2 Ricordare a Dave di fare i compiti prima che la mamma torni dal lavoro.

3 Andare a prendere la torta per il compleanno del babbo.

4 Ricordare a Tom di tagliare l'erba del prato.

5 Portare il cane a fare una passeggiata nel parco.

6 Sottolinea l'alternativa corretta.

1 William has promised to _lend me_ / _borrow me_ his scooter this evening.

2 Will you still _remind me_ / _remember me_ when you come back from New Zealand?

3 I've asked Dave if he'll _lend us_ / _borrow us_ his PlayStation for the day.

4 Helen had better wear her black shoes if she _borrows_ / _lends_ my new dress.

5 Look at that man! He really _reminds me_ / _remembers me_ of Hugh Grant.

6 Linda's mother always has to _remind_ / _remember_ her to take her medicine.

7 Julia has _borrowed_ / _lent_ her sister's MP3 player.

8 Would you _remember_ / _remind_ Darcy if you saw him again? You used to play together as children.

ALL IN ONE REVISION

1 I titoli dei giornali sono molto concisi e omettono alcuni elementi della frase per concentrarsi sulla sostanza della notizia. Che cosa significano questi titoli? Sotto ogni titolo, riscrivi la notizia in forma completa, evidenziando gli elementi della frase che sono stati omessi.

1 (At least six people believed injured in motorway crash last night)

At least six people **are** believed **to have been** injured in **a** motorway crash last night.

2 (FAMOUS HOLLYWOOD ACTOR SUSPECTED OF LAS VEGAS HOTEL ROBBERY)

....

3 (Pop celebrity to write her memoirs, say publishers)

....

4 (MINISTERS REPORTED TO BACK GENETICALLY MODIFIED CROPS IN UK)

....

5 (New MP considered 'cold and distant' reports UK survey)

....

425

2 Riscrivi le frasi seguenti inserendo all'inizio le espressioni tra parentesi, per dare enfasi al discorso. Fai tutti i cambiamenti necessari.

1 I had just got back home when it started raining. (*No sooner*)

No sooner had I got back home than it started raining.

2 Karen not only forgot my birthday, she didn't even make a fuss of me when I reminded her. (*Not only*)

3 You are not to tell Graham what I said about him under any circumstances. (*Under no circumstances*)

4 Grace has never been so upset by her exam results. (*Never*)

5 Michael only crashed his motorbike once in ten years of racing. (*Only*)

6 Mary had no sooner started her new job than the company went bankrupt. (*No sooner … than*)

7 Tim only started to get on with his younger brother when they both left home. (*Only when*)

8 You are not to leave my bicycle unlocked on any account. (*On no account*)

3 Riempi gli spazi con la forma appropriata di **lend** o **borrow**. Alcuni dei verbi sono negativi.

1 Look! You've got a flat tyre. Do you want to borrow my bicycle?

2 If Dan .... his tent, you could always ask Ben instead.

3 Why don't you .... Tom's laptop for a few days?

4 If I asked you very nicely, ... me twenty euros? Just until tomorrow.

5 My little brother really gets on my nerves. He's always .... my things.

6 You're only being nice to me because you want me .... my iPod.

7 I've told you before .... your things to Francis. He never gives them back.

8 Mandy needs .... something for her wedding day. I thought I .... her my blue wig!

4 Riscrivi le frasi seguenti usando una forma passiva diversa. Inizia le frasi con le parole in **neretto**.

1 It is believed that **Feltham Manor** is haunted by a ghost.

Feltham Manor is believed to be haunted by a ghost.

2 Critics say that **Zucchero's latest album** is his best so far.

3 It is known that **global warming** is partly responsible for extreme weather conditions.

4 People think that **Wayne Rooney** is one of England's best players.

5 It is thought that **the prisoners** escaped by means of a tunnel dug underground.

....

6 It is expected that **Ellie and David** will get married in 2008.

....

7 *Forbes* magazine reports that **nine of the world's fifty richest people** are women.

....

8 People expect the government to change **the pension scheme** radically in the next few years.

....

5 Quando era ancora uno studente universitario, Paul si è trasferito in Australia. Leggi quello che si dice di lui nella città dove è nato e riscrivi le frasi usando la forma passiva personale.

1 Paul Bowles, the Nobel Prize-winning scientist, was born in Daffodil Cottage at the end of East Lane. People say that he was a quiet, shy boy.

He is said to have been a quiet, shy boy.

2 They say he didn't mix easily with the other children.

....

3 They say he went to secondary school in York, where he happened to have Mr Lawrence Barnes for chemistry. ....

4 They believe that Barnes' lessons inspired the young Bowles because he then went on to study chemistry at Leeds University. ....

5 People report that after Bowles' mother died he moved with his father to Sydney, Australia.

....

6 People believe that at first it took him a long time to adapt to his new university.

....

7 They know he has travelled widely. ....

8 They believe he met his wife, Elena, in Mexico. ....

9 They report that he had the idea that led to his astounding discovery in cell biology while on a walk with Elena. ....

6 Traduci. Attenzione alle parole in **neretto**.

1 **Mai** mi sarei aspettato una cosa del genere da lui.

2 **A malapena** aveva finito di parlare quando tutti si alzarono in piedi e lo applaudirono.

3 **Solo** dopo una settimana la febbre è diminuita.

4 **Solo adesso** mi accorgo che Mr Franklin era un ottimo insegnante.

5 **Solo** con l'impegno si possono raggiungere buoni risultati.

6 **Per caso** eravamo a Dublino il giorno di San Patrizio. È stata un'esperienza indimenticabile.

7 **Mi è capitato** di incontrare il migliore amico di mio fratello sul traghetto per l'isola di Skye.

8 Se **per caso** vedi Angela, dille che ho bisogno di parlarle.

9 Che cosa faresti, se **ti capitasse** di vincere un milione di euro?

APPENDICE

FALSE FRIENDS

I *false friends* sono parole di due lingue diverse che si somigliano ma hanno un significato completamente differente. Qui sotto troverai una lista dei *false friends* di uso più comune in italiano e in inglese.

inglese	→ italiano	italiano	→ inglese
actually	→ realmente, in effetti	attualmente	→ at present, at the moment, now
addiction	→ dipendenza, assuefazione	addizione	→ adding (up), sum
(to) annoy	→ infastidire, seccare	annoiare	→ (to) bore
brave	→ coraggioso	bravo a …	→ good at …
camera	→ macchina fotografica	camera	→ room
canteen	→ mensa	cantina	→ cellar (= cantina di casa),
			→ wine shop (= negozio di vino)
code	→ codice	coda	→ tail
college	→ università, istituto superiore	collegio	→ boarding school
comprehensive	→ esauriente, completo	comprensivo	→ understanding
confidence	→ fiducia, sicurezza di sé	confidenza	→ intimacy, familiarity
convenient	→ comodo	conveniente	→ cheap, good value
corpse	→ cadavere	corpo	→ body
cucumber	→ cetriolo	cocomero	→ watermelon
delusion	→ illusione	delusione	→ disappointment
disposable	→ usa e getta	disponibile	→ available (= di prodotto),
			→ free, open-minded (= di persona)
(to) educate	→ istruire, fornire un'istruzione	educare, allevare	→ (to) bring up
educated	→ colto, istruito	educato	→ polite, well-behaved
eventually	→ alla fine	eventualmente	→ in case, if necessary
extravagant	→ spendaccione, con le mani bucate	stravagante	→ odd, bizarre
fabric	→ tessuto	fabbrica	→ factory
factory	→ fabbrica	fattoria	→ farm
firm	→ ditta	firma	→ signature
furniture	→ mobili, arredamento	fornitura	→ supplies
library	→ biblioteca	libreria	→ bookshop, bookseller's (= negozio)
			→ bookcase, bookshelves (= mobile)
morbid	→ morboso	morbido	→ soft
magazine	→ rivista	magazzino	→ warehouse, storehouse
nervous	→ agitato, inquieto, teso	nervoso	→ irritable
novel	→ romanzo	novella	→ short story
palette	→ gamma di colori	paletta	→ spade
parent	→ genitore	parente	→ relative, relation
phrase	→ espressione, modo di dire	frase	→ sentence
pretend	→ fingere	pretendere	→ (to) demand, (to) expect
(to) realise	→ rendersi conto	realizzare	→ (to) fulfil (= un sogno, aspettative)
			(to) carry out (= un esperimento)
romance	→ storia d'amore	romanzo	→ novel
rude	→ scortese	rude	→ rough
sensible	→ ragionevole, di buon senso, prudente	sensibile	→ sensitive
sympathy	→ comprensione, solidarietà, condoglianze	simpatia	→ like, be fond of
sympathetic	→ partecipe, solidale, comprensivo	simpatico	→ nice

Base form	Past simple	Past participle
arise *(sorgere)*	arose	arisen
be *(essere, stare)*	was/were	been
beat *(battere, picchiare)*	beat	beaten
become *(diventare)*	became	become
begin *(cominciare)*	began	begun
bend *(girare, piegare)*	bent	bent
bet *(scommettere)*	bet	bet
bite *(mordere)*	bit	bitten
bleed *(sanguinare)*	bled	bled
blow *(soffiare)*	blew	blown
break *(rompere)*	broke	broken
bring *(portare)*	brought	brought
broadcast *(trasmettere)*	broadcast	broadcast
build *(costruire)*	built	built
burn *(bruciare)*	burnt/burned	burnt/burned
burst *(scoppiare)*	burst	burst
buy *(comprare)*	bought	bought
catch *(prendere, afferrare)*	caught	caught
choose *(scegliere)*	chose	chosen
cling *(aggrapparsi)*	clung	clung
come *(venire)*	came	come
cost *(costare)*	cost	cost
creep *(muoversi furtivamente)*	crept	crept
cut *(tagliare)*	cut	cut
deal *(dare, distribuire)*	dealt	dealt
dig *(scavare)*	dug	dug
do *(fare)*	did	done
draw *(disegnare)*	drew	drawn
dream *(sognare)*	dreamed/dreamt	dreamed/dreamt
drink *(bere)*	drank	drunk
drive *(guidare)*	drove	driven
eat *(mangiare)*	ate	eaten
fall *(cadere)*	fell	fallen
feed *(nutrire)*	fed	fed
feel *(sentire, sentirsi)*	felt	felt
fight *(combattere)*	fought	fought
find *(trovare)*	found	found
fly *(volare)*	flew	flown
forbid *(proibire)*	forbade	forbidden
forecast *(prevedere)*	forecast/forecasted	forecast/forecasted
forget *(dimenticare)*	forgot	forgotten

Base form	Past simple	Past participle
freeze *(congelare, gelare, gelarsi)*	froze	frozen
get *(prendere, ricevere)*	got	got
give *(dare, regalare)*	gave	given
go *(andare)*	went	gone
grow *(crescere)*	grew	grown
hang *(appendere, essere appeso)*	hung	hung
have *(avere)*	had	had
hear *(sentire, udire)*	heard	heard
hide *(nascondere)*	hid	hidden
hit *(colpire)*	hit	hit
hold *(tenere)*	held	held
hurt *(ferire, fare male)*	hurt	hurt
keep *(tenere, conservare)*	kept	kept
kneel *(inginocchiarsi)*	knelt/kneeled	knelt/kneeled
know *(conoscere, sapere)*	knew	known
lay *(deporre, posare)*	laid	laid
lead *(condurre, portare)*	led	led
lean *(appoggiarsi)*	leaned/leant	leaned/leant
learn *(imparare)*	learned/learnt	learned/learnt
leave *(lasciare, partire)*	left	left
lend *(prestare)*	lent	lent
let *(lasciare, permettere)*	let	let
lie* *(giacere, stare sdraiato)*	lay	lain
light *(accendere)*	lit/lighted	lit/lighted
lose *(perdere)*	lost	lost
make *(fare, creare)*	made	made
mean *(significare)*	meant	meant
meet *(incontrare)*	met	met
pay *(pagare)*	paid	paid
put *(mettere)*	put	put
quit *(rinunciare, smettere)*	quit	quit
read *(leggere)*	read	read
ride *(cavalcare, andare es. bici/moto)*	rode	ridden
ring *(suonare, squillare, telefonare)*	rang	rung
rise *(alzarsi)*	rose	risen
run *(correre)*	ran	run
say *(dire)*	said	said
see *(vedere)*	saw	seen
sell *(vendere)*	sold	sold
send *(mandare, spedire, inviare)*	sent	sent
set *(sistemare, porre)*	set	set
sew *(cucire)*	sewed	sewn/sewed
shake *(scuotere)*	shook	shaken
shine *(brillare)*	shone/shined	shone/shined

* lie lied lied = *mentire, dire bugie (verbo regolare)*

Base form	Past simple	Past participle
shoot (sparare, girare un film)	shot	shot
show (mostrare)	showed	shown
shrink (far restringere, restringersi)	shrank	shrunk
shut (chiudere)	shut	shut
sing (cantare)	sang	sung
sink (affondare)	sank	sunk
sit (sedere, sedersi)	sat	sat
sleep (dormire)	slept	slept
slide (scivolare)	slid	slid
smell (sentire/avvertire odore, emanare/avere odore)	smelt/smelled	smelt/smelled
sow (seminare)	sowed	sown/sowed
speak (parlare)	spoke	spoken
spell (scrivere lettera per lettera)	spelt/spelled	spelt/spelled
spend (spendere, trascorrere)	spent	spent
spill (versare)	spilt	spilt/spilled
spit (sputare)	spat	spat
split (dividere, spaccare in due)	split	split
spoil (rovinare, viziare)	spoiled/spoilt	spoiled/spoilt
spread (stendere, spargere)	spread	spread
spring (balzare)	sprang	sprung
stand (stare in piedi)	stood	stood
steal (rubare)	stole	stolen
stick (conficcare, restare attaccato)	stuck	stuck
sting (pungere)	stung	stung
stink (puzzare)	stank	stunk
strike (colpire)	struck	struck
swear (giurare)	swore	sworn
sweep (spazzare)	swept	swept
swell (gonfiare, gonfiarsi)	swelled	swollen/swelled
swim (nuotare)	swam	swum
swing (dondolare, dondolarsi)	swung	swung
take (prendere)	took	taken
teach (insegnare)	taught	taught
tear (strappare)	tore	torn
tell (dire)	told	told
think (pensare)	thought	thought
throw (gettare)	threw	thrown
understand (capire)	understood	understood
wake (svegliare, svegliarsi)	woke	woken
wear (indossare)	wore	worn
win (vincere)	won	won
write (scrivere)	wrote	written

PHRASAL VERBS E LORO SIGNIFICATI PRINCIPALI

Qui sotto sono elencati i *phrasal verbs* di uso più comune.
Molti *phrasal verbs* hanno più di un significato.
Per una lista completa, e per tutti i significati di ogni *phrasal verb*, è
necessario consultare un buon dizionario. Puoi anche fare consultazioni
online all'indirizzo http://dictionary.cambridge.org

back	*back **out (of)***	tirarsi indietro, ritirarsi *You can't **back out** now, you've given your word.* ***Non puoi tirarti indietro** ora, hai dato la tua parola.*
	*back **up***	appoggiare, sostenere *My family **backed** me **up** throughout the court case.* * *La mia famiglia mi **ha appoggiato** durante tutto il processo.*
be	*be **into***	essere interessato a *Sheila **is** really **into** movies.* *Sheila **è** veramente **appassionata di** cinema.*
	*be **off***	partire, andare via *I must **be off**.* *Devo **andare**.*
	*be **up to***	stare combinando, avere in mente *What **are** the children **up to**?* *Che cosa **stanno combinando** i bambini?*
blow	*blow **up***	esplodere, saltare in aria *The bridge **was blown up** by the army.* *Il ponte **fu fatto saltare** dal nemico.*
break	*break **down***	guastarsi, rompersi (di macchine e simili); *His car **broke down** and he had to push it off the road.* *L'auto **si ruppe** e lui dovette **spingerla** al lato della strada.* crollare, avere una crisi (di persone) *When she heard the bad news, she **broke down** and cried.* *Quando le fu data la notizia, **crollò** e scoppiò a piangere.*
	*break **in***	penetrare, fare irruzione *The burglars **broke in** through the kitchen window.* * *I ladri **sono entrati** attraverso la finestra della cucina.*
	*break **off***	interrompersi, smettere; *She **broke off** in the middle of a sentence.* * *Si **interruppe** nel bel mezzo della frase.* interrompere, porre fine a *They **have broken off** their engagement.* * ***Hanno rotto** il fidanzamento.*
	*break **out***	scoppiare (di guerre) *War **broke out** in 1914.* * *La guerra **scoppiò** nel 1914.*
	*break **up***	lasciarsi (di coppie) *Jenny and George **have broken up**.* * *Jenny e George **si sono lasciati**.*

bring	bring **about**	causare, provocare *He **brought about** his company's collapse by his reckless spending.* * **Ha causato** il fallimento della sua ditta con le sue spese sconsiderate.
	bring **back**	riportare, restituire *Don't forget to **bring back** the books.* * Non dimenticarti di **restituire** i libri.
	bring **out**	rivelare, portar fuori *A crisis can **bring out** the best and the worst in people.* * Una crisi può **portar fuori** il meglio e il peggio delle persone.
	bring **round**	far rinvenire; *I gave him a sniff of smelling salts to **bring** him **round**.* * Gli ho fatto annusare dei sali per **farlo rinvenire**. convincere, far cambiare opinione; *At first he refused but I managed to **bring** him **round**.* * All'inizio rifiutò, ma sono riuscita a **fargli cambiare idea**.
	bring **up**	educare, crescere *She **was brought up** by her grandmother.* * **È stata allevata** dalla nonna.
call	call **for**	chiamare *They **called for** an ambulance, but it was too late.* **Chiamarono** un'ambulanza, ma era troppo tardi.
	call **in**	far venire, chiedere l'aiuto di *A new team of detectives **were called in** to conduct a fresh inquiry.* * **Fu fatta venire** un'altra squadra di investigatori per condurre una nuova inchiesta.
	call **off**	cancellare, disdire *The match **was called off** because of bad weather.* La partita **fu cancellata** a causa del maltempo.
	call (**in**) **on**	andare a trovare *I thought we might **call in on** your mother on our way.* * Ho pensato che potremmo **passare da** tua madre sulla strada.
carry	carry **off**	cavarsela, riuscire a fare (qualcosa di difficile) *I thought he **carried off** the part of Hamlet with great skill.* * Mi è sembrato che **se la sia cavata** con grande abilità nella parte di Amleto.
	carry **on**	continuare *I can't **carry on walking**, I'm too tired.* Non ce la faccio a **continuare a** camminare, sono troppo stanco.
	carry **out**	svolgere, eseguire *Nigel **is carrying out** research on early Christian art.* * Nigel **sta svolgendo** una ricerca sull'arte paleocristiana.
catch	catch **on**	cominciare a capire, afferrare *He doesn't take hints very easily, but he'll **catch on** eventually.* * Non coglie facilmente le allusioni, ma alla fine **comincerà a capire**.
	catch **up** (**with**)	raggiungere, mettersi in pari *I ran after her and managed to **catch up with** her.* * Le corsi dietro e riuscii a **raggiungerla**.
check	check **in**	registrarsi in arrivo *Please would you like to **check in** at the reception desk and sign your name in the book.* * Vi preghiamo di **registrarvi** al banco della reception e firmare il registro degli ospiti.
	check **out**	saldare il conto e andare via, lasciare libera la stanza; *We **checked out** at 5 am to catch a 7 am flight.* * Abbiamo **saldato** il conto alle 5 per prendere il volo delle 7. verificare, controllare *We'll need to **check out** his story.* * Dovremo **verificare** la sua storia.

▶

	check **up on**	fare indagini su, controllare *My mum **checks up on** me most evenings to see that I've done my homework.* * *Mia madre mi **controlla** quasi tutte le sere per essere sicura che ho fatto i compiti.*
clear	clear **out**	sgombrare, ripulire, svuotare *If we **clear out** the spare room, you can use it as a study.* * *Se **sgombriamo** la stanza per gli ospiti puoi usarla come studio.*
	clear **up**	chiarire, risolvere *They never **cleared up** the mystery of the missing money.* * *Non **hanno** mai **risolto** il mistero del denaro scomparso.*
come	come **across**	trovare per caso *He **came across** some of his old love letters in his wife's drawer.* * ***Trovò per caso** alcune sue vecchie lettere d'amore nel cassetto della moglie.*
	come **down**	scendere, venir giù (di prezzi, temperatura) *House prices **have come down** recently.* * *I prezzi delle case **sono diminuiti** ultimamente.*
	come **down with**	prendersi, contrarre (una malattia) *I think I'm **coming down with** flu.* * *Ho l'impressione che **mi sto prendendo** l'influenza.*
	come **forward**	farsi avanti *No witnesses to the accident **have come forward** yet.* * ***Non si è** ancora **fatto avanti** alcun testimone.*
	come **off**	riuscire, avere successo *I tried telling a few jokes but they **didn't come off** (=no one laughed).* * *Ho provato a raccontare delle barzellette, ma **non hanno avuto successo** (= **nessuno ha riso**).*
	come **out**	uscire, apparire, essere pubblicato *When **does** their new album **come out**?* * *Quando **esce** il loro nuovo album?*
	come **out in**	coprirsi di macchie, avere un'eruzione cutanea *This heat has made me **come out in** an itchy red rash.* * *Questo caldo mi ha fatto **ricoprire di** macchie rosse pruriginose.*
	come **round**	riprendere i sensi, rinvenire; *She **hasn't come round** from the anaesthetic yet.* * *Non si è ancora **ripresa dall'anestesia**.* andare a trovare, fare una visita ***Come round** tonight and we'll watch a video.* * ***Passa a trovarci** stasera e guarderemo un video.*
	come **up against**	incontrare (resistenza o difficoltà) *If you **come up against difficulties**, let me know and I'll help you.* * *Se **incontri** delle difficoltà, fammelo sapere e ti aiuterò.*
	come **up with**	proporre, suggerire, venir fuori con (piani, idee) *She's **come up with** some amazing scheme to double her income.* * ***È venuta fuori con** un progetto incredibile per raddoppiare il suo reddito.*
cut	cut **down**	tagliare, ridurre, limitare *I'm trying to **cut down** on caffeine.* * *Sto cercando di **ridurre** la caffeina.*
	cut **in**	intromettersi, interrompere *I was just talking to Jan, when Dave **cut in** (on us).* * *Stavo parlando con Jan quando Dave **si è intromesso**.*
	cut **out**	escludere, tagliar fuori qualcuno *They **cut** me **out** of the conversation.* * *Mi **hanno tagliato fuori** dalla conversazione.*

do	do **away with**	eliminare, abolire, liberarsi di *Computerization has enabled us to **do away with** a lot of paperwork.* * *L'informatizzazione ci ha consentito di **eliminare** un sacco di scartoffie.*
	do **out of**	defraudare, privare qualcuno di qualcosa *Pensioners **have been done out of** millions of pounds as a result of the changes.* * *I pensionati **sono stati defraudati di** milioni di sterline come conseguenza dei cambiamenti.*
	do **without**	fare a meno di *There's no mayonnaise left, so I'm afraid you'll just have to **do without**.* * *Abbiamo finito la maionese, così ho paura che dovrai **farne a meno**.*
draw	draw **in**	accorciarsi, far buio più presto *It's September, the days **are drawing in**.* *È settembre, le giornate **si stanno accorciando**.*
	draw **out**	allungare, prolungare *The director **drew** the meeting **out** for another hour.* * *Il direttore **prolungò** la riunione per un'altra ora.*
	draw **up**	accostare, avvicinare ***Draw up** a chair and I'll tell you all about it.* * ***Accosta** la sedia e ti racconterò tutto.*
drop	drop **by/in (on)**	passare a trovare *I **dropped in on** George on my way home from school.* * ***Passai a trovare** George mentre tornavo da scuola.*
	drop **off**	addormentarsi *I **dropped off** during the film.* ***Mi sono addormentata** mentre guardavo il film.*
	drop **out**	abbandonare, ritirarsi *He **dropped out** of the race after two laps.* * ***Si ritirò** dalla gara dopo due giri.*
fall	fall **back on**	ricorrere a *When the business failed, we had to **fall back on** our savings.* * *Quando l'azienda è fallita abbiamo dovuto **ricorrere ai** nostri risparmi.*
	fall **behind**	rimanere indietro *I've **fallen behind** with the mortgage payments.* * ***Sono rimasto indietro** con i pagamenti del mutuo.*
	fall **for**	innamorarsi di *She **has fallen for** a Spanish guy she met on holiday.* ***Si è innamorata** di uno spagnolo che ha conosciuto in vacanza.*
	fall **out with**	litigare, rompere *He left home after **falling out with** his parents.* * *Se ne andò di casa dopo **aver litigato con** i genitori.*
	fall **through**	andare a monte *My holiday plans **have fallen through**.* *I miei progetti per le vacanze **sono andati a monte**.*
feel	feel **like**	aver voglia di *Do you **feel like** a cup of tea?* ***Hai voglia di** una tazza di tè?*
	feel **for**	provare compassione / simpatia per *I know what it is like to be lonely, so I do **feel for** her.* * *So che cosa vuol dire essere soli, così **provo compassione per** lei.*

fill	fill **in/out**	riempire, compilare *Please **fill in** this form.* *Per favore riempia questo modulo.*	
	fill **out**	ingrassare, ingrossarsi *I started to **fill out** in the sixth month of my pregnancy.* * *Ho cominciato a **ingrossarmi** al sesto mese di gravidanza.*	
find	find **out**	scoprire *How **did** you **find out** about the party?* * *Come **sei venuto a sapere** della festa?*	
get	get **across**	comunicare, far recepire *This is the message that we want to **get across** to the public.* * *Questo è il messaggio che vogliamo **comunicare** al pubblico.*	
	get **along with**	andare d'accordo *I **don't** really **get along with** my sister's husband.* * ***Non vado** molto **d'accordo con** il marito di mia sorella.*	
	get **around**	diffondersi, circolare *News of Helen's pregnancy soon **got around** the office.* * *La notizia della gravidanza di Helen **si diffuse** nell'ufficio in un attimo.*	
	get **at**	punzecchiare, criticare, prendere di mira *He keeps **getting at** me and I really don't know what I've done wrong.* * *Continua a **punzecchiarmi** e non capisco proprio che cosa ho fatto di sbagliato.*	
	get **away**	liberarsi, andarsene, scappare *I just need to **get away** for a few days.* * *Ho bisogno di **andarmene** per qualche giorno.*	
	get **away with**	cavarsela, farla franca *If I thought I could **get away with** it, I wouldn't pay any tax at all.* * *Se pensassi che posso **farla franca**, non pagherei le tasse per niente.*	
	get **back**	tornare *If you **get back** in time, you can come with us.* * *Se **torni** in tempo puoi venire con noi.*	
	get **by**	sbarcare il lunario *How can he **get by** on so little money?* * *Come fa a **sbarcare il lunario** con così pochi soldi?*	
	get **down**	deprimere *This rainy weather **gets** me **down**.* *Questo clima piovoso mi **deprime**.*	
	get **down to**	dedicarsi a un compito, cominciare *I've got a lot of work to do, but I can't seem to **get down to** it.* * *Ho un sacco di lavoro da fare, ma mi sembra di **non riuscire a cominciare**.*	
	get **in**	entrare *They must **have got in** through the bathroom window.* * *Devono **essere entrati** dalla finestra del bagno.*	
	get **off**	scendere (da un mezzo di trasporto) ***Get off** at Camden Town.* * ***Scendi** alla fermata di Camden Town.*	
	get **on**	salire (su un mezzo di trasporto) *I think we **got on** the wrong bus.* * *Credo che **siamo saliti** sull'autobus sbagliato.* cavarsela, passarsela *How are you **getting on** in your new flat?* * *Come **te la passi** nel tuo nuovo appartamento?*	
	get **on with**	andare d'accordo *He **doesn't get on with** his daughter.* * ***Non va d'accordo** con sua figlia.*	

▶

437

	get **out**	uscire *We **don't get out** much since we had the children.** **Non usciamo** molto da quando abbiamo avuto i bambini.
	get **over**	riprendersi, guarire *It took him years to **get over** the shock of his wife dying.** Gli ci sono voluti anni per **riprendersi** dalla morte della moglie.
	get **round**	persuadere, convincere *See if you can **get round** your father to give you a lift to the cinema.** Vedi se riesci a **convincere** tuo padre a portarti al cinema in macchina.
	get **round to**	trovare il tempo di *I still **haven't got round to** fixing that tap.** **Non ho** ancora **avuto il tempo di** aggiustare quel rubinetto.
	get **through (to)**	contattare per telefono *I tried to phone her but I couldn't **get through**.** Ho provato a chiamarla ma non sono riuscito a **mettermi in contatto**.
	get **together**	riunirsi, incontrarsi ***Shall** we **get together** on Friday and go for a drink or something?** **Ci vediamo** venerdì per andare a bere insieme o qualcosa del genere?
	get **up**	alzarsi *I **got up** at five o' clock this morning!** **Mi sono alzato** alle cinque stamani!
give	give **away**	rivelare (volontariamente o involontariamente), lasciar trapelare *The party was meant to be a surprise, but Sharon **gave it away**.** La festa doveva essere una sorpresa, ma Sharon l'**ha lasciato trapelare**.
	give **back**	restituire *Has she **given** you those books **back** yet?** Ti ha **restituito** quei libri?
	give **in**	cedere, arrendersi *He nagged me so much for a new bike that eventually I **gave in**.** Mi ha assillato così tanto perché gli comprassi una bicicletta nuova che alla fine **ho ceduto**.
	give **out**	distribuire *They were **giving out** leaflets outside the school.** **Distribuivano** volantini davanti alla scuola.
	give **up**	rinunciare, smettere *I've **given up** trying to help her.** **Ho rinunciato** a cercare di aiutarla.
go	go **after**	inseguire *The police **went after** him but he got away.** La polizia lo **inseguì** ma lui riuscì a scappare.
	go **by**	passare, trascorrere *Hardly a day **goes by** when I don't think about her.** **Non passa** giorno che non pensi a lei.
	go **down**	diminuire (di prezzi, temperatura) *The temperature **went down** to minus ten last night.** La temperatura **è scesa** a meno dieci la scorsa notte.
	go **down with**	ammalarsi, prendere una malattia *Half of Martha's class **has gone down with** flu.** Mezza classe di Martha **si è presa** l'influenza.
	go **for**	preferire, scegliere *I **don't go for** war films in a big way (= very much).** **Non mi piacciono** molto i film di guerra.

	go **in for**	iscriversi, partecipare (esami, gare) *Are you planning to **go in for** the 100 metres race?** *Stai pensando di **partecipare** alla corsa dei 100 metri?*
	go **off**	andare a male (di cibo); *The milk **has gone off**.* *Il latte **è andato a male**.*
		suonare, squillare (di sveglia) *I'm sorry I'm late, the alarm clock **didn't go off**.* *Mi dispiace essere in ritardo, **non è suonata** la sveglia.*
	go **on**	continuare; *We really can't **go on** living like this.** *Non possiamo **continuare** a vivere così.*
		succedere *What's **going on** here?* *Che cosa **sta succedendo** qui?*
	go **out**	uscire; *Please close the door as you **go out**.** *Per favore chiudi la porta quando **esci**.*
		uscire con qualcuno, avere una relazione *How long **have** you **been going out** with him?** *Da quanto tempo **esci** con lui?*
	go **over/through**	controllare, esaminare *Remember to **go over** your essay checking for grammar and spelling mistakes before you hand it in to me.** *Ricordati di **controllare** se ci sono errori di grammatica o di ortografia nel tema prima di consegnarmelo.*
	go **through**	andare in porto *A council spokeswoman said that the proposals for the new shopping centre were unlikely to **go through**.** *Una portavoce del consiglio comunale ha detto che i progetti per il nuovo centro commerciale molto probabilmente non **andranno in porto**.*
	go **up**	aumentare (di prezzi, temperatura) *The price of petrol **has gone up** again.* *Il prezzo della benzina **è aumentato** di nuovo.*
	go **without**	fare a meno di *I'd rather **go without** food than work for him.** *Preferirei **fare a meno di** mangiare piuttosto che lavorare per lui.*
grow	grow **out of**	crescere troppo (per poter ancora indossare degli abiti) *William **has grown out of** the coat I bought him last year.* *William è cresciuto e il cappotto che gli ho comprato l'anno scorso **non gli sta più**.*
	grow **up**	crescere *I **grew up** in Scotland.** ***Sono cresciuto** in Scozia.*
hand	hand **in**	consegnare ***Have** you **handed in** your history essay yet?** ***Hai** già **consegnato** il saggio di storia?*
	hand **out**	distribuire *The teacher asked her to **hand out** the worksheets.** *L'insegnante le chiese di **distribuire** i worksheet.*
	hand **over**	consegnare, cedere *We were ordered to **hand over** our passports.** *Ci fu ordinato di **consegnare** i passaporti.*

hang	hang **around**	frequentare, passare il tempo *I spent most of my youth **hanging around** the bars of Dublin.** *Ho trascorso la maggior parte della mia gioventù (**passando il tempo**) nei bar di Dublino.*
	hang **on**	fermarsi, aspettare ***Hang on** a minute – I'll be with you in a moment!** ***Aspetta** un minuto – sarò con te tra un attimo!*
	hang **up**	riagganciare il ricevitore *Let me speak to Melanie before you **hang up**.** *Fammi parlare con Melanie prima di **riagganciare**.*
hold	hold **back**	trattenere *Sandbags **will hold** the flood waters **back** for a while.** *I sacchi di sabbia **tratterranno** l'inondazione per un po'.*
	hold **on**	restare in linea, aspettare ***Hold on**, I'll check in my diary.** ***Aspetta**, controllo sul mio diario.*
	hold **onto/on to**	tenersi aggrappato a ***Hold onto** the rope and don't let go.** ***Reggiti** alla corda e non lasciar andare la presa.*
	hold **up**	trattenere, bloccare *Traffic **was held up** for several hours after the accident.** *Il traffico **fu bloccato** per diverse ore dopo l'incidente.*
keep	keep **back**	nascondere, non dire *I suspect she's **keeping** something **back**.** *Ho il sospetto che **stia nascondendo** qualcosa.*
	keep **down**	reprimere, tenere a freno *It's all part of a conspiracy to **keep** women **down**.** *Fa tutto parte di un piano per **tenere sottomesse** le donne.*
	keep **off**	stare lontano *There was a notice saying: '**Keep off** the grass.'** *C'era un cartello che diceva: '**Non calpestare** l'erba.'*
	keep **on**	continuare *She **kept on** asking me questions the whole time.** ***Continuò** a farmi domande per tutto il tempo.*
	keep **out**	tenersi fuori ***Keep** me **out** of this.** ***Tienimi fuori** da tutto ciò.*
	keep **to**	attenersi a, rispettare *For heaven's sake **let's keep to** the point.** *Per l'amor del cielo **non divaghiamo**.*
	keep **up with**	restare al passo, tenersi al corrente *Wages are failing to **keep up with** inflation.** *Gli stipendi non riescono a **stare al passo** con l'inflazione.*
let	let **down**	deludere, abbandonare *You will be there tomorrow – you **won't let** me **down**, will you?** *Ci sarai domani – **non mi abbandonerai**, vero?*
	let **in**	lasciar passare *She opened the door and **let** me **in**.** *Aprì la porta e mi **fece entrare**.*
	let **off**	far esplodere *Don't **let off** fireworks near the house.** ***Non far esplodere** i fuochi d'artificio vicino a casa.*

live	live **on**	vivere di, alimentarsi di *I more or less **live on** pasta.* * Più o meno **vivo di** pasta.
	live **up to**	essere/dimostrarsi all'altezza di *The concert was brilliant – it **lived up to** all our expectations.* * Il concerto è stato fantastico – **è stato all'altezza di** tutte le nostre aspettative.
look	look **after**	occuparsi di, badare a *Don't worry about Mia – she can **look after** herself.* * Non preoccuparti per Mia – sa **badare a** se stessa.
	look **back (on)**	ricordare, riandare al passato *It wasn't such a bad experience when I **look back on** it.* * Non è stata poi una così brutta esperienza **a ripensarci**.
	look **for**	cercare *I'm **looking for** my car keys – have you seen them anywhere?* **Sto cercando** le chiavi della macchina. Le hai viste da qualche parte?
	look **forward to**	non vedere l'ora di, aspettare con impazienza *I'm **looking forward to** meeting him.* **Non vedo l'ora di** conoscerlo.
	look **in**	fare una capatina *I thought I might **look in** on Bob on my way to the shops.* * Pensavo di **fare una capatina** da Bob andando a far compere.
	look **into**	esaminare, indagare *We're **looking into** the possibility of merging the two departments.* * **Stiamo esaminando** la possibilità di unire i due dipartimenti.
	look **out**	stare attento ***Look out**! There's a car coming!* **Stai attento**! Sta arrivando una macchina!
	look **over**	esaminare rapidamente, dare un'occhiata *I had a few minutes before the meeting to **look over** what he'd written.* * Ho avuto alcuni minuti prima della riunione per **dare un'occhiata a** cosa aveva scritto.
	look **through**	esaminare con attenzione *I've **looked through** some catalogues.* * **Ho esaminato** alcuni cataloghi.
	look **up**	cercare qualcosa (in opere di consultazione, dizionari) *If you don't know what the word means, **look** it **up** in a dictionary.* * Se non conosci il significato della parola, **cercala** nel dizionario.
	look **up to**	rispettare, guardare con ammirazione *I've always **looked up to** my grandfather.* **Ho sempre ammirato** mio nonno.
make	make **for**	dirigersi verso *They **made for** the centre of town.* * **Si diressero verso** il centro della città.
	make **out**	capire (con difficoltà), distinguere (a fatica) *The numbers are too small – I can't **make** them **out** at all.* * I numeri sono troppo piccoli – non riesco a **decifrarli**.
	make **up**	inventare, escogitare *I **made up** an excuse about having to look after the kids.* * **Mi inventai** una scusa, che dovevo badare ai bambini.

▶

441

▶	make **up for**	compensare *No amount of money can **make up for** the death of a child.** **Nessuna somma di denaro può compensare** la morte di un bambino.
own	own **up (to)**	ammettere, confessare *No one **has owned up to** stealing the money.** **Nessuno ha ammesso** di aver rubato il denaro.
pull	pull **down**	abbattere, buttare giù *They **pulled down** the warehouse to build a new supermarket.** **Buttarono giù** il magazzino per costruire un nuovo supermercato.
	pull **in**	accostare e fermarsi (di veicoli) *He **pulled in** at the side of the road.** **Accostò** l'auto sul bordo della strada e si fermò.
put	put **aside**	mettere da parte, accantonare *Let's **put** our differences **aside** and make a fresh start.** **Cerchiamo di mettere da parte** le nostre differenze e ricominciare da capo.
	put **away**	riporre, mettere a posto *Please **put away** your toys tidily.* *Per favore, **mettete a posto** i giocattoli per bene.*
	put **by**	mettere da parte, risparmiare *I try to **put by** a few pounds every week.** *Cerco di **mettere da parte** un po' di sterline ogni settimana.*
	put **down**	umiliare, mortificare *Why did you have to **put** me **down** in front of everybody like that?** *Perché hai dovuto **umiliarmi** davanti a tutti in quel modo?*
	put **off**	rimandare *The meeting's **been put off** till next Wednesday.* *La riunione **è stata rimandata** a mercoledì prossimo.*
	put **on**	indossare ***Put on** your coat, it's freezing outside.* ***Mettiti** il cappotto, si gela fuori.*
	put **out**	spegnere *Firefighters have been called to **put out** the fire in the city centre.** *Sono stati chiamati i pompieri per **spegnere** l'incendio nel centro.*
	put **through**	mettere in comunicazione *Could you **put** me **through** to customer services please?** *Può **mettermi in comunicazione** con il servizio clienti per favore?*
	put **up**	alloggiare, dare un letto per la notte *Sally **is putting** me **up** for the weekend.** *Sally mi **ospiterà** il fine settimana.*
	put **up with**	sopportare, tollerare *I **won't put up with** bad behaviour in class.* ***Non tollererò** un comportamento scorretto in classe.*
run	run **down**	denigrare, criticare *He's always **running** himself **down**.** *Si **autodenigra** sempre. / Si **butta** sempre **giù**.*
	run **into**	incontrare, imbattersi in *Graham **ran into** someone he used to know at school the other day.** *L'altro giorno Graham **ha incontrato per caso** qualcuno che conosceva ai tempi della scuola.*
	run **out of**	esaurire, rimanere senza *We **have run out of** bread, can you buy some?* ***Siamo rimasti senza** pane, puoi comprarne un po'?* ▶

	run **over**	investire, travolgere *I'm afraid we **have** just **run** a rabbit **over**.* * **Ho paura che **abbiamo** appena **investito** un coniglio.**
see	see **about/to**	occuparsi di, provvedere a *It's getting late – I'd better **see about** lunch.* * **Si sta facendo tardi – farei meglio a **occuparmi del** pranzo.**
	see **off**	salutare qualcuno alla partenza *My parents **saw** me **off** at the airport.* * **I miei genitori mi **salutarono** all'aeroporto.**
	see **through**	capire le intenzioni, leggere in qualcuno *They were very friendly, but I quickly **saw through** them.* * **Erano molto amichevoli, ma **capii** subito le loro intenzioni.**
send	send **for**	mandare a chiamare *Do you think we should **send for** a doctor?* * **Pensi che dovremmo **mandare a chiamare** un dottore?**
	send **out**	emettere *The torch **sends out** a powerful beam of light.* * **La torcia **emette** un raggio di luce potente.**
set	set **back**	ritardare, rallentare *The opening of the new swimming pool **has been set back** by a few weeks.* * **L'apertura della nuova piscina **è stata ritardata** di alcune settimane.**
	set **off/out**	partire, mettersi in viaggio *They **have** just **set off** on a round-the-world cruise.* * ****Sono** appena **partiti** per una crociera intorno al mondo.**
	set **out**	esporre, presentare *The management board **has set out** its goals for the coming year.* * **Il consiglio di amministrazione **ha presentato** gli obiettivi per l'anno prossimo.**
	set **up**	avviare, intraprendere (un'attività) *She plans to **set up** her own business.* * **Ha intenzione di **avviare** un'attività in proprio.**
show	show **off**	ostentare, mettersi in mostra *She likes to wear short skirts to **show off** her legs.* * **Le piace indossare gonne corte per **mettere in mostra** le gambe.* ***
	show **up**	arrivare, farsi vivo *I invited him for eight o'clock, but he **didn't show up** until nine-thirty.* * **Lo invitai per le otto, ma **non arrivò** fino alle nove e mezzo.**
stand	stand **by**	sostenere, stare vicino *She has vowed **to stand by** her husband during his trial.* * **Ha giurato di **stare a fianco del** marito durante il processo.**
	stand **for**	essere l'abbreviazione di, significare; *What **does** N.A.T.O. **stand for**?* **che cosa **significa la sigla** N.A.T.O.?** essere a favore di, appoggiare *This party **stands for** low taxes and individual freedom.* * **Questo partito **è a favore** della riduzione delle tasse e della libertà individuale.**
	stand **in for**	sostituire *Paula **stood in for** Jane, while Jane was on holiday.* * **Paula **ha sostituito** Jane quando Jane era in vacanza.**
	stand **out**	risaltare, essere ben visibile *The black lettering really **stands out** on that orange background.* * **La scritta in nero **risalta** molto su quello sfondo arancione.**
	stand **up for**	difendere, intervenire a sostegno di *It's high time we all **stood up for** our rights around here.* * **È l'ora che tutti noi **cominciamo a difendere** i nostri diritti.**

►	*stand **up to***	opporsi, resistere a *He wasn't afraid to **stand up to** bullies.* * *Non aveva paura di **opporsi** ai prepotenti.*
switch	*switch **off***	spegnere *Don't forget to **switch off** the lights.* *Non dimenticarti di **spegnere** le luci.*
	*switch **on***	accendere ***Switch** the TV **on**, I want to hear the news.* ***Accendi** la televisione, voglio sentire il telegiornale.*
take	*take **after***	assomigliare (a qualcuno della famiglia) *He **takes after** his mother's side of the family.* * *Lui **assomiglia** tutto ai parenti di parte materna.*
	*take **away***	portare via ***Take** these chairs **away** – we don't need them.* * ***Porta via** queste sedie – non ne abbiamo bisogno.*
	*take **back***	ritrattare *All right, I **take** it all **back**: it wasn't your fault.* * *D'accordo, **ritiro** quello che ho detto: non è stata colpa tua.*
	*take **in***	ingannare *I can't believe she **was taken in** by him.* * *Non riesco a credere che **si sia fatta ingannare** da lui.*
	*take **off***	togliere, levarsi; *He **took off** his clothes and got into the bath.* * ***Si tolse** i vestiti ed entrò nella vasca.* decollare *The plane **took off** at 8.30 am.* * *L'aereo **decollò** alle 8:30 della mattina.* fare il verso di *She's really good at **taking** people **off**.* * *È bravissima a **fare le imitazioni**.*
	*take **on***	accettare, assumersi *She **took** too much **on** and made herself ill.* * ***Si è assunta** troppi impegni e questo l'ha fatta ammalare.*
	*take **over***	rilevare, acquisire (un'impresa) *The company he works for **has** recently **been taken over**.* * *La società per cui lavora **è stata acquistata** di recente.*
	*take **to***	prendere in simpatia *His wife **took to** her new neighbours at once.* * *Sua moglie **prese** subito **in simpatia** i nuovi vicini.*
	*take **up***	intraprendere, iniziare *Have you ever thought of **taking up** acting?* * *Hai mai pensato di **darti alla** recitazione?*
tell	*tell **off***	rimproverare ***Don't tell** him **off**, he didn't do it on purpose.* *Non **rimproverarlo**, non l'ha fatto apposta.*
think	*think **out***	studiare a fondo, elaborare nei particolari *The scheme **was** well **thought out**.* * *Il progetto **era stato** ben **studiato**.*
	*think **over***	riflettere su *I'll **think** it **over** and give you an answer next week.* * ***Ci rifletterò su** e ti darò una risposta la settimana prossima.*

try	try **on**	provarsi (un capo di vestiario) *Can I **try** that shirt **on**?* **Posso **provarmi** quella camicia?**
	try **out**	provare, sperimentare *Don't forget to **try out** the equipment before setting up the experiment.** * *Non dimenticare di **provare** l'attrezzatura prima di preparare l'esperimento.*
turn	turn **down**	abbassare; ***Turn down** the volume, will you?* ***Abbassa** il volume, per favore.* rifiutare *He **turned down** the job because it involved moving to Glasgow.* ***Rifiutò** il lavoro perchè comportava trasferirsi a Glasgow.*
	turn **out**	rivelarsi, risultare *The truth **turned out** to be stranger than we expected.* * *La verità **si è rivelata** più strana di quanto ci aspettassimo.*
	turn **over**	esaminare qualcosa da più punti di vista *His father **had been turning** the idea **over** in his mind for some time.* * *Suo padre **rifletteva** su quell'idea da un po' di tempo.*
	turn **up**	alzare ***Turn up** the radio, it's too low.* ***Alza il volume** della radio, è troppo basso.*
watch	watch **out**	stare attento ***Watch out**! We're going to crash!* ***Stai attento**! Stiamo per andare a sbattere!*
wear	wear **off**	affievolirsi, venir via *Most patients find that the numbness from the injection **wears off** after about an hour.* * *Quasi tutti i pazienti trovano che la sensazione di torpore dovuta all'iniezione **affievolisce** dopo circa un'ora.*
	wear **out**	consumarsi, logorare *You must rest a bit, you look **worn out**.* *Devi riposarti un po', hai un aspetto **sfinito**.*
work	work **out**	capire, trovare la soluzione *There will be a full investigation to **work out** what caused the accident.* * *Ci sarà un'inchiesta per **capire** che cosa ha causato l'incidente.*
	work **up**	eccitare, agitare, far infervorare *Try not **to work** yourself **up** about the exams.* *Cerca di non **agitarti troppo** per gli esami.*
write	write **down**	annotare *Did you **write down** Jo's phone number?* ***Hai scritto** il numero di telefono di Jo?*
	write **off**	rinunciare, abbandonare *The World Bank is being urged to **write off** debts from developing countries.* * *Vengono fatte pressioni sulla Banca Mondiale perché **cancelli** i debiti dei paesi in via di sviluppo.*

* Esempio tratto da *Cambridge Advanced Learners' Dictionary*, Second Edition, Cambridge University Press, 2005.

INDICE ANALITICO

ELENCO DELLE TRACCE DEI CD

CD1

Traccia	Registrazione
1	Title information
2	1a
3	1b
4	2a
5	2b
6	2c
7	3a
8	3b
9	4a
10	4b
11	5a
12	5b
13	6a
14	6b
15	7a
16	7b
17	7c
18	7d
19	8a
20	8b
21	9a
22	9b
23	9c
24	10a
25	10b
26	10c
27	10d
28	11a
29	11b
30	11c
31	11d
32	11e

CD2

Traccia	Registrazione
1	Title information
2	12a
3	12b
4	12c
5	12d
6	13a
7	13b
8	14a
9	14b
10	14c
11	15a
12	15b
13	16a
14	16b
15	17a
16	17b
17	18a
18	18b
19	19a
20	19b
21	20a
22	20b
23	20c
24	21a
25	21b
26	22a
27	22b
28	23a
29	23b